ALFA ROMEO GIULIETTA

WORKSHOP MANUAL
750 & 101 SERIES GIULIETTA
1300cc - 1955-1964
101 SERIES GIULIA
1600cc - 1962-1965

© 2021 Veloce Enterprises Inc., San Antonio, Texas USA
All rights reserved. This work may not be reproduced or transmitted in any form without the express consent of the publisher

Introduction

Welcome to the world of digital publishing ~ the book you now hold in your hand, was printed using the latest state of the art digital technology. The advent of print-on-demand has forever changed the publishing process, never has information been so accessible and it is our hope that this book serves your informational needs for years to come. If this is your first exposure to digital publishing, we hope that you are pleased with the results. Many more titles of interest to the classic automobile and motorcycle enthusiast, collector and restorer are available via our website at www.VelocePress.com. We hope that you find this title as interesting as we do.

Note from the Publisher

The information presented is true and complete to the best of our knowledge. All recommendations are made without any guarantees on the part of the author or the publisher, who also disclaim all liability incurred with the use of this information.

Trademarks

We recognize that some words, model names and designations, for example, mentioned herein are the property of the trademark holder. We use them for identification purposes only. This is not an official publication.

Information on the use of this Publication

This manual is an invaluable resource for those interested in performing their own maintenance. However, in today's information age we are constantly subject to changes in common practice, new technology, availability of improved materials and increased awareness of chemical toxicity. As such, it is advised that the user consult with an experienced professional prior to undertaking any procedure described herein. While every care has been taken to ensure correctness of information, it is obviously not possible to guarantee complete freedom from errors or omissions or to accept liability arising from such errors or omissions. Therefore, any individual that uses the information contained within, or elects to perform or participate in do-it-yourself repairs or modifications acknowledges that there is a risk factor involved and that the publisher or its associates cannot be held responsible for personal injury or property damage resulting from the use of the information or the outcome of such procedures.

Warning!

One final word of advice, this publication is intended to be used as a reference guide, and when in doubt the reader should consult with a qualified technician.

Measurements and Values

The metric system is the primary measurement method used in both the manufacture of these vehicles and in the production of the factory 'Mechanical Repair' and 'Technical' publications. As such, the reader is urged to verify that the conversion of those metric measurements to other forms of measurement is correct. All measurements and values contained within this compilation of the factory publications are made without any guarantees on behalf of the publisher, who also disclaims any and all liability incurred with the use of this manual.

SHOP MANUAL

S.p.A. *Alfa Romeo* MILANO

CENTRO ASSISTENZA CLIENTI

1 - TECHNICAL SPECIFICATIONS	page	3
2 - ENGINE AND AUXILIARY ENGINE EQUIPMENT	page	17
3 - CLUTCH - GEARBOX	page	89
4 - PROPELLOR SHAFT	page	109
5 - REAR AXLE AND SUSPENSION	page	115
6 - FRONT SUSPENSION	page	137
7 - STEERING SYSTEM	page	147
8 - BRAKES	page	159
9 - WHEELS AND TYRES	page	171
10 - ELECTRICAL EQUIPMENT	page	185
11 - COACHWORK	page	217
12 - LUBRICATION AND MAINTENANCE	page	237
13 - ACCESSORIES	page	247
14 - SPECIAL TOOLS AND EQUIPMENT	page	261
15 - APPENDIX	page	281

FOREWORD

The present shop manual provides, with its 14 parts, complete descriptive information, maintenanre and repair data on the Giulietta cars.

Assembly and disassembly procedures, of the various units or parts, which are given on this Manual, are the best for a better and faster result; of course an efficient servicing will be achieved, if the illustrated service tools would be used.

At the end of each part there is a page named « Information sheet reference », on this page shall be indicated the changes introduced on cars after the issue of the Manual and the instructions which will be given, step by step, to the Service Division by the « Sheets of Information » and by the « Improvement Bulletins ».

In this way the Manual will be brought constantly up to date, with remarkable advantage for a fine proceeding of the Workshops.

Centro Assistenza Clienti
Alfa Romeo

PART 1

TECHNICAL SPECIFICATIONS

INDEX

Main Data	page 5
Weights	» 5
Engine and chassis number	» 6
Overall dimensions	» 7
Tyres	» 7
Performance	» 7
Electrical equipment	» 8
Filling up	» 8
Distribution	» 9
Ignition	» 9
Carburation	» 9
Torque wrench data	» 10
PRINCIPAL DIMENSIONS FOR INSPECTION PURPOSES	» 10
Camshaft bearings and journals	» 10
Valves and valve guides	» 10
Valve lift	» 11
Valve cups	» 11
Valve springs	» 11
Cylinder head	» 11
Connecting rods	» 11
Pistons and liners	» 12
Crankshaft	» 12
Clutch	» 13
Gear box (Transmission)	» 13
Propeller shaft	» 13
Rear axle	» 14
Front suspension	» 14
Rear suspension	» 15
Brakes	» 15

Fig. 1 - Giulietta Berlina

Fig. 2 - Giulietta Sprint

PART 1

TECHNICAL SPECIFICATIONS

MAIN DATA

Number of cylinders		4
Bore and stroke (approx. 2.91 x 2.95 inches)		74 x 75 mm.
Total cylinder capacity		1290 cc.
Maximum power	Giulietta Berlina at 5200 r.p.m.	53 H.P.
	Giulietta t.i. at 5500 r.p.m.	65 »
	Giulietta Spider and Sprint at 6000 r.p.m.	80 »
	Giulietta Sprint Vel. and Spider Vel. at 6000 r.p.m.	90 »
Track	front	1286 mm. (4' 2½")
	rear	1270 » (4' 2")
Wheel base	Giulietta Berlina and t.i.	2380 » (7' 10")
	Giulietta Sprint and Sprint Veloce	2380 » (7' 10")
	Giulietta Spider and Spider Veloce	2200 » (7' 3")
Minimum turning circle	Giulietta Berlina and t.i.	11,000 » (36' 1")
	Giulietta Sprint and Sprint Veloce	11,000 » (36' 1")
	Giulietta Spider and Spider Veloce	9,600 » (31' 6")
Number of seats	Giulietta Berlina and t.i.	4
	Giulietta Sprint and Sprint Veloce	2
	Giulietta Spider and Spider Veloce	2
Fuel consumption per 100 km. (Italian Cuna Std. Spec.)	Giulietta Berlina	8,3 litres (1.825 gals.)
	Giulietta t.i.	8,5 » (1.869 »)
	Giulietta Sprint and Spider	9 » (1.979 »)
	Giulietta Sprint Veloce and Spider Veloce	11 » (2.419 »)

WEIGHTS

Weight of the car	Giulietta Berlina and t.i.	880 kg. (17 cwts 34 lbs.)
	Giulietta Sprint and Sprint Veloce	850 » (16 » 81 »)
	Giulietta Spider and Spider Veloce	830 » (16 » 37 »)

Fig. 3 - Giulietta Spider

ENGINE AND CHASSIS NUMBERS

Fig. 4 - The engine number is stamped on the left-hand side of the crankcase, and towards the front

Fig. 5 - The chassis number is stamped on the right-hand sinde of vertical panel below the scuttle.

OVERALL DIMENSIONS

Model	Maximum length		maximum width		maximum height	
	mm.	ft. in.	mm.	ft. in.	mm.	ft. in.
Giulietta Berlina and t.i.	3990	13' 1"	1555	5' 1¼"	1405	4' 7½"
Giulietta Sprint and Sprint Veloce	3980	13' 0½"	1535	5' 0½"	1320	4' 4"
Giulietta Spider and Spider Veloce	3850	12' 7¹⁴/₆₄"	1580	5' 2¼"	1250 lowered top / 1335 raised top	4' 1¼" / 4' 4½"

TYRES 155 x 15

Inflation pressures in Kg cm² (see part 9)

Model	Type									
	Pirelli Rolle		Pirelli Pordoi		Michelin S.D.S.		Pirelli Cinturato		Michelin X	
	front	rear	front	rear	front	rear	front	rear	front	rear
Giulietta Berlina	1.4	1.5	1.3	1.5	1.4	1.5	1.4 (1) / 1.5 (2)	1.5 (1) / 1.6 (2)	1.3	1.4
Giulietta t.i.	—	—	—	—	—	—	1.5 (1) / 1.6 (2)	1.6 (1) / 1.7 (2)	1.4 (1) / 1.5 (2)	1.5 (1) / 1.6 (2)
Giulietta Sprint and Spider	—	—	—	—	—	—	1.5	1.6	1.4	1.5
Giulietta Sprint Veloce and Spider Veloce	—	—	—	—	—	—	1.5 (3) / 1.7 (4) / 1.9 (5)	1.6 (3) / 1.8 (4) / 2.0 (5)	—	—

(1) For touring use and small loads
(2) For sports use and full loads
(3) For road use, up to 100 m.p.h.
(4) For road use, above 100 m.p.h.
(5) For race track use

kg/cm²	1.3	1.4	1.5	1.6	1.7	1.8	1.9	2.0
p.s.i.	18.2	19,5	21	22,5	24	25,2	26,8	28

PERFORMANCE

Model	Gear	Speed	
		in Km. p.h.	in m.p.h.
Giulietta Berlina: bevel drive ratio 9/41	1 st	42	26
	2 nd	72	45
	3 rd	104	65
	4 th	140	87
	reverse	41	25
Giulietta t.i.: bevel drive ratio 9/41	1 st	47	29
	2 nd	79	49
	3 rd	114	71
	4 th	155	97
	reverse	46	28,5
Giulietta Sprint and Spider: bevel drive ratio 9/41	1 st	48	30
	2 nd	82	51
	3 rd	118	72
	4 th	165	103
	reverse	49	30,5
Giulietta Sprint Veloce and Spider Veloce: bevel drive ratio 10/41	1 st	54	34
	2 nd	92	57
	3 rd	133	84
	4 th	180	112
	reverse	53	33

12 V. ELECTRICAL EQUIPMENT

1) **Main equipment**

	Marelli	Lucas
Generator	DN 44 A	C 39 PV 2
Control-box	IR 32 A	RB 106/1
Starter motor	MT 35 E MT 40 B	M 325 BZ 1 M 325 BZ 2
Distributor	S 71 B	DM 2
Coil	B 17 A	LA 12 - B 12/1
Battery — Giulietta Berlina and t.i. . . . . 38 A/h	
Battery — Giulietta Sprint, Spider, Sprint Veloce and Spider Veloce . . . . . 30 A/h	

2) **Sparking plugs**

Model	Plug type	Electrode gaps in mm.
Giulietta Berlina, t.i., Sprint and Spider	Marelli CW 225 G LODGE HLN	0.6 to 0.7 0.5 to 0.6
Giulietta Sprint Veloce and Spider Veloce	Marelli CBW 1000 B LODGE RL 47 LODGE 2 HLN	0.5 to 0.55 0.38 to 0.46 0.55 to 0.65

FILLING UP

	Berlina and t.i.		Sprint and Spider		Sprint Veloce and Spider Veloce	
	litres	gals.	litres	gals.	litres	gals.
Fuel tank capacity	40	8 6/8	53	11 5/8	80	17 ½
Water (engine and radiator)	7,5	1 ¾	7,5	1 ¾	7,5	1 ¾
	kg.	lbs.	kg.	lbs.	kg.	lbs.
Oil — engine in the sump	5	11	5	11	5	11
Oil — engine in the filter	0.7	1 lb. 3 oz.	0.7	1 lb. 3 oz.	0.7	1 lb. 3 oz.
Oil — gearbox	1.35	3	1.35	3	1.25	3
Oil — rear axle	1.25	2 lbs 12 oz.	1.25	2 lbs 12 oz.	1.25	2 lbs 12 oz.
Oil — steering box	0.25	9 oz.	0.25	9 oz.	0.25	9 oz.

DISTRIBUTION

		Giulietta Berlina, t.i. Sprint and Spider (see note)		Giulietta Sprint Veloce and Spider Veloce
Inlet valves	Start to open before T.D.C.	22°	25° 20'	34°
	Finish closing after B.D.C.	65°	68°	63°
Exhaust valves	Start to open before B.D.C.	55°	61° 20'	63°
	Finish closing after T.D.C.	12°	18° 40'	30°
Valve clearance when engine is cold, new valves	inlet min.	0.425 mm.	0,475 mm.	0.375 mm.
	inlet max.	0.45 »	0,50 »	0.40 »
	exhaust min.	0.475 »	0,525 »	0.535 »
	exhaust max.	0.50 »	0,55 »	0.56 »
Valve gap when valves are worn to the maximum	inlet min.	0.4 »	0,450 »	0.35 »
	inlet max.	0.475 »	0,525 »	0.425 »
	exhaust min.	0.45 »	0,50 »	0.51 »
	exhaust max.	0.525 »	0,575 »	0.585 »

REMARK: The data indicated in the second column concern engines with camshafts marked between first and second cams by a circle with a cross in the center.

IGNITION

Firing order	cylinders 1, 3, 4, 2
Contact gap when fully open	0.35 to 0.40 mm.
Fixed advance — Giulietta Berlina, t.i., Sprint and Spider	8°
Fixed advance — Giulietta Sprint Veloce and Spider Veloce	5° ÷ 8°
Maximum advance — Giulietta Berlina, t.i., Sprint and Spider	at 5000 to 5200 r.p.m. 44°
Maximum advance — Giulietta Sprint Veloce and Spider Veloce	» » » » » 46° ÷ 48°

CARBURATION

CARBURETTER	Solex 32 BIC (1) mm.	Solex 35 APAI-G (2) mm.	Solex 32 PAIAT (3) mm.	Solex 35 APAIG (4) mm.	Solex 35 APAI-G (5) mm.	Weber 40DC03 (6) mm.
Choke	21	—	—	—	—	28
Choke N° 1	—	24	22	24	24	—
Main jet	1.05	1.30	1.15	1.20	1.20	1.10 winter 1.05 summer
Idling jet	0.40	0.40	0.45	0.40	0.40	0.50
Emulsioner air jet	1.60	1.80	2.00	1.50	1.50	1.90
Idling air jet	1.00	1.00	1.00	1.00	1.00	1.75
Starter jet	1.30	1.60	1.50	1.60	1.60	—
Accelerator pump jet	—	0.60	0.45	0.60	0.60	0.40
Accelerator pump outlet jet	—	—	—	—	—	1.50
Choke N° 2	—	24	23	24	24	—
Main jet	—	1.55	1.35	1.50	1.50	—
Emulsioner air jet	—	1.10	1.10	1.40	1.90	—

(1) Fitted to Giulietta Berlina
(2) Fitted to Giulietta t.i.
(3) Fitted to the first 1000 Giulietta Sprint cars
(4) Fitted to Giulietta Sprint cars after the first 1000
(5) Fitted to Giulietta Spider
(6) Two carburetters are fitted on the Giulietta Sprint Veloce and Spider Veloce

TORQUE WRENCH DATA

Cylinder-head nuts	6.0 to 6.5 kgm.
Crankshaft bearing cap nuts	3.0 to 3.25 »
Con-rod big-end nuts { Giulietta Berlina and t.i.	3.0 to 3.25 »
{ Giulietta Sprint and Spider	3.7 to 4.0 »
{ Giulietta Sprint Veloce and Spider Veloce	3.9 to 4.1 »

PRINCIPAL DIMENSIONS FOR INSPECTION PURPOSES

NOTE: Except where specifically mentioned, the values given in the following tables are common to all types.

CAM-SHAFT BEARINGS AND JOURNAL
(see Part 2)

Cam-shaft journal diameter	26.959 to 26.980 mm.
Cam-shaft journal seat diameter	27.000 to 27.021 »
Clearance when new, between cam-shaft journal and their seats	0.020 to 0.062 »
Clearance between above members at maximum wear	0.10 »
Axial-play between cam-shaft and thrust bearing	0.10 »

VALVES AND VALVE GUIDES
(see Part 2)

Valves	diameter { inlet	37 mm.
	{ exhaust	34 »
	stem diameter { inlet	7.976 to 8.001 »
	{ exhaust	7.950 to 7.976 »
	total length { inlet	97.75 »
	{ exhaust	96.85 »
Valve guides	{ internal diameter when guides fitted	8.014 to 8.026 »
	{ external diameter when guides fitted	13.028 to 13.039 »
Play between guide and valve stem when guides are fitted	when new (and essembl.) { inlet . . .	0.013 to 0.050 »
	{ exhaust . .	0.038 to 0.076 »
	when worn to maximum { inlet . . .	0.10 »
	{ exhaust . .	0.13 »
Valve guide seats in the cylinder head	13.000 to 13.011 »
Interference between seats and valve guides	0.017 to 0.39 »

VALVE LIFT

Giulietta Berlina, Giulietta Sprint, Giulietta Spider	8 mm.
Giulietta Sprint Veloce	8.5 »

VALVE CUPS
(see Part 2)

Cup diameter	standard	32.479 to 32.495 mm.
	enlarged	32.679 to 32.695 »
Cup seat diameter	standard	32.500 to 32.516 »
	enlarged	32.700 to 32.716 »
Play when first assembled	. . . .	0.005 to 0.037 »
Play at maximum wear	. . . .	0.06 »

VALVE SPRINGS
(see Part 2)

Outer spring	Length (spring free)	43.0 to 44.6 mm.
	Length (compressed by load of 24/25 kg.)	22.5 »
Inner spring	Length (spring free)	39.35 to 40.95 »
	Length (compressed by load of 14/15 kg.)	21.0 »

CYLINDER HEAD

Head height	Giulietta Berlina, Giulietta Sprint, Giulietta Spider	103 mm.
	Giulietta Sprint Veloce	101.5 »

CONNECTING-RODS
(see Part 2)

Length of connecting-rod		132.955 to 133.045 mm.
Internal diameter of small-end bearing		20.005 to 20.015 »
Clearance between small-end bearing bore and gudgeon pins	prescribed	0.005 to 0.020 »
	max. wear	0.05 »
Diameter of bearing seat		48.658 to 48.671 »
Bearing thickness	for standard crank-shaft	1.822 to 1.829 »
	for 1st re-grind of crank-pins	1.949 to 1.956 »
	for 2nd re-grind of crank-pins	2.076 to 2.083 »
	for 3rd re-grind of crank-pins	2.203 to 2.210 »
Radial clearance between pins and bearings		0.025 to 0.064 »
Axial clearance between con-rods and their crank-pins		0.2 to 0.3 »

PISTONS & LINERS (see Part 2)

Cylinder liner, standard diameter			74.000 to 74.019 mm.
Ovality	with new liner (tolerance)		0.014 »
	with worn liner (maximum permissible limit)		0.05 »
Liner projection beyond the cylinder block			0.000 to 0.06 »
Piston: standard diameter (to be measured at a point 11 mm. from the skirt bottom)		Giulietta Berlina	73.935 to 73.965 »
		Giulietta Sprint and Spider	73.925 to 73.955 »
		Giulietta Sprint Vel. and Spid. Vel.	73.835 to 73.865 »
Clearance between cylinder liner and piston	prescribed, when coupled	Giulietta Berlina	0.04 to 0.059 »
		Giulietta Sprint and Spider	0.05 to 0.069 »
		Giulietta Sprint Vel. and Spid. Vel.	0.14 to 0.159 »
	at maximum wear	Giulietta Berlina, Sprint and Spider	0.12 »
		Giulietta Sprint Vel. and Spid. Vel.	0.18 »
Compression and oil scraper rings: standard diameter			74.00 »
Clearance between the ends of compression or oil scraper rings (when the rings are placed inside the liner)		compression	0.30 to 0.45 »
		oil scraper	0.25 to 0.40 »
		max. wear	1 »
Thickness of rings	compression		1.972 to 1.984 »
	oil scraper		3.958 to 3.970 »
Axial play between seats and rings	prescribed	compression	0.041 to 0.068 »
		oil scraper	0.045 to 0.072 »
	max. wear		0.10 »
Diameter of piston pins			19.994 to 20.000 »
Diameter of piston pin bore			20.000 to 20.003 »
Clearance between piston-pin and piston-pin bore	prescribed		0.000 to 0.008 »
	maximum wear		0.004 »

NOTE: The dimensions stated for pistons and liners are the outside limits; when assembling, the various parts must be selected so as to ensure the prescribed amount of play.

CRANKSHTFT (see Part 2)

Crankshaft	Crankshaft journal diameter	standard	57.074 to 57.086 mm.
		1st regrind	56.820 to 56.832 »
		2nd regrind	56.566 to 56.578 »
		3rd regrind	56.312 to 56.324 »
	Crank pin diameter	standard	44.963 to 44.975 »
		1st regrind	44.709 to 44.721 »
		2nd regrind	44.445 to 44.447 »
		3rd regrind	44.201 to 44.223 »
	Maximum permitted ovality of crank pins and crankshaft journal		0.05 »
	Maximum lack of alignment between crank pins and crankshaft journals		0.07 »
Diameter of crankshaft bearing seats			60.769 to 60.782 »
Thickness of crankshaft journals		standard	1.829 to 1.835 »
		1st regrind	1.956 to 1.962 »
		2nd regrind	2.083 to 2.089 »
		3rd regrind	2.210 to 2.216 »
Diametral clearance between crankshaft journal and bearing (prescribed)			0.013 to 0.050 »
Length of crankshaft centre journal		standard	30.000 to 30.035 »
		1st regrind	30.127 to 30.162 »
		2nd regrind	30.254 to 30.289 »
		3rd regrind	30.381 to 30.416 »
Thickness of thrust rings for the crankshaft centre journal		standard	2.311 to 2.362 »
		1st regrind	2.374 to 2.425 »
		2nd regrind	2.438 to 2.489 »
		3rd regrind	2.501 to 2.552 »
Axial play of the thrust rings for the crankshaft centre bearing (prescribed)			0.076 to 0.263 »
Axial play of the con-rods (prescribed)			0.20 to 0.30 »
Crankshaft journal fillets			2.00 »

CLUTCH

(see Part 3)

Internal diameter of the driven plate	130 mm.
External diameter of the driven plate	200 »
Clearance between the thrust ring and the disengaging ring — prescribed	2 »
— maximum wear	1 »
Thickness of the driven plate — with new linings	10 »
— maximum wear	6 »
Thickness of the clutch lining	3.5 »
Clearance between the flywheel and the thrust ring face	59 to 59.5 »
Clearance between the thrust ring face and the plane of the outer face of the cover	26 to 26.3 »
Number of springs	9 »
Length of uncompressed springs	43.5 to 45.5 »
Length of springs under load of 45/49 kg.	29 »
Free pedal movement	23 »
Maximum permissible lack of balance of the clutch unit	20 gr. cm.

GEAR BOX (TRANSMISSION)

(see Part 3)

Length of synchroniser springs when not compressed — 1st and 2nd gears	15.3 mm.
— 3rd and top gears	11.5 »
Spring length when loaded — at 1.6 to 1.8 kg. (1st and 2nd gears)	12.5 »
— at 1.9 to 2.1 kg. (3rd and top gears)	9 »
Ratios: 1st gear	1:3.313
2nd gear	1:1.959
3rd gear	1:1.354
top gear	1:1
reverse	1:3.365
N° of teeth on speedometer drive gear-wheel for rear-axle ratio of 10/41	9
N° of teeth on speedometer pinion for rear-axle ratio of 10/41	19
N° of teeth on speedometer drive gear-wheel for rear-axle ratio of 8/41	8
N° of teeth on speedometer pinion for rear-axle ratio of 8/41	22
N° of teeth on speedometer drive gear-wheel for rear-axle ratio of 9/41	9
N° of teeth on speedometer pinion for rear-axle ratio of 9/41	21

PROPELLER SHAFT

(see Part 4)

Maximum permissible lack of squareness between the rear shaft and the face of the front flange (measured at the flange extremities)	0.05 mm.
Maximum eccentricity of the intermediate bracket bearing seats	0.03 »
Maximum eccentricity of the rear shaft	0.02 »
Maximum permitted lack of balance of the rear shaft	10 gr. cm.

REAR AXLE
(see Part 5)

Type of bevel drive		Hypoid
Rear-axle ratio	Giulietta Berlina, t.i., Sprint and Spider	9/41
	Giulietta Sprint Veloce and Spider Veloce	10/41
Type of bearings for pinion and differential box		taper roller bearing
Type of rear-axles		half-floating axles
Backlash, pinion/crown wheel		0.13 to 0.18 mm.
Maximum crown-wheel eccentricity		0.025 »

FRONT SUSPENSION
(see Part 6 and 9)

* Wheel camber			0°
* Toe-in (measured at rims)			3 mm.
* King-pin slant			8° 35'
* King-pin caster angle	Giulietta Berlina	up to car N. 148810000 . .	10' ± 30'
		from car N. 148810001 .	30' ± 30'
	Giulietta t.i.		30' ± 30'
	Giulietta Sprint and Sprint Veloce . .		50' ± 30'
	Giulietta Spider and Spider Veloce . . .		1° 20' ± 30'
Steering angle	inner		36°
	outer		28° 30'
Length of springs when not compressed	Giulietta Berlina	up to car N. 148810000 . . .	389 ± 5 mm.
		from car N. 148810001 . . .	396 ± 5 »
	Giulietta t.i.		396 ± 5 »
	Giulietta Sprint	up to car N. 149302800 . . .	410 ± 5 »
		from car N. 149302801 . . .	394 ± 5 »
	Giulietta Spider		410 ± 5 »
	Giulietta Sprint Veloce	standard . . .	371 ± 5 »
		on request . . .	384 ± 5 »
	Giulietta Spider Veloce		364 ± 5 »
Lenght of springs under load	Giulietta Berlina	up to car N. 148810000, load 500 ± 15 Kg. . .	267 mm.
		from car N. 148810001, load 500 ± 15 Kg. . .	274 »
	Giulietta t.i., load 500 ± 15 Kg.		274 »
	Giulietta Sprint	up to car N. 149302800, load 525 ± 15 Kg. . .	267 »
		from car N. 149302801, load 505 ± 15 Kg. . .	267 »
	Giulietta Spider, load 465 ± 14 Kg.		267 »
	Giulietta Sprint Veloce, load 460 ± 13,8 Kg.		267 »
	Giulietta Spider Veloce, load 426 ± 12,8 Kg.		267 »

* All these data relate to vehicles fully loded

REAR SUSPENSION

(see Part 5)

Length of springs when uncompressed	Giulietta Berlina	up to car N. 148810000	471 5	mm.
		from car N. 148810001	463 5	»
	Giulietta t.i.		463 5	»
	Giulietta Sprint	up to car N. 149302800	461 5	»
		from car N. 149302801 to car N. 149304500	425 5	»
		from car N. 149304501	414 5	»
	Giulietta Spider	up to car N. 149501850	436 5	»
		up to car N. 149501850 (on request)	420 5	»
		from car N. 149501851 to car N. 149503250	433 5	»
		from car N. 149503251	418 5	»
	Giulietta Sprint Veloce	up to car N. 149304500	383 5	»
		up to car N. 149304500 (on request)	402 5	»
		from car N. 149304501	383 5	»
	Giulietta Spider Veloce		387 5	»
Length of spring under load	Giulietta Berlina	up to car N. 148810000, load 245 7.35 Kg.	260	mm.
		from car N. 148810001, load 245 7.35 Kg.	250	»
	Giulietta t.i., load of 245 7.35 Kg.		250	»
	Giulietta Sprint	up to car N. 149302800, load 210 6,30 Kg.	240	»
		from car N. 149302801 to car. N. 149304500, load 195 5,85 Kg.	240	»
		from car N. 149304501, load 195 5,85 Kg.	230	»
	Giulietta Spider	up to car N. 149501850, load 161,5 4,80 Kg.	240	»
		up to car N. 149501850 (on request) load 171 5.10 Kg.	240	»
		from car N. 149501851 up to car 149503250, load 161,5 4,84 Kg.	240	»
		from car N. 149503251, load 162 4,86 Kg.	240	»
	Giulietta Sprint Veloce, load 171 5.13 Kg.		240	»
	Giulietta Spider Veloce, load 155 4.65 Kg.		240	»

BRAKES

(see Part 8)

Internal drum diameter	front	266.7 to 266.8	mm.
	rear	254 to 254.1	»
Diameter of brake shoes	front	265.8 to 266.1	»
	rear	253.2 to 253.5	»
Type of lining		Ferodo MZ 41	
Useful width	front	57	mm.
	rear	44.45	»
Useful thickness	front	2.8	»
	rear	2.2	»
Hydraulic pump diameter		25.4	»
Brake cylinder diameter	front	25.4	»
	rear	22.22	»
Useful stroke of brake pedal		120	»

INFORMATION SHEET REFERENCE

ASSEMBLY	DATE	SHEET N.	SUBJECT

PART 2A

THE ENGINE

INDEX

DESCRIPTION	page 21
ENGINE TUNING	» 23
Group 1	» 23
Group 2	» 27
Group 3	» 29
ENGINE OVERHAUL	» 30
Work not requiring removal of the engine	» 31
1) Removing the valve cover	» 31
2) Timing chains	» 31
3) Valve timing	» 33
4) Checking and adjusting valve clearance	» 33
5) Removing the cylinder head from the crank-case	» 34
6) Dismantling and overhauling the cylinder-head	» 35
7) Removing the sump	» 41
Oil sump (for Giulietta Sprint Veloce and Spider Veloce)	» 42
8) The Oil pump	» 43
9) The Oil filter	» 44
10) Main and connecting-rod bearings	» 45
11) Cylinder liners, pistons, rings and connecting rods	» 46
12) The Front cover - The Timing reduction chain and sprockets	» 50
13) Engine suspension	» 52
14) Removing the engine gear-box unit from the car	» 53
Bench repairs	» 54
15) Dismantling the engine on a trestle	» 54
16) Replacing the ring gear on the flywheel	» 55
17) Crank-shaft	» 56
18) Refitting the engine	» 60
19) Valve gear timing	» 60
20) Running-in the engine on the test-bench	» 63

PART 2 B

AUXILIARY ENGINE EQUIPMENT

21) **The cooling circuit** . . . . page 65
    The Water pump . . . . » 65
    The Radiator . . . . » 67
22) **The fuel feed** . . . . » 69
    The Mechanical fuel pump . . . . » 69
    The Electric fuel pump . . . . » 70
    The Additional fuel filter . . . . » 71
    The Air cleaner . . . . » 71
23) **Carburation** . . . . » 71
    The SOLEX C 32 BIC Carburetter (for Giulietta Berlina cars) . . . . » 71
    The SOLEX C 35 APAIG Carburetter (for Giulietta t.i., Sprint and Spider) . » 75
    The SOLEX 32 PAIAT Carburetter (for Giulietta Sprint cars) . . . . » 79
    The WEBER 40 DCO 3 Carburetter (for Giulietta Sprint Veloce and Spider Veloce cars) . . . . » 79
    Starting when the engine is cold . . . . » 86
    Starting when the engine is hot . . . . » 86
24) **The exhaust side** . . . . » 86
    The Exaust manifold . . . . » 86
    The Exhaust pipe and silencer (muffler) . . . . » 86
    The Exhaust system (for Giulietta Sprint Veloce and Spider Veloce) . . » 87

Fig. 1 - Engine and gearbox (transmission) seen from the inlet side (Giulietta Berlina)

Fig. 2 - Engine and gearbox (transmission) seen from the exhaust side (Giulietta Berlina)

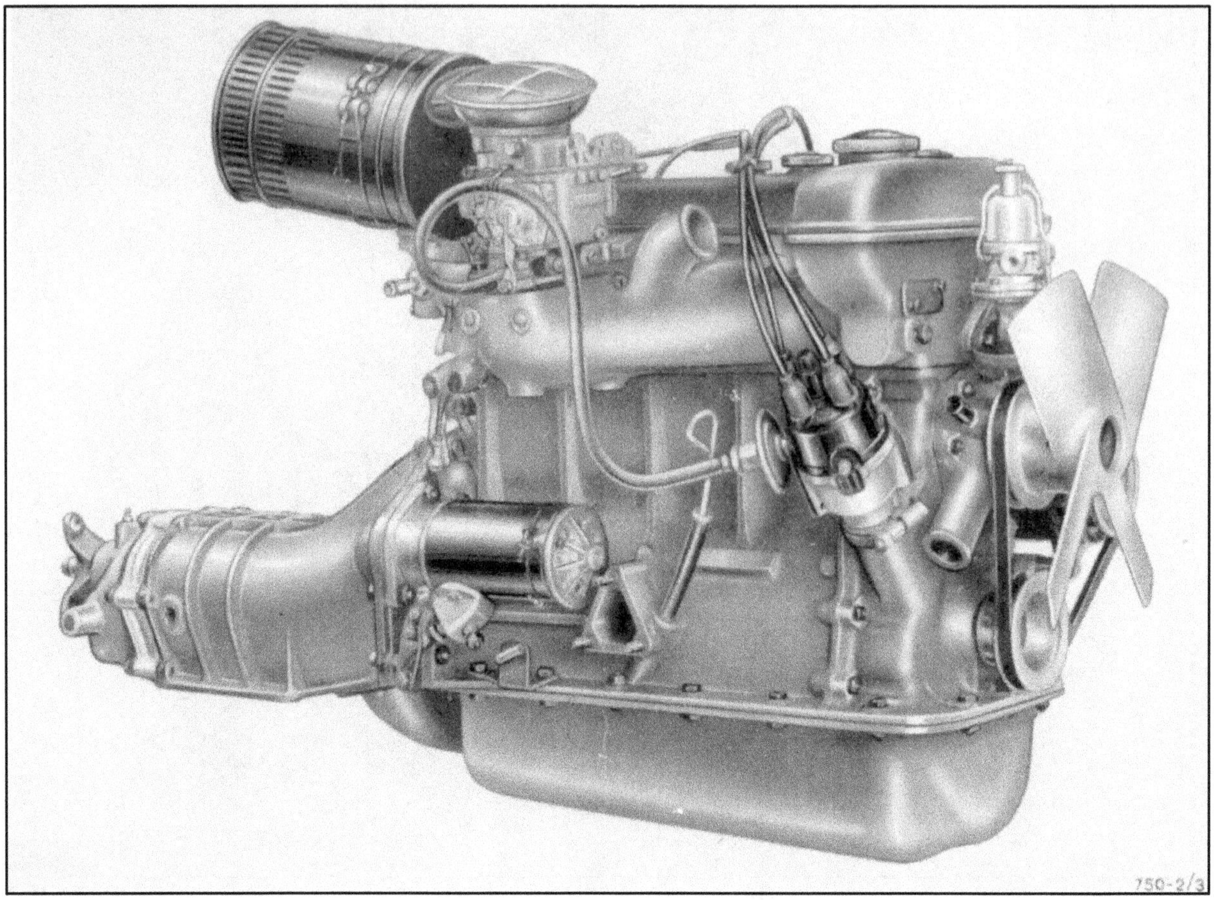

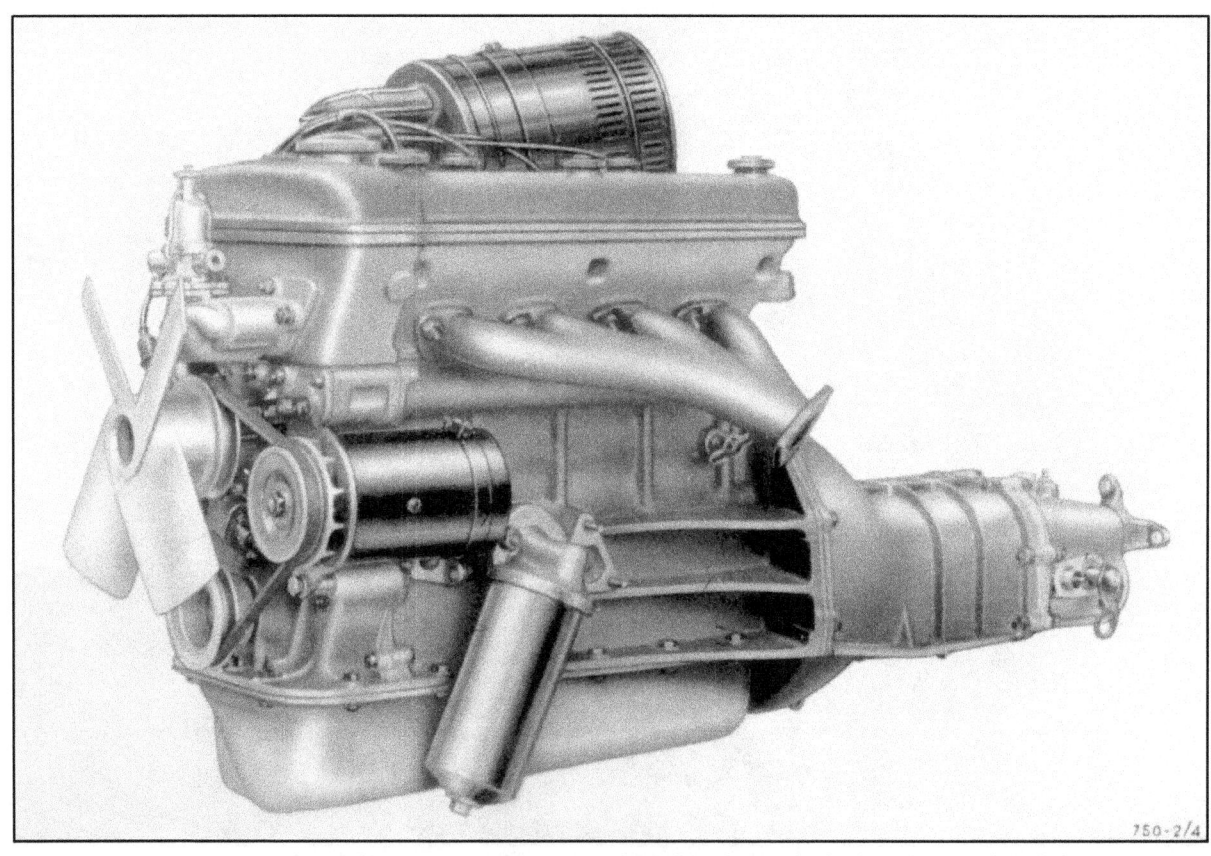

Fig. 3 - Engine and gearbox (transmission) seen from the inlet side (Giulietta Sprint and Spider)

Fig. 3 bis - Engine and gearbox (transmission) seen from the exhaust side (Giulietta Sprint and Spider)

PART 2A

THE ENGINE

DESCRIPTION

The Giulietta cars are powered by engines which reflect the traditional Alfa Romeo design; they thereby combine features of a low fuel consumption and a high power ratio.

The engines have 4 cylinders in line, hemispherical combustion chambers with sparking plugs located in the centre line of the combustion chamber, and large overhead, inclined valves directly operated by two camshafts (one camshaft for the inlet valves and one for the exhaust valves).

This orthodox Alfa Romeo timing system which has resulted in countless victories in world-wide sporting events, permits an unencumbered water circulation system to surround the entire combustion chamber so that the highest possible degree of thermal efficiency is obtained, with the resultant exceptionally good fuel consumption figures.

The aluminium alloy cylinder-head encloses the combustion chamber, and also houses the valves and camshafts. Pistons are in light alloy, with 2 compression rings (the top ring being chromium plated) and one oil scraper ring. The crank-case is in light high tensile alloy with cylinder liners made from special cast iron.

The crank-shaft, mounted on 5 main bearings, is fully balanced statically and dynamically, counterbalance weights being used for this purpose. The main and connecting-rod bearings are in steel faced with an anti-friction lead-indium alloy, and are easy to replace as they need no special fitting.

The carburetter on the Berlina is a Solex C 32 BIC, vertical down-draft with starting device.

The carburetter on the t.i., Sprint and Spider is a Solex 35 APAI-G, vertical, down-draft with double manifold, equipped with accelerating pump and starting device (on the first 1000 Sprint cars there is mounted the carburetter Solex 32 PAIAT with the same features).

On the Sprint Veloce and Spider Veloce cars there are assembled two carburetters type Weber 40 DCO3.

The battery-operated ignition system has a coil and distributor provided with a built-in centrifugal advance device completed, when operating at partial throttle openings, by a vacuum device connected to the carburetter, and which results in a considerable economy in fuel consumption.

Particular care has been given to air cleaning and oil filtering; the oil filter system uses a full-flow filter on the delivery circuit and a second filter on the oil pump suction side.

The cooling water circuit works under pressure; the radiator has been specially designed to withstand the high pressures and working temperatures demanded by the high thermal efficiency rating of the engine.

So that the engine may warm up quickly, the water circulation system is controlled by a thermostat through a capsule inserted in the water channel leading from the engine.

The various parts of the engine are described in greater detail in the chapters dealing wiht their overhaul.

As a general note regarding all the following chapters which describe the operations involved in the overhaul, maintenance and dismantling of the engine and its various units, it can be stated here that the fine performance of the Giulietta engine can be achieved and maintained unaltered over a long working life only if the engine and its accessory units are carefully adjusted and regularly maintained

The greatest care and attention should be given to the proper compliance with the instructions given in the following pages; these instructions faithfully reflect the practices and processes usd at the Alfa Romeo factory itself.

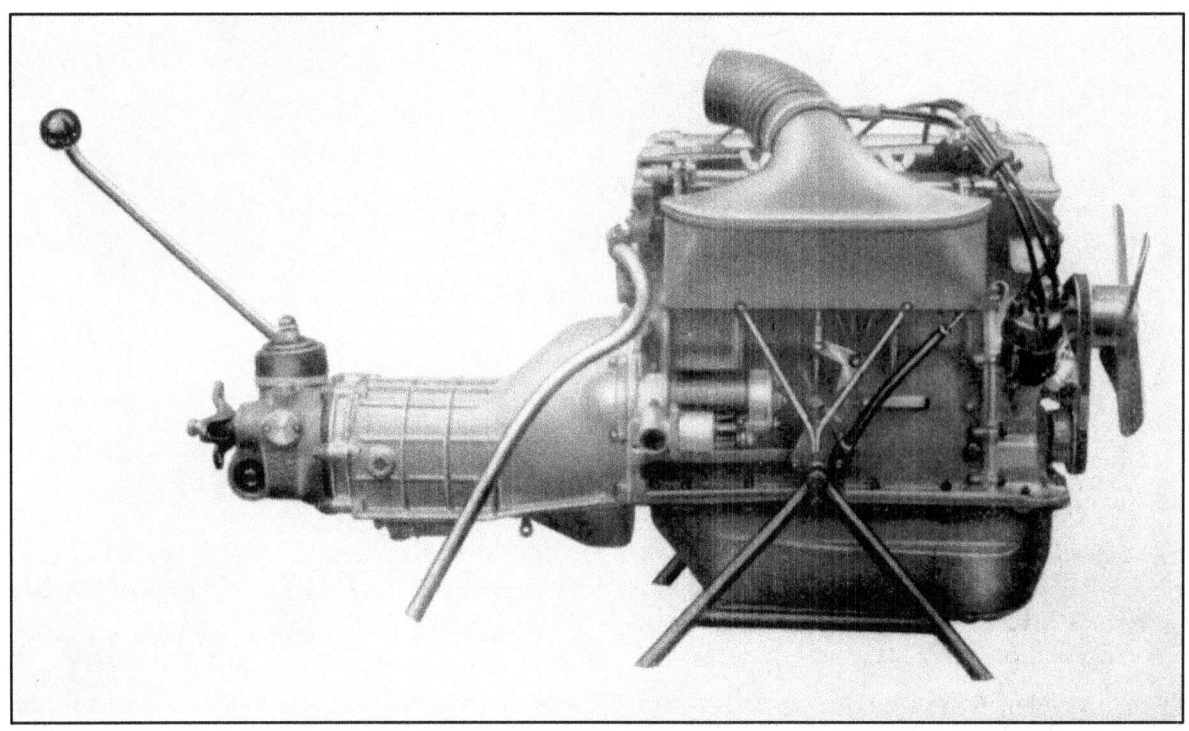

Fig. 4 - Engine and gearbox (transmission) seen from the inlet side (Giulietta Sprint Veloce and Spider Veloce)

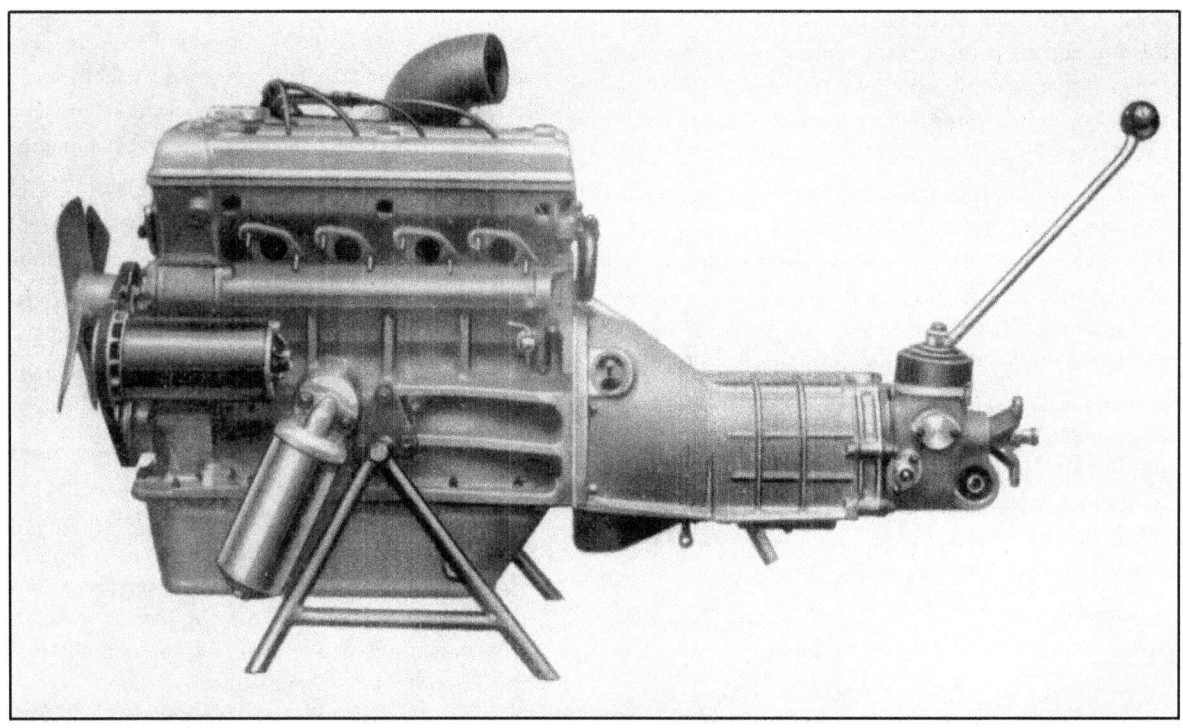

Fig. 4 bis - Engine and gearbox (transmission) seen from the exhaust side (Giulietta Sprint Veloce and Spider Veloce)

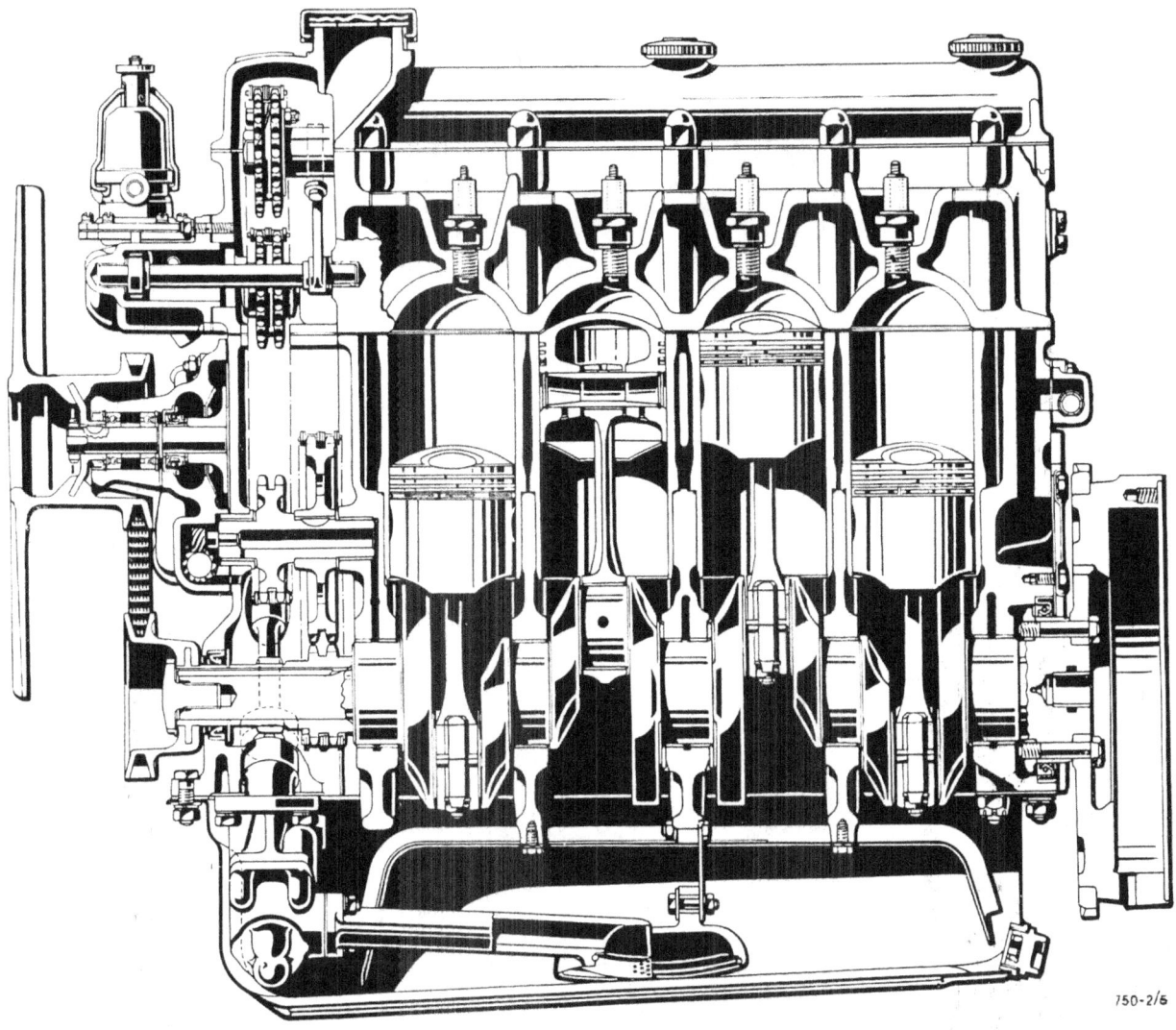

Fig. 5 - Longitudinal section through the engine

ENGINE TUNING

Engine tuning consists of a series of checks, measurements and adjustments designed to eliminate any cause of defective operation and to obtain maximum performance from both the engine and the rest of the car.

Such adjustment must be made at the time of the regular periodical inspections, and also whenever any major unit has to be replaced or a reasonably large repair effected.

Tuning operations may be divided into 3 groups as described hereunder. When the 1st group has been completed, carry out group 2, and group 3 if any defect is still noticeable in the running of the engine.

It is also advisable to carry out the three groups of adjustments whenever perfect engine tuning is required.

GROUP 1

a) **Check that all plugs produce a proper spark;** this can be done with the engine running by earthing the central electrode of the sparking plug by means of a screwdriver with an insulated handle (Fig. 7). II the plug is working properly, the engine speed will drop as soon as the screw-driver earths the plug, while the speed will remain the same if the plug is defective.

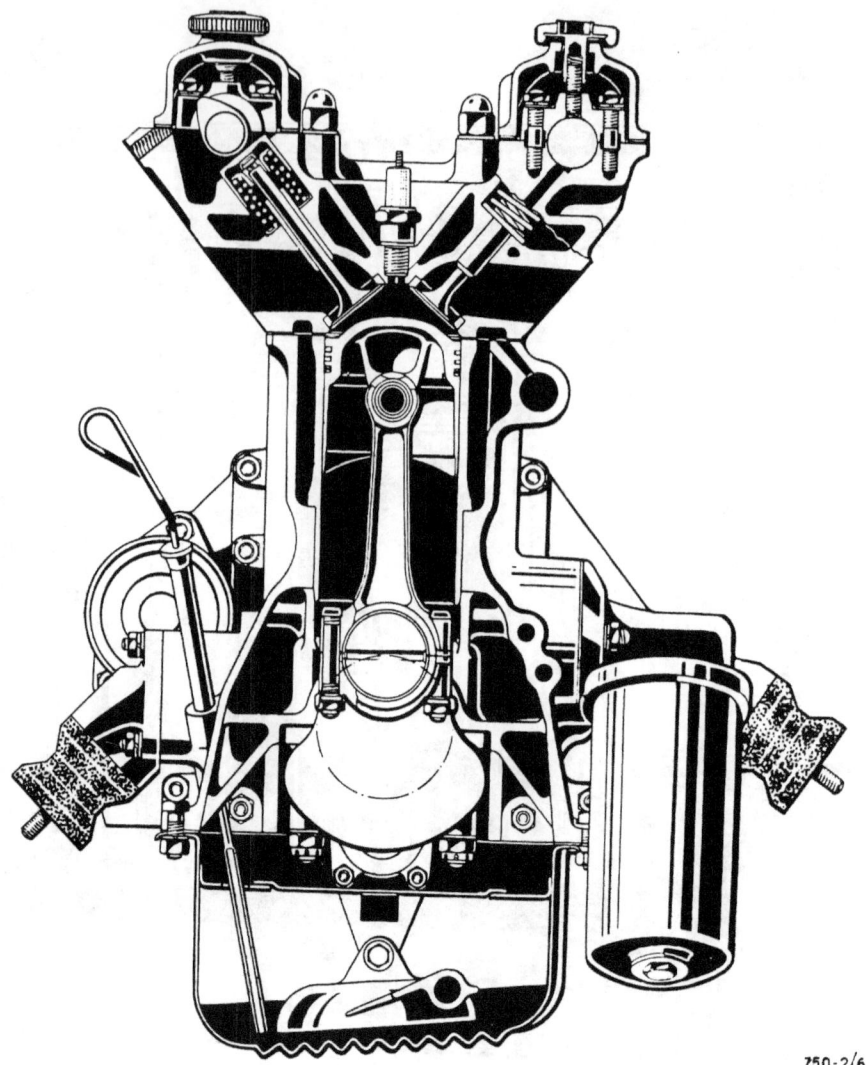

Fig. 6 - Cross section through the engine

Do not remove the plug lead or the distributor condensor may be damaged.

A more accurate inspection of sparking plug efficiency can be carried out on the test bench as described in part 10 under « Electrical Equipment ».

Sparking plug efficiency may also be reduced by the radio interference suppressors fitted to each plug; check that the suppressor resistance is in fact that stated on the casing. Remove the plugs, clean them and bring the electrode gap to 0.6 mm. (fig. 8).

Excessive electrode gap can cause faulty sparking with, as a consequence, a falling-off of engine power; if the electrode gap is less than 0.6 mm., dirty electrodes and irregular running at idling speeds will result.

b) **Check that the distributor cap** is free of cracks, corrosions, traces of carbon on the internal faces or condensation deposits. Check that the carbon contact slides freely inside the cap under the action of its spring (fig. 9).

c) **Check that the breaker contacts** are not corroded, rusted or blackened; check that the contact gaps are from 0.35 to 0.40 mm. (fig. 10). In addition, make

Fig. 7 - Testing the spark plugs with a screwdriver

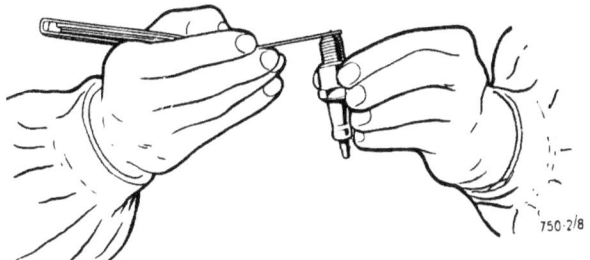

Fig. 8 - Checking the spark gap spark plugs

sure that the rotor arm is free to rotate around its pin even when the engine is cold; do not lubricate the rotor arm pin; for instructions regarding distributor lubrication see Part 10.

d) **Check the ignition timing**; this should be done with the stroboscopic device described in detail in Part 10 under « Electrical Equipement ». If this stro-

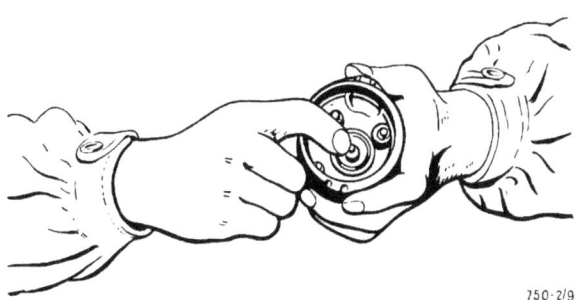

Fig. 9 - Checking the sliding of the carbon brush in its seat

boscopic instrument is not available, proceed as follows:

turn the crankshaft to bring the piston in cylinder 1 to the ignition phase; this position is reached when both valves are closed and the letters **« AF »** — cut into the flywheel — appear in the centre of the inspection windows. Check whether slight rotation of the engine in the proper operating direction (clockwise when seen from the front) causes the distributor contacts to begin to open.

This check must be made with a pilot lamp as follows:

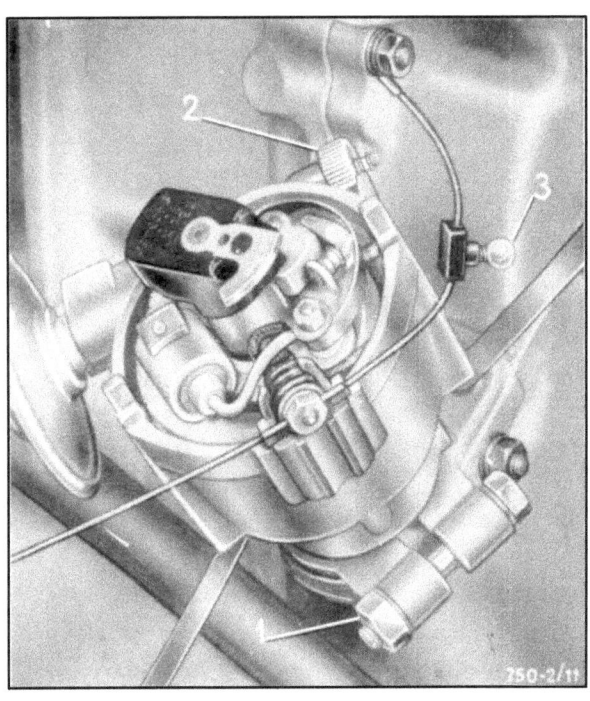

Fig 11 - Checking the instant the contact breaker points open:
1. Bolt locking the distributor - **2.** Knurled nut to correct the ignition advance - **3.** Test lamp for contact breaker points opening.

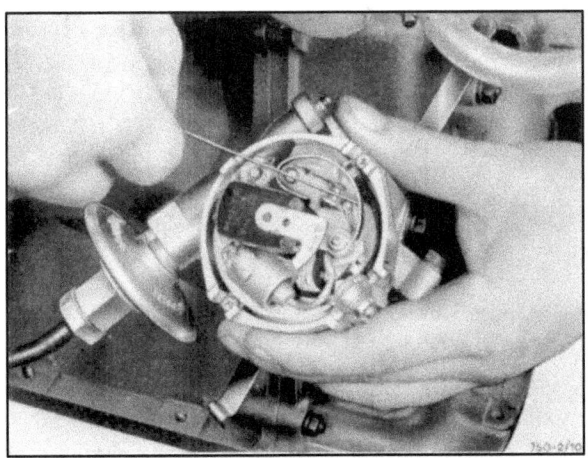

Fig. 10 - Checking the opening of the contact breaker points

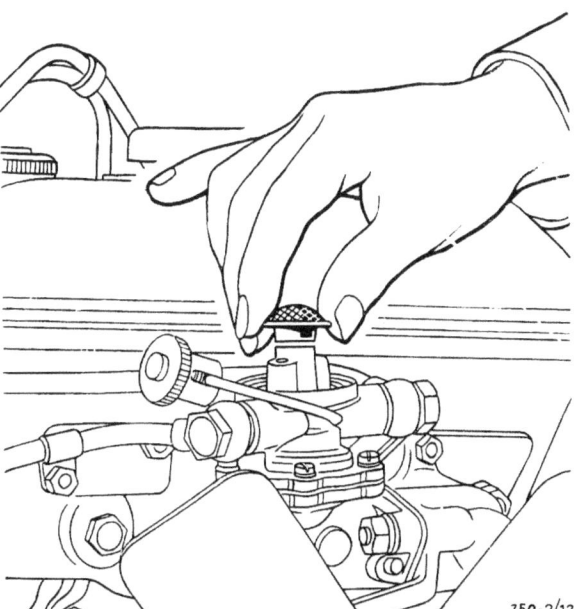

Fig. 12 - Removing the filter from the petrol (gasoline) pump

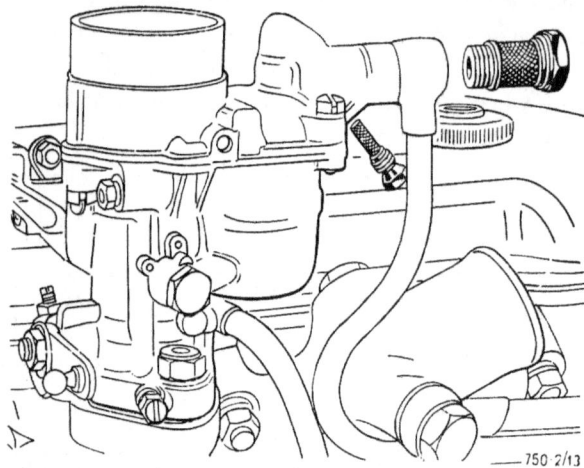

Fig. 13 - Carburetter Solex C 32 BIC for Giulietta Berlina: fuel filters

as shown in fig. 11, insert a 12 V. bulb between the feed terminal on the distributor and the earth; the bulb will light up immediately the contacts open.

Small timing corrections can be obtained by turning the knurled nut **2** (fig. 11); tightening or loosening the nut retards or advances the ignition. Corrections of greater magnitude are made as follows:

— slacken the nut on the locking bolt **1** (fig. 11);
— turn the distributor body clockwise to retard the ignition or anti-clockwise to advance it.

e) Remove the cup on the body of the fuel pump, **take out the gauze filter** and carefully wash it in petrol (fig. 12).

f) **Take out the fuel filters,** mounted on the cover of the Solex C 32 BIC carburetter fitted to the Giulietta Berlina, and wash them in petrol (fig. 13).

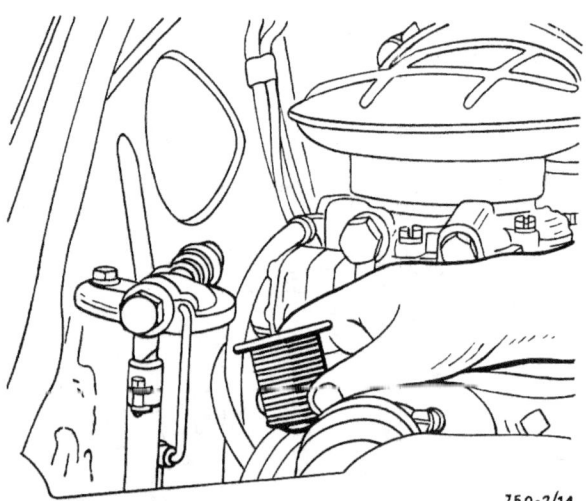

Fig. 14 - Additional Fuel filter for Giulietta Sprint

g) **Dismantle the element in the additional fuel filter** fitted to the Giulietta Sprint, and wash it in petrol (fig. 14).

h) **Remove the carburetter jet-holders** (figs. 15, 16 and 135) and clean the jets with compressed air; do not use a metal spike, as the orifice diameter must not under any circumstances be altered.

Fig. 15 - Carburetter Solex C 32 BIC for Giulietta Berlina
1. Main Jet - **2.** Idling Jet - **3.** Starter Jet

Fig. 16 - Carburetter Solex 35 APAIG for Giulietta t.i., Sprint and Spider.
1. Main jet of the choke tube N. 1 - **2.** Main Jet of the choke tube N. 2 - **3.** Idling Jet - **4.** Acceleration Pump Jet - **5.** Starter Jet.

i) **Adjust the engine idling speed** as described under « Carburation » in Part 2 B.

l) **Check the tension of the belt driving** the dynamo and the fan; belt tension can be increased by moving the dynamo outwards after first slackening the top nut on the tensioning device **1** (fig. 17) and the two nuts on the bottom bolts **2** (fig. 17) which fix the dynamo to the crank-case; in order not to make the belt too tight, as this would damage the dynamo and the water-pump bearings, make sure that the amount of slack shown in fig. 18 is not exceeded.

Fig. 17 - Tensioning the fan and dynamo driving belt:
1. Tensioning device - 2. Lower Pins

NOTE: To facilitate the slackening of the nuts on the bottom bolts, special plates designed to lock the bolts while the nuts are being loosened have recently been fitted to all new cars; we advise owners to fit these plates to all earlier models which were supplied without them.

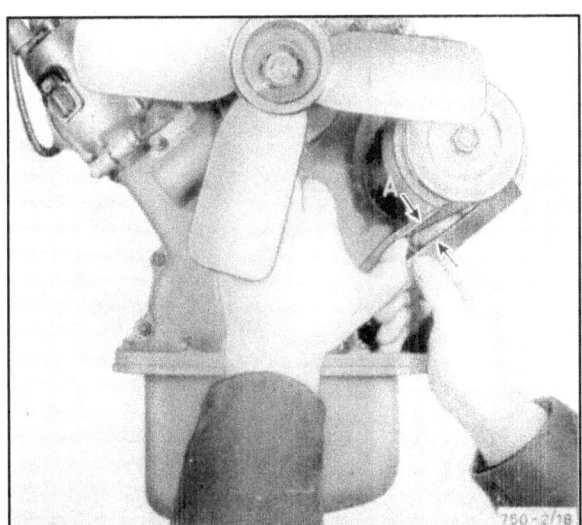

Fig. 18 - Checking the tension of the fan and dynamo driving belt
A $= 1 \div 1.5$ cm.

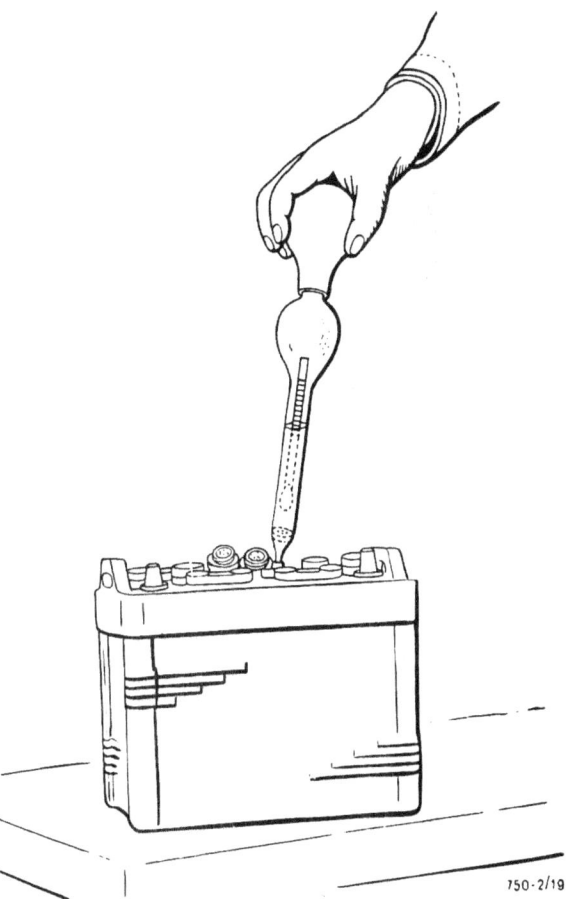

Fig. 19 - Checking the battery charge by means of a hydrometer

GROUP 2

a) **Check the battery**; its state and charge can be checked; after stopping the engine, by a densimeter (fig. 19); the electrolyte reading should be between

Fig. 20 - Individual-cell voltage tester

Fig. 21 - Restoring the electrolyte level in the battery

1.24 and 1.28 (equal to 27.9 and 31.5 Beaumé degrees).

If distilled water has been added, the specific gravity should be measured after mixing is complete; to speed up mixing, charge the battery for half an hour.

The charge in the various cells of the battery can be measured by means of a fork-type voltmeter (fig. 20); the cell is properly charged when the reading is between 1.5 and 1.9. V.

WARNING: As the cells tend to discharge when the voltmeter is applied to their terminals, the voltmeter should only rest on the terminals for a matter of seconds.

b) **Check that the terminals** on the battery leads are tightly secured; before being connected they should be coated with pure viscous vaseline.

c) **Check that the level of the electrolyte** in the battery is 4 to 5 mm. above the top of the plates; this can be checked by resting a wooden stick on the top of the plates. A special filler incorporating a nozzle with a valve preventing the passage of water when the above level is reached (fig. 21) allows the level to be checked at the time of topping up the battery.

d) **Check the condition of the high-tension leads** and make sure that they are undamaged; if their insulation is in any way defective, replace them. Check that they are properly connected to the distributor and to the sparking plugs.

e) **Check the condenser** fitted to the distributor; instructions will be found in Part 10 under « Electric Equipment »; a short-circuited condenser, or one with poor insulation, will mean insufficient voltage with, as a consequence, either a poor spark or no spark at all.

f) **Check the efficiency of the ignition coil** as described in Part 10 under « Electrical Equipment ».

g) **Check the engine compression** as follows: warm up the engine until it reaches the normal operating temperature, with the throttle fully open, and remove all the sparking plugs.

Connect the compression gauge to the various cylinders, one at a time, by screwing the connector into the sparking plug hole as shown in fig. 22.

Turn the engine by the starter motor, making sure that the connector is gas-tight, and read off the compression.

Before making the test, ensure that the battery is well charged so as to ensure a sufficient engine rotation speed.

If the compression readings for the various cylinders do not differ by more than 10% of the maximum reading it is considered that all the cylinders are in the same condition; on the other hand, if in one or more cylinders the compression reading is less than the above minimum, the reason must be found.

This is done by beginning with the valve seating and proceeding to an inspection of the compression rings and the pistons themselves.

The cylinder compression can also be measured by a recording instrument (fig. 23) which traces the maximum compression in each cylinder on a graph. The

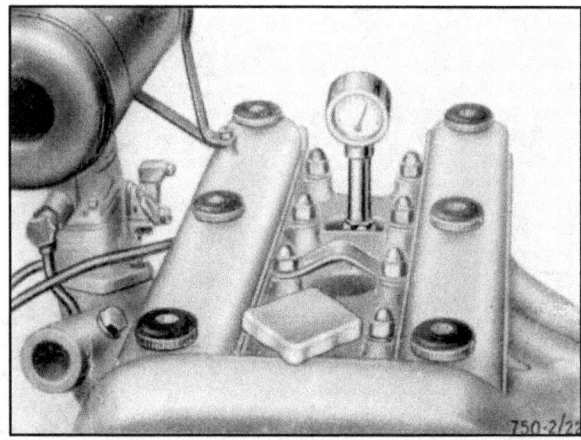

Fig. 22 - Checking the compression on the cylinder by means of a manometer

same procedure as described above for the compression gauge is also used in this case.

GROUP 3

a) **Ensure that the cylinder-head and inlet manifold nuts are tight.** Work on the engine when hot, and use a torque wrench as shown in figure 24. The torque load for the cylinder-head nuts is from 6 to 6.5 kgm. The nuts should be tightened in the order shown in fig. 25.

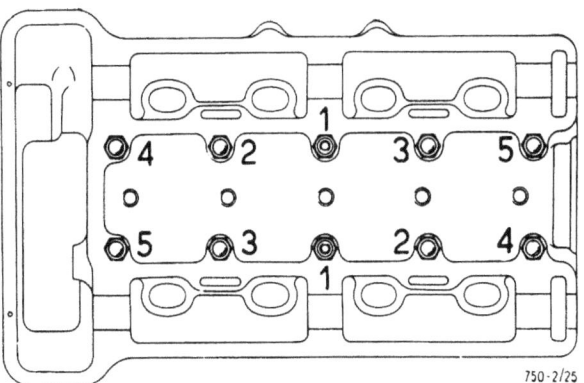

Fig. 25 - Locking order of the cylinder-head nuts

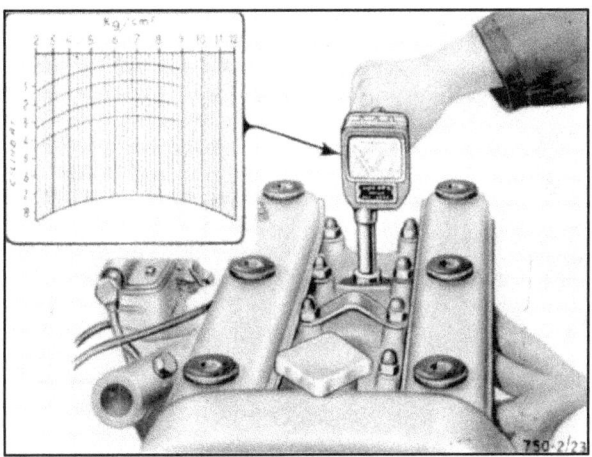

Fig. 23 - Cylinder compression test by means of a recording indicator

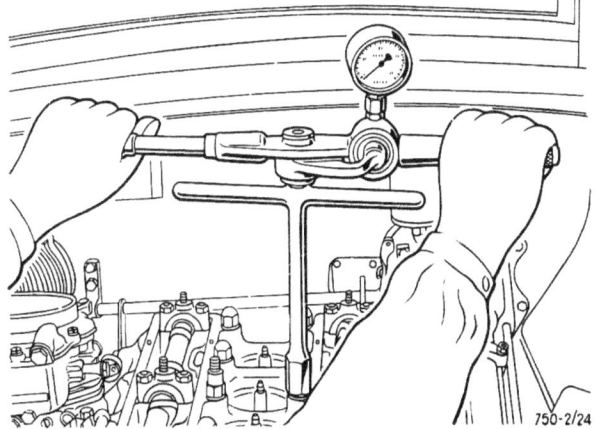

Fig. 24 - Checking the torque for tightening the nuts of the cylinder - head

b) **Check the gap between valves and tappets** as described in Chapter 4.

c) **Check the ignition timing** as described in Chapter 3.

d) **Clean the carburetter** as described in the Chapter entitled « Carburation » in Part 2 B.

e) **Check the operation of the fuel pump** as described in the Chapter entitled « Fuel Feed » in Part 2 B.

f) **Ensure that all joints in the fuel feed pipe are tight.**

g) **Check to ensure that the oil pressure** is as follows:
— max. pressure at max. revs.: 4.5 to 5 kg/cm^2
— min.   »   »   »   »   : 3,5 kg/cm^2
— »   »   »   min. »   : 0,5 to 1 kg/cm^2

If the oil pressure is not within the above limits the cause must be sought. In this connection the instructions in Chapter 2 regarding the oil pump and those in Chapter 10 regarding the main and big-end bearings must be carefully complied with.

On completion of the above adjustments, the vehicle must be roadtested to make sure that they have been properly performed.

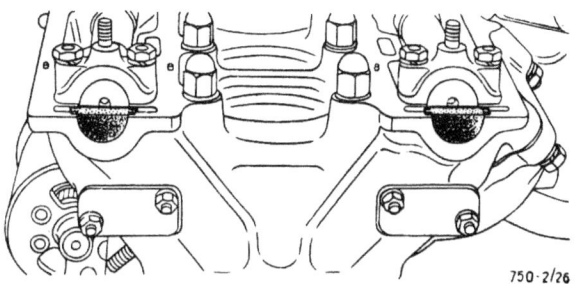

Fig. 26 - Oil sealings on the cylinder head in front of the rear camshafts ends

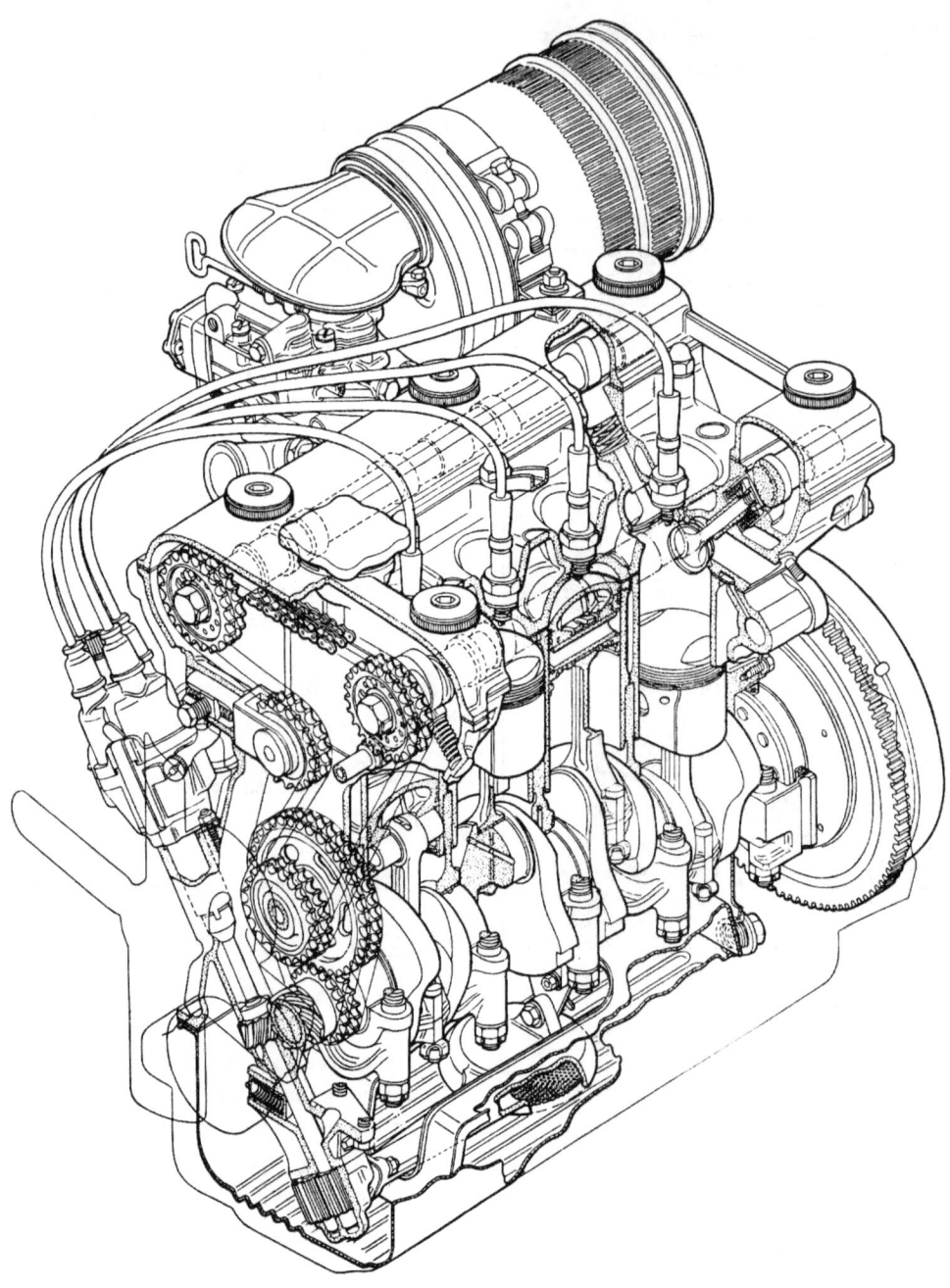

Fig. 27 - Section through the timing gear engine.

ENGINE OVERHAUL

By engine overhaul is meant the whole of the work which must be carried out after the car has covered a certain distance, with a view to replacing any worn parts. In this way the engine will regain its initial characteristics and will again develop its original power.

In all cases of major overhaul it is always necessary to remove the engine from the car and make the repairs while the engine rests on a stand designed for that purpose.

Sometimes, however, partial overhauls are necessary to eliminate some particular running defect; it may then be unnecessary to remove the engine from the car.

The following chapters will therefore deal firstly with those repairs which can be carried out without removing the engine, and secondly with those for which it is necessary to mount the engine on a special stand.

WORK NOT REQUIRING REMOVAL OF THE ENGINE

1 - REMOVING THE VALVE COVER

The cover must be removed for the following reasons:

- to replace the oil retaining gasket
- to check the valve timing
- to check the clearance between valves and tappets
- to replace a chain.

Dismantling

1) Remove the ignition leads
2) Remove the air cleaner
3) Loosen the round-headed nuts on the cover and lift off the cover itself.

Re-assembly

Repeat the above in reverse order, after first checking all mating surfaces.

WARNING

1) **Whenever the cover has to be re-fitted, no matter what the reason for its removal, we recommend the fitting of a new gasket which should first be smeared with grease or jointing compound.**

2) **Before re-assembly, examine the rubber seals used to close the holes through which the cam-shaft seats are bored (see fig. 26).**

2 - TIMING CHAINS

The cam-shafts are driven through two chains (fig. 27). The first chain serves to step down the engine speed; it is driven by a sprocket mounted on the front end

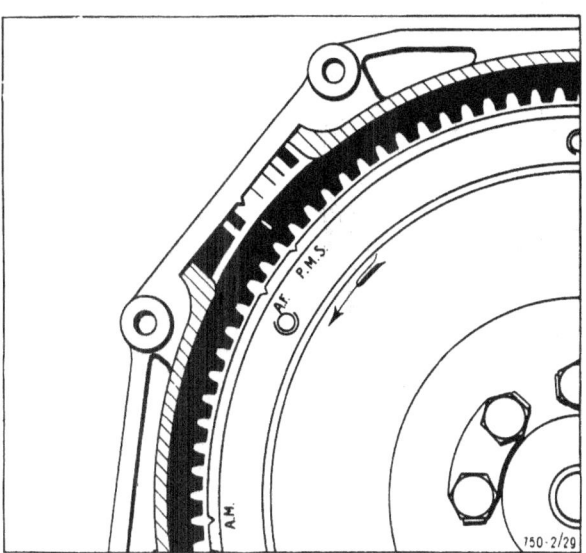

Fig. 29 - Timing marks stamped on the Flywheel:
P.M.S. Top Dead Center of Cylinder 1 at the ignition stroke - **A.F.** Fixed Advance of the distributor - **A.M.** Maximum Advance of the distributor

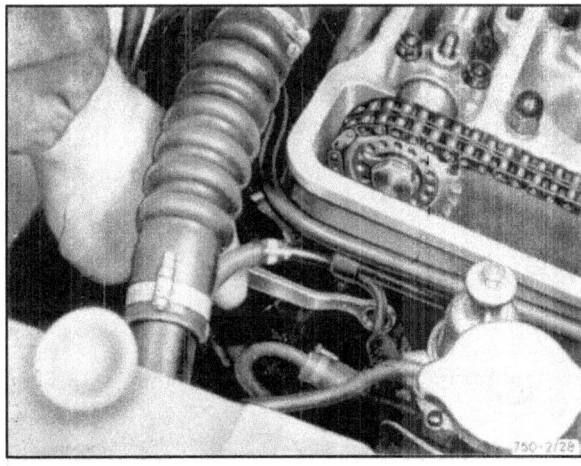

Fig. 28 - Loosening the screw locking the chain-tensioning

of the crank-shaft and drives the intermediate gear, while the second chain drives the cam-shaft.

A - THE CAM-SHAFT CHAIN

Adjusting chain tension

The tension of the chain must always correspond to the load of the spring on the chain tensioning device; it is adjusted as follows:

a) slacken the locking bolt on the tensioning device (fig. 28);

b) make sure that the tensioning device is not locked as a result of the earlier excessive tightening of the above bolt;

c) allow the engine to turn over at idling speed so that the tensioning device may tighten the chain; if the engine is not running, turn it over by hand or by means of the starter motor, after first replacing the sparking plugs by suitable perforated blank plugs which, while allowing the engine to rotate without cylinder compression, prevent foreign bodies from entering the cylinders;

d) tighten the above-mentioned locking bolt, taking care to avoid excessive tightening which might cause damage to the wedge beneath it and thereby impede the operation of the tensioning device.

NOTE: Instructions for dismantling and inspecting the chain tensioning device are given in Chapter 6.

Fig. 30 - Chain driving the cam-shafts: detail of the demountable link

Dismantling

1) Turn the engine until:

   a) piston No. 1 is at T.D.C. at ignition stroke (fig. 29);

   b) the separable link of the chain is between the two sprockets driving the cam-shafts (fig. 30).

2) Slacken the locking bolt on the chain tensioning sprocket, move the tensioning device outwards into the position of an un-tensioned chain, and lock it in that position.

3) To one end of the chain attach a copper wire approximately 1,5 m. in length; pull out the chain, in such a way that the wire trials behind it and follows its course; when the whole of the chain is removed, detach it from the wire which will remain in position so that the chain may later be easily replaced. Unless this is done, it will be impossible to re-fit the chain without dismantling the front end-cover.

WARNING: Until the chain is re-fitted the crank-shaft must not be rotated as the reference marks cut in the pinion keyed to the crankshaft and on the intermediate gear-wheel cannot be seen without removing the front end-cover, and this makes it impossible to return them to their proper positions.

Inspection

Cable stretch is checked by measuring the chain on the trestle firstly with the links close together and secondly pulled as far apart as possible; the difference between the two measurements must not exceed 6 mm.; if the difference is greater than 6 mm., a new chain must be fitted.

Re-assembly

a) with the crankshaft in the above-mentioned position, and with the camshaft in the position shown

Fig. 32 - Screw fastening a sprocket on its camshaft.

in fig. 31, fit the chain while carefully tensioning the two ends not subjected to the action of the tensioning device; then re-join the separable link;

b) again slacken the locking bolt on the tensioning device; then tighten it after the spring thrust has been applied.

B - DRIVING CHAIN FOR THE INTERMEDIATE SPROCKET

This chain should be dismantled and checked as described in Chapter 12.

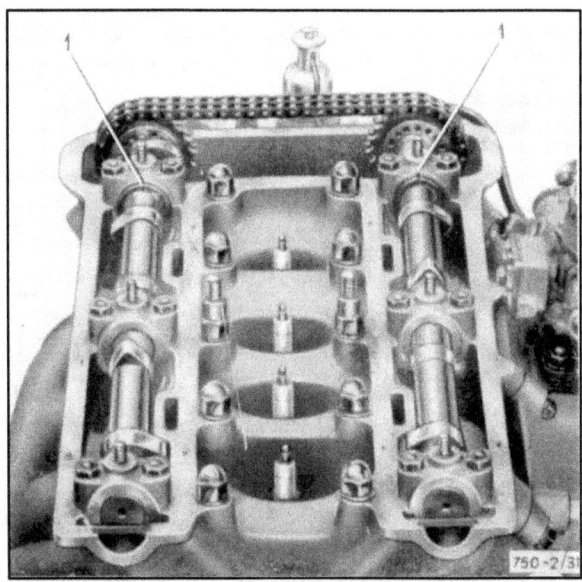

Fig. 31 - Timing marks (1) cut in the camshafts

3 - VALVE TIMING

Valve timing is correct when, with the No. 1 cylinder piston at T.D.C. on the ignition stroke, the reference line on the flywheel (marked P.M.S. = T.D.C.) is in line with the mark through the centre of the inspection hole (fig. 29) and the reference marks **1** (fig. 31) on the cam-shafts are in line with those on the front camshaft bearings. If due to cable stretch or any other cause, the marks on the camshaft (piston No. 1 being at T.D.C.) have moved out of alignment by an angle greater than 2° (or 1 mm), the following instructions should be followed:

1) Slacken the screw holding the sprocket on the cam-shaft (fig. 32);

2) remove the small bolt holding down the cam-shaft driving sprocket (fig. 33);

3) by means of the appropriate pin wrench (tool No. 6121.24.012 - fig. 34), rotate the cam-shaft until the reference marks are re-aligned;

4) re-fit the small bolt, tighten the screw and bend back the locking plate.

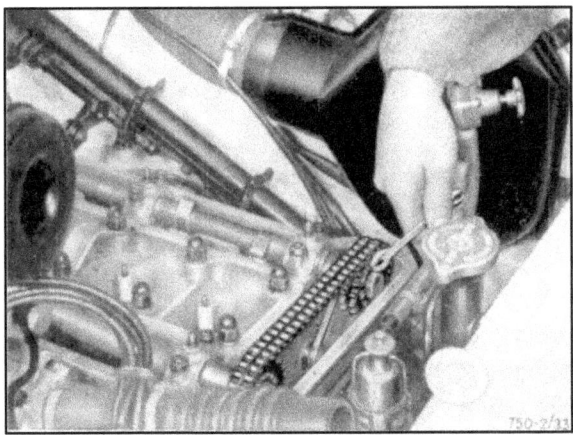

Fig. 33 - Bolt locking a sprocket on its camshaft.

4 - CHECKING AND ADJUSTING VALVE CLEARANCE

A) Checking the clearance

1) Rotate the cam-shaft until a portion of the quieting arc of the corresponding cam is in line with the valve.

2) With the engine cold, and using the appropriate feeler gauge, measure the clearance at each individual inlet and exhaust valve; make a note of each measurement.

3) If the clearance at any valve is greater or less by 0.025 mm. than the values shown in the under-

Fig. 34 - Making a camshaft rotate with regard to its driving sprocket by means of the tool 6121.24.012

noted table, the end cap fitted on the valve stem (fig. 36) must be replaced by another of suitable thickness.

Type of engine	Valve clearances			
	inlet		exhaust	
	when fitted mm.	at limit of wear mm.	when fitted mm.	at limit of wear mm.
Giulietta Berlina, t.i., Sprint and Spider	from 0.425 to 0.45	minimum clearance 0.40 maximum clearance 0.475	from 0.475 to 0.5	minimum clearance 0.45 maximum clearance 0.525

Note - For the complete data see also « **Distribution** » table on part 1.

Replacement end caps are supplied in all thickness from 1.5 to 2.5 mm., rising by 0.025 mm. so that the above-mentioned clearances can be obtained to within very fine limits.

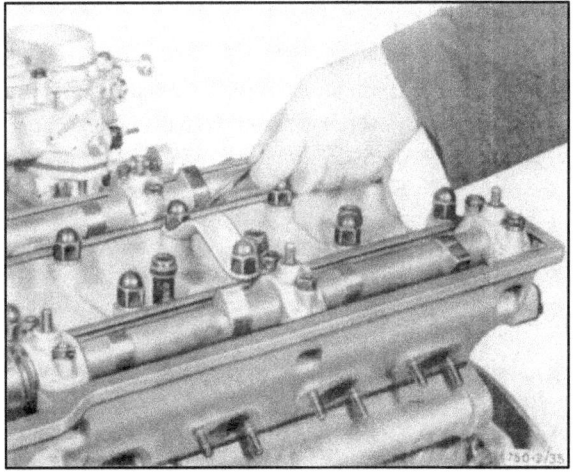

Fig. 35 - Checking with a feeler gauge the valve clearance.

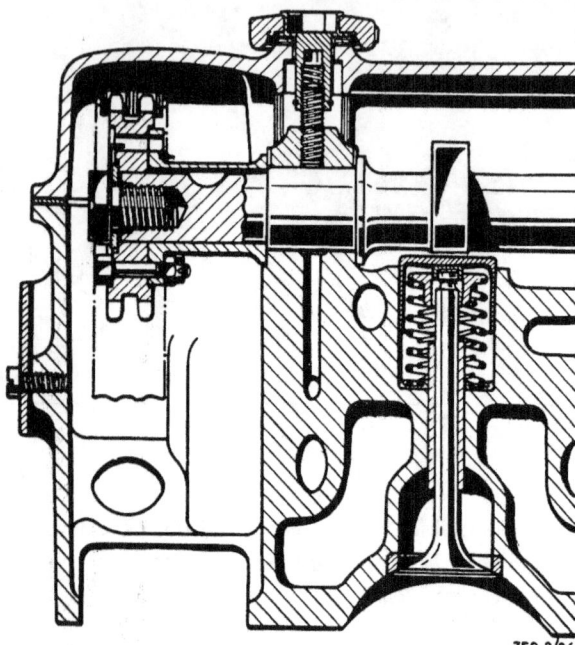

Fig. 36 - Details of the valve clearance adjustment

B) Adjusting valve clearances

When inspection has shown that end cap replacement is essential, adjustment is performed as follows:

1) Dismantle the valve gear as described in paragraphs 1) and 2) of Chapter 2, bearing in mind the warning given at the end of the description of the dismantling procedure.

2) At both ends of the chain fix a length of wire to prevent the chain from falling into the interior of the engine.

3) Disconnect the cam-shafts one at a time.

4) One at a time, dismantle the valve end caps to be changed; onto each valve stem place a new end cap of the correct thickness to that the difference between the new end cap and the old is the same as the difference between the clearance (as measured before dismantling the cam-shafts) and the correct value as given above; e.g., if the clearance measured is 0.60 mm. while it should be 0.45 mm., the thickness of the new end cap must be equal to the thickness of the end cap removed plus 0.60 minus 0.45 = 0.15 mm.

5) Re-assemble the cam-shafts and the chain as described in Chapter 2.

5 - REMOVING THE CYLINDER HEAD FROM THE CRANK-CASE

Dismantling

1) Drain the cooling water from the entire circuit.

2) Remove the rubber water hose from the cylinder head and the heater, and disconnect the vacuum ignition advance control from the distributor.

3) Disconnect the petrol feed pipe by unscrewing the pump terminal.

4) From the carburetter remove the air cleaner, the flexible cables leading to the easy starting control and the hand accelerator, and the rod links to the carburetter control rocker arm.

5) Remove the exhaust manifold, using the 14 mm. socket wrench (spanner) for the bottom nuts (this must be done from underneath) and the spanner with off-set handles for the top nuts. This manifold, after removal of the nuts, must be slid off the studs on which it rests; to do this the bracket (carrying the exhaust pipe and fitted to the gearbox) must be removed from underneath.

6) Remove the sparking plugs and replace them by suitable protective blanks.

7) Remove the cylinder-head cover as described in Chapter 2.

8) Disconnect the cam-shaft driving chain as described in Chapter 2, taking care first of all to turn the crankshaft until the No. 1 piston is at T.D.C. at the end of the compression stroke.

9) Remove the bolts holding the cylinder-head to the crank-case, reversing the order described in fig. 25; lift off the cylinder-head and remove the gasket.

WARNING

1) **The cylinder-head must never be removed from the cylinder block when the engine is hot as serious deformation might well be the result. Care should be taken at all times to avoid causing damage to the gasket between the cylinder-block and the cylinder-head.**

2) **Replace gaskets whenever damaged or when the internal edges of the holes corresponding to the cylinder show traces of burning. The best thing is to fit a new gasket every time the cylinder-head is removed.**

Inspection

Examination of the bearing surface of the cylinder-head must be carried out on a flat master template.

The maximum permissible gap between the cylinder-head and the crank-case is 0.05 mm.

Scrape where necessary, but only the essential minimum, or grind level.

Re-assembly

1) Place the gasket in position and slide the cylinder-head over the bolts set in the block.

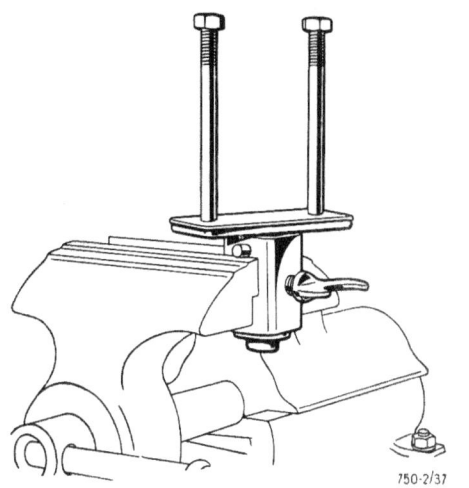

Fig. 37 - Tool No. 6121.01.274 to be employed with the vice for dismantling the cylinder-head

7) Refit the sparking plugs, re-connect the fuel pipe, water hose and ignition advance vacuum device, connect the link rods and flexible carburetter controls.

8) Re-fit the air cleaner.

9) Refill the radiator with water.

10) Check, with the engine hot, to ensure that no oil or water is leaking through the gaskets; check the oil pressure and water temperature.

6 - DISMANTLING AND OVERHAULING THE CYLINDER-HEAD

The following instructions must be complied with when:

— checking and replacing valves and valve parts;
— re-grinding valves and valve seats.

2) Tighten the cylinder-head nuts, using a torque spanner (fig. 24), before coldly with a 6 kgm torque loading and after hotly with a 6,5 kgm one; the tightening order is shown in fig. 25.

3) Re-fit the chain as described in Chapter 2.

4) Time the ignition as described in the chapter entitled « Engine Adjustment ».

5) Smear a little engine oil on the cam-shaft seats with a view to facilitating the sliding of the valve cups, and refit the cover.

6) After replacing the gasket, re-fit the exhaust manifold and lock the nuts securing it to the cylinder-head; refit the bracket holding the exhaust pipe to the gear-box (transmission).

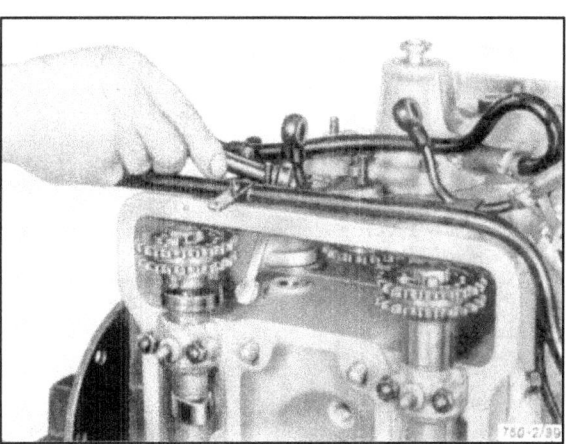

Fig. 39 - Dismantling the fuel pump rocker

Dismantling

To facilitate the above operations it is advisable to mount the cylinder-head on the special slewable bracket (tool No. 6121.01.274) which can be held in any vice (see fig. 37). Then proceed as follows:

1) Drain off the oil in the cam-shaft seats.

2) Remove the inlet manifold together with the carburetter.

3) Remove the fuel pump from its bracket.

4) Remove the caps on the cam-shaft bearings and remove the shafts.

NOTE: Before removing the exhaust valve cam-shaft it is necessary, using a screwdriver, to extract the return spring on the fuel pump rocker arm, taking care to prevent it from falling into the interior of the engine (fig. 38).

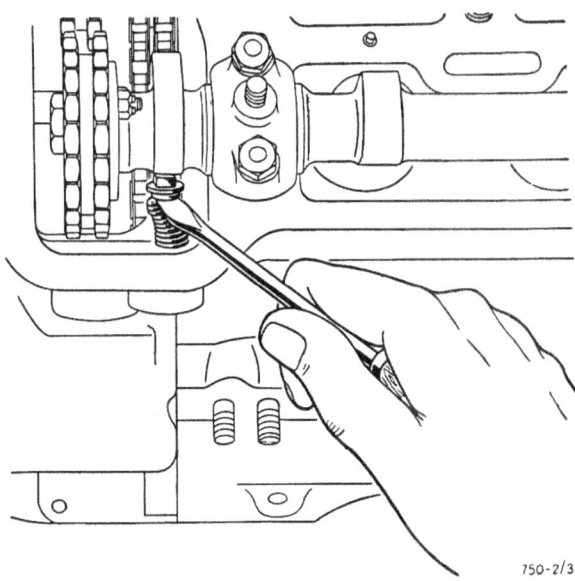

Fig. 38 - Dismantling the release spring of the rocker of the fuel pump

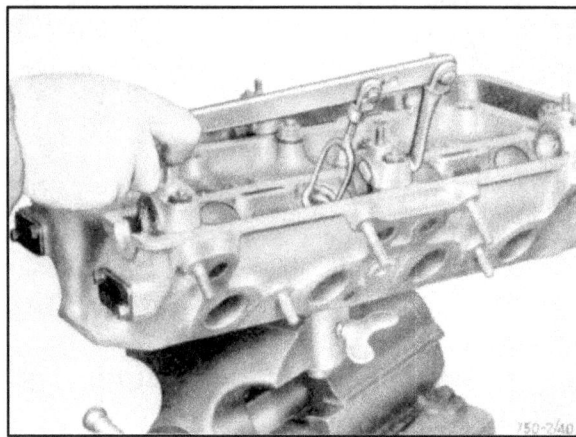

Fig. 40 - Dismantling the cotters of a valve by means of the tool 6121.15.011

5) Remove the fuel pump bracket and its driving shaft.

6) Remove the tappets and the valve clearance adjusting end-caps.

7) Refit the cam-shaft bearing caps and, using tool 6121.15.011 (as shown in fig. 40) on each valve, lower the upper spring seat and withdraw the cotters. Should any difficulty be encountered in removing the cotters apply pressure in the direction of the valve stems.
Extract the valve, remove the upper spring seat, springs and the lower spring seat.

8) Slacken the locking screw on the chain tensioning device (fig. 28) and slide the latter from its seat (fig. 41).

9) When inspection as described above reveals that it is necessary to remove the valve guides, they should be extracted by means of a suitable punch.

NOTE: If an abnormal noise suggests that a valve spring is broken the offending spring can be located and replaced, without removing the cylinder-head, as follows:

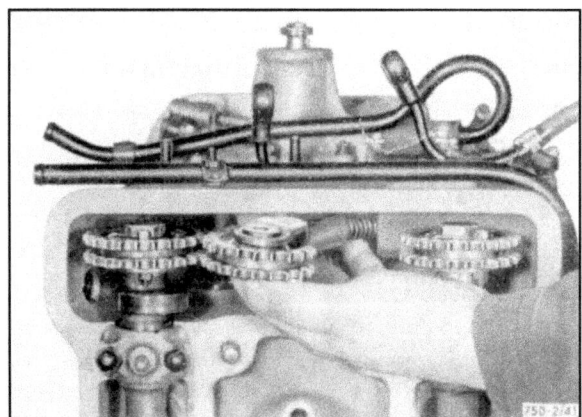

Fig. 41 - Taking off the chain tensioning device from its seating

a) remove the valve cover;

b) turn the engine so as to bring, cylinder by cylinder, the valve tappets into contact with the quieting arc of the cams;

c) using a suitable wooden rod, apply pressure to the tappets (to compare the load it is necessary to depress the tappets themselves), in and endeavour to find out which valve has a broken spring, and then dismantle the appropriate cam-shaft;

d) push into the corresponding spark plug orifice a tool similar to the one illustrated in fig. 43, and apply pressure against the valve head to prevent it from falling into the cylinder and at the same time to allow the cotters, upper spring seat and springs to be dismantled;

e) if, after dismantling, it is found that both springs on one valve have broken, it will be necessary to remove the cylinder-head to ascertain whether or not the piston has been damaged by the valve; it is also necessary to remove the cylinder-head in all case of uncertainty as to which valve spring has broken.

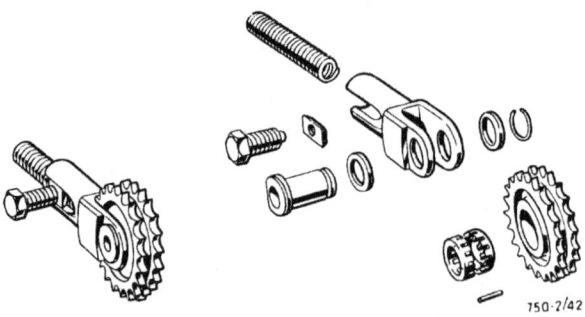

Fig. 42 - Chain tightener complete and in exploded view

Inspection

a) **Checking the condition of the cylinder-head surfaces.**

Examine for superficial or deep scratches; using a wire brush and a scraper, remove all carbon deposits from the combustion chamber and, where possible, the scale from the cooling circuit; wash the cooling circuit with a solution of water and washing soda or with a 15/20% solution of water and hydrochloric acid; the water circuit should then be carefully and repeatedly washed in running water (hot for preference) and then dried with compressed air. The passages-ways should then be tested with a jet of air or water. Smear oil on all bearing and internal surfaces if immediate assembly is not intended. See Chapter 5 for instructions regarding the inspection of the bearing surfaces between the cylinder-head and the cylinder block.

b) **Checking the tappets.**

Tappets which show signs of wear or deep scratching on their heads or rounded surfaces must be replaced at once.

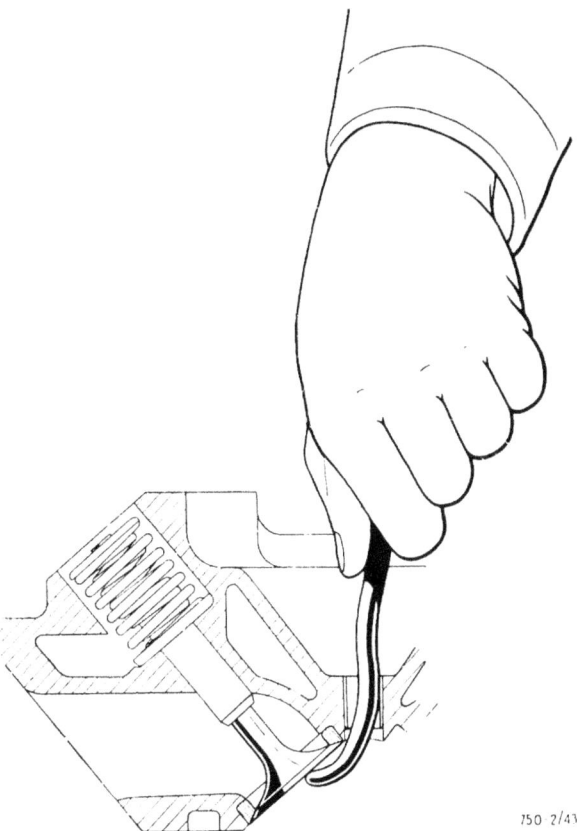

Fig. 43 - Taking off the springs of a valve without dismantling the cylinder head from the block

Tappets diameters **d** and seat diameters **D**, as well as the corresponding clearances, are shown in fig. 44.

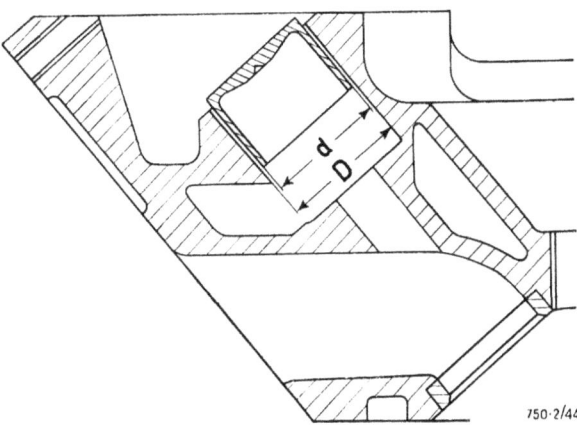

Fig. 44 - Tappets for valves and their seatings on the cylinder heads

Tappet Seat diameter	Normal **d**	32.479 ÷ 32.495 mm
	oversized **d1**	32.679 ÷ 32.695 »
Tappet Seat diameter	Normal **D**	32.500 ÷ 32.516 »
	oversized **D1**	32.700 ÷ 32.716 »
Mounting play **D-d** (or **D1-d1**)		0.005 ÷ 0.037 mm.
Clearance to the wear limit		0.06 mm.

Fig. 45 - Checking the thrust of the valve springs by means of a dynamometer

When the clearances exceed the limits of wear shown in the above-mentioned figure, it is necessary to fit new tappets the diameters of which are increased by **d1** and to re-bore their seats on the cylinder-head to a diameter **D1**.

The clearance must never be checked with a feeler gauge, but only by direct measurement on the tappet and its seat; the seat measurement must be made with a comparator gauge so as to reveal any tendency towards an oval shape. If the seat has worn oval, the clearance to be considered is that corresponding to the maximum diameter.

It is worth mentioning here that the external cylindrical surface of the tappets may have bright spots towards the top and bottom: they however are of no consequence.

NOTE: Giulietta Sprint engines, from. No. 1315.00.116 onwards, are fitted with tappets having an external diameter of 32.5 mm. On engines up to and including No. 1315.00.115 the diameter of the tappets was 32 mm. When replacing tappets on these earlier motors, the seats in the cylinder-head must be re-ground to bring the diameter to 32.5 to 32.516 mm.

c) **Checking the spring thrust.**

Whenever the valves are removed the springs must be checked with a dynamometer as in fig. 45 to ensure that their thrust values in relation to their length are those shown in fig. 46.

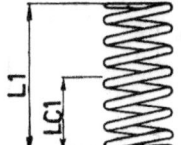
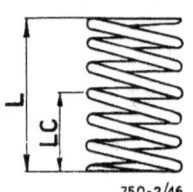
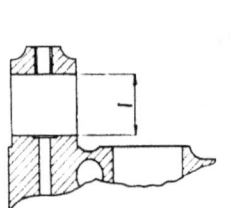

Fig. 46 - Checking data for valve springs

Outer spring	Lenght **LC** (24-25 kg. loaded spring)	43.0 ÷ 44.6 mm.
	Lenght **LC** (24-25 kg. loaded spring)	22.5 »
Inner spring	Lenght **L1** (free spring)	39.35 ÷ 40.95 »
	Length **LC1** (14-15 kg. loaded spring)	21.0 »

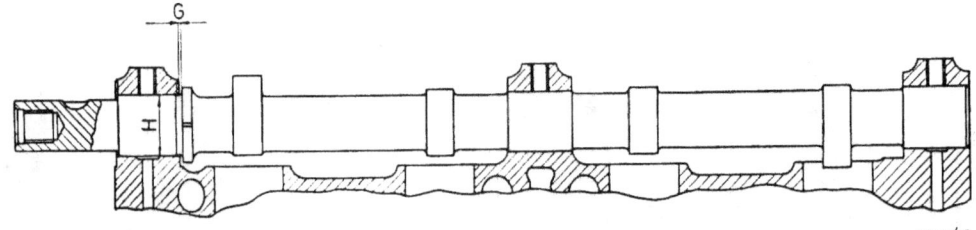

Fig. 47 - Sizes of cam-shaft bearings and pivots

Cam-shaft pivot diameter **H**	26.959 ÷ 26.980 mm.
Cam-shaft pivot seat diameter **I**	27.000 ÷ 27.021 »
Mounting clearance between shaft and pivot **I-H**	0.020 ÷ 0.062 »
Clearance to the wear limit	0.10 »
Axial-clearance between cam-shaft and thrust bearing **G**	0.10 »

d) Checking the cam-shafts.

All surfaces of pins and cams, and the internal surfaces of the bearings, must be smootht and free from scratches or any signs of seizing.

If such blemishes are superficial they may be removed with an abrasive block; if deep, the cam-shaft of bearing caps must be replaced.

The radial clearance between the pins and the bearing seats must conform with the values stated in fig. 47.

e) Checking the valve guides.

Make sure that surfaces of the bore are highly polished and free from scratches, traces of seizing or sticky or carbon deposits; if necessary clean the valve guides with a soft wire brush.

Using a plug gauge (tool 671.3153) as shown in figure 48, check the internal diameter of the valve guides; check the valve stem diameter with a micrometric gauge (fig. 49); the clearance between the guide (when mounted in the cylinder-head) and the valve stem must not exceed the wear limits shown in fig. 50; if that is not the case, replace as necessary.

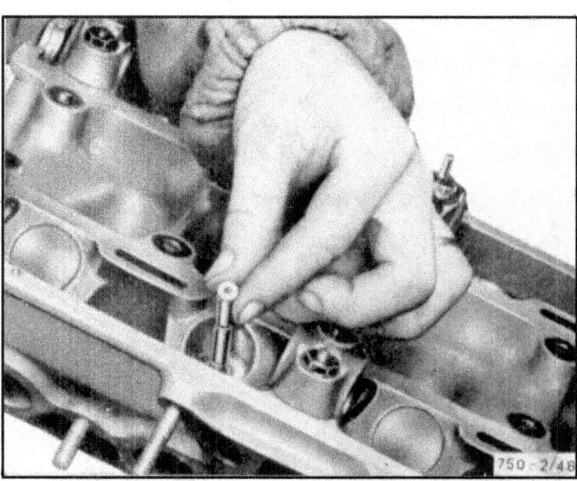

Fig. 48 - Checking the valve guide diameter with a plug gauge No. 671.3153

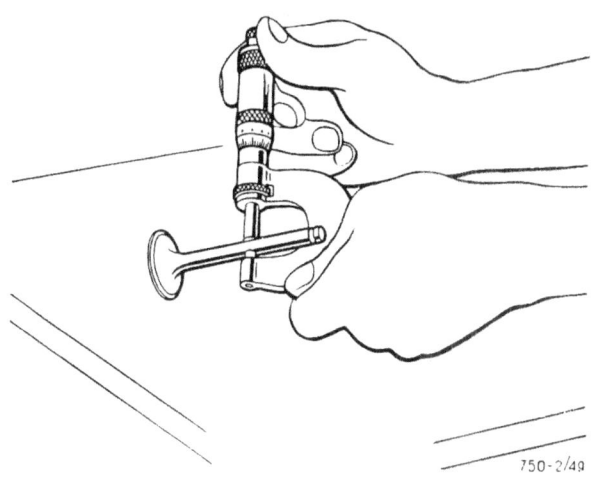

Fig. 49 - Checking the valve stem diameter with a micrometer gauge

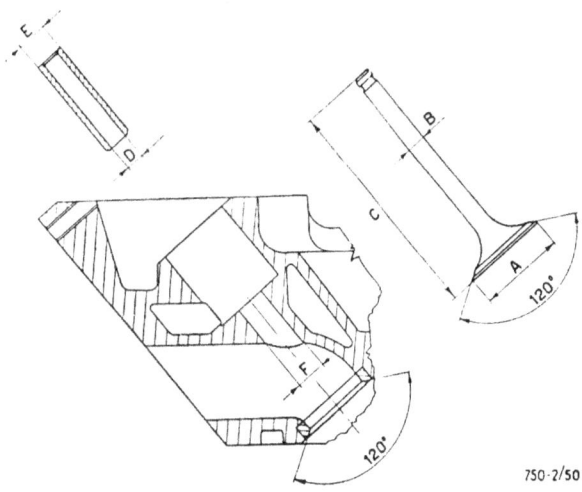

Fig. 50 - Sizes for checking the valves, valve guides and their seats

Valves	Diameter **A** Intake		37 mm.
	Exhaust		34 »
	Stem diameter **B** Intake		7.976÷8.001 »
	Exhaust		7.950÷7.976 »
	Total length **C** Intake		97.75 »
	Exhaust		96.85 »
Valve guides	Diameter **D** (guides fitted)		8.014÷8.026 »
	Diameter **E** (guides dismantled)		13.028÷13.039 »
Clearance between valve stem and guide **D-B**	original (when fitted together)	intake	0.013÷0.050 »
		exhaust	0.038÷0.076 »
	wear limit	intake	0.10 »
		exhaust	0.13 »
Guide seat on cylinder head, diameter **F**			13.000÷13.011 »
Interference between seats and guides **E-F**			0.017÷0.39 »

f) **Checking the valve seats.**

Ensure that the valve seating surfaces and the seats on the cylinder-head are perfectly uniform and free of steps, cracks, etc., so as to ensure perfect mating between the two surfaces.

In cases where the closed valves are not perfectly gas-tight or where the valve seats are slightly scratched or indented, the valves must be ground in.

The above operations are described in detail in the following paragraph.

If the valves or their seats are deeply scratched or indented, the parts concerned should be replaced immediately.

g) **Check the thrust of the chain tensioning spring**; when the spring is compressed to 58 mm., its thrust should be 11.4 to 12.6 kg.

h) Examine the condition of the surfaces of the **locking wedge of the chain tensioning device** and the surfaces of the tensioning device itself.

Grinding-in the valve seating surface.

a) **Valve seating surfaces**

Use a suitable grinding machine as shown in fig. 51; the inlet and exhaust valve angles of inclination are as shown in fig. 50.

Fig. 51 - Grinding the valve seats

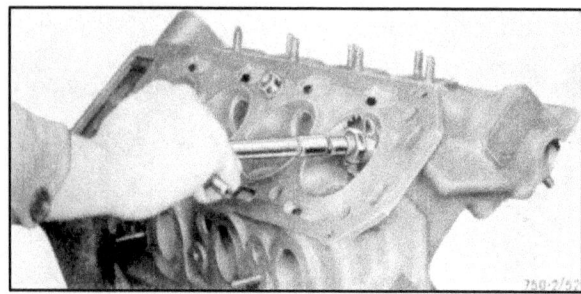

Fig. 52 - Hand grinding the valve seats on the cylinder head

Frequently renew the abrasive surface of the grinding wheel, trueing it from time to time with a diamond tip.

After re-grinding, check that the thickness of the metal in line with the maximum diameter of the valve head is not less than 0.5 mm. If that is not the case, replace the valve.

b) **Valve seats in the cylinder-head**

If the seats are only slightly grooved or pitted, it will be sufficient to re-grind them, otherwise they must be replaced.

Re-grinding requires the following:

1) Remove all carbon deposits with a wire brush.

2) Re-grind the seat by hand or by machine.

    When re-grinding by hand use mandril YA 20453/2 (fig. 52) on which the following cutters are mounted:

— 6549.432.2 in the case of inlet valves;

— 6549.499 in the case of exhaust valves.

    As these two tools actually remove metal as required they must be followed by a hand polishing process using tool 6121.90.006 (fig. 53).

    Re-grinding by machine can be performed with any of the wellknown machines (« Vibrocentric », etc.).

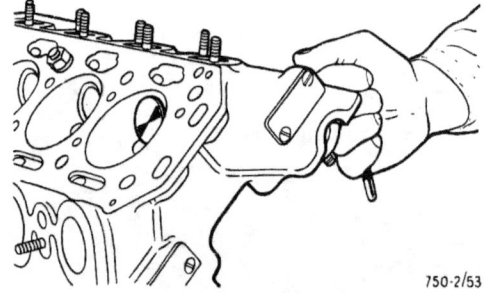

Fig. 53 - Hand emery buffing the valves on their seats, using tool No. 6121.90.006

The removal of valve seats (necessary in all cases of deep pitting or corrosion) requires the removal of the valve seat ring with a milling cutter; the hole diameter is then enlarged slightly.

Fitting the new ring is an operation which must be performed with great care; it has to be forced into the cylinder head as follows:

— machine the replacement ring, tapering it in such a way that the external diameter of the base is 0.1 mm. larger than the diameter of the hole in the cylinder-head, the diameter at the top being equal to the diameter of the hole (fig. 54);

— heat the cylinder-head in an oven to 100-110° C; if this is not possible, immerse it in boiling water;

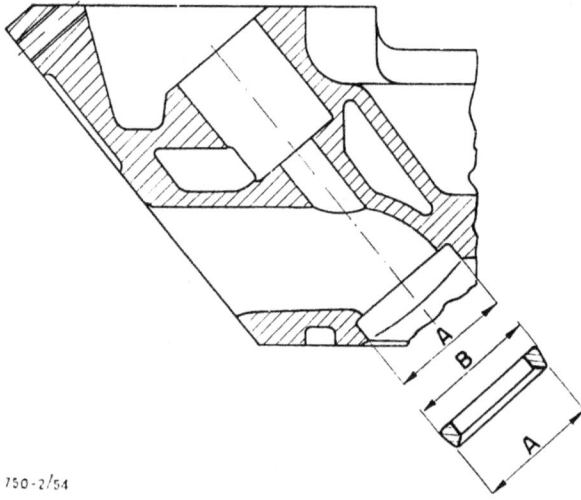

Fig. 54 - Valve seat sizes and their recesses in the cylinder head ($B = A + 0,1$ mm.)

— using the tool 6121.07.290 both for the inlet and exhaust valves, insert the ring in the seat; insert the largest end first in the manner of a dove-tail joint as shown in figure 54;

— then machine the tapered valve seat and polish it as described above.

Checking valves for a tight fit

When the valves are fitted in the cylinder-head, test them for tightness as follows:

1) Insert suitable close-fitting rubber plugs in the sparking-plug seats and pour petrol into the combustion chamber until the head of the valve under consideration is just covered.

2) Feed compressed air into the inlet and exhaust manifolds and look to see whether small bubbles form around the valve head (fig. 55).

    If any leaks are found, use the emery wheel a little more.

Re-assembling

1) Carefully wash the cylinder-head and valves with paraffin (Kerosene), check the oil channels for cleanliness and dry with compressed air.

2) Insert the valve guides (fig. 56) after first heating the cylinder-head in an oven to 100°C or by immersing it in boiling water. If after these operations the valve guide hole diameter should be found to have decreased below the values shown in fig. 50, enlarge it by means of a hand reamer.

3) Refit the valves, taking care that the numbers stamped on them agree with the numbers on the cylinder-head.

4) Fit the lower spring seats, springs, upper spring seats and cotters, and insert the adjusting end-caps and tappets.

WARNING: The adjusting end-caps must be chosen so as to obtain the appropriate valve clearances as described in Chapter 4.

5) Check the valves for a gas-tight fit as already described.

6) Place the cam-shafts in position, taking care that:
   - the timing marks cut on the shafts are in line with the marks on the front bearing cap (figure 31);
   - the cams operating the valves in cylinders 1 and 4 have their tips facing away from the engine.

7) Refit the induction manifold and the carburettor.

8) Refit the fuel pump, the return spring on the pump operating shaft and the shaft itself; during this assembly operation the driving cam must be in its position of minimum lift.

7 - REMOVING THE SUMP (PAN)

The sump is removed for the following operations:

- inspection and replacement of the oil pump and the pump filter;
- removal of pistons, piston rings and connecting rods;
- inspection of main and connecting-rod bearings.

Dismantling

1) Remove the lower front cross-member from the chassis.

2) Drain the oil from the sump by removing the drain plug; the plug should then be screwed back into

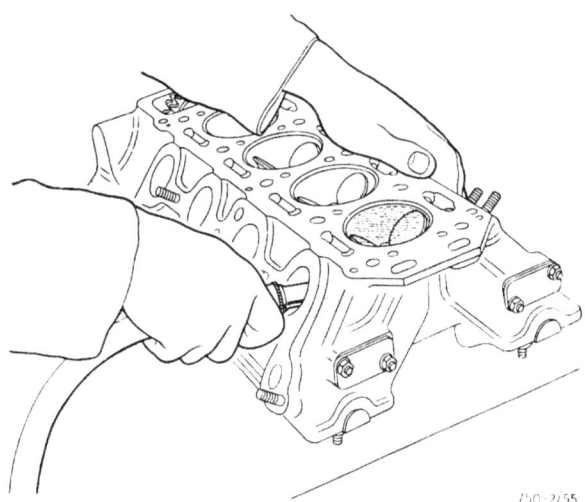

Fig. 55 - Checking valves for a tight fit

position before proceeding with the subsequent operations.

When fitted, the oil temperature thermometer bulb is to be removed.

3) Remove the lock-nuts on the sump and pull off the sump, sliding it towards the rear of the vehicle.

Re-assembly

Repeat the preceding operations in reverse order, taking care to insert the washers between the cross-member and the lower surface of the side members.

WARNING: Before refitting the sump, clean it carefully and replace the gasket.

The sump is connected to the crank-case at both ends via a flexible metal strap (see fig. 57) the purpose of which is to effect the uniform distribution of the pressure exerted by the nuts over the attachment edge; these spring straps should be fitted at the front of the sump even on engines on which they were not originally provided by the factory; in such cases the central bolt should be scrapped.

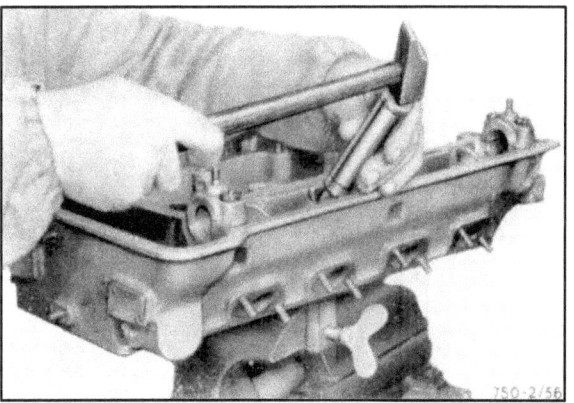

Fig. 56 - Assembling the valve guides with the tool No. 6121.07.291

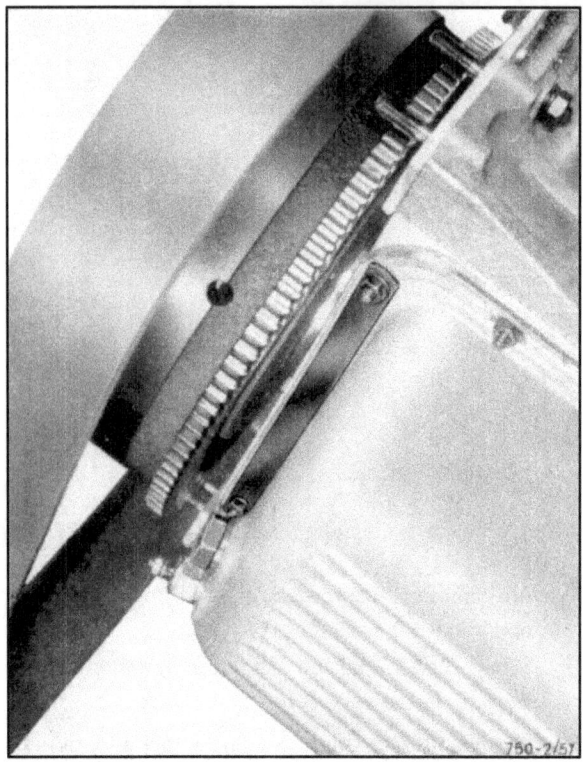

Fig. 57 - Flexible strap for oil sump (pan)

OIL SUMP (For Giulietta Sprint Veloce and Spider Veloce)

The oil sump (Fig. 57 bis) is in a light alloy and not in sheet metal. It consists of two units, a sump and a lower sump, and in addition is provided internally with a container fitted with flaps which open inwards so as to admit oil during violent brake or steering actions, and so as to prevent oil from leaving other than via the hole leading to the cooling labyrinth. The oil which returns from the engine to the sump is compelled to flow through a cooling labyrinth located in the lower sump and designed to increase the cooling surface in contact with the fluid.

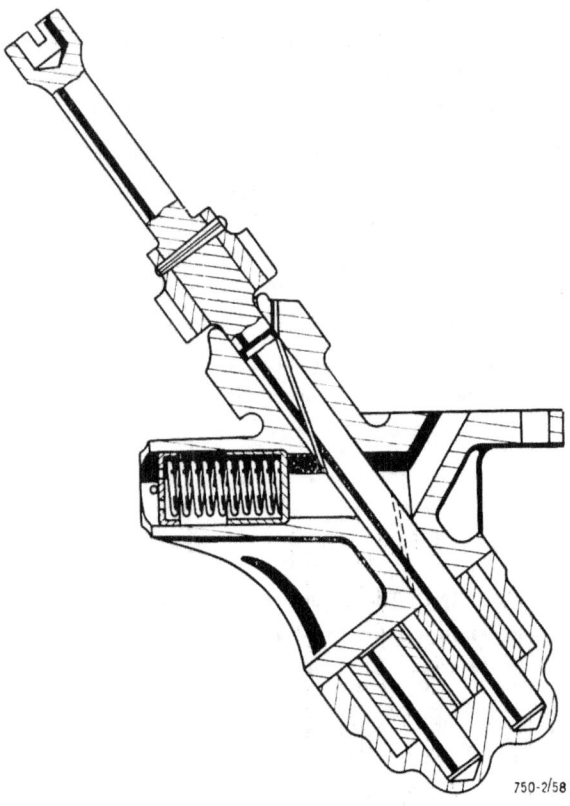

Fig. 58 - Oil pump sectional view

The sump is provided with a hole from which a hose leads to the pump. When fitting the sump care must

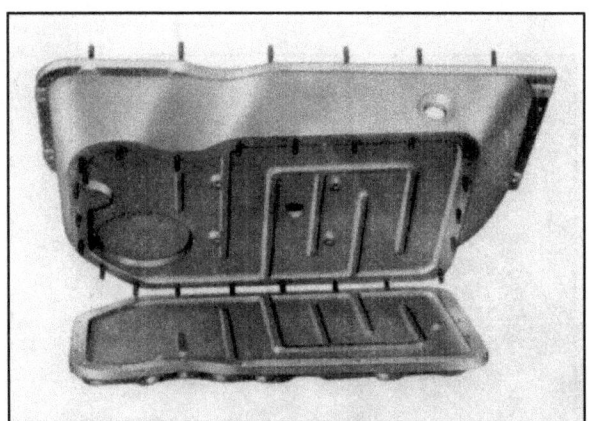

Fig. 57 bis - The oil sump and the sub-pump; the illustration shows the cooling labyrinth through which the oil must pass.

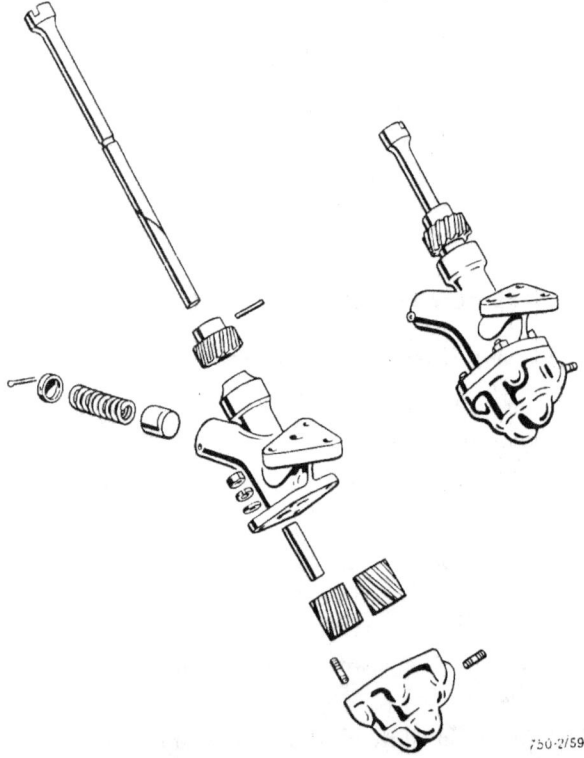

Fig. 59 - Assembled and exploded view of the oil pump

be taken to avoid damaging the rubber ring constituting the seal between the hose and the sump proper.

8 - THE OIL PUMP

The oil-pump shaft is driven by the pinion keyed to the crankshaft (fig. 58). The same pump shaft also turns the distributor the stem of which engages with the appropriate seat at the top of the said shaft. If follows, therefore, that the removal of the pump can easily upset the distributor timing; the ignition system should accordingly be re-timed after refitting the oil pump.

Removing the pump

When disconnecting the pump, after removing the sump, proceed as follows:

1) Turn the crankshaft to bring piston No. 1 to T.D.C. on the ignition stroke; this is necessary in order to facilitate the subsequent distributor adjustment.

2) Remove the bolts fixing the suction pipe to the cap of the central crankshaft bearing and remove the suction pipe itself.

3) Remove the 3 bolts holding the pump to the front cover and slide of the pump.

Dismantling the pump

1) After removing the retaining nuts take off the cover and slide off the bronze driven sprocket.

2) Remove the cotter, take off the cover and draw out the oil pressure relief valve spring.

Inspection

A falling-off of the oil pressure as shown on the gauge is due, if not to causes unconnected with the pump (such as abnormal wear of the bearings or journals, losses via the gaskets, etc.) to excessive play caused by wear of the pump gear-wheels or body.

Another cause of reduced oil pressure can be the failure of the return spring on the pressure relief valve or the poor fit of the valve on its seat.

It is accordingly necessary to check:

1) that the axial play of the gear-wheels is not much greater than the original figure of 0.2 to 0.5 mm. (fig. 60).

2) that the radial play between the gear-wheels and the pump body is not much greater than the original figure of 0.020 and 0.062 mm. (fig. 61);

3) that the pin of the driven sprocket is firmly fixed to its seat;

4) the state of the surfaces of the oil pressure relief valve and, where necessary, have them re-ground or (better still) replaced; in both cases it is essential to grind the valve into its seat on the pump;

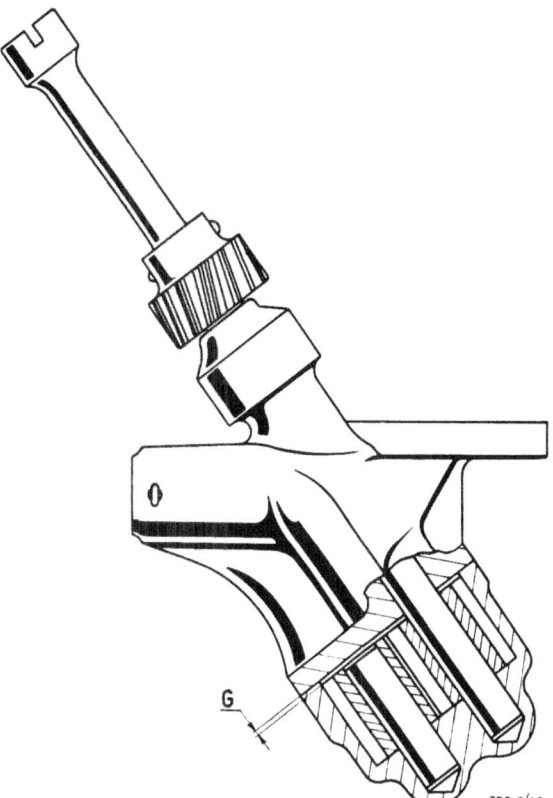

Fig. 60 - Axial clearance (**G**) between gears and oil pump body

5) the spring tension; the tension must be 15.2 to 16.2 kg. when the spring is compressed to a length of 32.25 mm.; the length of the spring before compression is 46.75 to 49.75 mm.

In the event that the play in paragraphs 1 and 2 is such that it reduces the oil pressure below the permitted limits (see the chapter on « Engine Tuning ») or that the pump driving gear is badly worn, the entire pump should be replaced.

Re-assembly

When re-assembling the pump, no particular instructions are necessary, though the following procedure

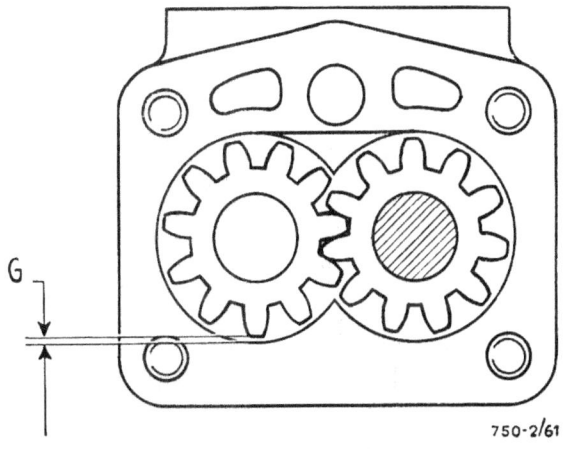

Fig. 61 - Radial clearance (**G**) between gears and oil pump body

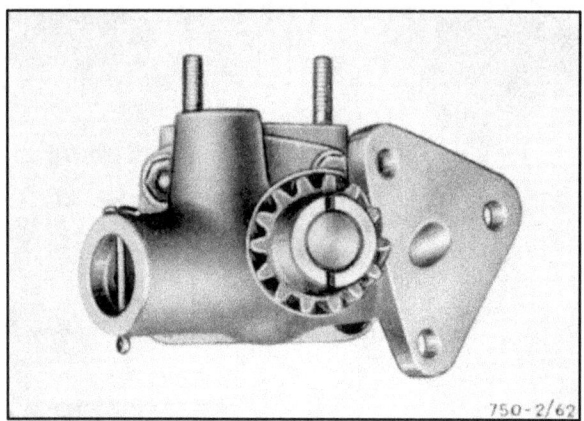

Fig. 62 - Position of the oil pump driving shaft before re-assembly on the engine cover

should be followed when fitting it to the engine, both to facilitate ignition timing and because the distributor has to occupy a specific position in relation to the engine.

It should be noted that the seat connecting the distributor to the oil pump shaft is eccentric to the axis of the shaft itself; if you look at the distributor shaft (which before you begin to dismantle the pump is in the position corresponding to that when the piston is at T.D.C. on the ignition stroke) you will see that the pawl is almost parallel to the longitudinal axis of the engine, and that the smaller arc faces away from the engine itself.

It is therefore necessary to rotate the pump shaft so that the seat is set at the same angle as the pawl (fig. 62) on the distributor shaft.

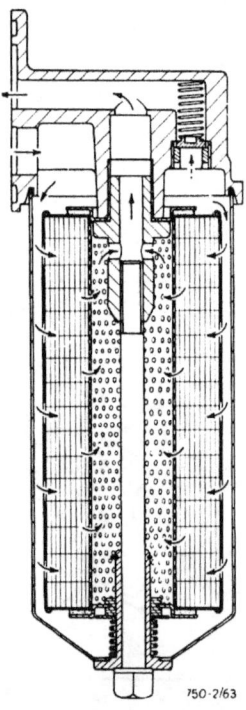

Fig. 63 - Sectional view of the oil filter

After having done this, mount the pump on its seat on the engine and, in the event that the pump shaft and distributor shaft cannot enmesh due to the disalignment of the seat, slide off the pump and rotate the shaft itself through an angle equal to one tooth on the driving sprocket, first in one direction and then in the other until the shafts mesh properly.

After mounting the oil pump it is always necessary to check the ignition timing in accordance with the instructions give in « Engine Tuning » or with the instructions in Part 10 (Electrical Equipment) if the distributor has to be removed.

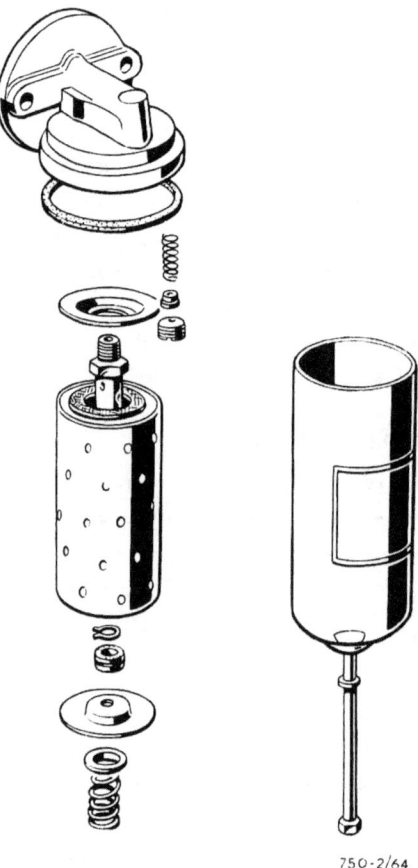

Fig. 64 - Exploded view of the oil filter

9 - THE OIL FILTER

Before it reaches the various parts of the engine, the oil is filtered by passing through a gauze filter situated on the pump suction pipe and then through a cartridge filter.

Engine lubrication is ensured even if the cartridge becomes entirely blocked, as at the top of the filter is a valve which then operates and thereby by-passes the cartridge when the oil can no longer pass through it. This, however, is a situation which never materializes if normal filter maintenance procedure is followed.

The filter cartridge (Fram filter) cannot be washed

clean; it must therefore be replaced after every 8000 to 10,000 Kms. The Fispa cartridge is, on the contrary, of a washable type and must be cleaned after the same above mileages.

The oil filter is removed from the engine merely by unscrewing the bolt fixing the filter body to the cover. When fitting a new cartridge, always wash the filter body with petrol and make sure that the valve in the filter cover is not blocked.

Examine the condition of the washer fitted between the body and the cover, and replace it if possible every time the filter is dismantled. Immediately the engine is re-started, check the washer and make sure that it is not leaking.

Do not over-tighten the bolt fixing the filter body to the cover, or deformation of the filter may be the result.

10 - MAIN AND CONNECTING-ROD BEARINGS

The main and connecting-rod bearings are of the steel thin-wall type plated with leaded bronze and covered with indium-lead antifriction alloy; the characteristics of the rubbing surfaces are such as to exclude any possibility of crankshaft wear if the leaded bronze is completely covered by the antifriction metal. The latter is applied in such thin amounts as to preclude any possibility of work on it with tools of any kind; its life is extraordinarily long always provided that assembly is performed as prescribed, the tightness of fit is as laid down elsewhere and lubrication instructions — including the proper maintenance of the oil filter — are carefully followed.

The main and connecting-rod bearings and journals are accessible from beneath the engine without having to dismantle the crankshaft; this means that all inspection and repair of these parts can be effected without removing the engine from the chassis.

However if during inspection it is found that the crankshaft is deeply scored or shows signs of seizure, it will be necessary to remove the engine from the chassis, dismantle the crankshaft and re-grind it.

Dismantling

1) in order to renew the connecting-rod bearings, it is necessary to remove the bearing caps and push the rods upwards.

2) To remove the main bearings, slacken all the cap lock-nuts, remove one group of 2/3 caps, inspect the bearings, and re-assemble them as below described. Then dismantle the remainder.

The half-bearings which adhere to the crank case can be removed by pushing them with a screwdriver on the side away from the stop and by facilitating their sliding by turning the crankshaft.

Fig. 65 - Numerals of the main bearing caps and connecting rod caps

NOTE: In order to slacken the Palmutter washers which lock the bearing cap nuts, the nuts themselves should first be slightly tightened.

Inspection

Inspection of the main and connecting-rod bearings is entirely a visual matter, as the extreme thinness of the indium-lead antifriction metal precludes any dimensional examination.

In the case of the main bearings, inspection will generally yield the following results:

a) the antifriction surface of the cap bearing is smooth and uniform except for possible circumferential scoring of moderate width and such that it does not appreciably reduce the area of the bearing surface; **in these cases the cap bearing can be refitted without any further inspection** of either the crank-pin or the upper half-bearing on the crank-case, as the latter is generally the less worn of the two;

b) the bearing surface of the cap bearing shows traces of the leaded bronze metal; **the cap bearing is then useless;** in addition to replacing the whole

Fig. 66 - Tightening the main bearing cap nuts with a torque spanner

Fig. 67 - Plate No. 6121.01.177 for fixing cylinder liners when taking off the pistons

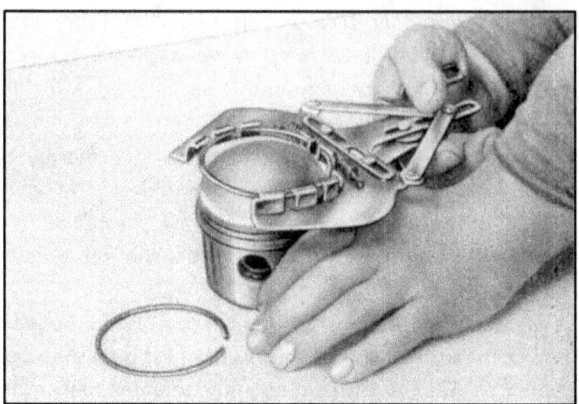

Fig. 68 - Dismantling the piston rings

bearing it will be necessary to check carefully to ensure that it has not caused scoring or wear of the corresponding crank-pin;

c) the condition of the cap bearing appears to justify replacement, although the leaded-bronze metal is not yet showing; in this case **it is necessary to check the half-bearing on the crank-case side** and make a quick check of the crank-pin.

In the case of the connecting-rod bearings, the same remarks apply; in cases of doubt it is better to replace them as they are subjected to greater stresses than the main bearings. The same remarks regarding inspection and wear also apply to the **axial thrust rings** mounted on the central main bearing.

Re-assembly

Fitting replacement bearings does not require any special instructions.

It is sufficient when assembling to repeat in reverse order the operation described for dismantling, through taking care to ensure that the numbers imprinted on the caps, con-rods and crank-case correspond (fig. 65). If slight traces, of seizure are found on the crankshaft and con-rod journals, first of all eliminate them, before re-assembling the bearings, by means of an abrasive block.

After re-assembly, tighten the nuts on the crankshaft studs and on the con-rod bolts; for this purpose use a torque spanner and the following ratings:

main bearings cap

studs: 3 to 3.25 kgm.

con-rod bolts
- 3 to 3.25 kgm. (Giulietta Berlina and t.i.)
- 3.7 to 4 kgm. (Giulietta Sprint and Spider)
- 3.9 to 4.1 kgm. (Giulietta Sprint Vel. and Spider Vel.)

Fit the Palmutter lock-nuts to the main bearing cap studs and tighten them until they touch the nuts proper; then give them an additional 90° turn.

11 - CYLINDER LINERS, PISTONS, RINGS AND CONNECTING-RODS

Dismantling

The earlier chapters have dealt with the dismantling of the cylinder head and of the con-rod bearing caps; after dismantling as described, proceed as follows:

1) As shown in fig. 67, insert the liner fixing tool No. 6121.01.177 over the studs holding the cylinder-head to the crank-case, and extract the whole of the piston and its connecting-rod from the top.

2) Remove the tool and pull out the liners by hand.

3) Remove the piston-rings with the special tool as shown in fig. 68.

4) Extract the piston-pin after first removing the spring clips (snap rings) which must be replaced when re-assembling. The piston pins can usually be extracted by hand or, if necessary, by a light blow with a wooden mallet.

Inspection

a) **Liners.**

The liners must be inspected for any surface damage, wear or oval deformity. If deep scratches, serious wear or ovalizing are encountered, the liner must be replaced.

Diameter and tolerance data are given in fig. 69. The diameter must be checked by means of a bar gauge as illustrated in figs. 70 and 71, at three positions approximately 15 mm. from the top edge, halfway along the liner and approximately 35 mm. from the lower edge. Two right-angle measurements will be taken in each position.

If any liner is worn or out-of-round by as much as 0.05 mm., the liner the piston and its rings must all be replaced.

b) **Pistons.**

Check for any signs of seizing or deep scoring; if such signs are encountered, replace the pistons.

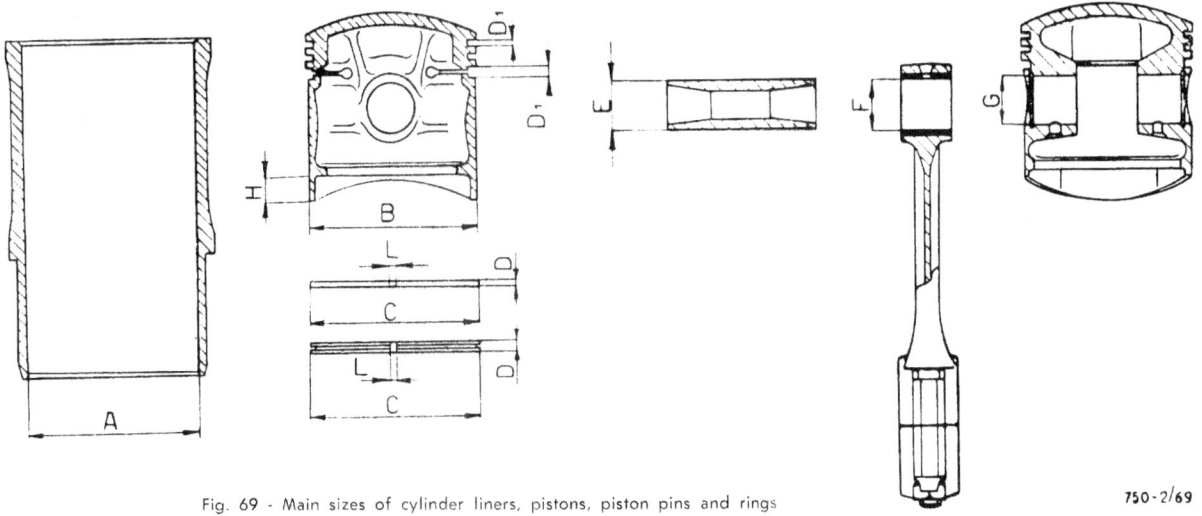

Fig. 69 - Main sizes of cylinder liners, pistons, piston pins and rings

750-2/69

Cylinder liner: normal diameter **A**			74.000÷74.019 mm.
Ovalisation	with a new liner (tolerance)		0.014 »
	with worn liner (max. limit allowable)		0.05 »
Piston: normal diameter **B** (to be measured at distance **H** = 11 mm.)		Giulietta Berlina	73.935 to 73.965 »
		Giulietta Sprint and Spider	73.925 to 73.955 »
		Giulietta Sprint Veloce and Spider Veloce	73.835 to 73.865 »
Clearance between cylinder and piston	original (fitted together)	Giulietta Berlina	0.04 to 0.059 »
		Giulietta Sprint and Spider	0.05 to 0.069 »
		Giulietta Sprint Vel. and Spider Vel.	0.14 to 0.159 »
	wear limit	Giulietta Berlina, Sprint and Spider	0,12 »
		Giulietta Sprint Veloce and Spider Veloce	0,18 »
Compression and oil rings: normal diameter **C**			74.00 »
Gap **L** between the ends of the compression and oil rings (with ring placed in the cylinder liner)		compression ring	0.30÷0.45 »
		oil ring	0.25÷0.40 »
		wear limit	1 »
Ring thickness: **D**	compression ring		1.972÷1.984 »
	oil ring		3.958÷3.970 »
Axial clearance between grooves and compression and oil rings: **D1-D**	original	compression ring	0.041÷0.068 »
		oil ring	0.045÷0.072 »
	wear limit		0.10 »
Inner diameter of con-rod small end bush: **F**			20.005÷20.015 »
Piston pin diameter: **E**			19.994÷20.000 »
Diameter of the hole for piston pin: **G**			20.000÷20.003 »
Clearance between con-rod small end bush and piston pin: **F-E**	original		0.005÷0.020 »
	wear limit		0.05 »
Clearance between piston pin and piston hole: **G-E**	original		0.000÷0.008 »
	wear limit		0.04 »

Note - The dimensions stated for pistons and liners are the outside limits; when assembling, the various parts must be selected so as to ensure the prescribed amount of play.

Check the piston diameter in order to determine the extent of the wear which, added to the liner wear, must be less than the permitted limits for the two members as shown under c) below. Piston dimensions are set out in fig. 69.

The diameter is checked by micrometer; the measurement must be made at a point 11 mm. from the lower edge and following the axis normal to the piston-pin hole (fig. 73).

Make sure that the piston-pin hole has not worn oval.

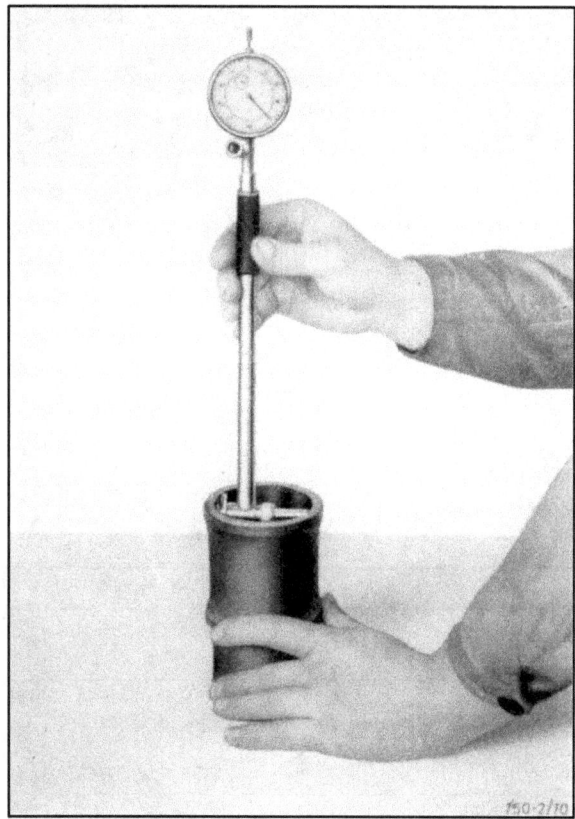

Fig. 70 - Measuring the cylinder liner diameter with a gauge

NOTE: The stamped pistons used for the Giulietta Sprint have been changed starting from engine No. 1315.01024 with chilled ones.

As the two types of pistons have different weights, care must be taken to ensure that no engine has mixed pistons. As, however, stamped pistons are no longer made or supplied as spares, it follows that when one piston on an engine with a number earlier

Fig. 72 - Piston, piston pin and rings

than 1315.01024 has to be changed, all the others must also be replaced.

c) **Clearance between piston and liner.**

The clearance must be kept within the following limits:

— clearance when fitted: 0.050 ÷ 0.069 mm.

Make sure that the piston pin surfaces are well polished and free of scoring of any kind; if they are worn or out-of-round they must be replaced.

Check the fit of the piston-pin in the piston and in the small-end of the connecting-rod; it should be possible to fit the piston-pin by hand, slightly forcing it into the piston hole but leaving it free (play of 0.005 to 0.02 mm.) in the small-end.

e) **Piston rings.**

As the metal from which the ring are made is rather brittle, care must be taken when removing them from the piston to stretch them as little as possible.

Check them for wear and inspect their surfaces; remove any carbon deposits.

Using a feeler gauge (fig. 74), check the clearance between the rings and the groove side; the play must

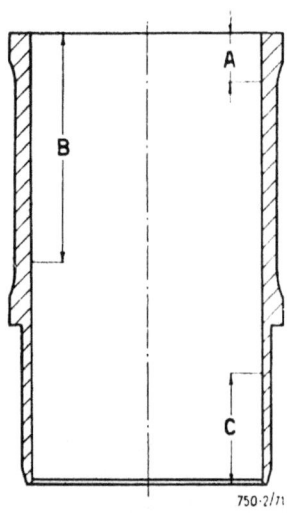

Fig. 71 - Positions for measuring the cylinder liner diameter:
A = 15 mm. **B** = 70 mm. **C** = 35 mm.

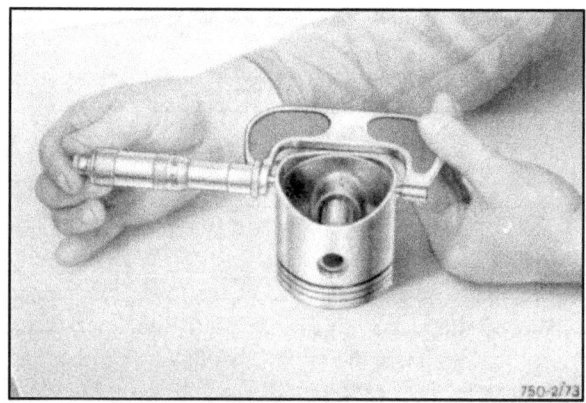

Fig. 73 - Checking the piston diameter

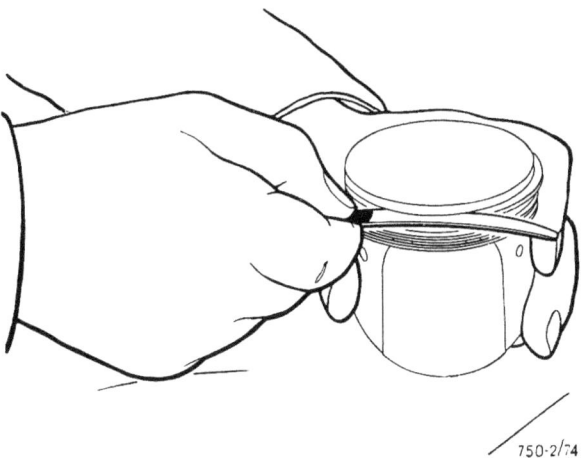

Fig. 74 - With a feeler gauge checking the clearances between rings and grooves of the piston

correspond to the values shown in fig. 69.
Check the gap (fig. 75) between the ends of the rings as follows:

— insert the ring to be checked into the liner in which it will be fitted and at a position 5 mm. from the cylinder-head, make sure that the ring lies at right-angles to the cylinder wall and, using a feeler gauge, check the play. The proper figures are 0.30 to 0.45 mm. for the compression rings and 0.25 to 0.40 mm. for the oils scraper rings.

f) **Connecting-rods.**

Inspect the internal surfaces of the small-end bushes; if they are worn or out-of-round, replace them.
In the manner shown in fig. 77, check to ensure that the big-end and small-end bores are parallel.
The maximum admissible difference is 0.03 mm. measured at a point 100 mm. from the rod.
If the difference is greater than 0.03, the rod must be straightened by means of a press or replaced if a proper degree of parallelism cannot be restored.

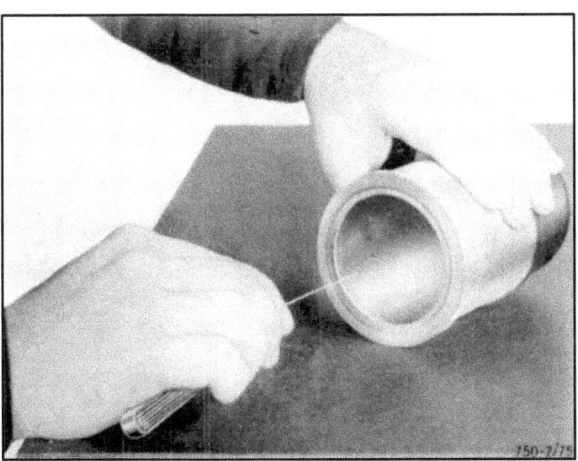

Fig. 75 - Checking the gap of the piston rings

Re-assembly

1) Insert the liners and their sealing rubber rings into the cylinder block and check if they project about $0 \div 0.05$ mm from the upper plane surface of the crankcase (fig. 78).

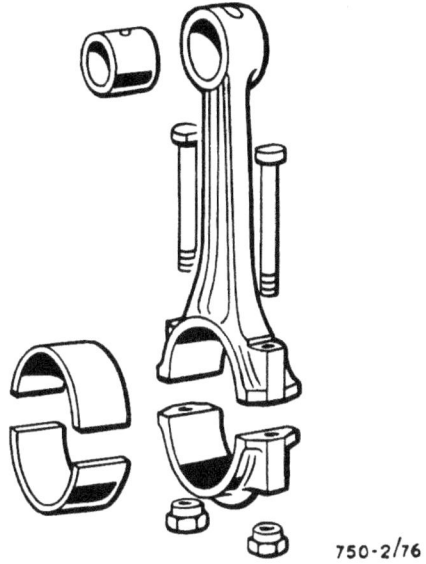

Fig. 76 - Connecting rod disassembled

2) Check the assembled weight of the con-rods with their caps, bearings and bolts fitted; the maximum difference between them must not exceed 2 gms.

3) This weight check must be repeated when the pistons and con-rods are assembled; the maximum difference must then not exceed 5 or 6 grams.

4) Insert the piston-rings in their appropriate grooves; use the special tool provided for this purpose (fig. 68).

5) Fit the pistons to the connecting rods.

6) Using the special collar (tool 6121.01.174) insert the pistons into the cylinder liners, taking care

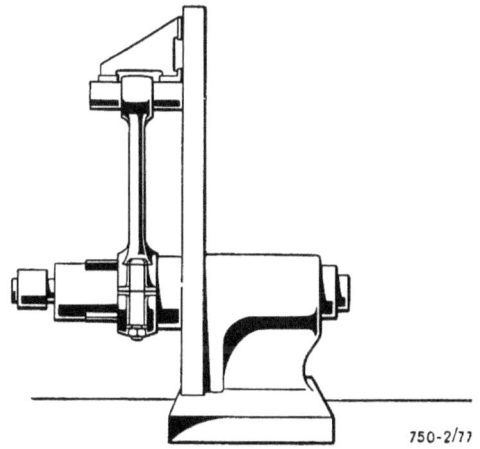

Fig. 77 - Checking the parallelism of small and big bores of the connecting rod

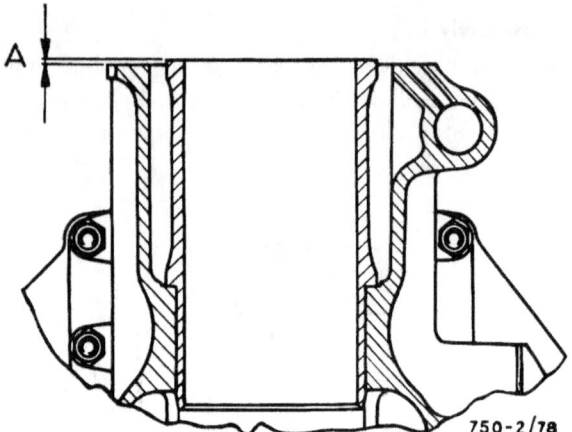

Fig. 78 - Checking the liner projection from the crankcase upper plane surface (**A** = 0,05 mm.)

that the ring ends are not vertically in line one with another.

7) After inspecting the con-rod bearings as described in the preceding chapter, fit the caps, nuts and bolts, and tighten them with a torque wrench to the torque ratings mentioned in that chapter.

Remember that the connecting-rods are asymmetrical and that they must therefore be assembled in the position shown in figure 81.

8) Fold over the locking plates on the con-rod nuts.

12 - THE FRONT COVER - THE TIMING REDUCTION CHAIN AND SPROCKETS

The following instructions must be complied with when:

1) Replacing the timing reduction chain, and the sprockets.
2) Replacing the oil-pump sprocket on the crankshaft.
3) Replacing the front oil seal on the crankshaft.

First remove:
— the radiator (part 2 B)
— the cylinder head (chapter 5)
— the oil sump (chapter 7)
— the oil pump suction pipe (chapter 8).

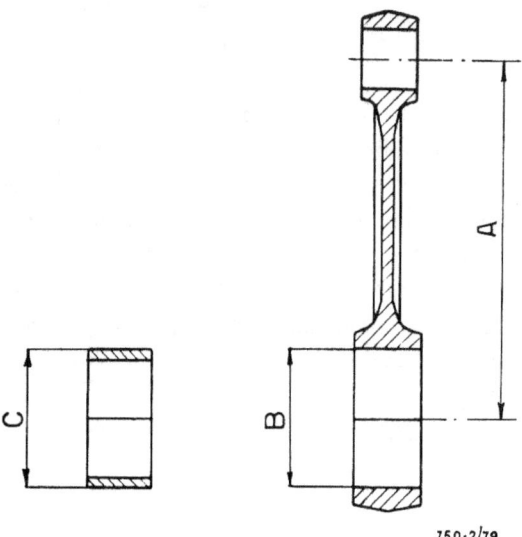

Fig. 79 - Connecting rod and its bearing main sizes

Length of connecting rod **A**	132.955÷133.045 mm
Bearing seat diameter **B**	48.658÷48.671 »
Bearing outer diameter **C**	48.671 »
Bearing thickness — for normal shaft	1.822÷1.829 »
— for first re-grinding of crankpin	1.949÷1.956 »
— for second re-grinding of crankpin	2.076÷2.083 »
— for third re-grinding of crankpin	2.203÷2.210 »
Radial clearance between journal and bearing	0.025÷0.064 »
Axial clearance between journal and con-rod	0.2÷0.3 »

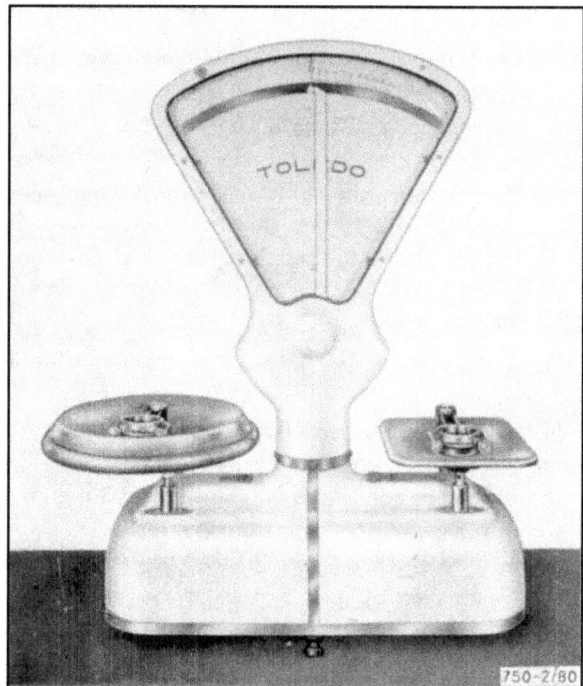

Fig. 80 - Checking the connecting rod weight with a balance

Dismantling

1) Slacken the belt and remove the fan.
2) Remove from the crankshaft the pulley which drives the auxiliary units (fig. 82).
3) Remove the water pump as described under « Engine Cooling » in part 2 B entitled: « Auxiliary engine equipment ».
4) Remove the distributor after slackening the screw which holds it on its bracket.
5) Take off the front cover complete with the oil pump.
6) Remove the sprockets (fig. 83) by sliding them off together with the chain.

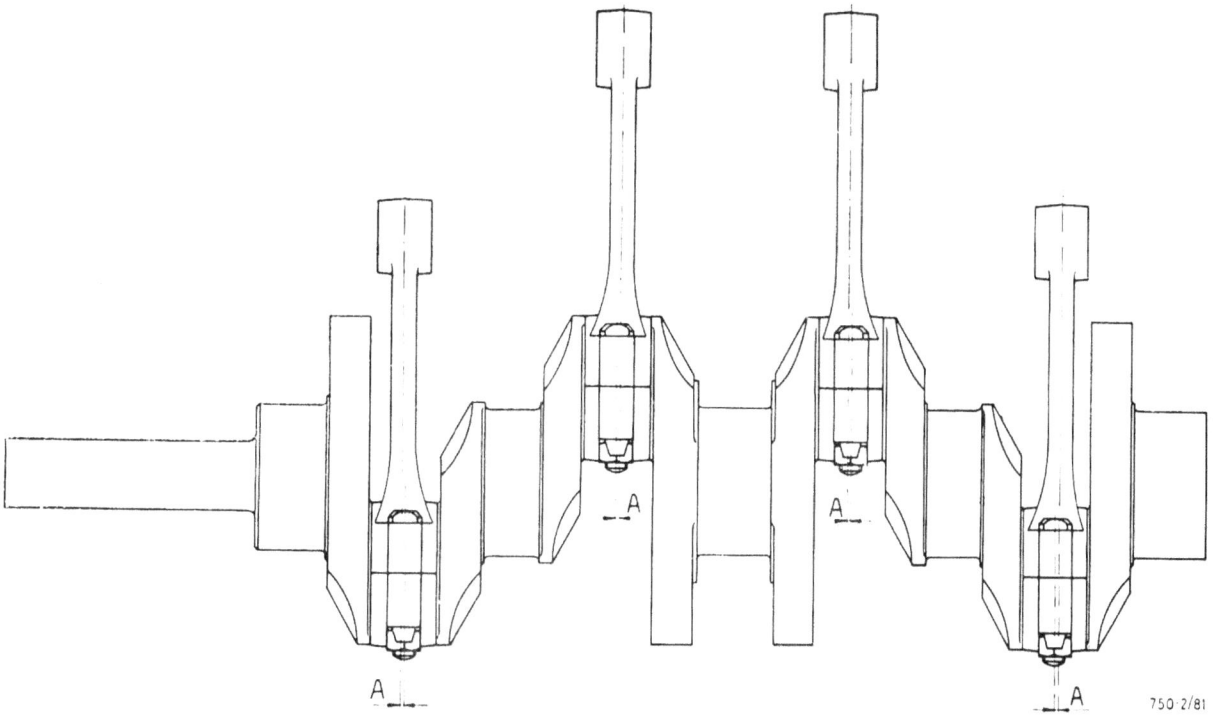

Fig. 81 - Assembly positions of the con-rods
A = Desplacement between the con-rod axis and journal center lines

Inspection

a) Examine the surface of the ignition gear shaft bushes for scoring; if necessary, replace them.

b) Make sure that the oil-ways are clean and free from any gummy deposits.

c) Examine the oil seal; replace it if necessary, using tool 6121.07.294 (fig. 85).

d) Inspect, and if necessary replace, the sealing rings between the oil pump body and front cover; also the sealing ring between the cover and the crankcase, and the gaskets between the cover and the crankcase and between the cover and the water pump.

e) Check sprocket tooth wear and replace if necessary.

f) Make sure that the chain rollers are unbroken and free from wear, and that the roller pins are firmly attached to their seats.

Fig. 82 - Dismantling the auxiliary part driving pulley from the crankshaft by means of the spanner 6121.20.040

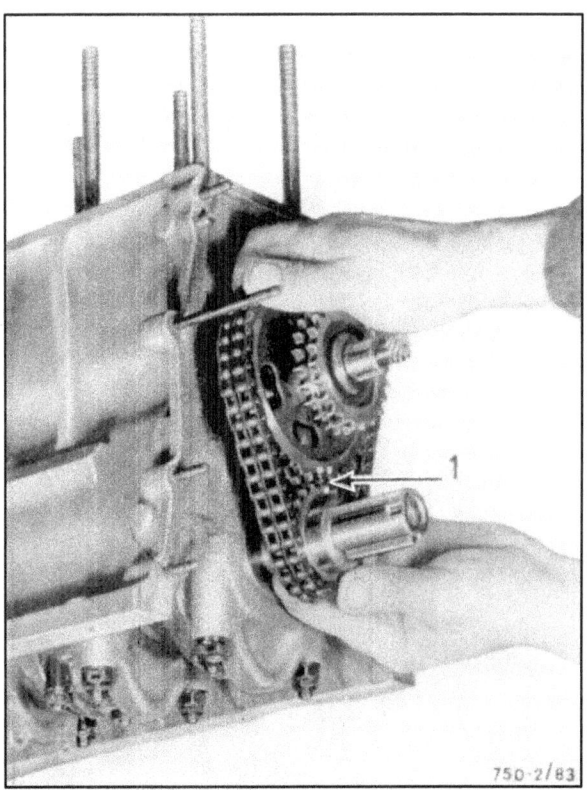

Fig. 83 - Dismantling the driving and reduction chain and sprockets
1. Timing marks for sprocket assembly

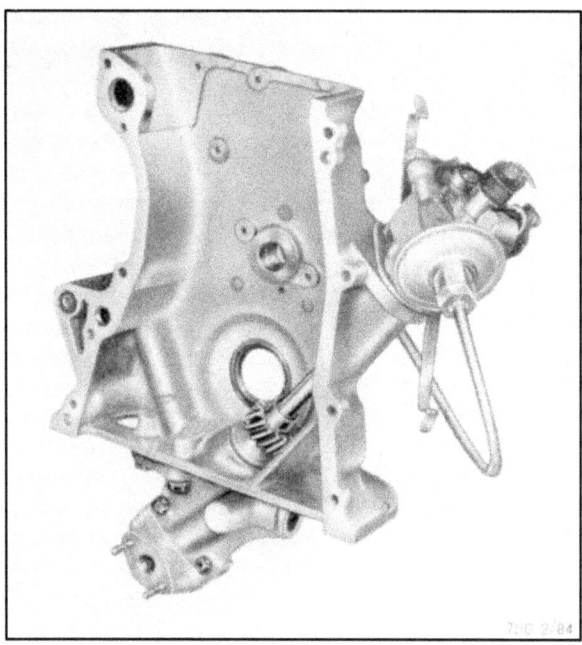

Fig. 84 - Front cover of the engine

NOTE: Block the hole in the crankcase (provided for lubricating the chain) with a plug if this has not already been done on the occasion of an earlier overhaul (fig. 86).

Re-assembly

1) Fit the chain and the sprockets together.
2) Fit the oil-pump and plunger to the cover.

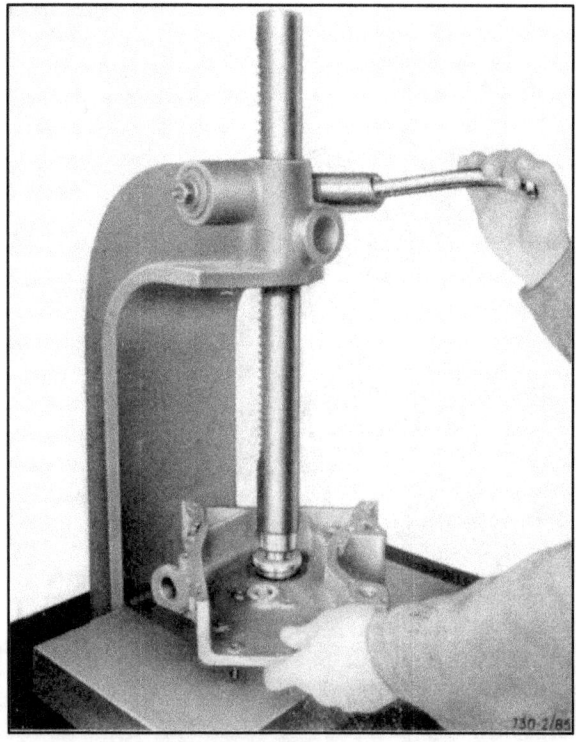

Fig. 85 - Inserting the oil seal into the front cover by means of the tool No. 6121.07.294

3) With the chain-driving sprockets in the position shown in fig. 83, mount the distributor on the cover and, after having positioned it as shown in fig. 87, lock the nut holding it to the engine; then turn the pump shaft so that the rotating brush in the distributor assumes the position also shown in fig. 87.

This must be done to ensure that the distributor is properly positioned in relation to the engine.

4) Fit the cover to the crankcase and check that the brush is in the position shown in fig. 88; if necessary, again remove the cover and rotate the pump shaft until the distributor brush is in the prescribed position.
5) Fit the water pump.
6) Fit the pulley for driving the auxiliary equipment, the fan, the sump and the cylinder head.
7) Re-time the ignition (see chapter 3).

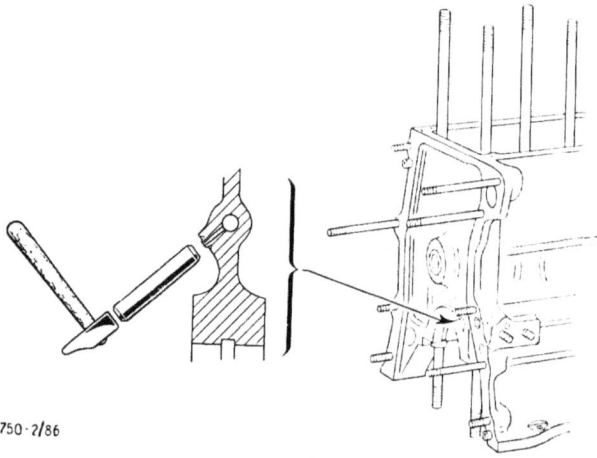

Fig. 86 - Closing the hole in the crankcase for the chain lubrication

8) Check the ignition timing as shown in the chapter entitled « Engine tuning ».

WARNING: The foregoing re-assembly of the front cover can be carried out only with taken off engine. With engine on car and to ease distributor timing, first fit the cover, then the oil pump complying with the suggestions set forth in chapter 8.

13 - ENGINE SUSPENSION

The engine is mounted on the vehicle through three rubber blocks, two of which are positioned approximately halfway along the cylinder-block and the third behind the gear-box (transmission).

The front supports are rubber blocks which rest on brackets welded to the sides of the structure carrying the car body (fig. 89 and 89 bis) and the rear support is a silentbloc fixed to the rear cross-member (fig. 90).

The following steps must be taken when replacing the front rubber pads:

1) Attach the hook of a hoist to the stirrup on the cylinder-head and raise the engine sufficiently to take all load off the pad.

2) Unscrew the nut from the bolt holding the engine to the frame and remove the washer.

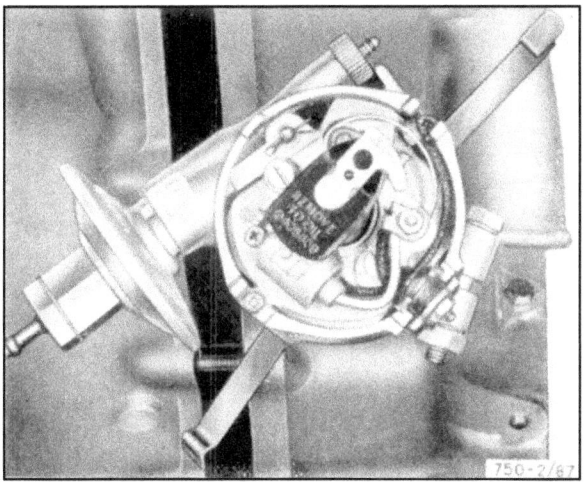

Fig. 87 - Position of the distributor body and of the rotating brush before mounting the front cover on the crankcase

3) Using a lever, move the cylinder-block a little to one side in order to release the engine mounting pad and unscrew it.

4) Insert a new pad and re-fix the whole assembly. When replacing the rear silentbloc the special tool, No. 6121.04.014, designed to facilitate both extraction and replacement of the pad (see part 3 under « Gearbox ») must be used.

NOTE

For reasons of space the engine on the Sprint Veloce and the Spider Veloce is set at an angle of inclination of 8°; this is done by fitting special engine supports. (Fig. 89 bis). The support on the inlet side is provided with silent blocs for the attachment of the carburetter supporting rods.

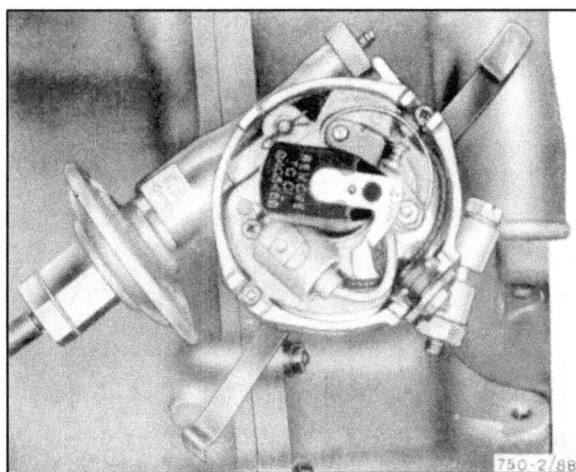

Fig. 88 - Position of the distributor body and of the rotating brush after mounting the front cover on the crankcase

Fig. 89 - Side rubber blocks of the engine

14 - REMOVING THE ENGINE-GEARBOX (TRANSMISSION) UNIT FROM THE CAR

1) Disconnect the earth cable from the battery (the positive pole);

2) With the car over a garage pit, disconnect:

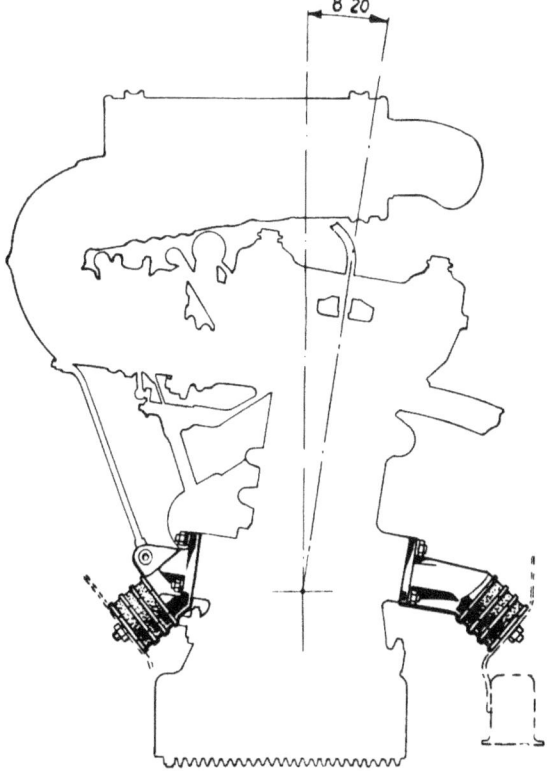

Fig. 89 bis - The side supports used to incline the engine at an angle of 8°. (Giulietta Sprint Veloce and Spider Veloce)

53

Fig. 90 - Silentbloc for rear support of the unit engine-gearbox (transmission)

- the front and rear cross-members connecting the frame side spars and fixing the engine rear;
- the gearbox and clutch controls;
- the connection for the oil-gauge tube (when re-assembling replace the copper washer);
- the return spring for the starter motor control;
- the electrical cables leading to the starter motor;
- the mileometer connector;
- the bracket carrying the exhaust pipe;
- remove the central propeller shaft bearing saddle and unscrew the nut on the sliding sleeve of the rear shaft;
- disconnect the exhaust pipe from the exhaust manifold (fig. 91);
- remove the nuts holding the flexible engine mounting pads to the body.

3) Remove the radiator, following the instructions given under « Engine Cooling » in Part 2 B.

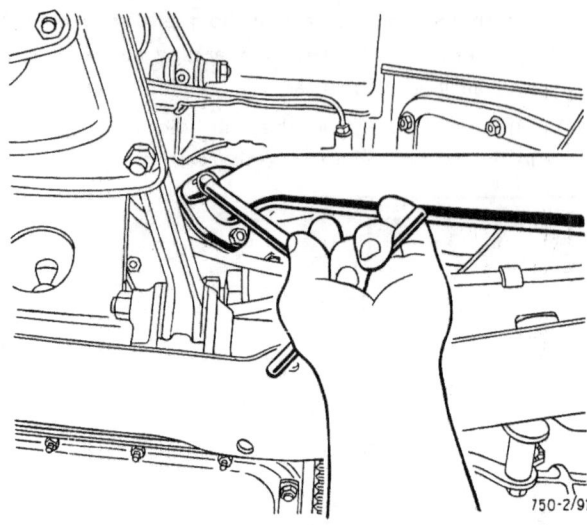

Fig. 91 - Dismantling the exhaust pipe from its manifold

4) Then:
- take off the bonnet by withdrawing the hinge pins;
- disconnect the carburettor controls, the heater hose-pipes, the dynamo leads, the pipe leading to the petrol pump, the distributor low and high-tension leads and also the r.p.m. indicator connection when it is fitted.

5) As shown in figure 92, insert a suitable hook into the engine lifting stirrup and lift the engine gearbox unit by means of a hoist; carefully guide the unit by hand as it is lifted.

6) Stand the engine on a suitable trestle (fig. 93), disconnect the clutch/gearbox unit (see part 3) and dismantle the engine as described in the following chapters.

BENCH REPAIRS

15 - DISMANTLING THE ENGINE ON A TRESTLE

After having removed:

- the cylinder-head (see Chapter 5),
- the sump (pan) and the oil pump suction pipe (see Chapters 7 and 8),
- the pistons, liners and con-rods (see Chapter 11),

complete the work of dismantling the engine as follows:

1) Slacken the belt and remove the fan.
2) Remove the water pump.
3) Remove the auxiliary drive pulley mounted on the crankshaft.
4) Disconnect the dynamo by drawing off the fixing bolts.

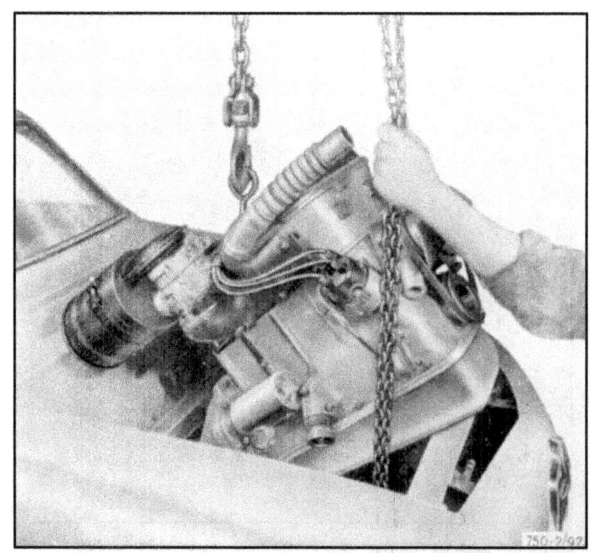

Fig. 92 - Taking off the unit engine-gearbox (transmission) from the car

NOTE: To facilitate this operation, disconnect the dynamo only after having turned the engine on the trestle so that the dynamo is located at the top.

5) Remove the starter motor.
6) Take off the front cover (see Chapter 12).
7) Remove the oil filter.
8) Draw off the flywheel, loosening the locking bolts.
9) Remove the sprocket driving the distributor and the oil pump.
10) Remove the intermediate sprockets together with the chain as shown in fig. 83.

Fig. 93 - Engine on a trestle

11) Remove the crankshaft bearing caps (figs. 94 and 95).
12) Take off the crankshaft.
13) Remove the plate attaching the gearbox (transmission) to the engine, the rear cover and the connection for the breather tube.

16 - REPLACING THE RING GEAR ON THE FLYWHEEL

Dismantling

1) Bring the No. 1 piston to T.D.C. as indicated when the mark cut on the flywheel is in line with the reference mark on the plate (fig. 96).

Fig. 94 - Dismantling the rear bearing cap by means of the tool No. 6121.11.004

2) Remove alternatively 4 of the 8 bolts connecting the flywheel to the crankshaft; screw in their holes 4 studs to avoid the fixing rings of the flywheel moving from their seats; remove the other bolts and draw the flywheel.
3) Press off the flywheel ring gear without pre-heating it.

Re-assembly

1) Heat the replacement ring-gear in an oil bath at 100° C and press fit it to the flywheel.
2) After aligning the reference marks on the flywheel and on the plate (and with the No. 1 piston at T.D.C.), fit the flywheel to the crankshaft and bolt it in position.

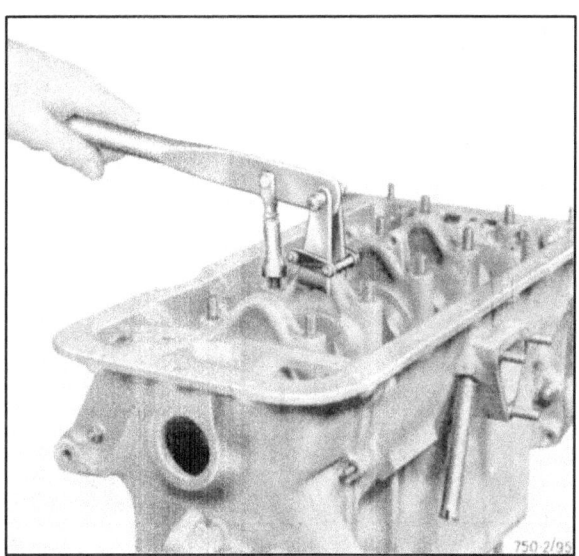

Fig. 95 - Dismantling the intermediate bearing caps

Fig. 96 - Timing marks cut on the flywheel and rear plate

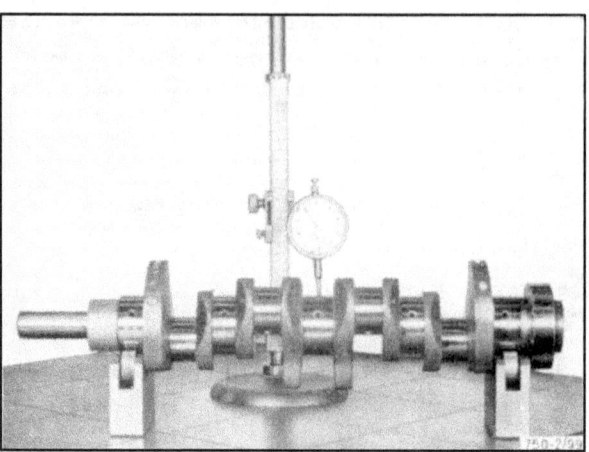

Fig. 98 - Checking the journal alignment by means of a micrometer comparator

17 - CRANKSHAFT

After removing the crankshaft as described in Chapter 15, inspection and checking should be performed as follows.

Inspection

a) **Checking the crankshaft and con-rod journals for wear.**

The surfaces of all crankshaft and con-rod journals must be free from scoring or signs of seizing. Any slight traces of seizing or superficial scoring can be removed with a fine-grain oil-stone; deep scoring may be removed by re-grinding, though this will mean that bearings with a smaller internal diameter will have to be fitted.

Surface roughness of the journals after re-grinding must never exceed 10 thousandth of an inch R.M.S.

b) **Checking crankshaft and con-rod journals for oval wear.** This check must be made with a micrometer as shown in fig. 97.

If a journal is out of round by more than 0.05 mm., it must be re-ground and re-fitted together with bearings of a smaller internal diameter.

Figure 101 shows the diameters for con-rod and crankshaft journals and also other dimensions which must be respected during re-grinding operations.

After re-grinding and polishing the journals, the crankshaft must be carefully washed with petrol and

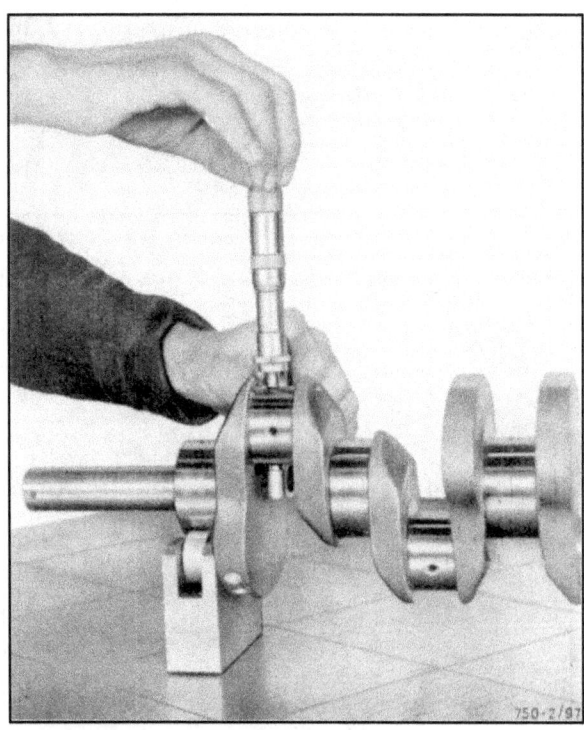

Fig. 97 - Checking the journals diameter by means of a micrometer gauge

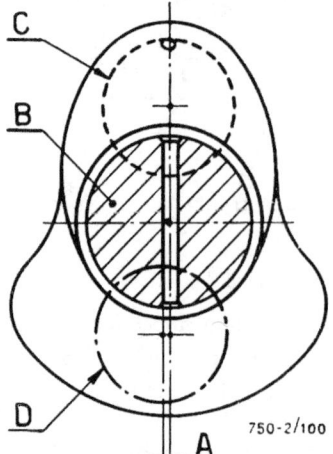

Fig. 99 Alignment of the con-rods journals

A. maximum allowable displacement = 0,07 mm. - **B.** Crankshaft journals - **C.** Con-rods journals of cylinders No. 2 and 3. - **D.** Con-rods journals of cylinders No. 1 and 4.

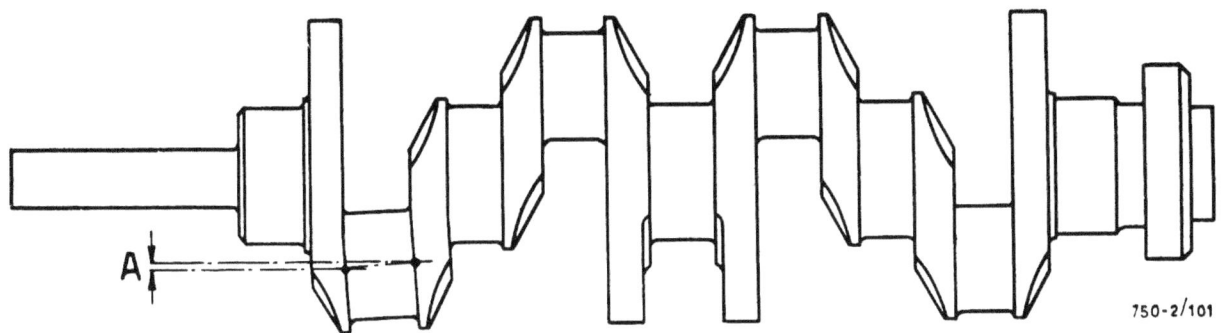

Fig. 100 - Parallelism of the crankshaft and con-rods journals
Maximum allowable tolerance **A** = 0.015 mm (0,03 wear limit)

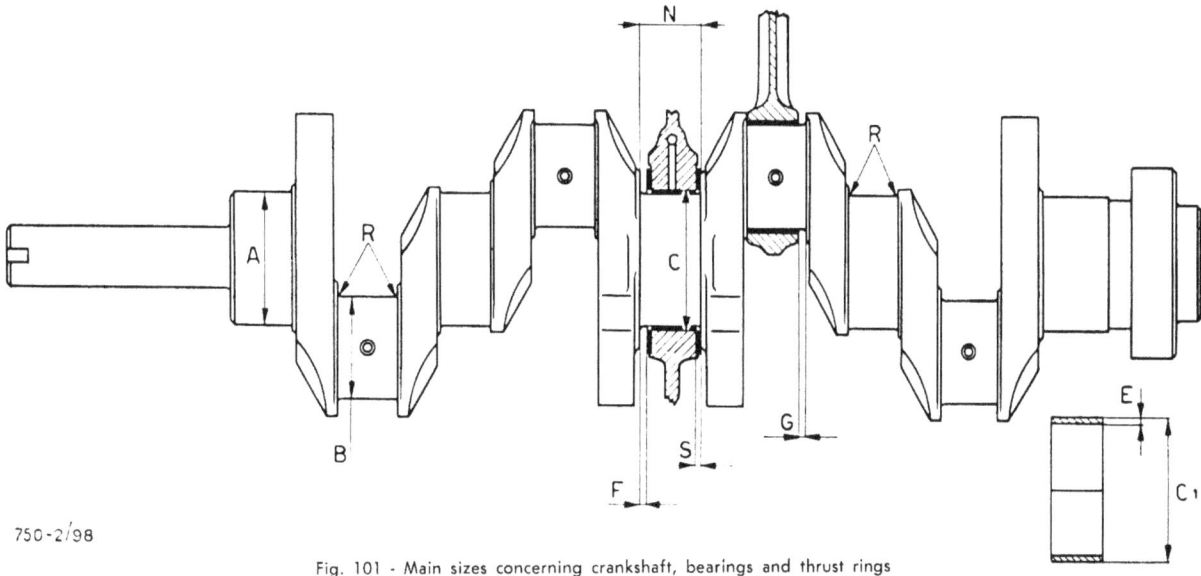

Fig. 101 - Main sizes concerning crankshaft, bearings and thrust rings

Crankshaft	Cranshaft journals diameter: **A**	standard 1st re-grinding 2nd re-grinding 3rd re-grinding	57.074÷57.086 56.820÷56.832 56.566÷56.578 56.312÷56.324	mm. » » »
	Con-rod journals diameter: **B**	standard 1st re-grinding 2nd re-grinding 3rd re-grinding	44.963÷44.975 44.709÷44.721 44.445÷44.447 44.201÷44.223	» » » »
	Maximum allowable ovalisation of the journals		0.05	»
Main bearing seat diameter: **C**			60.769÷60.782	»
Outer diameter of the main bearings: **C1**			60.845	»
Main bearing thickness: **E**		standard 1st re-grinding 2nd re-grinding 3rd re-grinding	1.829÷1.835 1.956÷1.962 2.083÷2.089 2.210÷2.216	» » » »
Diametral clearance between journals and their bearings (**C1-2E**) - **A** (recommended)			0.013÷0.050	»
Length of the central crankshaft journals: **N**		standard 1st re-grinding 2nd re-grinding 3rd re-grinding	30.000÷30.035 30.127÷30.162 30.254÷30.289 30.381÷30.416	» » » »
Thickness of thrust rings of central crankstaft journals: **S**		standard 1st re-grinding 2nd re-grinding 3rd re-grinding	2.311÷2.362 2.374÷2.425 2.438÷2.489 2.501÷2.552	» » » »
Axial clearance of thrust rings for central crankshaft support: **F** (recommended)			0.076÷0.263	»
Axial clearance of connecting rods: **C** (recommended)			0.20÷0.30	»
Fillets **R**			2.00	»

Fig. 102 - Checking the balancing of the crankshaft

compressed air in order to remove any particles of metal or abrasive. This washing process must include the oil-ways (using a 6 mm. drill) and the aluminium caps which close the ends of the oil-ways. When cleaning is completed, the oil-ways must be closed with new caps which will be caulked home.

c) **Checking journal alignment.**

This check must be made with a micrometer and with the crankshaft on suitable supports as shown in fig. 98.

The alignment tolerance for the crankshaft journals is 0.008 mm., with a new crankshaft and 0.05 at the moment of maximum wear. The alignment tolerance for the pairs of con-rod journals is 0.07 mm. in both directions (fig. 99). The tolerance for parallelism in the case of the crankshaft and con-rod journals in relation to their longitudinal axis is measured over their length and is 0.015 mm. (0.03 at the moment of maximum wear - fig. 100).

If the above limits are exceeded the crankshaft must be re-straightened in a press. This can only be done by a specialist workshop.

d) **Balance test.**

This must only be done in the case of crankshafts which have been re-ground and after the above checks have been made, or after the flywheel ring gear has been replaced.

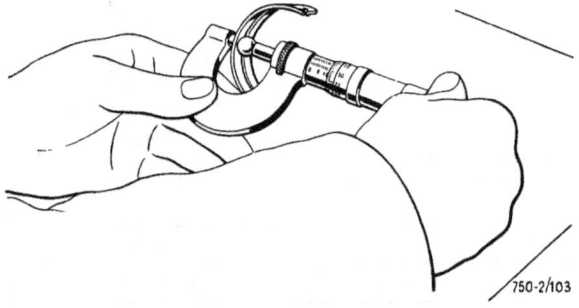

Fig. 103 - Measuring the thickness of a bearing with a micrometer

Proceed as follows:

Position the crankshaft as shown in figure 102, and ensure (using a spirit level) that the supporting flat surface is perfectly horizontal. If the shaft is in a state of balance it will not move, but if it tends to rotate, stick a temporary wad of putty on the side opposite that which tends to rotate downwards; the weight of the putty stabilises the whole assembly. Then, with a grinding wheel, remove from the counter-weights of crankshaft an amount of metal of equivalent weight to that of the putty, or bore weight-reducing holes in the flywheel. This must be done at a position diametrically opposed to the position at which the putty was affixed. The maximum permitted lack of balance is 32 gr/cm.

If the necessary equipment is available, it is advisable to balance the crankshaft dynamically as well, particularly in the case of engines used for racing.

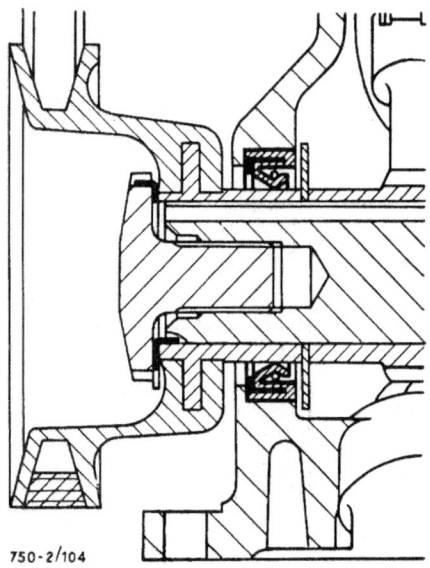

Fig. 104 - Front oil seal

e) **Checking clearance**

1) **Radial play** between crankshaft and con-rod journals and their bearings must be checked by finding the difference between the diameter of the bearing housing and the sum of the journal diameter and twice the thickness of one half-bearing.

Radial play limits and the thicknesses of the con-rod and crankshaft bearings are shown respectively in figures 79 and 101.

The thickness of a half-bearing must be measured with a micrometer and with a 10 mm. ball as shown in fig. 103. The purpose of this is to prevent errors and to avoid damaging the antifriction bearing surface.

2) **Axial play** of the crankshaft must be checked by measuring the difference between the length of the central journal measured between the shoulders of the crankshaft itself and the sum of the thickness of the intermediate bearing and the thickness of the two thrust rings.

The play when assembled must be between 0.076 and 0.263 mm.

The dimensions of the standard and oversize thrust rings are as shown in figure 101.

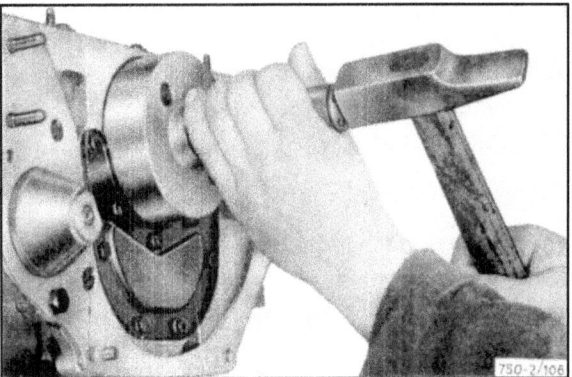

Fig. 106 - Mounting the rear oil seal with the tool No. 6121.07.293

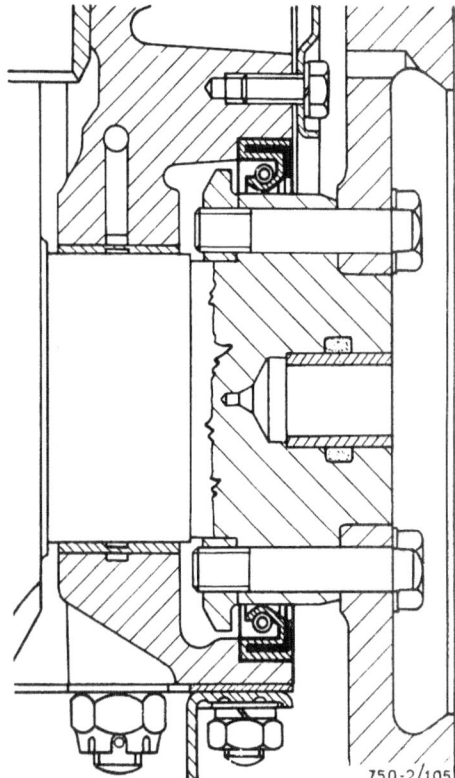

Fig. 105 - Rear oil seal

cooling it to room temperature in the open air. The wollen felt ring located in the housing on the crankshaft (and which surrounds the bush) must also be replaced with another which has been impregnated for 1 hour in engine oil at 45°C and then left to cool. The bush is pressed on by means of a special tool provided with an end-of-stroke stop.

i) Check that the two rubber oil seals (fig. 107) located between the rear bearing cap and the bearing itself are undamaged; replace them if necessary.

Assembly

1) Fit the crankshaft half-bearings and the halved thrust rings to the crankcase.

2) Put the crankshaft on its seats together with the half-rings wich will fix the flywheel, kept by the four studs mentioned in chapter 16.

3) Fit on the lateral bearing caps after first fitting

3) The fillet between the crankshaft and con-rod journals and the crankshaft shoulders must be 2 mm.

f) **Checking wear of the flywheel ring gear.**

If this ring gear is badly worn it should be replaced as described in Chapter 16.

g) **Inspect the front and rear oil seals** and replace them where necessary. Tool 6121.07.293 should be used for the rear seal as shown in fig. 106; see Chapter 12 regarding the front seal.

h) **Ensure that the clutch shaft centring bush** on the crankshaft is well impregnated with oil; if it is found to be dry it must be replaced.

The new bush must first be impregnated by immersing it for 4 hours in engine oil at 120°C and then

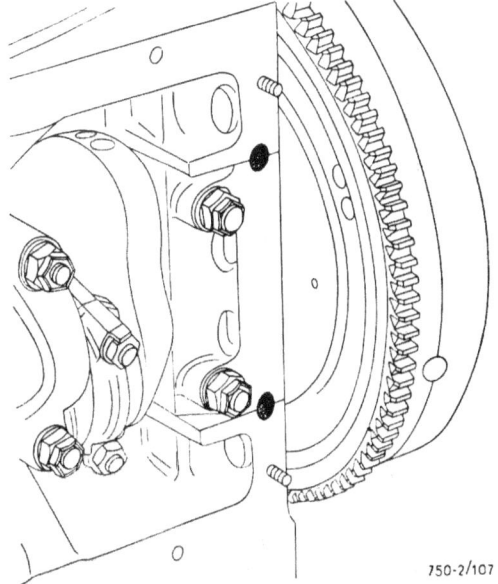

Fig. 107 - Rubber bushes for rear support oil seal

the half-bearings, and then the centre cap together with the halved thrust ring; fix the caps by tightening the nuts with a torque spanner as described in Chapter 10.

4) Fit the « Palmutter » lock-nuts and tighten them as described in Chapter 10.

NOTE: When fitting the rubber oil seals between the rear bearing cap and the crankcase, tool 6121.06.002 must be used as shown in figure 108.

18 - REFITTING THE ENGINE

Before the engine is refitted all the main units must be prepared and assembled as described in the respective sections above, namely:

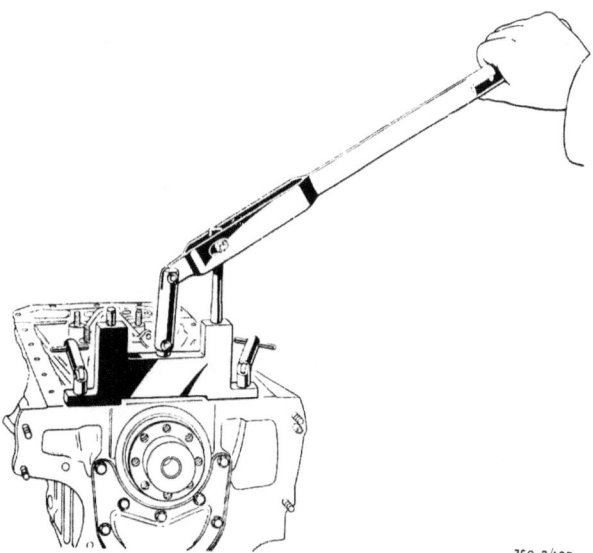

Fig. 108 - Fitting the rubber bushes of rear support oil seal

1) **Crankshaft** (chapter 17).
2) **Front cover** (chapter 12).
3) **Pistons, rings, con-rods** (chapter 10).
4) **Cylinder-head,** complete with inlet manifold, carburetters, etc. (chapter 6).
5) After fitting the gasket, fix the front cover, the steel plate and the breather tube connection.
6) Fix the front oil seal by means of the special tool 6121.07.293.
7) Rotate the crankshaft so that the con-rod journal for piston No. 1 is in the T.D.C. position.
8) With the crankshaft in the position described in 7) above, fit the flywheel; take care that the T.D.C. mark on the flywheel is in line with the mark cut on the gear-box attachment plate (figure 16); then lock the retaining bolts.

9) Insert the cylinder liners as described in Chapter 11.
10) After first inserting the adjusting washer on the intermediate shaft, simultaneously fit the auxiliary driving sprockets and intermediate sprocket in their respective seatings. Before doing this, however, fit the chain over the sprockets in such a way that the zero mark on the gear-wheel mounted on the crankshaft is located between the two similar marks on the intermediate sprocket as shown in fig. 83.
11) Fit the distributor and pump driving sprockets onto the crankshaft.
12) Fit the seal and the front cover complete (see Chapter 12).
13) Assemble the pistons, rings and connecting-rods as described in Chapter 11.
14) Fit the cylinder-head and its cover as described in Chapters 1 and 5.
15) Fit the pulley (for auxiliary drive) onto the crankshaft, and also the fan, the dynamo and the starter motor.
16) Fit the sump (pan) and the oil filter.
17) Check the distributor and ignition timing.
18) Tune the engine and, where necessary (such as, for example, after replacing pistons, bearings, etc.), run in the engine anew as described in Chapter 20.

19 - VALVE GEAR TIMING

The following operations are performed only in cases of the absence of any one of the reference marks designed to facilitate the simple procedure described in the Chapter 3.

WARNING: Before the engine is properly tuned, it is always necessary to rotate the crankshaft slowly by hand in order to ascertain the relative piston valve positions. The pistons and valves may be damaged by rapid rotation of the crankshaft.

While bearing this in mind, proceed as follows:

1) Stand the graduated quadrant (tool 6123.45.003) on the crankcase and rotate the crankshaft until the mark cut in the flywheel comes into line with the zero mark on the quadrant (fig. 109).

   Into the spark-plug socket for piston No. 4 screw the device for checking the T.D.C. position and bring the gauge on this instrument to the zero position.

2) Turn the flywheel 5° to the right and to the left of the datum position and record the gauge read-

Fig. 109 - Working out the T.D.C. by means of a graduated sector (tool No. 6123.45.003) and comparator gauge

Fig. 110 - Working out the valve opening and closing angles by means of a graduated sector and tool No. 6121.01.053

ing for each of the two positions. If the T.D.C. piston position coincides with the flywheel T.D.C. position, the gauge will show an equal reading for both of the flywheel positions.

3) If that is not the case, rotate the graduated quadrant until — by bringing the mark cut on the flywheel to a position where it coincides, both on the right and on the left, with the 5° positions on the quadrant — equal values are shown on the gauge. Test these gauge readings several times and then lock the graduated quadrant in position.

4) With the crankshaft in the T.D.C. position determined as above, fit the camshafts and bring them into the position shown in figure 31. Then connect them to the driving sprocket as described in Chapter 3.

NOTE: By way of explanation of the operations described hereunder, it is worth mentioning that the camshafts are provided — in order to achieve particularly quiet performance — with a type of cam of an unusual design; the cam shape makes it difficult to determine, using standard workshop equipment, the exact cam angles corresponding to the opening and closing of the inlet and exhaust valves. Experience has, however, shown that such determination can be replace quite satisfactorily by noting the height of lift corresponding to a given angular position of the crankshaft.

5) Then check the valve opening and closing angles: for this purpose, place in line with cylinder No. 1 tool 6123.01.053 which is provided with two gauges whose ends (fig. 110) are arranged to rest on the valve tappets.

6) Rotate the crankshaft through one turn until the cams assume positions corresponding to the end of the exhaust stroke and the beginning of the induction stroke at cylinder No. 1. Then, for each of the two cams, rotate the crankshaft until the sector angle — in which the gauge pointer remains stationary — is found; that sector corres-

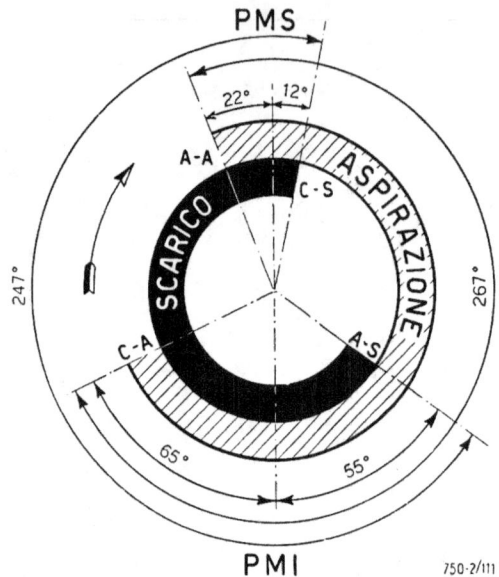

Fig. 111 - Timing diagram
P.M.S. = T.D.C. - **P.M.I.** = B.D.C. - **Scarico** = Exhaust - **Aspirazione** = Inlet - **A.A.** = Inlet opening - **C.A.** = Inlet closing - **A.S.** = Exhaust opening - **C.S.** = Exhaust closing.

ponds, on the cam face, to the quieting arc. Take the gauge reading in any position within this sector. After having determined the quieting position of the cam, slowly rotate the crankshaft in the normal direction in order to line up the cam operating the inlet valve (and in the opposite direction when dealing with the cam operating the exhaust valve) until a gauge reading shows movement of:

0.15 mm. for the exhaust valves
0.20 mm. for the inlet valves.

The distributor angles shown in figure 111 are correct if, with the above readings, the graduated quadrant shows the following crankshaft rotation values:

5° advance in inlet valve opening
5° retard in exhaust valve closing.

The remaining cam positions are checked in the above manner after the engine has been turned until the camshaft has been rotated through 180°. With the camshaft in this new postion, the zone in which the gauge pointer remains stationary must be found, the readings made and the engine rotated until the gauge shows the following movement:

0.15 mm. for the exhaust valves
0.20 mm. for the inlet valves.

The crankshaft must have been rotated through the following arcs as read off the graduated quadrant:

48° retard in inlet valve closing
48° advance in exhaust valve opening.

NOTE: With regard to the above timing requirements, a tolerance of ± 1½° is permitted.

If the above tolerance limit is exceeded, proceed as follows:

1) Slacken the screw fixing the sprocket to the camshaft and remove the corresponding bolt (see Chapter 3).

2) Using the appropriate pin wrench (tool No. 6121.24.012) rotate the camshaft forward or backward as follows:

   a) for inlet opening and exhaust opening advance, rotate the camshaft forwards in the proper direction of rotation if negative angular values are encountered, and backwards if these angular values are excessive.

   b) for inlet closing and exhaust closing retard, rotate the camshaft forwards if excessive angular values are encountered, and backwards if these angular values are insufficient.

Replace the bolt and tighten the screw.

Another and simpler way of timing the valve gear is as follows:

— give 0.60 to 0.65 play to the valves of cylinder No. 1. (With excess play it is easier to determine the moment when the cam touches the valve tappets);

— fit the chain in such a way that, with the No. 1 piston at T.D.C. on the ignition stroke, the camshafts take up the position shown in fig. 31;

— check (using the graduated quadrant which rests on the crankcase as shown in fig. 109) that the valve opening and closing takes place as shown in the following conventional diagram:
inlet valves
    opening begins: 5° 30′ before T.D.C.
    closing ends: 48° 30′ after B.D.C.
exhaust valves
    opening begins: 48° 30′ before B.D.C.
    closing ends: 5° 30′ after T.D.C.

— if and when valve opening and closing occurs at different angles, the camshafts must be rotated (while their driving sprockets are held still) until the above values are obtained;

— when the above valve opening and closing angles have been achieved, remove the camshafts and adjust all valves until they have the amounts of play shown in the table given in Chapter 4;

with an electric stylus cut reference marks as shown in figure 31 on both the camshafts and on the front bearing caps.

Running-in cycle for the Giulietta Berlina engine

Minutes at		Speed in r.p.m.	Power in H.P.
individual powers	Cumulative time		
5'	5'	1000	—
10'	15'	2000	3
15'	30'	3000	10
25'	55'	3500	16
35'	1h.30'	4000	25
40'	2h.10'	4500	35
5'	2h.15'	5000	48
15'	2h.30'	5000	48-50

20 - RUNNING-IN THE ENGINE ON THE TEST-BENCH

During the initial operational period, overhauled engines offer perceptible resistance to rotation; this is particularly the case when pistons and crankshaft bearings have been replaced.

For this reason overhauled engines should be tested on a special bench equipped with a hydraulic brake and the necessary checking instruments.

If the new parts and the new working surfaces are to bed down properly and gradually, it is essential for test-bench running-in to be performed as set out below:

Running-in cycle for the Giulietta Sprint and Spider engine

Minutes at		Speed in r.p.m.	Power in H.P.
individual powers	Cumulative time		
10'	10'	1.000	—
10'	20'	2000	3
10'	30'	3000	10
20'	50'	3500	16
25'	1h.15'	4000	25
35'	1h.50'	4500	35
15'	2h.5'	5000	48
5'	2h.10'	5500	55
5'	2h.15'	6000	60
15'	2h.30'	6000	63-65

The following checks must be made during the running-in period:

a) **Oil pressure, water and oil temperatures.** The pressure and temperature must be as follows:

Oil pressure:
 at maximum r.p.m. : 4.5-5 kg/cm^2
 at minimum r.p.m. : 0,5-1 kg/cm^2
Temperature of water leaving engine: 75°C.
Temperature of oil in sump (pan) : 80 to 85°C.

b) **Checking the ignition advance**
(to be done with an engine speed of 5000 r.p.m.).

Using the stroboscopic instrument described in the chapter entitled « Ignition » in Part 10 (« Electrical Equipment ») check the maximum centrifugal advance (43° to 45°); while reading off the advance, cut out the vacuum advance. If the desired value is not obtainable, disconnect the distributor and correct as appropriate.

Then repeat the reading at an engine speed of 500 r.p.m. in order to ensure that even at low speeds the advance is maintained at the proper values (6° to 8°).

c) **Power and fuel-consumption check**

During the 15 minutes at which the engine runs at maximum power carry out power and fuel consumption tests and also make the various acceleration tests to check the operation of the carburettor.

Fuel consumption at maximum power should be 240/250 grams per H.P. per hour.

d) **Checking slow-running and the exhaust fumes**
After removing the exhaust manifold, bring the carburetter to its lowest slow-running setting and estimate the strength of the mixture on the basis of the colour of the exhaust gas.

On returning the engine to maximum r.p.m. check the exhaust fumes.

e) **Oil consumption**
Oil consumption is only checked if the exhaust fumes appear excessive. The procedure to be adopted is as follows:

— draw off the engine oil, allowing it to drain for 15 minutes, weigh it and return it to the engine;
— run the engine at 4,500 r.p.m. and at full power for 30 minutes, endeavouring to maintain the oil and water temperatures constant and equal to the permitted values as set out in the above table;
— again draw off the oil, allowing it to drain for 15 minutes; re-weigh it.

The difference between the two weights gives the oil consumption which should be between 2 and 4 grams per H.P. per hour. This corresponds to 50 to 100 grams of oil consumed during the above 30-minute test.

f) **Checking for leaks**
After switching off the engine, examine it for signs of oil, fuel or water leaks.

WARNING

1) The maximum speeds indicated above, for the brake test of Giulietta Sprint and Spider engines, are also valid for engines used for racing and to which certain modifications designed to increase their power have been made. The maximum speed of **6400-6600 r.p.m.** for these engines is not to be considered as an operating speed but only as a speed which must never be exceeded and not even maintained for long; if this fact is ignored, fractures will develop and will lead, generally during normal operation, to the total destruction of the damaged part.

2) This test-bench process is not to be considered as completing the running-in of the engine. The following conditions must therefore be observed during the next **3000 km**.
   a) do not exceed the following speeds:

Distance covered		Max. permissible speeds in km/h.			
		1st. gear	2nd. gear	3rd. gear	gear 4th.
first 1000 km.	Berlina	29	48	70	95
	t.i., Sprint and Spider	33	55	80	110
	Sprint Vel. and Spider Vel.	38	64	93	126
from 1000 to 3000 km.	Berlina	35	59	85	115
	t.i., Sprint and Spider	40	65	100	135
	Sprint Vel. and Spider Vel.	46	78	113	153

b) on starting:
— switch off the starter as soon as the engine fires;
— before moving off, allow the engine to run at about 1500 r.p.m. for 3 minutes in summer and 5 minutes in winter.

c) while moving:
— do not maintain the maximum speeds for long periods;
— never press the accelerator to the floorboards, and release it from time to time.

PART 2 B

AUXILIARY ENGINE EQUIPMENT

21 - THE COOLING CIRCUIT

Engine cooling is effected by a forced circulation system using a centrifugal pump (see diagram in figure 112).

To obtain rapid engine warming on starting, a thermostat valve (fig. 118) is fitted on the engine outlet pipe and only opens when the water in the engine reaches a temperature of 80 to 85°C. Only then is the radiator brought into use.

In the interests of high thermal efficiency, the water temperature should be between 105° and 110°C; the water circuit is therefore under pressure even in the radiator.

THE WATER PUMP

The water pump is of the centrifugal low-pressure type and is incorporated in the fan bracket; it is driven from the belt which also drives the fan and the dynamo.

The cast-iron impeller is shrunk onto its shaft.

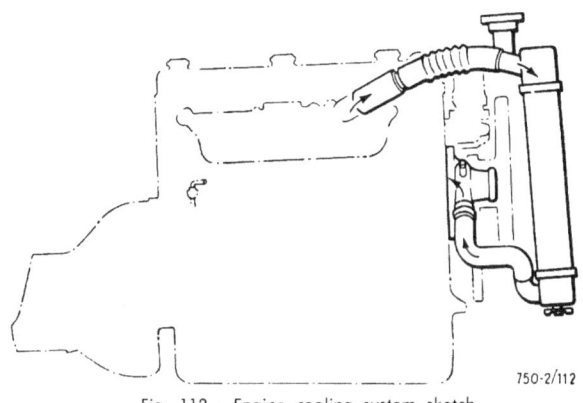

Fig. 112 - Engine cooling system sketch

Removing the water pump from the engine

1) Remove the radiator as described in the next chapter.

2) When it is fitted remove the hose leading from the engine to the heater.

3) Unscrew the nuts retaining the tensioning bracket and the dynamo bottom bracket, and rotate the dynamo in order to slacken the fan belt.

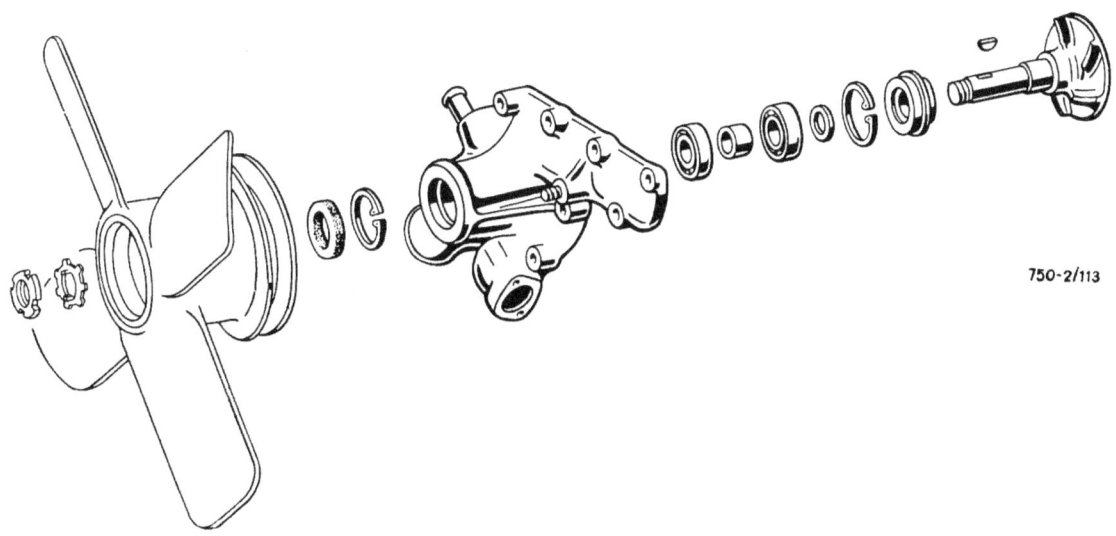

Fig. 113 - Exploded view of the water pump

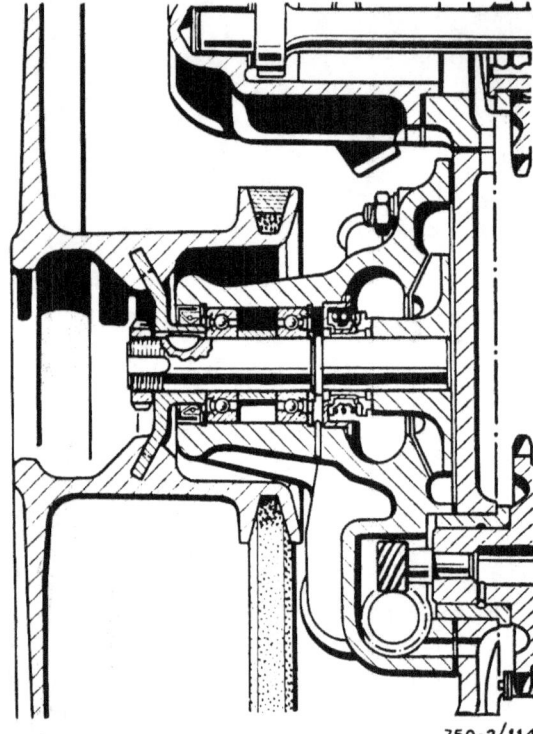

Fig. 114 - Sectional view of Giulietta Models water pump. Notice please that Berlina is not provided with intermediate gears for the tachometer as other models.

4) Remove the fan, taking off the safety plate and the locking nut.

5) Remove the key coupling the impeller shaft to the fan.

6) Remove the pump body from the engine.

Dismantling the water pump

1) Remove the shaft with its impeller, using a small hand press.

2) Remove the water seal, the front oil seal and the bearing-retaining spring rings; by means of tool 6121.07.308 remove the bearings and the distance-piece from the pump body.

3) When fitted remove the flexible muff coupling and the r.p.m. indicator driven gear.

Inspection

1) Check (or preferably replace) the oil retaining ring and the water-seal ring.

2) Check that the key on the fan drive shows no sign of damage; replace it if necessary.

3) Check that the surface of the impeller has no holes due to corrosion.

4) Check that the spring rings used to retain the bearings are in good condition; replace them if necessary.

5) Check that the impeller shaft bearings are undamaged; replace them if necessary.

6) For all Giulietta engines, excluding Berlina model, check that the r.p.m. indicator (tachometer) driven gear (fig. 115) is sound and that there is no excessive tooth wear. Replace it if necessary.

A similar check must be made in the case of the r.p.m. indicator driving pinion located on the reduction gearing shaft.

WARNING: In the case of Giulietta Sprint engines from No. 1315.00472 onwards, the water pump sealing ring has been replaced by another of different size. If the seal on the earlier engines proved defective, ring seats must be re-bored in order to bring the internal diameter A and the depth B to the dimensions shown in fig. 116.

Re-assembling the water pump

1) Refit the rear spring ring which retains the bearings in the pump body.

2) Using tool No. 6121.07.308, refit the bearings and the distance piece after first greasing them and filling the space between them with grease.

3) Refit the front spring ring which retains the bearings. Using tool N. 6121.07.310, refit the water seal ring; the adjusting washer for the internal ring of the rear bearing can be made to stick to the water seal ring by smearing it with a little grease.

4) Using tool No. 6121.07.312, refit the front oil seal.

5) Slide on the shaft together with the impeller.

6) For all Giulietta engines, excluding Berlina model, refit the r.p.m. indicator (tachometer) driven gear and the muff coupling.

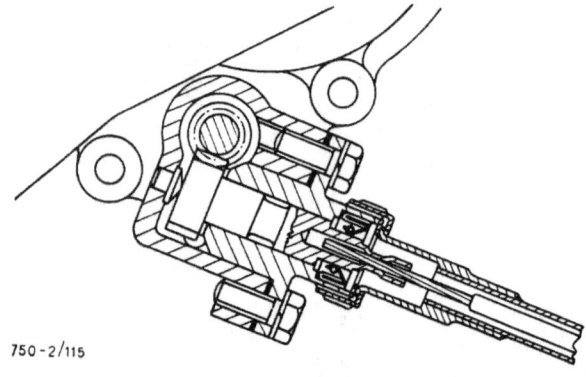

Fig. 115 - Sectional view of the Tachometer driving gear for all Giulietta models, excluding Berlina.

7) Refit the pump body to the front cover of the engine.

8) Refit the fan and the fan belt. Tighten the belt by means of the tensioning arrangement on the dynamo bracket. Then lock the nuts on the bottom dynamo bracket.

9) Re-fit the radiator as described in the next section.

THE RADIATOR

The radiator, which is of the vertical tube type, is located in front of the engine and is fixed to the body through four bolts and four rubber pads.

A drain tap is provided at the bottom of the radiator; the filler is provided with a special type of cap incorporating a pressure-reducing valve.

Removing the radiator from the car.

1) After removing the filler cap, draw off the water by opening the drain tap located at the bottom of the radiator.

2) Take off the 4 anchor bolts and the rubber pads.

3) Loosen the straps on the rubber hose joining the radiator to the cylinder-head and pull the hose off the nozzle.

4) Loosen the straps on the rubber hose joining the radiator to the water pump, and pull the hose off the nozzle.

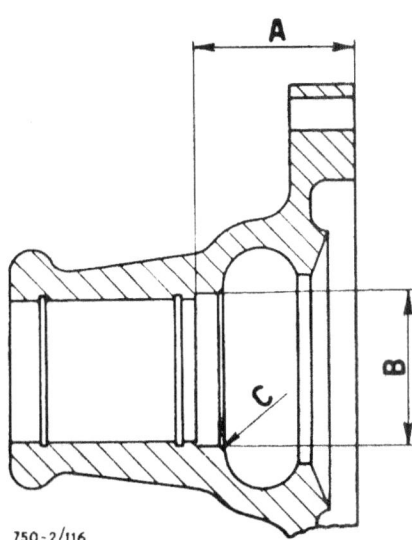

Fig. 116 - Sizes for the water seal bore in the water pump body

(The boring to be effected only on engines Giulietta Sprint up to No. 1315.00471).
Recess depth **A** = 37.85÷38 mm. - Inner diameter **B** = 36.425÷36.450 mm. - Chamfer **C** = 0.5 mm.

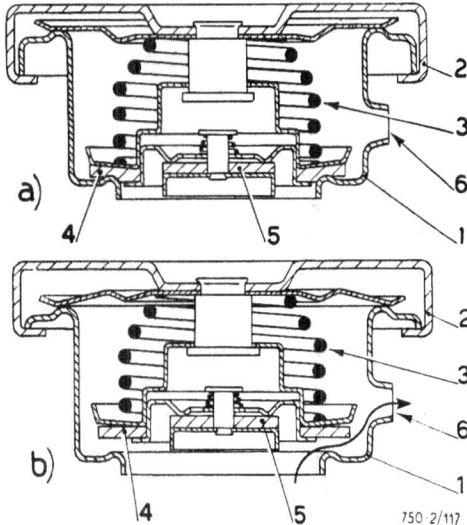

Fig. 117 - Radiator cap
a) Cap closed and radiator under pressure - b) Cap opened as far as the first catch (that is rotated about 1/4 turn) for steam release.
1. Fitting of the radiator - **2.** Cap - **3.** Adjustment spring - **4.** Gasket - **5.** Vacuum valve - **6.** Steam release

5) Lift out the radiator while inclining it slightly towards the back of the car and taking care not to knock it against the fan.

Inspection

1) Make sure that the radiator fins are in good condition.

2) Examine the welds of the brackets, the lateral straps and the nozzles.

3) Make sure that excessive scale has not formed inside the radiator. If such scale deposits have formed, carefully wash out the radiator with a solution of water and household soda as follows and after re-fitting the radiator to the car:

— fill the radiator and the engine with a solution consisting of 8 litres of water and 300 grams of sodium carbonate (household soda), and run the engine slowly for at least ten minutes;

— switch off the engine and leave the solution in the radiator for about half an hour;

— drain off all the solution;

— when the engine has cooled, and after opening the drain taps on both the radiator and the cylinder block, wash out the entire cooling system with a copious flow of running water;

— re-fill the system with clean water, run the engine for a few minutes, drain off the water once more and re-fill with fresh water.

Re-fitting the radiator to the car

1) Re-fit the rubber pads and place the radiator in position; tighten the four bolts.

2) Attach the rubber hose leading from the radiator to the cylinder-head and from the pump to the radiator, and tighten the respective straps. Before re-fitting the hose in question, examine it carefully and replace it if it is not in perfect condition.

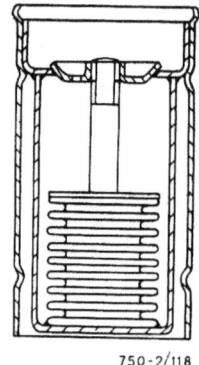

Fig. 118 - Section of the thermostat valve

WARNING:

1) **As the temperature of the cooling water may exceed 100°C at high engine speeds, the water circuit will be under pressure, even within the radiator. When checking the water level while the engine is still hot, it is essential that, on unscrewing the radiator cap, it is only given an initial quarter turn (when a « stop » will be felt) so that the pressure may be reduced. The water level should only be checked where a supply of fresh water is available.**

2) **In winter, and if an anti-freeze solution has not been added to the water, the radiator and the cooling circuit must be drained immediately the engine is switched off.**

3) **Users are reminded that, when for any reason the cooling circuit is re-filled after having been partly or completely emptied, the engine must be run for a few minutes with the radiator full, the heater tap open and the filler cap off. The purpose of this is to allow any air entrapped in the heater to escape; the water in the radiator must then be topped up and the filler cap tightly closed.**

Thermostatic valve

As mentioned above, a thermostatic valves is fitted to the water circuit on the outlet side of the engine.

Recommended anti-freeze solutions

Glycerine	Freezing point	Alcohol	Freezing point
20%	— 6°C	12%	— 5°C
30%	—11°C	20%	—10°C
40%	—18°C	25%	—15°C
		30%	—20°C

Remarks - Alcoholic solutions require periodical topping up with alcohol to compensate the losses due to evaporation.

This facilitates the rapid warming-up of the engine. To make sure that this valve is working properly, immerse it in water and check whether it begins to open when the temperature of the water reaches 82-87°C and opens fully (7 mm.) when the temperature reaches 90-95°C.

22 - THE FUEL FEED

Fuel is fed to the carburettor by means of a mechanical diaphragm-type pump mounted on a bracket affixed to the cylinder-head (Berlina, t.i., Sprint and Spider engines) or by means of an electric pump (Sprint Veloce and Spider Veloce engines).

The pump draws fuel from the tank located at the back of the car and delivers it to the carburettor bowl.

Fig. 119 - Fuel pump

THE MECHANICAL FUEL PUMP

Description

The FISPA fuel pump (model SUP 60) is driven via a rocker arm which in turn receives its motive power from a cam located on the exhaust valve cam-shaft. The pump comprises a top compartment and a bottom compartment (fig. 120).

The top compartment houses the bowl, the wire gauze filter (pump screen), the fuel inlet and outlet channels and the suction and delivery valves.

In the bottom compartment is located the diaphragm incorporating a central driving rod with its return spring. Also in the bottom compartment is the lever operating the diaphragm.

Operation

The rotation of the cam (mounted on the front end of the cam-shaft which controls the exhaust valves) operates a rocker arm which in turn operates a rocker **1**; the latter, oscillating on a pin **2**, drives a link **3** attached by means of a tie-rod **4** to the diaphragm **5** mounted between the plates **6**.

When the diaphragm descends it compresses a spring **7** and creates a vacuum in chamber **8**; the fuel is then drawn in by the suction valve **10** and is filtered by the fuel filter **9**.

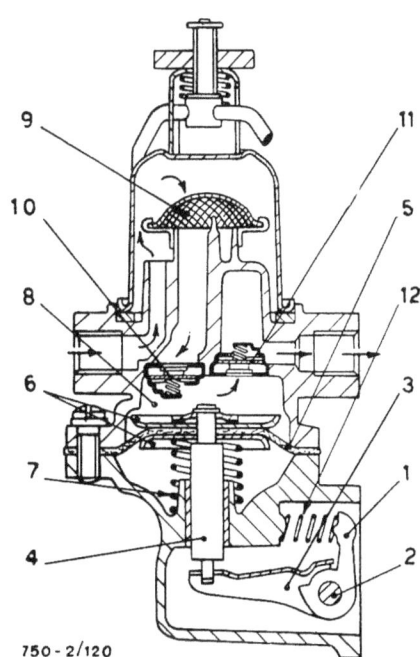

Fig. 120 - Sectional view of the mechanical fuel pump.

1. Driving rocker arm - 2. Rocker pin - 3. Link - 4. Tie-rod - 5. Diaphragm - 6. Diaphragm plates - 7. Diaphragm spring - 8. Vacuum and pressure chamber - 9. Fuel filter - 10. Suction valve - 11. Outlet valve - 12. Rocker arm spring.

The rocker arm, following the profile of the cam, allows rocker **1** to return to its original position; the spring **7** thereby expands and pushes the diaphragm **5** upwards, thus applying pressure on the fuel which is then forced into the carburettor bowl via the delivery valve **11**.

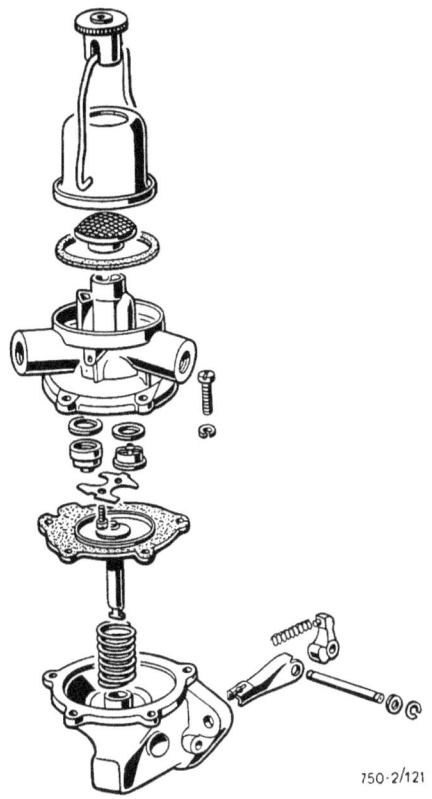

Fig. 121 - Exploded view of the fuel pump

When the fuel in the carburettor bowl reaches the prescribed level, the float closes the inlet valve and creates a differential pressure within the pump chamber **8**; this compels the diaphragm **5** to remain in the bottom position, thus compressing the spring **7**.

When the fuel level in the bowl falls, the float re-opens the inlet valve and allows fuel to enter chamber **8** again. A pressure drop therefore takes place within this chamber **8** and this enables the diaphragm to move upwards again under the thrust of the spring **7**; more fuel is thus injected into the carburettor bowl. It should be noted here that the link **3** is coupled to the rocker **1** in order to allow the rocker to control the variable stroke of the diaphragm **5** as determined by the greater or lesser pressure existing in chamber **8**. The spring **12** serves only to keep the rocker **1** in contact with the driving rocker arm.

Pump maintenance

The pump does not **normally** require any special attention, but it is advisable to **inspect it periodically**;

Fig. 121 bis - The electric pump fitted to the car; electrical connections to be made.

it should be examined whenever maintenance work is done on the carburetter.

Every 3000 km.

a) Remove the top compartment, lift out the gauze filter and clean it carefully with petrol.

b) Make sure that the rubber gasket is undamaged.

Whenever the engine is overhauled

a) Remove the top pump body, take out the valve seat retaining plate, withdraw the valves and wash them with petrol (gasoline). If they show even minor signs of wear, replace them.

b) Make sure that the diaphragm and spring are in proper working order.

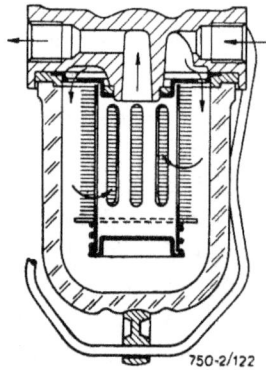

Fig. 122 - Cross section through the additional fuel filter

c) Remove the bottom compartment from its bracket and examine the rocker arm for wear; also check the efficiency of the corresponding spring.

d) Wash the diaphragm driving mechanism with paraffin and lubricate it with a thin oil.

THE ELECTRIC FUEL PUMP

Fuel is fed to the two Weber 40 DCO 3 carburetters by means of an electric pump (fig. 121 bis) located on the fuel pipe below the car floor adjacent to the rear body crossmember.

Operation

The pump is brought into action when the ignition key is turned to its first position; it continues to operate until the engine is switched off.

The pump includes a vertical cylinder, in whose airlock chamber is installed an electric solenoid having one piston in the center.

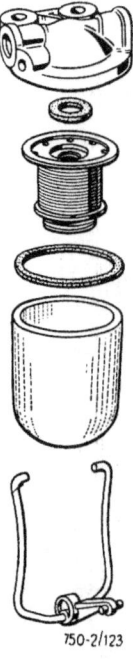

Fig. 123 - Exploded view of the additional fuel filter

The fuel enters in the pump by the lower end and flows out by the upper one passing through a piston duct.

At the bottom end, are located the wire gauze filter and the suction-and delivery valves.

At rest, the piston is kept in top position by a spring; turning the key the electric circuit is closed and the pison is sucked back by the solenoid. This piston movement causes the opening of the electric circuit and the return of the piston to top position due to the spring action, and therefore the new closing of the electric circuit: and the operating cycle starts again.

The pump must never be intered with if perfect operation is required.

In the event of the irregular or insufficient flow of fuel, check the electrical connections and ensure that

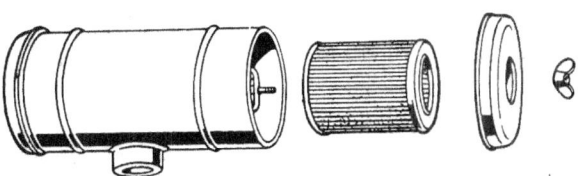

Fig. 124 - Air cleaner for Giulietta Berlina and t.i.

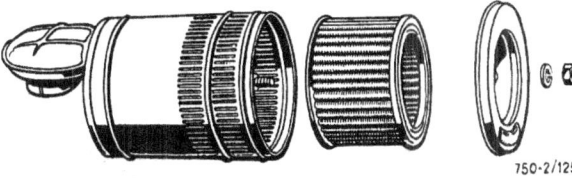

Fig. 125 - Air cleaner for Giulietta Sprint and Spider.

all are tight; removing the lower cover also check the filter.

If internal pump wear is found, replace the pump.

THE ADDITIONAL FUEL FILTER

The Giulietta Sprint is provided with an additional FISPA fuel filter (fig. 122) of the multi-disc type, the filter element is made of special paper.

The maintenance of this filter requires that every 3000 km. (and whenever the carburetter is cleaned) the filter element should be removed and — while compressing the spring used to separate the discs — washed with petrol (gasoline).

If the discs are found to be damaged, the entire filter element should be changed.

Examine the gasket for damage and replace it if necessary.

THE AIR CLEANER

Description

The cleaner (figs. 124 and 125) is made up of a sheet steel body containing the filtering element.

The cleaner has a stirrup for fixing it to the cylinderhead; its outlet end is strapped to the carburetter.

The filtering element is made of a special fabric device designed in the form of a star in order to increase the cleaning surface.

Maintenance

Every 8000 to 10000 km: remove the cover from the cleaner body, withdraw the filter element, blow through it carefully with low-pressure compressed air and clean it with petrol (gasoline). When dry, smear it with engine oil, replace it in the cleaner body and refit the cover.

It is advisable to clean the air filter in this way whenever maintenance work is done on the carburetter.

23 - CARBURATION

THE SOLEX C 32 BIC CARBURETTER (FOR GIULIETTA BERLINA CARS)

Operation

Constant-level bowl

The fuel arriving at the connection **19** shown in figure 127 passes through a needle valve incorporated in the seat **18** wich is closed by the float **21** as soon as the carburetter reaches a determined level within the bowl.

Starting the engine

The carburetter is provided with a variable easy-starting device which facilitates starting when the engine is cold and gives a richer mixture during the first few minutes after the engine is started, and while the engine reaches its proper working temperature. This is particularly useful in winter. This starting device is controlled by pulling out a knob on the dashboard. The knob controls a lever **4** which, set at an intermediate stage between its two extreme positions, regulates the quantity and strength of the mixture admitted to the engine.

The starting device is operated as follows:

1st. position - knob pulled right out

(starting the engine from cold)

The considerable negative pressure on the engine side of the throttle (which is almost closed) causes an energetic supply of petrol to issue from the feed wells **15** and **17**, and causes the petrol to mix with the air entering through the orifice **16** and flow into the

Fig. 126 - Carburetter Solex C 32 BIC for Giulietta Berlina
1. Starter control lever - **2.** Idling jet - **3.** Throttle maximum opening adjustment screw - **4.** Throttle control lever - **5.** Throttle minimum opening adjustment screw - **6.** Idling mixture adjustment screw. - **7.** Main jet - **8.** Filter - **9.** Fitting with filter, fuel inlet - **10.** Starter jet.

chamber of the starting device where it mixes still further with the air entering through the air jet **2**; this produces a very rich mixture.

This rich mixture passes through the port **5** in the disc, enters the duct **6** and flows into the inlet manifold.

By keeping the knob out to its maximum position (the « rich mixture » position) the petrol in the wells **15** and **17** becomes exhausted and automatically causes a weakening of the mixture, since the only fuel reaching the chamber in the easy-starting device is that which passes through the jet of the device itself **22**.

The mixture becomes still weaker due to the greater quantity of air which then enters via the wells.

2nd. position - knob in the intermediate position
(during the first few minutes after starting)

So that the engine will perform properly during the first few minutes after it is started from cold, particularly in winter, a fairly rich mixture must continued to be supplied.

This mixture must nevertheless be weaker (both insofar as concerns quantity and strength) than that used at the actual moment of starting as described above. The control knob is therefore then placed in an intermediate position. This setting rotates the disc in the starting device and simultaneously modifies the degree of opening of the mixture outlet port and the orifice admitting fuel into the chamber of the starting device. By varying the position of the control knob it is thus possible gradually to reduce the strength of the mixture as the engine warms up.

If the engine has not cooled down completely it can be re-started with the control knob in approximately the half-way position.

Idling

When the engine is idling, the throttle is almost completely closed, and the negative pressure created by the engine draws fuel from channel **12**. This fuel passes through the jet **14** and there mixes with air entering via the idling air calibrator **13**; it then passes through the orifice **27** and enters the inlet manifold.

The quantity of mixture which passes through port **27** is controlled by a screw **25** and in this way the engine idling speed is controlled. Any opening of the throttle automatically reduces the suction beyond it, and this reduces the idling speed. Until the main jet comes into operation the mixture enters the engine via port **26**.

Normal operation

Opening the throttle gives rise to a depression in the restricted zone of the choke tube (venturi) **7** and this sucks across the air bleed holes **8** of the bleed tube **9**

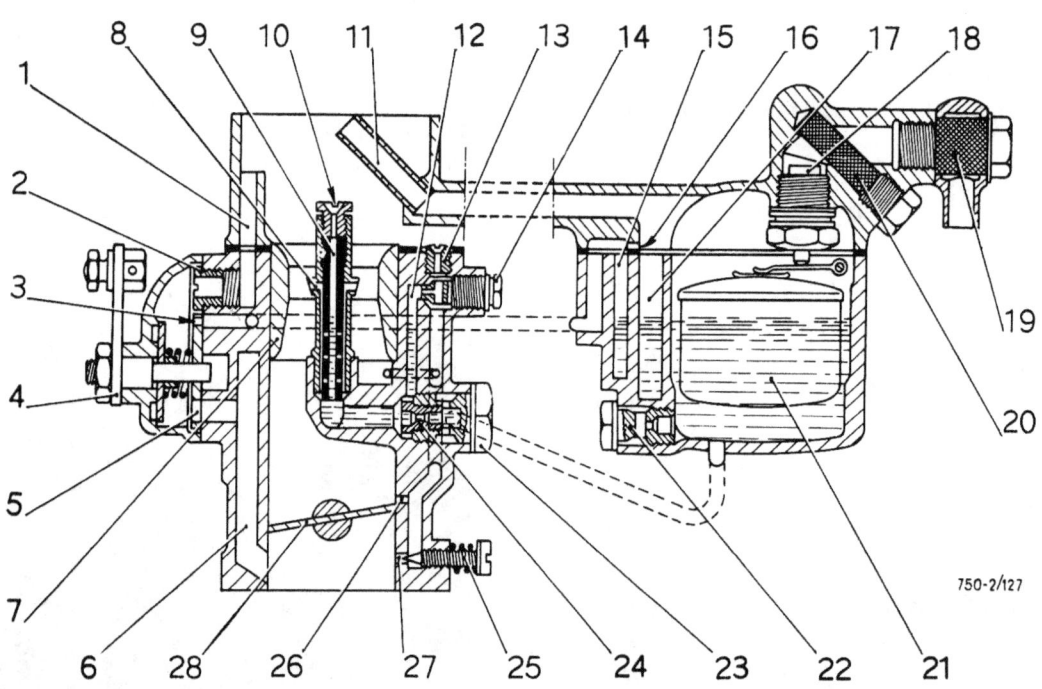

Fig. 127 - Schematic sectional view of the Carburetter Solex C 32 BIC for Giulietta Berlina

1. Starter air intake - 2. Starter air jet - 3. Hole of the rotating disc for fuel flow into the starter - 4. Starter control lever - 5. Hole in the disc for mixture flow into the intake duct - 6. Mixture passage duct - 7. Choke tube (venturi) - 8. Bleed holes - 9. Bleed tube - 10. Bleed tube plug - 11. Vent tube - 12. Low speed (idling) mixture channel - 13. Low speed air plug - 14. Low speed jet - 15. Starting device well - 16. Air passage to the well 15 - 17. Well of the starting device - 18. Fuel intake needle seat - 19. Union with filter for fuel intake - 20. Filter - 21. Float - 22. Starter jet - 23. Main jet holder - 24. Hain jet - 25. Low speed mixture adjustment screw - 26. Progressive hole for low speed - 27. Low speed mixture passage hole - 28. Throttle

the fuel contained in the well on the bleed tube itself and which reached there via the main jet **24**.

The mixture is kept constant by the fact that by increasing the fuel supply, the fuel level in the bleed tube 9 drops and uncovers a greater number of holes through which the air introduced through the bleeder cap hole **10** then passes. In this way the petrol/air ratio remains constant.

Maintenance

WARNING:

1) **If the carburetter is to function properly, it is extremely important that all maintenance and overhaul work is performed by skilled mechanics and that the instructions given in this manual are strictly observed.**

2) **When cleaning jets, orifices, channels, ducts and filters, never use needles or any other metal tools: only compressed air must be used.**

Minor overhaul

Minor overhaul can be performed as follows without removing the carburetter from the engine:

1) Take off the air cleaner and wash the filtering element with paraffin (Kerosene).
2) Unscrew the fuel feed pipe, take out the filter and clean it by blowing air through it.
3) Remove the cover-retaining screws and take off the cover.
4) Lift off the bowl gasket and the clip, withdraw the float and clean the bowl.
5) Unscrew the jet-holders and the jets, the idling air calibrator and the bleeder cap, slide off the bleed tube, wash them all with petrol (gasoline) and blow through with compressed air.
6) Blow through all the carburetter channels with compressed air.
7) Unscrew the seat of the needle in the cover, wash it, and carefully blow through it. Check to ensure that it is a close fit.
8) Unscrew the inclined screw located beneath the cover, extract the strainer and blow through it; prevent the small ring forming the seat from falling off.
9) Remove the screws holding down the starting device; using compressed air, blow thorugh the seat, the tubes and the cover.

Then re-assemble the various parts, taking care to fit the gaskets properly after checking to ensure that they are sound.

WARNING: Make sure during the above operations that nothing falls into the inlet manifold.

Major overhaul

Removing the carburetter from the engine

To remove the carburetter from the engine proceed as follows:

1) Slacken the screw on the strap affixing the air cleaner to the carburetter;
2) remove the nut from the bolt holding the air cleaner to the cylinder-head; remove the cleaner;
3) remove the two screws which attach the control cable leading to the starting device; and disconnect the cable;
4) disconnect the petrol feed pipe connection;
5) disconnect the advance correction tube;
6) remove the stop from the throttle-control lever;
7) remove the nuts from the studs connecting the carburetter to the manifold, and lift off the carburetter.

Dismantling the carburetter

1) Remove the three screws connecting the carburetter cover to the body, and lift off the gasket.
2) Unscrew the inclined screw holding down the filter, together with the seat and the inlet needle
3) Remove the float arm and the float itself.
4) Unscrew and take off the various jets and jet holders.
5) Unscrew the bleeder cap and draw off the bleed tube.
6) Remove the four screws which join the easy-starting device to the carburetter body.
7) Unscrew the idling adjustment screw.
8) Unscrew the idling air calibrator.
9) Disconnect the throttle control unit.
10) Remove the throttle fixing screws and take out the throttle.
11) Take out the throttle spindle.
12) Slacken the fixing nut on the choke tube (venturi) and remove the latter.

Inspection

1) **When the engine has been unused for long periods:**

Dismantle all the various parts as described above, carefully wash them in petrol (gasoline), blow through them with compressed air and check to make sure that the jet diameters correspond with the prescribed values.

2) **After a long period of use:**

a) check the degree of wear of the throttle. If excessive, replace the throttle;

b) check the play of the throttle spindle in both seats. If excessive play is encountered, bore out the seats and fit a larger spindle. When this is impossible, fit bushes in the carburetter body;

c) check the jet diameters with suitable gauges;

d) check the fuel inlet needle and its operation. If the stem of the needle is worn, replace it together with its seat;

e) check the efficiency of the filters, the float and the float arm;

f) check the wear of the variable disc of the starting device and also of its spindle.

After having performed the above operations, and before re-assembling the carburetter, wash all parts carefully with petrol (gasoline) and blow through them with compressed air.

3) **If the carburetter has been dismantled because of incorrect operation:**

Proceed as described in the preceding paragraph, and then make the following inspection:

— check the internal ducts for gas-tight
— check the cover for a flat fit
— check all gaskets for soundness.

And lastly, make sure that:
— the body and the cover are not cracked;
— that the choke tube is as prescribed;
— that the diameters of the idling air calibrator, bleeder cap hole and the bleed tube have not been altered;
— that all screwed holes are undamaged;
— that the float has not been deformed or damaged.

WARNING: When maintenance work is performed on the carburetter it is advisable to inspect and overhaul the fuel pump and to clean the air cleaner, the fuel pipes and the fuel tanks.

Re-assembling the carburetter

The assembly operation should be the reverse of those described above for the dismantling of the carburetter. In addition the following should be borne in mind:

1) thin gaskets should be used with flanges; thick gaskets deform flanges;

2) the screws fixing the various parts of the carburetter should not be tightened to excess;

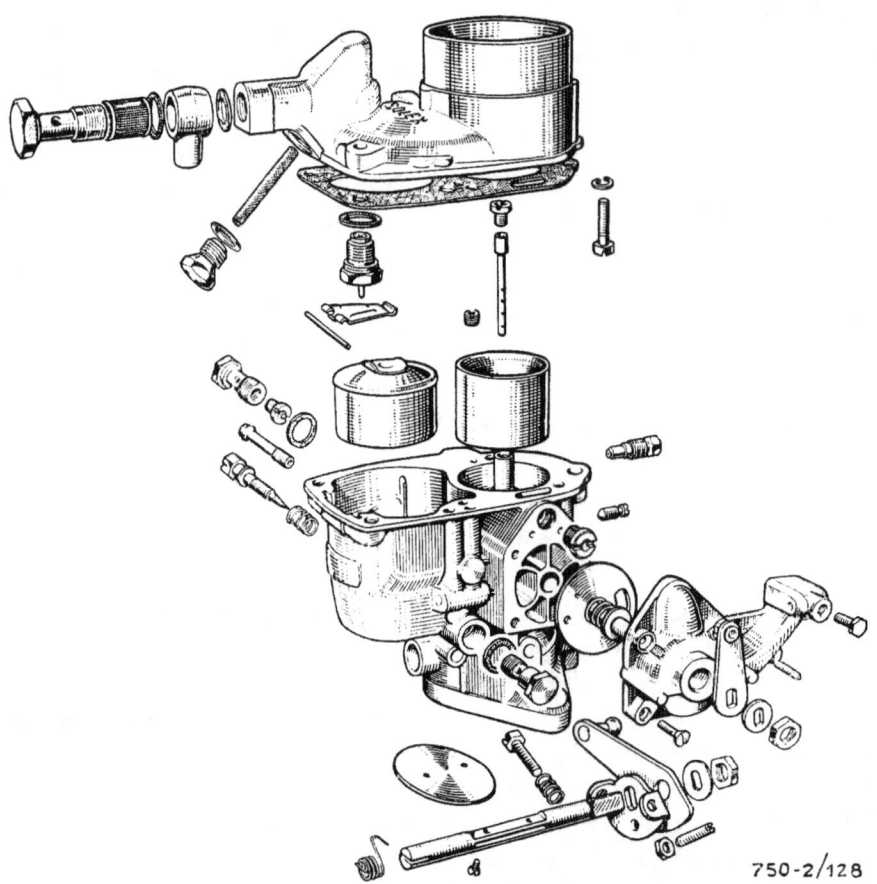

Fig. 128 - Exploded view of carburetter Solex C 39 BIC for Giulietta Berlina

3) check to ensure that the throttle opens and closes perfectly;
4) when tightening the nuts holding the carburetter to the manifold, tighten the nuts gradually and alternately in order not to deform the flange. These nuts should be provided with locking washers;
5) take extreme care when fitting the accelerator control rods, and be certain that the clearance between all jointed sections is correct;
6) when fitting the easy-starting device control cable sheath, avoid sharp bends. Fix the cable to the lever so as to allow the control knob to have an initial movement of 5 mm. before acting on the device;
7) after completing assembly, check that all joints are tight and that there are no leaks on the fuel feed line.

Slow-running adjustment (idling)

If the engine operates irregularly when idling, or if it tends to stall, make sure first of all that the sparking plugs are working properly; then adjust the carburetter as follows, **with the engine running and when the engine is hot:**

- slightly screw in the screw adjusting the throttle opening **5** (fig. 126) in order to increase the engine speed;
- screw out the idling mixture screw **6** until the engine begins to race; then screw it in gradually until the engine runs smoothly;
- very slowly screw out the throttle regulating screw **3** until the engine speed is approximately 450 r.p.m.;
- if the engine again begins to race slightly tighten the idling mixture screw; **under no circumstances must this screw be turned right home.**

Calibration data for the Solex C 32 BIC carburetter:
choke tube diameter . . . . 21 mm.
main jet diameter . . . . 1.05 »
slow-running jet diameter . . . . 0.40 »
easy-starting jet diameter . . . . 1.30 »
bleeder cap hole diameter . . . . 1.60 »
idling air calibrator diameter . . . 1.00 »

THE SOLEX C 35 APAIG CARBURETTER (FOR GIULIETTA t.i., SPRINT and SPIDER CARS)

Description

The C 35 APAIG SOLEX carburetter with its acceleration pump is a two-stage dual carburetter.

It differs from the usual dual carburetter in that both bodies discharge into a single feed pipe; while the engine is idling or running at lower power, only the right-hand half is used, but when running at high

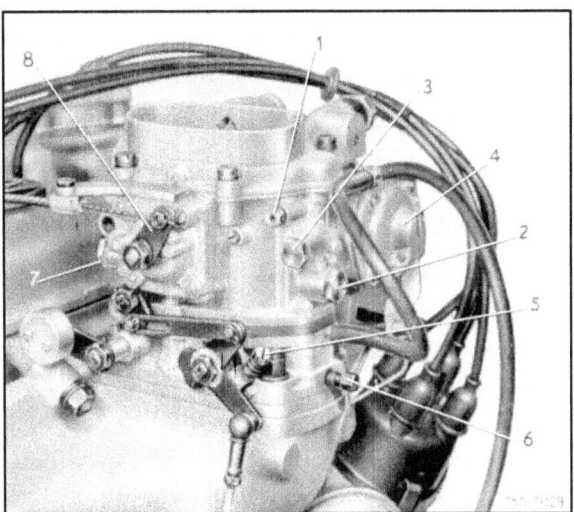

Fig. 129 - Carburetter Solex C 35 APAIG for Giulietta t.i., Sprint and Spider cars.

1. Low speed jet - **2.** Main jet for n. 1 choke tube (venturi) - **3.** Acceleration pump jet - **4.** Acceleration pump - **5.** Throttle minimum opening adjustment screw - **6.** Low speed air adjustment screw - **7.** Main jet for n. 2 choke tube (venturi) - **8.** Starter control lever.

power the second half — that is, the member on the left (nearest the engine) — is also brought into play. Another particular feature of this carburetter is that the throttles in the two shells do no open simultaneously.

The throttle in the right-hand shell is connected to the accelerator pedal, while the left-hand throttle is connected to the first by means of a lever system such that the second throttle begins to open when that in the first shell is a little more than half open. Beneath the throttle in the second shell is a third throttle wich operates under the influence of differential pressure; this third throttle is connected to a calibrated counterweight and opens automatically when — with the second throttle at least partially opened — the degree of vacuum within the inlet manifold reaches a predetermined value.

The choke tubes (venturi) in the two carburetter bodies have different diameters in the narrowed zone; the right hand choke tube is the wider.

The bleed tube in the right-hand body follows the longitudinal axis of the choke tube, while that in the left-hand body is located in a special housing in the body of the bowl itself, and discharges into the choke tube (venturi) by means of an atomiser tube.

The SOLEX C 35 APAIG carburetter is illustrated in fig. 130 and comprises the following essential parts:
- main body with bowl;
- cover for the body and the bowl, with a breather tube (vent);
- variable easy-starting device;
- acceleration pump.

Operation

Starting the engine

The easy-starting device fitted to this carburetter is similar in design and operation to that used with the Solex C 32 BIC single-body carburetter described in the preceding chapter.

The device is used as follows:

— **starting the engine from cold:** the control knob is pulled out as far as it will go; in this position the richest mixture is obtained;

— **idling when engine is cold:** when the engine fires the knob is pushed back to an intermediate position which reduces the strength and quantity of the mixture. In this way the engine gradually warms up and ultimately reaches the optimum operational temperature;

— **re-starting before the engine has quite cooled down:** the control knob is moved into the intermediate position as demanded by the temperature of the engine.

Idling

The idling control fitted on the right-hand side of the carburetter is similar to that used with the Solex C 32 BIC carburetter already described.

Normal engine operation

The accelerator pedal directly operates throttle **1** (figure 130) located within the right-hand body of the carburetter; this throttle in turn operates throttle **2** in the left-hand body via a lever system. The control rod **3** for throttle **2** is provided with a port which prevents the two throttles from opening simultaneously.

In the right-hand shell, beneath throttle **2**, there is a third throttle **4** excentrically mounted on its own control spindle and which is kept closed by the action of a suitable counterweight. This third throttle is opened automatically by the depression which develops within the engine as the engine speed increases at higher powers.

1) **Operation at low and medium power ratings**

At this stage only the right-hand half of the carburetter is used, the principle then being the same as in the case of the Solex C 32 BIC.

When the accelerator pedal is depressed, throttle **1** opens and brings the bleed tube **5** into action; the bleed tube supplies the engine with the necessary quantity of mixture for ordinary operation.

2) **Operation at high power ratings**

The assistance of the left-hand body of the carburet-

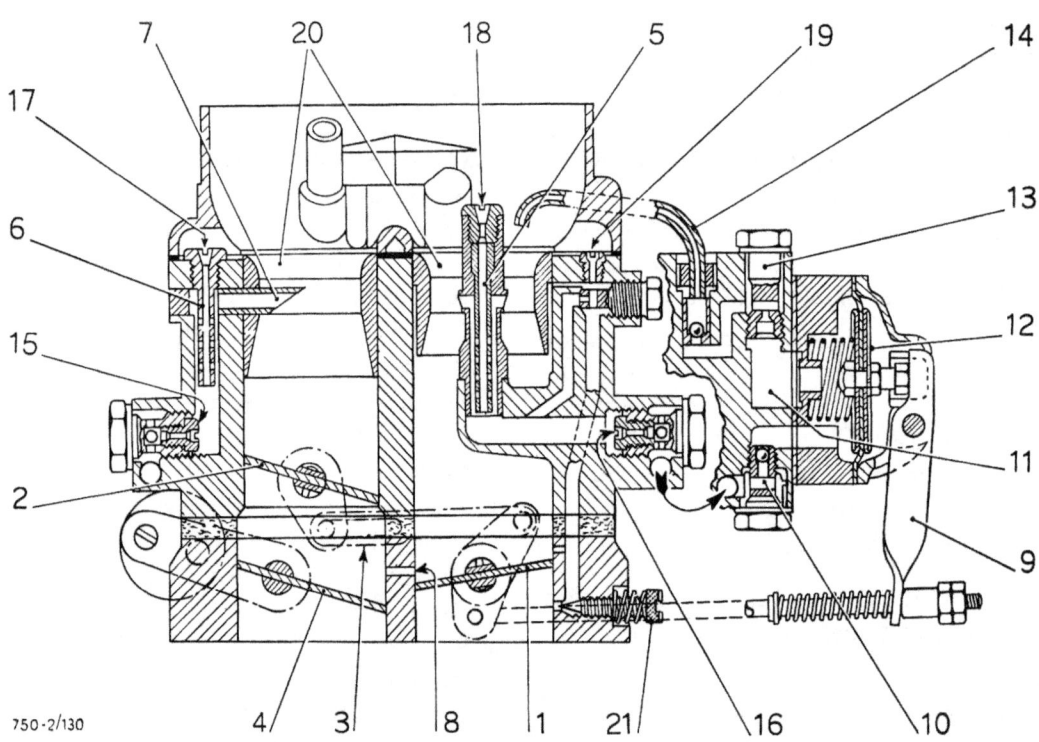

Fig. 130 - Schematic sectional view of the carburetter Solex C 35 APAIG for Giulietta t.i., Sprint and Spider cars.

1. Throttle of the right body - **2.** Throttle of the left body - **3.** Throttle control rod, left body - **4.** Automatic opening throttle - **5.** Bleed tube of the right body - **6.** Bleed tube of the left body - **7.** Spray tube of the left body - **8.** Drilling between left and right bodies - **9.** Pump control lever - **10.** Pump inlet (suction) valve - **11.** Pump pressure chamber - **12.** Pump diaphragm - **13.** Pump jet - **14.** Injector - **15.** Main jet of the left body - **16.** Main jet of the right body - **17.** Bleed tube plug, left body - **18.** Bleed tube plug of the right body - **19.** Low speed air plug - **20.** Choke tubes (venturi) - **21.** Low speed mixture adjustment screw.

ter is added to the action of the right-hand body as follows:

when throttle **1** has opened by a little more than one half, and when the accelerator pedal is still further depressed, the control rod **3** causes throttle **2** in the left-hand body to open. The bleed tube **6** then comes into action and — via spray tube **7** — supplies the extra mixture required to develop the greater power. As the automatic throttle **4** is still closed at this stage, the extra mixture is compelled to pass into the right-hand shell hrough port **8** and cannot reach its peak value.

3) Operation at maximum power

The increase in the degree of vacuum beyond throttle **4** as the engine speed increases towards the maximum causes the throttle in question to open and allows the mixture to pass directly into the inlet manifold.

The bleed tube **6** is then in a position to supply the maximum amount of petrol air mixture needed to allow the engine to develop its maximum power.

Acceleration pump

The acceleration pump is affixed to the side of the bowl of the right-hand carburetter chamber; its purpose is to inject into the right-hand choke tube the additional fuel required for acceleration.

The operation of this pump takes place simultaneously with the opening of the right-hand throttle, and is achieved via lever **9** which is elastically con-

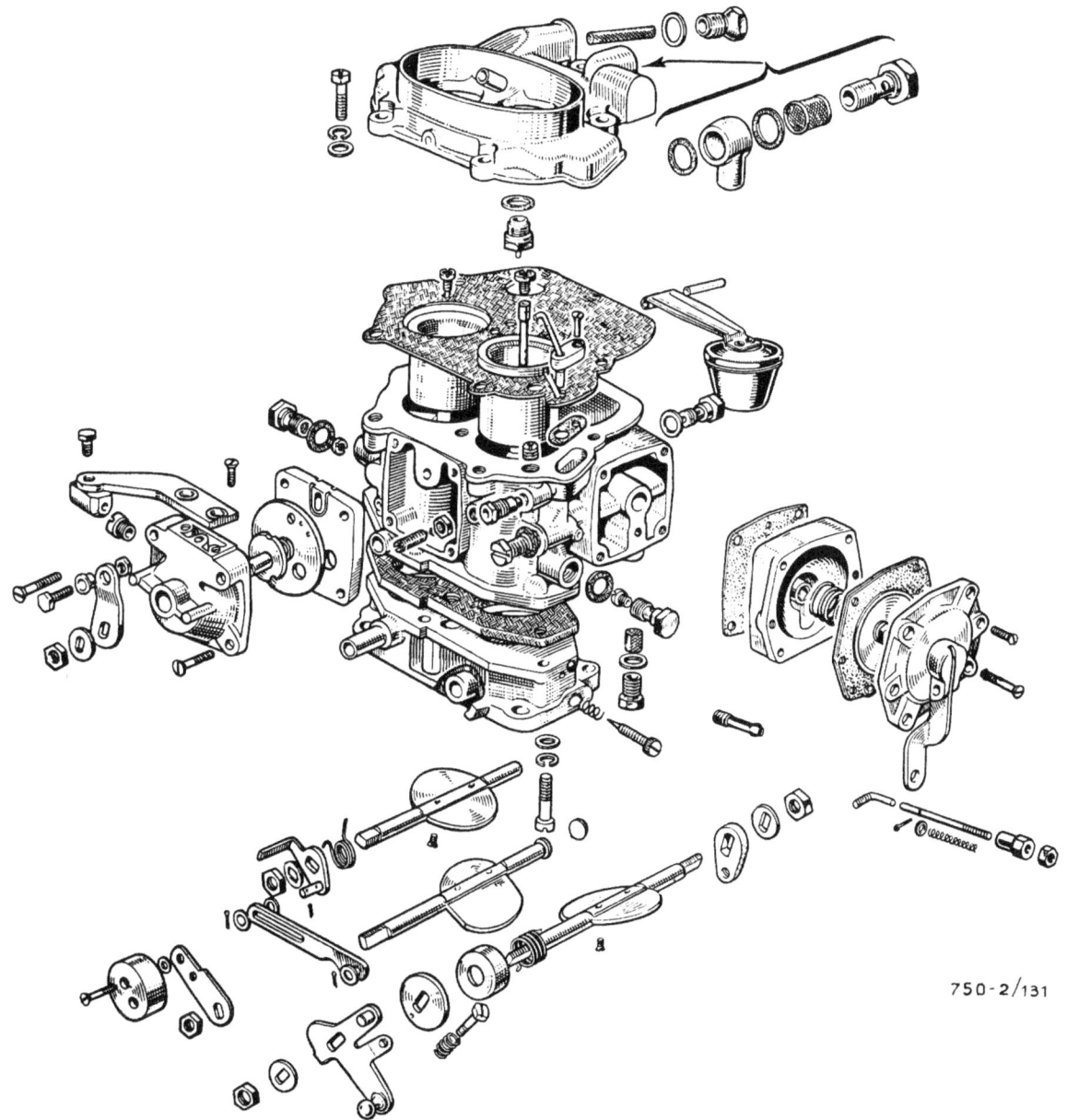

Fig. 131 - Exploded view of the Carburetter Solex C 35 APAIG for Giulietta t.i., Sprint and Spider cars.

nected to the throttle by means of a spring which prolongs the injection of fuel.

While the throttle **1** is released the fuel can flow, via check valve **10**, into the pressure chamber **11**; when the accelerator is depressed the lever **9** acts against the diaphragm **12** and causes the displacement of the diaphragm; this displacement forces the fuel through the jet **13** and the injector **14** into the right-hand choke tube.

It should be noted that when throttle **1** is wide open, a certain amount of fuel flows from the injector **14** the whole time, and for this reason the pump jet **13** must not under any circumstances be altered; this fuel flow ceases when the throttle is less than half-way closed.

Maintenance

WARNING: When cleaning jets, orifices, ducts and filters, needles or other metal tools must never be used but only compressed air.

When cleaning operations are completed, check to ensure that the diameters of the jets and calibrators correspond; the proper gauges should be used for this purpose.

A) Minor overhaul

The instructions given for the Solex C 32 BIC carburetter should first be followed; the work will then be completed by the following:

— Unscrew and remove the idling air calibrator, the left-hand bleeder cap with the bleed tube, and the pump injector tube; wash them with petrol and blow through them with compressed air.

— Take off the cover from the accelerator pump. Remove the diaphragm, the check valve and the jet. Wash them and the suction and delivery channels of the pump with petrol (gasoline) and blow through them carefully with compressed air.

B) Major overhaul

Dismantling the carburetter

1) Remove the screws holding the cover to the bowl, and take of the cover.
2) Remove the retaining screw on the fuel inlet filter and the needle with its seat.
3) Remove the idling air calibrator, the left-hand bleeder cap with the corresponding bleed tube and the fuel injection tube.
4) Remove the gasket from the bowl body.
5) Lift out the float.
6) Disconnect the complete acceleration pump from the bowl body.
7) Disconnect the complete left-hand and right-hand throttle control lever system.

Fig. 132 - Carburetter Solex 32 PAIAT for Cars Giulietta Sprint

1. Low speed jet - **2.** Main jet for n. 1 choke tube (venturi) - **3.** Acceleration pump jet - **4.** Acceleration pump - **5.** Throttle minimum opening adjustment screw - **6.** Low speed air adjustment screw - **7.** Main jet for n. 2 choke tube (venturi) - **8.** Starter control lever.

8) Unscrew the screw connecting the bowl and body to the bottom body with its to shells, and remove the bottom body complete with its heat-resisting gasket.
9) Unscrew and remove the various jets and jet-holders, the right-hand bleeder cap and the corresponding bleed tube.
10) Remove the easy-starting device complete.
11) Remove the lever with the automatic throttle counterweight.
12) Unscrew the idling control screw.
13) Unscrew the throttle fixing screw, remove them and take out the control spindles.
14) Slacken and remove the screws fixing the choke tubes.

Inspection

Proceed as described for the Solex C 32 BIC carburetter, remembering to inspect both carburetter bodies and also the acceleration pump.

In addition, check to ensure that:

— the acceleration pump diaphragm is sound and that its spring is working properly;
— the heat-resisting gasket is sound;
— the counterweight calibration remains unaltered.

Re-assembling the carburetter

The various operations described for dismantling should be performed in the reverse order.

Re-fitting the carburetter to the engine

After assembly, check to ensure that all joints are tight and that there are no leakages in the pipe circuit.

WARNING: At the time of all major carburetter overhauls, it is always advisable to clean out all fuel pipes and the fuel tanks; the air cleaner, fuel pump and the acceleration pump should also be overhauled at the same time.

Slow-running adjustment

Adjustment of the idling controls is carried out as described for the Solex C 32 BIC carburetter.

Calibration data for the Solex C 35 APAIG carburetter.

A) **Right-hand body:**

choke tube diameter	24 mm.
main jet diameter \ t.i.	1.30 »
/ Sprint and Spider .	1.20 »
idling jet diameter	0.40 »
bleed tube-cap \ t.i.	1.80 »
hole diameter / Sprint and Spider .	1.50 »
idling air calibrator diameter . . .	1.00 »

B) **Left-hand body:**

choke tube diameter	24 mm.
main jet diameter \ t.i.	1.55 »
/ Sprint and Spider .	1.50 »
bleed tube-cap \ t.i.	1.10 »
hole diameter \ Sprint	1.40 »
/ Spider	1.90 »

C) **Easy-starting device:**

jet diameter . . . . 1.60 mm.

D) **Acceleration pump**

jet diameter . . . . 1.00 mm.

THE SOLEX 32 PAIAT CARBURETTER (FOR GIULIETTA SPRINT CARS)

The Solex 32 PAIAT carburetter shown in fig. 132 was fitted to all Giulietta Sprint cars up to No. 1315.00970. This two-stage carburettor also had two bodies, an easy-starting device and an acceleration pump. In addition to the normal bowl, this carburettor also has a second bowl alongside the first, its purpose being to ensure perfect fuel feed when cornering.

The Solex 32 PAIAT carburetter is, except for several small differences, similar from the constructional point of view to the Solex C 35 APAIG already illustrated; the details regarding operation and maintenance are the same for both types.

Idling control adjustment is also the same as in the case of the Solex C 35 APAIG carburetter.

Calibration data for the Solex 32 PAIAT carburetter:

A) **Right-hand body:**

choke tube diameter	22 mm.
main jet diameter	1.15 »
idling jet diameter	0.45 »
bleed tube-cap hole diameter . . .	2.00 »
idling air calibrator diameter . . .	1.00 »

B) **Left-hand body:**

choke tube diameter	23 mm.
jet diameter	1.35 »
atomiser air calibrator diameter . .	1.10 »

C) **Easy-starting device:**

jet diameter . . . . 1.50 mm.

D) **Acceleration pump:**

jet diameter . . . . 0.45 mm.

NOTE: In the case of engines on cars owned by racing drivers who have lowered the cylinder-head by 1 mm., the alteration to the Solex 32 PAIAT carburetter settings is as follows:

Right-hand body

choke tube diameter	25 mm.
main jet diameter	1.35 »
bleeder cap hole diameter	1.80 »

Left-hand body

choke tube diameter	27 mm.
jet diameter	1.80 »
bleeder cap hole diameter	1.00 »

THE WEBER 40 DCO 3 CARBURETTER (For Giulietta Sprint Veloce and Spider Veloce cars)

Operational diagram

Fig. 133 shows that the air enters horizontally, passes through the centring devices **23** where it is mixed with the fuel emerging from the jet tubes **22**; then, after passing through the choke tube **25**, it is conveyed, through the throttle valves **27**, to the engine cylinders. From the fuel-feed pipes, connected to the carburetter by means of a suitable connector and filter, the fuel arrives, via the needle valve **12**, in the bowl **16** where the float **15**, hinged on the fulcrum screws **14**, controls the needle opening and thus maintains the liquid at a constant level.

From the bowl the fuel passes via the appropriate channels to the communication bushes **19**; it is then measured by the main calibrated jet **6** and passes into the emulsion bowl **7**.

After mixing with the air which arrives from the calibrated brake screw **8** through the emulsion holes in bowls **7** and the jet tubes **22**, the fuel reaches the carburation area consisting of the mixture centring devices **23** and the choke tube **25**. The centring arrangements **23** serve to increase the negative pressure (caused by the engine suction) on the jet tubes **22** and to bring the emulsified fuel to the centre of the choke tube **25** so as to make the mass more homogeneous.

Running the engine at idling speed

The fuel, is conveyed from the bowl **16**, via appropriate ducts, to the calibrated idling jets **10** through the lateral hole in bushes **19**. After being emulsified with the air arriving via the calibrated hole in screws **11** through the channels **18** and the idling feed ports **29** (adjustable by means of the taper tipped screws **31**) the fuel reaches the fuel ducts downstream of throttle **27** where it is mixed with the air which can be sucked in by the engine through the small ports located between the duct walls and the throttle when the latter is in the idling position.

The mixture then passes via channels **18** to the fuel ducts and through the progression ports **28** which are located in line with the throttle or which serve to permit a regular increase in the angular speed of the motor, beginning at the idling speed, when the throttles are opened.

Acceleration pump

This pump serves to provide a regular increase in the angular velocity of the engine even when the throttles are suddenly opened.

In the case of the Weber 40 DCO 3 carburetter the pump consists of a metal piston **21** driven, via an arrangement of levers and springs, by the shaft carrying the throttles.

When the throttles are closed, the lever arrangement frees a sliding rod which, under the action of the spring **5**, raises the piston **21**; the fuel is thus sucked from the bowl **16** into the pump cylinder through the inlet (suction) valve **17** and the duct **20**. When the throttles are opened, the lever arrangement lowers the sliding rod, by overcoming the action of the spring **5** and by pressing the piston **21** downwards; this piston movement is controlled by the pumping extension spring located inside the sliding rod; the fuel is then conveyed via the channel **33**, through the needle valve **4** to the calibrated pump jets **3** by which it is injected into the main ducts in the carburetter.

In order to be able to vary the quantity of fuel discharged by the acceleration pump, the carburetter is provided with a calibrated drain screw **1** which, via channels **26** and **30** drains off excess fuel into the

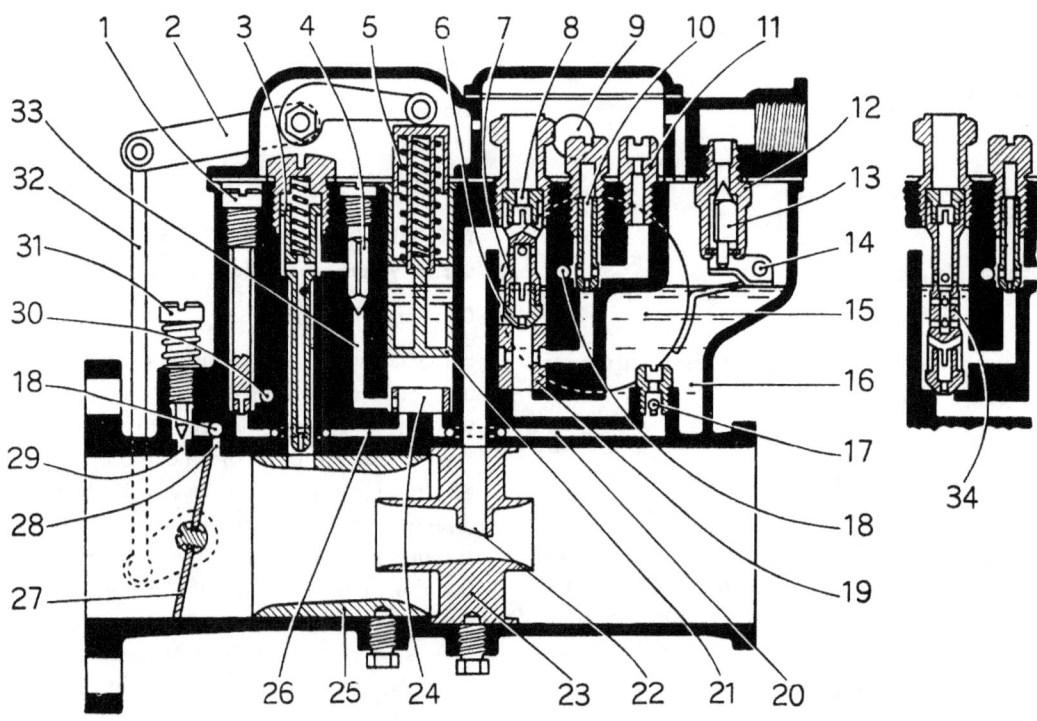

Fig. 133 - Schematic-section of the Weber 40 DC03 Carburetter.

1. Pump drain screw - **2.** External pump operating lever - **3.** Pump jet - **4.** Delivery needle valve - **5.** Piston return spring - **6.** Main jet - **7.** Emulsion bowl - **8.** Air brake screw - **9.** Dynamic air intake attachment - **10.** Idling jet - **11.** Idling air screw - **12.** Needle valve - **13.** Valve needle - **14.** Float fulcrum screw - **15.** Float - **16.** Carburetter bowl - **17.** Pump suction valve - **18.** Idling mixture channel - **19.** Idling communication bushes - **20.** Pump suction pipe - **21.** Pump piston - **22.** Jet tube - **23.** Mixture centring device - **24.** Piston stroke reducing distance-piece - **25.** Choke tube - **26.** Pump drain pipe - **27.** Throttle - **28.** Progression port - **29.** Idling port - **30.** Pump drain channel - **31.** Screw for adjusting idling mixture - **32.** Pump operating rod - **33.** Pump inlet pipe - **34.** Emulsion bowl.

bowl; in order not to reduce the speed with which the pump comes into action this variation in the quantity of fuel discharged can also achieved by limiting the stroke of piston **21**; this is done by inserting a distance-piece **24** in the cylinder of the acceleration device.

Pump Jets

These jets (**3**) operate as a high speed device, in as much as the negative pressure in the carburetter ducts reaches a sufficient value to lift the needles **4** from their seats; a certain quantity of fuel is drawn into the main ducts via the inlet valves **17**, the channels **20** and **33**, and the pump jets **3**; the mixture drawn into the engine is thus enriched.

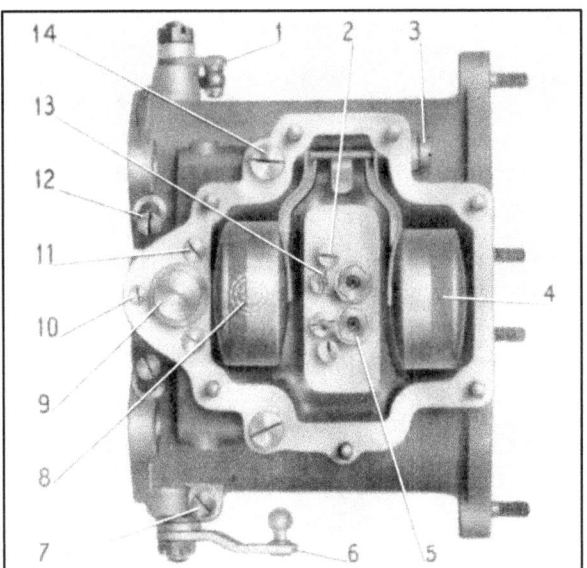

Fig. 135 - Top view of the Weber 40 DCO 3 carburetter without its cover.

1. Main pump-operating lever - **2.** Idling jets - **3.** Float fulcrum pin - **4.** Float - **5.** Complete main jet wells and air brake screws - **6.** Throttle-operating lever - **7.** Idling adjustment screw - **8.** Pump suction valve - **9.** Acceleration pump - **10.** Pump drain screw - **11.** Delivery pump valves - **12.** Idling mixture control screws - **13.** Idling air brake screws - **14.** Pump jets.

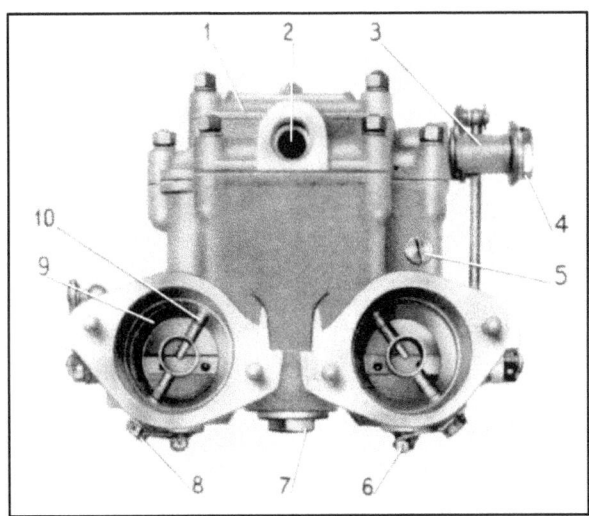

Fig. 134 - Front view of the Weber 40 DCO 3 Carburetter.

1. Jet inspection cover - **2.** Connection for dynamic air inlet - **3.** Fuel filter - **4.** Filter plug - **5.** Float fulcrum pin - **6.** Screws retaining the centring devices - **7.** Bowl drain plug - **8.** Screws retaining the centring devices - **9.** Choke tubes - **10.** Mixture centring devices.

Removing and refitting the air inlet bowl

When removing the nuts (**2**) fitting the air inlet bowl to the carburetter (Fig. 138), use a 10 mm flat crowsfoot spanner not more than 5 mm thick.

When removing the nuts (**1**) the special spanner No. 6121.18338 must be used.

Work on the Weber 40 DCO 3 carburetter when fitted to the car

To remove the carburetter proceed as follows:

1) remove the two clips and the corrugated hose between the air cleaner and the air intake bowl cover;

2) remove the air intake cover by unscrewing the two wing nuts;

3) detach the air inlet bowl as described in the next paragraph;

4) remove the cover with the Weber box spanner. Access can then be had to the bowl supports carrying the emulsion bowl, the air brake jet and the main jet, the idling jet and the idling air brake jet.

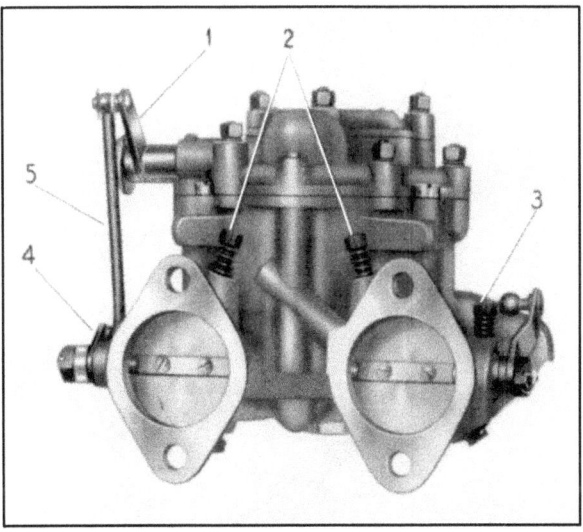

Fig. 136 - Rear view of the Weber 40 DCO 3 carburetter.

1. Outer pump-operating lever - **2.** Idling mixture control screw - **3.** Idling adjustment screw - **4.** Main pump operating lever - **5.** Pump-operating rod.

Removing and refitting the carburetter

Radiator end: When removing the top nuts securing the carburetter to the flexible joints (item **7**, Fig 140), the special spanner 6121.23027 must be used. When removing the lower nuts (item **3**, Fig. 139), the special spanner 6121.23029 must be used.

Steering-wheel end: When removing the top nuts securing the carburetter to the flexible joints (item **8**, Fig. 140) the spanner 6121.23028 must be used.

When removing the lower nuts (item **4**, Fig. 139) use spanner 6121.23029.

Removing and refitting the inlet manifold to the cylinder head

When removing the lower nuts (**5**) securing the manifold to the flexible joints (Fig. 139) the special spanner 6121.23026 must be used.

When removing the lateral nuts (**6**) securing the manifold to the flexible joint (Fig. 139) and the bolts (**9**) securing the manifold to the cylinder head (Fig. 140) the 12 mm wrench and the 14 mm, 100 mm long, offset spanner must be used.

Test-bench inspection & repair of the carburetter

The data in Part 1 must be observed. Take great care not to draw air into the zone between the carburetter and the cylinder head, and make sure that the needle valves sit perfectly on their seats.

These carburetters require very accurate adjustment, it is particularly important to check:

a) **the level of the fuel in the bowl**

To make sure that the level of the fuel to the carburetter bowls is as prescribed, proceed as follows:

Fig. 137 - View of the engine mounted in the car (Sprint Veloce and Spider Veloce).

1. Air cleaner - **2.** Corrugated hose - **3.** Air bowl cover.

1) remove the small covers with the 6 mm box spanner and leave the large covers;

2) remove the man jet-holder emulsifier unit;

3) operate the fuel pump;

4) by means of a syringe remove the petrol from the main jet bowl (Fig. 141) so as to make a definite reduction in level;

5) allow the fuel to find its own level and check it;

6) if the level is found to be at other than 24 ÷ 25 mm from the level of the cover support, the cover must be removed; the needle

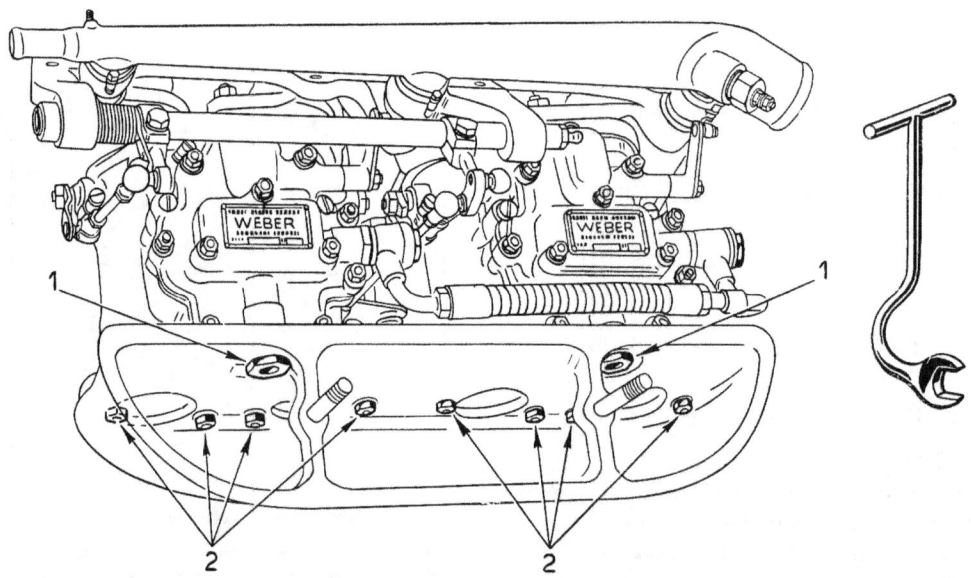

Fig.138 - Fuel feed system seen from the top, showing the special spanner No. 6121.18338 to remove the nuts. **1.**

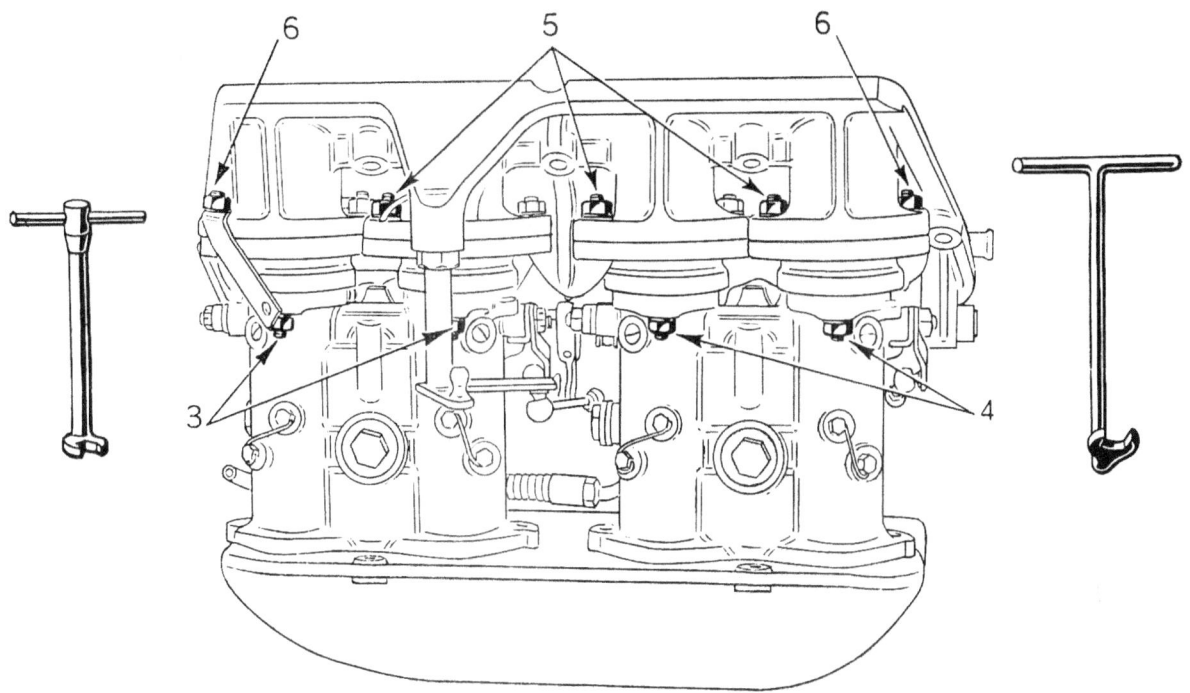

Fig. 139 - Fuel feed system seen from below, showing the special spanners 6121.23026 and 6121.23029 needed to remove the nuts **3, 4** and **5**.

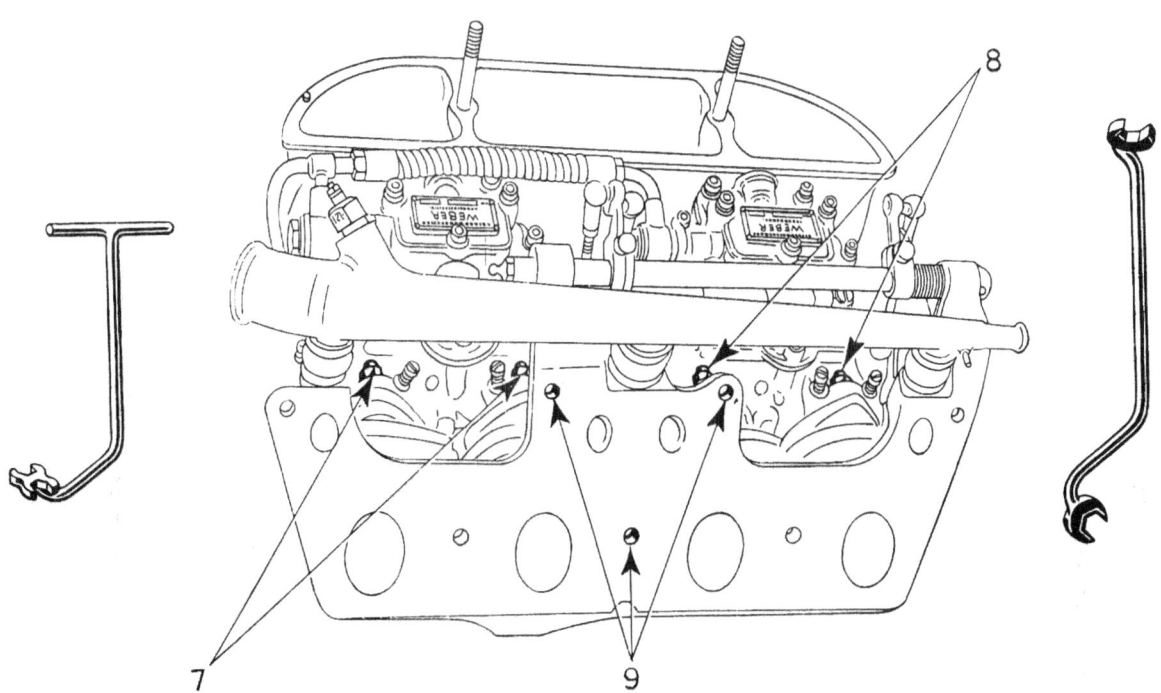

Fig. 140 - Fuel feed system seen diagonally from the top (3/4) on the inlet manifold side, showing the special spanners 6121.23027 and 6121.23028 for removing the nuts **7, 8** and **9**.

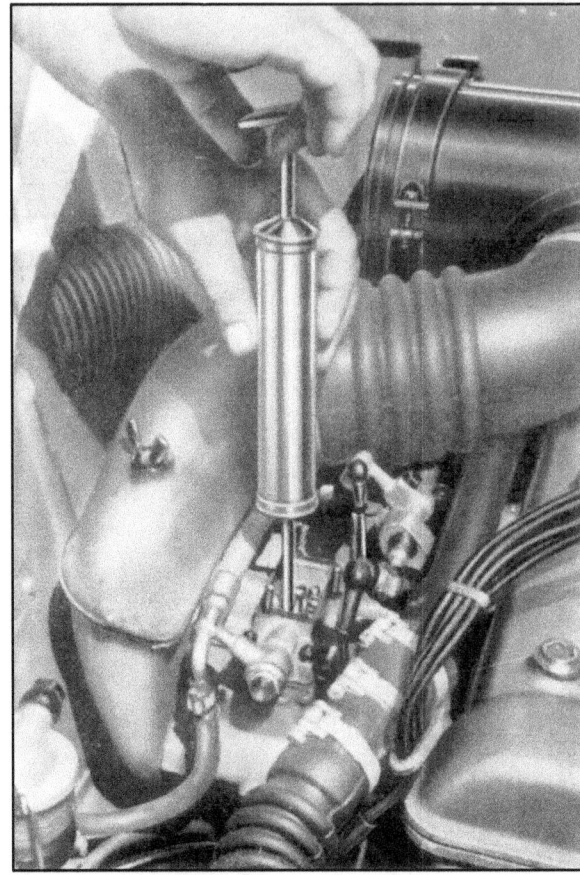

Fig. 141 - Drawing of petrol from the main jet bowl when checking the level in the bowl.

valve must then be removed, checked and if necessary replaced. To remove the carburetter covers it is necessary to remove the throttle control link after having detached the ball joint; unscrew the feed connections and remove all the bolts securing the cover. The float with tongue and the needle valve will then be accessible;

7) if the needle valve is a perfect fit, and if the level is still not correct, bring it to the prescribed level by altering the position of the float tongue.

b) **linked throttle operation**

To ensure the harmonious joint operation of the two carburetters, and to make sure that the links are accurately set, proceed as follows:

1) slacken the clamp securing the throttle control levers to the intermediate shaft on the inlet manifold.

2) bring the fuel feed rate to that required for engine idling by turning the mixture screws and the throttle setting screws in the appropriate direction, with the linkage freed. A good rule to adopt is to begin this check by unscrewing the mixture adjustment screw by 1½ turn ad by screwing the throttle adjustment screw (Fig. 142) inwards half a turn from the positions in which these screws make contact with the appropriate levers on the throttle spindle when the throttles are fully closed.

3) make sure that the two levers on the throttle spindle make contact with the tips of the idling adjustment screws. After a small rotation of the driving shaft, having the purpose to avoid eventual precedent impressions, retighten the clamps on the levers on the driving shaft, taking great care not to alter their positions once they are correctly set.

4) Recheck the throttle alignment and reset the idling screws. Make sure that the position of the accelerator when at rest corresponds to the idling position of the throttle. The throttles have to be kept at idling position under a slight pre-load.

5) Lastly check that with the accelerator depressed to the floor the throttles are fully open, but make sure that the pressure applied to the pedal does not overload the rods. To prevent this, adjust the pedal stroke by means of the adjustable stop provided for the purpose.

Fig. 142 - Adjusting the throttle idling position.

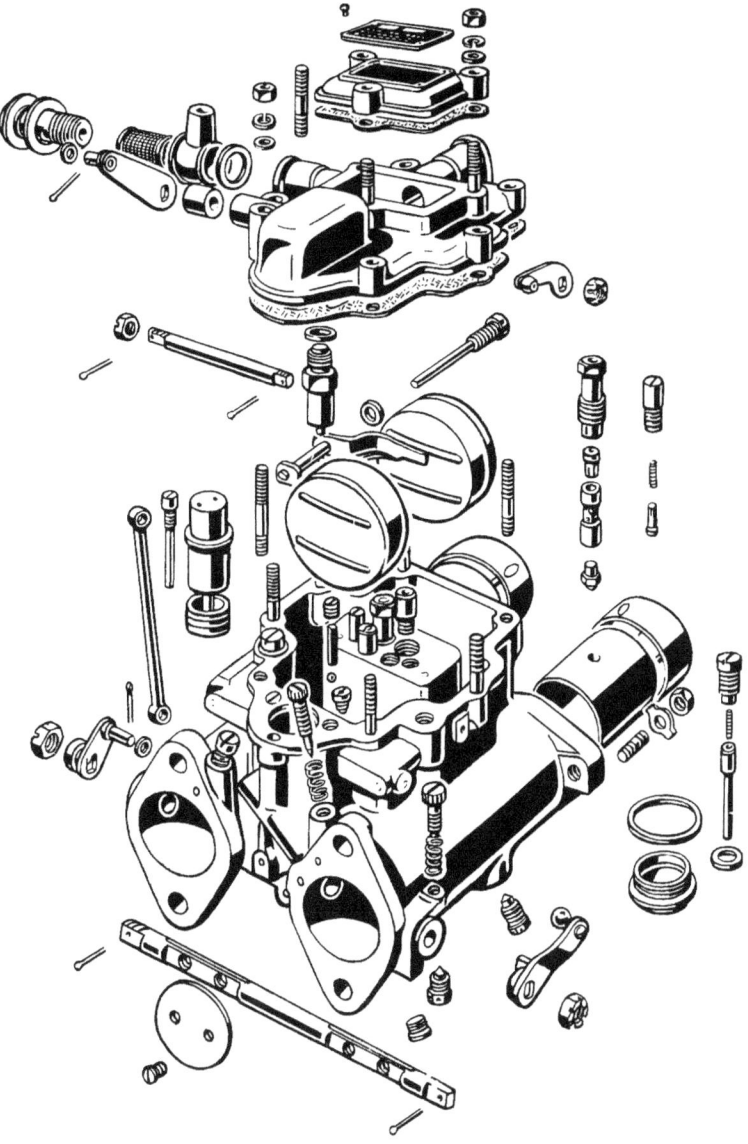

Fig. 143 - Exploded view of the carburetter Weber 40 DCO 3.

General overhaul of the carburetter unit

Such overhaul is necessary when causes of uneven running cannot be attributed to ignition defects or incorrect fuel levels, throttle alignment and link settings. Proceed as follows:

— dismantle the carburetter unit into its component parts: carburetters, flexibles flanges, manifold;
— completely dismantle the carburetters, wash them with petrol, clean and blow through the ducts and passages;
— check the following:
  a) that the two throttles on the carburetters are perfectly parallel;
  b) that there is no excessive play in the throttle bearings;
  c) that the valves and the acceleration pump seats are in good condition, that the piston slides properly in its cylinder and is efficiently returned by the springs;
  d) that the two tie-rods linking the levers on the throttle spindle and the link spindle are 95 mm long from the centre line of each ball-joint;
  e) that the mating surfaces on the carburetter, the flexible joints and the manifold, are all clean and perfectly smooth.

Instructions for reassembling the carburetters

— check the rubber gaskets and make sure that they are undamaged; properly clean all bearing surfaces;
— check the inlet manifold and make sure:

1) that there is no excessive play in the carburetter intermediate shaft bearings;
2) that the reaction of the return spring on the shaft is sufficient;
3) that the mating surfaces are smooth and clean;

— assemble the fuel feed system and fit new gaskets smeared with a sealing compound;
— check the carburetter level using a feed pressure of approximately one third of an atmosphere. Observe the requirements and values set out under « fuel level ».
— fit the water tube, using suitable lengths of rubber hose, securing them with hose clips.
— fit the unit to the engine, making sure that the gasket is not damaged.

STARTING WHEN THE ENGINE IS COLD

As the carburetters are not fitted with an easy starting device it is necessary, when starting from cold, to inject fuel into the feed ducts by operating the acceleration pump connected to the pedal.
Proceed as follow:

1) place the gear lever in neutral;
2) insert the ignition key, turn it to the right to energise the coil, and operate the electric fuel pump;
3) depress the clutch pedal in order to cut out the gear-box drag caused by the cold oil (while actually starting only);
4) pump the accelerator pedal three or four times, and then hold it down about one centimetre;
5) start the engine by turning the key as far as it will go. As soon as the engine fires, help it by rapid, short strokes with the accelerator pedal.

STARTING WHEN THE ENGINE IS HOT

Proceed as for a cold engine, but exclude item 4; do not pump the accelerator pedal before starting the engine.

24 - THE EXHAUST SIDE
THE EXHAUST MANIFOLD

The exhaust manifold should be overhauled at the same time as the rest of the engine. The recommended procedure is as follows:

Dismantling

1) Disconnect the exhaust pipe bracket fixed to the gear box.
2) After having removed the exhaust pipe connecting bolts, disconnect the manifold from the cylinder-head.
3) Remove the old gaskets and replace them with new ones.

Inspection

1) Clean the inside of the manifold with a wire brush driven by an electric motor through a flexible shaft.
2) Check to ensure that the manifold is not cracked or distorted.
3) Examine the condition of the flange connecting it to the engine.

WARNING: In order to give proper protection against dangerous leakage of exhaust fumes, it is essential that the gasket between the manifold and the exhaust pipe should be made of annealed copper. It is emphasised that in the case of such leakage, the exhaust gas might penetrate the hydraulic brake system with the consequent failure of the brakes.

Re-assembly

1) Carefully clean the gasket bearing surfaces.
2) Insert the annealed copper gasket (see warning above) between the exhaust pipe and the manifold, and connect the two members.
3) Fit new gaskets to the cylinder-head and fit the manifold.

THE EXHAUST PIPE AND SILENCER (MUFFLER)
Dismantling

1) Disconnect the exhaust pipe from the manifold.
2) Slacken the bolts connecting the exhaust pipe to the stirrup on the gear-box (transmission).
3) Remove the bolts from the rubber straps holdings the silencer and the exhaust pipe.
4) Remove the exhaust pipe.

Inspection

Chek to ensure that the silencer, the pressure surge dampers and the pipes are not blocked or holed, or damaged in any other way which might interfere with the proper operation of the exhaust equipment; replace any defective sections.

When re-fitting the exhaust pipe, proceed in the reverse of the order described for dismantling.

NOTE: Make sure that the exhaust pipe straps on all Giulietta Sprint cars are made of rubber, and that a heat-insulating pad is inserted between each strap and its corresponding stirrup, and welded to the exhaust pipe or silencer.

Any straps made of rubberised fabric should be replaced.

Remember that the pair of straps in line with the rear pressure surge damper, needs the 2-piece retainer designed to limit lateral movement of the exhaust pipe.

THE EXHAUST SYSTEM (For Giulietta Sprint Veloce and Spider Veloce)

The exhaust system (Fig. 144) on the Veloce version consists of two manifolds which are connected to a forked member immediately preceeding the first silencer on the exhaust pipe.

The two manifolds each comprise two forked tubes which respectively connect the first and fourth cylinders and the second and third. This arrangement has been adopted to prevent excessive pressure of the exhaust gases.

Dismantling

Remove the bolts connecting the two flanges to the exhaust pipe, using the 14 mm wrench, remove the connecting nuts for the flanges on the cylinder-head studs. Working from the bottom, first of all slip off the narrow forked tubes and then the wide forked tubes.

Inspection

Check that there are no cracks or leakages in the exhaust system, as they could result in the dangerous conditions of an overheated brake fluid pump, with disastrous results.

Assembly

Work in the reverse order, and carefully tighten all nuts after first fitting them all. Make sure that the pipes properly match the exhaust manifold orifices and that the mating surfaces are free from roughness and scratches.

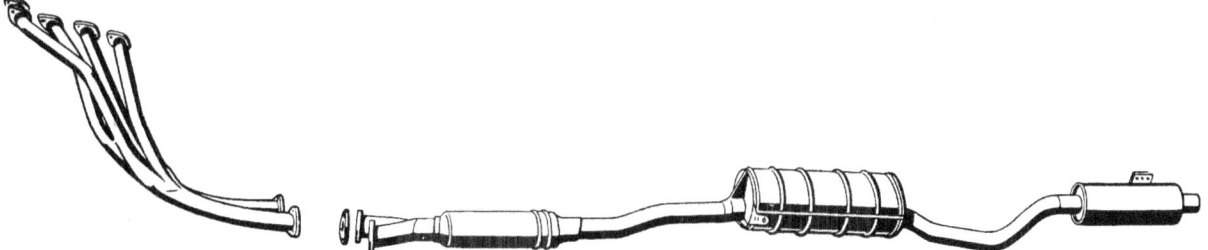

Fig. 144 - The 2-piece manifold and the exhaust pipe. (Giulietta Sprint Veloce and Spider Veloce)

INFORMATION SHEET REFERENCE

ASSEMBLY	DATE	SHEET N.	SUBJECT

PART 3

CLUTCH-GEARBOX

INDEX

CLUTCH	page	91
Description	»	91
1) Checking clutch operation without removing the clutch from the car	»	92
2) Removing the clutch from the car	»	92
3) Dismantling the clutch	»	93
4) Checking the clutch	»	93
5) Reassembling the clutch	»	94
GEAR-BOX (TRANSMISSION)	»	96
Description	»	96
6) Checks to be made with gear-box in place on the car	»	98
7) Removing the gear-box from the car	»	99
8) Dismantling the gear-box	»	101
9) Inspection and checking	»	102
10) Reassembling the gear-box	»	103
11) Replacing the gear-box in the car	»	106
12) Gear-box controlled by ball gear shift lever	»	106

PART 3

CLUTCH

DESCRIPTION

The single plate dry type of clutch used on the Giulietta cars consists of (Fig. 3):

1) A driven plate
2) A pressure plate
3) A cover
4) Springs and retainers
5) Rocking levers
6) A thrust ring
7) A cloutch disengaging ring

The clutch is attached to the engine flywheel by means of the cover **3** bolted on with 6 set-screws.

The clutch disengaging levers **5** with their return springs are connected to the pressure plate **2** by bolts and nuts.

The complete driven plate **1** is mounted directly on the gear-box drive-shaft.

The pressure plate **2** is actuated, through three rocking levers **5** and the thrust ring **6**, by the disengaging ring **7** and a ball bearing which has a graphite packing ring. The bearing is operated through the links by the clutch fork which transmits the thrust from the clutch pedal (Fig. 4).

When the clutch is engaged (pedal fully released), the spring **4** pressing against the pressure plate **2**, forces the driven plate **1** against the face of the flywheel and thus transmits power to the gear-box direct drive shaft.

Pressure on the clutch pedal disengages the clutch; the clutch disengaging ring acts on the pressure plate and the rocking-levers to withdraw the thrust ring and release the driven plate.

Clutch actuation, from the pedal to the withdral ring **7** control lever is by means of jointed levers and rods so that the pedal is unaffected by vibration from the engine and gear-box unit.

Fig. 1 - Clutch.

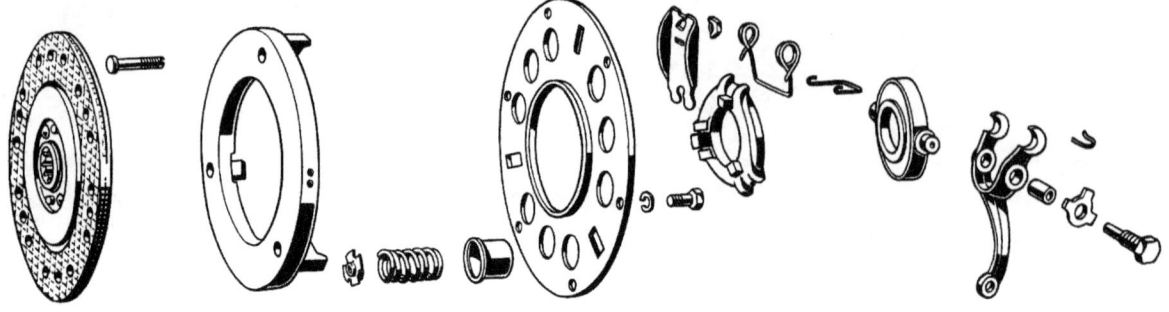

Fig. 2 - Details of clutch.

1 - CHECKING CLUTCH OPERATION WITHOUT REMOVING THE CLUTCH FROM THE CAR

The clutch pedal should have free travel of 23 mm. measured at the centre of the pedal before it makes contact with the disengaging ring. The distance between the two rings **6** and **7** is 2 mm.

When, as a result of wear on the driven plate lining, the free travel has been reduced to less than 10÷12 mm., the original degree of free travel must be restored. To do this, unscrew the adjusting nut **1** (Fig. 4). and re-set the pedal travel as shown in Fig. 5.

When the correct adjustment has been made, lock the nut with its lock-nut.

If, after making the above adjustment, it is still not possible to obtain the full travel of 23 mm, it must be concluded that wear on the clutch lining has become excessive and that the lining must be replaced; always provided, of course, that the various control rods are not out of adjustment or damaged.

2 - REMOVING THE CLUTCH FROM THE CAR

Remove the gear-box as described in Section 7 and then remove the clutch as follows:

1) Mark the position of the clutch in relation to the flywheel so that it can be reassembled without altering the conditions under which the complete engine-flywheel-clutch unit was originally balanced.

2) Remove the studs holding the cover to the flywheel and draw off the clutch, taking care not to drop the driven plate.

Fig. 3 - Section through clutch - Data and measurements:
1. Driven plate - **2.** Pressure plate - **3.** Cover - **4.** Springs - **5.** Rocking levers - **6.** Thrust ring - **7.** Clutch disengaging ring.

A.	Clearance between thrust ring and disengaging ring	Min. limit of wear	2 mm 1 mm
B.	Thickness of driven plate	with new lining limit of wear	10 mm 6 mm
C.	Distance from flywheel to thrust ring face		26-26.3 mm
D.	Distance from thrust ring face and the face inside the cover		59-59.5 mm
L.	Length of spring not compressed		43.5-45.5 mm
Le.	Length of spring with load of 45-49 kg		29 mm

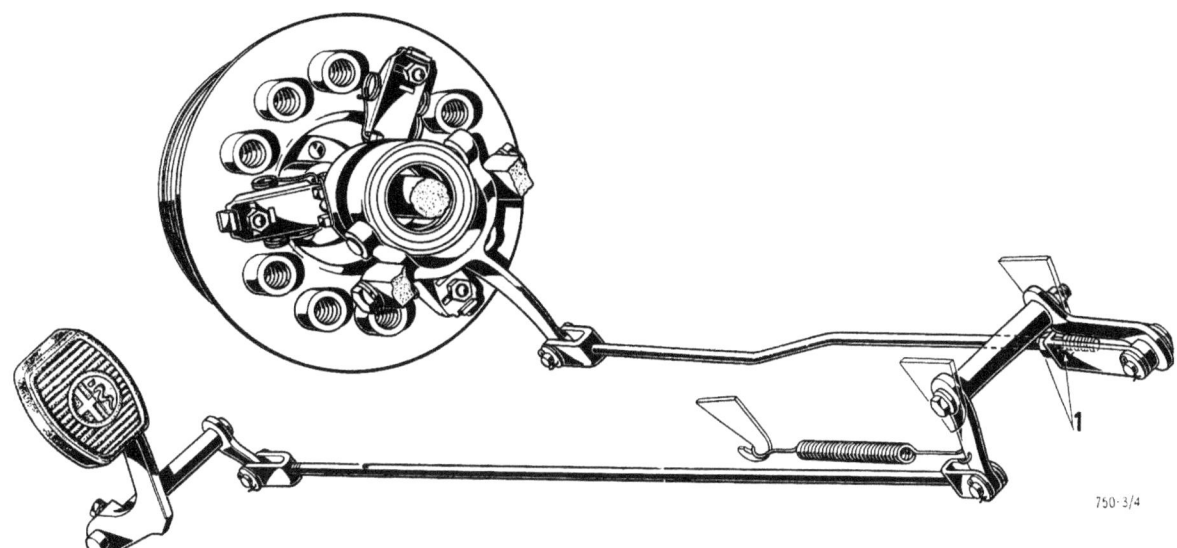

Fig. 4 - Clutch with its controls: 1. control nuts.

3 - DISMANTLING THE CLUTCH

It is usually unnecessary to separate the cover from the pressure-plate or to remove the springs and rocking levers from the cover.

However, in the rare cases in which it is necessary to replace the spring or to check its tension, the clutch should be dismantled in the following way:

1) Mark the position of the pressure-plate in relation to the cover so that the two parts may later be returned to their original position without altering the conditions under which the unit was balanced.

2) Bolt the clutch cover to a suitable fixture so that it is held in the same way as when it is mounted on the flywheel so as to place as little load as possible on the studs which hold the pressure plate on the spring-holding plate. The flywheel itself may be used, but in that case the driven-plate must be placed between them.

3) Disconnect the thrust ring from the rocking-arms.

4) Remove the rivet packing between the nuts and studs holding the rocking-levers and, without turning the nuts, screw out the studs with a screwdriver; the pressure-plate levers can be dismantled in this way.

5) Remove the bolts which hold the cover on the fixture (or to the flywheel) and lift off the cover itself.

4 - CHECKING THE CLUTCH

1) The clutch linings must always be thoroughly dry; if they have oil merely on the surface, wash with petrol and roughen the surface with a wire brush. If they are badly impregnated, they must be replaced.

Check the wear by comparing thickness **B** with the figures given in Fig. 3.

2) Make sure that the driven plate is firmly fixed on its boss and that the lining rivets fit firmly; tighten them if necessary.

3) With an abrasive stone remove any unevenness on the edges of the splines in the driven plate boss and smooth out any roughness.

4) Check the clearance between the lateral faces of the splines in the driven plate boss and the gearbox direct-drive shaft; **when newly assembled, this should be 0.03 to 0.11 mm. and the maximum amount of wear permissible is 0.3 mm.**

The driven plate should slide freely lengthways on the splined shaft; very slight rubbing or

Fig. 5 - Measuring the clutch pedal travel.

Fig 6 - Checking the centring of the driven clutch plate.

sticking may prevent the clutch from operating properly.

5) Check that the driven-plate is not running out of true **(tolerance: 0.5 mm)** by means of a comparator after fixing the plate on the clutch shaft, and mounting the shaft between 2 centres (Fig. 6). If necessary, centre the plate by pressure on the plate surfaces only.

6) When a new lining has been mounted, make sure that the rivets are fitted by a specialist; it should furthermore be noted that each rivet will only do its work properly if it can cause pressure so as to produce, between the lining and the plate on which it is fixed, a frictional effort capable of preventing the lining from moving in relation to the plate; this applies even to the most powerful forces to which the clutch may be subjected.

In particular, this condition will not be realised if the centre line of the rivet is not exactly at right angles to the lining and if it is not sunk as far down as the hole in the lining allows.

7) When a new lining has been fitted, the driven-plate must be statically balanced by mounting it on a suitable shaft fitted in turn onto the special fixture 6123.13.001 (Fig. 7). After being gently rotated the driven plate should not always come to rest with one particular point at the bottom; if necessary, remove enough metal from the edge to achieve a state of balance.

8) Check the condition of the pressure-plate surface and true it up on a grinder, if required. This can be done without removing the plate from the cover if a suitably equipped grinder is available.

9) Make sure that the thrust ring is not scored on the face in contact with the levers.
It is particularly important, if the seating is to be level, that any such scoring should be to a uniform depth.
If this is not the case, replace the thrust ring.

10) Check to ensure that the threads on the bolts and nuts have not been damaged during the dismantling operations, and replace them if necessary.

11) Check that the bush in the flywheel is effectively centring the gear-box drive shaft as described in part 2A, Section 17, para h.

12) Check that the pressure-plate springs have not become distorted and make sure of their effectiveness by verifying that the values **L** and **LC** agree with those given in Fig. 3.
If the springs are too weak, they must be replaced.

13) Check that the ball-bearing and the graphite thrust-ring are in order; should one or the other need changing, replace the complete unit.

5 - REASSEMBLING THE CLUTCH

A) REASSEMBLING ON THE BENCH

Proceed as follows:

1) Mount the caps on the pressure-plate **2** (Fig. 3) and position the springs with their retainers.

2) Place the clutch cover on the assembled pressure plate in the position marked before dismantling

Fig. 7 - Checking the static balance of the driven plate.

Fig. 7 bis
Checking the static balance of the clutch, without driven plate.

(Section 3, para 1); assemble the rocking levers with their pins and nuts and fix the thrust ring in position.

3) Mount the clutch on the fixture mentioned in Section 3. Adjust the position of the three levers by means of their pins so that they fulfil the following conditions:

   a) The sliding face of the thrust ring will be exactly parallel with the face of the flywheel.

   b) The distance **C** between these two surfaces will be that shown in Fig. 3. The distance **D** (fig. 3) from the surface of the thrust ring to the outside face of the clutch cover can only be taken as a first approximation.

4) Place the assembled clutch on a press and check that the figures shown below are correct:

   Displacement of thrust ring for a load of { 115-120 Kg. . . 3 mm.
   140-145 Kg. . . 8 mm.

   Any discrepancy is caused by the behaviour of individual springs.

   It should be noted that the angle of the rocking levers has no effect on the values given above.

5) When everything is in order, lock the nuts on the bolts to prevent any risk of the levers getting out of adjustment.

6) Check the stating balance of the clutch, without driven plate, by mounting it on the plate 6123.10 052 fitted in turn onto the special tool 6123.10.001 (fig. 7 bis). After being rotated the clutch should not always come to rest with one particular point at the bottom; if necessary remove enough metal by drilling the exterior surface of the pressure plate to achieve a state of balance.

7) To facilitate re-fitting the clutch to the chassis it is advisable to insert 3 mm distance-pieces between the ends of the rocking levers and the clutch-cover when the clutch is removed from the fixture.

B) RE-FITTING THE CLUTCH TO THE CAR

1) Wash the friction surfaces on the flywheel and the pressure-plate with a rag moistened in petrol.

2) Mount the complete clutch on the flywheel, centring it with a bar (Fig. 8) similar to the clutch shaft and making sure that the reference marks made when dismantling coincide (see Section 2, para. 1).

3) The distance pieces fitted between the flywheel and the clutch cover may only be removed when the distance **C** (Fig. 3) is not less than that shown there.

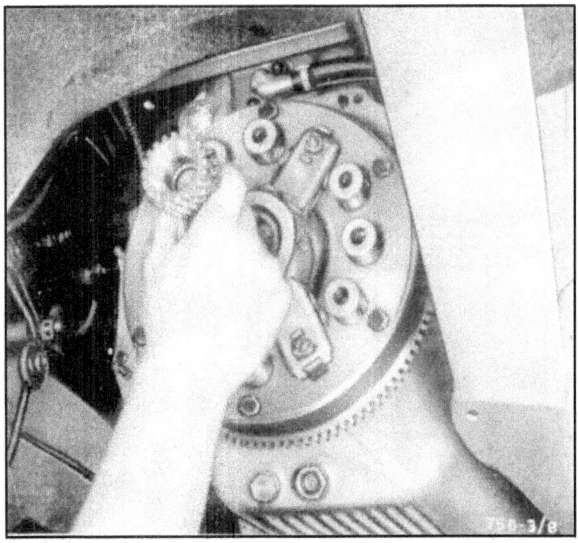

Fig. 8 - Checking the centring of the clutch on the flywheel

4) Bolt the clutch to the flywheel with the studs; the distance pieces mentioned in the previous section **A**, para. 6, will fall off during assembling, when the studs are practically screwed home.

5) Replace the gear-box as explained in Chapter 12.

6) Assemble the clutch control rod and adjust its length so that the distance **A** (Fig. 5) is correct. The length of travel for complete disengagement, from the position of rest, is:

Thrust ring . . . . 8 mm.
Disengaging ring . . . . . 10 mm.
End of withdrawal lever . . . 33 mm.

7) Replace the bottom protective cover.

GEAR BOX (TRANSMISSION)

DESCRIPTION

The gear-box, which forms a unit with the clutch, comprises a lightmetal housing bolted to the crankcase with a steel ring between them for the purpose of ensuring that the starting motor is properly centred.

A number of carefully-located studs connects the unit to the engine.

The housing is divided into three parts, the first containing the clutch with its controls, the second the forward gears and the third the reverse gear and the speedometer drive as well as gear-changing levers.

The three sections are separated by walls carrying the ball bearings on which the gear shafting is mounted.

While the first two sections are cast in one piece, the third consists of a rear cover secured to the main casting by a flange.

This arrangement facilitates easy assembly of the units forming the gear-box and gives a particularly compact clutch gear-box design.

The gear-box has four forward speeds with helical gears in all cases while the reverse is by spur pinions.

The gear-box direct-drive shaft transmits power to the secondary shaft through a pair of intermediate gear-wheels, the driving wheel of which is integral with the direct drive shaft.

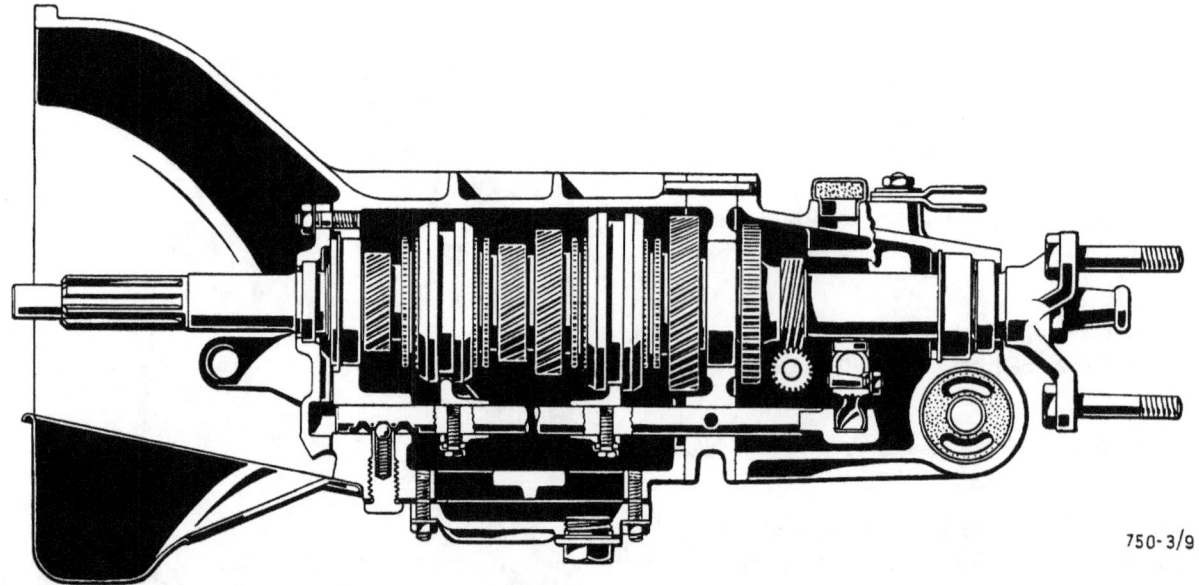

Fig. 9 - Longitudinal section of gear-box.

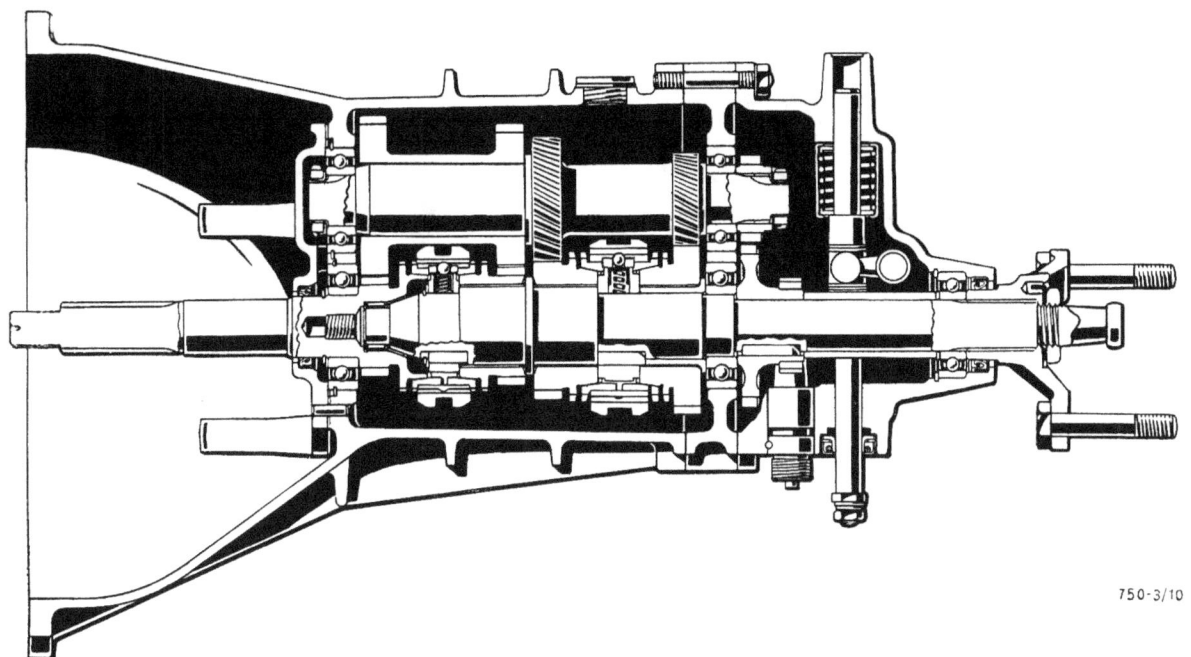

Fig. 10 - Sectional plan view of gear-box.

In the earlier types of Giulietta Sprint, the intermediate shaft gears were made integral with the shaft itself.

In current models, the intermediate shaft pinion, together with 3rd gear driving pinion, forms part of a single sleeve keyed onto the secondary shaft. This shaft also carries the 2nd and 1st gear driving pinions the latter also being in one piece.

The corresponding driven gears are mounted loose on the primary shaft. Their engagement, for the different speeds, is obtained by the axial movement of the synchronising sleeves.

The primary shaft is in line with the direct-drive shaft; the two are locked by moving one of the sleeves, and direct drive (4th gear) is thus engaged.

The outer synchro sleeves are coupled to the driven gears by splines cut on the inside of the sleeves and the outside of the gear wheel bosses. Synchronisation of the different gears is effected by means of a floating ring with teeth on the outside (the teeth engage with the outer sleeve) and with a grooved tapered surface internally which surrounds the cone on the driven-gear.

The operation of the synchro unit is as follows:
With the gear engaged and the car in motion, the complete synchro unit, being integral with the primary shaft, rotates at a speed proportionate to that of the car.

Starting from neutral and with movement of the gear-lever, the gear-box fork moves the synchronising sleeve endways. Its internal teeth press on the balls, force them to rotate and thus carry forward the thrust pads and with them the sliding sleeve.

As the speed of the external sleeve is approximately twice that of the thrust pad, there is first of all engagement between sleeve and the teeth on the sliding ring and subsequently contact between the internal coned surface of the ring and the outside of the driven-gear boss.

The friction between these surfaces is such that the driven gear adopts the rotational speed of the synchro sleeve.

Under this circumstance, the internal teeth in the sleeve can easily engage the external teeth on the driven-gear boss and the two become solid, via the sleeve, with the primary shaft and thus with drive. Suitable tooth angles for the floating ring sleeve and for the gear-wheel bosses facilitate the sliding on of the sleeve.

The reverse is through two spur gears keyed onto the rear ends of the primary and secondary shafts and an

Fig. 11 - Details of gear-box: synchro-mesh mechanism in sectional plan view.

intermediate idle pinion which slides endways on its shaft.

As mentioned above, the reverse is in the third section of the housing.

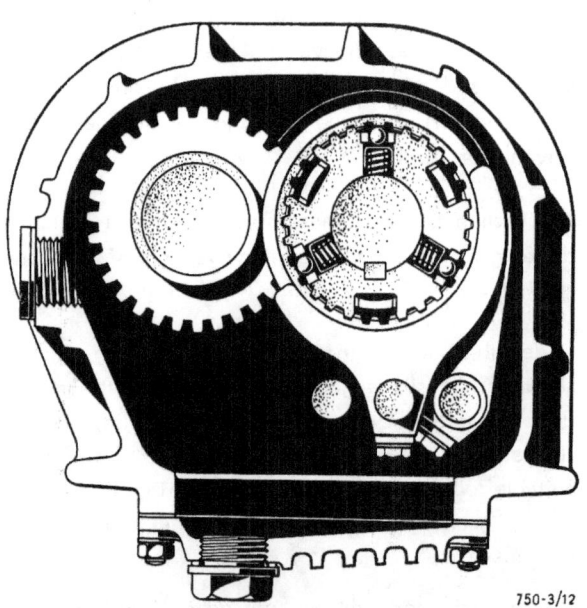

Fig. 12 - Details of gear-box: synchro-mesh mechanism in cross-section.

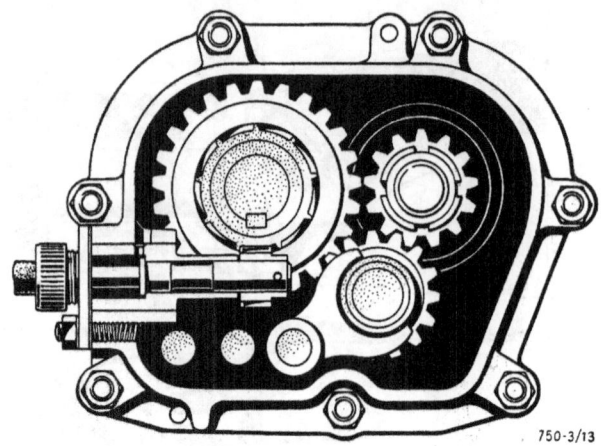

Fig. 13 - Cross-section through reverse and speedometer drive.

A magnetised oil drain plug ensures that the oil is freed from all metallic particles which may contaminate it.

The gear ratios are as follows:

1st gear	3.313 : 1
2nd »	1.959 : 1
3rd »	1.354 : 1
4th » (top)	1 : 1
Reverse	3.365 : 1

Overall ratio (gear-box rear axle) with 9/41 bevel ratio:

1st gear	15.090 : 1
2nd »	8:923 : 1
3rd »	6.167 : 1
4th » (top)	4.555 : 1
Reverse	15.327 : 1

6 - CHECKS TO BE MADE WITH THE GEAR-BOX IN PLACE IN THE CAR

A) Checking for oil leaks

Make sure that oil does not leak from the bottom cover.

B) Checking the oil level

Check the oil level; it should not be more than 1 cm below the filler plug. This check should be made every 5.000 km.
The types of oil to be used are shown in Part 12.

C) Checking the controls

Check that no bolts to the external control mechanism

have become loose or show signs of turning and especially make sure that the brazed joint at the end of the flexible gear-selection control sheath is in order.

D) Checking the operation of the gear-change control

1) Gear selection control

a) When the gear-lever **1** (Fig. 16) is moved, the actuating rod **2** should be able to move a further distance **A** = 3 mm approximately (Fig. 17) after the 1st or the 2nd speeds have engaged, before making contact with the edge of the steering column bracket.

If this extra travel is not available, adjust the length of the flexible control cable by turning the nuts **3** (Fig. 16) which position the threaded end of flexible control itself.

b) If on the other hand the flexible control has to be dismantled or replaced, the following sequence should be followed when reassembling.

— Remove the carpet above the gear-box and take off the rubber cap.

— Attach the threaded end of the flexible control to the bracket **4** for the actuating rod. The nuts **3** should be in the centre of the threaded end.

— Bring the gear-lever into the position of the 1st gear as explained in para a).

— Place the lever **5** on the gear-box in the position for 1st and 2nd speeds and engage the 1st speed gears.

— Push the flexible cable onto its seating on the lever **5** and tighten the locking nut, taking care to hold the bottom nut to prevent the cable being bent and damaged (Fig. 18).

— Check that selection gear is working correctly, as explained in para a) and adjust any inaccuracies.

2) Gear Engagement control

It is important to check the angular travel of the hand-operated gear-lever when, with a gear already engaged, it is pushed as far as it will go.

This additional travel ensures that the synchro sleeve concerned will move the full length necessary for correct engagement.

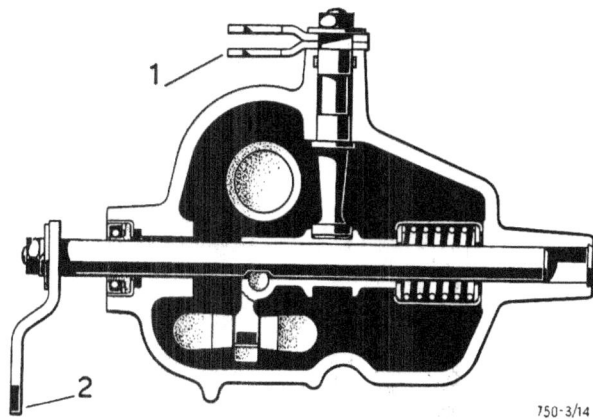

Fig. 14 - Cross-section through selector rods and gear engagement
1. Gear selection arm - **2.** Gear engaging arm.

It is therefore essential to check that this extra movement is the same on all four gears; any adjustment needed should be made on the top operating rod **6** (Fig. 16).

In other words, if the gear-lever travel is greater with gears 1 and 3 engaged than with gears 2 and 4, the actuating rod **6** must be shortened, screwing it into the top fork, and lengthening it if the travel is too short.

7 - REMOVING THE GEAR-BOX FROM THE CAR

To remove the gear-box from the car, proceed as follows:

1) Remove the central clutch actuating rod.

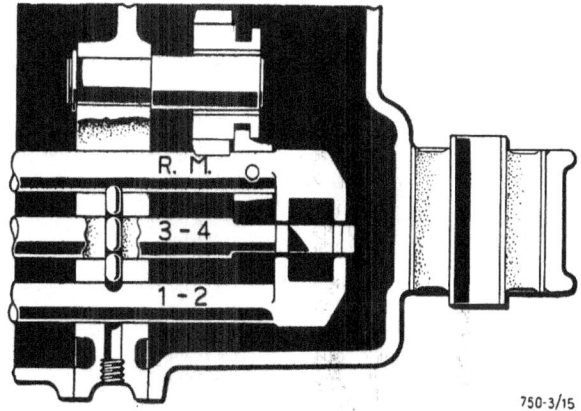

Fig. 15 - Partial section through speed-change operating rods.

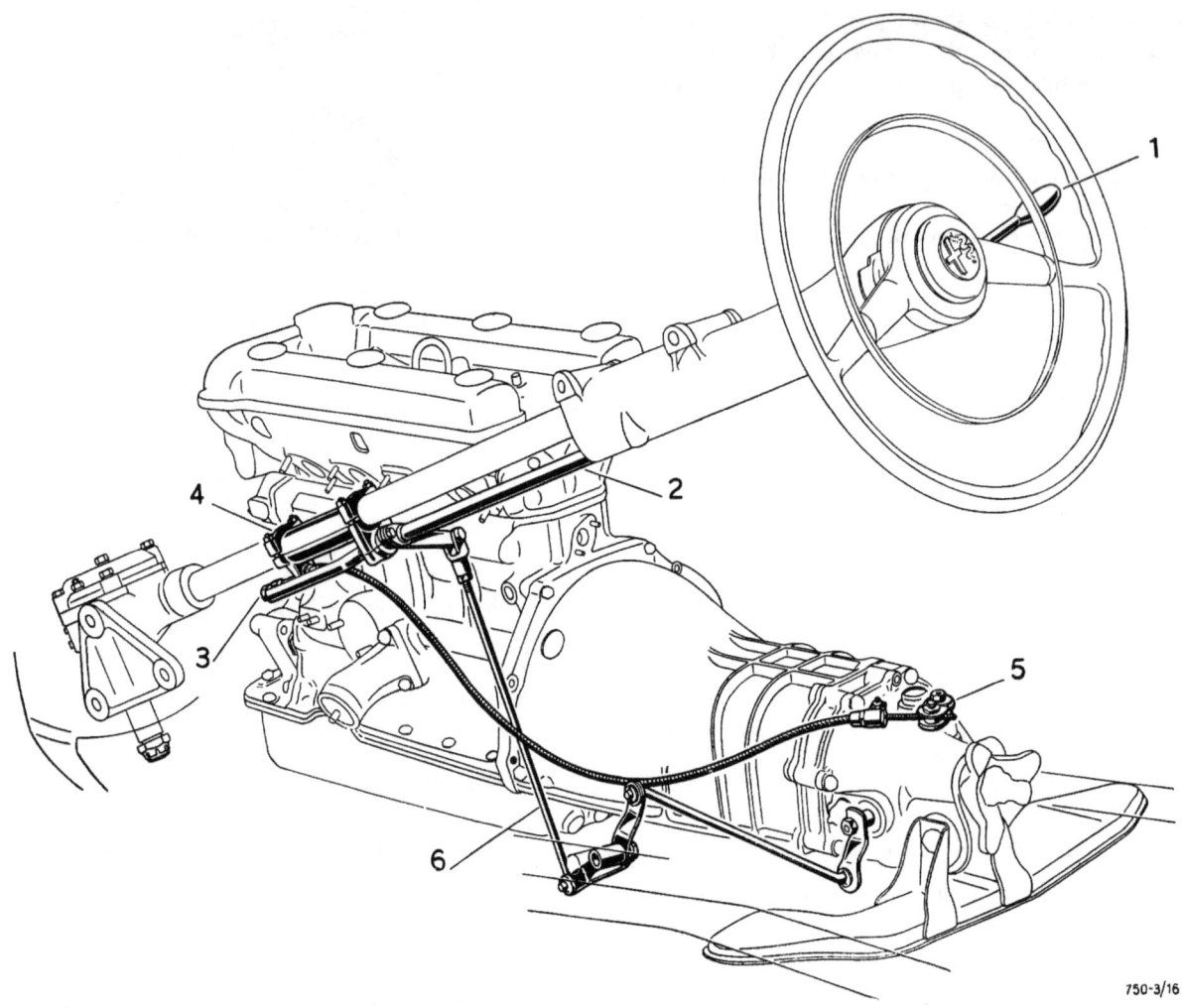

Fig. 16 - Gear-box controls.

1. Gear lever - **2.** Rod operating gear selection and engagement - **3.** Gear selector adjustment nuts - **4.** Lower rod bracket - **5.** Gear selector arm - **6.** Gear engagement control and adjustment rod.

2) Take off the bottom clutch protection cover.

3) Disconnect the lower gear actuating rod.

4) Disconnect the speedometer drive connection by unscrewing the knurled nut; take care not to lose the washer.

5) Remove the clip holding the engine breather pipe on the gear-box.

6) After having gripped the rubber transmission joint in a suitable hexagonal band, remove the bolts which hold it on the gear-change fork and detach the transmission shaft (together with the joint) from the gear-box.

7) Remove the centre support for the transmission shaft and attach the free end of the shaft to the body.

8) Remove the bracket attaching the exhaust pipe.

9) Remove the front chassis cross-member.

10) Disconnect the gear-box from the rear chassis cross-member.

11) Remove the rear chassis cross-member.

12) Allow the engine/gear-box unit to drop downwards by its own weight; disconnect the clip holding the flexible gear selection control to the gear-box.

13) Disconnect the flexible shaft from the gear selector fork.

14) Remove the bolts and nuts holding the gear-box on the crankcase and lift off the gear-box. (If the inclined position occupied by the engine/gear-box by virtue of its own weight does not give sufficient slope to make removal possible, the angle can be increased by using a jack).

Fig. 17 - Gear lever in correct position for engaging 1st and 2nd speeds. **A = 3 mm** (gap between the rod and the steering column bracket).

NOTE: In cases where it is essential that the gear-box when removed should have the selector-fork lever with it, the latter can be slid off its own pin and left connected to the flexible control contrary to the instructions given in 13 above. This has the advantage that the length of the flexible control does not need adjusting when the gear-box is replaced.

8 - DISMANTLING THE GEAR-BOX

1) Completely drain the oil from the gear-box by unscrewing the drain plug.

2) Remove the clutch fork and the front cover from the gear box.

3) Remove the centring pin (wrench 6121.19.025) and the rear fork forming the connection with the transmission.

4) Remove the rear cover complete.

5) Remove the cages with their springs and balls positioning the gear-change rods.

6) Remove the bottom cover and loosen the studs which hold the gear-forks on the sliding rods.

7) Remove the reverse gear-change rod with the idling intermediate pinion and then the sliding rods for the forwards speeds. Draw off the sleeve-actuating forks.

8) Remove the driven reverse pinion from the primary shaft, using tool 6121.12.062 (Fig. 19).

9) Block the reverse driving pinion with tool 6121.01.181 and unscrew the two end screw-rings (front and rear) from the secondary shaft, using the wrench 6121.00.038 (front screw-rings) or 6121.20.024 (rear screw-ring; fig. 20); then remove the reverse driving pinion.

10) Remove the spring washer and the distance piece from the front end of the primary shaft. Draw off the intermediate flange with the bearings, using tool 6121.12.091; remove the safety catches on the flange.

11) Using tool 6121.12.092, withdraw the two shafts from the front gear-box bearings.

12) Withdraw the two ball bearings from the gear-box, pushing them forwards with tool 6121.07.238 in the case of the secondary shaft bearing and tool 6121.07.239 in the case of the primary shaft.

NOTE: Dismantling the unit on the bench does not require any special instructions. It is, however, advisable to mark the different parts so as to be able to reassemble them in the proper relative positions.

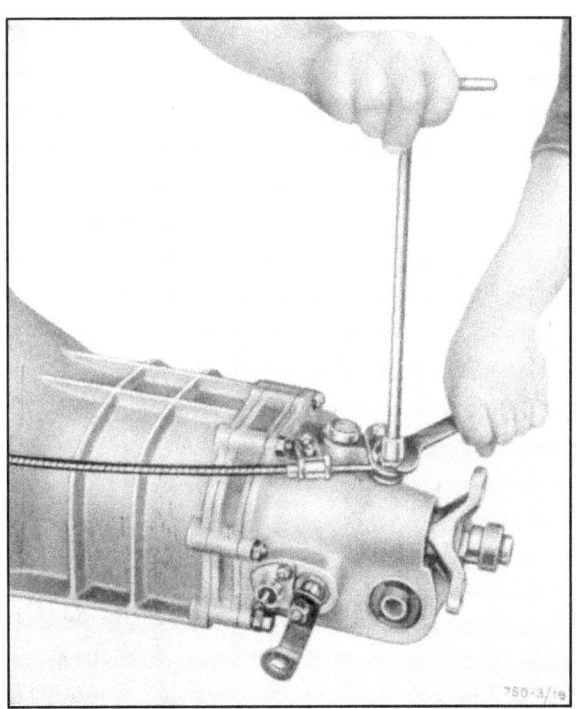

Fig. 18 - Attachment of flexible cable to gear selector arm.

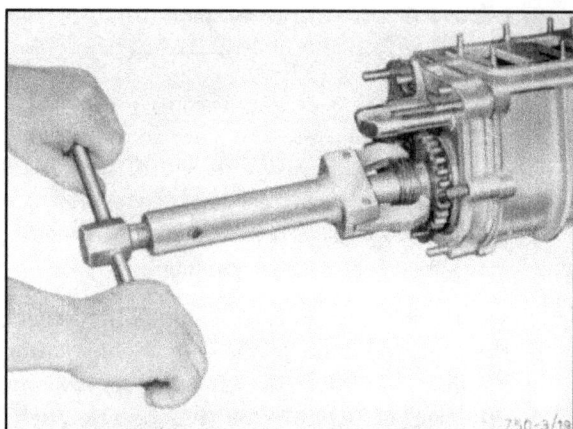

Fig 19 - Removal of the driven reverse pinion from the gear-box primary shaft, using tool 6121.12.062.

9 - INSPECTION AND CHECKING

Wash all the individual gear-box parts with paraffin.

1) Check to ensure that the gear-box housing, the flange and the cover show no signs of cracks and that there is no damage to the ball bearing seatings which would prevent the outside bearing rings from revolving.

2) Make sure that the ball bearings are in perfect order; they must be replaced if any roughness or noise is caused by the races being damaged.

   The surface on which the rollers between the gear-box direct-drive shaft and the primary shaft run must be perfectly smooth.

   Ensure that no longitudinal grooves have been worn by the rollers.

   The rollers should be perfectly round; replace them if they show signs of damage or faceting.

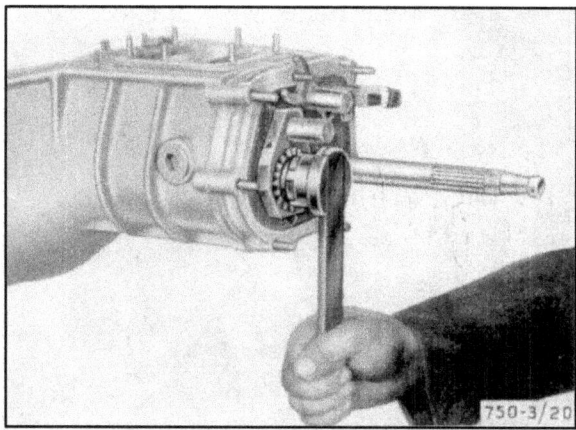

Fig. 20 - Removal of the rear ring-nut from the secondary shaft; use wrench 6121.20.024 while preventing the shaft from turning with tool 6121.01.181.

3) Check that both the shafts are turning true by mounting them between centres. Check the eccentricity with a comparator; it should not exceed two-thousandths of an inch (0.05 mm). If this figure is found to be exceeded the shafts must be straightened in a hydraulic press.

4) Check the gear-box direct drive shaft and the primary shaft on centres while they are turning as one on the roller bearings between them. The total side play between the end of the primary shaft and the roller seating should not be more than 0,04 mm.

5) Make sure that the surfaces of the gear teeth do not show any signs of seizure where they have meshed, or undue wear. Their contact surfaces should be smooth and any minor wear should show that contact is uniform and wide over the whole length of the teeth.

6) Check that the clearance between the outside grooves on the synchro sleeve and the fork are within the following values:

   Clearance when new: 0.04 to 0.28 mm.
   Limit of wear : 0.4 mm.

7) Check that the springs for the selector rod locking balls in the synchro unit and those for synchronisation have the values shown below:

   Spring for 1st and 2nd gear synchro unit
   Length not compressed . . . 15.3 mm.
   Length with load of 1,6 to 1,8 kg   12.5 mm.

   Spring for 3rd and 4th gear synchro unit
   Length not compressed . . . 11.5 mm.
   Length with load of 1.9 to 2,1 kg   9.0 mm.

   Spring for ball locking gear-selector rod
   Length not compressed . . . 22.0 mm.
   Length with load of 2,8 to 3,2 kg   17.0 mm.

8) Check to ensure that the floating rings do not show any signs of damage on their edges and that the grooving on the cones is in order.

   It is generally found that synchronising defects are due to the floating synchro unit being out of order.

   Check that when the floating synchro rings are fully home on the bosses of the gears, the distance **A** (Fig. 11) between the faces of each gear and its ring is not less than 0.5 mm.

9) Check that the rollers on the rod seating slide freely (Fig. 15). Should the gears not engage and disengage properly, increase the radius of the notch in the rod with a file or replace the pawls if they are defective.

10) Check that the synchro sleeves more freely on their hubs and that the splines show no dents.

11) Check the wear on the hollow in which the ball engages in the synchro sleeve, the action of the key pressure and the angles on the engaging edges of the gear teeth on the floating ring.

12) Check that the clearance between the diameter of the driven-gear boss and the corresponding bushes does not exceed 0.12 mm.

FURTHER CHECKS

1) Check that the gear-shifting arm is of the type hardened on the end subjected to the action of the pin on the gear-selector lever; if not, replace it even if it is not worn.

2) Check that the silent-bloc located at the back of the engine/gear-box unit and mounted on the rear cover is not cut or perished and has not turned in its seating; the correct position is shown in Fig. 9.

Use tool 6121.04.014 for extracting and inserting the silent-bloc unit.

3) Check all oil-retaining gaskets and washers; they should be replaced as often as they show any damage or defects, however slight.

10 - REASSEMBLING THE GEAR-BOX

PREPARATION OF THE DIFFERENT UNITS

A) Gear-box casing

Insert the two front bearings in their seatings, using tool 6121.07.239 for the primary shaft bearing and tool 6121.07.238 for the secondary shaft.

B) Intermediate flange

Insert the rear primary shaft bearing in its seating (tool 6121.07.239) and, if it has been previously removed, the spindle for the sliding reverse pinion.

C) Rear cover

First mount the silent-bloc attachment, using tool 6121.04.014, and then the oil seal on the gear control shaft (tool 6121.07.274), the rear oil seal on the primary shaft (tool 6121.07.275) and the corresponding bearing, securing the latter with the spring ring.

Mount the gland for the selector arm spindle and the gear engagement control shaft, sliding onto the latter the spring, its cap and the gearshifting arm which is fixed by means of a locking pin. It is advisable to mount the support for the speedometer drive-shaft only when the complete gear-box has been assembled.

D) Primary shaft

1) Grip the shaft in a vice or, preferably, with tool 6121.01.179, fit the two keys for the synchro hubs in their seatings and make sure that the corresponding keyways in the hubs are wide enough to take the keys; if they are not, file them out to the minimum necessary.

2) With tool 6121.01.178, place the shaft vertically in a vice, with the front end uppermost.

Drive on the 3rd speed driven gear, the floating ring and the hub by means of tool 6121.07.236; fit the distance piece the thickness of which is obtained as shown in Fig. 21 so that there is no end play. Mount the spring washer, insert the three sleeves (plungers) with their springs, the pressure keys and the balls and complete the assembly by means of the synchro sleeve for the 3rd and 4th speeds.

Fig. 21 - Determining the thickness of the packing washer to be inserted between the synchro hub for engaging 3rd and 4th speeds and the spring ring on the primary shaft.

Fig. 22 - Checking the centring of primary shaft mounted in the rear cover with intermediate flange.

ficient, check whether the faces of the driven reverse pinion are parallel.

NOTE: If the parts already marked (mentioned above) have been replaced, new marks must be made after the correct positions have been determined.

RE-ASSEMBLING THE GEAR-BOX

1) Press the roller bearing onto the front end of the primary shaft (tool 6121.07.240) and insert it in the direct-drive shaft.

   Insert the two shafts into the gear-box, with the intermediate flange, grip the front ends of the two shafts with tool 6121.05.036 (Fig. 23) and press the front bearings into place while supporting the opposite end; the intermediate flange will thus be forced along and will engage with the studs.

   Great care must be taken to prevent jamming of the flange on the studs or dowels which would pull the primary shaft off its rear bearing.

2) Press the rear secondary shaft bearing onto its seating with a suitable tool. Assemble the driving reverse pinion on the secondary shaft and attach it with tool 6121.01.181 so as to prevent the rotation of the pinion and of the two shafts as well. Mount the plate and nut, lock them with the wrench 6121.20.024 and bend over the washer. Lock the front end of the shaft in the same way (with the wrench 6121.20.038). Check that the shafts are rotating freely.

3) Reverse the shaft, grip it in the vice in tool 6121.01.179 and mount the 2nd speed gear-wheel with the floating ring: press the synchro hub into position on the shaft, using tool 6121.07.237, mount the sleeves with their springs, the pressure keys, the balls, the sleeve and the 1st gear floating ring. Press the 1st gear-wheel on and insert the distance piece. Press into the shaft the ball bearing which is already assembled by being forced against the intermediate flange and fit the key for the driven reverse pinion.

4) If the shaft or any of the parts mounted on it have been replaced, proceed as follows: mount the driven reverse pinion, push on the distance piece, taking care to march up the file mark made on it when the gear-box was originally assembled and the reverse pinion key. Place a distance piece in position and mount the rear cover. The bearing is forced onto the shaft by inserting the fork into the spline (which should be placed with the hole for the plate matching up with the file mark on the end of the shaft) and blocking the centring nut. Before screwing the latter right home, temporary locating pins are placed in position between the rear cover and the intermediate flange.

5) As shown in Fig. 22, place the rear cover in a vice and check that, when turned, the opposite end of the shaft does not move more than 0.05 mm. Any correction needed can be obtained by rotating the distance piece between the reverse pinion and the rear cover or the transmission connecting fork. If this is not suf-

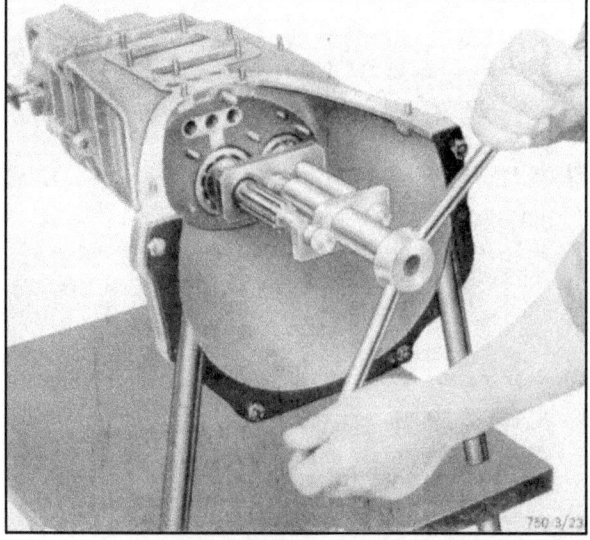

Fig. 23 - Setting of the primary and secondary shafts into the gear-box casing front bearings; use tool 6121.05.036.

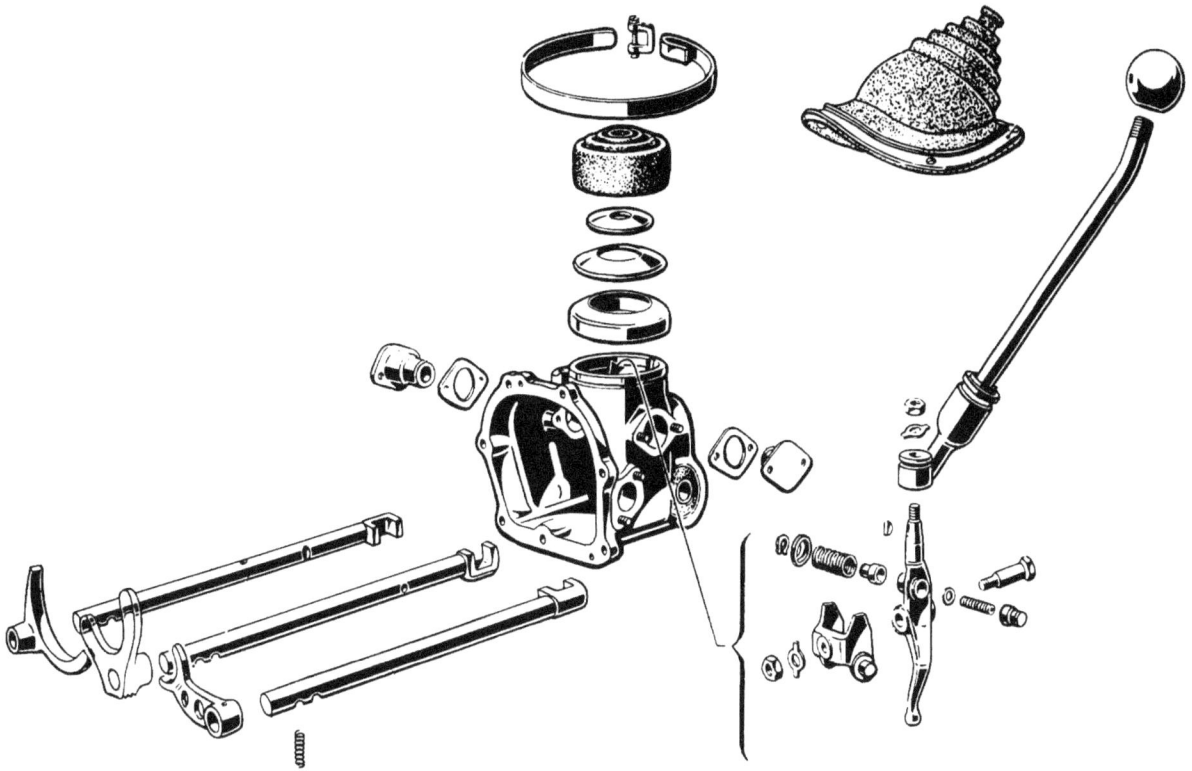

Fig. 24 - The gear-box for the Giulietta Sprint Veloce, Spider and Spider Veloce.

3) On the front end of the gear-box direct-drive shaft mount a washer of suitable thickness (this is to be found as shown in Fig. 21) and the spring ring.

4) Mount the oil seal in the front cover, using tool 6121.07.247. Place the gasket and the front cover on the front of the gear-box casing, after having placed a sleeve with a rounded end to prevent the oil seal from damaging the shoulder on the shaft; fit the corrugated washer, put on the nuts and tighten up.

5) Place the fork for operating the synchro sleeve in its groove. Insert the rollers, after lubricating them in their holes in the intermediate flange and fit the driven reverse pinion.

Insert the gear change rod for 3rd and 4th speeds then the rod for 1st and 2nd and finally the rod for the reverse with the intermediate pinion. Assemble in position (tool 6121.22.041) the gear change rods with their positioning sleeves, balls and springs suitably lubricated with grease.

NOTE: To prevent jamming of the sleeves on the casing from breaking off material with the consequent bedding in of the sleeves and their interference with the rods, it is advisable to fit plate No. 1365.17.071 between the sleeves and their seating in the casing. To do this, replace the 33 mm long sleeves by others 1 mm longer (the same applies to the thickness of the plate).

6) Replace the distance piece between the driven reverse pinion and the bearing in the rear cover in its final position mentioned under 4 in the preceding paragraph and an adjusting washer. Mount the complete rear cover, the fork, the plate and the nut and tighten up.

With a pair of calipers (tool 672.5300) check that the height **B** (Fig. 11) is from 45.75 to 46 mm and, if necessary, adjust it to this value by replacing the packing washer between the distance piece and the rear primary shaft bearing with another of suitable thickness.

7) Attach the corrugated washer on the gear engaging fork with set-screws and locking plates. Check that the distance **C** between each synchro sleeve and its gears (Fig. 11) is 0.1 mm. Also check that, with the gears engaged, the distance between the front faces of the gears and the sleeves involved is not less than 0.1 mm. Check that there is a cer-

tain clearance for each rod between the position when the gear is engaged and the end of its travel so as to ensure that the sleeve can actually reach the engaging position.

8) Place the gasket and the bottom cover in place and then fit the speedometer drive support.

9) Mount the clutch fork, complete with the clutch withdrawal ring, on its bracket.

11 - REPLACING THE GEAR-BOX IN THE CAR

Remount the gear-box in the car by carrying out in reverse the procedure described in Chapter 7.
Remember that the checks described in Chapter 6 should be made when making the outside connections to the gear-box controls.

12 - GEAR BOX CONTROLLED BY BALL GEAR SHIFT LEVER (for Giulietta Sprint Veloce, Spider and Spider Veloce models).

It derives from gearbox with gear shift lever under steering wheel in which the whole rear part relative to speed engagement has been replaced.

Dismantling

When previous operations indicated for gearbox with gear shift lever under steering wheel have been carried out, the group comprising main driving shaft, counter shaft, intermediate flange, gear selector rods, can be quickly drawn out from gearbox using tool N. 6121.12092.

When the group will be fixed in the vice, inspection and overhaul can be performed.

THE GEARBOX SUPPLEMENT THAT WAS INCLUDED IN THE PREVIOUS (1957) PUBLICATION OF THIS MANUAL WAS OMITTED FROM THIS 1958 EDITION. FOR THE SAKE OF COMPLETENESS IT IS INCLUDED IN THE APPENDIX AT THE END OF THIS MANUAL

INFORMATION SHEET REFERENCE

ASSEMBLY	DATE	SHEET N.	SUBJECT

INFORMATION SHEET REFERENCE

ASSEMBLY	DATE	SHEET N.	SUBJECT

PART 4

PROPELLOR SHAFT

INDEX

Description . . . . page 111

1) Inspection without removing the shaft from the car . . . . . » 112

2) Removing the shaft from the car . . . . » 112

3) Dismantling . . . . » 112

4) Inspection . . . . » 112

5) Reassembling . . . . » 113

6) Replacing the shaft in the car . . . . » 114

PART 4

PROPELLOR SHAFT

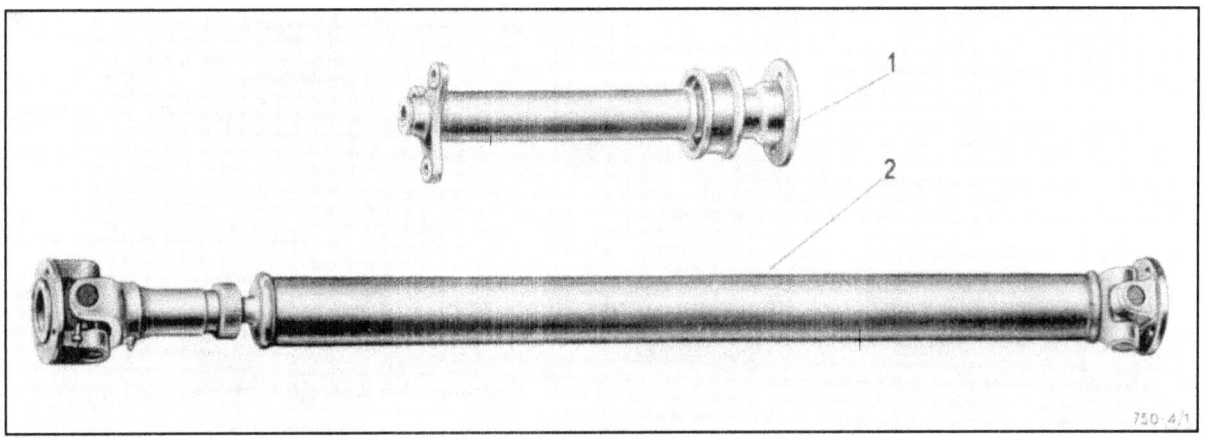

Fig. 1 - Propellor shaft
1. Forward half of shaft - 2. Rear half of shaft.

DESCRIPTION

The propellor shaft is in two halves as follows:
— the forward half, which is connected to the gearbox by a rubber joint.
— the rear half, which has roller bearing cardan joint at both ends and is connection to the bevel pinion by a sleeve.

The two shafts are joined together by a central flanged joint which is mounted on the front half of the shaft by means of a tapered sleeve for ensuring correct centring of the joint. The front cardan joint is integral with a sleeve sliding on a splined shaft. The rear cardan joint is fixed.

The rear end of the forward half is fixed to the body through a flexible support fitted with a ball bearing.

Fig. 2 - Details of propellor shaft.

1 - INSPECTION WITHOUT REMOVING THE SHAFT FROM THE CAR

1) Checking the front flexible joint.

Check that the outside of the joints is not damaged.

2) Checking the packing on the centring pin in the front flexible joint.

Check the effectiveness of the packing seal **6** (Fig. 4) and replace it if it is worn.

3) Checking the play.

While holding the gear-box shaft fork with a tool to prevent it from moving, revolve the sliding sleeve and check that there is no excessive play in the front cardan joint; repeat the operation, holding the cardan joint fork on the bevel pinion to prevent it from moving and revolving the rear half of the shaft.

2 - REMOVING THE SHAFT FROM THE CAR

1) Remove the three bolts holding the shaft to the gear-box shaft fork.

2) Remove the 4 bolts holding the cardan fork to the bevel pinion.

3) Remove the 2 screws holding the saddle carrying the centre bearing and withdraw the inner shaft.

3 - DISMANTLING

1) Remove the studs attaching the flanged joint on the forward shaft to that on the rear half.

2) Unscrew the bolts attaching the rubber joint on the forward half on the propellor shaft.

3) Remove the nut securing the flange to the forward half of the shaft, the flange, the keys and the centre bearing support.

4) Slide the sleeve off the rear half shaft after screwing out the ring holding the seal.

5) Dismantle the two cardan joints in the following order:

   a) Remove the four spring washers (Fig. 3);
   b) Remove the lubricator;
   c) Slide out the roller cages with the rollers to free the pins;
   d) Remove the spider.

6) Wash with paraffin except for the rubber joint.

4 - INSPECTION

1) Checking the rear half-shaft for straightness

Mount the shaft between centres and check with a gauge to ensure that it is straight. Eccentricity should not exceed 0.5 mm (fig. 6). If this figure is exceeded straighten the shaft in a hydraulic press or replace it.

2) Checking the cardan joints

Check the cork seals, the roller bearing seatings and the play between the pins on the spider and the roller cages; the limit of wear is 0.20 mm.

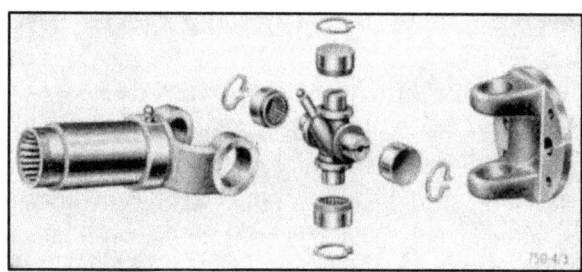

Fig. 3 - Details of a cardan point.

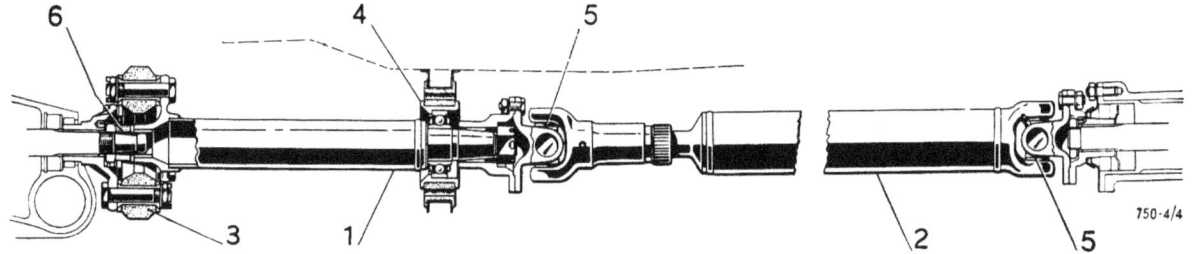

Fig. 4 - Complete propellor shaft:
1. Forward half of shaft - 2. Rear half of shaft - 3. Flexible rubber joint - 4. Intermediate support - 5. Roller bearing cardan joints - 6. Seal on rubber joint centring pin.

3) Checking the splined shaft

Check that the play between the splining in the sleeve and the splines on the rear half of the shaft does not exceed the limit of wear of 0.3 mm (Fig. 5).

4) Miscellaneous checks

Check that the flexible joint shows no signs of turning, and that the centring sleeve on the gearbox shaft has no internal roughness. If necessary replace the parts.

Check that the bearing carrying the centre support is not defective and replace it if necessary.

5 - REASSEMBLING

1) Assemble the components of cardan joints, lubricating them well when doing so.

2) Mount the cardan shaft sleeve on the rear half of the shaft, taking care that the reference marks on the shaft and sleeve match up.

3) Slide the central bearing with its flexible support into position with tool 6121.07.327, insert the key and sleeve, and tighten up the nut.

4) Mount the flexible joint on the forward hal-shaft.

5) Connect up the front and rear shafts.

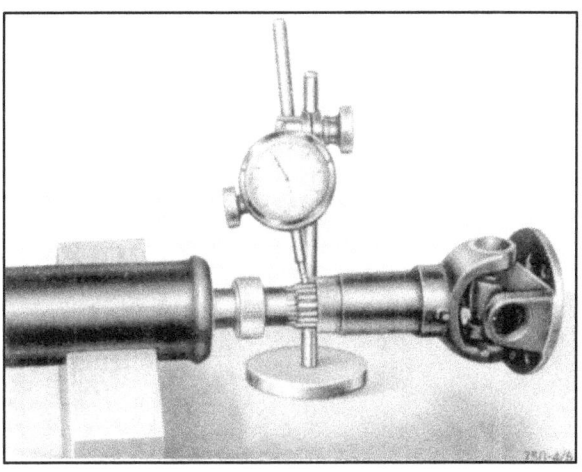

Fig. 5 - Checking the play between the splines in the sliding sleeve and on the rear shaft

Fig. 6 - Checking the rear shaft for straightness.

6) If any parts have to be replaced, it is advisable to re-balance the complete shaft unit dynamically.

6 - REPLACING THE SHAFT IN THE CAR

When replacing the shaft in the car proceed as described in Section 2 but in the reverse order, remembering to grease the bushing for centering the propellor shaft with the primary gear-box shaft, and to tighten up the nuts in order and uniformly.

Lubricate the bolts in the rubber joint to prevent their pulling their bushes round when tightened up and thus damaging the joint.

INFORMATION SHEET REFERENCE

ASSEMBLY	DATE	SHEET N.	SUBJECT

PART 5

REAR AXLE AND SUSPENSION

INDEX

Description . . . . page	118
Rear Axle . . . . »	119
1) When replacing rear axle shafts, bearings and oil seals . . . . »	119
2) Removing the rear axle unit . . . . »	121
3) Dismantling and inspecting the differential . . . . . . »	121
4) Re-assembling the differential . . . . »	123
Rear Suspension . . . . »	130
5) Replacing the rebound straps . . . . »	130
6) Dismantling and checking the rear suspension units . . . . »	130
7) Removing the rear shock-absorbers . . . . »	131
8) Hydraulic shock-absorbers . . . . »	131
Appendix . . . . »	134

PART 5

REAR AXLE AND SUSPENSION

Fig. 1 - Rear axle and suspension.

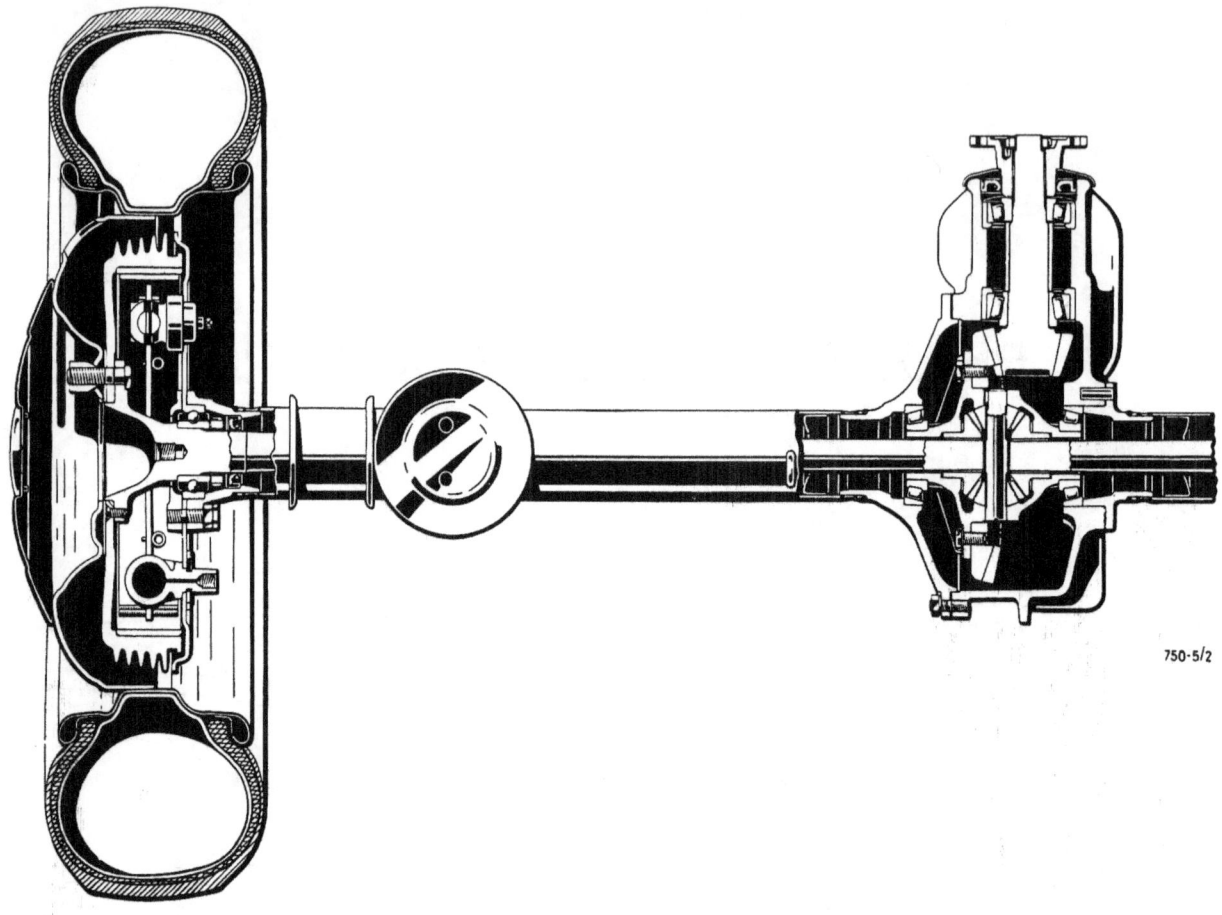

Fig. 2 - Section through rear axle.

DESCRIPTION

The rear suspension is of the rigid rear-axle type with vertical coil springs (Fig. 1).

The differential and the hypoid bevel drive are enclosed in an aluminium housing to which are bolted the two drawn steel tubes in which the axle shaft revolve.

This system has the advantage of reducing the weight of the unit and of improving the springing through the decrease in the influence of the unsprung units. The rear axle is attached to the body as follows:

— by longitudinal arms carried on rubber (silentbloc) supports and designed to transmit the direct stresses (transmission and braking) along the axis of the vehicle;

— by a triangular torque rod to take the transverse forces; this rod also has rubber supports on the body and a spherical joint on the rear axle;

— by a flexible system comprising two vertical coil springs, integral with the hydraulic shock-absorbers and coaxial with them.

The rear axle has one of the two following ratios:

— 9/41 for standard models

— 8/41 and 10/41 on request

The rear axle shafts are of the « semi-floating » type. The rear axle casing has a magnetised drain plug so that it retains metal chips and particles suspended in the oil.

The greatest care is taken when assembling the bevel drive and differential at the factory to ensure that silent running is obtained.

It is of the utmost importance to comply exactly with the following instructions when overhauling and reassembling the axle.

REAR AXLE

Fig. 3 - Dismantling a rear axle shaft with tool 6121.12.055.

1 - WHEN REPLACING REAR AXLE SHAFTS BEARINGS AND OIL SEALS

Dismantling

- Jack up the car.
- Remove the wheel.
- Remove the brake-drum after removing the locking set-screws.
- Remove the brake-shoes and tie up the cylinders with wire to prevent the pistons dropping out.
- Bend back the lock-washers and unscrew the studs securing the brake-shoe back-plates and the wheel bearing housings to the axle tubes.

Fig. 4 - Checking that a rear axle shaft is running true.

- Disconnect the pipes from the brake cylinders and close their ends with blind nuts (3/8", 24 t.p.i.), taking care to put a washer in the bottom of the nuts to prevent the ends being damaged.
- Disconnect the hand-brake cables.
- Remove the brake-shoe back-plates.
- If it is only a question of removing the axle shafts, it is not necessary to remove the bracke-shoe back-plates or to disconnect the piping.
- Using the tool No. 6121.12055, withdraw the rear axle shaft (Fig. 3) with the bearing, the nut and the collar holding the bearing still in place. While withdrawing the shaft from the tube be careful not

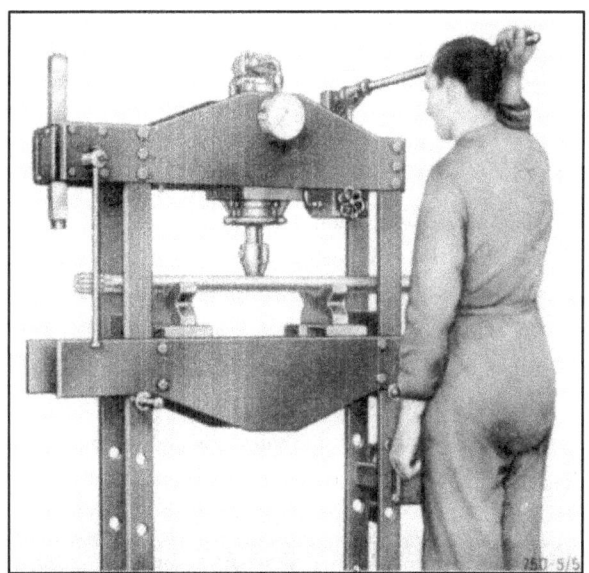

Fig. 5 - Straightening a rear axle shaft in a hydraulic press.

to let it scrape on the oil-seal ring and damage it. If the brake-shoe back-plates have not been removed, they should be supported and care should be taken not to damage the brake piping; when the half-shafts have been removed, fix the plates to the axle tubes by means of two screws.

- If the bearing has to be removed from the axle shaft, lift the tab securing the collar and unscrew the latter with tool No. 6121.20.036; then draw off the bearing with tool No. 6121.12.087.

If necessary, remove the oil-seal ring from the tube.

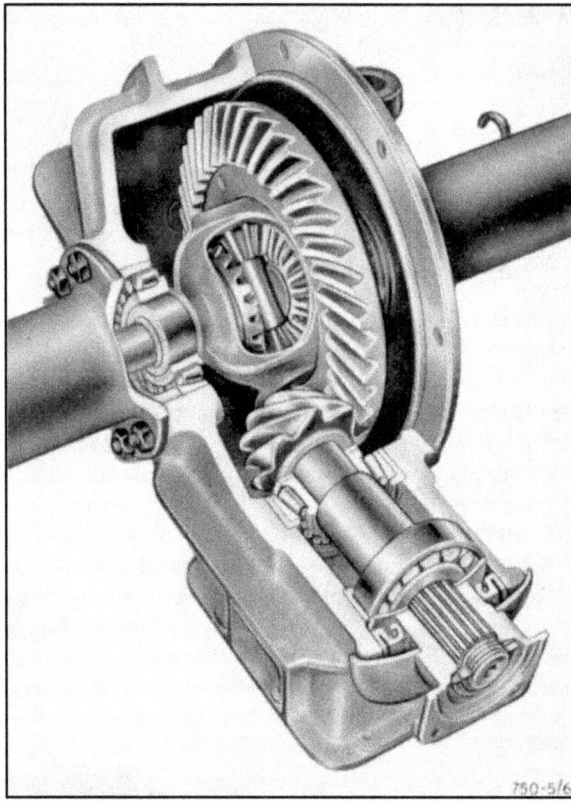

Fig. 6 - Section through the differential.

NOTE: On cars with numbers higher than 1488.02001 for the Giulietta Berlina and 1493.01851 for the Giulietta Sprint, the brake-shoe back-plates and the bearing retaining collars are secured to the axle tubes by studs fixed to the collar so that it is not necessary to remove the brake shoes from the back-plate in order to withdraw the axle shafts.

WARNING: To ensure that the brakes operate properly, the brake shoes must be reassembled in their original position and it is therefore advisable to mark them as they are removed.

Inspection

— Check the condition of the oil-seal ring and, if necessary, replace it.

— Check that the bearings and shaft are free from defects, scoring, dents, etc.

— Check that the rear axle shafts are not bent (Fig. 4); if they are, measure their eccentricity (which should not exceed 0,10÷0,15 mm (4÷6 thousandths) and straighten them if necessary in a hydraulic press. (Fig. 5).

— Check the play between the splines of the shafts and the planet pinions.

Reassembling

The paragraphs below describe how to reassemble one rear axle shaft; the other shaft is re-fitted in an exactly similar manner.

— Insert the oil-sealing ring in the axle tube, using tool No. 6121.07.057.

— Thread the collar onto the shaft, insert the bearing with tool No. 6121.07.219, slip on the lock-washer, screw on the ring nut with tool 6121.20.036 and bend over the locking tab.

— Re-fit the brake-shoe back-plate (if it has been removed) and then push in the axle shaft, bringing it to engage with the splined hole in the planet pinion. Take care, while doing this, not to damage the oil-sealing ring and the oil guard welded inside the axle tube near the flange to which the differential bracket is bolted.

— Drive the axle shaft right home with a hammer after placing a piece of aluminium on the axle end.

— Turn the bearing retaining collar so that the oil drain-hole is at the bottom and opposite the hole in the back-plate; place the lock-washer in position (with the tabs slightly bent up to facilitate their final bending), tighten the studs and fold the tabs over.

— Re-fit the brake shoes, beginning with the rear shoes. Make sure that the pull-off springs are on the inner side, mounting the one with the two separated spirals on the side of the brake actuating cylinder.

— Using tool 6123.29.007, check that the faces of the brake linings are at right angles to the axle shaft collar and, if necessary adjust them by means of the regulating studs located at the rear of the brack-shoe back plate (see Part 8 - Brakes).

— Re-fit the brake drums, screwing up the two locking screws.

— Re-fit the wheels and lower the car from the jack.

— If the brake piping has been detached when dismantling, it will be necessary to bleed the circuit.

2 - REMOVING THE REAR AXLE UNIT

— Wash and dry the rear axle and suspension.

— Remove the complete exhaust pipe.

— Disconnect the flexible brake-fluid tube from the union attached to the body and empty it of oil or close the union with a threaded plug.

— Disconnect the hand-brake operating rods from the cylinders and from the rear axle bracket.

— Unfasten the rear axle anti-sway straps.

— Disconnect the shock-absorbers from the rear axle; in order to remove the axle it is unnecessary to disconnect the shock-absorbers from the car; it is sufficient to push them down and leave them in the end-of-compression position.

— Loosen the nuts holding the wheels on the axle shafts.

— Disconnect the triangular torque arm from the axle, unscrewing the nut which secures the shank of the ball-headed pin to the latter. Take care not to damage the thread on the pin while removing it.

— Place a car jack under the axle tubes and raise the car.

— Block up the car on supports placed under the seatings for the jack supplied with the car. Remove the rear wheels.

— Gently lower the jack and remove the rear springs.

— Disconnect the longitudinal radius rods from the body.

— Disconnect the propellor shaft from the bevel pinion and remove the axle.

3 - DISMANTLING AND INSPECTING THE DIFFERENTIAL

Dismantling

1) Drain the oil from the rear axle.

2) Remove the rear axle shafts as described in Chapter 1.

3) Detach the right and left-hand axle tubes from the central axle bracket.

4) Remove the differential casing.

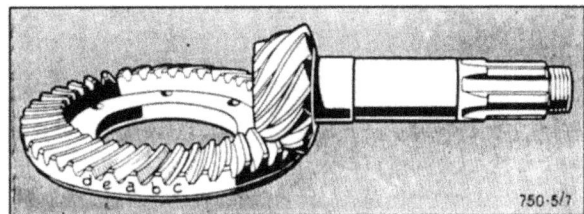

Fig. 7 - Marks of wear on the crown wheel teeth.
a. Correct meshing - **b.** Excessive pressure near the base of the teeth - **c.** Excessive pressure at the top of the teeth - **d.** Excessive pressure on the outside edges of the teeth - **e.** Excessive pressure on the under part of the point of the teeth.

Inspection

1) **Checking the condition of the gear teeth**

   Make sure that the surface of the teeth is smooth and not ridged. Should there be signs of undue wear, the bevel pinion and crown wheel must be replaced.

   WARNING: The crowns and pinions are matched together at the factory; no one member of the bevel gear must be changed on its own. The whole unit must be replaced complete.

2) **Checking the contact between the teeth.**

   Contact should be uniform over the whole length of the crown-wheel teeth.
   The following conditions may be found (Fig. 7):

   — **normal state:** the lateral surface will be as shown on tooth **a**;

Fig. 8 - Withdrawal of the bevel pinion oil seal, using tool 6121.04.015.

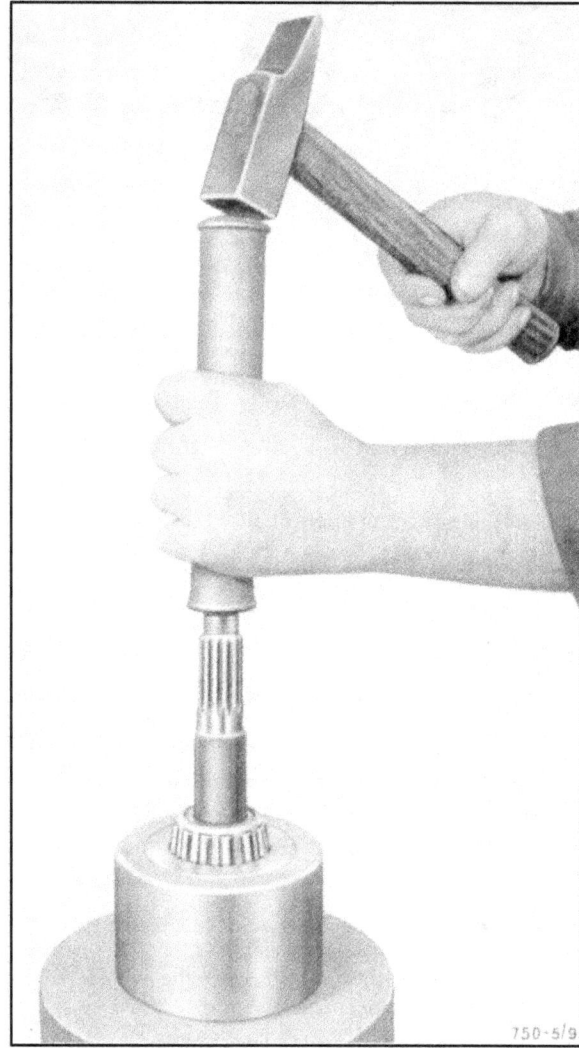

Fig. 9 - Withdrawal of the inner race of the rear bevel pinion bearing, using tool 6121.13.019.

- **excessive pressure near the base of the crown wheel teeth (b)** due to the bevel pinion being too close to the crown wheel;

- **excessive pressure towards the tips of the crown wheel teeth (c)** due to the pinion being too far from the crown wheel.

  With either of the conditions **b** or **c**, check the position of the two bevels, testing the play with a gauge as explained under the chapter 4;

- **excessive pressure at the sides of the teeth and towards the outside (d)**, due to the distance between the crown wheel centre and the plane of the pinion being too great, or to the bevels not being properly aligned, or to the teeth being distorted;

Fig. 11 - Withdrawal of the outer race of the front bevel pinion bearing, using tool 6121.12.057.

- **excessive pressure on the tips of the teeth towards the inside (e)**, caused by the crown wheel being too close to the pinion, or to the bevels not being properly aligned, or to the teeth being distorted.

  In cases **d** and **e** (which are very rarely met with in practice) the pair of gears must be replaced.

3) **Removing the bevel pinion from the housing**

- Apply tool 6121.01.166 to the propellor shaft fork to prevent the bevel pinion turning and, with wrench 6121.20.035, unscrew the ring holding the pinion (Fig. 20);

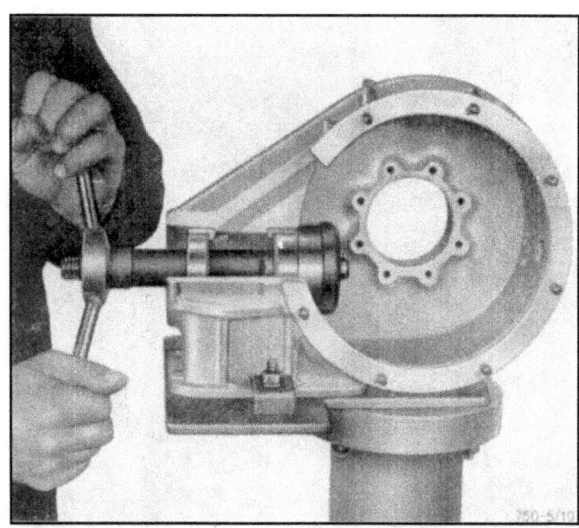

Fig. 10 - Withdrawal of the outer race of the rear bevel pinion bearing, using tool 6121.04.015.

- remove the propellor shaft fork, pull the pinion out of its housing and, with tool 6121.04.015, withdraw the oil-sealing ring together with the inner race of the outer bearing (Fig. 8);
- in cases where the bevel pinion bearings have to be replaced, withdraw the inner race of the rear bearing, using tool 6121.13.019 (Fig. 3);
- withdraw the outer race of the rear bearing with tool 6121.04.015 (Fig. 10) and the outer race of the front bearing with tool 6121.12.057 (Fig. 11).

4) **Inspection**

Check the condition of the teeth and of the roller bearings.

5) **Dismantling the differential casing**

Remove the crown wheel and withdraw the inner races of the bearings (Fig. 12), using tool No. 6121.12.052; remove the planetary pinion spindle and the sun gears.

6) **Removing the outer race of the differential housing bearings and the left hand axle tube.**

To extract the outer race of the right-hand differential housing bearing, use tool 6121.07.141; use tool 6121.12.054 (Fig. 13) for the outer race of the left-hand tube bearing.

4 - RE-ASSEMBLING THE DIFFERENTIAL

The correct operation of the differential and, in particular, the absence of noise, can only be obtained if

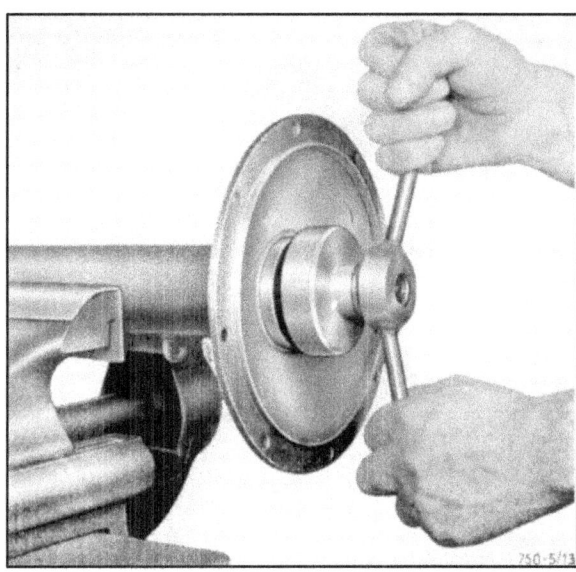

Fig. 13 - Withdrawal of the outer race of the taper roller bearing from the left-hand rear-axle tube, using tool 6121.12.054.

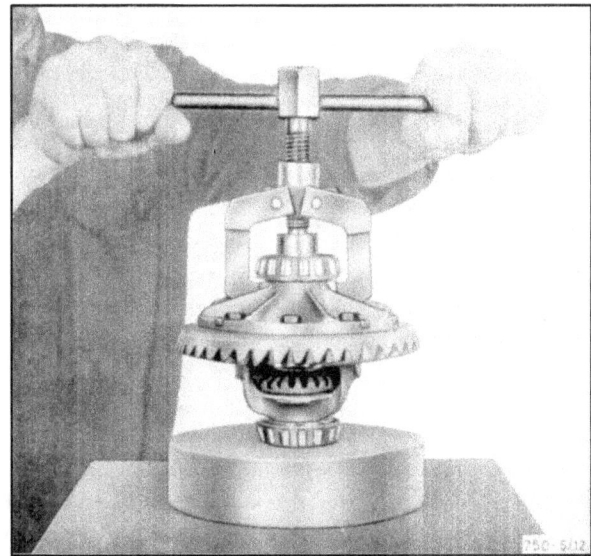

Fig. 12 - Withdrawal of the inner races of the differential casing taper roller bearings, using tool 6121.12.052.

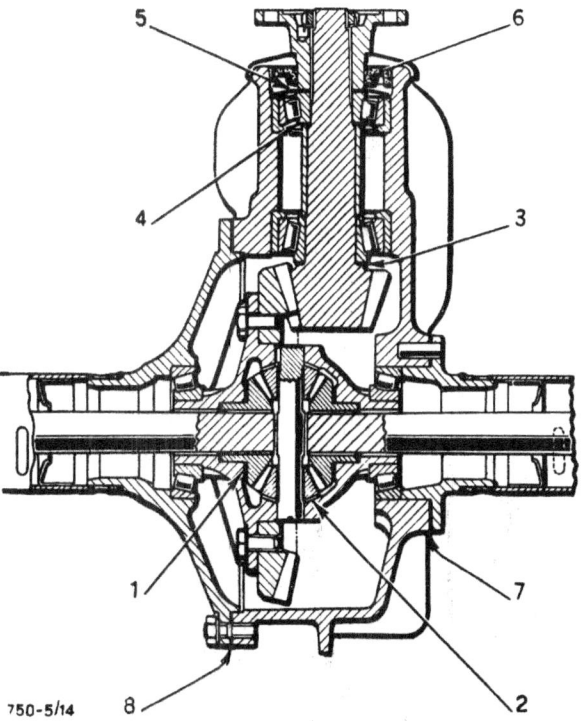

Fig. 14 - Section through the differential.
1. Sun wheel packing washers - 2. Spherical planet wheel washers - 3. Packing washer for adjusting distance between bevel pinion and crown wheel - 4. Packing ring for adjusting pre-load on bevel pinion bearings - 5. Oil-seal plate - 6. Oil-seal washer - 7. Packing ring for right-hand axle tube - 8. Packing ring for left-hand axle tube.

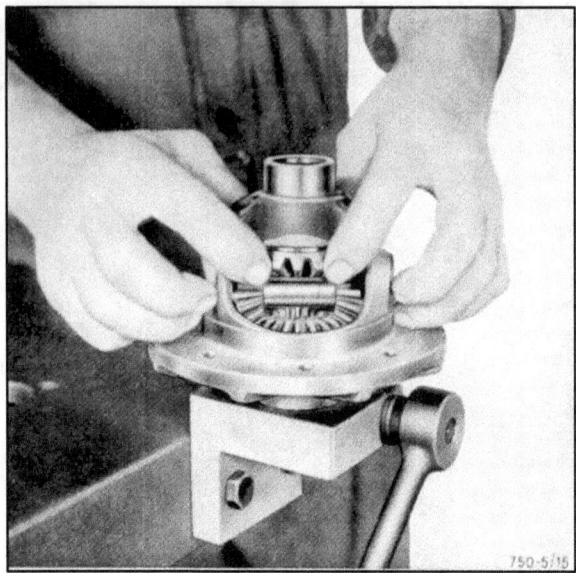

Fig. 15 - Checking the backlash between sun and planet pinions.

the same procedure is adopted when assembling and overhauling as was used at the factory, and if the same checks and tools are used.

The differential is reassembled in sections and in accordance with the procedure mentioned below.

1) **Differential casing**

   Assemble the packing rings **1** (Fig. 14), the two sun gears and the planet pinions, their spherical washers **2** and the spindle in the casing. Check that the back-lash between the teeth is about 0.05 mm (2 thousandths), for which purpose it is sufficient to ensure that the gears revolve freely when turned by hand (Fig. 15).

Fig. 16 - Mounting the outer race of the rear bevel pinion bearing in the differential housing, using tool 6121.04.015.

Should there be excessive resistance or should the meshing be too slack, correct by inserting packing washers of different thicknesses between the sun gears and the casing.

Fit the key in the planet pinion spindle, place the crown wheel in position and lock it with the bolts and the lock-washers.

2) **Bevel pinion**

   First mount the outer races of the taper roller bearings in the bevel pinion housing, using tool No. 6121.04.015 for the rear race (Fig. 16) and No. 6121.07.287 for the front race (Fig. 17).

   Mount an 0.8 mm (0.315") packing washer **3** (Fig. 14) on the pinion shaft (for adjusting the correct

Fig. 17 - Mounting the outer race of the front bevel pinion bearing in the differential housing, using tool 6121.07.287.

distance from the crown wheel), then the inner race of the rear bearing, using tool No. 6121.07.220 (Fig. 18), the distance piece between the two pinion bearings and a 0,8 mm (0,315") packing ring **4** for setting the preload on them. Next insert the bevel pinion thus assembled in its housing and hold it in position in the housing by means of a wood block; put the inner race of the outer bearing on the pinion, using tool 6121.07.221 (Fig. 19), then fit the oil sealing ring **5** (Fig. 14), the cardan joint sleeve (do not include the rubber oil seal) and tighten up the unit with the outer locking ring, using tool No. 6121.01.166 and wrench 6121.20.035. (Fig. 20).

WARNING: Before replacing the pinion note must be taken of the reference mark stamped on it; this shows which packing rings to select, as described in Section 4 (« Checking the distance between the end of the pinion and the crown wheel centre »).

3) **Checking the preload on the bevel pinion bearings**

The « preload » is the name given to the torque in kgm offered by a taper roller bearing when it is rotated after being mounted and tightened up on its shaft and before it has done any work.

To measure this preload fit tool No. 6123.15.006 (as shown in Fig. 21) on the cardan-joint sleeve and attach a 500 g (1 lb. 1 5/8 oz) weight to the end of the lever 250 mm (9.842") long, this lever

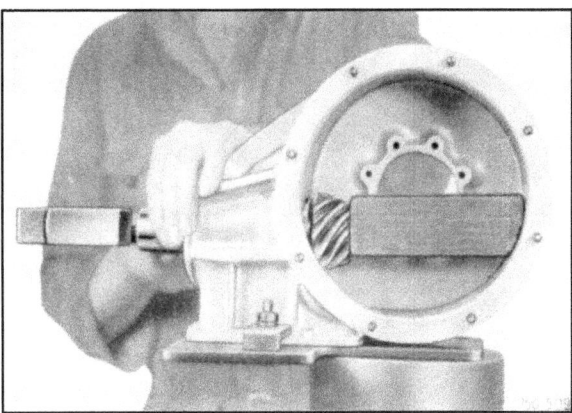

Fig. 19 - Mounting the inner race of the front bearing on the bevel pinion, using tool 6121.07.221.

Fig. 18 - Mounting the inner race of the rear bearing on the bevel pinion, using tool 6121.07.220.

(2.244"), plus or minus the amount marked on the pinion shaft; if this value is preceded by the + sign, the distance should be 57 mm plus the figure and, if it is preceded by the — sign, 57 mm minus the distance indicated on the pinion. A check is made as follows:

— Insert tool 6123.27.028 into the housing of the right-hand differential casing bearing as shown in Fig. 23.

— Apply tool 6123.41.111, provided with an indicator (which has been previously set to zero with gauge 6123.26.217), to the end of the pinion as shown in Fig. 24.

Fig. 20 - Locking the round nut on the bevel pinion, using tool 6121.01.166 and wrench 6121.20.035.

should move spontaneously; if necessary, start the movement with slight finger pressure. If the lever offers resistance it is because the preload is too high while if the lever starts to turn quickly it shows that the preload is insufficient.

Adjustment of the preload is obtained by replacing the packing washer **4** between the front bearing and the distance piece (Fig. 14) with a thinner or thicker one as the case may require.

4) **Checking the distance between the end of the pinion and the crown wheel centre**

The distance **A** or **A1** (Fig. 22) should be 57 mm.

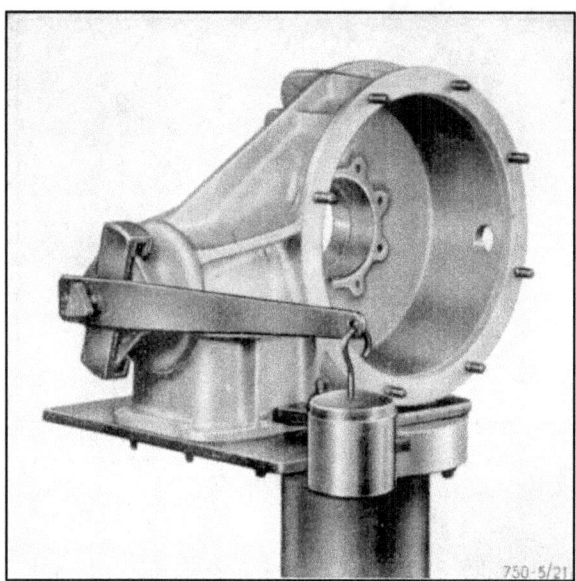

Fig. 21 - Checking the pre-load on the bevel pinion bearings, using tool 6123.15.006.

suitable thickness between the pinion and the rear bearing.

WARNING:

1) **When productions was started, pinions H1 = = 32.5 mm (1.278″) in height, Fig. 22, were fitted; the distance A1 should therefore be 59 mm (2.322″). The fixture shown in Fig. 24 has two flat surfaces, and the appropriate surface should be used to correspond with the figure involved. It should be noted that the heights of the flat surfaces above the base of the fixture are actually 70 mm (2 3/4″) for pinions having H = 34.5 mm (1.357″) and 72 mm (2.834″) for those having H1 = 32.5 mm (1.278″) so as to take into account the diameter (26 mm) of the centre pin on which the gauge of fixture 6123.27.028 rests.**

— Read the measurement on the indicator; it should be the same as the figure marked on the shaft, preceded by a + or — sign. If this is not so, insert a packing washer **3** (Fig. 14) of

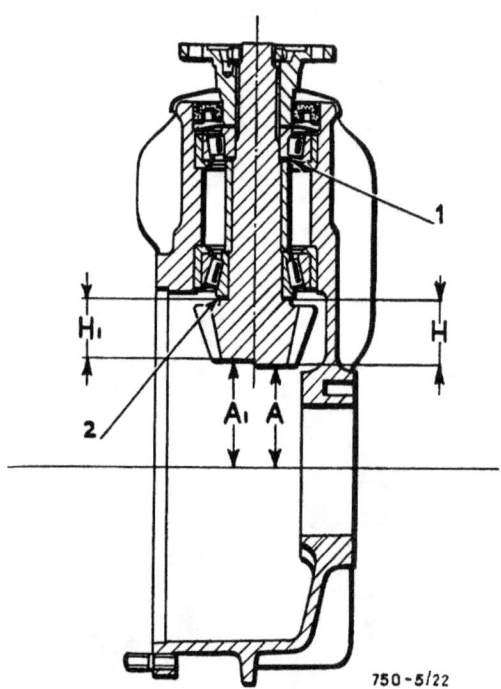

Fig. 22 - Mounting the bevel pinion in the differential housing.
1. Packing ring for adjusting the play in the taper roller bearings - **2.** Packing ring for adjusting backlash between the bevel and crown wheel - **A.** Distance between pinion and crown wheel centre (for pinion with a tooth depth of H. - **A1.** Distance from bevel pinion to crown wheel centre (with pinion having a tooth depth of H1) - **H.** Pinion tooth depth of 34.5 mm. - **H1.** Pinion tooth depth of 32.5 mm.

Fig. 23 - Checking the distance between the bevel pinion and crown wheel centre, using tool 6123.27.028 and a comparator gauge 6123.41.111

2) **Determination of the preload on the taper roller bearings (paragraph 3) and the distance from the pinion to the centre of the crown wheel (Section 4) can be effected, at least in part, at the same time so as to reduce the number of times the bevel gear has to be removed from its housing.**

5) **The differential unit**
After the checks described above, proceed as follows:

— mount the outer race of the bearing (Fig. 25) in the right-hand side of the differential housing, using tool 6121.07.222, and both the inner races in the differential casing, using tool 6121.07.217 (Fig. 26);

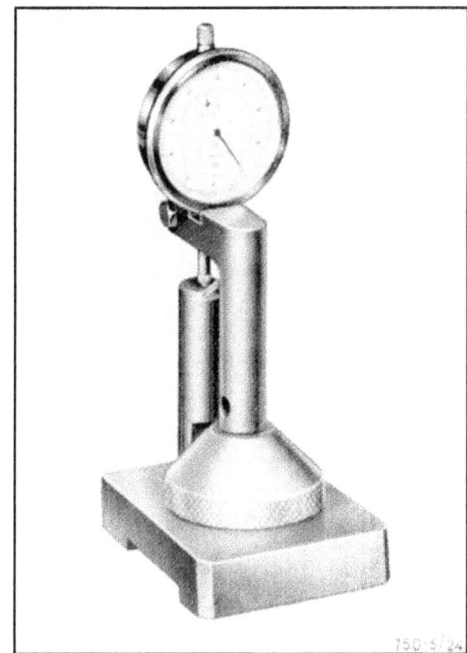

Fig. 24 - Setting the gauge to zero for checking the distance between the bevel pinion and crown wheel centre.

- mount the part of the tool 6123.27.025 which is fitted to the right-hand side of the differential housing (Fig. 27);

- fit the complete differential with its casing into the differential housing;

- place the outer race of the bearing on the other part of the fixture 6123.27.025 and fit the fixture thus assembled onto the near side of the housing;

- push the crown wheel towards the pinion, moving it by the handles **3** shown in Fig. 28;

- attach the fixture 6123.13.006 to the cardan-joint fork for the purpose of checking the total preload which should be 600 g (21 oz 2 1/2 dr)

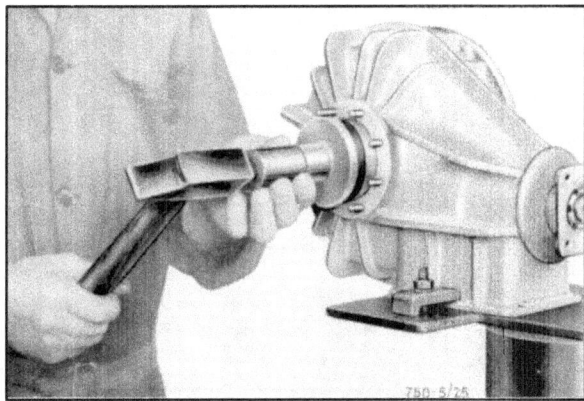

Fig. 25 - Mounting the outer bearing race on the right-hand side of the differential casing, using tool 6121.07.222.

and the backlash between pinion and crown wheel teeth; this should be between 0.05 and 0.10 mm (2 to 4 thousandths);

- the preload is checked as explained in paragraph 3. For checking the backlash with a gauge, place its actuating rod at a distance of 45 mm from the centre-line of the pinion (Fig. 28);

- block the crown wheel by screwing the pin into the oil filler hole in the differential housing, and oscillate the fixture. If the play shown on the gauge is from 0,18 to 0,30 mm (7 to 11 thousandths) this will give the backlash figure mentioned above. If the play shown on the

Fig. 26 - Mounting the inner bearing race on the differential casing, using tool 6121.07.217.

gauge is greater than the figure laid down, screw up the small right-hand hand-wheel and unscrew the left-hand hand-wheel to an equal extent; if the play is less, unscrew the right-hand wheel and screw up the left-hand wheel by an equal amount.

WARNING: The play should be checked at four positions of the crown wheel by turning the pinion one revolution after each reading, and by locking the crown wheel in each position with the pin as mentioned above.

- when the requisite conditions of play and preload have been achieved, lock the sliding parts of the two fixtures with the pins **4** (Fig. 28); remove the fixture from the right-hand tube

Fig. 27 - Fixture 6123.27.025 mounted on the differential housing.

side and read off the value «a» and «b» (shown in Figs. 29 and 30) using gauge 670.1655 for the purpose. The difference between these two figures gives the value of the thickness to which the packing ring **7** to be inserted between the differential casing and the right-hand axle tube (fig. 14) should correspond as closely as possible;

— check that the outer bearing race is bedding on its seating in the tube;

— remove the fixture from the left-hand axle tube side and take out the outer race of the

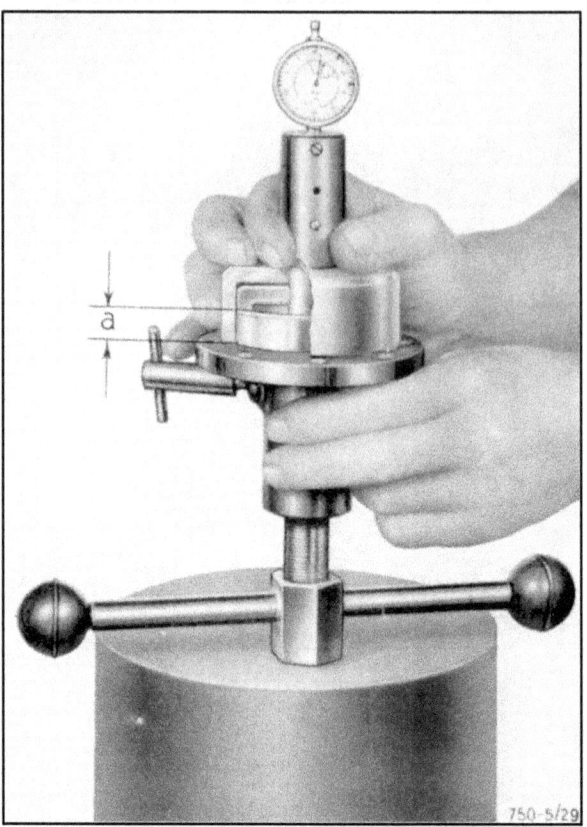

Fig. 29 - Measuring the value «a» for determining the thickness of the packing ring between the right-hand axle tube and the differential casing, using gauge 670.1655 and fixture 6123.27.025.

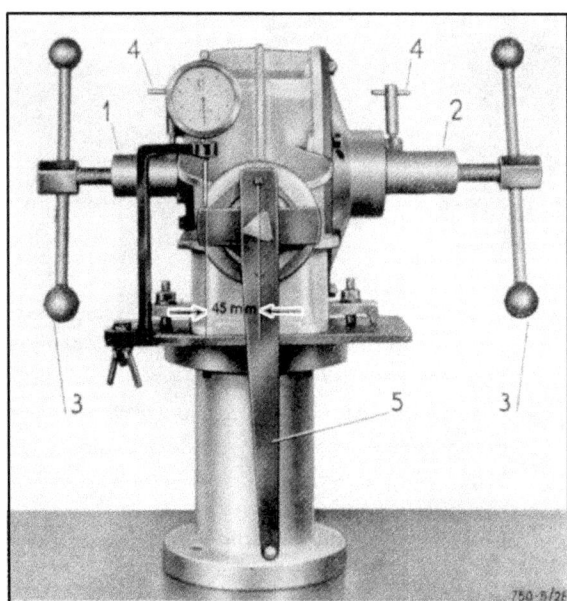

Fig. 28 - Fixture 6123.27.025 mounted on the differential housing for adjusting the backlash between pinion and crown wheel and the preload on the differential casing bearings.
1. Right-hand part of tool - **2.** Left-hand part of tool - **3.** Handles for setting the bearing preload - **4.** Dowels for locking the handles 3 - **5.** Fixture 6123.15.006 for checking the bearing preload and adjusting the backlash between the bevel and crown wheel teeth. The figure shows the fixture while the backlash is being measured with the gauge.

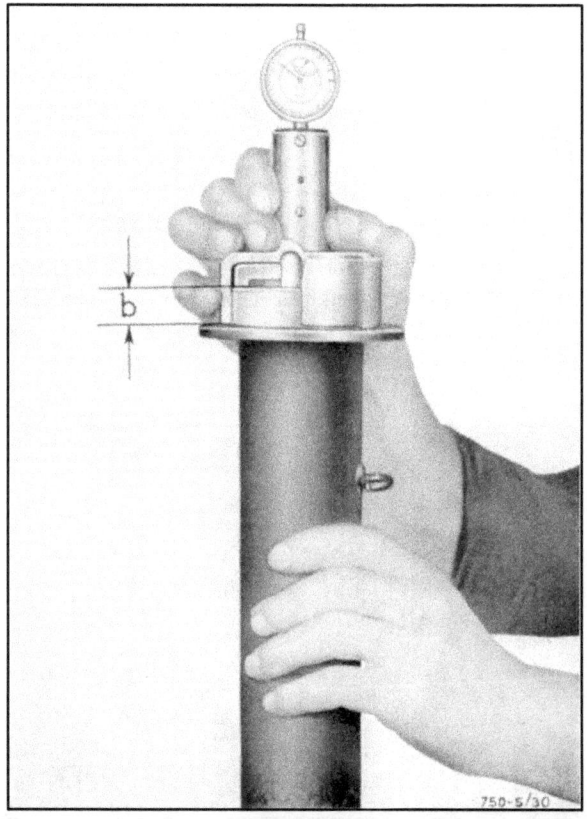

Fig. 30 - Measuring the value «b», with gauge 670.1655, to determine the thickness of the packing ring between the right-hand axle tube and the differential casing.

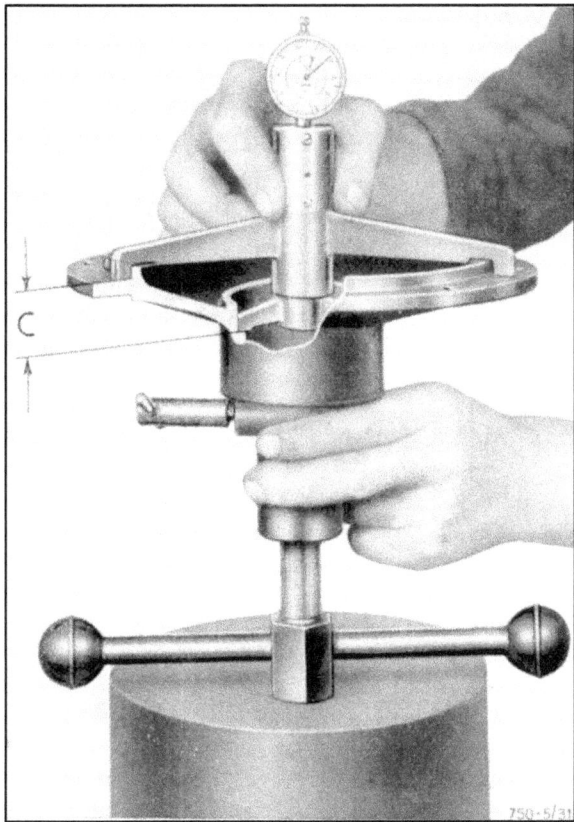

Fig. 31 - Measuring the value « c », with gauge 670.1654 and fixture 6123.27.025, to determine the thickness of the packing ring between the left hand axle tube and the differential casing.

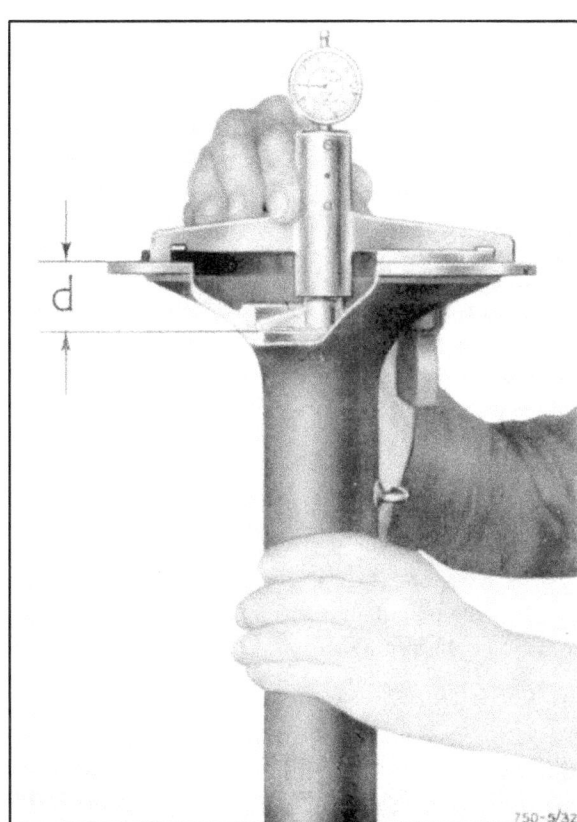

Fig. 32 - Measuring the value « d », with gauge 670.1654, to determine the thickness of the packing ring between the left-hand axle tube and the differential casing.

Fig. 33 - Mounting the outer taper roller bearing race for the differential casing in the left-hand axle tube.

bearing in the fixture. Do the same thing for right-hand side and then read the values « c » and « d » (shown in Figs. 31 and 32), using the gauge 670.1654 for that purpose; fit a suitable packing ring **8** (Fig. 14) having a thickness equal to **d - c + 0.05** mm. (see warning above);

— mount the outer bearing race in the left hand tube, using tool 6121.07.141 (Fig. 33) and make sure that the race is well home in its seating;

— fit the left-hand tube and tighten up the nuts without turning up the tabs on the lockwashers;

— again check the preload and the play;

— if the resulting play is not within the limits given above, the packing rings between the

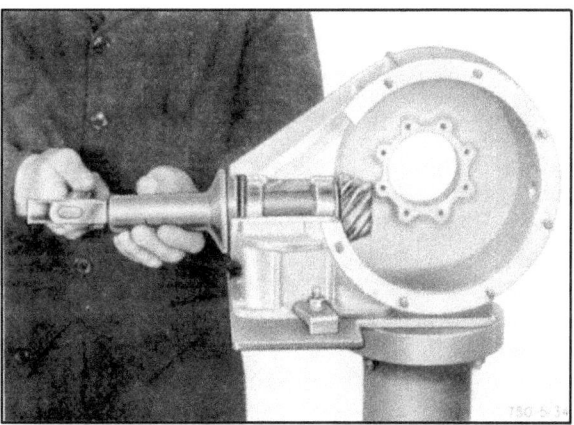

Fig. 34 - Mounting the bevel pinion oil seal, using tool 6121.07.223.

tubes and the differential casing must be replaced and, more particularly:

When the play is less than the value prescribed ($+ 0.05$ mm), increase the thickness of the left-hand packing-ring and reduce that of the right-hand one by an equal amount; if the play is greater than the maximum value laid down ($+ 0.10$ mm) the right-hand thickness must be increased and the left-hand one reduced to the same extent. Then re-check the preload. Bend up the tabs on the lock-washers on both sides of the casing; place the oil seal **6** (Fig. 14) in position, using tool 6121.07.223 (Fig. 34); place the transmission sleeve and the lock-washer; tighten up the round nut; bend over one tab on one lock-washer.

WARNING:

1) **Increasing the thickness of the packing ring is necessary because, while the outer bearing race is free on the tool, it is forced into the left-hand axle tube and as a consequence of being pressed up during mounting, the backlash between the bevels is reduced. It is therefore necessary to increase the thickness of the ring to obtain the backlash originally determined with the fixture 6123.27.025 (paragraph 5).**

2) **The packing rings are of the laminated type, with layers 0.05 mm thick; this means that the thickness required can be obtained by removing the requisite number of laminations.**

REAR SUSPENSION

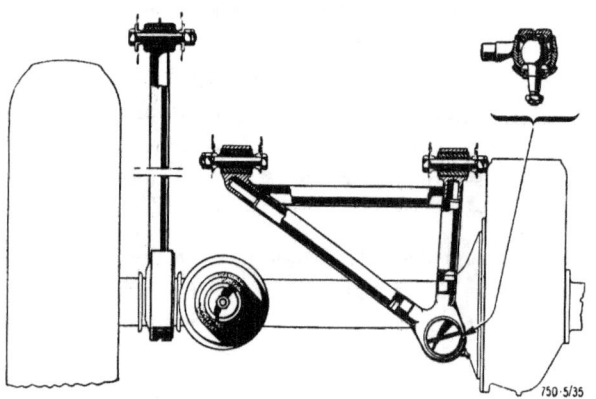

Fig. 35 - Rear suspension: Detail of the central rear axle drive.

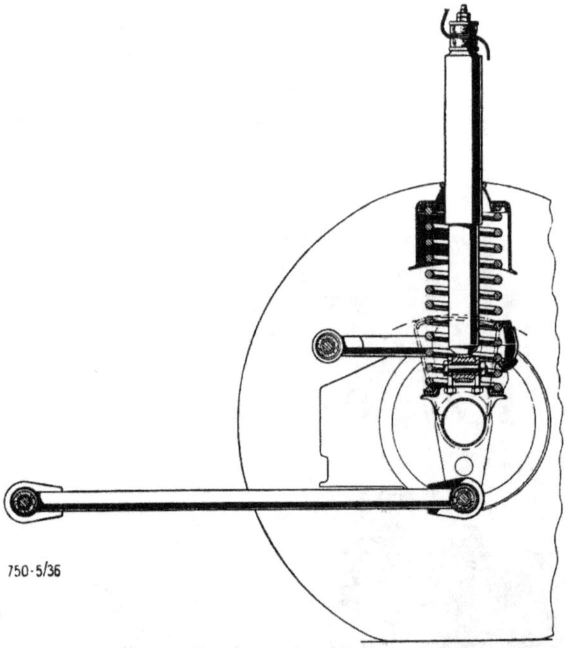

5 - REPLACING THE REBOUND STRAPS

1) Remove the bolts from the strap connections. This operation is greatly facilitated if the body is lowered by being suitably loaded.

2) Remove the screws fixing the rubber pad and the strap to the frame.

3) Replace the strap and reassemble in the reverse order to the above.

6 - DISMANTLING AND CHECKING THE REAR SUSPENSION UNITS

The dismantling of the longitudinal radius rods, the central triangular torque arm and the springs is described in Chapter 2. The shock-absorbers will be dealt with in Chapter 7.

Inspection

a) The silent-bloc units should be inspected each time the parts on which they are fitted are dismantled; any silentblocs in which the rubber is damaged should be replaced.

b) Check the working surfaces of the spherical torque-arm end. The upper threaded ring should be tightened against the lower half-cup. Axial play is always taken up by the spring and no adjustment is therefore needed. If there is excessive wear on either the spherical end or on one of the half-cups, both parts must be replaced.

Fig. 36 - Rear suspension: Details of shock-absorber and coil spring assembly.

c) The following dimensions should be respected when checking the springs:

Length of spring with no load:

Giulietta Berlina
    up to car N. 148810000 . . . . 471 mm.
    from car N. 148810001 . . . . 463 »

Giulietta t.i. . . . . 463 »

Giulietta Sprint
    up to car N. 149302800 . . . . 461 »
    from car N. 149302801 to car
    N. 149304500 . . . . . . 425 »
    from car N. 149304501 . . . . 414 »

Giulietta Spider
    up to car N. 149501850 . . . . 436 »
    up to car N. 149501850 (on request) 420 »
    from car N. 149501851 to car
    N. 149503250 . . . . . . 433 »
    from car N. 149503251 . . . . 418 »

Giulietta Sprint Veloce
    up to car N. 149304500 . . . . 383 mm.
    up to car N. 149304500 (on request) 402 »
    from car N. 149304501 . . . . 383 »

Giulietta Spider Veloce . . . . 387 »

Length of spring under load:

Giulietta Berlina
    up to car N. 148810000, load
    245 ± 7.35 Kg. . . . . . 260 mm.
    from car N. 148810001, load
    245 ± 7.35 Kg. . . . . . 250 »

Giulietta t.i. load 245 ± 7.35 Kg. . 250 »

Giulietta Sprint
    up to car N. 149302800, load
    210 ± 6.30 Kg. . . . . . 240 »
    from car N. 149302801, to car
    N. 149304500, load
    195 ± 5.85 Kg. . . . . . 240 »
    from car N. 149304501, load
    195 ± 5.85 Kg. . . . . . 230 »

Giulietta Spider
    up to car N. 149501850, load
    161.5 ± 4.80 Kg. . . . . . 240 »
    up to car N. 149501850 (on request)
    load 171 ± 5.10 Kg. . . . . 240 »
    from car N. 149501851 to car
    N. 149503250, load
    161.5 ± 4,84 Kg. . . . . . 240 »
    from car N. 149503251,
    load 162 ± 4.86 Kg. . . . . 240 »

Giulietta Sprint Veloce, load
    171 ± 5.13 Kg. . . . . . 240 »

Giulietta Spider Veloce, load
    155 ± 4.65 Kg. . . . . . 240 »

7 - REMOVING THE REAR SHOCK-ABSORBERS

1) Remove the nuts which hold the shock-absorber on the spring seat cup welded to the rear axle tube (Fig. 36). Press the bottom cylinder upwards and leave it in the end-of-compression position.

2) Free the shock-absorber top attachment from the body;

3) Remove the shock-absorber; in the case of both versions this is done from inside the car after removing the rear seat.

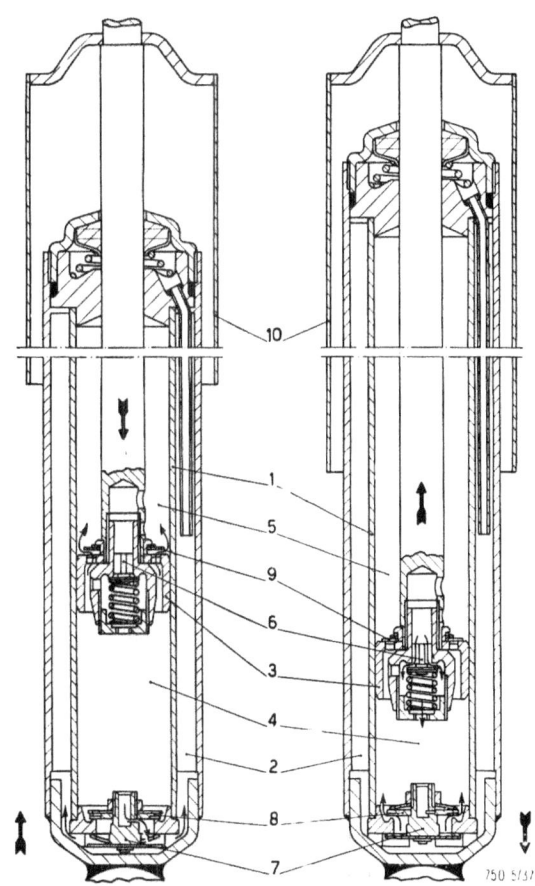

Fig. 37 - Section through shock-absorber during compression and extension phases.

1. Working cylinder - 2. Compensating reservoir - 3. Piston - 4. Chamber under pressure during the compression phase - 5. Chamber under pressure during the extension phase - 6. Extension valve - 7. Compression valve - 8. Compensation valve - 9. Transfer valve - 10. Protective sheath.

8 - HYDRAULIC SHOCK-ABSORBERS

Description

The Girling shock-absorbers consist essentially of a cylinder comprising two coaxial tubes the inner one of which is the working cylinder **1** (Fig. 37); the outer one encloses the compensating tank **2**.

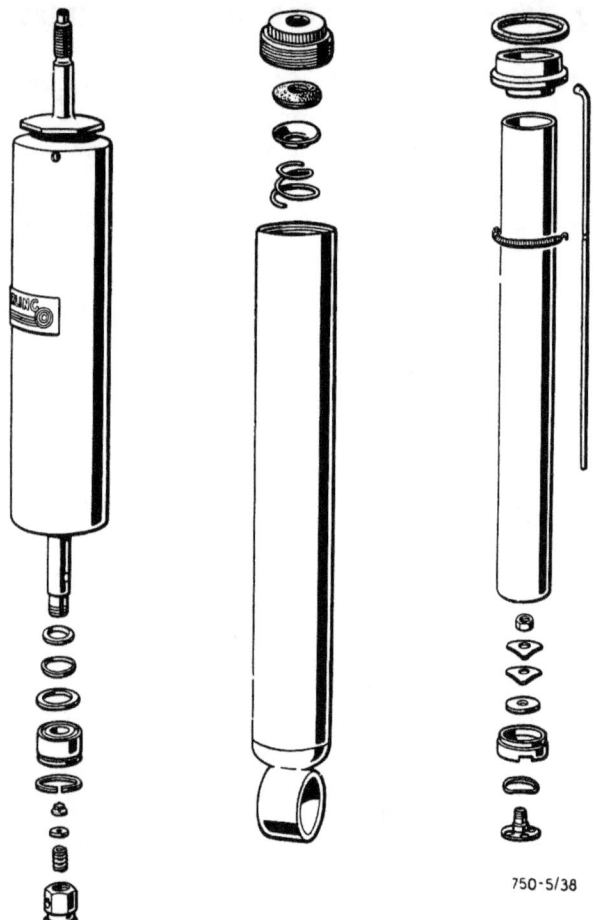

Fig. 38 - Details of shock-absorber.

A third tube **10** outside the cylindrical body protects the piston-rod from external damage.

The cylindrical body is closed at the top by a cap provided with an oil seal. The piston-rod passes through this seal and has an attachment at the top for connecting the shock-absorber to the body-work while, at the bottom, it has a piston **3** carrying the transfer valve **9**, and the extension valve **6**. The inner tube **1** is closed at the bottom by a plug carrying the compression valve **7** and the compensation valve **8**.

1) **Operation**

   a) **The Compression phase**

   This phase occurs while the shock-absorber closes and the piston moves downwards. The oil passes from the chamber **4**, through the transfer valve **9**, and into the chamber **5**, but, since the latter has a volume less than that of chamber **4** (due to the space occupied by the piston-rod) part of the oil is driven into the compensation tank **2** through the compression valve **7**.

   Altering the rating of the return spring operating valve **7** varies the damping effect of the shock-absorber during the compression stroke.

   b) **The Extension phase (recoil)**

   During this phase the shock-absorber extends. The oil passes from the chamber **5** into the chamber **4** through the extension valve **6**. The negative pressure caused by the upwards movement of the piston draws the oil from the tank **2** and drives it into the chamber **4** through the compensation valve **8**.

   Altering the rating of the extension valve spring modifies the braking effect of the shock-absorber during the extension phase (recoil).

2) **Maintenance**

   No special maintenance is required. The large reserve of oil in the compensating chamber makes it possible to cover long distances without the need for topping up.

   Incorrect action of the shock-absorbers is shown by noise or by changes in the damping effect. Noise which is initially attributed to the shock-absorbers may arise from other causes and it is therefore advisable to carry out the following checks before dismantling the shock-absorbers:

   — Carefully inspect the whole of the suspension system, paying special attention to the connections between the shock-absorbers, the body and the axle.

   — Check that all rubber parts are in perfect order.

   — Make sure that no part of the shock-absorber touches any other metal part of the suspension.

   Noise from the shock-absorbers may be due to insufficient oil (shock-absorbers « knocking ») or to deformation of the fluid pipes caused by knocks or, more rarely, by stones flung up from the road.

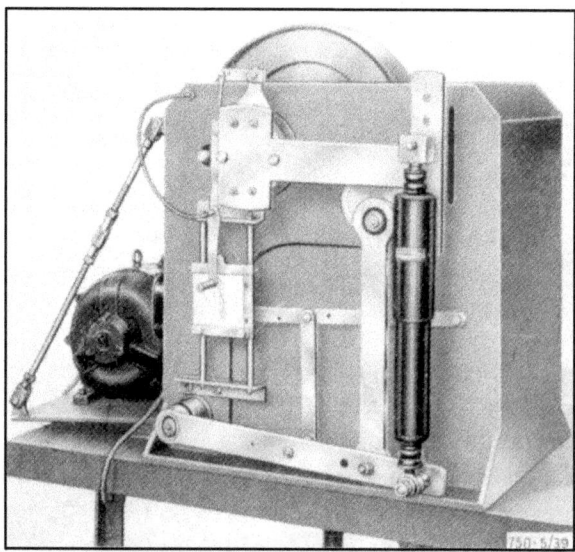

Fig. 39 - Shock-absorber test bench.

The damping effect of the shock-absorbers may be reduced or increased.

An increase in the damping effect (very rarely met with) may be due to the oil having become thicker or to the enhanced sealing action of the valves as they bed down on their seats. A reduction in the damping effect may be attributable to the following causes:

— insufficient oil;
— valves sticking;
— defective seating of the valves (perhaps grit on the seat)
— wear on the piston and inner tube;
— failure of internal parts.

WARNING: All shock-absorber overhauls should be carried by a specialist garage where the necessary equipment for the work, including the test bench, is available. This test bench (Fig. 39) makes it possible to check the efficiency of the shock absorbers at different operational speeds.

3) **Inspection**

— Make sure that the pipes and the protective casing have not been damaged by knocks or by stones thrown up from the road.
— Check that the outer casing does not rub against the cylindrical body.
— By comparing them with new ones check briefly that the shock-absorbers are working efficiently.

If the comparison proves unsatisfactory, drain off the oil and check that the piston moves smoothly inside its cylinder, though without any play which would reduce the damping effect. When the shock-absorbers have been dismantled (by specialised mechanics, of course) the parts should be carefully washed with petrol or paraffin; care should then be taken to ensure that:

— all the valves are seating properly,
— the piston-rod packing is in perfect order,
— the amount of wear on the inside diameter of the inner tube and on the piston.

4) **Topping-up the shock-absorbers**

The shock-absorbers require refilling when hand testing shows some absence of resistance over most of the piston stroke.
To refill proceed as follows:

— Extend the shock-absorber as far as possible, until the outside protective tube uncovers the top plug in the cylindrical body (in the case of the front shock-absorbers, lift up the cap on which the pad rests); unscrew the sealing ring and withdraw the piston.

— Fill the central cylinder to the three-quarter level and the compensating reservoir to the half-way level. The following quantities of oil are required:

Front shock-absorber, 1 inch model about 110 cm^3

Rear shock-absorber, 1 inch model about 170 cm^3

After refilling, replace the plugs and check that there are no leaks when the shock-absorbers are operated.

APPENDIX

DIFFERENTIAL GROUP ADJUSTMENT

The systems of distance washers, for the right settlement of rear axle wheelworks, has been modified beginning from Giulietta Berlina car n. 148803686, Giulietta Sprint n. 149302585, Giulietta Spider and Spider Veloce n. 149500373 and Giulietta Sprint Veloce n. 149300658.

This new system appears in the sectional view of the differential post modification, as shown in fig. 40.

In consequence, while the fitting up of the pinion on the cage is unvaried (see Caution 1), on the contrary the assembling procedure of the differential group is changed for post-modification axles. Therefore it is different from the other procedure notified on chapter 4.

The new procedure is the following:

1) assemble the outside ring of the bearing in the right side of the support by means of implement n. 6121.07.141, inserting a mm 1 (in. 0.0394) distance washer between the seat rabbot and the ring. When it is about a support already used, then it will be better to insert the same washer previously assembled.

2) Introduce the complete differential carrier in the support.

3) Fasten the outside ring of the bearing on the left side wall of implement n. 6123.27.025. Said implement, so prepared, is to be applied on the left side of the support.

   Note: With new axles it is necessary to utilize only the left side of implement n. 6123.27.025.

4) Draw the ring gear nearer to the pinion operating on the proper handles **3** (fig. 28) and make the ring gear turn some revolutions, by hand, up to settle the bearings.

5) Assemble implement n. 6123.15.006 on the transmission sleeve of the pinion for the control of total pre-load and clearance between teeth of crown wheel and pinion. Said clearance must result between mm 0,05 and mm 0,10.

   The pre-load is controlled by hooking a gr. 600 (lb. 1,322) weight at the end of the lever. With said weight test if the lever, placed in horizontal position, attempts to move by itself.

   If the lever moves too freely then it is necessary to operate on handles of implement n. 6123.27.025 in screwing wise up to get given conditions.

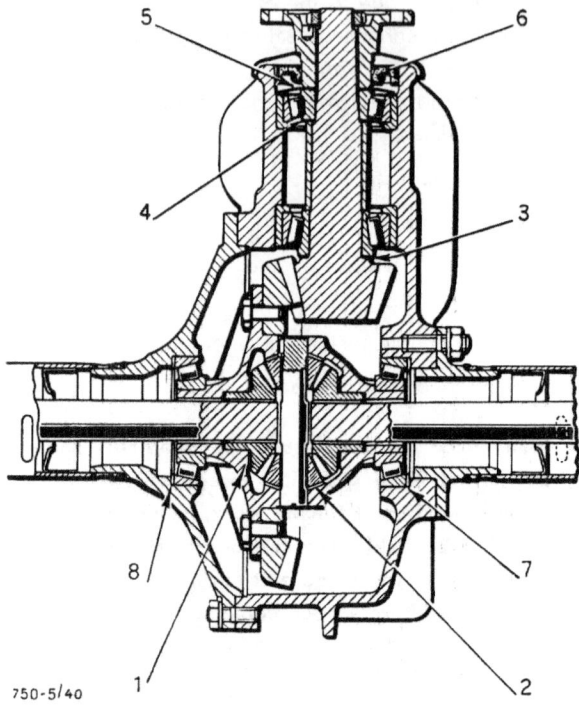

Fig. 40 - Section through the differential.
1. Sun wheel packing washers - **2.** Spherical planet wheel washers - **3.** Packing ring for adjusting distance between bevel pinion and crown wheel - **4.** Ring for adjusting pre-load on bevel pinion bearings - **5.** Oil seal plate - **6.** Oil seal washer - **7.** Ring for adjusting clearance on differential rightside bearing - **8.** Ring for adjusting clearance on differential leftside bearing.

On the contrary, if the lever stands, it may depend upon two causes: either the right side washer is too thin (easily recognizable for the reason why of no clearance between the pinion and ring gear) or handles of implement are screwed too much.

In the first case the washer is to be replaced after having pulled out the outside ring of the bearing by means of post-modification implement n. 6121.12.054 (see Caution 3).

6) Once the proper pre-load is obtained then verify again, by means of a comparator, the clearance between the pinion and crown wheel.

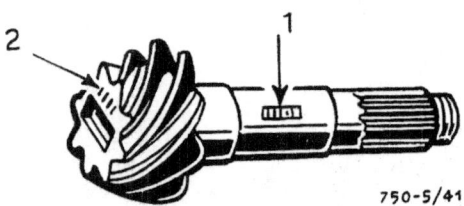

Fig. 41 - Position mark for the right settlement of the pinion.
1. Old position mark - **2.** New position mark.

Whenever the new clearance is higher than mm 0,05 ÷ 0,10 it is necessary to reduce thickness of the right side washer or to increase it if the clearance is lower than mm 0,05 ÷ 0,10.

In other words modifying the right side washer or, according to cases, operating on the handles, through some attempt, it will be possible to obtain the right value of pre-load and clearance.

Clearance is to be controlled in four positions of the crown wheel by giving one turn to pinion after each reading and locking the crown wheel in each position by means of the proper pin.

7) Realize the given conditions of clearance and pre-load, lock the sliding part of implement n. 6123.27.025. Dismount the implement and remove the outside ring of its bearing.

8) Through dial gauge n. 670.1654 survey the heights « c » and « d » of the implement and left side tube shown in fig. 31 and fig. 32, with proper choice, arrange that shim **8** of adjustment to given clearance (fig. 40) will be equal to « d » - « c » - mm 0,05 (see Caution 2).

9) Settle the outside ring of the bearing in the seat of left side tube in the usual way and assemble the tube by locking it, without bending borders of the safety shims.

10) Verify again the pre-load of bearings and clearance between pinion and crown wheel as well. If clearance is lower than the minimum given value, while pre-load is regular, it is necessary to oversize the right side washer and undersize the left side one; on the contrary, undersize the right side washer and oversize the left side one if clearance is higher than the maximum given value.

If clearance is regular, then the pre-load is adjusted by oversizing or undersizing both the washers in equal proportions in accordance with the case: either the pre-load is to be increased or reduced.

11) Once the adjustment operations have been performed then bend the lock shims of nuts at both sides of the support.

CAUTIONS

1) **We inform that the mark determining the exact position of the pinion, engraved previously on the spindle, has been engraved at head side of the pinion on a second time (fig. 41).**

   Other marks are engraved on the spindle but they are used only for the assembly line at the Factory. In consequence the new pinions, that of course can be used on old and new axles indifferently, are engraved with three marks but, for assembly in outside workshops, the top mark only has to be used.

2) **Undersizing of left washer (in place of oversizing as in case of pre-modification axle) for the adjustment of given clearance, is necessary for the same reasons valid for pre-modification axles. This is due to the fact that while the outside ring of the bearing is free on the implement, it is forced in the left side tube of the axle and in consequence shrunken in assembling.**

   Therefore, if thickness of washer is not undersized then clearance between teeth of pinion crown wheel couple, previously given, would be reduced with increase of pre-load.

3) **Implement n. 6121.12.054 may be used also for pulling out the outside ring of the right side bearing, duly bending the arms in proper way.**

   At any rate the operation may also be carried out by using a tube with outside diameter mm 61,5 (2"27/64) and operating on at outside of the support.

INFORMATION SHEET REFERENCE

ASSEMBLY	DATE	SHEET N.	SUBJECT

PART 6

FRONT SUSPENSION

INDEX

| **Description** | page | 139 |

1) Removing the front suspension system . . . . » 140

2) Dismantling one suspension unit . . . . » 140

3) Refitting the wishbones to the stub axles . . . . » 142

4) Refitting the suspension units to the car . . . . » 143

5) Checking and re-setting front-wheel camber . . . . . . » 143

6) Removing the wheel hubs from the stub axles, and re-fitting them . . » 143

7) Dismantling and checking the stabiliser rod . . . . . . » 144

PART 6

FRONT SUSPENSION

DESCRIPTION

Fig. 1 - Front suspension.

The front wheels are independently sprung attached to the car by means of transverse wish-bones.

Coil springs and double-acting telescopic hydraulic shock-absorbers, these being particularly effective on the rebound of the car, are fitted between the lower wishbones and the body.

The suspension system is completed by a transverse stabiliser rod which improves stability on curves.

Upwards pivoting of the wishbones is limited by pads on the shock-absorbers; downwards pivoting is limited by a steel cable affixed to the body and the lower wishbones.

Fig. 2 - Stabiliser rod.

1 - REMOVING THE FRONT SUSPENSION SYSTEM

The following instructions relate to the removal of the system for one wheel only; the procedure for the other wheel is identical.

1) Raise the car from the ground by means of a jack located at the centre of the front cross-member, and take off the wheel.

2) Unscrew the nuts on the pins which attach the lower wishbones to the stabiliser rod links; remove the cups and the corresponding rubber pads.

3) Remove the to brackets holding the stabiliser rod to the body and take the links with it.

4) Unscrew the nut and lock-nut fixing the top of the shock-absorber to the body, unscrew the two small bolts fastening the shock-absorber bottom bracket and slide out the shock-absorber from below.

5) Remove the springs and the spring-retaining plates, using tool No. 6121.04.016 (Fig. 3).

6) Unscrew the nut holding the ball joint to the lever on the stub axle and disconnect the lateral track rod from the lever itself.

7) Disconnect the brake fluid pipe after first applying a clip to the rubber tube.

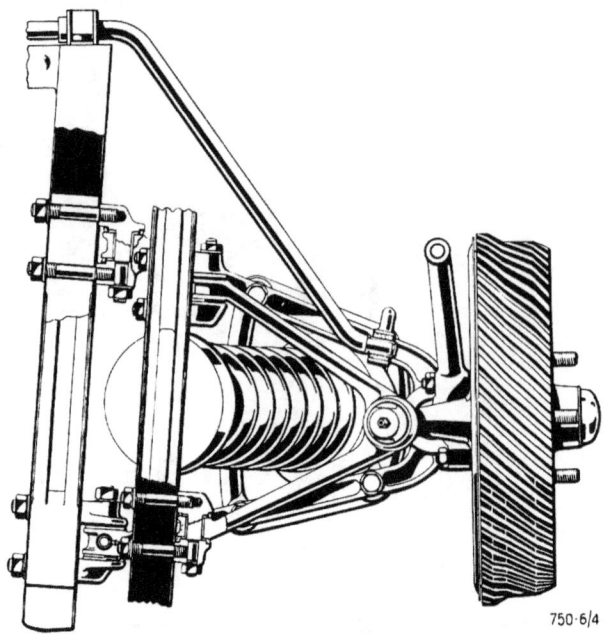

Fig. 4 - Front suspension - horizontal view.

8) Unscrew the nuts on the studs connecting the upper and lower wishbones to the body, and remove the suspension unit.

2 - DISMANTLING ONE SUSPENSION UNIT (RIGHT-HAND OR LEFT-HAND)

THE LOWER WISHBONE

1) Disconnect the ball joint from the stub axle.

2) Take off the retaining ring and, using spanner No. 6121.25.009, unscrew the nut; withdraw the lower spherical half-seat, the ball pin and the upper spherical seat.

3) Dismantle the inner bearings, the outer bearings and the oil seals.

4) If necessary take out the wishbone bushes.

THE UPPER WISHBONE

1) Disconnect the ball joint from the stub axle.

2) Unscrew the nut, withdraw the spring, the upper spherical halfseat, ball pin and the lower spherical seat.

3) Dismantle the outer bearings, the inner bearings and the oil seals.

4) If necessary take out the wishbone bushes.

Fig. 3 - Dismantling the front suspension springs, using tool No. 6121.04.016

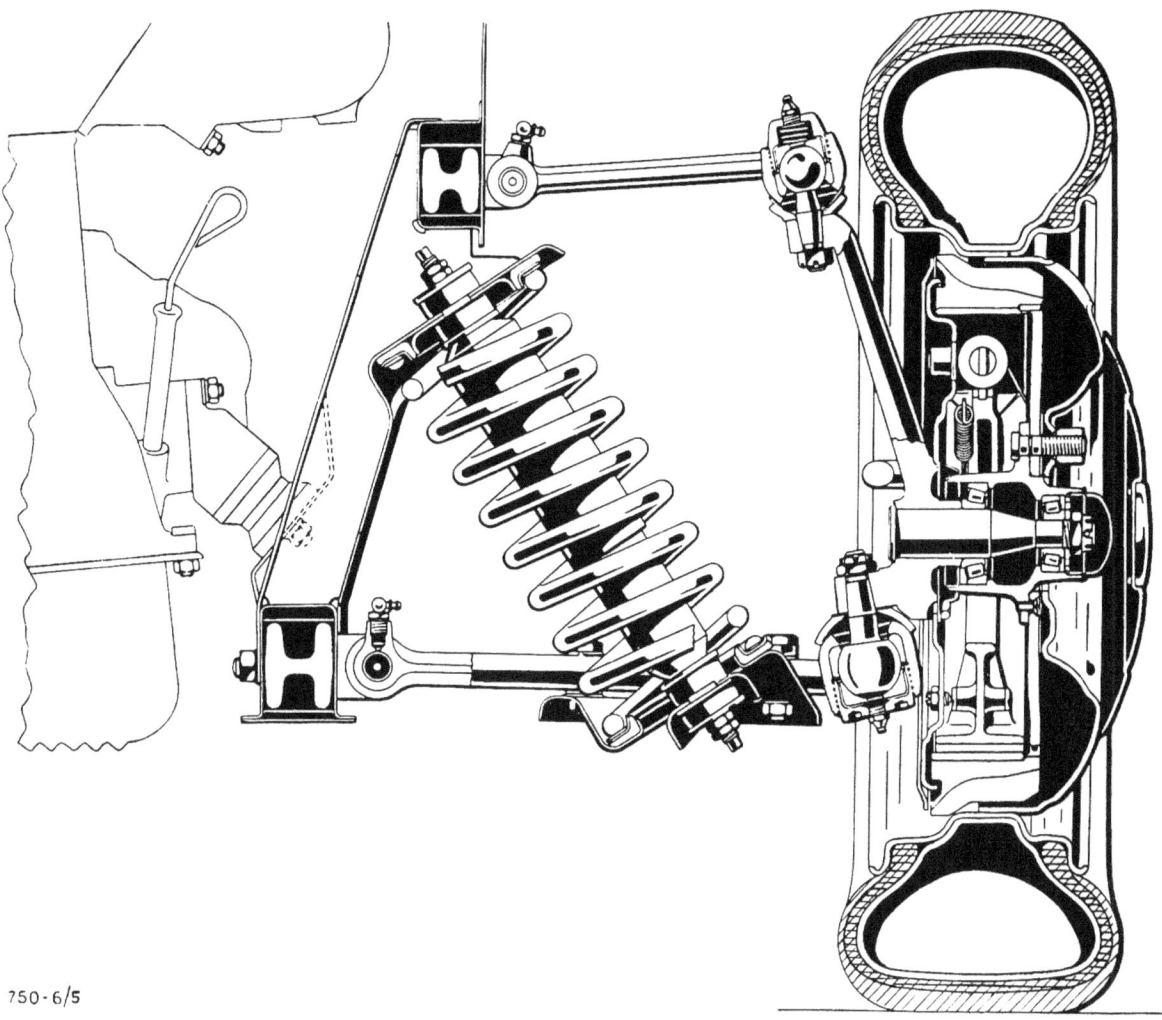

Fig. 5 - Front suspension - section and transversal view.

Inspection

1) Using a mandril, check the alignment of the holes for the pins for the brakets provided for attaching the upper and lower wishbones to the body.

2) Check the working surfaces on the ball pins and their seats; replace any parts which are scored or worn.

3) After having removed the grease cups, check the radial and axial play of the pins used to attach the wishbones to the body. Replace the bushes and adjusting rings in the case of excessive play.

4) Check the efficiency of the front shock-absorbers, using the same procedure as in the case of the rear shock-absorbers.

5) Check the condition of the silentblocs and the rubber pads on the stabiliser rod; replace any which are defective.

6) Check the springs, bearing in mind the following values:

Length with no load
Giulietta Berlina
  up to car N. 148810000 . . . 389 mm.
  from car N. 148810001 . . . . 396 »
Giulietta t.i. . . . . 396 »
Giulietta Sprint
  up to car N. 149302800 . . . . 410 »
  from car N. 149302801 . . . . 394 »
Giulietta Spider . . . . 410 »
Giulietta Sprint Veloce
  standard . . . . 371 »
  on request . . . . 384 »
Giulietta Spider Veloce . . . . . 364 »

Length under load
Giulietta Berlina
  up to car N. 148810000, load
    500 ± 15 Kg. . . . . 267 »
  from car N. 148810001, load
    500 ± 15 Kg. . . . . 274 »

141

Giulietta t.i., load 500 ± 15 Kg. . . 274 mm.

Giulietta Sprint
up to car N. 149302800, load
525 ± 15 Kg. . . . . . . 267 »
from car N. 149302801, load
505 ± 15 Kg. . . . . . . 267 »

Giulietta Spider, load 465 ± 14 Kg. . . 267 »

Giulietta Sprint Veloce, load
460 ± 13.8 Kg. . . . . . 267 »

Giulietta Spider Veloce, load
426 ± 12.8 Kg. . . . . . 267 »

NOTE:

1) **During the early stages of production, and in the case of the Giulietta Berlina only, shorter springs were fitted and aluminium rings were placed between the springs and the plates fixed to the lower wishbones; when replacing one or both springs of the old type, the aluminium rings must be scrapped when the new type springs are used.**

2) **Both springs on a given car must have the same coloured mark (red or white).**

3) **When fitting springs with a red mark, both in the case of the Giulietta Berlina and the Giulietta Sprint, 4 washers 3 mm thick must be placed over the bolts and between the lower wishbone and the spring supporting plate.**

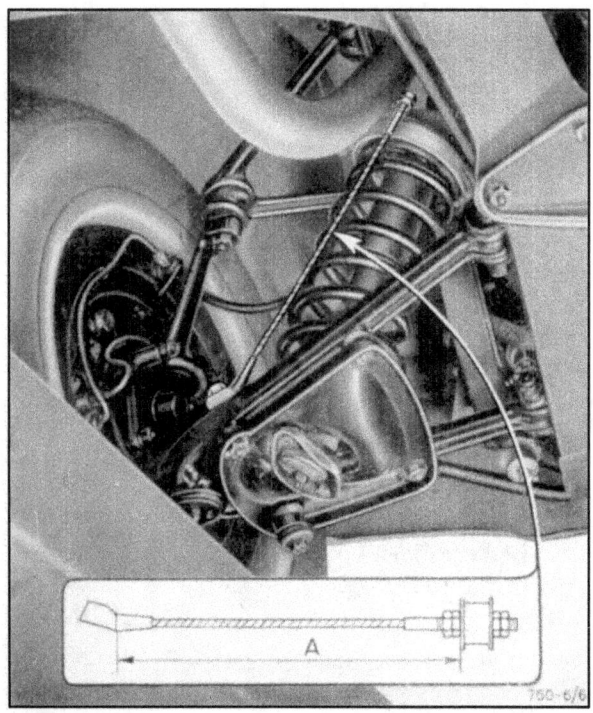

Fig. 6 - Front suspension; checking the length of the metallic cord limiting the downwards travel of the wishbones.

3 - RE-FITTING THE WISHBONES TO THE STUB AXLE

THE LOWER WISHBONE

1) Using tool No. 6121.07.265, fit the oil seals for the outer bearings.

2) Using tool N. 6121.07.266 fit the oil seals for the inner bearings.

3) Using a suitable tool, insert the bushings (if replaced) in their seats on the wishbones.

4) Fit the inner and outer bearings after first inserting the adjusting washers (see warning).

5) Insert the upper half of the spherical seat for the stub-axle, add the dust-cap, the ball pin, the lower half of the spherical seat and an adjusting washer, and tighten the ring nut with spanner No. 6121.25.009.

6) Connect the wishbone to the stub axle - and to the latter fix the ball joint stem; then tighten the nut.

7) Check to ensure that the wishbone rotates freely but without any appreciable play; if that is not the case, remove the adjusting washer located between the upper hemispherical seat and the nut ring and replace it with another of suitable thickness.

THE UPPER WISHBONE

1) Using tool No. 6121.07.268, fit the oil seal for the outer bearings.

2) Using tool No. 6121.07.267, fit the oil seal for the inner bearings.

3) Using a suitable tool, insert the bushings (if replaced) in their seats on the wishbone.

4) Fit the inner and outer bearings after first inserting the adjusting washers (see warning).

5) Insert the upper half of the spherical seat for the stub axle, add the dust-cap, the ball pin, the upper half of the spherical seat and the spring; then tighten the ring nut.

6) Fit the wishbone to the stub axle, making sure that it rotates freely and that, after being raised, it falls by the effect of its weight alone.

WARNING

1) **The very greatest care must be taken in correctly tightening the joints between the wishbones and their respective pins; suitable adjusting washers must be used.**

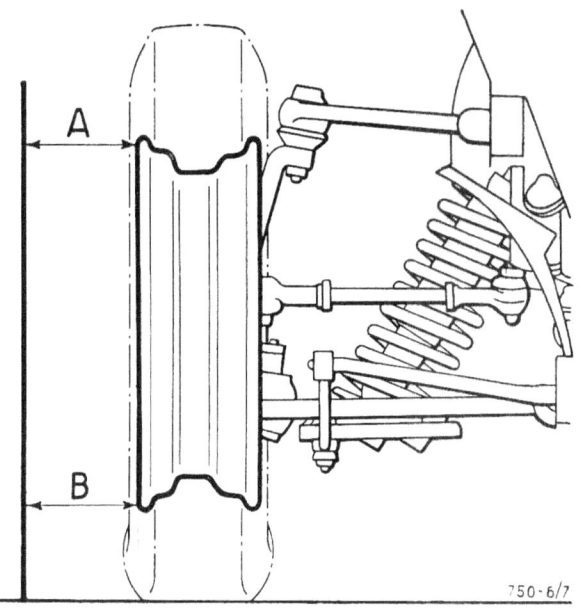

Fig. 7 - Front-wheel camber with full load car: **A = B**.

In this connection each wishbone will be trial fitted to its corresponding bearing without the appropriate oil seals.

The degree of tightness is correct (and the proper adjusting washers have been used) when the wishbone - after being placed in the horizontal position and released there - slowly descends.

2) **When the replacement of the adjusting washer is not necessary, care must be taken to refit them in their original order.**

3) **When re-assembling the ball joints, copiously lubricate the pins and their seats.**

4 - RE-FITTING THE SUSPENSION UNITS TO THE CAR

1) Insert the upper and lower wishbone bracket studs in their seats on the body.
2) Check that the movement of the wish-bones is unimpeded.
3) Connect the lateral track rod to the lever on the stub axle.
4) Fit the springs and the spring-supporting plates, using tool No. 6121.04.016; connect the metallic cord limiting the suspension movement, keeping the length between connections to 312 mm (Fig. 6).
5) Fit the stabiliser rod link-pins.
6) Fit the shock absorbers.
7) Attach the brake fluid tube to the nipple.

5 - CHECKING AND RE-SETTING THE FRONT WHEEL CAMBER

After fitting the suspension wish-bones to the body, the camber of the front wheels must be checked. This angle is variable according to the car load.

When the car has a full load (4 persons and a full petrol tank) the wheels must be vertical; this can be checked as shown in Fig. 7.

Correction is effected by inserting one or more washers (internal diameter 10,5 mm, external diameter 30 mm, thickness 2 mm) between the body and the brackets for the upper wish-bones.

6 - REMOVING THE WHEEL HUBS FROM THE STUB AXLES AND RE-FITTING THEM

Dismantling

1) Remove the wheel.
2) Remove the brake drums and shoes.
3) Remove the hub cap.
4) Unscrew the nut and remove the washer; then, using tool No. 6121.12.063, draw off the hub (Fig. 8).
5) Using tool No. 6121.12.066, withdraw from the stub axle the inner race of the inner bearing.
6) Using a suitable tool, draw the outer race of the outer bearing from the wheel hub.
7) Using tool No. 6121.12.057, simultaneously withdraw from the hub the outer race of the inner bearing and the oil-seal ring.

Fig. 8 - Removing the front-wheel hub from the stub axle, using tool 6121.12.063.

Inspection

1) Check the condition of the bearings and replace them if the roller paths are worn or scored.

2) Ensure that the oil-seal ring is tight; the ring should always be replaced after removal.

Assembly

See Part 8 for instructions regarding the assembly of the brake shoe back-plate, the brake shoes and the drums, and also regarding the adjustment of the gap between the brake linings and the drum.

1) Using tool No. 6121.07.277, fit the outer race of the outer bearing onto the wheel hub.

2) Using tool No. 6121.07.278, fit the outer race of the inner bearing to the wheel hub; using tool No. 6121.07.276, fit the oil seal.

3) Fit the inner race of the inner bearing onto the stub axle.

4) Fill the hub chamber with grease and spread grease copiously over the bearing roller paths.

5) Using tool No. 6121.05.041, fit the hub on the left-hand stub axle; use tool No. 6121.05.042 for the right-hand hub.

6) Fit the inner race of the outer bearing and the washer, and tighten the nut in such a way as to eliminate all play, but at the same time allowing the hub to rotate freely.

Checking the preload

7) Apply lever No. 6123.15.007 (470 mm long) to the wheel set-screws as shown in Fig. 9. Then apply a weight of 700 grams to the end of the lever. The lever should then tend to move spontaneously (if necessary help the movement by applying light finger pressure).

If the lever resists, it means that the preload is excessive, if on the other hand, the leve rotates rapidly, it means that the preload is insufficient. The preload is adjusted by screwing the lock-nut inwards or outwards.

Fig. 9 - Checking the preload on front wheel bearings using tool 6123.15.007.

8) After having adjusted the preload and tightened the lock-nut, the proper adjustment of the bearings is obtained by unscrewing the nut one notch and by inserting the split pin in that position.

9) Fit the cap to the wheel hub.

10) Fit the brake drum.

11) Adjust the gap between the drum and shoe as described in Part 8.

12) Fit the ball pins for the upper and lower wishbones.

7 - DISMANTLING AND CHECKING THE STABILISER ROD

1) Unscrew the lower nuts from the link-pins and remove the cup and rubber pads.

2) Remove the two attachments fixing the rod to the body, and take off the rod and the links.

Inspection

1) Check to ensure that the silentblocs and the rubber pads are sound.

2) Check to ensure that the two stabilizer rod arms lie in the same plane.

Refitting the stabilizer rod

To re-fit the rod, proceed in the reverse order.

INFORMATION SHEET REFERENCE

ASSEMBLY	DATE	SHEET N.	SUBJECT

INFORMATION SHEET REFERENCE

ASSEMBLY	DATE	SHEET N.	SUBJECT

PART 7

STEERING SYSTEM

INDEX

Description	page 149
1) Adjustment of play between the taper rollers and helical worm . . .	» 149
2) Adjustment of front wheel toe-in	» 150
3) Removing the steering wheel and the horn/light-signal controls . .	» 150
4) Removing the steering column and the steering box from the car . .	» 152
5) Dismantling and inspecting the steering box	» 153
6) Re-fitting the steering box	» 154
7) Dismantling, inspecting and re-assembling the ball joints, and the intermediate steering-arm bracket	» 154
8) Re-fitting the steering box, steering-arms and track-rods to the car . .	» 155

PART 7

STEERING SYSTEM

DESCRIPTION

The steering gear is of the helical worm and taper roller type; as the worm turns, so the taper roller moves along the worm and causes the rotation of the shaft on which the operating rocker lever is keyed. This type of steering, besides being very smooth in operation, ensures the automatic return to the centre position after a corner is turned.

Steering is absolutely accurate and independent of the spring movement.

1 - ADJUSTING OF PLAY BETWEEN THE TAPER ROLLER AND THE HELICAL WORM

Before adjusting the play between the taper roller and the helical screw (when the car is over a garage pit, on a stand or otherwise raised) the central and left-hand track-rods must first be detached from the steering arm and the transverse bolt which holds the steering column to the bracket must be slackened off.

A feature of the roller and helical screw type of steering is that the play between the two members is as the minimum when the roller is in the centre, and at the maximum when it is at the worm ends. Play must therefore be adjusted only when the steering-wheel is in the position of straight-ahead travel.

When the above preliminaries have been carried out, the steering arm must be subjected to short but sharp angular rotation so that the mechanic may recognise the moment of contact between the sides of the roller and the sides of the worm grooves.

The amount of the possible angular travel between the two positions at which resistance is met makes it possible to assess the play both with the steering-wheel in the position corresponding to straight-ahead travel, and in a position very close thereto.

After having accurately determined the lever position of minimum play, keep the wheel at this position and turn the adjusting screw **2** (fig. 2) until the minimum play is brought to nothing; then lock the adjusting screw by tightening the nut.

When that is done, check that this locking motion has not affected the adjustment, as it is of paramount importance that the taper roller is not forced to move when gripped between the groove walls.

This check must be performed as follows:
turn the steering-wheel slowly by hand; on passing the position corresponding to the absence of play between the taper roller and the groove somewhat greater resistance will be noticed; this will indicate whether the adjustment has been properly made; excessive resistance will mean that the roller has to be forced within the groove, while too little resistance will mean excessive play.

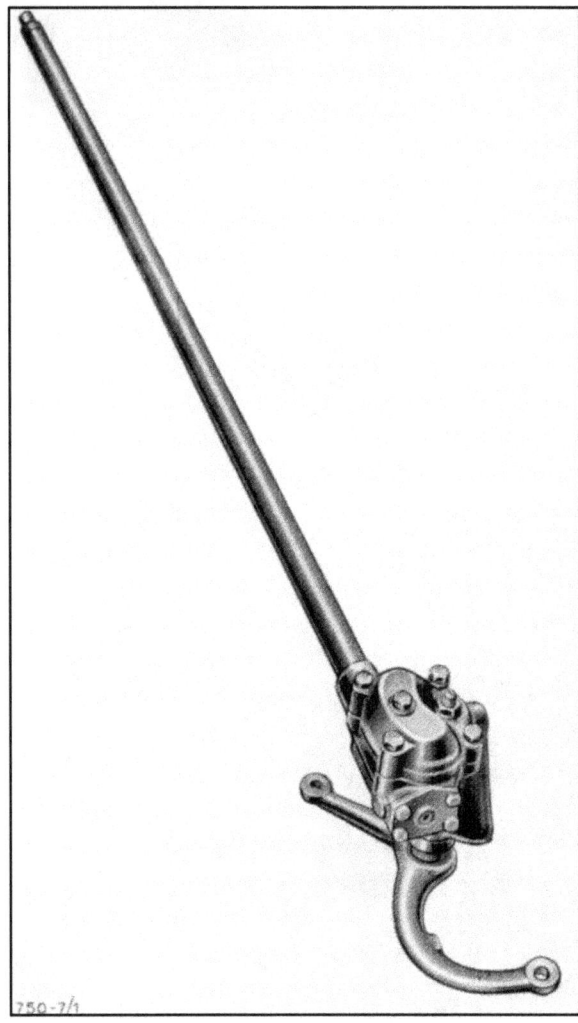

Fig. 1 - The Steering gear.

2) using the left-hand lateral track rod (on the driver's side), place the left-hand wheel in the straight-ahead position (position of no toe-in);

3) measure the resulting length of the left-hand lateral track rod and bring the right-hand lateral track-rod to the same length;

4) place the right hand wheel in the straight-ahead position by adjusting the central track road;

5) reduce the two lateral track rods by identical amounts so as to obtain the prescribed degree of toe-in.

3 - REMOVING THE STEERING-WHEEL AND THE HORN/LIGHT SIGNALS CONTROLS

1) Remove the battery earthing lead (from the positive pole).

2) Using tool No. 6121.06.007 (Fig. 5) remove the push-button switch seat ring and the push-button itself.

3) Remove the spoke cover by unscrewing the 3 fixing screws.

This increase in resistance must always be restricted to one steering wheel position only which, as stated above, must correspond to the position of no roller play.

2 - ADJUSTMENT OF FRONT-WHEEL TOE-IN

The amount of front-wheel toe-in must be as shown in Fig. 4.

Checking and, if necessary, adjusting toe-in must be performed when the car is loaded with the equivalent of 4 passengers and a full fuel tank, but without luggage.

Proceed as follows:

1) lock the steering-wheel in the straight-ahead position, that is, with the two spokes arranged symmetrically in relation to the vertical;

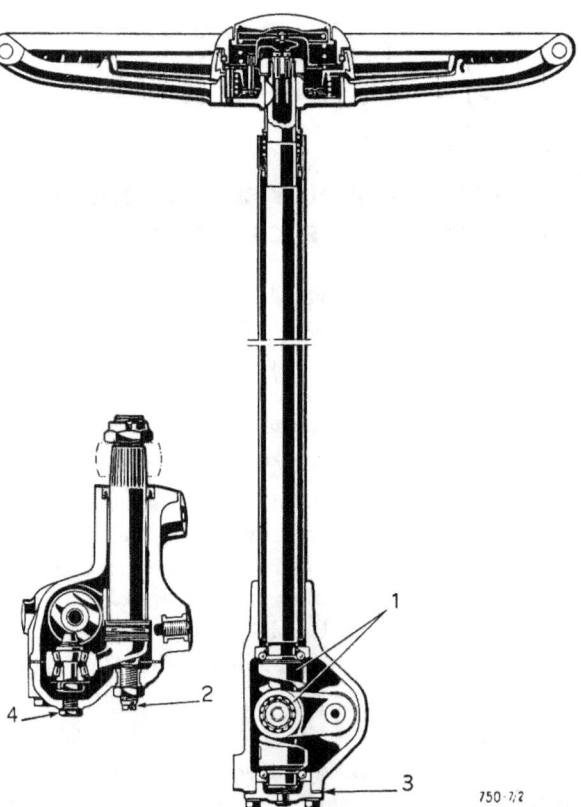

Fig. 2 - Section through the steering gear.

1. Worm/roller unit - **2.** Screw for taking up play in the worm/roller unit - **3.** Shim to take up play in the worm bearings - **4.** Oil filler plug.

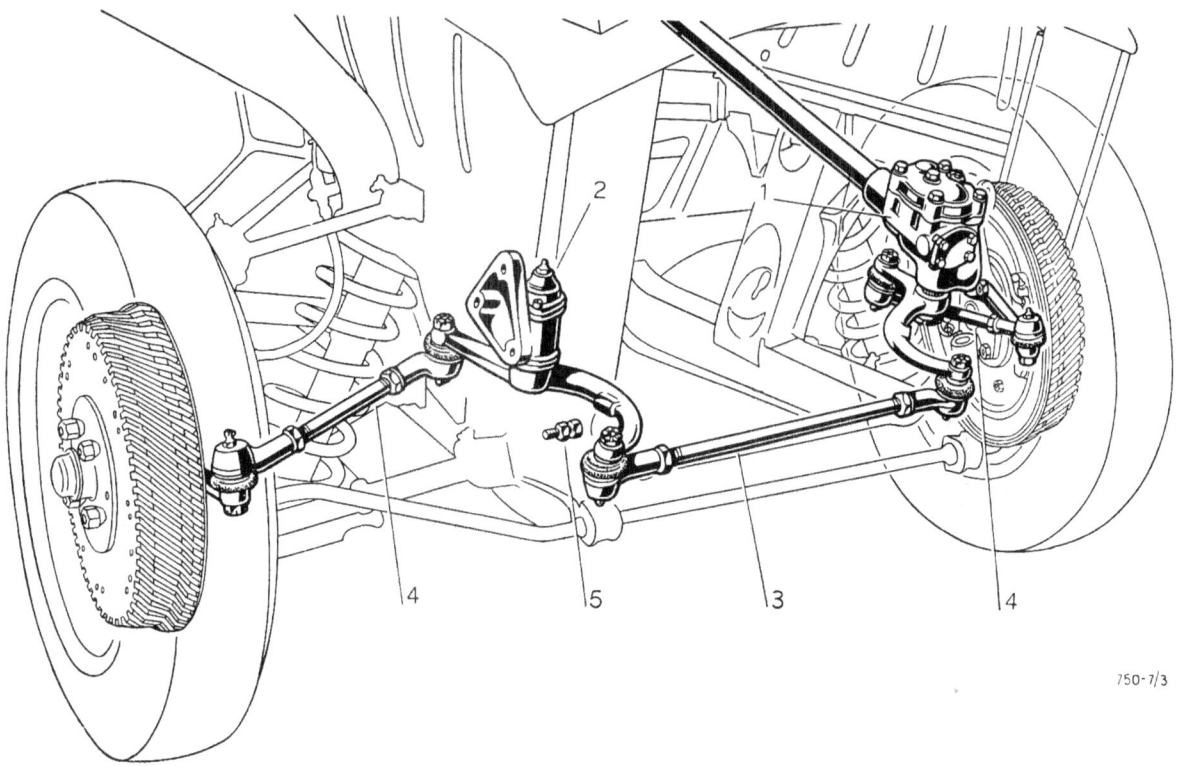

Fig. 3 - Steering system diagram.
1. Steering box - 2. Intermediate steering arm bracket - 3. Track rod connecting the steering arms - 4. Lateral track rods - 5. Screws for adjusting the maximum turning circle.

4) Withdraw as a whole unit the switches for the hornlight signals.

5) Withdraw the two pressure caps which are connected to the conductor ends; pull out the conductors from the steering-box side and remove the rubber seals from their seat.

6) Unscrew the nut holding the steering-wheel to its shaft.

7) Screw a thread-protection on to the steering-wheel shaft and draw off the steering-wheel, using tool No. 6121.12.090 (Fig. 6).

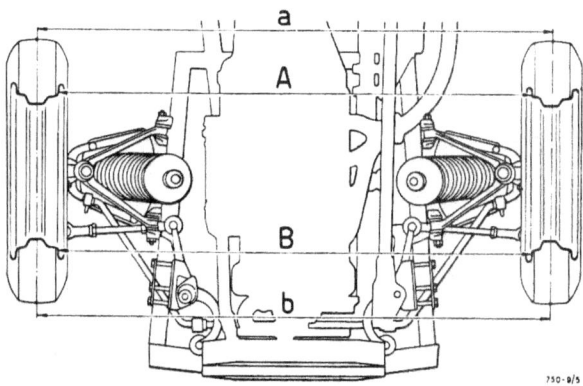

Fig. 4 - Front-wheel toe in (with full loaded car).
A = B + 3 mm.   **a = b + 4 mm.**

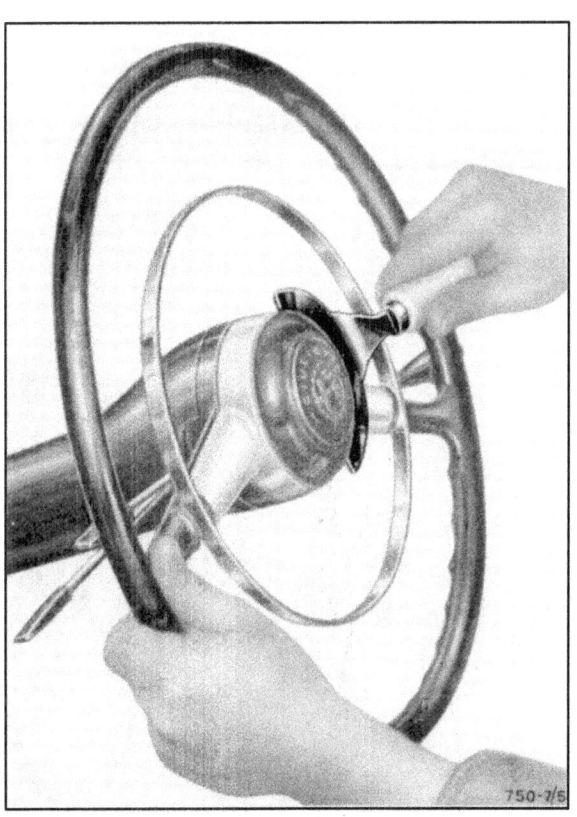

Fig. 5 - Withdrawing the push-button for the light signals, using tool No. 6121.06.007.

8) Remove the steering-wheel key.

9) Unscrew the three lock-nuts for the control switch cable clamps; remove the screw holding the two switches to the bracket, and the nut connecting the two switches together.
Slacken the three head-lamp switch cable clamps and withdraw the cables; remove the screw fixing the switch to the steering-column bracket and withdraw the conductors from the steering-column. When re-assembling, the foregoing instructions must be performed in the reverse order, and the following warning borne in mind:

WARNING

1) The assembly of the switches for the trafficator and head-lamps is only possible provided that the electrical conductors in the space between the two control plates are accurately positioned.

2) The switch unit cup must be mounted in such a way that it does not become locked by the spoke cover fixation screws.

3) When fitting the rubber ring for fixing the push-button seat ring, only talc must be used; under no circumstances must oil or grease be used.

4) After re-assembling the electrical equipment, and before fitting the steering-wheel, connect the circuit to the battery and check that the connections have been made properly.

4 - REMOVING THE STEERING-COLUMN AND STEERING-BOX FROM THE CAR

After removing the steering-wheel as described in the preceding section, proceed as follows:

Fig. 6 - Removing the steering-wheel from the steering column, using tool No. 6121.12.090.

1) Mark the steering-column to show the position of the column bracket; this is done by drawing a reference mark in line with the end of the top boss of the bracket.

2) Remove the gear-change lever after having unscrewed the threaded ring fixing it to the gear-change rod.

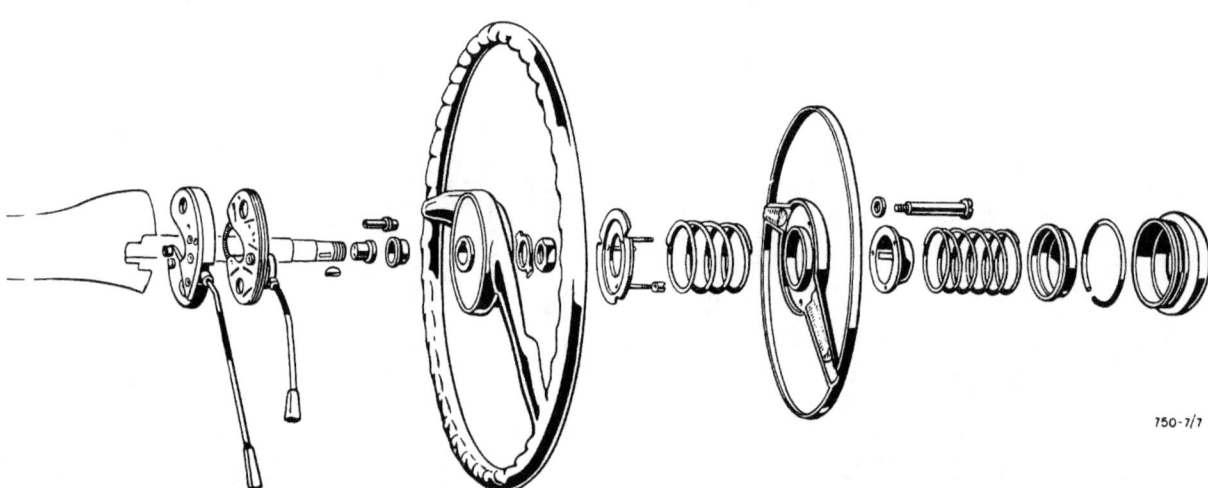

Fig. 7 - Details of the steering wheel and the horn/light signal controls.

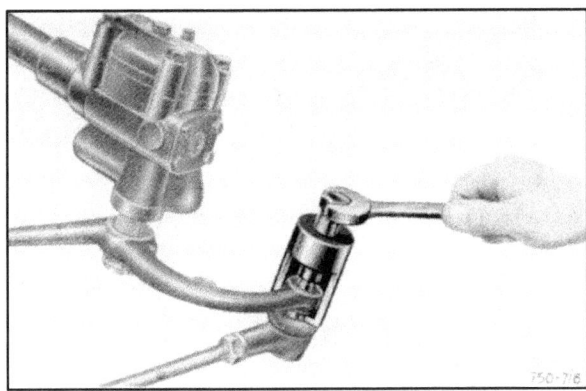

Fig. 8 - Removing a ball joint, using tool No. 6121.12.086.

3) Slacken the screw holding the steering-column bracket to the column itself.

4) Unscrew the two bolts fixing the steering-column bracket to the body.

5) Disconnect the hand-brake lever.

6) For guidance purposes when re-assembling, mark the steering-column to show the position of the gear-change rod bearing and remove the bearing caps.

7) Remove the steering-column bellows.

8) Remove the bracket carrying the switch for the reversing light, taking care to mark its position on the steering-column for ease of assembly; detach the two horn cables fixed to the bottom of the steering-box.

9) Remove the actuating lever ball joint by means of tool No. 6121.12.086 (Fig. 8).

10) Unscrew the three bolts fixing the steering-column to the body, and take out the column.

5 - DISMANTLING AND INSPECTING THE STEERING-BOX

1) Drain off the oil.

2) Disconnect the steering actuating lever, using tool No. 6121.12.085 (Fig. 9).

3) Unscrew the 4 bolts which hold the cover in place.

4) Withdraw the actuating pin.

5) Withdraw the oil seal and the actuating pin bushings but only if they have to be replaced.

6) By removing the front cover it is possible to remove the worm, its shaft and the ball-bearings.

7) Dismantle the taper roller bearing, straighten the retaining lug and unscrew the lock-nut.

WARNING

The top end of the worm shaft is provided with balls which centralise the shaft in relation to the steering column. When withdrawing the shaft it is therefore necessary to make sure that the balls and their bushing (which stays in the steering column tube) are not lost.

Also take care that the ring provided to retain the ball-bearing at the bottom of the worm does not fall from its seats as this would cause the jamming of the shaft or the displacement of the balls, with the possible loss of some of the balls.

Inspection

1) Check the degree of wear and examine the worm for damage.

2) Check the balls and their seats for wear.

3) Examine for wear the taper portion of the pin which engages with the worm.

4) Check the play in the taper bearing on the pin which engages with the worm.

5) Check the play between the actuating pin and its bushes.

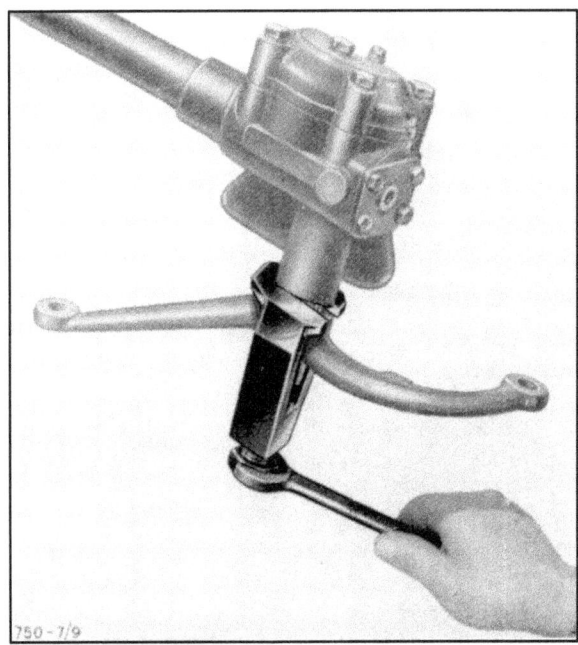

Fig. 9 - Removing the steering actuating lever from the steering box, using tool No. 6121.12.085.

6 - RE-FITTING THE STEERING-BOX

1) Fit the cage with 13 ball-bearings at the top of the steering column and the upper bearing ring in the steering-box.

2) Fit the cage of ball-bearings and the seat for the bottom bearing onto the worm, and fix the seat with the locking ring; insert the steering-wheel shaft thus assembled into the column.

3) Fit a shim for adjusting the play in the helical-worm bearing, and the bottom cover, and lock the latter in position with the screws provided.

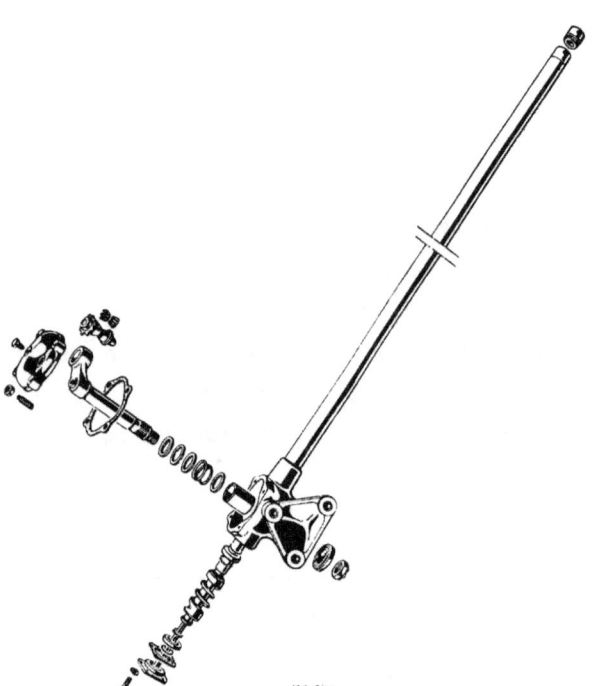

Fig. 10 - Details of the steering system.

4) Check the bearings for the proper degree of tightness; the worm must be able to rotate without any play when applying the power of one hand to the top of the steering-wheel shaft.

If the tightness of the bearings fails to give this result, replace the shim by one of suitable thickness.

5) Fit the taper roller bearing on the actuating pin. There must be no play between the rollers and their taper housing.

6) Fit the actuating shaft bushings and oil seal to the steering-box.

7) Hold the steering-box in a vice in the horizontal position and with the side of the flange (provided for fixing it to the body) in the vertical position. To the top of the actuating rod fit the stop ring for the ball cage, the spring and the spring thrust bush. Temporarily fit the steering wheel in position and ensure that the spokes occupy the appropriate position (in relation to the steering-box) that they will occupy when the column is returned to the car; while holding the steering-wheel in this position, insert the actuating pin, complete with the spring and the two washers, into its housing.
Fit the gasket and the cover, and adjust the play in accordance with the instructions given in Chapter 1.

7 - DISMANTLING, INSPECTING AND RE-ASSEMBLING THE BALL JOINTS AND THE INTERMEDIATE STEERING-ARM BRACKET

Dismantling

There is no particular problem in taking down the various ball joints provided that tool No. 6121.12.086 is used (Fig. 8); the same applies to the removal of the intermediate steering arm bracket from the body, and the separation of the latter into its component parts (Figs. 11, 12 and 13).

Inspection

a) Check the play in the ball joints; they are of a type which cannot be separated. Proceed as follows:

— hold the joint in a vice.

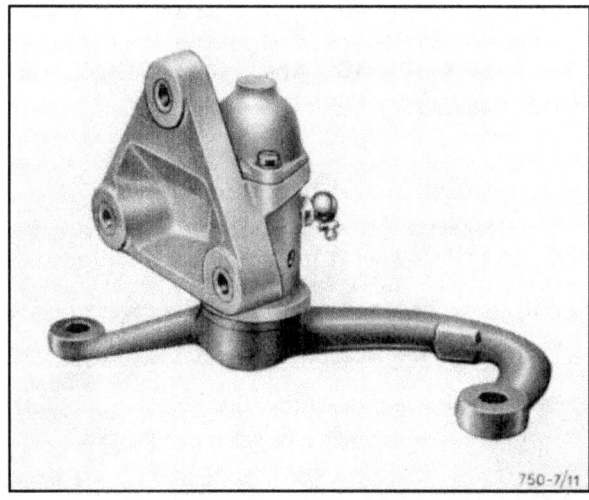

Fig. 11 - Intermediate steering-arm bracket.

Attach a threaded stem to the threaded part and, by means of this stem, apply thrust and rotational pressure to the ball pin, thus ascertaining the extent of the play. If play is excessive the ball joint must be replaced.

b) Check the radial play between the bushing and the intermediate steering arm pin (original play 0.01 to 0.03 mm, maximum wear 0.1 mm).

c) Make sure that the grease nipples are working properly and check the oil seal for efficiency.

Re-assembly

When re-assembling the bracket unit, the axial play of the pin itself must be checked after having locked its nut; play should be from 0.01 to 0.03 mm, otherwise it should be brought to that figure by varying the thickness of the adjusting washer inserted beneath the nut in question.

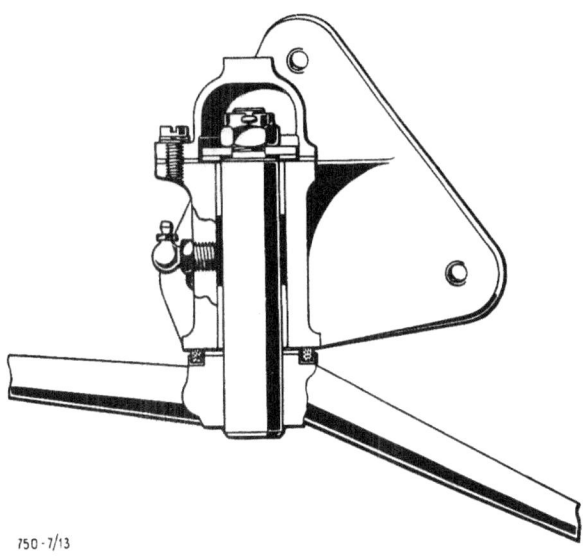

Fig. 13 - Cross-section through the intermediate steering-arm bracket.

8 - RE-FITTING THE STEERING BOX, STEERING ARMS AND TRACK RODS TO THE CAR

1) Fit the steering column to the body, tightening but not locking the three bolts which hold down the steering box.

   NOTE: These bolts must be 65 mm long; they must be shortened if they are found to be longer, as if they touch the bottom of the hole in the box, it would be impossible to tighten the box to the body.

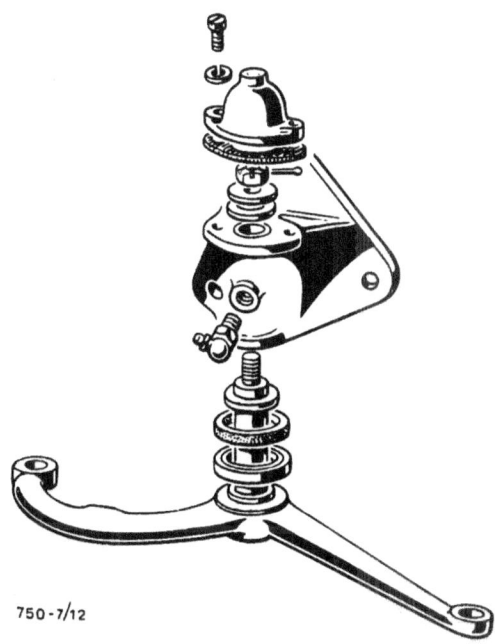

Fig. 12 - Details of the intermediate steering-arm bracket.

2) Fit the steering column bracket to the body and lock the bracket to the column itself after having placed it in such a position it does not interfere with the free rotation of the steering-wheel.

3) Lock the three bolts which affix the steering-box to the body.

4) Re-fit the gear-change rod and its two bearing caps; tighten the bearing to the column, making sure that it is at the position marked on the column at the time of removal.

5) Return the steering-column bellows to its position on the body.

6) Re-fit the hand-brake lever.

7) Re-fit the gear-change lever.

8) Attach the intermediate steering-arm bracket to the body.

9) Attach the lateral track rods to the steering arm on the stub axle.

10) Connect the central track rod to the steering-arm and the intermediate steering-arm.

11) Pass the cables for the flashing warning lamps through the steering column tube and attach the horn and trafficator cables to the steering-column bracket.

12) Insert the two warning lamp conductors into the holes in the rubber bushing and fit the capped terminals to the ends. Insert the bushing in its housing on the steering-column tube.

13) Fit the head-lamp switch (Fig. 14) and the switch

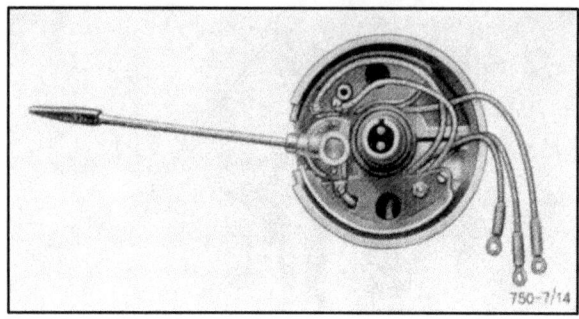

Fig. 14 - Fitting the switch for full and anti-dazzle lighting.

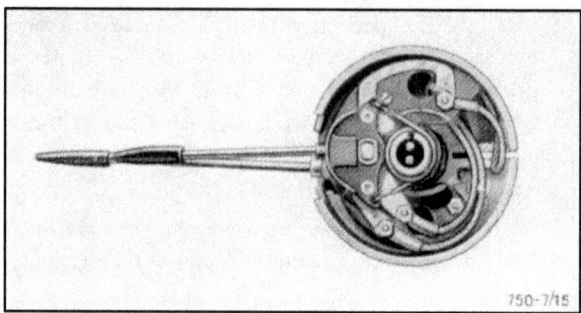

Fig. 15 - Fitting the trafficator switch.

for the trafficators (Fig. 15) and connect the cables to same.

14) Fit the steering wheel and lock it in place on the steering-column by means of the nut provided; bend over the nut one lip of the safety plate.

15) Insert the switch unit for the horn light signals and horn return spring.

16) Fit the spoke cover, insert the spring for the flashing-signal push-button, the button and the button seat ring, after first placing the rubber washer in position.

17) Fit the reversing lamp switch and lock it in the position as marked at the time of its removal.

18) Connect up the horn light signal cables to the special plate at the bottom of the steering column, and fix them in position.

INFORMATION SHEET REFERENCE

ASSEMBLY	DATE	SHEET N.	SUBJECT

INFORMATION SHEET REFERENCE

ASSEMBLY	DATE	SHEET N.	SUBJECT

PART 8

BRAKES

INDEX

Description . . . . page 161

1) Fitting new brake linings . . . . » 162

2) Brake drums . . . . » 165

3) Adjusting the brake shoes . . . . » 165

4) Removing the hydraulic pump from the car . . . . . . » 166

5) Dismantling and re-assembling the wheel cylinders on the back plates . . » 166

6) Bleeding the hydraulic system . . . . » 167

PART 8
BRAKES

DESCRIPTION

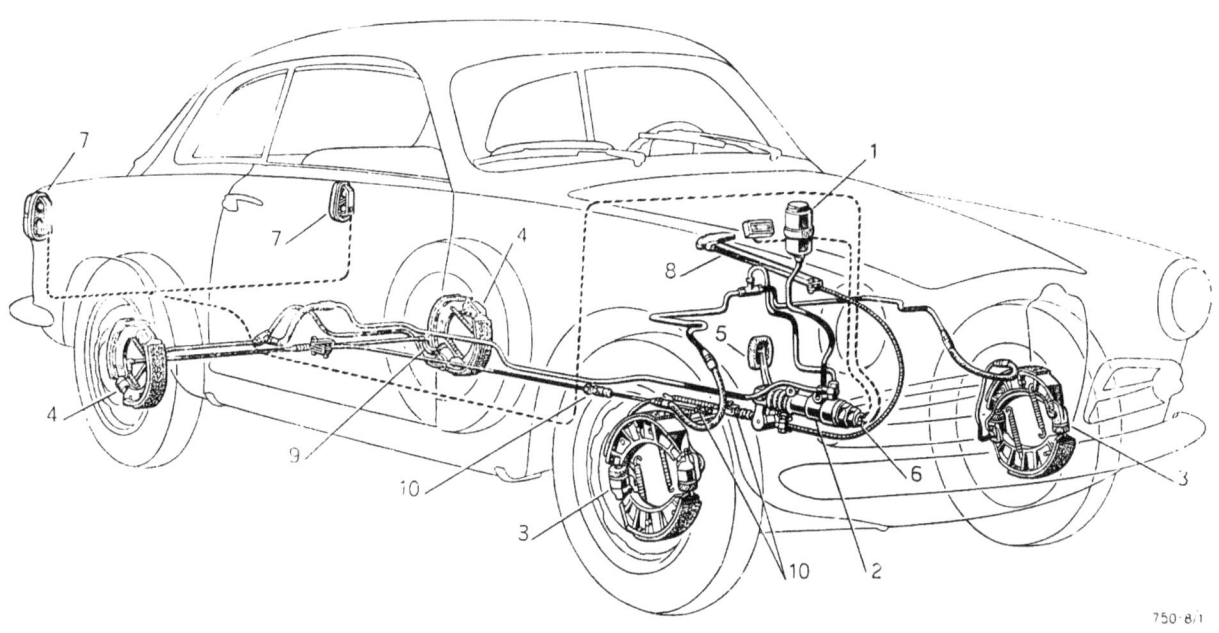

Fig. 1 - Diagram of the hydraulic and mechanical braking system.

1. Feed tank - **2.** Hydraulic pump - **3.** Front-wheel brake cylinders - **4.** Rear wheel brake cylinders - **5.** Pedal operating the hydraulic pump - **6.** Switch for the rear stop lamps; this switch operates by hydraulic pressure - **7.** Rear lights - **8.** Lever for manually-controlled rear-wheel brakes - **9.** Control lever for the rear cylinders.

The braking system comprises the hydraulic circuit operating on all four wheels through the actuating pedal, and the hand-brake which acts on the rear wheels only.

THE HYDRAULIC BRAKE

The controls for the hydraulic brakes comprise the fluid feed tank, the hydraulic pump and the wheel cylinders which actuate the brake-shoes.

THE HYDRAULIC PUMP

The hydraulic pump (Fig. 3) comprises the body **1** in which the piston **2** slides under the action of the rod **3**. The oil enters the pump body via the connector **4** and, following the route shown by the arrow, enters chamber **5** in front of the piston; the chamber connects, via the outlet connector **6**, with the pipes leading to the brake-actuating wheel cylinders.

As the piston **2** advances under the thrust of the rod, the ports **7** move in front of the seal **8** and the oil in the chamber **5**, being unable to return to the tank, is forced into the pipes leading to the wheel cylinders. When the pedal pressure is released, the piston is returned to its inactive position by the return spring **9** and by the release springs on the brake shoes; communication with the tank is then re-established.

The pump is completed by the hydraulic switch **10** (which operates the stop lamps) and the rear piston seal **11**.

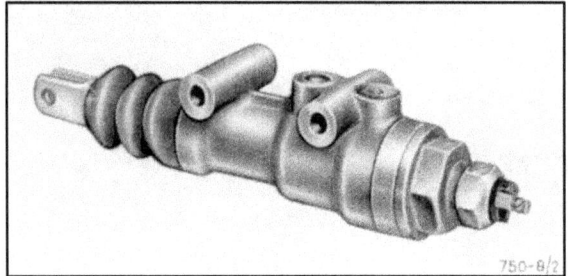

Fig. 2 - Hydraulic pump.

WHEEL CYLINDERS

The brake cylinders on the front wheels are single-acting; this means that on each wheel there is a cylinder which acts on one of the two shoes, both of which are leading shoes.

The rear-wheel brake cylinders are double-acting; this means that there is simultaneous action by both shoes of each wheel; in fact, while one shoe is actuated by the piston, the other is actuated, by reaction, by the body of the wheel cylinder which slides over the back-plate.

Each wheel cylinder comprises a body inside which there is a piston and seal; each wheel cylinder has two connectors, one for the oil inlet and one for bleeding the circuit.

THE HAND-BRAKE

The hand-brake, which acts on the rear-wheel brake blocks, is designed essentially to prevent the vehicle from moving when left on a slope, and may be con-

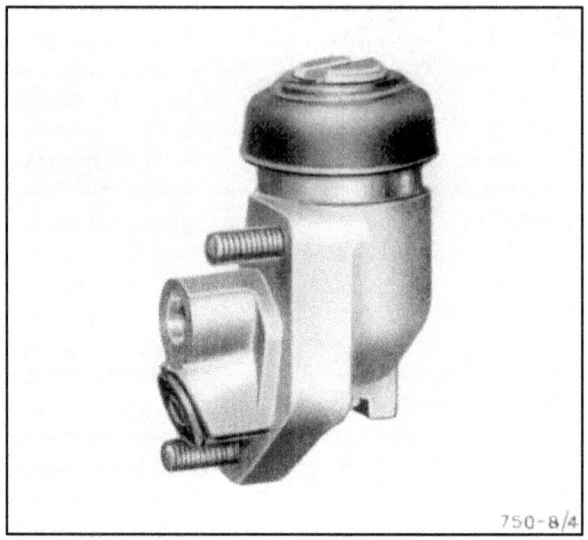

Fig. 4 - Front-wheel brake cylinder.

sidered as an emergency brake for use when the vehicle is in motion.

The brake-shoes are actuated as follow:

A control lever is connected by cables to the body of the wheel cylinder; one end of the cylinder is connected to the control cable and the other acts on the lower shoe; when the lower shoe comes into contact with the drum, the wheel cylinder moves, by reaction, and in turn actuates the other shoe.

1 - FITTING NEW BRAKE LININGS

The linings must be of the make and type approved by Alfa Romeo. This approved type is:

Ferodo MR. 41 for the rear brakes

Ferodo MZ. 41 for the front brakes.

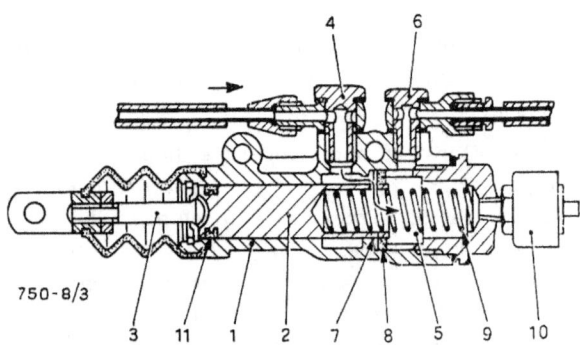

Fig. 3 - Cross-section of the hydraulic pump.

1. Body - **2.** Piston - **3.** Actuating rod - **4.** Oil inlet connector - **5.** Pressure chamber - **6.** Oil outlet connector - **7.** Port in the piston allowing oil to pass - **8.** Front seal - **9.** Piston return spring - **10.** Hydraulic switch for the stop lamps - **11.** Rear seal.

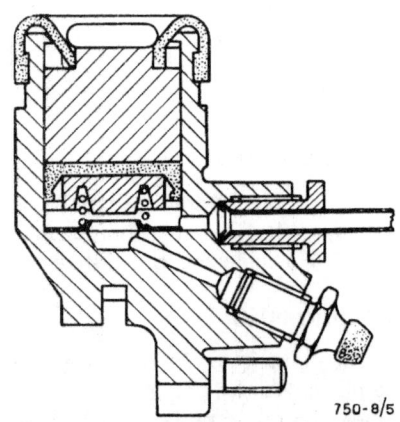

Fig. 5 - Cross-section through the front-wheel brake cylinder.

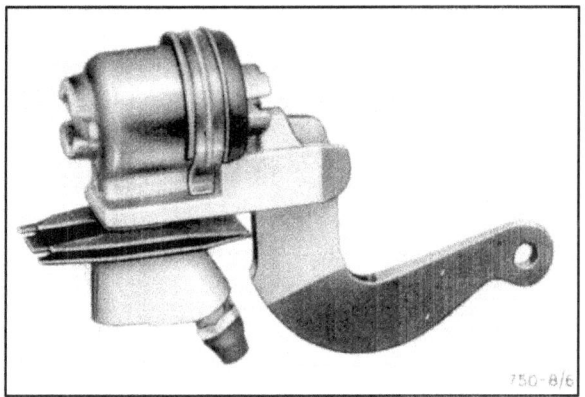

Fig. 6 - Rear-wheel brake cylinder.

1) Remove the wheels.
2) Remove the brake drums.
3) Remove the brake shoes from the wheel cylinder and tie up the latter to prevent the piston from falling out.

   The shoes must generally be disconnected by hand, without the use of a tool; should that prove impossible because of earlier mishandling (over-strong springs or distorted actuating rods) the use of screwdrivers, levers, etc. against the actuating rods or their seats on the brake-shoe must nevertheless be avoided.
4) Remove the rivets holding the old lining to the shoe.
5) Fit the new lining to the shoe:
   a) tool No. 6121.70.009 must be used to fix the linings to the front-wheel shoes, and tool No. 6121.70.011 for the rear wheels (Fig. 10);

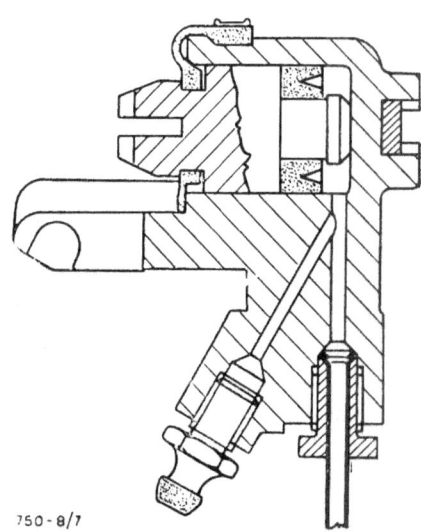

Fig. 7 - Cross-section through the rear-wheel brake cylinders.

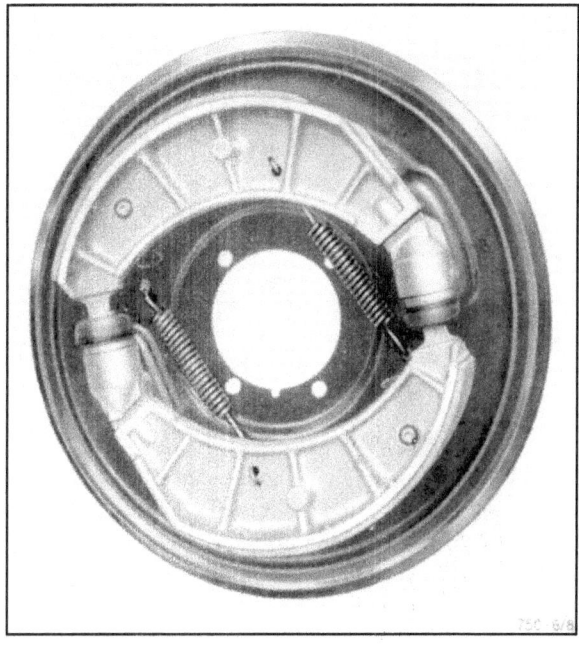

Fig. 8 - Right-hand front-wheel brake.

otherwise it will be extremely difficult to obtain perfect adherence between the shoe and the new lining.

This adherence must be checked by tapping the entire lining surface with a hammer; the resulting noise is different where adherence is imperfect.

b) The lining rivets must also be checked to ensure that the rivet heads are sunk in the lining to a uniform depth of 2 to 2.2 mm.

6) Re-grinding the linings:

Fig. 9 - Right-hand rear-wheel brake.

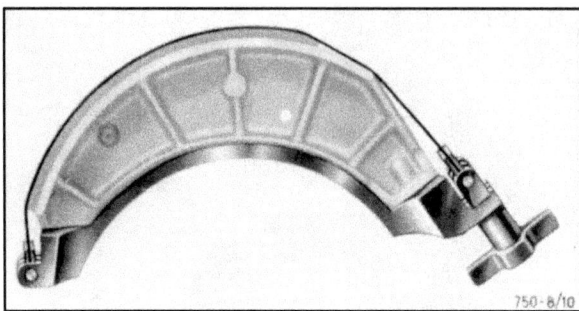

Fig. 10 - Rivetting the lining to the front-wheel shoes, using tool No. 6121.70.009.

a) It is absolutely necessary to re-grind the linings in order to bring them to the dimensions shown in the illustration. This re-grinding must be performed after placing the front-wheel brake shoes on tool No. 6112.01.330 (Fig. 11) and the rear-wheel shoes on tool No. 6112.01.323.

After this re-grinding, which must be very accurately performed, the working surface of the lining must not be touched up in any way.

b) Only in cases where linings have been soiled with grease is it necessary to clean them, using a clean rag soaked in petrol.

Abrasives (emery-cloth, files, etc.) must under no circumstances be used.

c) The dimensions of the bevels cut at the ends of the front-wheel linings must be as shown in Fig. 12. The rear-wheel linings are un-bevelled.

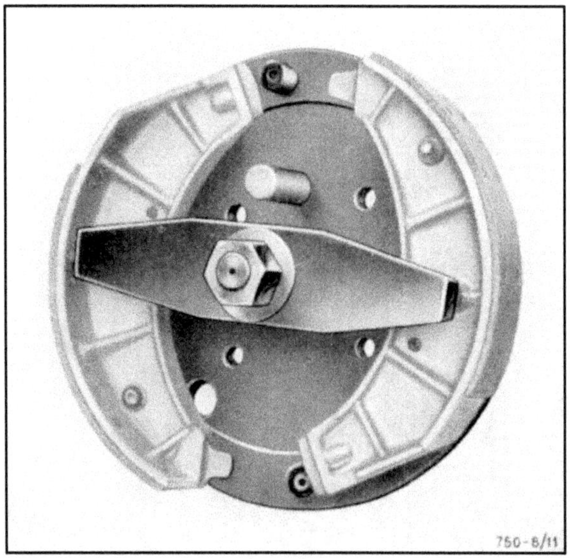

d) In the event that un-bored linings are fitted, we recommend that, in order to eliminate difficulties, the length of lining beyond the last rivet does not exceed in length the value shown in Fig. 12.

7) Check the efficiency of the brake-shoe return spring.

8) Fit the shoes in their original positions. Before assembly, check that:

— the rubber tube located in the holes provided in the front wheel shoe back-plates for hooking on the shoe return spring is undamaged, as water might otherwise enter through the holes and have a serious effect on braking;

— the two actuating rods on each shoe are in perfect condition and perfectly in line;

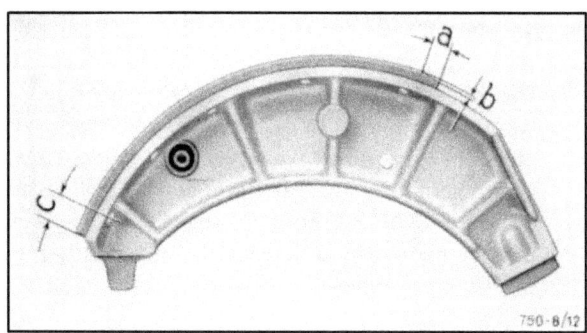

Fig. 12 - Bevel cuts for the front-wheel brake-shoe linings.
Length of bevel: $a = 8$ mm - Height of bevel: $b = 0,5$ to 1 mm. - Distance from the centre of the rivet to the end of the shoe: $c = 12$ mm.

— the bearing surface of the screw for adjusting the quadrature of the individual shoes shows no sign of tool marks or other damage.

Before assembling the brake shoes, the ends of the actuating rods and the surface bearing on the adjusting screw must be lightly smeared with grease.

The individual shoes are assembled by first positioning the rod which acts on the wheel cylinder, and then the one acting on the pivot.

A check must then be made to ensure that the rods slide freely in their seats and that the shoes, when mounted, are quite free to move both axially and vertically; this means that there must be no interference from the back-plate.

The accurate inspection of the fit of each shoe is of paramount importance, and for this purpose the appropriate square (tool No. 6123.29.007) should

Fig. 11 - Front-wheel brake-shoe mounted on tool No. 6112.01.330 for re-grinding.

be fitted to the hub flange, the latter first being carefully cleaned (Fig. 13).

This operation is performed as follows:

— bring to the zero position the cams for adjusting play between shoe and drum;

— position the square so as to make the check along the centre line of the shoe;

— make sure that the surface of the lining lies exactly along the edge of the arm of the square.

— in the event that the lining does not exactly fit the contour of the square, operate the adjusting screw until the fit is perfect.

— then fasten the adjusting screw with the locknut and repeat the fit test described above.

2 - BRAKE DRUMS

Inspection

a) Check that the inner band of ferrous metal has not separated in one or more places from the external part in light alloy; such separation can be assessed by any lack of uniformity in the sound emitted when the inner ring is lightly tapped all over with a hammer. If necessary replace the drum.

b) Check the drums for ovality, eccentricity or rake; the following values are permissible:

ovality   : 0.03 mm. on the diameter
eccentricity : 0.07 mm. on the radius
rake   : 0.02 mm. on the diameter.

If the said defects exceed the figures given above, the drums must be re-ground in order to remove the necessary material to eliminate the trouble.
The maximum depth of re-grind is 1 mm. off the diameter of the drum when new. The original drum diameter in the case of the front wheels is 266,7 to 266,8 mm.; the original rear wheels drums diameter is 254 to 254,1 mm.
The requisite degree of roughness is 40 to 60 (average ground finish); do not use emery paper or make the surface specular.

Fig. 13 - Checking the front-wheel shoe quadrate, using tool No. 6123.29.007.

c) If the drum is scored or burned, or shows signs of spots or cracks, it must be re-ground as described in the preceding paragraph.

d) If the drum appears uniformly brightened but does not require regrinding, it will suffice to rub it over with emery cloth, taking care to ensure that the four drums on any one car have the same degree or roughness.

3 - ADJUSTING THE BRAKE SHOES

Front wheel shoes

Place both adjusting cams **1** (Fig. 18) in such a position that the wheel can rotate freely.

Work on one cam only until the corresponding shoe touches the drum.

Turn the cam back over 1 to 3 (probably 2) notches so that the drum can again rotate freely.

Repeat the operation on the cam for the second shoe.

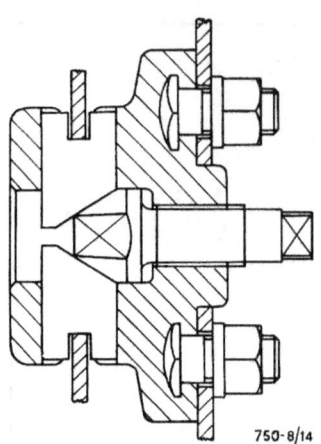

Fig. 14 - Pin for adjusting the play between the rear-wheel brake-shoe and drums.

Rear-wheel shoes

Lock the shoes by working on the adjusting pin **1** (Figs. 19 and 14); and then turn the screw backward until the drum begins to be free.

Care must be taken to ensure that the release system connects the pin itself in a stable position (that is, that it is not in an intermediate position between the two notches). In the event that more than three notches are necessary to free the drum, the cause must be sought; it is probably one of the following:

— the shoes are not square
— the shoes are not centralised in relation to the drum;
— the shoe actuating rods are jammed in their seats.

4 - REMOVING THE HYDRAULIC BRAKE PUMP FROM THE CAR

Unscrew the joint connecting the feed tank to the pump and drain the oil from the tank; disconnect the oil delivery tube from the pump.

Disconnect the electric cable for the stop-light.
Disconnect the rod attached to the clutch pedal.

Unscrew the bolts holding the pedal bracket to the body and take it off together with the pump.

When re-assembling, the above instructions should be followed in the reverse order.

Taking the hydraulic pump down into its component parts (Fig. 15) involves no particular difficulties.

Inspection

Check the wear and the condition of the internal surfaces of the pump body and the piston.

Make sure that the seals are neither worn nor swollen by the absorption of oil; in cases of doubt, replace them.

Check the efficiency of the piston return spring.
Ensure that the dust-cover bellows are in good condition.

When re-assembling, take the greatest care not to damage the seals; if it has been removed, tighten the lock-nut which fixes the brake pedal link fork to the actuating rod.

5 - DISMANTLING AND RE-ASSEMBLING THE WHEEL CYLINDERS ON THE BACK-PLATES

a) Front-wheel-cylinders

— Remove the wheel.
— Remove the drum.
— Disconnect the shoes from the cylinders.
— Unhook the shoe return spring from the back-plate.

When re-assembling, repeat the above procedure in the reverse order.

After tightening the cylinders on the back-plates, smear a little sealing compound over the back-plates in order to prevent water from reaching the brake drums.

Fig. 15 - Details of the hydraulic pump.

Fig. 16 - Details of the front-wheel brake cylinders.

b) Rear-wheel cylinders

— Remove the wheel.

— Remove the drum.

— Disconnect the shoes from the cylinders.

— Slide off the outer flexible plate, then lower the two teeth on the inner plate so as to release the intermediate plate; it will then be possible to slide off both these plates which serve to fix the cylinder to the back-plate.

— Remove the hand brake lever and the rubber dust cover; remove the cylinder.

When re-assembling repeat the above procedure in the reverse order.

Separating the front and rear cylinders into their component parts (Fig. 16 and 17) presents no particular difficulties.

Inspection

As in the case of the hydraulic pump, the cylinder body and piston must be checked for signs of abnormal wear or scoring.

The rubber seals must be neither worn nor swollen through the absorption of oil; in all cases of doubt they must be replaced.

6 - BLEEDING THE HYDRAULIC SYSTEM

Whenever brake repairs involving the removal of the tubing or cylinders are necessary, or whenever the car has been left unused for long periods, the hydraulic circuit must be bled; it is also necessary to bleed the circuit whenever brake pedal travel becomes excessive or spongy.

Bleeding must be performed with the maximum care, and the following instructions scrupulously observed:

1) Fill the feed tank with the appropriate type of oil, and take care during the bleeding operation that the oil level does not fall below the quarter-full level;

2) Bleed the two rear-wheel cylinders separately as follows (Fig. 18):

Fig. 18 - Bleeding the rear-wheel brake cylinders and adjusting the play between the shoes and drums.
1. Cams for adjusting the play between the shoes and the drum -
2. Screws for adjusting the shoe quadrature in relation to the drum
3. Bleeding connection.

— slacken the drain screw after having attached to it a rubber tube; the other end of the tube will be placed in a glass jar suitable for the collection of the brake fluid;

— operate the brake pedal several times, allowing it to return slowly to its zero position; continue until the oil leaving the tube no longer contains air bubbles;

— close the air release screw;

3) Bleed the front wheel cylinders as follows (see Fig. 19):

— turn the shoe adjusting cylinders inwards so as to move the shoe as far away from the drum as possible;

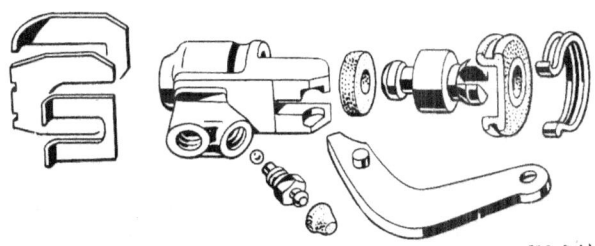

Fig. 17 - Details of the rear-wheel brake cylinders.

Fig. 19 - Bleeding the front-wheel brake cylinders and adjusting the play between the shoes and drum.

1. Pin for adjusting the play between the shoes and drum - **2.** Screws for adjusting the brake-shoe quadrature in relation to the drum - **3.** Bleeding connection.

Fig. 20 - Lay-out of the rear-wheel handbrake arrangements. (Giulietta Sprint Veloce and Spider Veloce cars).

— proceed as for the rear wheels, taking care, however, to operate the brake pedal with greater force and closing the cylinder release screw before releasing the pedal;

— when bleeding is completed, the brake shoes must be re-set by means of the cams.

If the above bleeding operations have been carefully performed, it will be found that when the pedal is depressed, the action on the brake fluid will be noticed, without any sponginess, immediately after the initial free travel of the pedal.

The free travel of the brake pedal, before actuating the hydraulic pump must be such that the actuating rod moves through 1 to 1.5 mm.

The brake pedal must be adjusted whenever, due to lining wear, the free pedal travel is greater than one third of the total possible travel.

Scouring the hydraulic system.

Only methyl alcohol must be used to scour the brake system.

Petrol, paraffin or petroleum must never be used or the rubber parts will be damaged.

7 - BRAKES FOR GIULIETTA SPRINT VELOCE AND SPIDER VELOCE CARS

Braking system is the same that the one employed in other Giulietta models. The difference among these models and the other ones consists in a different designe of front wheels shoes, in a different location of rear wheels shoes and in a different setting of hand brake control.

INFORMATION SHEET REFERENCE

ASSEMBLY	DATE	SHEET N.	SUBJECT

INFORMATION SHEET REFERENCE

ASSEMBLY	DATE	SHEET N.	SUBJECT

PART 9

WHEELS AND TYRES

INDEX

Introduction	page 173
Description	» 176
Wheels	» 176
Tyres and tubes	» 176
1) Inflation pressures	» 176
2) Maintenance	» 177
3) Fitting and removing tyres	» 179
4) Balancing wheels with tyres fitted	» 180
a) Static balance	» 180
b) Dynamic balance	» 181
c) Wheel-balancing machines	» 181

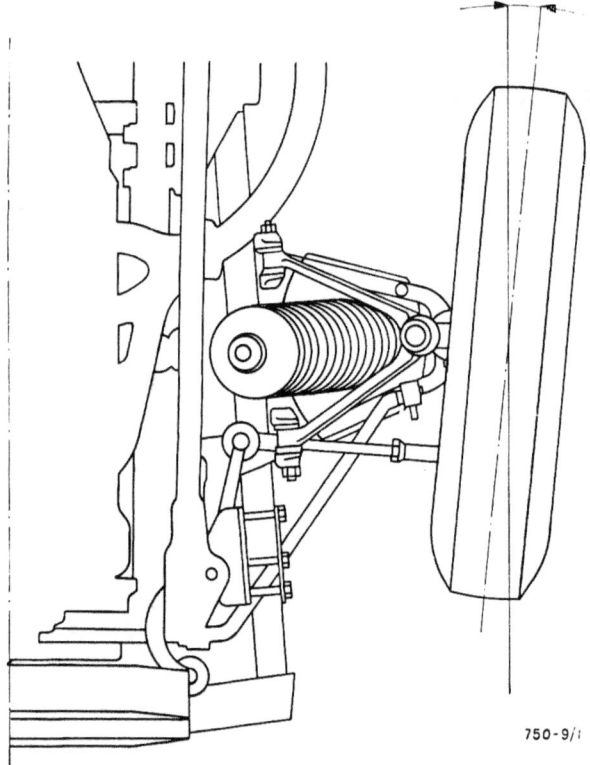

Fig. 1 - Front-wheel toe-in.

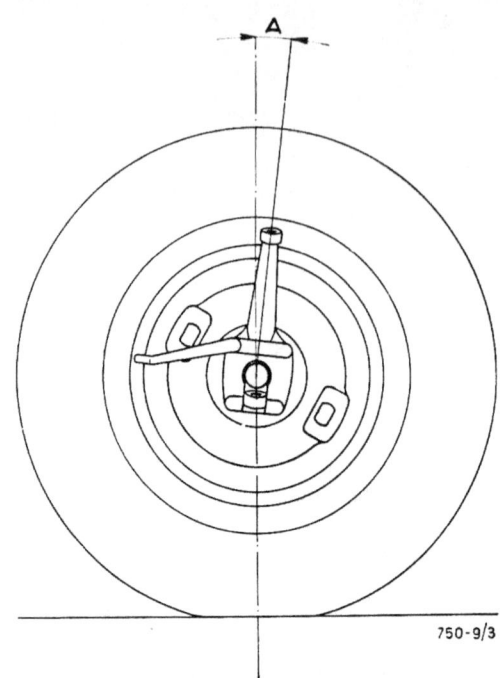

Fig. 3 - King-pin caster angle (Angle of inclination of the King-pin in relation to the vertical and measured according to the longitudinal axis of the vehicle).

$$A = \begin{cases} 10' \pm 30' & \text{(Berlina up to car N. 148810000)} \\ 30' \pm 30' & \text{(Berlina from car N. 148810001)} \\ 30' \pm 30' & \text{(t.i.)} \\ 50' \pm 30' & \text{(Sprint and Sprint Veloce)} \\ 1°20' \pm 30' & \text{(Spider and Spider Veloce)} \end{cases}$$

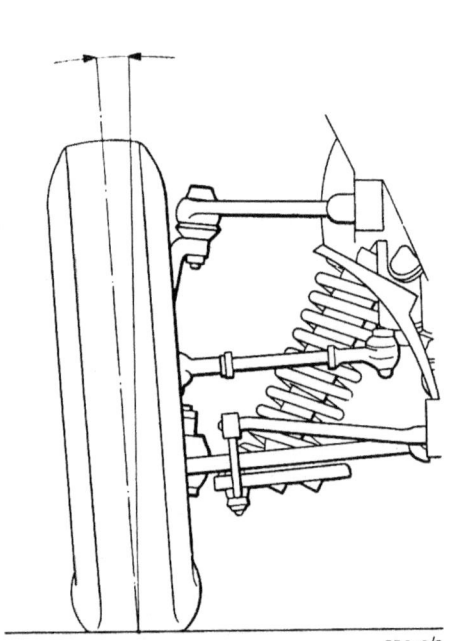

Fig. 2 - Front-wheel camber.

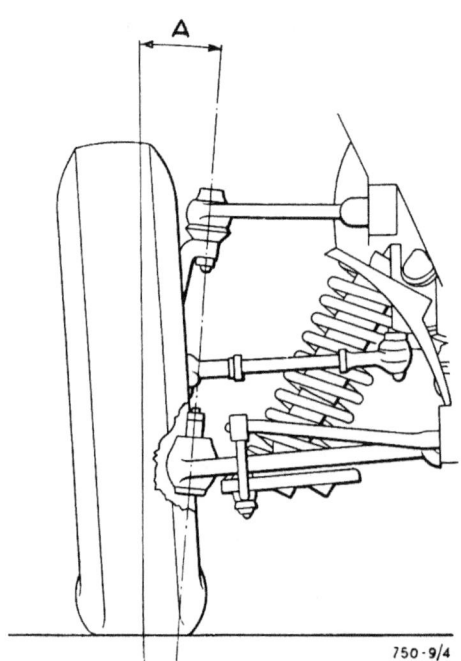

Fig. 4 - King-pin slant. (Angle of inclination of the King-pin in relation to the vertical and measured according to the transverse axis of the vehicle) $A = 8°\,35'$

PART 9

WHEELS AND TYRES

INTRODUCTION

In view of the importance of the effect of the perfect adjustment and setting of the front wheels on tyre consumption and road-holding qualities, we feel that the subject deserves more detailed attention than the brief references made to it on Parts 6 and 7.

The accurate positioning of the front wheels demands the observance of the under-noted requirements for:

— front-wheel toe-in (Fig. 1)
— front-wheel camber (Fig. 2)
— King-pin caster and slant (Figs. 3 and 4 respectively).

The first two factors can be varied by means of simple adjustment operations, but king-pin caster and slant depend on the geometrical dimensions of the king-pins and suspension arms.

When the prescribed dimensions or angles are not maintained, the deformed members (which will generally be found to have been damaged as the result of knocks or collision) must be replaced of the arrangements anchoring them to the body checked.

As a final check when inspecting or adjusting wheel position, the alignment between the rear axle and the front wheels should also be checked.

For these checks to be accurate it is essential:

— to drive the car onto a perfectly level and horizontal floor;
— to ensure that the tyre pressures are those prescribed;
— to check that the steering system ball joints are not worn and that there is no excessive play bet-

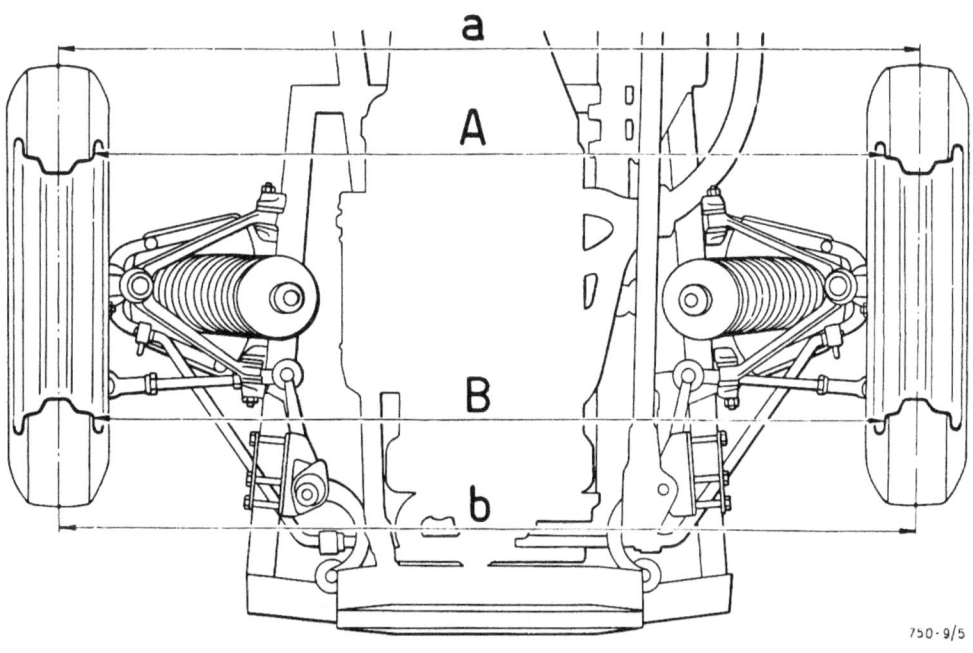

Fig. 5 - Front-wheel toe-in (car with full load)

A = B + 3 mm.   **a = b + 4 mm.**

Fig. 6 - Measuring front-wheel toe-in, using the wheel rims as reference points.

ween the worm and the roller in the steering box;

— to check that the front wheel bearing play is that prescribed;

— to check that all bolts holding the steering-gear and suspension arms to the body are tight;

— to carry out all checks when the car has a static load, that is, when the fuel-tank is full, with 4 persons aboard (each weighing approximately 75 kgs.) in the case of the Giulietta Berlina and t.i., and 2 persons in the case of other types.

This check can be made by uniformly distributing sand-bags over the seats and the floor to a total weight of 300 or 150 kgs. and by placing sand-bags in the luggage boot to a weight equal to that of the petrol needed to fill the tank.

Fig. 5 shows the front-wheel toe-in values as follows: the values **A = B + 3 mm.** refer to the toe-in measurement made in accordance with the arrangements illustrated in figures 6 and 7 in which the wheel rims are used as reference points:

Fig. 7 - Measuring front-wheel toe-in with the wheel rims taken as reference points.

the values **a = b + 4 mm.** refer to the toe-in measurement made in accordance with the arrangements illustrated in Fig. 8 in which the tyres are used as reference points.

When measuring toe-in as shown in figures 6 and 7 it is essential to ensure that the rims are not distorted through knocks; in all cases the same measurement should be made at two or three points around the rim. When measuring toe-in as shown in figure 8 the following procedure must be followed:

Fig. 8 - The reference line marked on the tyre for the measurement of the front-wheel toe-in.

— jack up the front wheels;
— place a surface gauge on the centre-line of the tyre and revolve the wheel by hand; in this way a fine line will be left on the tyre tread. Do the same thing with the other wheel.
— lower the jack and load the vehicle as described above;
— by referring to the lines drawn on the tyres, perform the necessary operations to obtain the prescribed degree of toe-in.

Toe-in adjustment must be performed as follows:

— lock the steering-wheel in the straight-ahead position, that is, with the two spokes arranged symmetrically in relation to the vertical;

Fig. 9 - Measuring front-wheel camber (vehicle fully loaded).

— by moving the lateral track rod (on the steering-wheel side) move the corresponding wheel into the straight-ahead (zero toe-in) position;

Fig. 10 - Measuring front-wheel camber (vehicle fully loaded).

- measure the length of the left-hand lateral track rod thus obtained and bring the length of the right-hand track rod to the same amount;
- place the right-hand wheel in the straight-ahead position by adjusting the central track rod;
- reduce the two lateral track rods by identical amounts so as to obtain the prescribed degree of toe-in.

The length of the lateral track rods measured from centre to centre of the ball joints, must be 266 to 274 mm., the length of the central track rod must be 476 to 484 mm. on the Giulietta Berlina and t.i., and 466 to 474 on the Giulietta Sprint, Sprint Veloce, Spider and Spider Veloce. If these dimensions cannot be obtained the reason must be located; it will probably lie in damage to the car body resulting from a collision.

Front-wheel camber should be zero degrees when the vehicle is fully loaded and can be checked as shown in figure 9 or by means of a suitable instrument applied to the wheel rims (Fig. 10).

DESCRIPTION

WHEELS

The pressed-steel disc wheels are fitted with 4½ J x 15 rims.

TYRES AND TUBES
1 - INFLATION PRESSURES

For long tyre life only 155-15 (155 x 380) tyres should be used; the inflation pressures (when cold) should be as follows:

Giulietta Berlina cars

Pirelli « Pordoi » tyres:
front 1.3 kg/cm² (18.2 p.s.i.);
rear 1.5 kg/cm² (21 p.s.i.)
Pirelli « Rolle » tyres:
front 1,4 km/cm² (19.5 p.s.i.);
rear 1.5 kg/cm² (21 p.s.i.)

Pirelli « Cinturato » tyres:
front 1.4 kg/cm² (19.5 p.s.i.) (^{1});
rear 1.5 kg/cm² (21 p.s.i.) (^{1});
front 1.5 kg/cm² (21 p.s.i.) (^{2});
rear 1.6 kg/cm² (22.5 p.s.i.) (^{2})

Michelin « S.D.S. » tyres:
front 1.4 kg/cm² (19.5 p.s.i.);
rear 1.5 kg/cm² (21 p.s.i.)

Michelin « X » tyres:
front 1.3 kg/cm² (18.2 p.s.i.);
rear 1.4 kg/cm² (19.5 p.s.i.)

Giulietta t.i. cars

Pirelli « Cinturato » tyres:
front 1.5 kg/cm² (21 p.s.i.) (^{1});
rear 1.6 kg/cm² (22.5 p.s.i.) (^{1});
front 1.6 kg/cm² (22.5 p.s.i.) (^{2});
rear 1.7 kg/cm² (24 p.s.i.) (^{2})

Michelin « X » tyres
front 1.4 kg/cm² (19.5 p.s.i.) (^{1});
rear 1.5 kg/cm² (21 p.s.i.) (^{1});
front 1.5 kg/cm² (21 p.s.i.) (^{2});
rear 1.6 kg/cm² (22.5 p.s.i.) (^{2})

Giulietta Sprint and Spider cars

Pirelli « Cinturato » tyres:
front 1.5 kg/cm² (21 p.s.i.);
rear 1.6 kg/cm² (22,5 p.s.i.)

Michelin « X » tyres:
front 1.4 kg/cm² (19.5 p.s.i.);
rear 1.5 kg/cm² (21 p.s.i.).

Giulietta Sprint Veloce and Spider Veloce cars

Pirelli « Cinturato » tyres:
front 1.5÷1.6 kg/cm² (21÷22.5 p.s.i.) (^{3});
rear 1.6÷1.7 kg/cm² (22.5÷24 p.s.i.) (^{3})
front 1.7÷1.8 kg/cm² (24÷25.6 p.s.i.) (^{4});
rear 1.8÷1.9 kg/cm² (25.6÷27 p.s.i.) (^{4})
front 1.9÷2.0 kg/cm² (27÷28.4 p.s.i.) (^{5});
rear 2.0÷2.1 kg/cm² (28.4÷29.8 p.s.i.) (^{5})

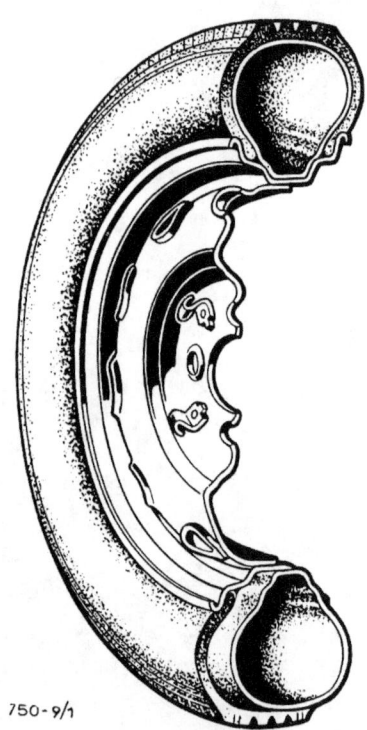

(^{1}) For touring use with light load
(^{2}) For sporting use with full load
(^{3}) For road use, up to 100 m.p.h.
(^{4}) For road use, above 100 m.p.h.
(^{5}) For race track use

Fig. 11 - Sectional view of a wheel, tyre and tube.

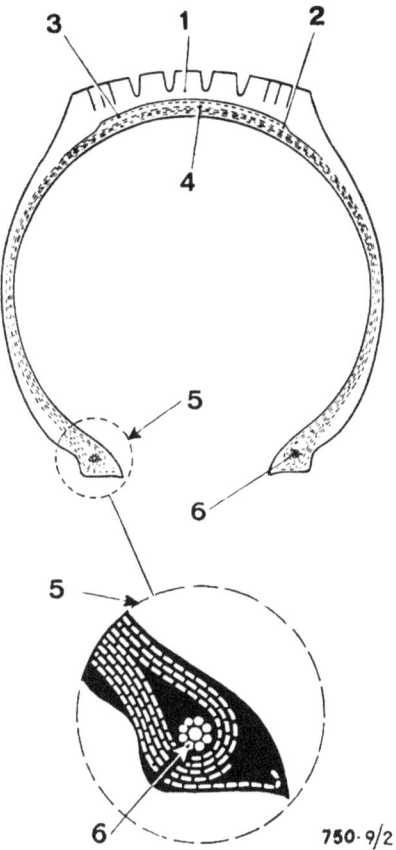

Fig. 12 - Tyre section.
1. Tread - **2.** Undertread - **3.** Breaker strip **4.** Cord - **5.** Bead wire.

2 - MAINTENANCE

So that users may understand the necessity for observing the recommendations made with a view to obtaining long tyre life, let us now examine the various factors which influence tyre efficiency.

Figures 11 and 12 show the component parts of a modern tyre and tube.

a) an insufficiently inflated tyre

The tyre bulges abnormally; the load is not distributed over the whole tread but is concentrated on the outside edges, the result being premature wear (Figs. 13 and 14).

Fig. 13 - **1.** Correct inflation - **2.** Insufficient inflation.

Fig. 14 - Comparison of wear between correctly-inflated and insufficiently-inflated tyres (premature wear at the side of the tread).

Furthermore, the tyre walls are excessively stressed; the result is the generation of greater heat, an increase in the internal temperature, the disintegration of the entire structure of the tyres, and the separation of the tread from the carcass, the separation of the individual plies (Fig. 15) and the breakdown of the fabric lining (Fig. 16).

Cracks develop in the tyre walls and gradually turn into real cuts leading to the fracture of the plies and tyre bursts.

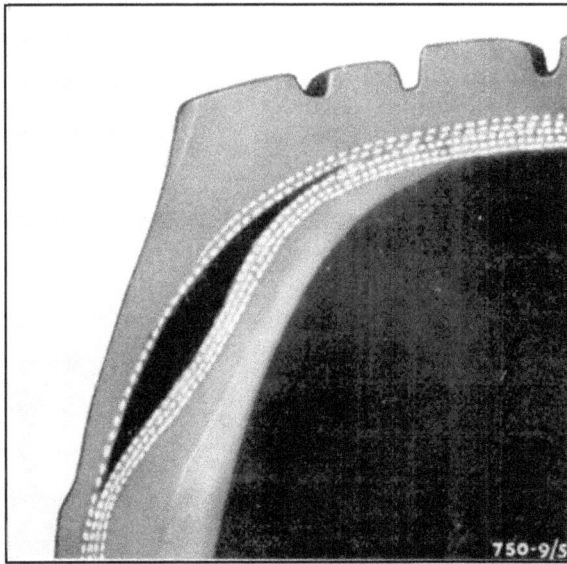

Fig. 15 - Separation of plies in the case of an insufficiently-inflated tyre.

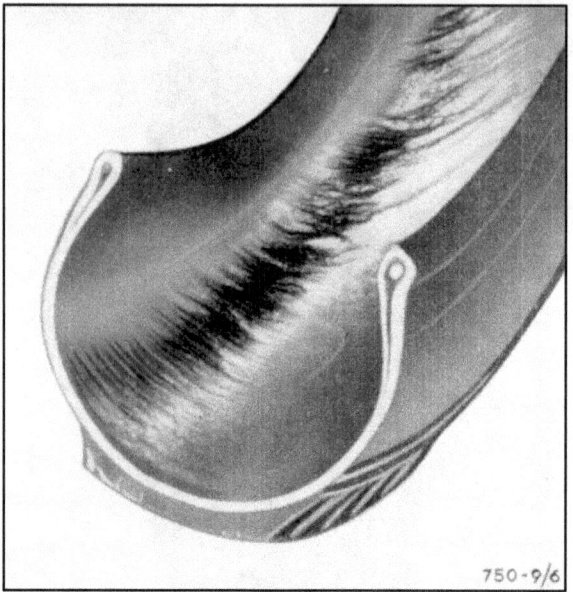

Fig. 16 - Ply thread breakdown in the case of an insufficiently-inflated tyre.

Steering becomes difficult and heavy, and the unpleasant rolling motion result in a less comfortable ride.

b) an over-inflated tyre

An excessively inflated tyre reduces passenger comfort, impedes the operation of the suspension system and detracts from the road-holding qualities of the car on corners.

Tyre life is shortened as the centre of the tread wears away quickly due to the reduced area in contact with the road. (Figs. 17 and 18).

The ply fabric is overstressed and is thus more vulnerable to the knocks resulting from rough roads; the danger of ply collapse and burst tyres is very real.

The tread rubber, being abnormally stressed, lacerates more easily.

Punctures, cuts and tread-groove cracks are also encouraged by excessive tyre pressures.

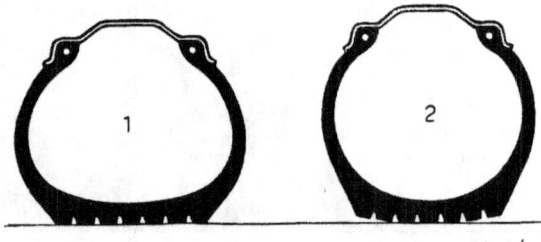

Fig. 17 - **1.** Correct inflation - **2.** Excessive inflation.

Fig. 18 - Comparison of wear between correctly-inflated and over-inflated tyres.

c) over-loaded tyres

An excessive load causes the abnormal flexion of the cord; this gives rise to the generation of great heat which may cause the separation of the plies at the top of the tyre walls, with the consequent risk of tearing or bursts.

Such an abnormal load may also cause the collapse of the plies under the tread and simple knocks may result in sidewall cuts.

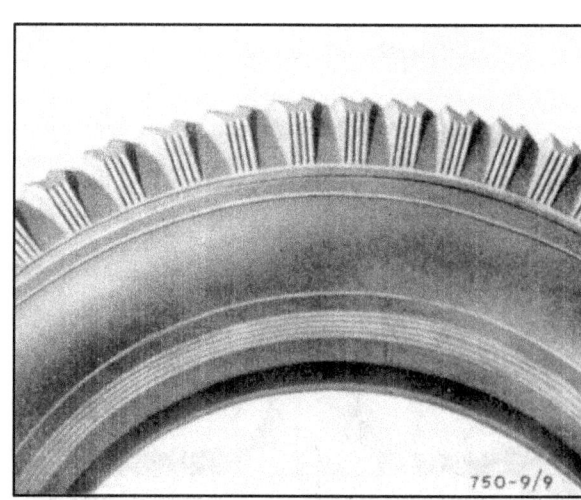

Fig. 19 - « Saw-tooth » tyre wear.

Fig. 20 - Spot wear.

d) other factors which shorten tyre life

Vicious acceleration or braking, high-speed cornering, frequent town stops and intermittent acceleration on main roads in heavy traffic - all these factors reduce tyre life.

The saw-tooth wear shown in Fig. 19 is one of the characteristic effects of skidding on corners, and is accentuated by incorrect suspension adjustment as well as by insufficient inflation pressures.

« Spot wear » (Fig. 20) is usually caused by sliding over the road surface as a result of sharp braking; sometimes it may be caused by a local repair or by a loose patch.

Tyre temperature, whether due to the ambient temperature, to the heat generated by the flexion of the tyre itself or to the vehicle speed, plays a prominent part in tyre life; all other circumstances being equal, tyre wear in summer is approximately double that in winter.

And lastly, tyre life can be seriously shortened by mechanical faults on the car, specific examples of which are:

— out-of-balance wheels
— mal-adjusted brakes
— incorrect front-wheel toe-in or camber
— front and rear axles out of parallel
— excessive play in the steering-box members and in the steering system ball joints.

Change-over of tyre positions

Even if every rule for long tyre life is strictly observed, it is still difficult to arrange for all four tyres to wear out at the same rate; this is due to the different tasks the tyres perform according to their positions on the car.

To ensure uniform wear, the tyres (including the spare) should be changed round every 2/3,000 miles in the order shown in Fig. 21.

3 - FITTING AND REMOVING TYRES

Fitting

— clean the rim, using a wire brush if necessary;
— give the inside of the cover and the beads a generous dusting with talc;
— fit the first bead into the rim well;
— insert the inner tube after inflating it slightly and dusting it with talc;
— fit the second bead; to do this, insert a tyre lever to the right of the valve and position the bead a little at a time, with a second lever which must be pushed to the right by some 8 to 10 cm. at a time. During this operation the portion of the tyre bead already fitted over the rim must be pushed into the well base; in this way it will be found easier to force the remainder of the tyre bead over the rim edge;
— it will also be found easier to fit the tyre bead in position alongside the valve if the valve is pushed back a little through its hole in the rim;
— inflate the tyre gradually, using the special tool for beating the tyre walls to facilitate the proper bedding down of the beads;
— make sure that both beads are properly in position and check that the centring ridge on the tyre walls lies uniformly in line with the rim edge;
— inflate the tyre to the prescribed pressure.

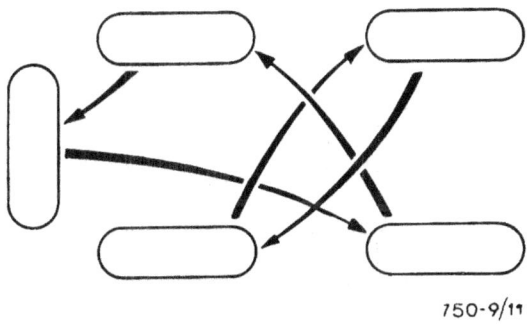

Fig. 21 - Tyre rotation plan.

Tyre removal

— After having deflated the tyre, push the tyre bead clear of the rim by pressing against the walls;

— insert a tyre lever to the left of the valve and draw the bead over the rim edge, at the same time pressing on the opposite portion of the tyre so as to force the bead into the well base;

— insert the second lever to the right of the valve and continue forcing the bead over the rim edge;

— when the first bead has been extracted, remove the inner tube from the cover, beginning with the portion opposite the valve. Then press the valve out of its housing so that the tube can be completely removed;

— turn the wheel over and press the second bead into the rim well; then, using a tyre lever, remove the cover entirely from the wheel.

4 - BALANCING WHEELS WITH TYRES FITTED

It should be remembered that even new wheels and tyres should be brought into a proper state of balance. In actual practice it is often found that wheel tyre units can lose their original balance either through uneven wear or because of tyre repairs.

As a consequence steering becomes uneven, and tyre and steering-gear wear increases. Wheels (complete with tyres and tubes) must therefore always be checked to ensure perfect static and dynamic balance.

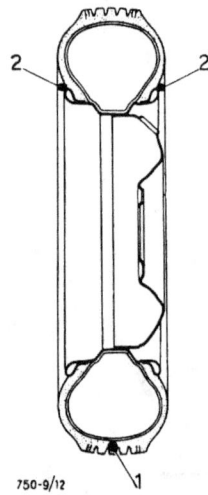

Fig. 22 - Diagram of a wheel statically out of balance.
1. Weight causing lack of balance - **2.** Balance weights.

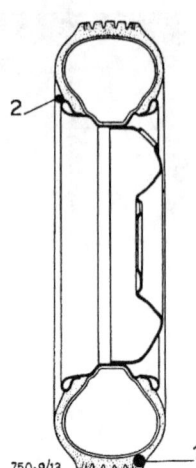

Fig. 23 - Diagram of a wheel dynamically out of balance.
1. Weight causing lack of balance - **2.** Balance weights.

Wheel balance must always be restored whenever tyre repairs are made or when the car is fitted with new tyres.

a) STATIC BALANCE

A wheel is balanced statically if its weight is uniformly distributed around its axis of rotation.

If an out-of-balance wheel is mounted, complete with tyre and tube, on a horizontal shaft in such a way that it can rotate freely, it will be found that it always stops with its centre of gravity below the axis of rotation.

Balance is restored to a wheel-and-tyre unit by attaching two weights (together equal to the lack of balance) to the rim (Fig. 22).

b) DYNAMIC BALANCE

A wheel is balanced dynamically if its centre of gravity is on the axis of symmetry of the wheel. If the centre of gravity has moved to one side, lateral wheel thrust will develop with consequential wheel rock wich increases with speed. This type of lack of balance is compensated by fitting a weight on the rim in a position diametrically opposite (referred to the vertical axis of the wheel) (Fig. 23).

c) WHEEL-BALANCING MACHINES

Several types of machine are available for balancing wheels both statically and dynamically.

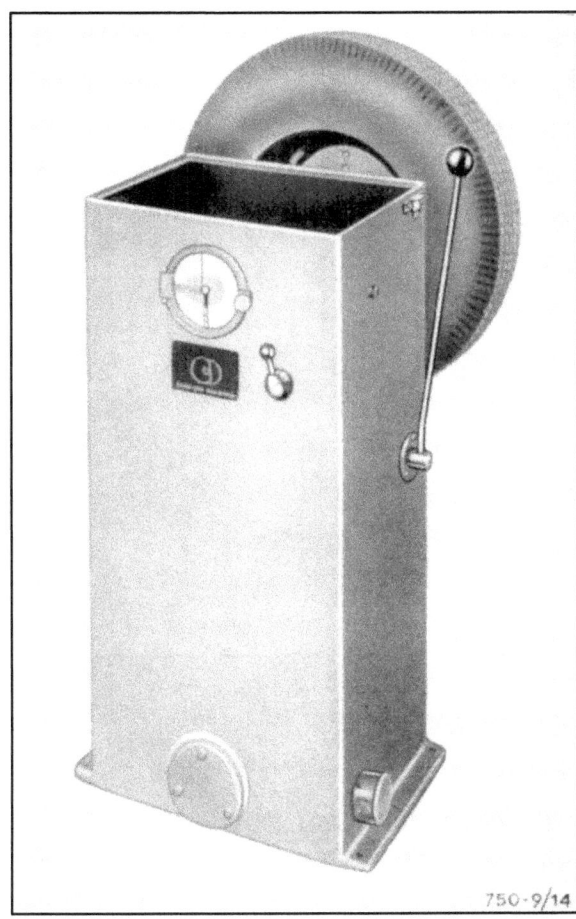

Fig. 24 - Hofmann wheel-balancing machine.

As an example we will briefly describe the operation of the Hofmann machine (Fig. 24); additional details are available from the makers.

After mounting the wheel on the machine in accordance with the makers' instructions, it can be balanced in two successive phases (Fig. 25):

1) balance in plane 1
2) balance in plane 2

Phase 1:

Start the electric motor and rotate the wheel until it reaches the maximum speed; switch off the current; the wheel will then rotate freely.

The wheel reaches the critical speed after several seconds; the movement caused by the vibrations is recorded on the recorder disc (Fig. 26). Reverse the direction of rotation of the wheel and repeat the record on the disc.

The two diagrams on the recording disc will be partially superimposed.

Rotate the wheel so that the intersection between the two diagrams becomes perfectly vertical, and read — on the scale cut on the door — the maximum value of the lack of balance (Fig. 26).

By means of a table supplied with the machine, determine — for each type of wheel — the value of the weight to be applied to the outside edge of the rim in the direction of the lack of balance (divergence from the vertical).

Phase 2

Slowly rotate the wheel and allow it to stop; when the wheel swings to a stop the centre of gravity will be found to be exactly beneath the axis of rotation.

Make a chalk mark on the inner edge of the rim at the top and vertical to the wheel centre.

Attach one of the magnetic blocks (supplied with the machine) to the rim in line with the chalk mark and turn the wheel through 90°; according to the direction of rotation of the wheel, and after allow-

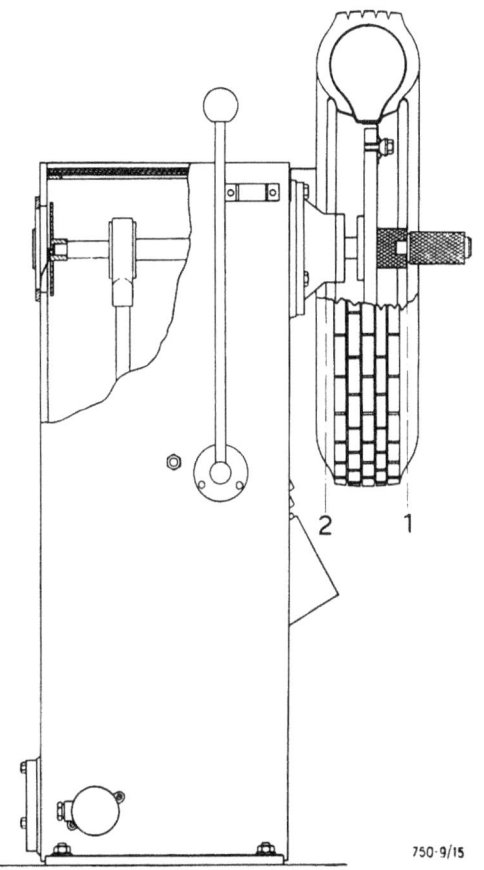

Fig. 25 - Diagram illustrating the Hofmann wheel - balancing machine.
1. External wheel plane - **2.** Internal wheel plane.

ing it to come to rest, it can be ascertained whether the weight of the magnetic block fitted is the correct one or not; if not, try alternative weights until the wheel remains stationary when moved through 90°.

Check again to make sure that the wheel remains stationary in all positions.

The magnetic block can then be replaced by a permanent block of the same weight.

On completion of the two sets of tests, the wheel will be statically and dynamically balanced.

WARNING

After fitting permanent balancing blocks to the inner rim edges as described above, a careful check must be made to ensure that when the front wheels are turned (or when they are bounced to the suspension limits) the balance weights do not touch the flexible brake-fluid pipes, as this could have serious consequences.

Contact between the flexible pipes and the balance weights can only take place in cases in which the pipes themselves have been twisted somewhat during their assembly; such twisting results in a spontaneous tendency for the pipe to approach the rim edge.

In such a case, slacken the nut fixing the top end of the flexible pipe to the bracket welded to the body, allow the pipe to assume a spontaneous position, make sure that it is not twisted and — while

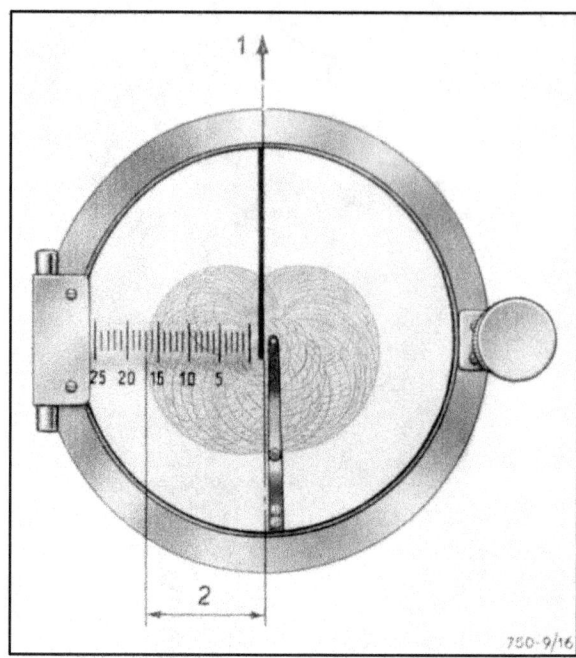

Fig. 26 - Recording disc.
1. Direction of lack of balance - 2. Value of maximum lack of balance.

holding the hexagonal nut integral with the pipe — tighten the lock-nut.

It should be remembered that a slight lack of wheel balance is better than the risk of damaging the brake-fluid pipes as a consequence of fitting balance weights.

In cases of doubt it is advisable to remove all balance weights from the rim and to balance the wheel statically (not dynamically) by applying balance weights only to the outer edge of the rim.

INFORMATION SHEET REFERENCE

ASSEMBLY	DATE	SHEET N.	SUBJECT

INFORMATION SHEET REFERENCE

ASSEMBLY	DATE	SHEET N.	SUBJECT

PART 10

ELECTRICAL EQUIPMENT

INDEX

Description	page 187
Battery	» 187
Generator	» 193
1 - General	» 193
2 - Normal maintenance	» 193
3 - Operating characteristics	» 193
4 - Faults and repairs	» 194
a) Locating charging circuit faults	» 194
b) Dismantling	» 195
c) Commutator	» 195
d) Armature	» 196
e) Field coils	» 196
f) Ball-bearings and bushes	» 197
g) Re-assembly	» 198
Control box	» 198
1 - General	» 198
2 - Adjustment data	» 199
3 - Locating and repairing faults	» 200
a) Locating faults in the charging circuit	» 200
b) Adjusting the regulator	» 200
c) Adjusting the cut-out	» 201
Starter Motor	» 202
1 - General	» 202
2 - Operating characteristics	» 204
3 - Normal maintenance	» 204
4 - Inspection and repair	» 204
a) Testing the motor in position	» 204
b) Test bench-checks and examination of brushes and commutator	» 204
c) Dismantling	» 205
d) Brushes replacement	» 205
e) Commutator	» 205
f) Armature	» 205
g) Field coils	» 206
h) Replacing motor end plate bushes	» 206
i) Re-assembly	» 206
Ignition Coil	» 206
Distributor	» 207
1 - General	» 207
2 - Normal maintenance	» 208
3 - Characteristic data	» 208
4 - Locating and repairing faults	» 209
a) Locating faults causing irregular ignition	» 209
b) Tracing causes of ignition failure	» 210
c) Low-tension circuit	» 210
d) High-tension circuit	» 210
e) Dismantling	» 211
f) Replacing the bush	» 211
g) Re-assembly	» 212
h) Replacing contacts	» 212
i) Timing the distributor	» 212
Sparking Plugs	» 213
Maintenance and testing of spark plugs	» 214

PART 10

ELECTRICAL EQUIPMENT

DESCRIPTION

The electrical equipment (Figs. 1 to 5) comprises the installation for starting the engine, for the ignition and lighting circuits and for the electrically-operated accessories.

This section will be devoted solely to the engine starting and ignition equipment; the lighting circuits and accessories will be dealt with in Part 13 entitled « Accessories ».

Every unit (except the starter motor and the ignition circuit) is protected by a fuse on the fuse panel shown in Fig. 6.

The electrical equipment used on the Giulietta cars has been designed to provide long life with a minimum of maintenance. Neverthelese, in the interests of efficient operation certain units require a small amount of periodical attention.

The following paragraphs, therefore, include brief descriptions of the various units, their operation and appropriate methods for their checking and repair.

Attention is drawn to the fact that the positive of Lucas or Marelli electric equipment is grounded, except the Sprint Veloce and Spider Veloce cars on which the negative is grounded.

BATTERY

The level of the liquid (electrolyte) in the battery cells must be approximately 4÷5 mm above the top edge of the plates. When topping up employ a glass filler and only use distilled water which has not been stored in a metal container.

When replacing spilled electrolyte, use only chemically-pure sulphuric acid (battery type) and bring the solution to the proper specific gravity in a non-metallic container, remembering pour the acid into the distilled water and not vice versa.

If the starter motor should revolve too slowly to rotate the engine easily, the battery charge should be checked and the battery recharged if necessary.

The battery charge can be checked by measuring the specific gravity of the electrolyte with a suitable hydrometer, always provided that the battery has been properly maintained as described above.

The relationship between the specific gravity and the battery charge is:

— specific gravity 1.28 (32° Baumé) - battery is charged;

— specific gravity 1.23 (27° Baumé) - battery is half discharged;

— specific gravity 1.11 to 1.14 (15 to 18° Baumé) - battery is fully discharged.

After adding distilled water to the elctrolyte, the specific gravity reading should anly be made when the mixing process is complete.

Make sure that the cable lugs are thoroughly tight on the battery terminals, thus ensuring proper contact, and from time to time smear them with sufficient vaseline to provent corrosion.

Do not place spanners or other metal objects on the battery or the cables, or short-circuiting may take place.

See Part 2 for additional battery maintenance hints.

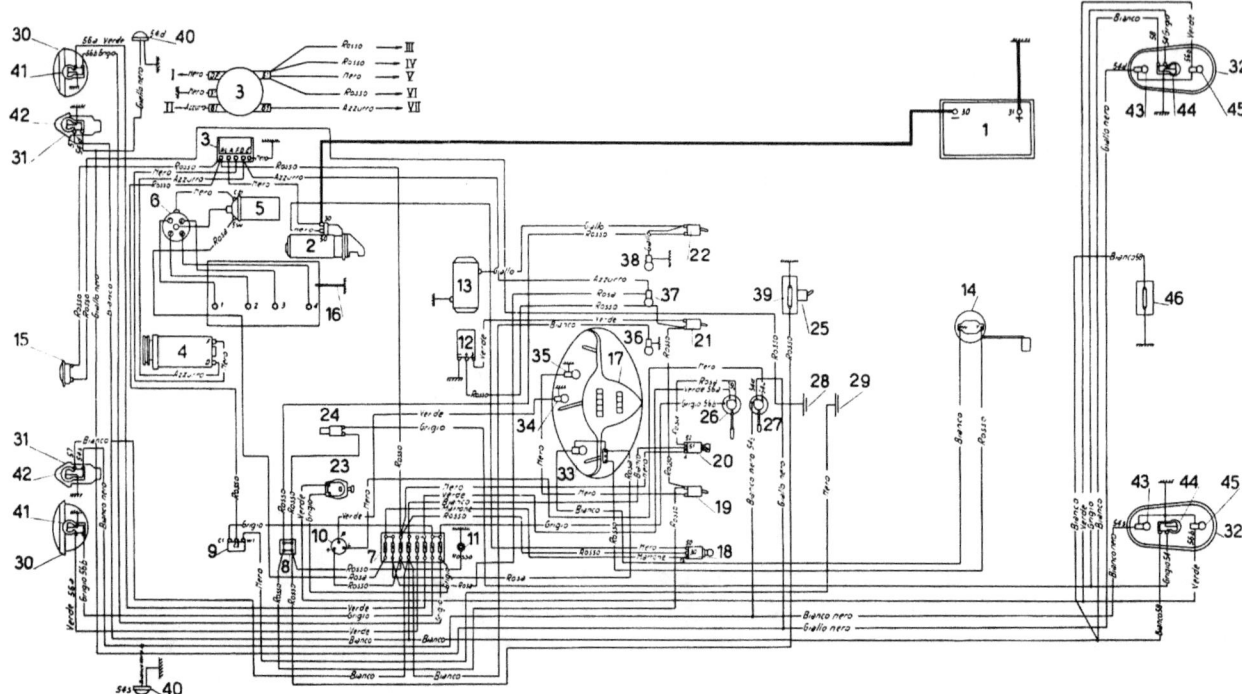

Fig. 1 - Circuit diagram of the electrical system (Giulietta Berlina).

I. To dynamo. - II. To dynamo. - III. To horn. - IV. - To fuses. - V. To starter motor. - VI. To electromagnetic change-over switch. - VII. To generator tell-tale lamp.

1. Battery.
2. Starter motor.
3. Control box.
4. Generator.
5. Ignition coil.
6. Distributor.
7. Eight fuses box.
8. Terminal board.
9. Electromagnetic change-over switch for trafficators.
10. Automatic device for blinking.
11. Socket for inspection lamp.
12. Windshield wiper motor.
13. Heater.
14. Float of petrol level indicator.
15. Electric horn.
16. Ground connection, engine to coach.
17. Instrument panel.
18. Ignition switch.
19. Switch for instrument panel lights.
20. Switch for headlamps and parking lights.
21. Switch for windshield wiper motor.
22. Switch for heater motor.
23. Reverse signal switch.
24. Stop signal switch.
25. Rooflight.
26. Switch for full and anti-dazzle lighting.
27. Trafficator switch.
28. Push-button for horn.
29. Push-button for headlights blinking.
30. Headlights.
31. Front lamps.
32. Rear lamps.
33. 12 V - 2.5 W tell-tale lamp for petrol reserve.
34. 12 V - 2.5 W tell-tale lamp for trafficators.
35. 12 V - 2.5 W lamps for instrument panel lighting.
36. 12 V - 2.5 W tell-tale lamp for anti-dazzle lighting.
37. 12 V - 2.5 W tell-tale lamp for generator.
38. 12 V - 2.5 W tell-tale lamp for heater.
39. 12 V - 3 W lamp for roof light.
40. Side blinking lamps.
41. 12 V - 45 W - 40 W lamps for headlights.
42. 12 V - 3 W - 20 W lamps for front lamps.
43. 12 V - 20 W lamps for rear blinking lights.
44. 12 V - 3 W - 20 W lamps for rear lamps.
45. 12 V - 20 W lamps for reverse signal.
46. 12 V - 5 W lamp for rear license plate.

Rosso	= Red	Giallo	= Yellow	Bianco	= White
Nero	= Black	Grigio	= Grey	Marrone	= Brown
Azzurro	= Blue	Verde	= Green	Rosa	= Pink
Bianco-nero	= Black and white			Giallo-nero	= Black and yellow

I. To dynamo. - **II.** To dynamo. - **III.** To horn. - **IV.** To fuses. - **V.** To starter motor. - **VI.** To electromagnetic change-over switch. - **VII.** To generator tell-tale lamp.

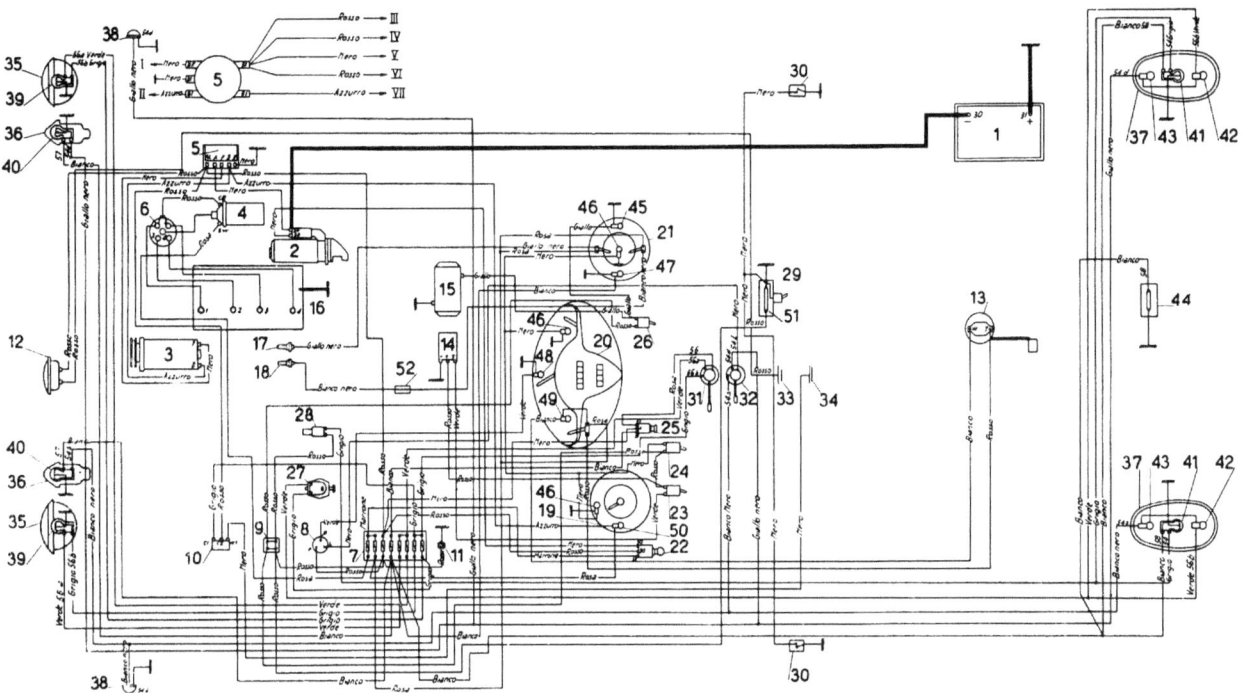

Fig. 2 - Circuit diagram of the electrical system (Giulietta t.i.).

1. Battery.
2. Starter motor.
3. Generator.
4. Ignition coil.
5. Control-box.
6. Distributor.
7. Eight fuses box.
8. Automatic device for blinking.
9. Terminal board.
10. Electromagnetic change-over switch for trafficators.
11. Socket for inspection lamp.
12. Horn.
13. Float of petrol level indicator.
14. Windshield wiper motor.
15. Heater.
16. Ground connection, engine to coach.
17. Bulb for water thermometer.
18. Bulb for oil thermometer.
19. Revolution counter.
20. Instrument panel.
21. Oil and water thermometers.
22. Ignition and starter switch.
23. Switch for windshield wiper motor.
24. Switch for instrument panel lights.
25. Switch for headlamps and parking lights.
26. Switch for heater motor.
27. Reverse signal switch.
28. Stop signal switch.
29. Rooflight.
30. Rooflight switch on doors.
31. Switch for full and anti-dazzle lighting.
32. Trafficator switch.
33. Push-button for horn.
34. Push-button for headlights blinking.
35. Headlights.
36. Front lamps.
37. Rear lamps.
38. Side blinking lamps.
39. 12 V - 45 W lamps for headlights.
40. 12 V - 3 W - 20 W lamps for front lamps.
41. 12 V - 3 W - 20 W lamps for rear lamps.
42. 12 V - 20 W lamps for reverse signal.
43. 12 V - 20 W lamps for rear blinking lights.
44. 12 V - 5 W lamp for rear license plate.
45. 12 V - 2.5 W tell-tale lamp for heater.
46. 12 V - 2.5 W lamps for instrument panel lighting.
47. 12 V - 2.5 W tell-tale lamp for anti-dazzle lighting.
48. 12 V - 2.5 W tell-tale lamp for trafficators.
49. 12 V - 2.5 W tell-tale lamp for petrol reserve.
50. 12 V - 2.5 W tell-tale lamp for generator.
51. 12 V - 3 W lamp for rooflight.
52. Resistance in oil circuit.

Rosso	= Red	Giallo	= Yellow	Bianco	= White
Nero	= Black	Grigio	= Grey	Marrone	= Brown
Azzurro	= Blue	Verde	= Green	Rosa	= Pink
Bianco-nero	= Black and white		Giallo-nero	= Black and yellow	

I. To generator. - II. To generator. - III. To horn. - IV. To fuses. - V. To starter motor. - VI. To electromagnetic change-over switch. - VII. To generator tell-tale lamp.

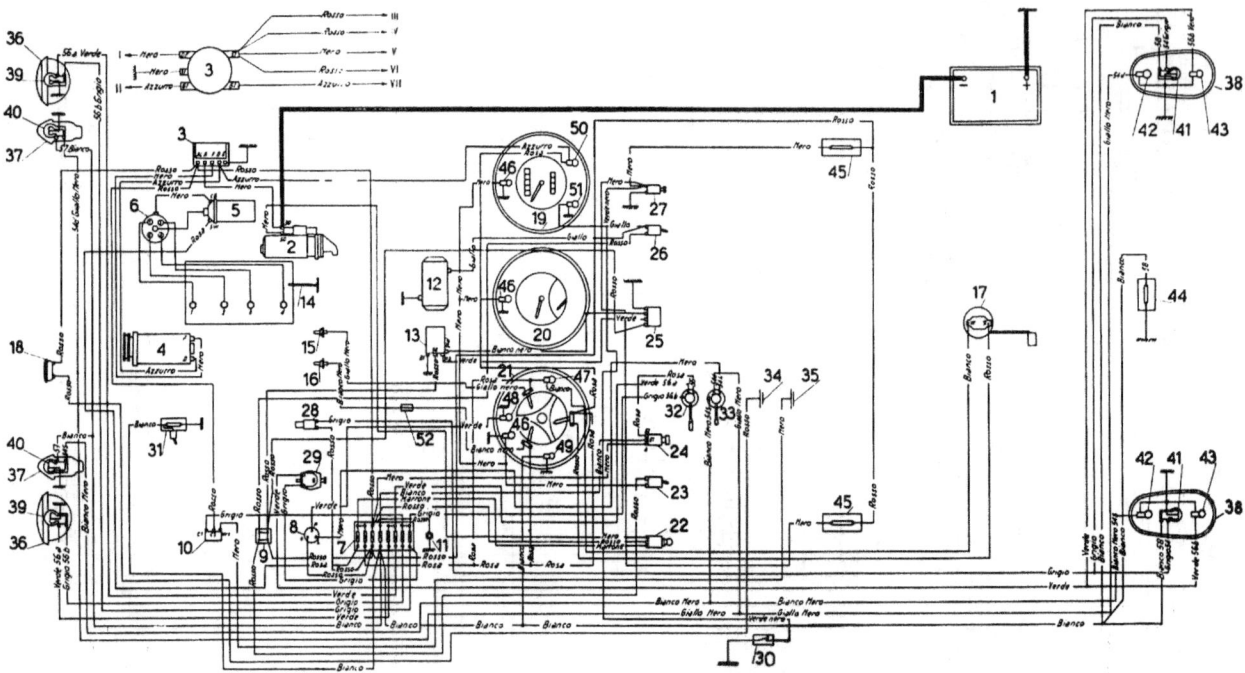

Fig. 3 - Circuit diagram of electric system (Giulietta Sprint).

1. Battery.
2. Starter motor.
3. Control-box.
4. Generator.
5. Ignition coil.
6. Distributor.
7. Eight fuses box.
8. Automatic device for blinking.
9. Terminal board.
10. Electromagnetic change-over switch for trafficators.
11. Socket for inspection lamp.
12. Heater.
13. Windshield wiper motor.
14. Ground connection, engine to coach.
15. Bulb for water thermometer.
16. Bulb for oil thermometer.
17. Float of petrol level indicator.
18. Horn.
19. Speedometer.
20. Revolution counter and oil gauge.
21. Oil and water thermometers and petrol gauge.
22. Ignition switch.
23. Switch for instrument panel lights.
24. Switch for headlamps and parking lights.
25. Switch for windshield wiper motor.
26. Switch for heater motor.
27. Rooflight switch.
28. Stop signal switch.
29. Reverse signal switch.
30. Rooflight switch on door.
31. Bonnet light with switch.
32. Switch for full and anti-dazzle lighting.
33. Trafficator switch.
34. Push-button for horn.
35. Push-button for headlights blinking.
36. Headlights.
37. Front lamps.
38. Rear lamps.
39. 12 V - 45 W - 40 W lamps for headlights.
40. 12 V - 3 W - 20 W lamps for front lamps.
41. 12 V - 3 W - 20 W lamps for rear lamps.
42. 12 V - 20 W lamps for rear blinking lights.
43. 12 V - 20 W lamps for reverse signal.
44. 12 V - 5 W lamp for rear license plate.
45. 12 V - 3 W lamp for rooflight.
46. 12 V - 2.5 W lamps for instrument panels lighting.
47. 12 V - 2.5 W tell-tale lamp for petrol reserve.
48. 12 V - 2.5 W tell-tale lamp for trafficators.
49. 12 V - 2.5 W tell-tale lamp for anti-dazzle lighting.
50. 12 V - 2.5 W tell-tale lamp for generator.
51. 12 V - 2.5 W tell-tale lamp for heater.
52. Resistance in oil circuit.

Rosso	= Red	Giallo	= Yellow	Bianco	= White
Nero	= Black	Grigio	= Grey	Marrone	= Brown
Azzurro	= Blue	Verde	= Green	Rosa	= Pink
Bianco-nero	= Black and white		Giallo-nero	= Black and yellow	

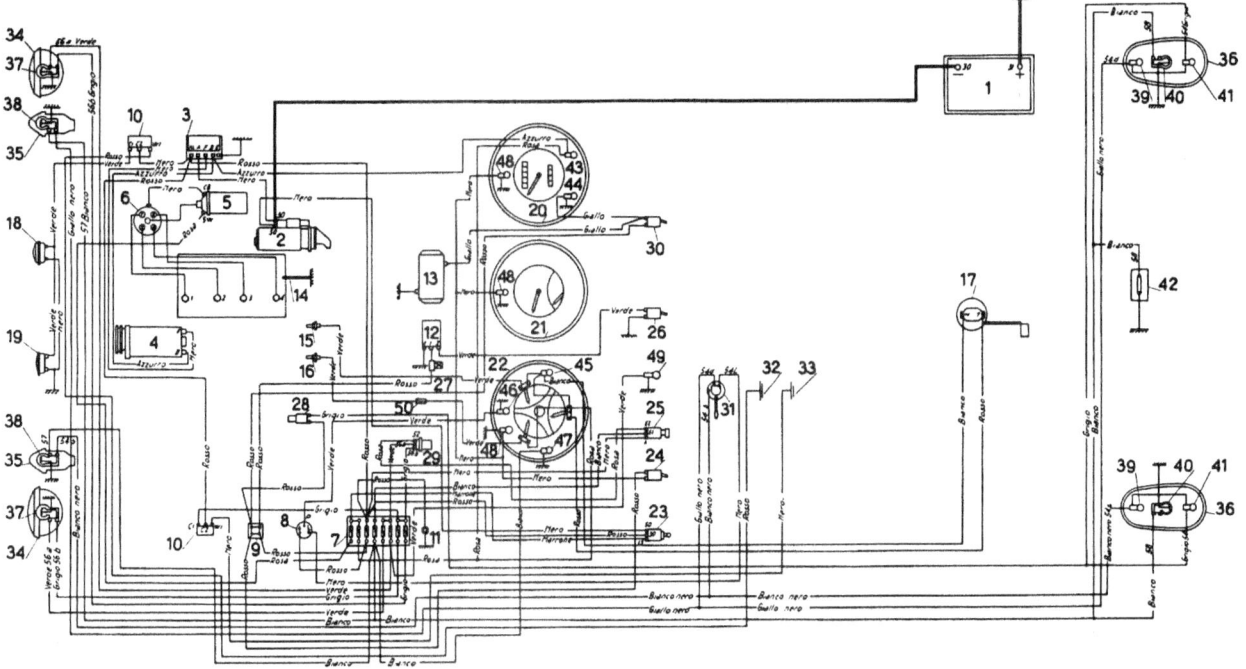

Fig. 4 - Circuit diagram of electric system (Giulietta Spider).

1. Battery.
2. Starter motor.
3. Control-box.
4. Generator.
5. Ignition coil.
6. Distributor.
7. Eight fuses box.
8. Automatic device for blinking.
9. Terminal board.
10. Electromagnetic change-over switch.
11. Socket for inspection lamp.
12. Windshield wiper motor.
13. Heater.
14. Ground connection, engine to coach.
15. Bulb for water thermometer.
16. Bulb for oil thermometer.
17. Float of petrol level indicator.
18. Electric horn.
19. Electric horns.
20. Speedometer.
21. Revolution counter and oil gauge.
22. Oil and water thermometers and petrol gauge.
23. Ignition switch.
24. Switch for instrument panel lights.
25. Switch for headlamps and parking lights.
26. Switch for windshield wiper motor.
27. Thermal switch.
28. Stop signal switch.
29. Pedal switch for headlamps lights.
30. Switch for heater motor.
31. Trafficator switch.
32. Push-button for horns.
33. Push-button for headlights blinking.
34. Headlights.
35. Front lamps.
36. Rear lamps.
37. 12 V - 45 W - 40 W lamps for headlights.
38. 12 V - 3 W - 20 W lamps for front lamps.
39. 12 V - 20 W lamps for rear blinking lights.
40. 12 V - 3 W - 20 W lamps for rear lamps.
41. 12 V - 20 W lamps for stop signal.
42. 12 V - 5 W lamp for rear license plate.
43. 12 V - 2.5 W tell-tale lamp for generator.
44. 12 V - 2.5 W tell-tale lamp for heater.
45. 12 V - 2.5 W tell-tale lamp for petrol reserve.
46. 12 V - 2.5 W tell-tale lamp for trafficators.
47. 12 V - 2.5 W tell-tale lamp for anti-dazzle lighting.
48. 12 V - 2.5 W lamp for instrument panel lighting.
49. 12 V - 2.5 W tell-tale lamp for headlamps lighting.
50. Resistence in oil circuit.

Rosso = Red	Giallo = Yellow	Bianco = White
Nero = Black	Grigio = Grey	Marrone = Brown
Azzurro = Blue	Verde = Green	Rosa = Pink
Bianco-nero = Black and white		Giallo-nero = Black and yellow

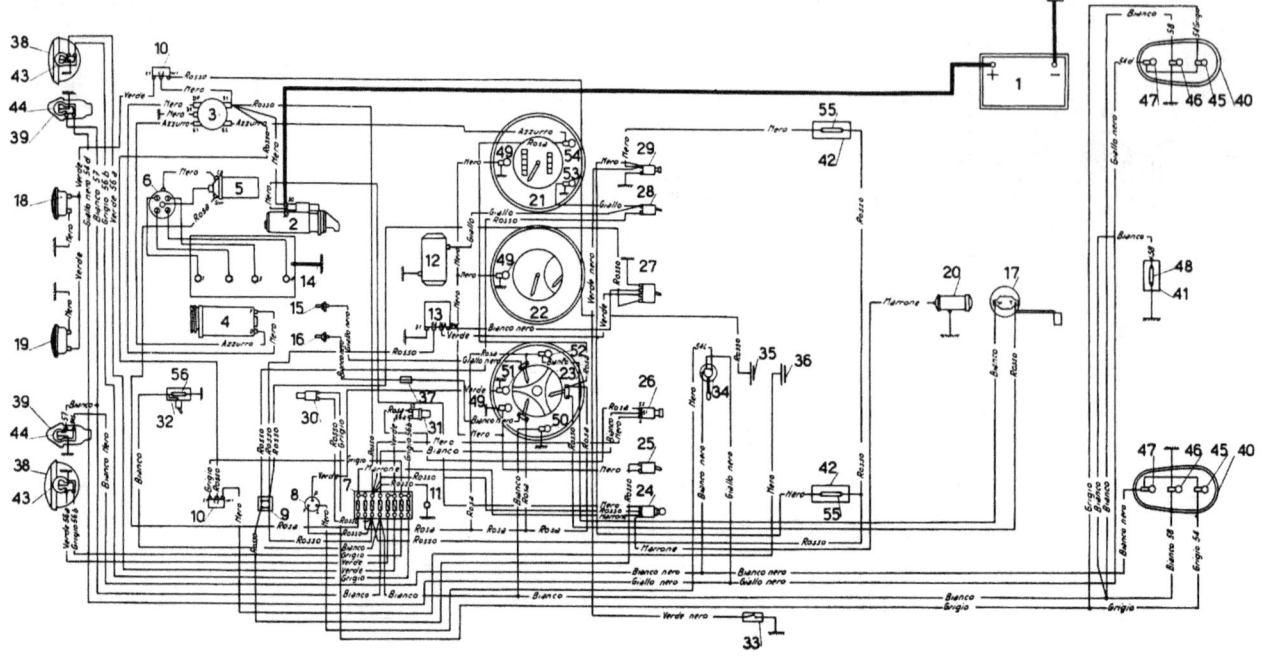

Fig. 5 - Circuit diagram of electric system (Giulietta Sprint Veloce and Spider Veloce).
Note - On Spider Veloce cars there is not the rooflight.

1. Battery.
2. Starter motor.
3. Control-box.
4. Generator.
5. Ignition coil.
6. Distributor.
7. Eight fuses box.
8. Automatic device for blinking.
9. Terminal board.
10. Electromagnetic change-over switch for trafficators.
11. Socket for inspection lamp.
12. Heater.
13. Windshield wiper motor.
14. Ground connection, engine to coach.
15. Bulb for water thermometer.
16. Bulb for oil thermometer.
17. Float of petrol level indicator.
18. Horn.
19. Horn.
20. Petrol pump.
21. Speedometer.
22. Revolution counter and oil gauge.
23. Oil and water thermometers and petrol gauge.
24. Ignition switch.
25. Switch for instrument panel lights.
26. Switch for headlamps and parking lights.
27. Switch for windshield wiper motor.
28. Switch for heater motor.
29. Rooflight switch.
30. Stop signal switch.
31. Pedal switch for headlamps lighting.
32. Bonnet light with switch.
33. Rooflight switch on door.
34. Trafficator switch.
35. Push-button for horn.
36. Push-button for headlights blinking.
37. Resistence in oil circuit.
38. Headlights.
39. Front lamps.
40. Rear lamps.
41. Rear license lamp.
42. Rooflight.
43. 12 V - 45 W - 40 W lamps for headlights.
44. 12 V - 3 W - 20 W lamps for front lamps.
45. 12 V - 20 W lamps for stop signal.
46. 12 V - 20 W lamps for parking lights.
47. 12 V - 20 W lamps for rear blinking lights.
48. 12 V - 5 W lamp for rear license plate.
49. 12 V - 2.5 W lamps for instrument panels lighting.
50. 12 V - 2.5 W tell-tale lamp for anti-dazzle lighting.
51. 12 V - 2.5 W tell-tale lamp for trafficators.
52. 12 V - 2.5 W tell-tale lamp for petrol reserve.
53. 12 V - 2.5 W tell-tale lamp for heater.
54. 12 V - 2.5 W tell-tale lamp for generator.
55. 12 V - 3 W lamp for rooflight.
56. 12 V - 3 W lamps for bonnet light.

Rosso	= Red	Giallo	= Yellow	Bianco	= White
Nero	= Black	Grigio	= Grey	Marrone	= Brown
Azzurro	= Blue	Verde	= Green	Rosa	= Pink
Bianco-nero	= Black and white		Giallo-nero	= Black and yellow	

GENERATOR

1 - GENERAL

The C 39 PV-2 Lucas generator is of the 2-brush, two-pole, shunt-wound type designed to operate in conjunction with a control box unit. A fan, integral with the driving pulley, directs a stream of cold air over the dynamo through inlet and outlet vents provided in the dynamo end covers.

The output from the dynamo is controlled by the control box and is dependent on the state of the battery charge and the load due to the electrical equipment. When the battery is discharged, the output is high, but when the battery is fully charged the output is reduced to a rate sufficient to maintain the charge while preventing any possibility of over-charging.

The control box also provides for an increased output when necessary to make good the current drawn by the lamps or other accessories in operation, and also for a large increase in the charge for several minutes immediately after the self-starter has been used.

2 - NORMAL MAINTENANCE

Lubrication

Every 10.000 Kms. (6.000 miles) inject a few drops of medium-viscosity (S.A.E. 30) engine oil through the hole marked « OIL » at the armature bearing-support end on the commutator side (Fig. 7).

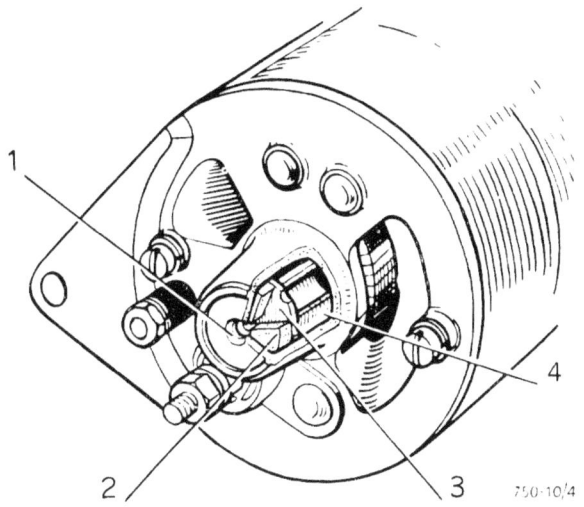

Fig. 7 - Dynamo lubrication.
1. Oil hole - 2. Felt washer - 3. Aluminium plate - 4. Porous bronze bush.

Inspecting the commutator and brushes

Remove the metal cover to inspect the brushes and the commutator.

Make sure that the brushes move freely in their holders; for this purpose, push back the brush springs and carefully pull on the flexible leads (Fig. 8). If a brush tends to stick in its holder, draw it out and clean its sides with a rag moistened in petrol. Make sure that each brush is returned to its own position in order to ensure that no changes have been made.

Any brushes which have worn shorter than 8.5 mm. must be replaced.

The commutator must be kept clean, bright and free of oil. If found to be dirty, it should be cleaned by pressyng against it a soft, dry rag while rotating the armature slowly by hand. If the commutator is very dirty, moisten the rag with petrol.

Adjusting belt tension

Check the belt tension from time to time, and adjust it if necessary to correct any undue slackness. Take care to avoid overtightening the belt; the tension should be just sufficient to prevent belt slip.

Make sure that the dynamo is properly lined up with the engine centre line as there would otherwise be excessive stress on the bearings. (See also Part 2).

3 - OPERATING CHARACTERISTICS

Speed at which charging begins: 1050-1200 r.p.m. with the 13 V dynamo.

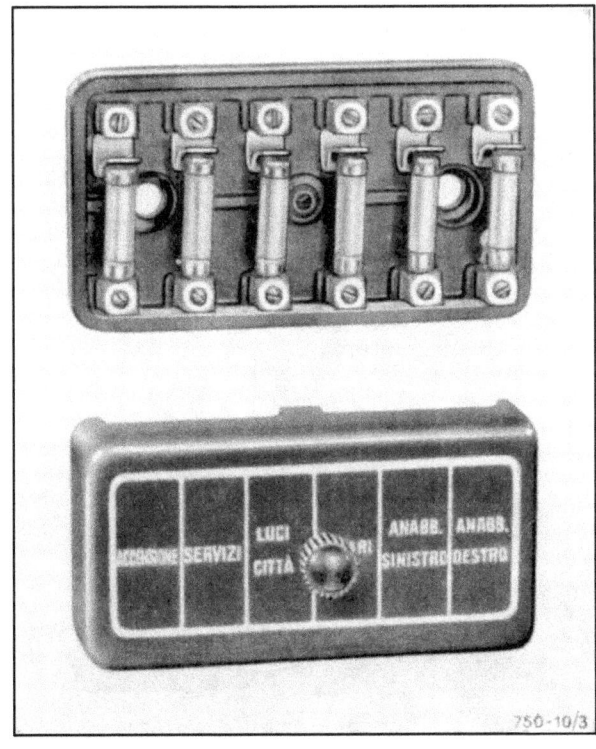

Fig. 6 - Fuse box.

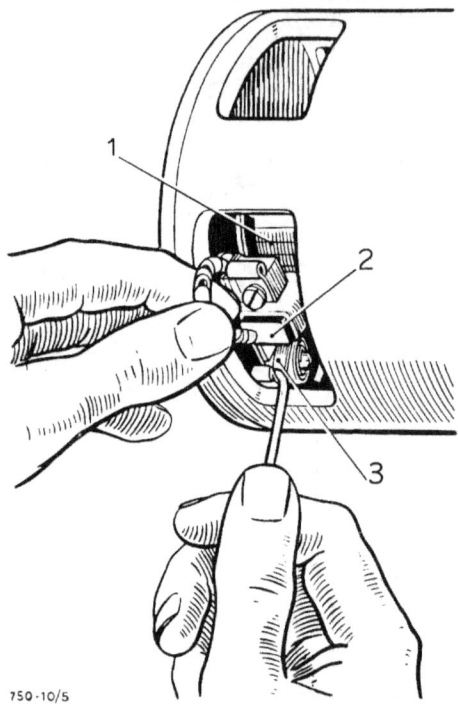

Fig. 8 - Inspecting the dynamo commutator and brushes.
1. Commutator - 2. Brush - 3. Brush spring.

Maximum output: 19 amps for 1900-2150 r.p.m. at 13.5 V and with the dynamo connected into a charging resistance of 0.7 ohms.

Field resistance: approximately 6 ohms.

4 - FAULTS AND REPAIRS

a) **Locating charging circuit faults**
Proceed as follows:

1) Check the belt tension and adjust it if necessary.

2) Check that the dynamo and the control box are properly connected. Make sure that the larger dynamo terminal is connected to terminal **D** on the control box, that the smaller dynamo terminal is connected to terminal **F**, and that terminal **E** on the control box is connected to earth.

3) Disconnect all lamps and accessories, detach the leads from the dynamo terminals and short-circuit the two screw terminals by means of a piece of wire.

4) Run the engine at the normal idling speed.

5) Connect the negative lead of a moving-coil voltmeter (with a range of 0 to 20 volts) to one dynamo terminal and the other lead to any well-earthed part of the dynamo casing.

6) Gradually accelerate the engine in such a way that the swing of the voltmeter pointer is fast and uniform; the voltmeter must not be allowed to reach 20 volts, nor must the engine speed be increased too much in order to achieve an increase in voltage; it is sufficient to revolve the dynamo at a speed of 1000 r.p.m.

If the voltmeter gives no indication, check the brushes as shown in the following paragraph.

If the meter reading is low (approximately ½ to 1 volt) the field coil is probably faulty (see paragraph 4e). If the voltmeter shows approximately half the nominal voltage, the armature winding is probably faulty (see paragraph 4d).

7) Remove the inspection cover and check brushes and commutator. Pull back the spring retaining each brush and withdraw the brush by pulling gently on the flexible lead. (Fig. 8).

If the brush is too tight a fit, withdraw it and file its sides slightly with a very smooth file; when re-fitting the brush make sure thet it is returned to its original position.

II as a result of wear a brush is less than 8.5 mm. long it must be replaced, as any further

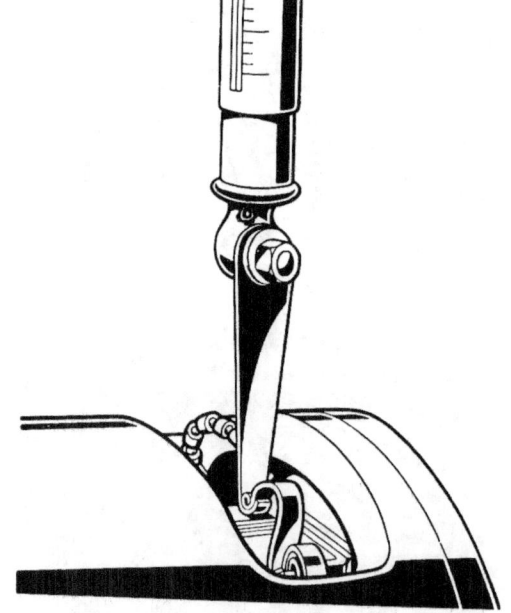

Fig. 9 - How to use the spring tension tester.

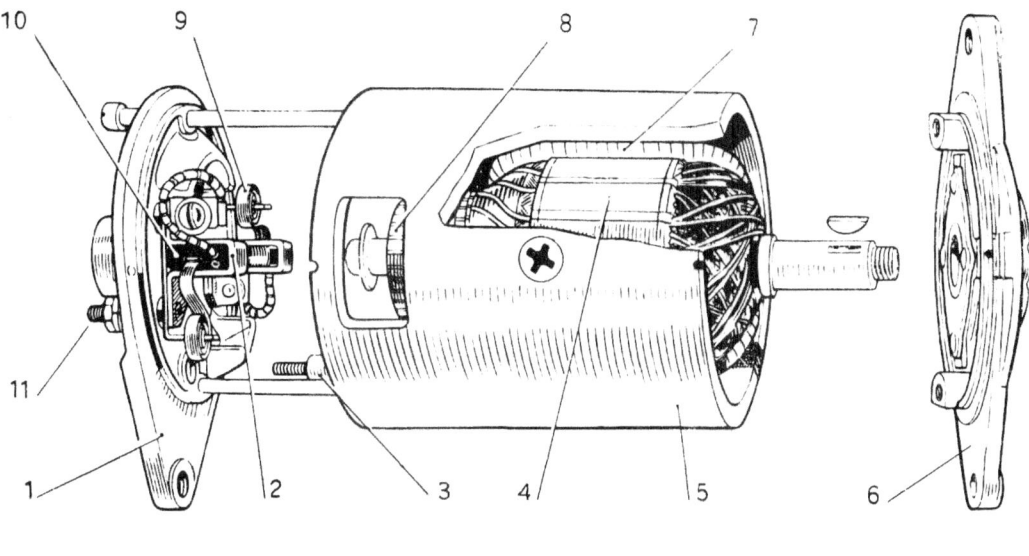

Fig. 10 - Dynamo details.

1. Brush-holder end-plate - **2.** Brush holder - **3.** Terminal to be connected to terminal **F** on the control box - **4.** Armature - **5.** Casing - **6.** Driving side end-plate - **7.** Field coil - **8.** Commutator - **9.** Brush-retaining spring - **10.** Brush - **11.** Terminal to be connected to terminal **D** on the control box.

wear would bring the flexible lead into contact with the commutator and damage it.

Check the tension exerted by the brush-holder spring with a spring tension tester (see Fig. 9); the tension of a new spring is 625 to 710 grammes but after a long period of use, it may fall to 425 grammes below which figure it should be replaced.

If the commutator is blackened or dirty, clean it by pressing against it a rag moistened with petrol while slowly turning the armature round by and.

Again check the dynamo as described in paragraph 6. If there is still no reading on the voltmeter, the cause will be some defect which will involve dismantling the dynamo and inspecting it internally (see paragraph 4b).

8) If the dynamo is operating properly, remove the shortcircuiting wire from the terminals and re-make the original connections, taking care, of course, to connect the larger dynamo terminal **D** on the control box and the smaller dynamo terminal to terminal **F**.

b) **Dismantling**

1) Remove the driving pulley.

2) Remove the inspection cover, raise the brush-retaining springs and remove the brushes from their holders.

3) Slacken and remove the through-bolts.

4) Remove the commutator-side end-plate from the dynamo casing; take care not to lose the fibre thrust washer.

5) Slide off the drive-side end-plate together with the armature.

6) The drive-side end-plate, after having been pulled away from the dynamo casing together with the armature and the ball-bearing, need not be drawn off the shaft unless damage to the bearing is suspected (requiring inspection of the bearing) or unless the armature must be replaced. In this event the armature can be withdrawn from the end-plate by pressing it out with the hand.

c) **Commutator**

To be in perfect working order a commutator must be smooth and free from scratches or burned areas.

Clean the commutator with a rag moistened in petrol; if that is insufficient, press fine glass-paper lightly against it while rotating it.

a Correct

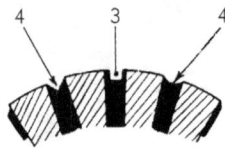
b Incorrect

Fig. 11 - Undercutting the insulating separators between the commutator segments.

1. Insulation - 2. Segment - 3. and 4. Incorrect undercutting.

To true-up an excessively worn commutator, mount the armature (with or without the drive-side endplate) on a lathe, revolve it at high sped and skim it up with a very sharp tool; do not remove more metal than is absolutely necessary.

Undercut the insulating separators between the commutator segments (Fig. 11) to a depth of 0.75 mm., using a hand saw (Fig. 12).

d) **Armature**

Testing the armature winding involves the use of instruments for measuring the voltage drop and checking short-circuits; when such instruments are not available the armature must be replaced.

In no case should the armature core be machined, nor should a bent armature shaft be straightened.

To remove the armature from the drive-side endplate and from the bearing, firmly hold the plate carrying the bearings and withdraw the shaft from the bracket by prising it out.

e) **Field Coils**

Measure the resistance of the field coils (without removing them from the dynamo casing) with an ohmmenter connected between the field terminals and the casing.

The ohmmeter should register approximately 6 ohms; if no ohmmeter is available, connect a 12 V D.C. source between the field terminals and the dynamo casing with an ammeter in series; the ammeter should register about 2 amps.

If the ammeter indicates « zero » or if the ohmmeter shows « infinity », there is a break in the field coil. If on the other hand the ammeter indicates values higher than 2 amps, or if the ohmmeter reading is less than 6.2 ohms, the field coil insulation is damaged.

In either case, unless another dynamo casing in good order is available, the field coils must be replaced; replacement is effected as follows:

1) Remove the rivet which secures the end of the field coil to the dynamo casing and unsolder the connections.

2) Remove the piece of insulating material which prevents the field coil ends from earthing against the dynamo casing.

3) Suitably mark the dynamo casing and the pole shoes so that the latter can be returned to their original positions.

4) Using a suitable hand-wheel operated screwdriver, remove the two screws which retain the pole shoes.

5) Remove the pole shoes and coils from the casing and slide the coils off the pole shoes.

6) Fit the new field coils on the pole shoes and return them to the dynamo casing, taking care that the insulating binding round the field coils does not entangle with the pole shoes and the casing.

7) Place the pole shoes and field coils in position and slightly tighten the fixation screws.

8) Using a hand-wheel operated screwdriver (Fig. 10), tighten up the fixing screws and seal them with some suitable compound.

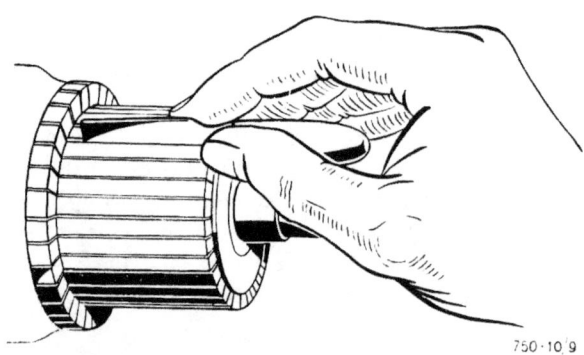

Fig. 12 - Undercutting the insulating separators between the commutator segments.

9) Replace the insulating material between the field coil connections and the dynamo case.

10) Solder the field coil terminals to the connections and rivet the whole unit to the dynamo casing.

f) **Ball-bearings and bushes**

Ball-bearings and bushes must be replaced if they become worn to such an extent as to allow lateral movement of the armature shaft.

To change the bush on the commutator side, proceed as follows:

— run a 3/8 in. screw tap a short distance into the bush and then withdraw the two together, taking care not to damage the end-plate.

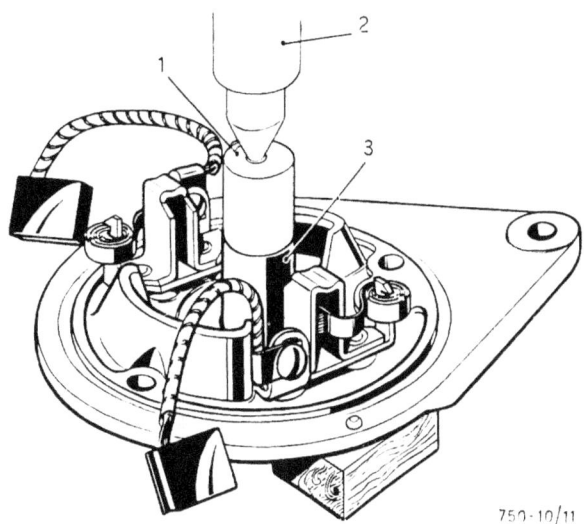

Fig. 14 - Inserting the bush in the brush-holder support.
1. Mandrel with accurately machined shoulder - 2. Hand press. - 3. Porous bronze bush.

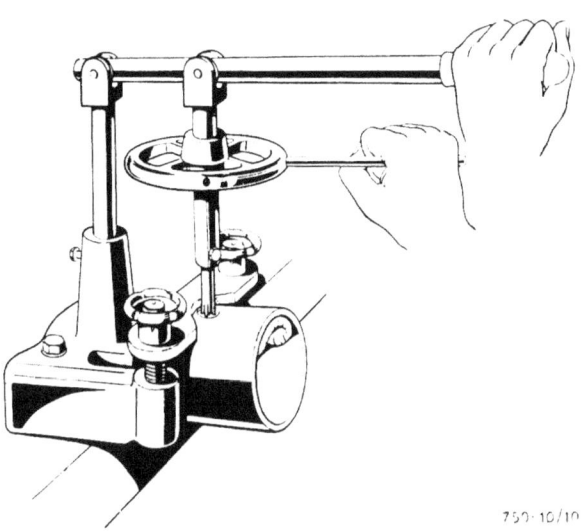

Fig. 13 - Tightening the pole shoe attachment screws.

The drive-side ball bearing is replaced as follows (Fig. 12):

1) Remove the rivets securing the ball-bearing retention plate to the end-plate and then detach the plate.

2) Press the ball-bearing out of its seating and remove the corrugated washer, the felt ring and the oil-seal.

3) Before fitting the new bearing, make sure that it is absolutely clean and smear it with high melting-point grease.

4) Fit the oil-seal, the felt ring and the corrugated washer in the bearing seating in the end-plate.

Place the felt washer and the aluminium plate in the seating in the end-plate and then insert the new bush; to do this use a pressure pad with an accurately finished shoulder (Fig. 14); the pressure pad must have the same diameter as the shaft which will run in the bush. The bush will be absolutely flush with the inner face.

WARNING: The porous bronze bush must not be reamed out after being inserted or its porosity may be affected. Prior to its insertion the new bush must be immersed in engine oil for 24 hours to allow the pores of the bush to absorb the oil.

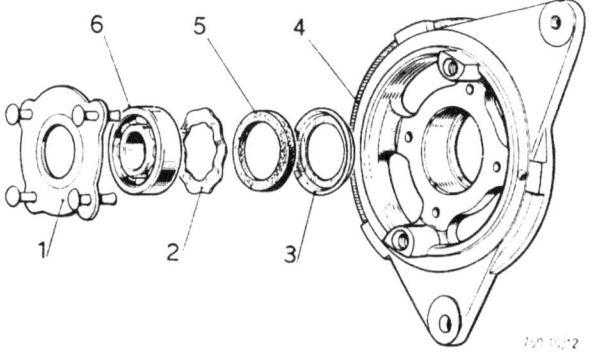

Fig. 15 - Exploded view of the drive-side bracket and bearing.
1. Bearing retention plate - 2. Corrugated washer - 3. Oil-seal - 4. End-plate - 5. Felt ring - 6. Ball bearing.

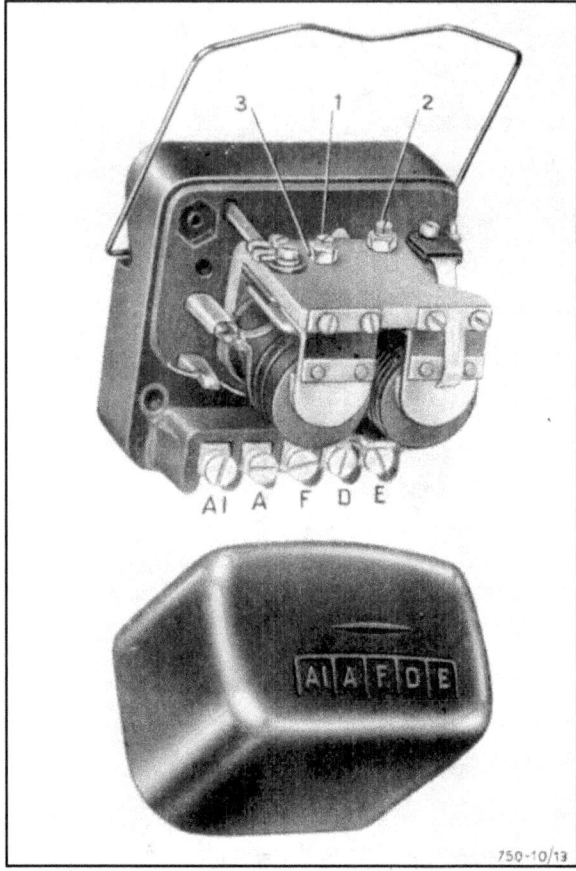

Fig. 16 - Control box.

1. Voltage adjustment screw - **2.** Screw for adjusting voltage of under-voltage connection and disconnection control - **3.** Lock-nut.

5) Place the ball bearing in its seating.

6) Replace the bearing retention plate; insert the new rivets from inside the end-plate and rivet them over with a punch so that the plate is held firmly.

g) **Re-assembly**

When re-assembling the dynamo proceed in the reverse order to that described in paragraph 4b above. After assembly, lubricate the bush on the commutator side and the ball-bearing; see paragraph 2 for the procedure to be adopted.

CONTROL BOX

1 - GENERAL

The Lucas RB 106-1 control box illustrated in Fig. 16 consists of two units; a voltage regulator and an under-voltage cut-out. Although mounted in a single unit, the regulator and the cut-out are electrically separate.

Both are correctly set at the factory, and the protective cover should not be removed unnecessarily.

The regulator

The regulator is set to maintain an almost constant voltage at the dynamo terminals at all speeds above that at which battery-charging begins, with the field current controlled by the automatic cutting in and out of a resistance in the dynamo field circuit.

When the dynamo voltage reaches a predetermined value, the magnetic flux in the regulator core (due to the shunt or voltage windings) becomes sufficiently strong to attract the armature towards the core.

This causes the contacts to open, thereby inserting the resistance into the generator field circuit.

The resulting reduced field current lowers the voltage at the dynamo terminals and this in turn weakens the magnetic flux in the regulator core. The armature thereupon returns to its initial position and the contacts close, thus again increasing the dynamo voltage to its maximum value.

This cycle is then repeated; the armature is kept in a state of oscillation with the result that the dynamo voltage is constant.

When the generator speed exceeds the speed at which the regulator comes into operation, the frequency with which the contacts open and close increases with the result that the average dynamo voltage remains practically the same as soon as this rotation speed is reached.

The series (or current) winding has a conpensating effect on the control system since if control were arranged entirely on the basis of voltage there would be a risk of seriously overloading the generator when the battery was in its discharged condition, particularly if all the lights were on.

When the battery voltage is very low, the output for the dynamo to the battery increases; if it were not for the series (or current) winding, the dynamo working voltage would then be much greater than normal.

The magnetism due to the series winding then helps the shunt winding so that, when the dynamo supplies an appreciable current to the battery, the regulator comes into action at a somewhat lower voltage, thus limiting the output from the generator.

As shown in Fig. 17, which illustrates a split series winding, terminal **A** is connected to the battery and terminal **A 1** to the lighting and ignition switch.

By adding a temperature-compensation device, the voltage characteristics of the dynamo can be varied in such a way as to adapt themselves more closely to the battery demand whatever the climatic conditions.

In cold weather the voltage required to charge the battery increases, whilst in warm weather the voltage of the battery is lower.

The compensation device consists of a bi-metallic spring mounted behind the tension spring on the regulator armature. Since the bi-metallic spring controls the voltage increase in cold weather and the voltage drop in hot weather, it compensates the battery characteristics which vary with the temperature, and prevents any abnormal fluctuation in the charging current.

The bi-metallic spring also compensates the effects caused by the increased resistance of the copper windings under low temperature conditions.

The cut-out

This cut-out is an electro-magnetic switch connected in the charging circuit between the dynamo and the battery. It is designed to connect the dynamo automatically to the battery when the dynamo voltage is sufficient to charge the latter, and to disconnect it when the dynamo is stationary or when its voltage falls below the battery voltage level, thus preventing the battery from discharging and protecting the dynamo windings from damage.

The cut-out consists of an electro-magnet provided with an armature which operates a pair of contacts.

The electro magnet has two windings, the shunt winding with many turns of thin wire, and the series winding comprising only a few turns of thicker wire.

The contacts are normally held apart and only close when the pull of the magnet on the armature is sufficient to overcome the tension of the adjusting spring, that is, when the voltage generated by the dynamo is greater than the battery voltage.

The under-voltage cut-out operates as follows:

The shunt coil is connected to the dynamo. When the vehicle is started the engine speed (and thus the dynamo voltage) increased until the electromagnet is sufficiently magnetised to overcome the tension of the spring and to close the cut-out contacts. This in turn closes the circuit between the battery and the dynamo via the cut-out and the contacts.

The charging current which passes through the cut-out windings creates a magnetic field which follows

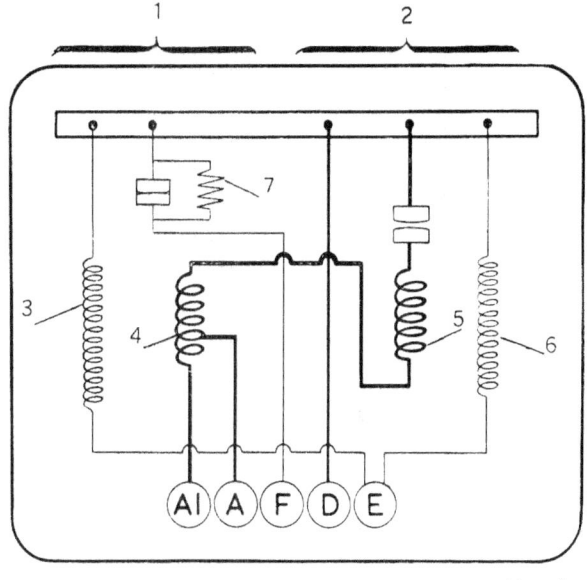

Fig. 17 - Diagram of control-box.

1. Regulator - 2. Cut-out - 3. Regulator shunt coil - 4. Regulator series coil - 5. Cut-out series coil - 6. Cut-out shunt coil - 7. Field resistance.

the same direction as that produced by the shunt winding.

This phenomenon causes the pull on the armature to increase so that the contacts remain firmly closed; they cannot be separated by vibration.

When the vehicle stops, the dynamo speed falls until its voltage is less than the battery voltage; current then passes from the battery, through the cut-out series winding, to the dynamo in the opposite direction to that taken by the charging current; this reverse current will produce a differential effect between the two windings and will partly demagnetise the electromagnet.

The spring which is under constant tension then pulls off the armature and separates it from the magnet thus opening the circuit. Opening the contacts prevents any further discharge from the battery through the dynamo.

A bi-metallic spring is provided for minimising temperature effects both on the cut-out and on the regulator itself.

2 - ADJUSTMENT DATA

a) **Regulator**

Open circut setting at 20°C and with the dynamo turning at 1500 r.p.m., 15.6 to 16.2 V.

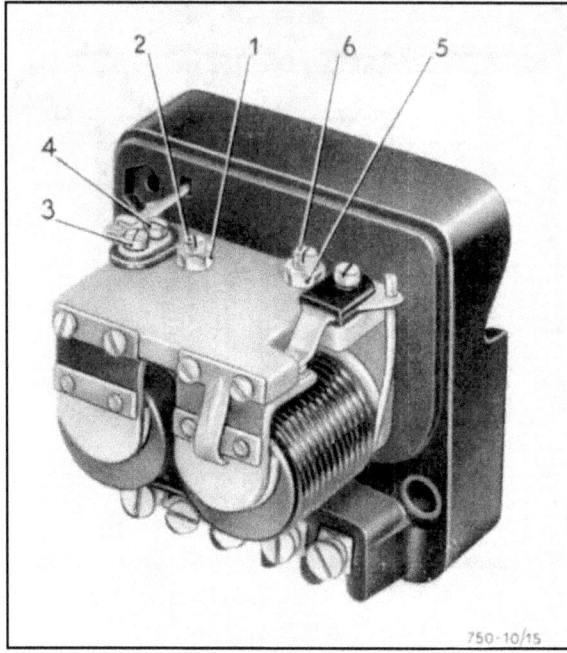

Fig. 18 - Control box.

1. Lock-nut for the voltage-regulating screw - **2**. Voltage-regulating screw - **3**. and **4**. Fixed regulator contact securing screws - **5** and **6**. Cut-out screw and lock-nut.

NOTE: If the ambient temperature is other than 20°C, the following allowances must be observed when making the above adjustment:

— **For every 10°C above 20°C, deduct 0.3 V.**
— **For every 10°C below 20°C, add 0.3 V.**

b) **Cut-out**

Cut-in voltage: 12.7 to 13.3 V.
Drop-off voltage: 8.5 to 11 V.
Reverse current: 3.5 to 5 Amp.

3 - LOCATING AND REPAIRING FAULTS

a) **Locating faults in the charging circuit**

If the generator and battery are in order, check as follows:

1) Make sure that the connections between the battery and the regulator are in order; for this purpose disconnect the wire from the terminal **A** on the control box and connect it to the negative terminal of a voltmeter.

Connect the positive terminal of the voltmeter to a suitable earthing point on the chassis. If the voltmeter pointer moves, the connection is sound, and the fault must then be sought in the regulator itself.

2) If the voltmeter pointer does not move, examine the connections, between the battery and the control box, for defective cables or loose connections.

3) Re-connect the lead to terminal **A**.

b) **Adjusting the regulator**

The regulator is accurately adjusted at the factory, and as a general rule no further adjustment should be necessary after it has been set.

If, however, the battery does not maintain its charge, or if the output from the dynamo does not drop off when the battery is fully charged, the setting must be checked, and, if necessary, corrected.

Before starting to adjust the regulator setting, make sure that the failure to charge is not due to some defect in the battery itself or to a slipping fan belt.

1) **Electrical adjustment**

When inspecting the regulator it is essential that a highly sensitive **moving-coil voltmeter** be used (0-20 Volts). The electrical check can be made without removing the control box cover.

Disconnect the cables from terminals **A** and **A1** on the control box, and connect the two together.

Connect the negative voltmeter lead to terminal **D** on the control box and the other lead to terminal **E**.

Slowly increase the engine speed until the voltmeter pointer first oscillates and then remains steady; this should occur when the reading on the instrument is between the limits given in paragraph 2a, according to the ambient temperature.

If the instrument readings are outside these limits, the regulator requires adjustment.
Stop the engine and remove the control box cover.

Slacken nut **1** (Fig. 18) on adjusting screw **2** and turn the screw clockwise to increase the voltage or anticlockwise to reduce it. The screw should only be given a fraction of a turn; the lock-nut should be tightened.

Repeat the above procedure several times until the correct reading is obtained.

The measurement of the open-circuit regulator voltage must be completed within 30 seconds otherwise the shunt windings will overheat and give incorrect readings.

Re-make the connections as before.

A dynamo which runs at high speed generates a high voltage; for this reason take care not to run the engine with the throttle more than half open when checking the regulator.

2) **Mechanical adjustment**

Measure the regulator air gap as shown in Fig. 19; the gap is correctly set before the instrument leaves the factory and, unless the armature which carries the moving contact has been tampered with, it requires no further adjustment.

If, however, the armature has been tampered with, the instrument must be re-set as follows:

Slacken the two screws holding the armature and the adjusting screw **2** (Fig. 15); then insert an 0.5 mm. feeler-gauge between the rear of the armature and the regulator bracket; the width of the gap should as shown at **A** (Fig. 19) vary from 0.45 to 0.46 mm.

With the feeler-gauge in position, press the armature against the regulator frame and tighten the two screws which secure the armature in position.

Remove the feeler-gauge and check the gap between the face of the armature and the top of the core.

This gap **B** (Fig. 19) must be between 0.3 and 0.5 mm. If these limits are exceeded the gap should be corrected by carefully bending the fixed contact bracket.

Remove the feeler-gauge and press the armature downwards; the gap **C** (Fig. 19) between the contacts must now be 0.15 to 0.43 mm.

3) **Cleaning the contacts**

After long periods of operation, it may become

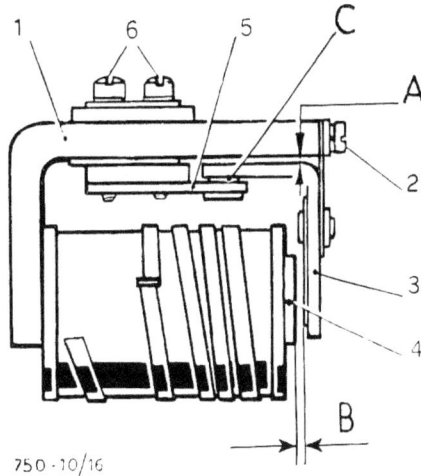

Fig. 19 - Adjusting the regulator.

1. Regulator bracket - **2.** Armature retaining screws - **3.** Armature - **4.** Core - **5.** Fixed contact - **6.** Fixed contact retaining screws - **A.** Gap between armature and bracket: 0.45 to 0.46 mm. - **B.** Gap between armature and core: 0.3 to 0.5 mm - **C.** Gap between contacts: 0.15 to 0.43 mm.

necessary to clean the contacts. Access can be obtained to them by slackening the screws holding the fixed contact; it will be necessary to slacken screw **3** slightly more than screw **4** (Fig. 18) so that the contact arm may be moved outwards. Clean the contacts, using a fine grain carborundum stone or very fine emery cloth.

Carefully remove any traces of dust or other foreign matter, using methylated spirit.

Re-fit the fixed contact bracket and tighten up the holding-down screws.

c) **Adjusting the cut-out**

1) **Electrical Adjustment**

If after the regulator has been correctly set the battery still does not charge, it may be that the cut-out is not properly adjusted.

In order to check the voltage at which the cut-out operates, remove the control box cover and connect the voltmeter across terminals **D** and **E** (Fig. 16).

Start the engine and slowly increase its speed until the cut-out contacts are seen to close. At that point note the voltage shown on the instrument; it should be between 12.7 and 13.3 V.

If the cut-out contacts close at some voltage outside the above limits, the switch requires adjustment as follows:

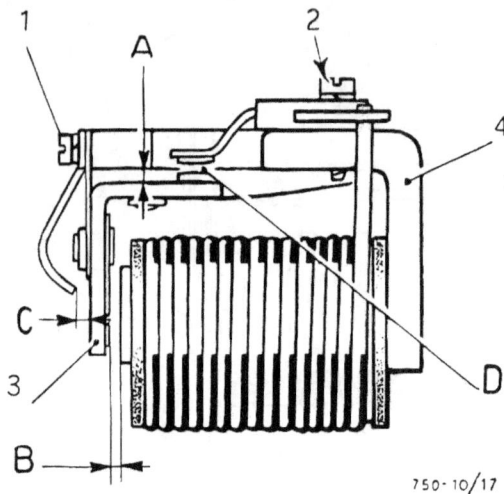

Fig. 20 - Adjusting the cut-out.

1. Armature retaining screws - 2. Screws retaining the fixed contacts. 3. Armature - 4. Bracket - **A.** Gap between the armature and bracket: 0.35 mm - **B.** Gap between armature and core: 0.29 to 0.38 mm - **C.** Gap between armature and stop: 0.76 to 0.86 mm - **D.** Gap between contacts: 0.05 to 0.15 mm (with an 0.63 mm feeler-gauge between armature and core).

Slacken lock-nut **5** (Fig. 15) and turn screw **6** clockwise to increase the voltage or anti-clockwise to reduce it; give the screw a fraction of a turn only and tighten lock-nut **5**.

After each adjustment, increase the engine speed and note the voltmeter reading at the moment the cut-out contacts close.

These electrical settings (as in the case of the regulator) must be made as quickly as possible because of temperature rise effects.

If the cut-out fails to operate the cause may be an interruption in the cut-out and regulator connections. The whole unit must then be removed and examined or replaced.

2) Mechanical adjustment

If for any reason it should be necessary to remove the cut-out armature from the frame, care must be taken when re-assembling it to ensure that the gap (Fig. 20) is correct. The following procedure should be adopted:

Slacken the two screws which secure the armature, the adjusting screw **6** (Fig. 18) and the fixed contact retaining screw. Insert an 0.35 mm. feeler gauge in space **A** (Fig. 20) between the rear of the armature and the frame.

The air-gap **B** between the front face of the core and the armature must be 0.29 to 0.38 mm. If this is not the case, fit a new armature. Press the armature against the feeler-gauge and tighten the armature fixing screws **1** (Fig. 20) with the feeler-gauge still in place; bring the gap **C** between the armature and the stop to 0.76 to 0.86 mm. by carefully bending the stop plate.

Remove the feeler-gauge and tighten the fixed contact retaining screw.

Insert an 0.63 mm. feeler-gauge between the core face and the armature. Press the armature against the feeler-gauge; the distance **D** (Fig. 20) between the contacts must be 0.05 to 0.15 mm. and the voltage must be within the limits shown in paragraph 2b. If it should be necessary to adjust the gap between the contacts, carefully bend over the fixed contact blade.

3) Cleaning the contacts

If the cut-out contacts are found to be roughned or burnt, rub a sheet of fine glass-paper between them; this should be repeated several times, the rough side of the paper being turned towards each contact in turn. Then remove any trace of powder or other foreign matter, using a hair-free rag dipped in methylated spirit.

Do not use emery cloth or carborundum stone when cleaning cut-out contacts.

STARTER MOTOR

1 - GENERAL

The Lucas M 325 starter motor (Fig. 21) is a 4-brush, 4-pole type with a pinion designed to mesh with the flywheel gear-ring before the armature torque develops.

An extension of the armature shaft carries a starter-pinion assembly controlled by a lever.

In the event of failure to mesh, and because the teeth on the pinion would then strike against those on the flywheel ring, a spring is compressed while the starter motor control lever cuts off the current so that the armature may rotate thus allowing the pinion to mesh with the crown ring.

The motor is prevented from over-running by a roller clutch incorporated in the drive assembly. This clutch ensures that torque is transmitted from the motor to the flywheel but not inversely; this means that should the pinion remain in mesh with the flywheel after the engine has started, no damage will be done to the starter motor.

The drive assembly require no servicing; if faulty it must be replaced complete.

The cover on the commutator side contains a braking device comprising two friction discs, one solid with the end plate and the other with the armature.

A return spring on the control lever causes the two discs to rub aginst each other, thus stopping the armature quickly as soon as the lever is released.

Operation

When the starter motor is operated, a forked lever presses the drive assembly outwards and along the thread cut on the armature shaft so that the pinion engages with the flywheel ring; the final movement of the forked lever operates a switch located on the starter motor.

Closing the switch contacts connects the starter motor to the battery; the armature then rotates, thus initiating the starting phase.

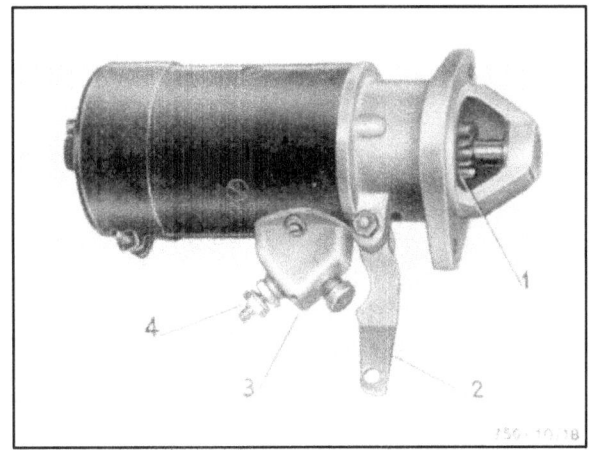

Fig. 21 - The starter motor.

1. Pinion - 2. Pinion drive lever - 3. Switch - 4. Terminal leading to the negative battery pole.

When the engine fires and the forked lever is released, the switch contacts open and the drive assembly returns to the « disengaged » position.

The pressure of the friction disc keyed to the armature against the disc fixed to the end-plate on the commutator side quickly brings the starter motor to a standstill.

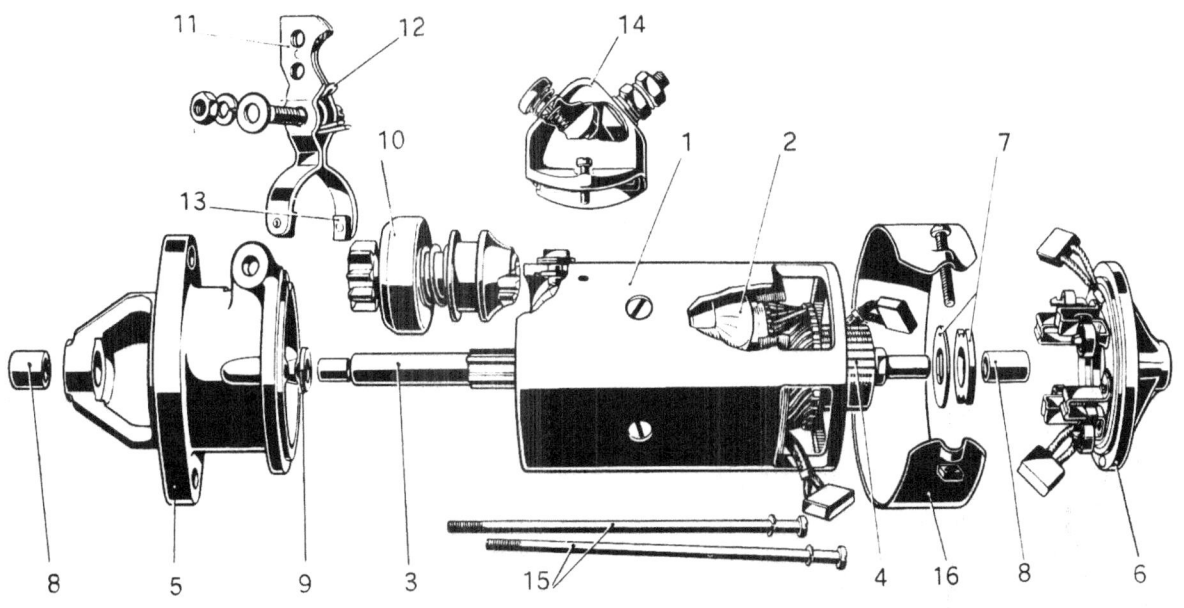

Fig. 22 - Exploded view of the starter motor.

1. Casing - 2. Field coil - 3. Armature shaft - 4. Commutator - 5. Drive end bracket - 6. Commutator end cover - 7. Friction discs - 8. Porous bronze bush for the armature shaft - 9. Thrust washer - 10. Drive assembly - 11. Forked lever - 12. Return spring - 13. Shoes - 14. Switch - 15. Through-bolts - 16. Cover band assembly.

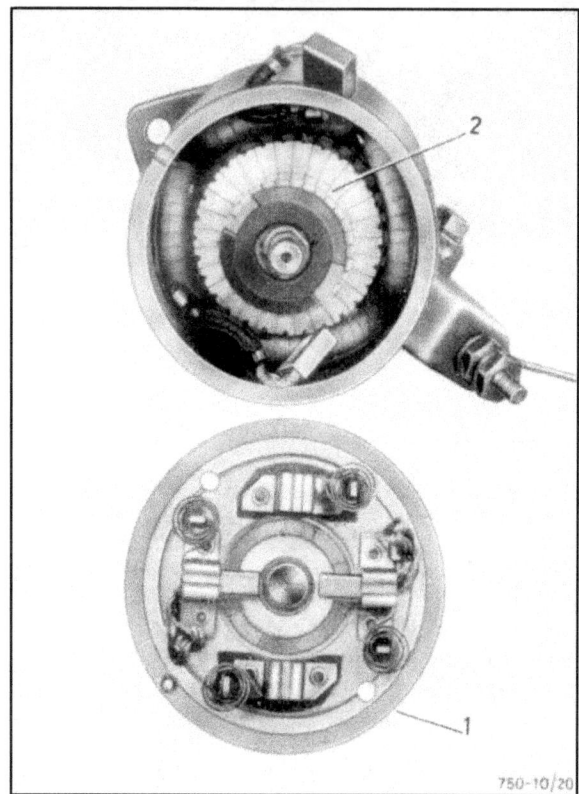

Fig. 23 - End views of the starter motor.
1. Front cover, with the positive brushes (earthed) and the brush springs - **2.** Commutator and negative brushes (insulated).

2 - OPERATING CHARACTERISTICS

Maximum torque	1.27 kgm.
Current	400 Amp.
Starter terminal voltage	9 V.
Torque at 1000 r.p.m.	0.795 kgm.
Current	200 Amp.
Starter terminal voltage	9.9 V.

3 - NORMAL MAINTENANCE

The only maintenance the starter motor requires is the checking, approximately once every six months, of the brush-holders and the commutator. This is better done after temporarily removing the starter motor from the engine.

Clean the outside of the motor before removing the metal cover band.

Check to ensure that the brushes move freely in their holders; this can be done by raising the brush springs and pulling lightly on the flessible leads.

If a brush tends to stick, remove it from its holder and clean the sides with a rag moistened with petrol. Take care to return the brush to the exact position it occupied previously so as to maintain the original assembly arrangement. Any brushes which are worn to such an extent that they are less than 9.5 mm. in lenght must be replaced.

Any oil or dirt must be wiped off the commutator. If it is dirty, clean it by pressing a soft rag against it while the armature is rotated by hand from the pinion end. If the commutator is very dirty, dip the rag in petrol.

4 - INSPECTION AND REPAIR

a) **Testing the motor in position**

1) If the motor rotates but fails to start the engine the pinion assembly will be found to be worn; remove the starter motor for examination.

2) If the motor fails to rotate, connect a voltmeter (reading from 0 to 20 V) across the battery terminals (the battery must of course be well charged) and try to rotate the starter motor. If the voltmeter indicates approximately 6 volts, the inference is that though the current is passing through the motor windings, but that the armature will not rotate. Remove the motor for examination.

3) If the voltmeter shows a constant value of about 12 V when an attempt is made to start the motor, check whether the lead from the battery to the motor is damaged or disconnected. Verify the connections.

4) If the motor is sluggish, or only rotates at slow speed, the cause may be loose connections in the starter motor circuit.

To inspect the motor switch contacts, disconnect the motor cable from the switch and slacken the two retaining screws; the housing can then be lifted off the yoke and contacts examined.

b) **Test-bench checks and examination of brushes and commutator**

1) The following procedure should be adopted when removing the starter motor from the engine:

— Disconnect the battery to prevent short-circuiting.

— Disconnect the cable from the starter motor switch terminal.

— Free the motor lever from the other parts.

— Slacken the two securing bolts and remove the starter motor from the engine.

2) Place the starter motor in a vice and connect it by two suitable cables to a 12 V battery. One cable must go to the switch terminal and the other be held firmly against the case. Then press the motor switch. As there is no load on the motor it should spin freely at approximately 8500 r.p.m.

3) Should the motor not operate satisfactorily under the above conditions, remove the cover band and examine the brushes and the commutator.

Lift the spring on each brush and withdraw the brush by pulling gently on the flexible lead. It a brush is found to be sticky, pull it out of its holder and clean the sides with a very smooth file. Brushes must always be replaced in their own holders.

The minimum brush length permitted is 9.5 mm.

Check the brush spring tension with a spring tension tester. The correct tension is between 425 and 710 grammes; if less the spring should be replaced.

Blackened or dirty commutators must be cleaned by pressing a petrol-moistened rag against them while rotating the armature.

4) Again check the starter motor as described in paragraph 4b/2. If still unsatisfactory it must be dismantled and subjected to detailed inspection as follows.

c) **Dismantling**

1) Remove the cover band and, while lifting the brush springs, slide the brushes from their holders.

2) Screw out the two screws which hold the switch to the motor case, and remove the switch.

3) Screw out the two bolts holding the commutator side endplate; then remove the bracket together with the braking device from the casing.

4) Remove the end-plate on the pinion side, complete with the operating lever and the drive assembly on the armature shaft extension.

5) Slide the armature out of the casing.

d) **Brush replacement**

The flexible leads are soldered to terminal lugs; two leads are connected to the brush-holders and two to the free ends of the series field coils. Unsolder these flexible leads and solder them to new brushes.

The new brushes must first of all be bedded perfectly onto the commutator.

e) **Commutator**

If the commutator is in good working order it will be found to be bright, free from stains, scratches or burned patches. Clean it with a rag moistened in petrol. If that is insufficient, carefully polish with a strip of fine glass paper while rotating the armature; then remove all traces of abrasive powder with a blast of dry compressed air. (Never use emery paper).

If the commutator shows serious signs of wear, mount it on a lathe, rotate it at high speed and skim it up with a very sharp tool, taking care not to remove more metal than absolutely necessary then finish it off with very fine glass-paper.

The insulators between the commutator segments must not be beneath the level of the latter.

f) **Armature**

Causes of faulty operation can be traced by examining the armature.

1) If it is found that the armature conductors are higher than the commutator ends, the cause will be the excessive speed of the motor; the fault will lie in the drive assembly which should be replaced.

2) If the armature rubs against the pole shoes, this is due to worn bearings or a damaged armature shaft. If the armature is damaged, it must always be replaced. Never regrind it or straighten a damaged shaft.

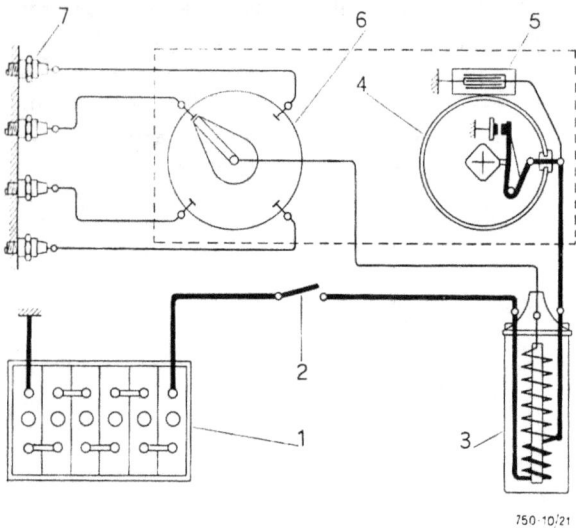

Fig. 24 - Ignition and battery circuit diagram.
1. Battery - 2. Switch - 3. Coil - 4. Contact breaker - 5. Condenser - 6. Distributor cover - 7. Sparking plugs.

g) Field coils

1) Check the continuity of the coils and make sure that there are no breaks; for this purpose use a 12-volt test bulb and a battery connected between the insulated contact switch on the casing and each brush (the armature and the switch are removed from the yoke).

Make sure that neither brush is in contact with the casing.

2) Use a lamp and connect the coil to the A.C. mains; check the insulation between the switch contact and the casing; remember that the voltage used must not exceed 110 V; insert a suitable transformer if necessary.

If the lamp lights up it means that the insulation between one or more coils is defective. To locate the defective coil, unsolder the joint connecting them to the terminal and check each coil individually; replace any found defective.

3) While carrying out the examination described in paragraph 2), also check the insulated pair of brush-holders located on the commutator terminal bracket after first removing any traces of carbon deposit.

Connect the 110 V test lamp between each insulated brush-holder and the bracket; if the lamp lights up, the insulation is defective and the bracket must be replaced.

h) Replacing motor end-plate bushes

The armature shaft is carried on two porous bronze bushes, one at each end.

If the bushes are worn to such an extent that they allow the armature shaft excessive end play, they must be replaced as follows:

1) The bush at the drive end can be removed by pressure; that on the commutator end can be easily removed by screwing a tap into the bush and then by removing the tap and the bush together.

2) New bushes are fitted by means of an accurately finished punch having the same diameter as that of the shaft over which the bush must be fitted.

The porous bronze bushes **must not be reamed out after they are fitted**, as such treatment would reduce their porosity.

**WARNING: Before fitting a new porous bronze bush, take care to soak it completely in clean engine oil (SAE, 30-40) for 24 hours.
In emergency the soaking period can be reduced by immersing the bush in oil a 100°C (212°F) for two hours, and allowing the oil to cool before removing the bush from the bath.**

i) Re-assembly

When all parts have been cleaned, the starter motor may be re-assembled by repeating the dismantling instructions in reverse; first of all, however, make quite sure that:

1) The friction discs on the braking device are in the same place as before the motor was dismantled;

2) The pivoted shoes on the fork pins must be returned to their original positions when re-assembling the operating fork unit;

3) The ends of the return-spring on the operating fork must be firmly positioned in the two slots in the end of the switch box; (this only applies if the fork has been removed).

IGNITION COIL

The ignition coil (Fig. 25) transforms the low voltage supplied by the battery (12 V) into a high tension current of 10,000 to 15,000 V.

It consists of two windings (primary and secondary)

would round a laminated mild steel core, and is housed in a metal casing filled with insulating material.

The cover, which is also in insulating material, is provided with two lateral low-tension terminals and one central high-tension terminal. One of the lateral terminals on the Lucas coil is marked « SW », and one end of the primary coil is connected to it; this terminal is connected to the battery via the ignition switch and the fuse-board. The lateral terminal marked CB (which takes the other end of the primary winding) is connected to the cable leading to the distributor contact-breaker.

NOTE: As soon as the engine stops the ignition key should be turned anti-clockwise to prevent serious damage being caused through overheating of the ignition coil.

DISTRIBUTOR

1 - GENERAL

The Lucas DM2 distributor (Fig. 27) comprises the contact-breaker, the capacitor, the centrifugal ignition advance device and the vacuum spark advance correcting unit.

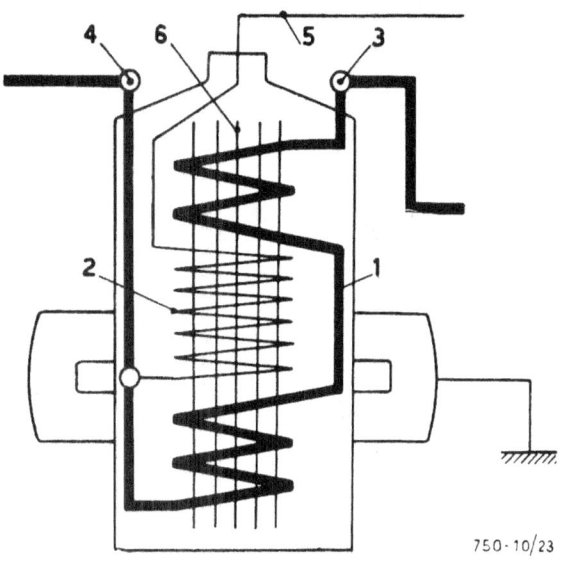

Fig. 26 - The ignition coil.

1. Primary winding - **2.** Secondary winding - **3.** Terminal to connect to ignition switch and battery - **4.** Terminal to connect to distributor contact-breaker - **5.** High-tension terminal - **6.** Core.

The centrifugal ignition advance device is mounted on the distributor shaft immediately above the contact-breaker. It consists of a pair of spring loaded governor weights connected by a lever to the contact-breaker cam. The centrifugal force — which increases as the engine speed rises — tends to separate the weights and counteract the effect of the return springs; the position of the contact-breaker in relation to the distributor shaft thus changes so that the ignition timing is advanced.

A vacuum operated timing control is also mounted on the distributor; it gives additional advance at part-throttle settings.

The engine inlet manifold is connected to the vacuum control the vacuum thus created depresses a diaphragm and through a lever mechanism causes the contact-breaker plate to turn around the driving shaft cam, thus advancing the spark when the engine is being run at partially-closed throttle settings.

There is also a micrometer adjustment for the fixed advance setting; this makes possible small changes of the distributor position; screwing in the micrometer screw retards the ignition, while screwing it out advances the spark.

The metallised paper capacitor is completely enclosed. Should the dielectric break down the metal film around the point of rupture is melted by the heat of the spark and thus prevents a permanent short-circuit. Defective capacitors are rare.

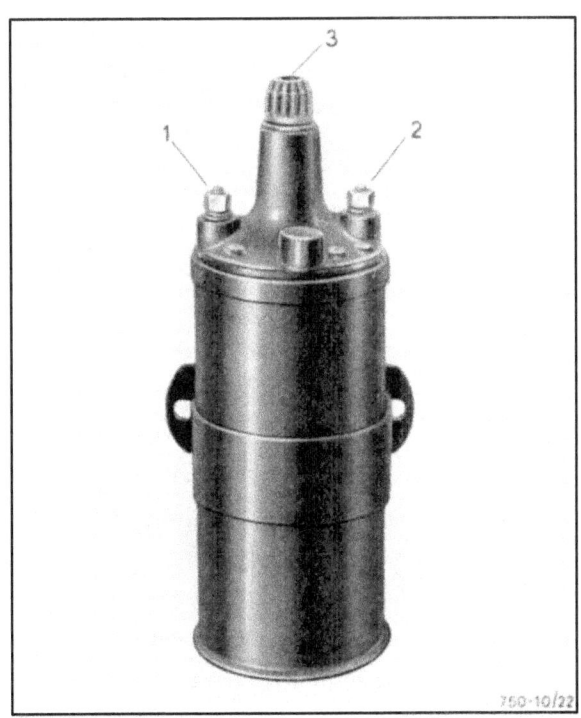

Fig. 25 - The ignition coil.

1. Terminal for cable leading to the ignition switch and to the battery - **2.** Terminal to connect to the distributor contact breaker - **3.** High-tension cable terminal.

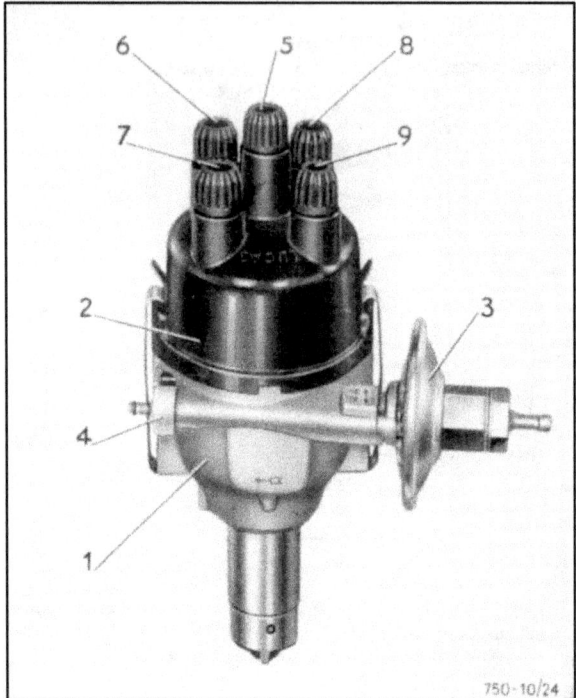

Fig. 27 - Lucas DM2 Distributor.
1. Body - **2.** Cover - **3.** Vacuum control unit - **4.** Knurled nut for minor distributor timing adjustments - **5.** High-tension terminal from coil - **6.** Cylinder No. 1 terminal - **7.** Cylinder No. 2 terminal - **8.** Cylinder No. 3 terminal - **9.** Cylinder No. 4 terminal.

The central carbon brush in the distributor cap is in two parts; the top is made of a tough composition while the bottom is of softer carbon to prevent wear on the rotor arm. The tougher part — which is in series with the coil and the distributor — reduces radio interference. Under no circumstances should the short, soft carbon be replaced with a long hard one.

2 - NORMAL MAINTENANCE

In general no attention other than lubrication and cleaning is necessary.

a) Lubrication (every 2,500 miles)

Inject several drops of thin engine oil through the aperture at the edge of the contact-breaker; this will lubricate the centrifugal advance device. Smear a little Mobilgrease No. 2 on the cam. Pull off the rotor arm and inject several drops of oil at the top of the camshaft. The screw need not be removed as a space is provided to allow oil to pass.

Take great care to prevent oil or grease from touching the contacts.

Carefully push on the rotor arm, making sure that the projection enters the slot provided on the spindle.

b) Cleaning (every 6,000 miles)

Wipe the inside and outside of the distributor cap with a soft dry cloth, paying particular attention to the spaces between the metal electrodes. Make sure that the small carbon brush works freely in its holder.

Then examine the contact-breaker. The contacts must be free from grease or oil. If they are burned or blackened, clean them with a fine carborundum stone or very fine emery cloth, afterwards wiping away any trace of dirt or metal dust with a petrol-moistened cloth. Cleaning the contacts is made easier if the contact breaker lever is removed. Before replacing the rotor arm, smear its spindle with Mobilgrease No. 2.

After cleaning, check the contact-breaker setting by turning the driving shaft until the contacts are opened to their widest positions (0.35 to 0.40 mm).

If the measurement is incorrect (with the engine in the position giving maximum contact opening) slacken the two screws which secure the fixed contact plate. Now move the plate and adjust its position to give the required gap. Tighten the screws an then re-check the gap in other contact-breaker positions.

WARNING: With a new car the contact-breaker gap should be adjusted after the first 500 miles, as during the running-in period the breaker arm contact beds down; after the first 500 miles contact wear is practically nil.

3 - CHARACTERISTIC DATA

a) Firing angles: 0°, 90°, 180°, 270°, ± 1°.
   Closing: 60° ± 3°
   Opening: 30° ± 3°

b) Contact-breaker gap: 0.35 to 0.40 mm.

c) Contact-breaker spring tension measured at the contacts: 0.5 to 0.65 kg.

d) Capacitor: 0.2 microfarad (.2 mF).

e) Rotation: anti-clockwise (seen from the drive end).

f) Checking the centrifugal and vacuum timing controls:

1) **Centrifugal advance:**

   Adjust to spark at 0° at less than 100 r.p.m.

Rotate the distributor at 3,000 r.p.m. At that speed the advance should be between 17° and 19°.

Check the advance at the following distributor deceleration speeds.

Speed R.p.m.	Advance (degrees)
2375	16 to 18
1500	8 ½ to 10 ½
550	½ to 2 ½
375	0 to 1

2) **Vacuum advance**

With a vacuum of 457 mm. mercury column the advance must be between 4 ½° to 5 ½° (distributor).

As the vacuum decreases so does the advance; the rate is as follows:

Vacuum	Advance (degrees/Distrib.)
305 mm. mercury column	4 to 5
228 mm. mercury column	3 to 4
165 mm. mercury column	½ to 2 ½

Below 63 mm. mercury column, the ignition advance is nil.

4 - LOCATING AND REPAIRING FAULTS

Before attempting to locate faults, make sure that the battery is not fully discharged, otherwise results similar to those signifying ignition circuit defects would be encountered.

a) **Locating faults causing irregular ignition**

Run the engine at a fairly fast idling speed.

If possible, short-circuit the plugs in turn, using a screwdriver with an insulated handle; if the short-circuited plug is defective, there will be practically no change in the engine running. On the other hand, short-circuiting will cause the engine a pronounced increase in roughness.

If it is impossible to short-circuit plugs fitted with shrouded cable connector remove each plug connector in turn.

The disconnection of the cable leading to the defective cylinder will have no effect on the running of the engine; however, the engine will increase in roughness when the other cables are disconnected.

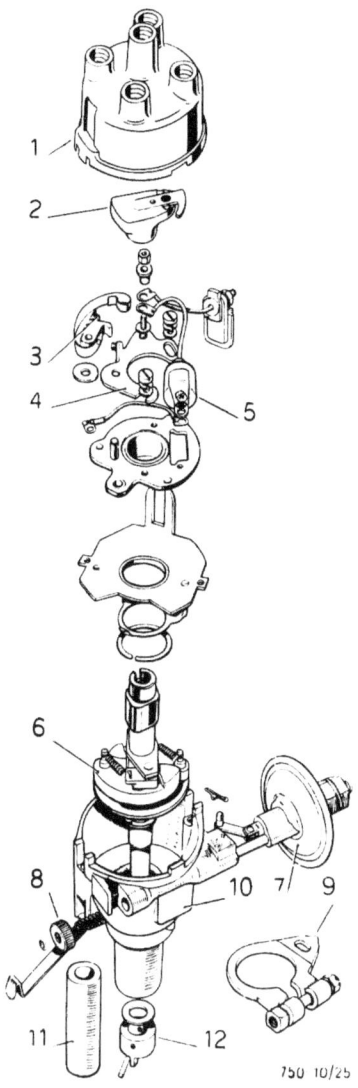

Fig. 28 - Exploded view of the Lucas DM2 Distributor.
1. Cover - **2.** Rotor arm - **3.** Contact-breaker moving contact - **4.** Contact-breaker plate - **5.** Capacitor - **6.** Centrifugal advance control **7.** Vacuum control unit - **8.** Knurled nut for minor distributor timing adjustments - **9.** Clamping plate - **10.** Distributor body - **11.** Porous bronze bush between the shaft and the body - **12.** Distributor driving coupling.

On locating the defective cylinder as described above, switch off the engine and disconnect the cable leading to the appropriate sparking plug.

Restart the engine again and hold the cable 4 to 5 mm. away from the cylinder-head.

If sparking is strong and regular the fault will lie in the sparking plug which should then be discarded or removed, cleaned and adjusted. If there is

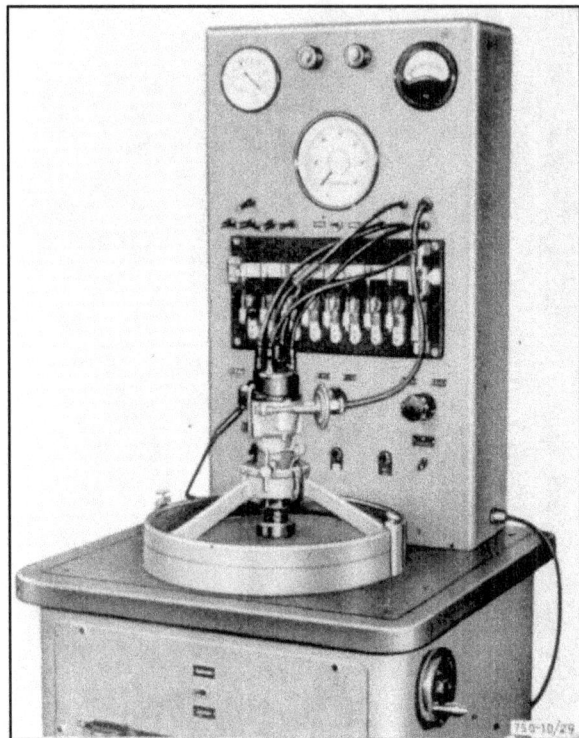

Fig. 29 - Distributor test-bench.

no spark, or if the spark is weak and uneven, examine the cable leading from the distributor cover to the plug and make sure that the insulation is not defective. Replace the cable if the rubber is cracked or damaged.

Clean the cover and check to ensure that the small carbon brush moves freely. It it is necessary to replace the brush, make sure that it slides freely in its seating. If a fine black line is found to connect two or more electrodes or one electrode and the earth, this signifies electrical leakage and the distributor cover should be discarded and replaced.

b) **Tracing causes of ignition failure**

Start the engine; while it is idling, note the reading obtained with an ammeter connected in series with the cable from the battery.

If the low-voltage circuit is in order, the instrument reading must rise and fall in harmony with the closing and opening of the contacts.

If the reading is steady, the cause may be a short-circuit or permanently-closed contacts.

If the reading is nil, the low-tension circuit is disconnected or the contacts are either dirty or incorrectly set.

Remove cover cap by releasing the two lateral springs; pull off the rotor arm, levering it off with a screwdriver if necessary, though taking care not to damage it.

Make sure that the contacts are clean and that the contact gap is as provided in paragraph 2b.

Make sure that the contact-breaker arm moves freely on its spindle. If the movement is too slow, remove the arm and clean the spindle with very fine emery cloth.

Smear Mobilgrease No. 2 on the spindle and return the contact-breaker arm to its operating position. If the defect continues, proceed as follows:

c) **Low-tension circuit**

1) **No reading in ammeter test.**

Refer to wiring diagram and check that its connections are not broken or loose, including the connections to the ignition switch.

Test the ignition coil, temporarily substituting a replacement for comparison purposes.

2) **Steady reading in ammeter test.**

Refer to the wiring diagram and check for short-circuits.

Examine the capacitor (either by substituting it or using a suitable testing instrument).

Test the ignition coil by temporarily substituting it.

Check the contact-breaker insulation.

d) **High-tension circuit.**

If the low-tension circuit is free from defects:

— disconnect the high-tension lead from the centre terminal on the distributor cover;

— switch on the ignition and rotate the engine with the starter motor until the contacts close;

— raise the contact-breaker arm while holding the high-tension coil lead about 4 mm. from the cylinder block.

If the ignition system is in order there will be a strong spark.

If there is no spark the secondary winding of the ignition coil will be defective; the coil must then be replaced.

The high-tension leads must be examined; they should be replaced if the rubber is cracked or perished.

The method of connecting high-tension cables to the ignition coil or the distributor cover is to thread the moulded terminal nut over the cable, bore the end of the cable for about ¼ in., thread the wire through the brass washer (removed from the old cable) and bend back the strands. Finally screw the moulded terminal onto the coil or the distributor cover.

The cables leading from the distributor to the sparking plugs must be connected in the correct firing order.

e) **Dismantling.**

Before dismantling a distributor, carefully note the relative positions of the various parts so that they will occupy the same positions when re-assembled. If the driving pinion has to be removed, note the relative positions of the pinion and the rotor arm; they must be adhered to when re-assembling.

Push off the spring clips and lift off the distributor cover and the rotor arm.

Break the connection between the vacuum control device and the moving contact plate and remove the two screws at the edge of the contact-breaker base. The complete contact-breaker, together with the outer terminal, can now be lifted off (see next paragraph).

Remove the circlip fitted at the end of the micrometer adjustment screw, and turn the micrometer nut proper until the screw and the vacuum control device are free.

Take care not to lose the ratchet and the coil type springs fitted beneath the micrometer nut.

The shaft assembly, complete with the centrifugal advance device, and the cam foot may now be removed from the distributor body.

1) **The contact-breaker.**

To dismantle the contact-breaker, unscrew the nut and slide off the insulating member and the connection from the bolt to which the contact-breaker spring is secured.

Slide off the plastic terminal and lift the contact-breaker lever as also the insulating washers fitted beneath it.

Remove the screws which secure the fixed-contact plate, and also — together with the spring — the corresponding plain steel washers and the plate.

Remove the screw which secures the capacitor and (in the case of older models) the contact-breaker earth lead.

Remove the contact-breaker base assembly by turning the base plate in a clockwise direction while pulling on it to free it from the moving-contact plate.

2) **Driving shaft and plate.**

Continuing, remove the screw inside the cam and draw off the cam and the cam foot. The weights, spring and toggles of the centrifugal timing device may then be raised and removed from the driving plate.

It should be noted that a distance collar is fitted on the spindle beneath the driving plate.

f) **Replacing the bush.**

The only porous bronze bush in the distributor can be removed from its seating with a punch.

A new bush must be fitted whenever it is necessary to remove the old one. Before fitting, the new bush must be completely immersed in medium-viscosity motor oil (S.A.E. 30-40) for at least 24 hours.

In cases of extreme urgency, this period may be reduced by immersing the bush for two hours in oil at 100°C; the oil must then be allowed to cool before the bush is removed from the bath.

The bush can then be inserted by means of a shouldered, polished mandrel having a nose diameter 0.01 mm. less than that of the shaft in it in order to prevent the mandrel withdrawing the bush when it is pulled out.

Under no circumstances must the internal diameter of the bush be altered by reaming or any other process, as this would reduce the porosity of the bushing and interfere with its lubrication characteristics.

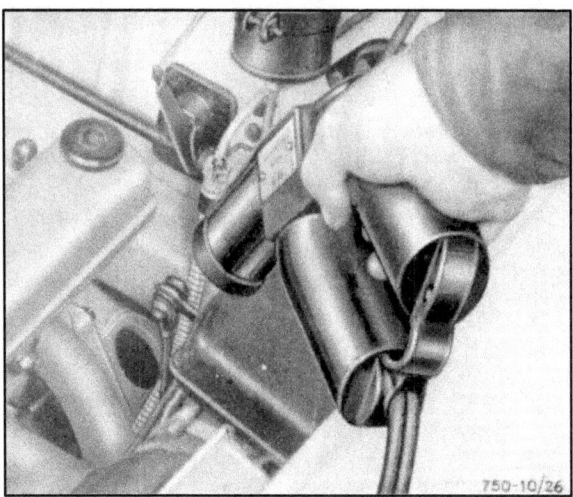

Fig. 30 - Timing the distributor with a stroboscopic gun.

g) **Re-assembly.**

The following instructions apply when the distributor has been completely dismantled.

1) Fit the distance collar on the shaft; smear a little light engine-oil on the latter and insert it in its seating.

2) Refit the vacuum unit in its housing and fit the springs, the knurled adjusting nut and the safety circlip.

3) Refit the centrifugal timing control taking care that the springs are not stretched or damaged. Fit the cam unit on the shaft, carefully engaging the projections on the cam foot with the weights.

4) Before re-assembling the contact-breaker base assembly, smear it with a little Mobilgrease No. 2.

Place the moving contact-breaker plate on the base plate and fix it position by reversing the dismantling procedure.

Refit the contact-breaker base in the distributor body; engage the vacuum unit link.

Tighten the screws which secure the baseplate; one of the screws also secures one end of the contact-breaker earthing cable.

5) Refit the capacitor. Place the fixed contact plate in position and slightly tighten the retaining screws. A plain washer and a spring washer must be inserted beneath the retaining screws.

6) Place the insulating washers, etc., over the contact-breaker spindle and on the pin on which the contact-breaker spring is fixed. Refit the contact-breaker lever and its spring.

7) Slide the terminal block into its slot.

8) Fit the low-tension lead and the condenser eyelets over the insulating member and place the latter over the pin which secures the end of the contact-breaker spring. Refit the washer and the nut.

9) Adjust the gap between contacts to between 0.35 to 0.40 mm. and tighten the screw which secures the fixed contact.

10) Push on the rotor arm, taking care that the projection on its side enters the slot in the socket. Refit the distributor cover.

h) **Replacing contacts.**

When contacts are so worn as to require replacement, both must be replaced, not one only. After the first 500 miles with new contacts, the gap must be checked and brought to 0.35 to 0.40 mm. In this way the initial bedding-down of the contacts can be compensated for.

i) **Timing the distributor.**

The necessary instructions for timing the distributor are to be found on Part 2 (« The engine »).

More accurate timing can be obtained with a stroboscopic gun.

Bearing in mind that due to the action of the centrifugal timing control the maximum advance is 44°, the advance can be checked with a stroboscopic gun in the following way:

— Run the engine from 5,000 to 5,200 r.p.m. and direct the light from the gun onto the flywheel (Fig. 30) through the orifice provided;

— if the engine is accurately timed, the distinguishing mark with the letters AM (stamped on the flywheel) will be seen on the centreline of the orifice;

— if it is found that the advance is greater or less than 44°, adjust the fixed advance device accordingly; it is better to have correct degree of advance at high speeds than at low speeds.

SPARKING PLUGS

Sparking plugs are subjected to very severe and sudden changes in pressure and temperature which develop inside the cylinders; the insulating material used in their manufacture must also be suitable for withstanding high voltages. In addition, all the materials from wich they are made are subjected in use to the corrosive action of the combustion gas, this action being more pronounced with the increased use of anti-knock additives in the fuel.

The sparking plugs used must therefore comply with high standards of thermal, electrical and mechanical efficiency, and must be perfectly gas-tight.

Specific characteristics required are:

a) good thermal conductivity to ensure rapid heat dissipation;

b) ability to withstand extreme and rapid temperature fluctuations;

c) excellent insulation and dielectric strength, even when the engine is hot, so as to prevent current leakage and disruptive discharges;

d) good mechanical strength to eliminate breakage during assembly or in use;

e) perfect gas-tight properties.

The thermal characteristics obviously determine the choice of the plugs; for every type of engine the plug

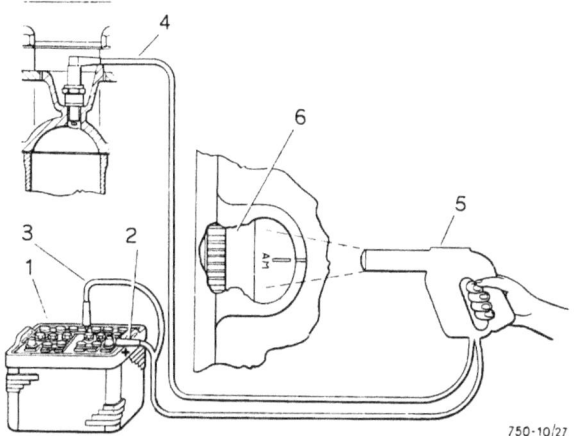

Fig. 31 - Connections for the 6 volt SUN stroboscopic gun, model X 14.
1. Battery - **2.** Red lead - **3.** Black lead - **4.** Blue lead connected to plug in No. 1 cylinder - **5.** Gun - **6.** Flywheel.

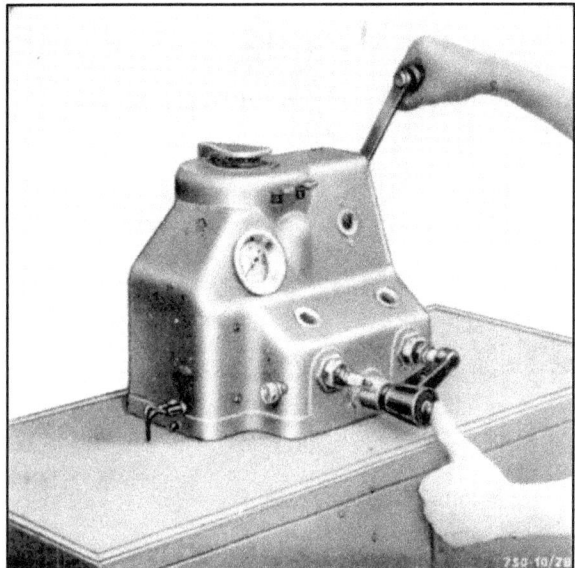

Fig. 32 - Plug testing instrument.

used must operate over a wide temperature range, the two limits being known respectively as the « self-cleaning temperature » and the « pre-ignition temperature ».

The thermal behaviour of sparking plugs is normally defined according to the « thermal rating » which is a figure giving the number of seconds needed for the plug to cause pre-ignition on a test engine.

As a consequence, plugs with a high thermal rating are called « cold plugs » and, conversely, those with a low thermal rating are called « hot ».

High speed engines with high compression ratios (or supercharged engines) therefore require « cold » plugs, i.e. plugs with a high thermal rating.

Engines with intermediate characteristics should always be fitted with plugs with a corresponding intermediate thermal rating.

When a plug becomes so hot as to cause pre-ignition, change to the same type but to one having the next higher thermal rating; if, on the other hand, the plug in use becomes oiled up or carbonised, replace it with one having the next lower termal rating.

It is even advisable to use plugs with two different thermal ratings for any given engine; the plugs with the lower rating during the running-in period, in winter or when the running conditions tend to cause fouling of the plugs; plugs with the higher thermal rating after the running-in period, in summer and whenever

higher engine performance is required.
The plugs recommended are:

Marelli CW 240 B or Lodge HLN (for Giulietta Berlina, t.i., Sprint and Spider);

Marelli CBW 1000 B, or Lodge RL 47, or Lodge 2 HLN (for Giulietta Sprint Veloce and Spider Veloce).

Plugs with thermal ratings different from the above should not be used.

One method (somewhat empirical perhaps, but often used by experts) of determining the identity of a type of plug is to examine the colour of the insulator.

Whitish colour: fit colder plugs.

Blackish, oily colour: fit hotter plugs.

Brownish colour: the plug is of the correct termal efficiency.

Maintenance and testing of spark plugs.

The standard methods of testing spark plugs are described in Part 2.

After long use, or when otherwise necessary, plugs should be carefully tested and cleaned on a suitable test-instrument (Fig. 32).

First of all fit the plug in its seating and check to ensure that with a pressure of 6 to kg/cm^2 the spark jumps correctly between the two electrodes. If the spark is in order it is only necessary to clean the electrodes with a wire brush and adjust the gap (0.6 mm.).

If, on the other hand, the spark is erratic, the plug should be cleaned with a wire brush and — but only if the trouble persists — by sand blasting followed by a blast of compressed air. The sand-blasting machine should not be used to excess.

INFORMATION SHEET REFERENCE

ASSEMBLY	DATE	SHEET N.	SUBJECT

INFORMATION SHEET REFERENCE

ASSEMBLY	DATE	SHEET N.	SUBJECT

PART 11

COACHWORK

INDEX

DESCRIPTION . . . . page 219

1 - Dashboard instruments and controls . . . . » 220

2 - Removing and refitting the windshield and rear window glass . . . » 221

3 - Doors and their accessories . . . . » 224

4 - Body repairs . . . . » 228

5 - Equipment for body inspection . . . . » 229

6 - Washing and cleaning the car . . . . » 234

PART 11

COACHWORK

DESCRIPTION

Fig. 1 - 4-seater Giulietta Berlina.

The body of the Giulietta Berlina and t.i. is designed to provide a high degree of roomy comfort for four passengers. The wide windows ensure a clear field of vision in all directions.

The Giulietta Berlina and t.i. are of monocoque construction. The four doors, bonnet and boot cover are easy to remove for replacement as necessary.

The front mudguards may be replaced by merely removing the bolts and screws securing them to the frame and to the door posts, and by cutting the welds between the corner of the bonnet opening and the door posts.

In the same way the rear wings may be replaced by making suitable cuts in the coachwork so as to remove the damaged portion.

Dust exclusion and water-proofing is effected by fitting a specially shaped strip of sponge rubber around the doors. This rubber moulding is merely glued in position and is easy to replace.

The panel carrying the various instruments may easily be removed as it consists of a single sheet metal unit screwed onto the top cross-member and the side posts.

All controls and instruments may easily be replaced without removing the dash-board.

Fig. 2 - 2-seater Giulietta Sprint

The front seat is removed by sliding it off the two guides fitted to the floor.

The rear seat is separate from its back, and both portions can easily be removed for replacement as necessary.

Satisfactory thermal and sound insulation is provided by fitting « Ultralite » to the bonnet, the roof and the scuttle; felts is fitted to the floor, and anti-drum varnish is sprayed under the floor and inside the boot.

With this type of insulation the temperature of car interior remains fairly constant even if exposed for long periods to the sun or to the rigours of winter.

The door-closing arrangements are of the most modern and practical types; the doors open easily by means of a press-button located alongside the external door-handle.

The luggage compartment is at the back of the car and has a capacity of 0.7 cubic metres (24 cubic feet); it also houses the spare wheel and the battery.

The body of the Giulietta Sprint and Sprint Veloce is also of monocoque construction and is in all respects similar to that of the Giulietta Berlina except in that its external line and its streamlining are somewhat different, it seats two instead of four, and the capacity of its luggage boot is much greater.

The repair instructions given in the following pages relate to the Giulietta Berlina and t.i. cars; they are, however, applicable in general to the Giulietta Sprint and Sprint Veloce as well.

1 - DASHBOARD INSTRUMENTS AND CONTROLS

Removing the instrument panel

Proceed as follows:

— disconnect the negative battery lead;

— slacken the screws securing the oil gauge tube and speedometer cable duct (Fig. 4) and then loosen the strap fixing the speedometer cable to the heater air pipe;

— remove the oil tube (Fig. 5);

— remove the three knurled nuts which, by means of three clips, fix the instrument panel to the dashboard (Fig. 6);

— remove the panel and disconnect the speedometer cable and all the electrical leads to the panel instruments (Fig. 7);

— the panel then being completely freed, carry out the necessary repairs or replacements.

Re-fitting the instrument panel

Follow the above instructions in the reverse order:

— re-fix the speedometer cable and connect the various electrical leads;

Fig. 3 - 2-seater Giulietta Spider.

— place the panel in its housing; make sure that it is correctly positioned and that the VIPLA strip at the top of the panel is properly tensioned (Fig. 8);

— fix the panel in position with the three clips and knurled nuts;

— engage the oil pressure-gauge pipe;

— tighten the clip which secures the speedometer cable to the heater air duct;

— re-fix the oil gauge tube and speedometer cable duct;

— connect the negative battery lead;

WARNING: When cleaning the plexiglas instrument-panel cover, use only cold water and soap and a chamois-leather or suitable rag.

Re-placing the control knobs.

The following control knobs are located beneath the instrument panel: the headlamp knob, the hand accelerator control, the starter motor knob and the heater motor knob.

The following procedure should be followed when replacing hand accelerator knob and starter motor knob:

— release the grub screw as shown in Fig. 9 and unscrew the knobs.

For head-lamp knob the procedure is:

— with a suitable spike push in the spring dowel (Fig. 10) and at the same time pull off the knob.

For heater motor knob:

— release the grub screw and pull off the knob.

2 - REMOVING AND REFITTING THE WINDSHIELD AND THE REAR WINDOW GLASS

The windshield and rear window glass should only be removed for the following purposes;

— to replace the car roof fabric lining;

— to remove dents in the coachwork;

— to replace the glass, the rubber moulding or the aluminium frames;

— to re-cellulose the entire car.

Removal

Bearing in mind that the foregoing instructions apply to both the windshield and the rear window:

— using a wooden tool, remove the rubber moulding from its seat, taking care not to cut it;

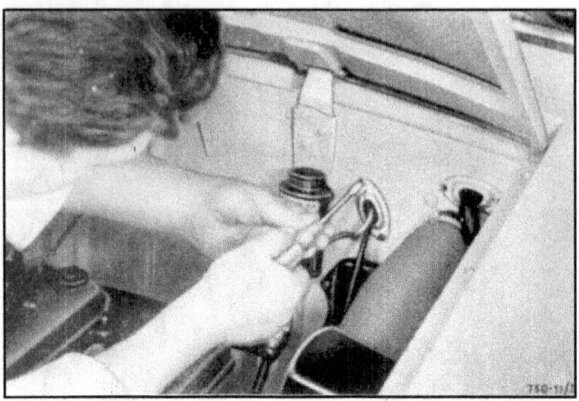

Fig. 4 - Removing the conduit for the oil-gauge tube and the flexible speedometer cable.

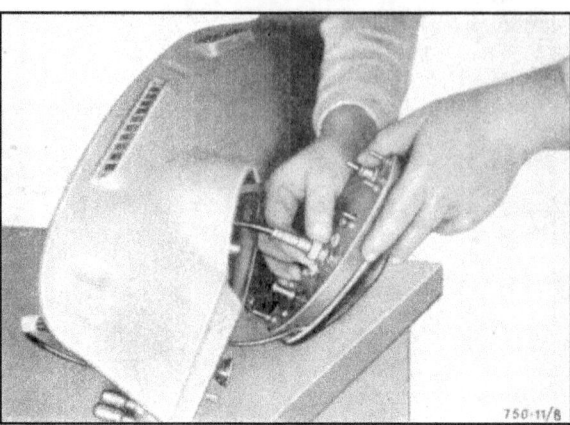

Fig. 7 - Disconnecting the flexible speedometer drive cable from the instrument panel.

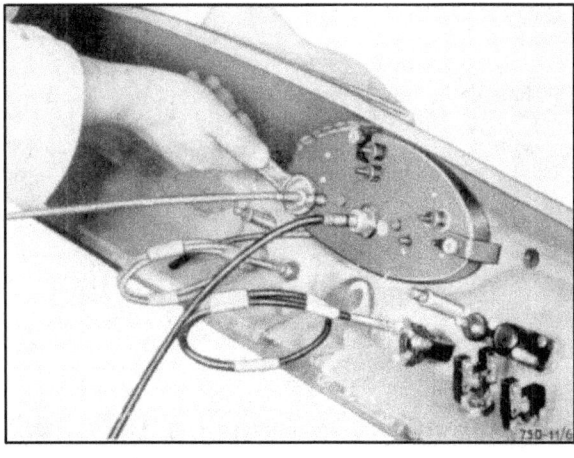

Fig. 5 - Disconnecting oil-gauge tube from the instrument panel.

— apply pressure with the palm of the hand and push the glass (from inside the car) so that the rubber moulding leaves its seat on the car body (fig. 11);

— with the glass on a suitable trestle, push off the aluminium frame joint cover and remove the aluminium frame;

— remove the rubber moulding.

Refitting

— place the glass on a suitable trestle;

— fit the rubber moulding with a suitable tool as shown in Fig. 13;

— lubricate, using liquid soap, the shaped portion of the rubber moulding designed to take the aluminium frame;

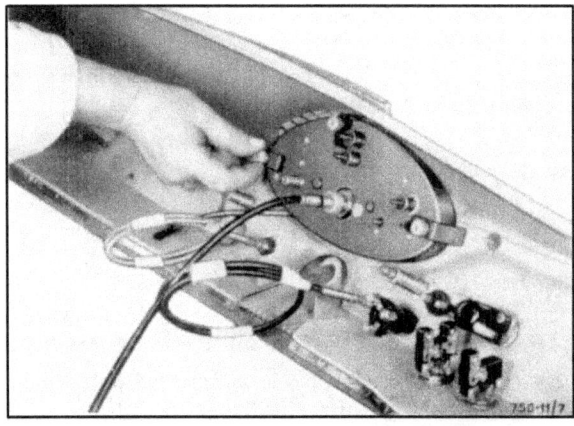

Fig. 6 - Removing the knurled nuts holding the instrument panel in position.

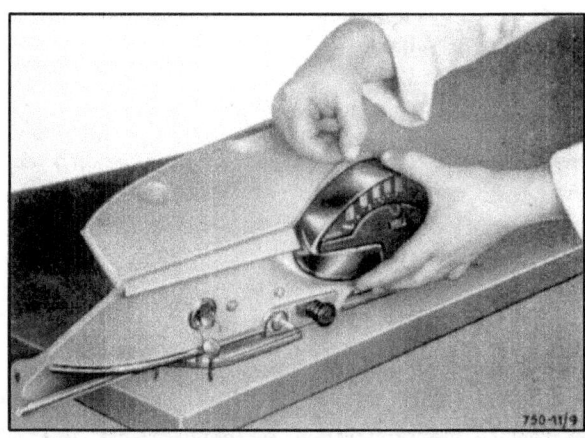

Fig. 8 - Refitting the instrument panel.

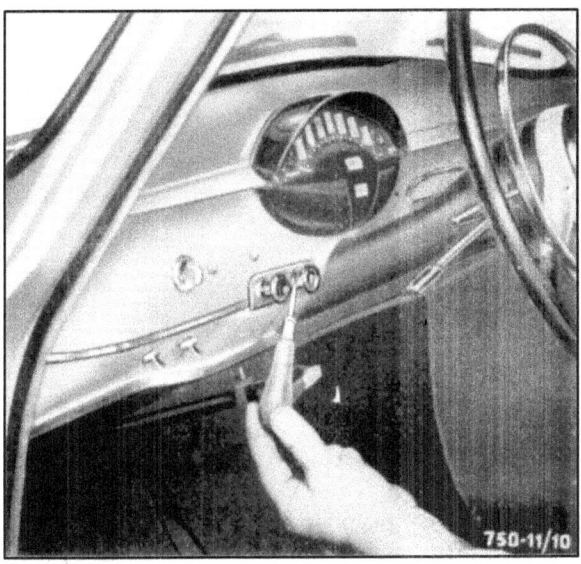

Fig. 9 - Removing the hand accelerator control knob.

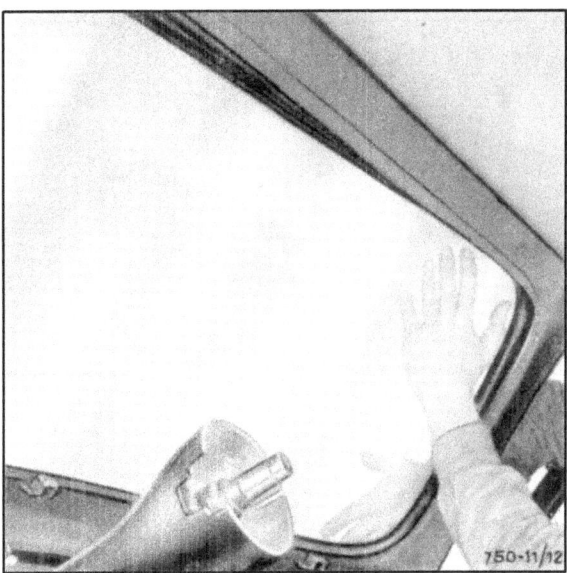

Fig. 11 - Removing the windshield glass.

— fit the aluminium frame after having expanded its housing in the rubber moulding by means of a suitable tool (Fig. 14);

— attach the joint cover to one end of the aluminium frame and cover the joint as shown in Fig. 15;

— turn the glass over and insert a cord in the groove in the rubber moulding, that is, in the groove designed to receive the metal edge of the coachwork window opening (Fig. 16).

The ends of the cord must overlap by a short distance and protrude by approximately 15 to 20 cm. from the rubber moulding. The cord will be used to fit the glass to the car body;

— place the glass in position alongside its seat on the car body and, using a rubber mallet, tap it firmly (from the outside) into place; while so tapping it, another mechanic working inside the car must pull on the cord (inserted as described above) in order to pull inside the car body the rubber lip designed to grip the inside of the steel coachwork (fig. 17);

— using a suitable gun, inject sealing compound into the joint (Fig. 18) in order to prevent water penetrating to the car interior;

— remove any excess of compound with petrol.

Fig. 10 - Removing the driving-light switch knob.

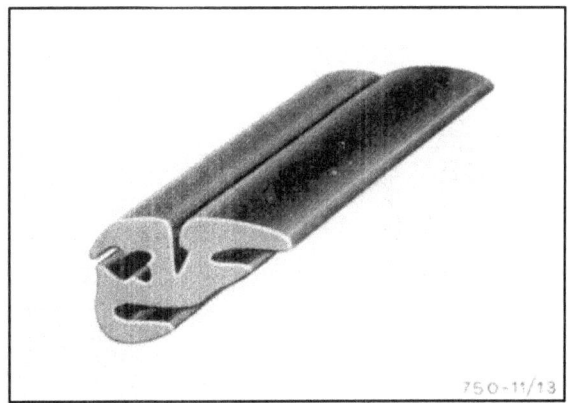

Fig. 12 - Sectional view of the windshield and rear-window rubber moulding.

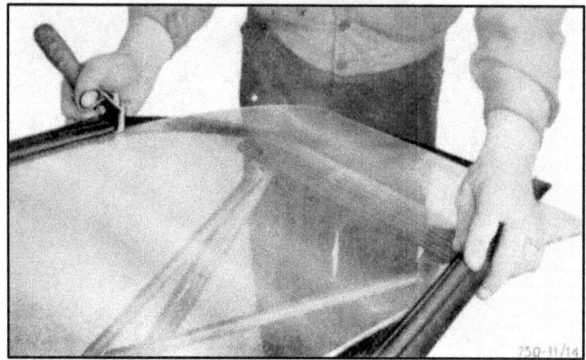

Fig. 13 - Fitting the rubber moulding to the windshield.

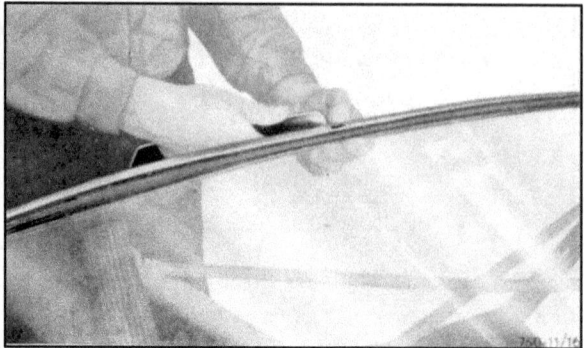

Fig. 15 - Fitting the aluminium joint cover.

3 - DOORS AND THEIR ACCESSORIES

The following operations can be performed (and the undernoted inconveniencies eliminated) without removing the doors from the car:

— the defective operation or replacement of locks;

— the entry of water and/or dust;

— dismantling the window-raising mechanism to correct defective operation;

— removing the window glass for replacement when broken or excessively scratched or to repair damaged or defective mouldings;

— adjusting the door opening stop rod;

— replacing the moulding.

Replacing locks

To remove a front door lock proceed as follows:

— fully raise the window, remove the window-raising handle, the internal lock handle, the internal door panel (Fig. 19) and partially remove the transparent plastic sheet glued to the internal metal wall of the door;

— remove the three screws **1** (Fig. 20) which secure the lock and the two screws **2** which secure the window guides;

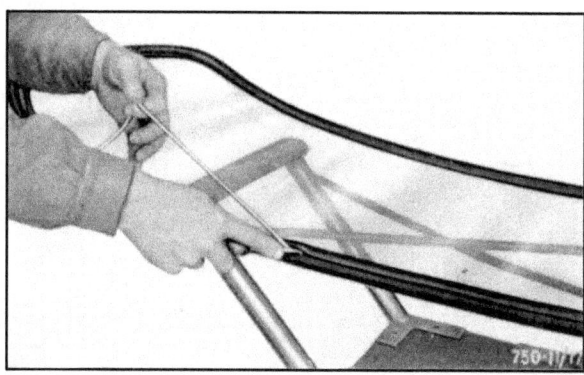

Fig. 16 - Inserting the cord in the window groove in the rubber moulding.

— draw off the lock after first removing the rod **3** (Fig. 21) which connects the lock to the internal operating handle.

To remove the external handle, remove the rear screw (Fig. 22) and the front screw by means of a jointed screwdriver (Fig. 23).

The locks and handles of rear doors are removed in the same way.

Removing the window-raising mechanism

Different procedure is used for removing theから and rear door window-raising mechanisms.

Fig. 14 - Fitting the aluminium frame to the windshield rubber moulding.

When it is necessary to remove the front door mechanism, first of all remove the panel, the two screws which secure the window limit bracket and then the bracket itself (Fig. 24). Then:

— lower the window until the mechanism levers disengage from the window guides;

— remove the four screws **1** (Fig. 24) which secure the mechanism and slide the mechanism out at the bottom as shown in Fig. 25. At the same time support the glass by hand.

In the case of the rear door mechanism, first remove the panel; then bring the handle levers into the horizontal position, remove the securing screws and slide the mechanism horizontally backward and forwards in order to disengage the levers from the window guides. Then proceed as in the case of the front doors and withdraw the window-raising mechanism.

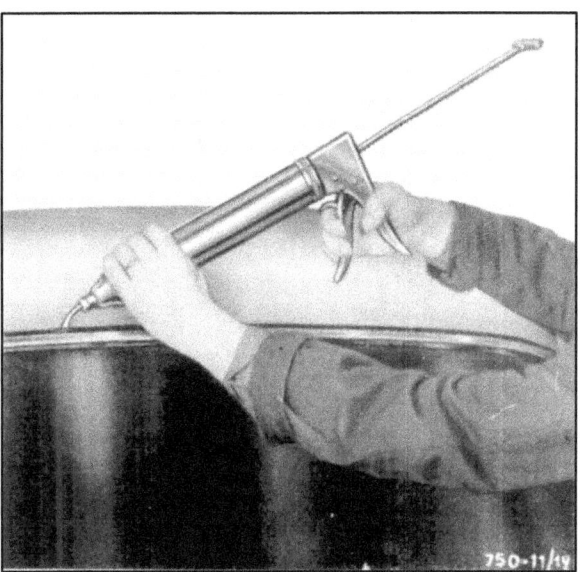

Fig. 18 - Applying sealing compound around the inner edge of the window rubber, using a special injection gun.

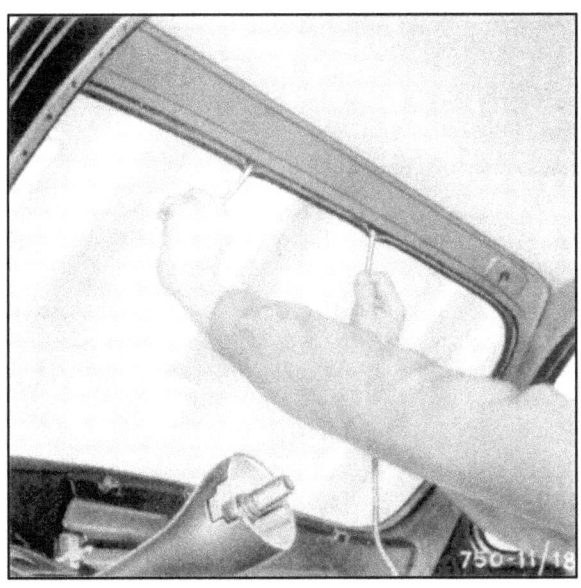

Fig. 17 - Simultaneously removing the cord and fitting the rubber surround over the edge of the opening in the car body.

Removing the window glass from a door

First of all remove the two window frames, using a wooden block and a hammer.

Proceed as shown in Fig. 27, starting with the joint at the top of the frame.

Repeat the operations for removing the window-raising mechanism as far as the disengagement of the glass from the operating lever. Then raise the glass, rotate it and withdraw it as shown in Fig. 28.

Preventing water and dust from entering the car

If water or dust enters the car due to the perishing of the door sealing rubber, proceed as described under « Replacing the foam rubber door seal ». If, however, the cause is deformation of the door due to a knock or a strained door, proceed as follows:

— insert a sheet of paper between the door and its

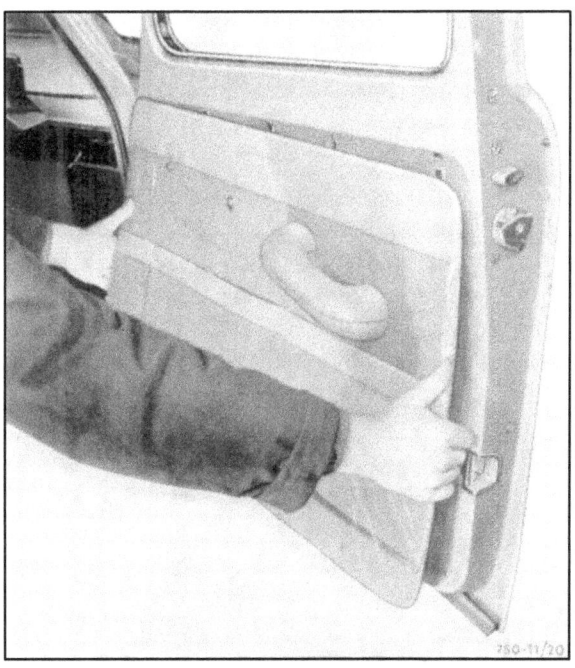

Fig. 19 - Removing a door trim panel.

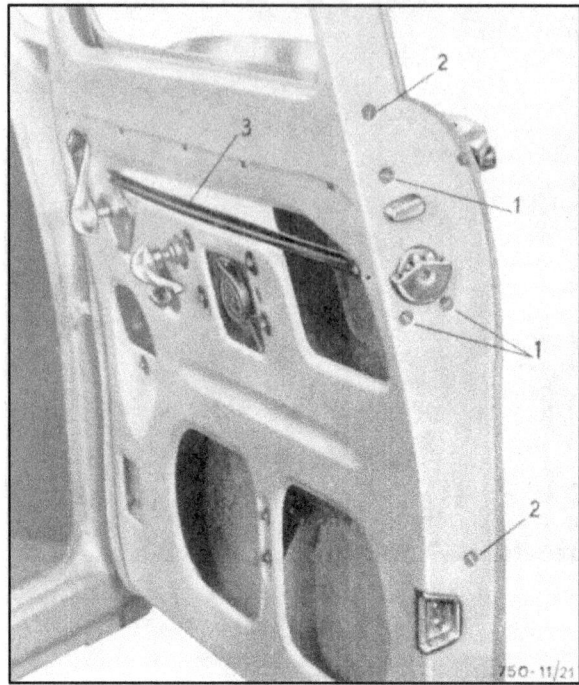

Fig. 20 - Removing a front-door lock.
1. Screws securing the lock - 2. Screws securing the window guides
3. Rod connecting the lock to the external handle.

Fig. 22 - Removing the front screw securing the external handle of a front door.

— if dust and water enter at the bottom of the door, insert the wood block at the top and apply pressure (inwards) at the bottom. By suitably locating the wood block in the centre of the door, the entire door trim can be re-set if necessary (Fig. 31).

seat (Fig. 29) and — on the basis of the force needed to pull out the sheet — determine the point or points at which the door no longer touches its seat;

— if the part which fails to make contact is at the top, insert (between the door and its seat) a block of wood at the bottom of the door (as shown in Fig. 30) and force (using manual pressure only) the top of the door inwards until the desired degree of fit is obtained;

Adjusting the door-opening stop rod

It may so happen that on opening a rear door it strikes against its corresponding closed front door. This is caused by the excessive deformation of the internal rubber block which serves as a shock-absorber. The trouble may be corrected by removing the split pin from the rod (Fig. 32) and either by inserting it in another hole in the rod or by fitting a leather distance-piece between the rod and the thrust surface on the door.

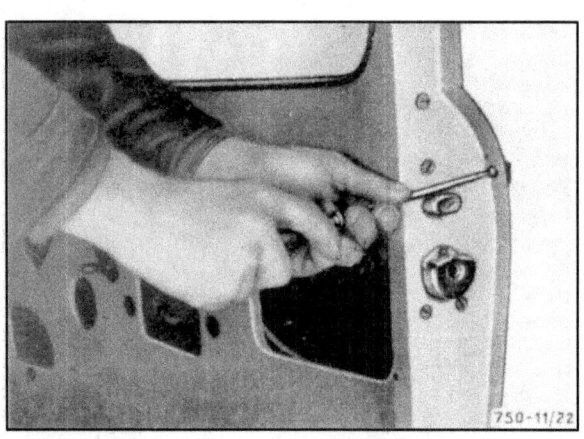

Fig. 21 - Removing the rear screw securing the external handle of a front door.

Fig. 23 - Front door.
1. Lock - 2. Window control - 3. Connecting rod.

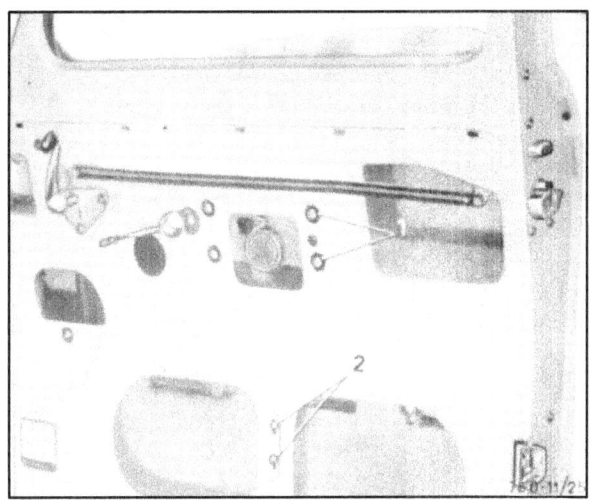

Fig. 24 - Front door.
1. Screws securing the window-raising mechanism - 2. Screws securing the window-lowering limiting bracket.

Fig. 26 - A front-door - the window-raising mechanism.

Removing the doors

When is becomes necessary to remove a door, proceed as follows:

— remove the screws securing the internal trimming panels;

— remove the split pin from the door-opening stop rod and withdraw the two pegs from the hinges (Fig. 34).

When refitting the door, proceed in the reverse manner. Then check to ensure that the doors fit properly when closed, and adjust as described above if necessary.

WARNING: Remember to oil the door hinges regularly

Replacing the foam rubber door seal

The purpose of the foam rubber fitted around the doors is to prevent water and dust from entering the car.

When refitting a new rubber seal, first clean the rubber and the door with petrol and then smear both the rubber and the door edge with suitable glue (Fig. 34). Allow the glue three or four minutes to become tacky and then press tre rubber surround in place.

Then, with a cotton rag moistened with petrol, remove any excess glue from the door edge **while taking every care not to touch the rubber surround.**

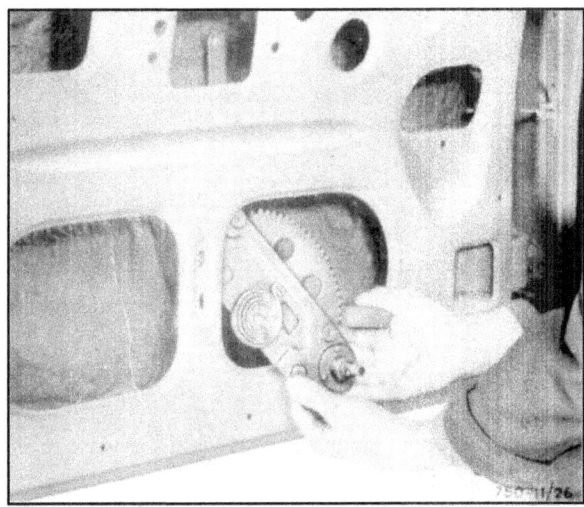

Fig. 25 - Removing the window-raising mechanism from a front door.

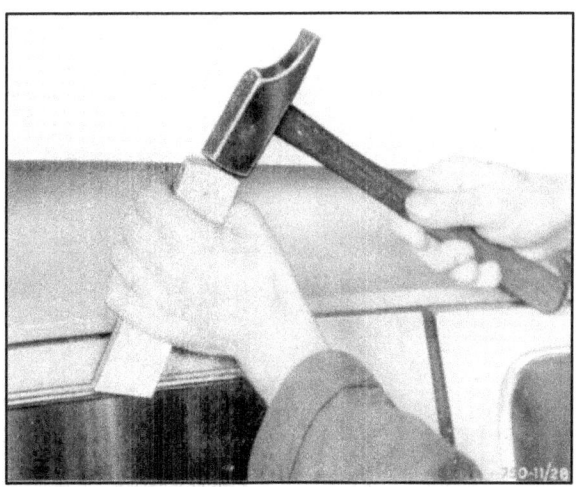

Fig. 27 - Removing the metal frame from a side window.

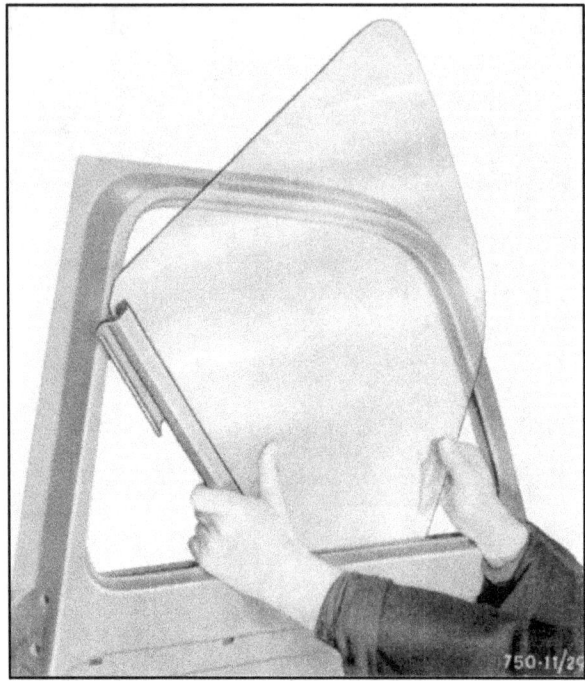

Fig. 28. - Removing a door window.

4 - BODY REPAIRS

Removing a front wing

Slight dents in the wing caused by knocks or scraping can often be repaired without removing the wing from the car.

When, however, more serious damage requires the removal of the wing, proceed as follows:

— remove the doors;

— remove the bumpers;

— remove the screws which secure the wing to the chassis;

— lift the front part of the wing by hand.

This will cause the welded joint on the scuttle to crack; if the joint fails to break, saw off the wing along the welded joint shown in Fig. 35.

Refitting the front wing

Place the wing in position on the body and fit all securing bolts.

Fig. 30 - Correcting a badly-fitting door to ensure that the rubber seal adequately excludes water and dust.

Clean the members and then arc-weld the wing to the scuttle (Fig. 35).

Radius the welded parts and re-paint as necessary.

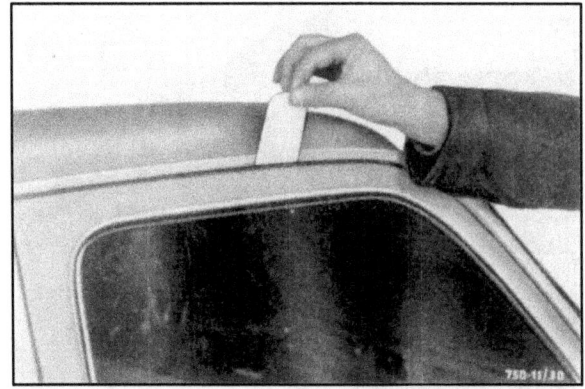

Fig. 29 - Checking the fit of the rubber door seal.

Rear Wings

The rear wings are welded over the whole joint connecting them to the body; they should be replaced in whole or in part according to circumstances.

Removing the bonnet and the luggage - compartment lid

The removal of these members is very easy. It is only necessary to remove the screws securing them to the body as shown in Figs. 36 and 37.

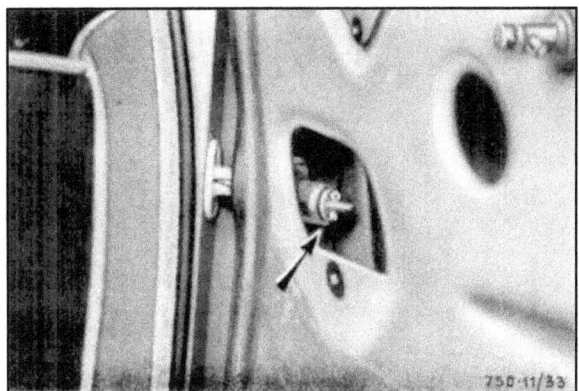

Fig. 32 - Stop rod limiting the extent of door opening.

The body must be inspected in all cases of damage or collision (even if not serious) so as to locate any possible twisting or bending of the attachment members securing the various mechanical units and to facilitate any necessary repairs.

Instructions for using the special tools and equipment

Rest the body on the chassis 6123.91001 (Fig. 44) and let it stand on the rear jacks **1** and the front crossbeam **2**, the latter serving merely to facilitate the positioning of the body on the chassis.

Then adjust the rear jacks **1** until the rear-axle differential tie-rod front attachment brackets engage with the rods **3**.

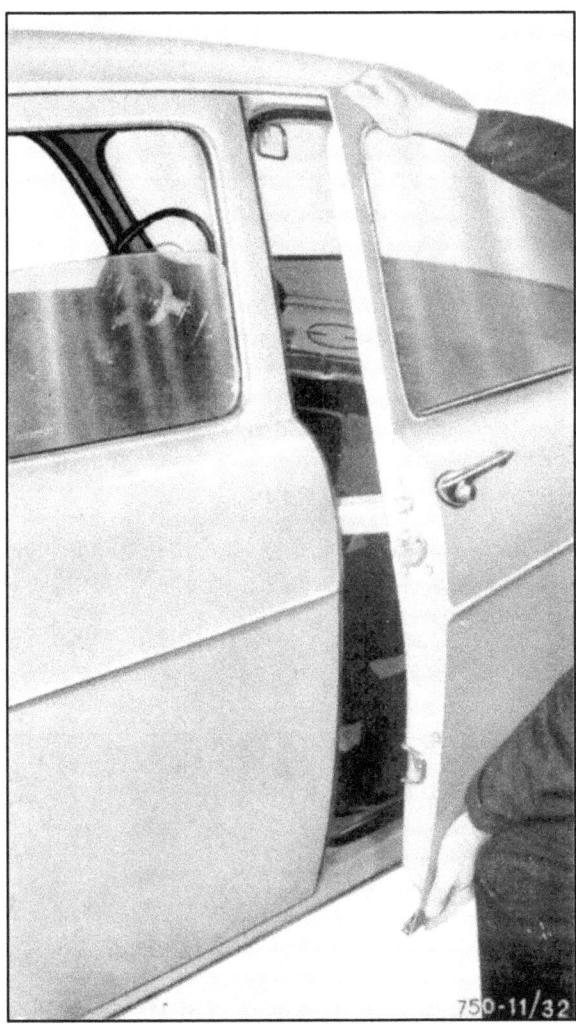

Fig. 31 - Correcting a warped door to ensure a close fit.

Figures 38, 39, 40, 41, 42 and 43 show various coachwork parts which can be supplied as body spares.

5 - EQUIPMENT FOR BODY INSPECTION

A set of special tools has been designed for inspection purposes and to ensure that the body is in good shape.

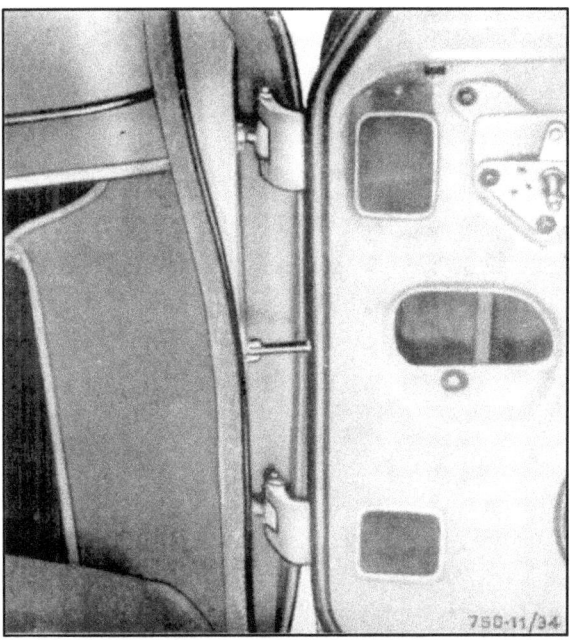

Fig. 33 - Door hinges.

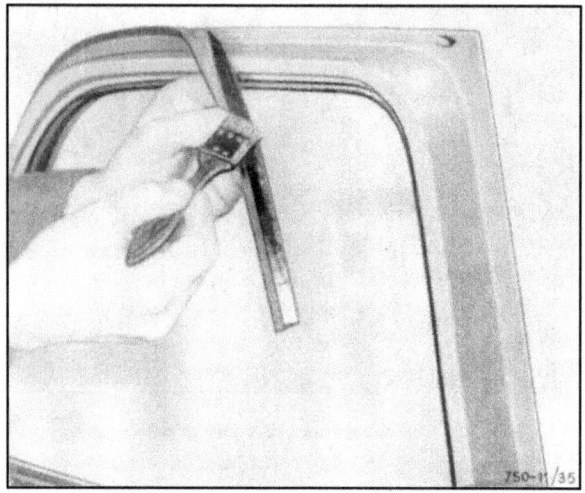

Fig. 34 - Glueing the rubber door seal in position.

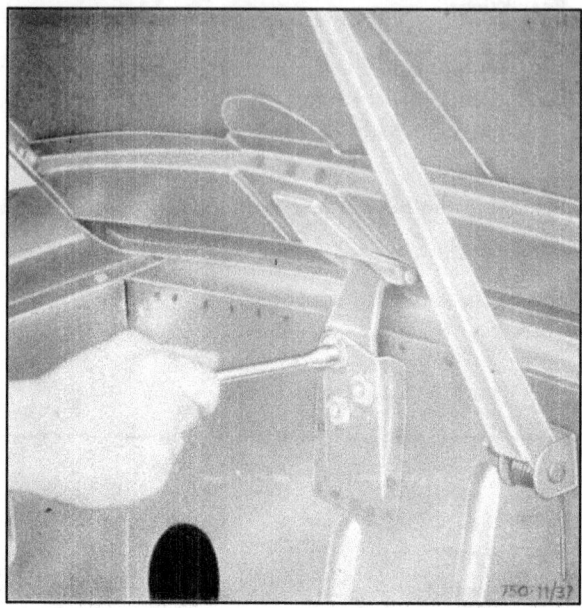

Fig. 36 - Removing the bonnet.

Adjust the front jacks **4** until the holes in the frame side member (which serve to connect the suspension arms) are in line with those on the lattice members **5** mounted at the front of the chassis; it should be remembered that there should be a gap of 4 mm. per side between the supports (top and bottom, front and rear) of the lattice members on the chassis side beams and the chassis beams itself.

During welding operations it is therefore necessary to interpose 8 **S** plates 4 mm. thick.

As the front jacks are raised it will be found that the front lower chassis side members will rise above the cross-member **2**; the body will then no longer rest on the latter.

If the chassis is not twisted it will be possible to insert the pins which fix the top rear-axle triangular spar joint to the lattice member **6** and the pin which fixes the engine/gear box rear bracket cross-member to the vertical rod **7**.

If it is found that the said pins cannot be inserted, the body will be twisted or deformed, and suitable repairs will have to be made.

Fig. 45 and 46 shaw tool assemblies No. 6123.91002, 6123.91003 and 6123.91.004 the use of which is stated in the figure captions.

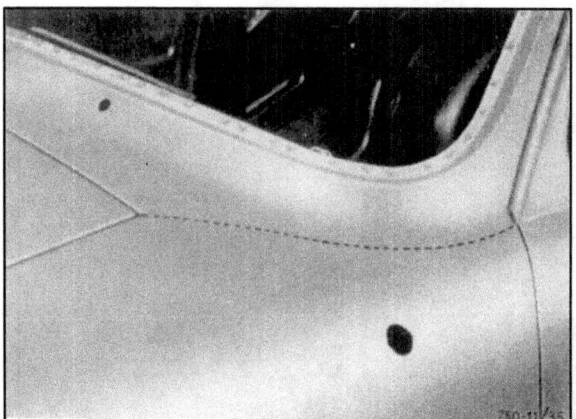

Fig. 35 - The welding line at the junction of the wing and the scuttle.

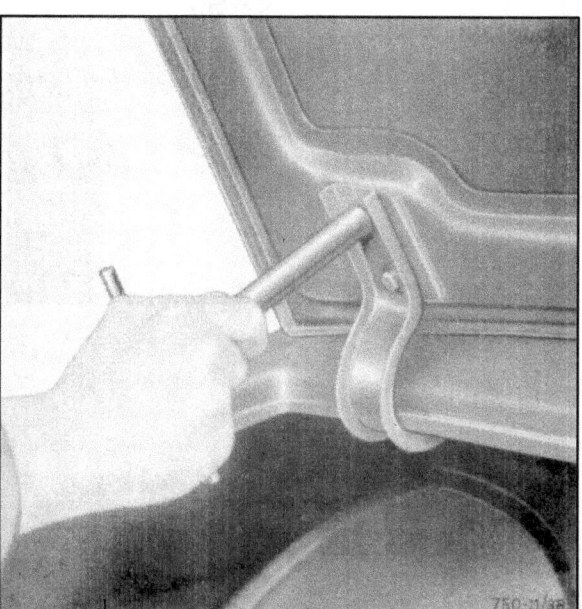

Fig. 37 - Removing the luggage compartment cover.

Fig. 38 - Spare parts to effect body repairs to the Giulietta Berlina and t.i.

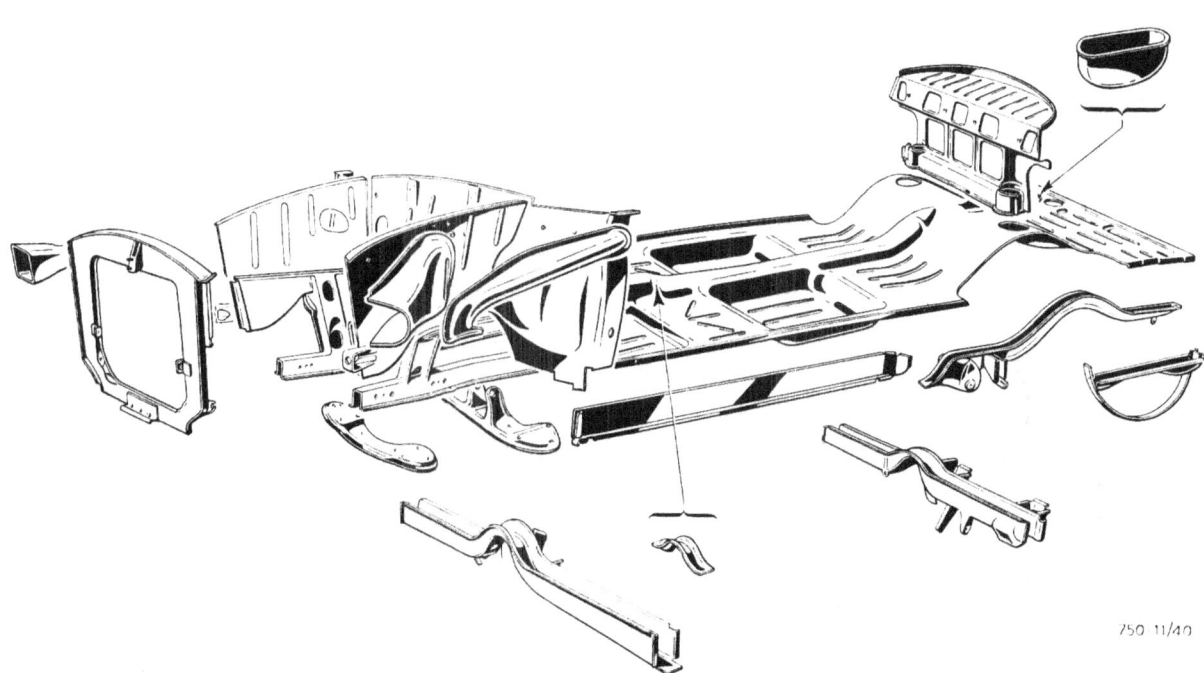

Fig. 39 - Spare parts to effect body repairs to the Giulietta Berlina and t.i.
Note: When ordering spare parts please refer to tables from 100 to 107 in the catalogue.

Fig. 40 - Spare parts to effect body repairs to the Giulietta Sprint and Sprint Veloce.

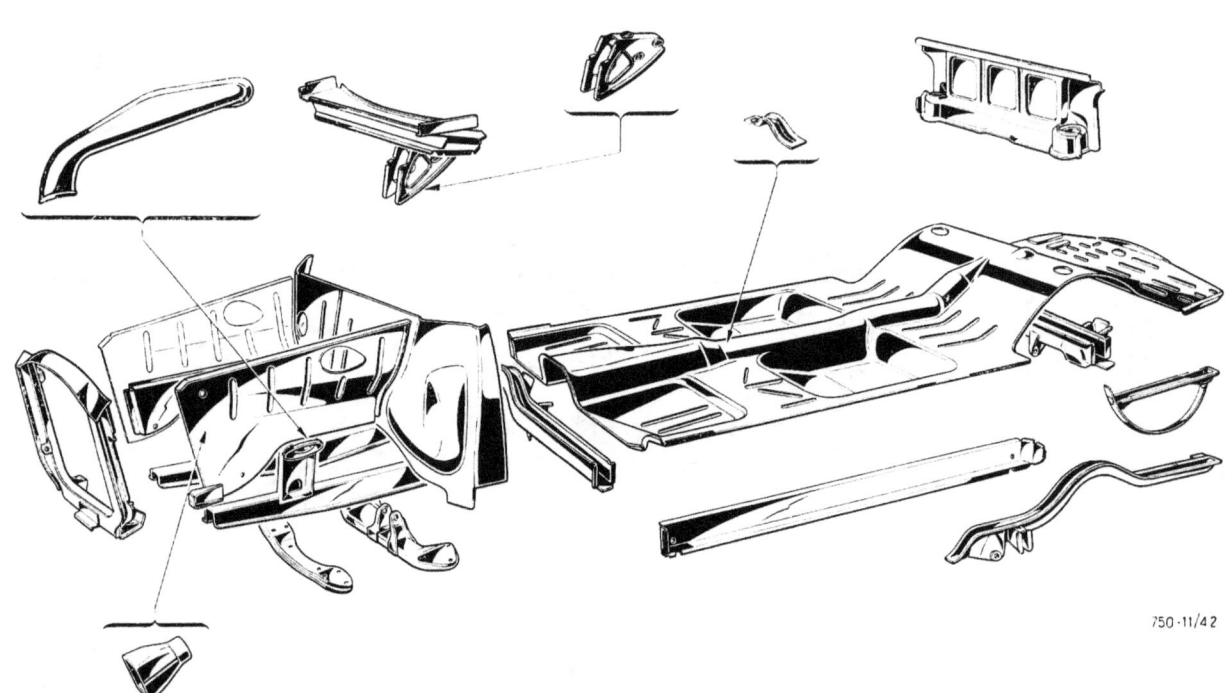

Fig. 41 - Spare parts to effect body repairs to the Giulietta Sprint and Sprint Veloce.
Note: When ordering spare parts please refer to tables from 108 to 115 in the catalogue.

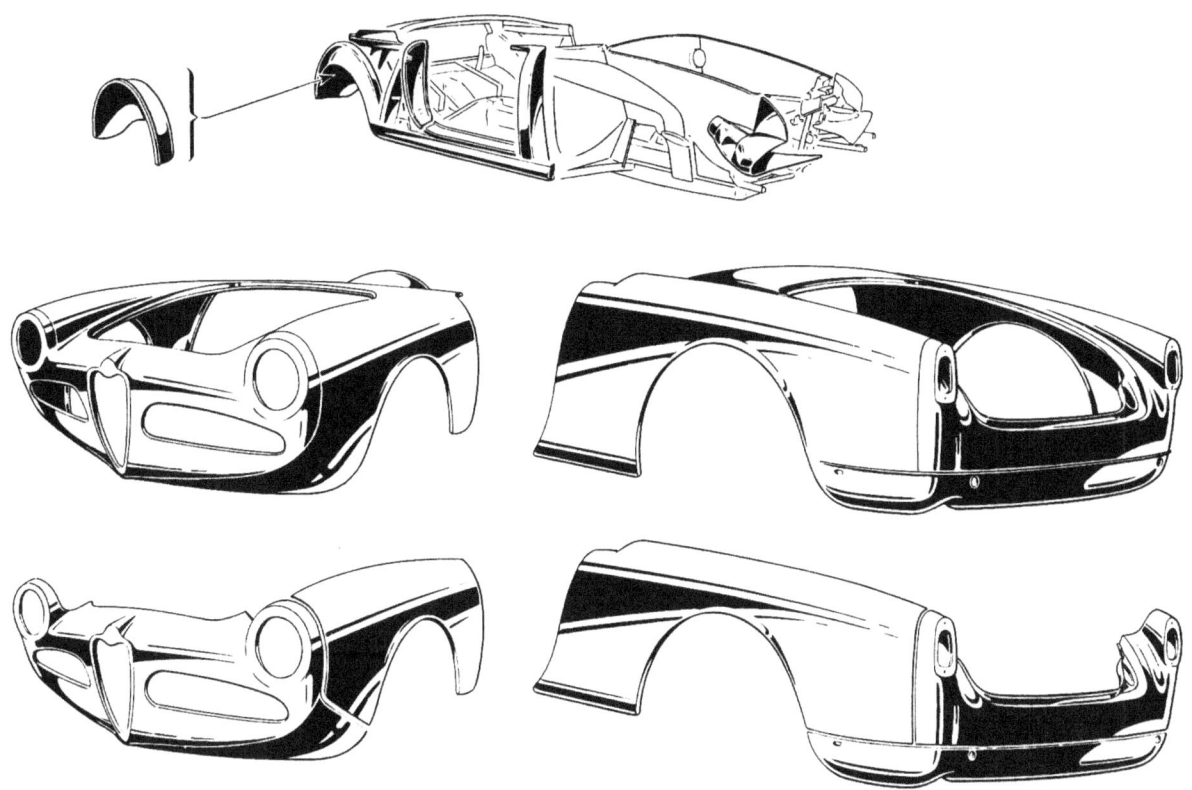

Fig. 42 - Spare parts to effect body repairs to the Giulietta Spider and Spider Veloce.

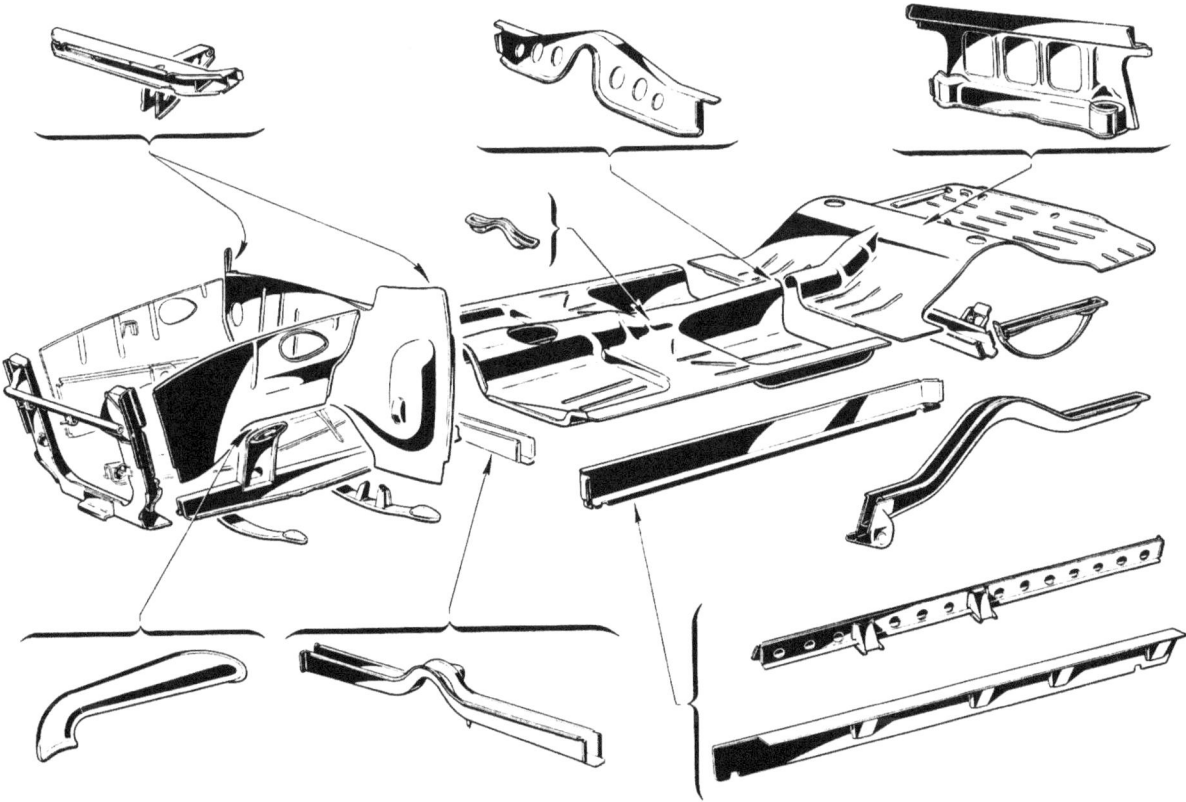

Fig. 43 - Spare parts to effect body repairs to the Giulietta Spider and Spider Veloce.
Note: When ordering spare parts please refer to tables from 116 to 122 in the catalogue.

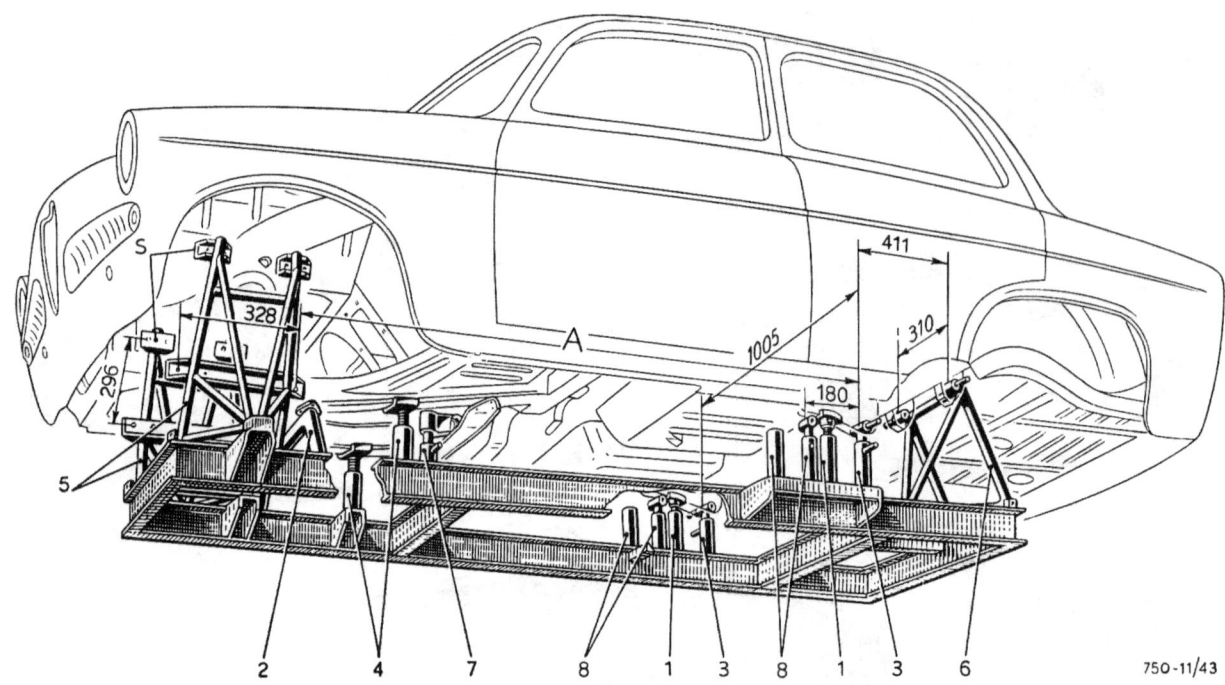

Fig. 44 - Complete chassis 6123.91001 and the principal body dimensions to be considered during inspection

The distance, measured over the longitudinal axis of the car, between the rear holes in the bottom frame member (for the connection to the front suspension arms) and the differential tie-rod attachments:

$$A = \begin{cases} 1644 \text{ mm. for vehicles with 2380 mm. wheelbase.} \\ 1464 \text{ mm. for vehicles with 2200 mm. wheelbase.} \end{cases}$$

Figures 44 also shows the vertical rods **8** which are used to check vehicles with a 2200 mm. wheelbase.

The figures also include several major dimensions with a view to facilitating a summary examination of the body when the special equipment is not available.

6 - WASHING AND CLEANING THE CAR

Washing: Frequent washing is one of the best ways to preserve the paintwork. Only plain water should be used; many commercial products of the shampoo type are harmful to cellulose.

The car should preferably be washed with cool engine and away from the direct rays of the sun. The best method is to use a sponge and a liberal water supply followed by a drying rub with a chamois leather.

Removal of dirt: If the coachwork is badly soiled with grease, road tar and oil products, etc., they must be removed with a solvent such as benzine.

Ordinary petrol should never be used as it contains tetraethyl of lead which is poisonous.

Polishing cellulosed surfaces: A fine protective surface can be obtained by the application of a suitable polish at least once a year or preferably twice; before applying the polish remove all dirt from the coachwork and wash the car carefully as described above.

The type of polish used should be chosen with care; highly abrasive (abrasive pastes, etc.) corrosive (containing nitrocellulose solvents or plastifiers) or overgreasy (wax) products mus not be used.

The methods of application are usually supplied with the polish. As a general rule the polish should be spread on with light pressure; the final shine is then obtained by a brisk rubbing with another clean cotton rag.

Cleaning fabric and plastic upholstery and carpets:

When cleaning upholstery, carpets, the dashboard, etc., use suitable solvents of terpentine type. Ordinary petrol must not be used as it contains tetraethyl of lead which is poisonous and less easily dried.

Woollen carpets must be washed with standard commercial detergents or dry-cleaned with trichloroethylene;

Rubber carpets should be cleaned with suitable commercial products which revive the colour and the shine.

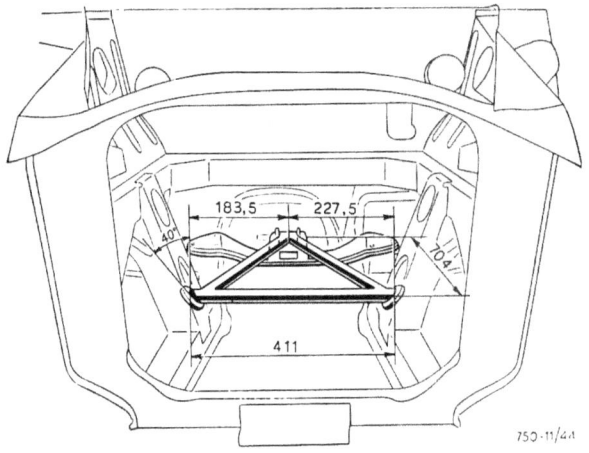

Fig. 45 - Tool assembly No. 6123.91002 for checking rear and lateral engine/gear-box mounting points.

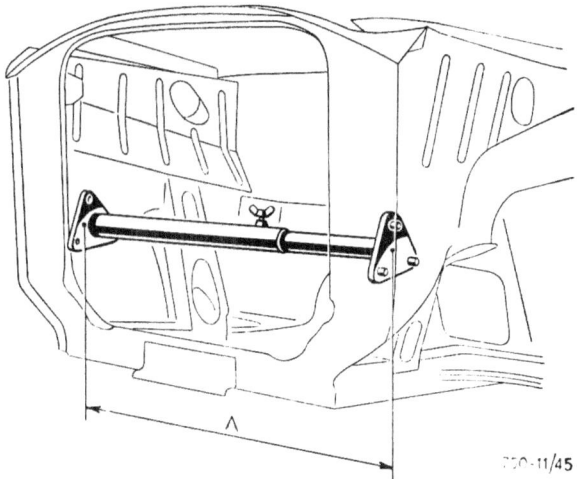

Fig. 46 - Tool assembly No. 6123.91003 and No. 6123.91004 for checking the positions of the steering-box and steering-arm bracket attachment points.

$A = \begin{cases} 620 \text{ mm. for the Giulietta Berlina.} \\ 617 \text{ mm. for the Giulietta Sprint.} \end{cases}$

Cleaning chromium-plating: Chromium-plating must be cleaned by suitable commercial products.
Take care that the product selected is not excessively abrasive or corrosive.

It is advisable to protect chromium-plating with wax or resin base products. Such products must of course be absolutely transparent and allow the natural brightness of the chromium-plating to remain visible.

This protective treatment should be given once or twice a year and should be preceded by careful cleaning and after having removed the old protective coating. In this way the chromium-plating will retain its perfect finish for many years.

Cleaning and protecting the under-surfaces of the car

After carefully washing the under-surface of the car, they should be sprayed with a water-repellant product which leaves a protective film. The efficiency of the anti-drum paint applied particularly to reduce noise and to prevent damage to the paint-work by stones thrown up under the mudguards must also be carefully checked.

Painting operations

When sheet metal members are damaged, or when various parts of the body have to be touched up, nitrocellulose enamel should be used.

Rust preventive priming, stopping and undercoats may be of the nitro-synthetic or nitrocombined types.
These products can be allowed to dry under normal atmospheric temperatures or by the use of infra-red ray lamps.

Drying ovens at temperatures greater than 60°C must not be used.

INFORMATION SHEET REFERENCE

ASSEMBLY	DATE	SHEET N.	SUBJECT

PART 12

LUBRICATION AND MAINTENANCE

INDEX

LUBRICATION INSTRUCTIONS . . . . page 239

1 - Engine lubrication . . . . » 240

    Changing the engine oil . . . . » 240

2 - General lubrication . . . . » 240

3 - Special instructions for the use of Energol Visco-Static Oil . . . . » 240

PERIODICAL MAINTENANCE . . . . » 242

PART 12

LUBRICATION AND MAINTENANCE

LUBRICATION INSTRUCTIONS

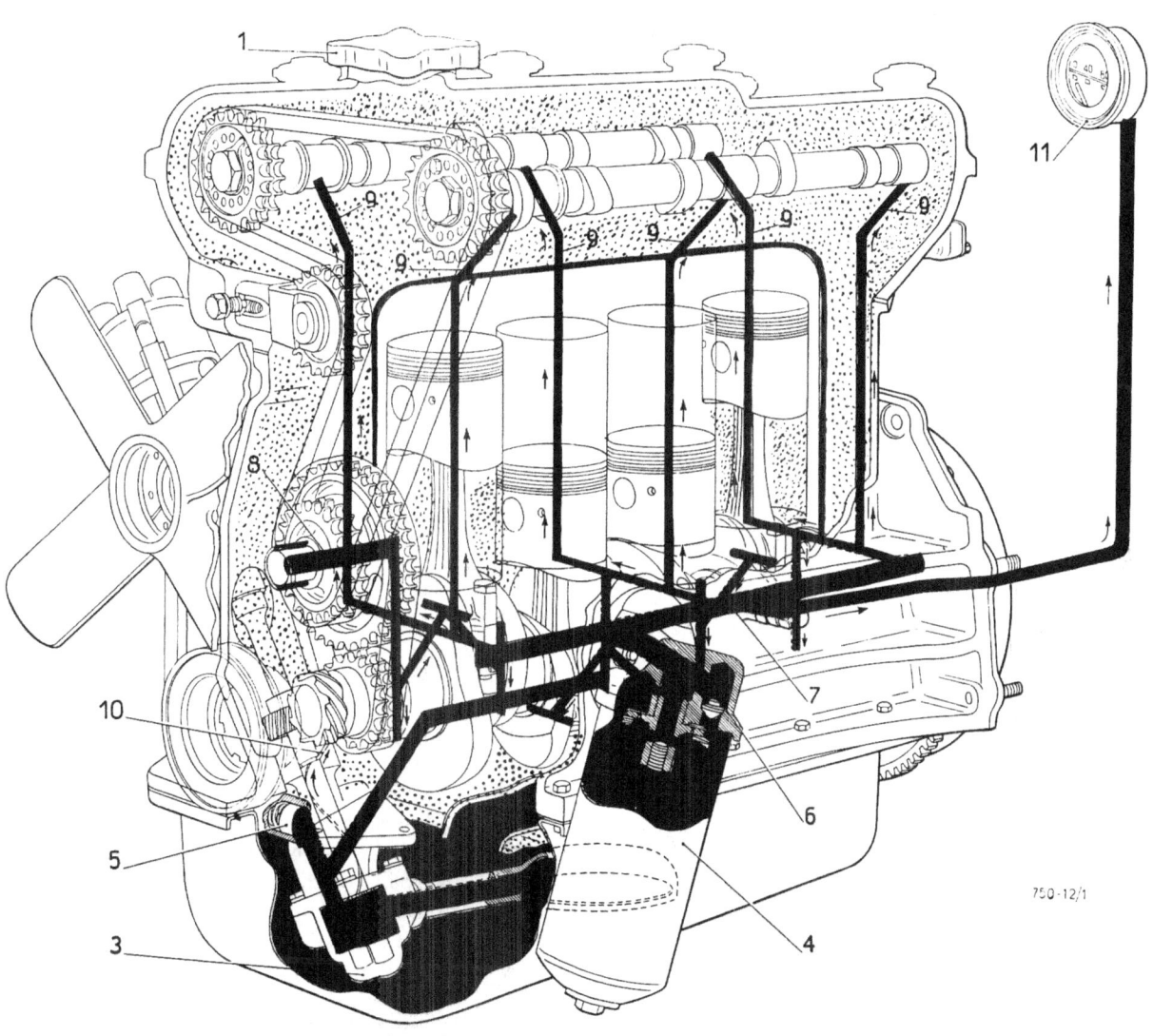

Fig. 1 - Engine lubrication circuit diagram.

1. Oil filler plug - **2.** Oil intake from sump, with strainer - **3.** Oil pump - **4.** Oil filter - **5.** Safety valve - **6.** By-pass valve which opens if filter becomes clogged - **7.** Main oil distribution pipe - **8.** Oil line to intermediate camshaft gearing - **9.** Oil lines to camshafts - **10.** Oil line to distributor driving gear - **11.** Oil pressure gauge.

1 - ENGINE LUBRICATION

The engine is force-lubricated by means of a gear-wheel pump installed at the front of the crankcase.

The pump is immersed in the sump oil and driven by a pair of helical gear-wheels, one of which is keyed to the front of the crankshaft.

There are no pressure-regulating valves on the oil circuit other than the safety valve on the pump body.

The maximum permissible oil pressure is 4.5 to 5 kg/cm² (64 to 71 p.s.i.)

If the pressure drops below the following minimum values, the cause must be located at once:

— minimum pressure at maximum revs, with a hot engine: 3,5 kg/cm² (50 p.s.i.);

— minimum pressure when idling with a hot engine: $0.5 \div 1$ kg/cm² ($7 \div 14$ p.s.i.).

CHANGING THE ENGINE OIL

In the case of new or re-built engine, the sump should be drained and refilled more frequently than is necessary after the engines have been properly run in. The recommended oil changes are as follows:

1st - after the first 800 km. (500 miles)

2nd - after the next 2000 km. (1250 miles)

3rd - after the next 4000 km. (2500 miles)

4th - then after every 4000 km. (2500 miles).

The oil filter cartridge (with « Fispa » filter) must be replaced after the first 4000 km. (2500 miles) and then after every 4000 km. (2500 miles).

With « Fram » filters the cartridge should be carefully washed, after the first 4000 km. (2500 miles) and then after every 4000 km. (2500 miles) when changing the engine oil.

Users are reminded that the periodic replacement or washing of filter cartridges, and the perfect cleanliness and careful fitting of the filter, are essential factors in trouble-free engine operation.

2 - GENERAL LUBRICATION

The various parts of the car must be lubricated as shown in Fig. 2.

The following SHELL or AGIP lubricants are recommended:

Engine (All cars but Sprint Veloce and Spider Veloce):

— Special Energol Visco-Static

— Shell X 100 M.O. 20 W 40

Engine (Only for Sprint Veloce and Spider Veloce cars):

above 10 °C (50 °F) — Energol 40 / Shell X 100 M.O. 40

below 10 °C (50 °F) — Energol 30 / Shell X 100 M.O. 30

Gear-box — Energol SAE 90 for gear-boxes and differentials / Shell - Dentax 90

Differential and Steering box — Energol EP-SAE 90 for gear-boxes and differentials / Shell Spirax 90

Ball joints on front and rear suspension and steering arms / Front suspension arm pins / Universal joints on propeller shaft — Energrease A 1

Front-wheel bearings / Brake circuit feed tank — Energrease L 3 / Energol brake fluid

Shock-absorbers — Energol shock-absorber oil / Shell Donax

3 - SPECIAL INSTRUCTIONS FOR THE USE OF ENERGOL VISCO-STATIC OIL

Energol Visco-Static engine oil has a very high detergent capacity; when it is used in engines which have already operated with other types of oil the undernoted instructions must be carefully observed.

This is made necessary because when subjected to the action of detergents, any carbon deposits adhering to the various parts of the engine tend to break away and can quickly clog the oil filter with consequent damage to the crankshaft and connecting-rod bearings and to other parts lubricated by the circulating oil.

1) **Draining off the old oil**

— Run the engine until its normal working temperature is reached;

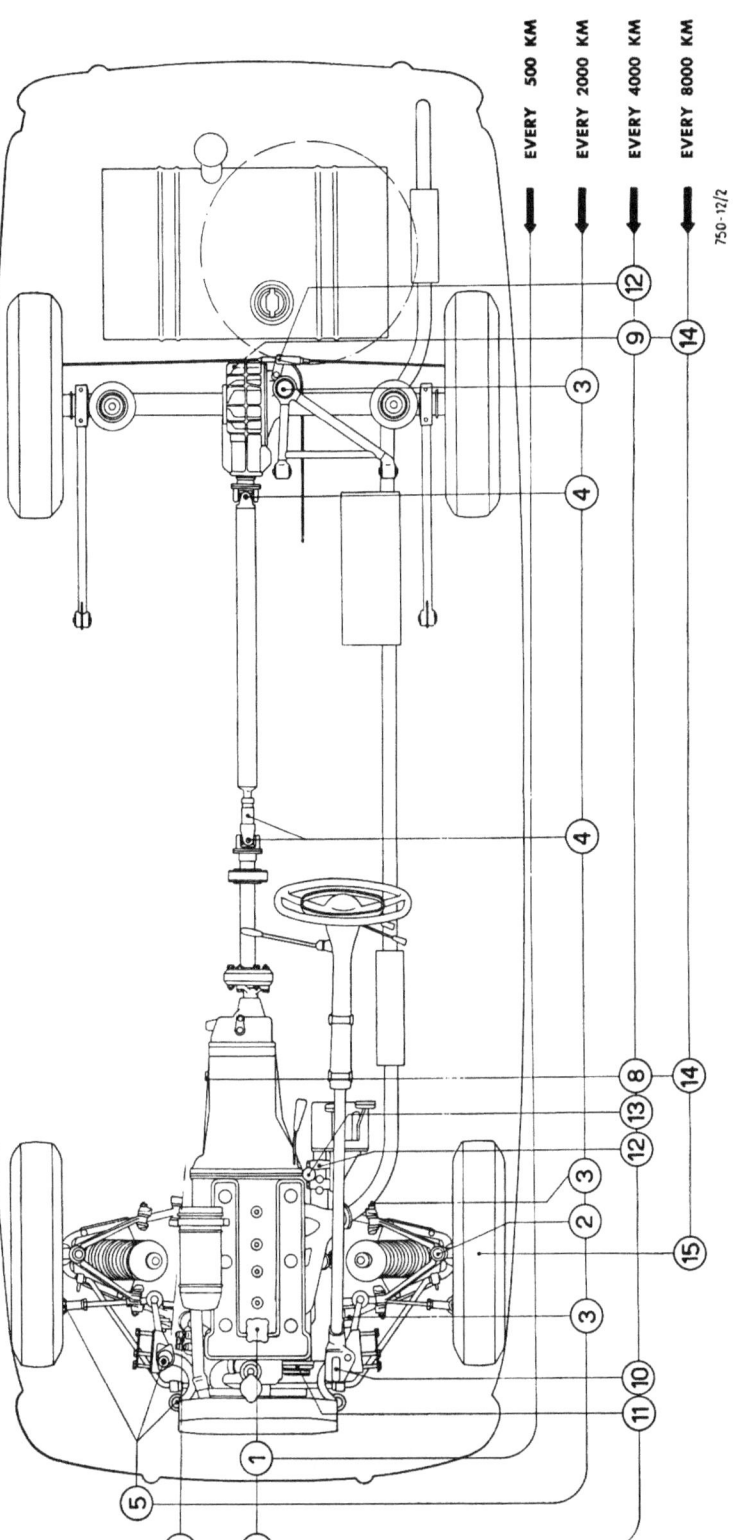

Fig. 2 - General lubrication diagram.

Periodical lubrication.

Every 500 km. (approximately 300 miles)

1 - Check the engine-oil level.

Every 2000 km. (approx. 1250 miles)

2 - Lubricate top and bottom ball joints of steering knuckle
3 - Lubricate connecting bolt arms of front and rear suspensions
4 - Lubricate universal joints of cardan shaft
5 - Lubricate ball joints of steering system rods.

Every 4000 km. (approx. 2500 miles)

6 - Change the engine oil

Supply with lubricant or grease the following parts:

7 - Ignition distributor (see Part 10)
8 - Gear-box
9 - Rear axle casing
10 - Steering box
11 - Generator (see Part 10)
12 - Clutch controls, hand-brake controls, hydraulic-brake controls and carburettor linkage
13 - Brake system feeding tank
— Hinges and locks of doors and hoods.

Every 8000 km (approx. 5000 miles)

14 - Change the oil in the gear-box and in the rear axle casing
15 - Grease bearings of front wheels.

— Raise the front of car a few inches to facilitate the complete draining of oil;

— Drain the oil from the sump;

— Dismantle the filter and empty it of oil and sludge;

— Examine the filtering element, which should be in perfect condition. If not, either replace the cartridge (in the case of the Fram filter with cardboard cartridge) or wash the felt filtering element (in the case of the Fispa filter with a felt element).

2) **Fill up with Visco-Static oil**

3) **Substitution**

— After 200/500km. (125/300 miles) according to the total mileage covered by the vehicles, empty the sump and filter as described in 1. above. Cars which have done more than 30.000 km. (approximately 20.000 miles) must be filled up every 200 km. (125 miles) while newer cars need filling only every 500 km. (300 miles).

— Replace the Fram filter or carefully wash the filtering element in the Fispa filter.

— Fill up with fresh Visco-Static engine oil.

WARNING

A) **While it is permissible to add ordinary oil (that is, oil without detergents, or detergent oils made by other firms) to an engine containing Energol Visco-Static oil, it is quite inadvisable to add Energol Visco-Static oil to engines containing ordinary oil. This is because, as stated above, the highly detergent action of Visco-Static could lead to the rapid clogging of the filter.**

B) **The above warning regarding Visco-Static oil is equally applicable to all other high detergent capacity oils now available on the market.**

PERIODICAL MAINTENANCE

EVERY 500 KM. (approx. 300 miles)

— Check the level of the engine oil (see Fig. 2).

1) Check the level of the water in the radiator. Special instructions to be observed in winter and when de-scaling the radiator are given in Part, 2, Chapter 21.

2) Check the type pressures.
Part 9 sets out the proper inflation pressures, describes the effects of running with excessively or insufficiently inflated tyres, and gives instructions for balancing wheels and tyres.

EVERY 2000 KM. (approx. 1250 miles)

3) Check the level of the battery electrolyte.
The electrolyte should not cover the top of the battery plates by more than ¼ in.; nor should it leave the plates uncovered.

A method of checking the electrolyte level is shown in Part 2.

Ways of prolonging battery life are described in Part 10.

EVERY 4000 KM. (approx. 2500 miles)

— Lubricate the car as shown in Fig. 2.

4) Check the valve clearances and adjust if necessary. Valve clearance data and adjustment instructions are given in Part 2.

Perfect valve clearances mean ideal engine performance and long valve-seat life.

5) Adjust spark-plug gaps and remove carbon deposits. Part 2 shows how to check this important piece of equipment and keep it efficient.

6) Adjust the distributor contact gap. See Part 2 and Part 10 for instructions in this connection.

7) Adjust the tension of the belt driving the fan and the generator.

Correct belt tension is essential, as too tight a belt may damage the generator bearings, while too slack a belt will cause the generator to slip with the result that it will fail to charge the battery properly.

Part 2 shows the method of adjusting belt tension and gives the appropriate data.

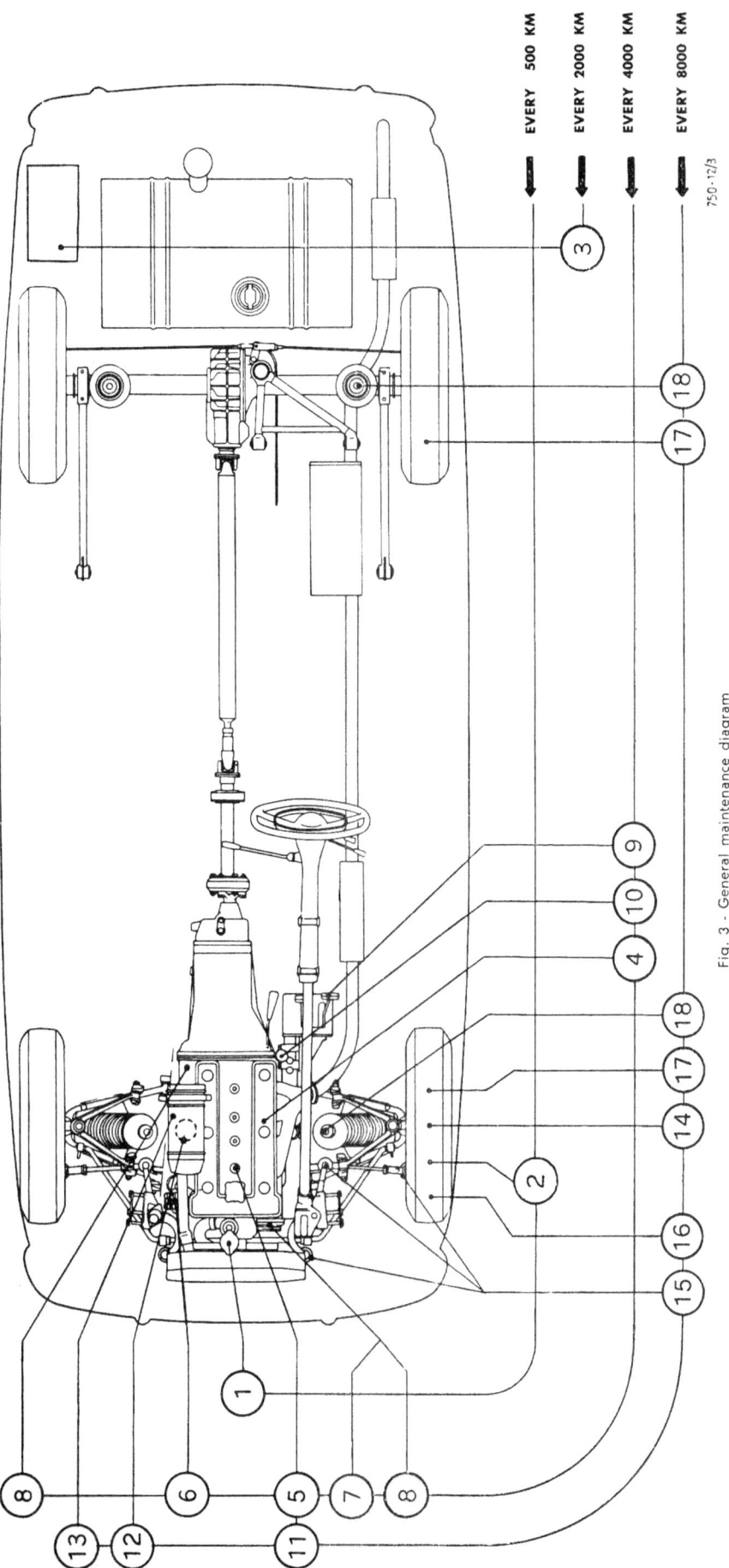

Fig. 3 - General maintenance diagram

Every 500 km. (approx. 300 miles)
— Check the engine oil-level.
1 - Check the radiator water-level
2 - Check the tyre pressures.

Every 2000 km. (approx. 1250 miles)
3 - Check the level of the battery electrolyte

Every 4000 km. (approx. 2500 miles)
— Lubricate the car as described in Fig. 2
4 - Check valve clearances and adjust as necessary
5 - Check and adjust sparking-plug electrode gaps and remove any carbon deposits
6 - Adjust the distributor contact gap
7 - Adjust the generator and fan-belt tension
8 - Inspect the generator and starter-motor brushes and commutator
9 - Check the clutch pedal free travel
10 - Check the level of the brake fluid in the feed tank.

Every 8000 km. (approx. 5000 miles)
— Lubricate the car as described in Fig. 2
11 - Fit new sparking plugs or adjust the electrode gaps
12 - Clean the fuel filters and the carburettor bowl
13 - Clean the air filter
14 - Check the front-wheel bearings for wear
15 - Check the steering-arm ball joints for wear
16 - Check front-wheel toe-in
17 - Check the brake linings and shoes for wear
18 - Inspect the shock-absorbers

Note: Certain of the above instructions must be observed more frequently according to the season of the year and according to the extent to which the car is used; for example, the battery electrolyte level should be checked more often in summer, and the radiator water level more often when the car is used in mountainous or hilly country.

8) Examine the generator brushes and commutator.

The brushes must be perfectly clean, and must slide freely in their seats; the sliding surface of the commutator must be cleaned with a rag dipped in petrol; the brush pressure springs must be efficient.

Part 10 give suitable maintenance instructions, for brushes and generator.

9) Adjust the free travel of the clutch pedal. Adjustment details are given in Part 3.

10) Check the level of the brake fluid in the feed tank. The oil level must never fall below the quarterfull mark; top up only with the recommended type of fluid.

EVERY 8000 KM. (approx. 5000 miles)

— Lubricate the car as shown in Fig. 2.

11) Fit new sparking plugs if necessary, and in any event adjust the electrode gaps.

12) Clean out the fuel filters and bowl. This must be done more frequently if necessary.

The appropriate instructions are given in Part 2.

13) Clean the air filter (see Part 2).

14) Check the play in the front-wheel bearing (see Part 6).

15) Check the wear in the steering-arm ball-joints (see Part 7).

16) Check front-wheel toe-in (see Part 7).

17) Check the brake-linings and shoes for wear (see Part 8).

18) Inspect the shock-absorbers (see Part 5).

INFORMATION SHEET REFERENCE

ASSEMBLY	DATE	SHEET N.	SUBJECT

INFORMATION SHEET REFERENCE

ASSEMBLY	DATE	SHEET N.	SUBJECT

PART 13

ACCESSORIES

INDEX

1 - Electric Horn . . . . page 249

2 - MARELLI Windscreen Wiper, model TGE-41 A . . . . » 251

3 - AVOG Windscreen Wiper . . . . » 252

4 - SWF Windscreen Wiper, model BSW . . . . » 253

5 - Panel instruments . . . . » 254

6 - Lighting equipment . . . . » 254

7 - Car interior heating and air-conditioning equipment . . . . » 257

8 - Windscreen washing unit . . . . » 260

PART 13

ACCESSORIES

1 - ELECTRIC HORN

Description

The main components of the Marelli horn are:

— **the diaphragm** which is caused to vibrate by the electromagnet and which emits the sound;

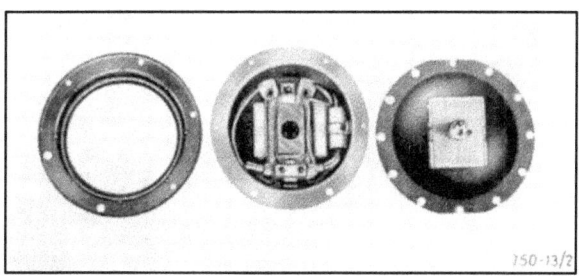

Fig. 2 - The Marelli electric horn.

— **the elctromagnet** designed to cause the diaphragm to vibrate.

The diagram in Fig. 1 clearly demonstrates the operation of the horn; by closing the circuit in practice effected by pressing on the horn ring on the steering-wheel) a magnetic field is created by means of the electromagnet wihch then attracts the armature **4** connected to the diaphragm **10**.

By moving towards the electromagnet, the armature operates circuit-breaker **6** in such a way as to open the electric circuit; the magnetic effect then fails and the armature returns to ist initial position.

When the armature thus returns to its original position, the circuit-breaker contacts-close and restore current to the circuit. The cycle is then repeated.

The very frequent repetition of the opening and closing of the electromagnetic circuit cause the diaphragm to vibrate and the horn sound. The tone of the horn depends on the frequency of the oscillations.

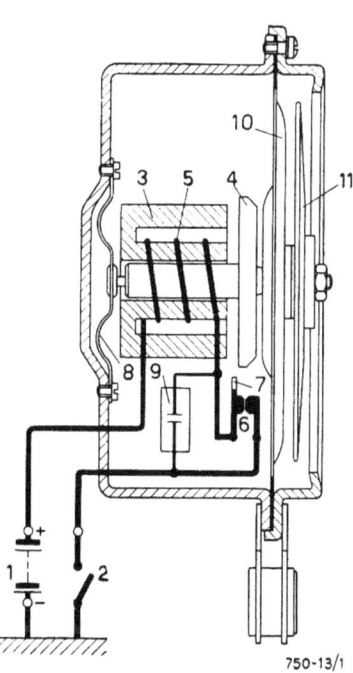

Fig. 1 - The electric wiring diagram of the Marelli electric horn.
1. Battery - **2**. Push-button - **3**. Electromagnetic core - **4**. Electromagnet armature - **5**. Electromagnet coil - **6**. Circuit breaker - **7**. Contact spring - **8**. Leaf spring - **9**. Condenser - **10**. Diaphragm - **11**. Loudspeaker cone.

Fig. 3 - An exploded view of the Marelli electric horn.

How to trace faults

If the horn does not work, the defect may be due to the following causes:

— a damaged horn;

— broken electric leads;

— a faulty earth connection;

— irregular closing of the earth circuit through faulty operation of the horn ring on the steering-wheel.

Causes of damage to the horn may be as follows: excessive wear of the electromagnet contacts;

— broken or burned-out windings or connections;

— deformation or breakage of the diaphragm.

As a general rule the latter three cases of damage require the horn to be discarded and replaced.

When the circut-breaker contacts wear or corrosion is not excessive, the contacts may be cleaned with a fine file and re-set by means of the adjusting screw.

After checking to ensure that the horn itself is in working order, the related equipment should be examined.

— First check, using a test bulb, that current is reaching the horn. If the bulb lights up, the trouble will lie between the horn and the horn ring;

— by earthing the other terminal with a suitable lead, the horn should sound;

— If the horn then sounds, check the horn equipment on the steering column.

Causes of faulty operation of the horn may be a broken wire or poor contact between the terminal strip and the steering column surface due to dirt or oxidation. When the horn emits an irregular sound after the said contacts have been cleaned, alter the setting of the adjusting screw.

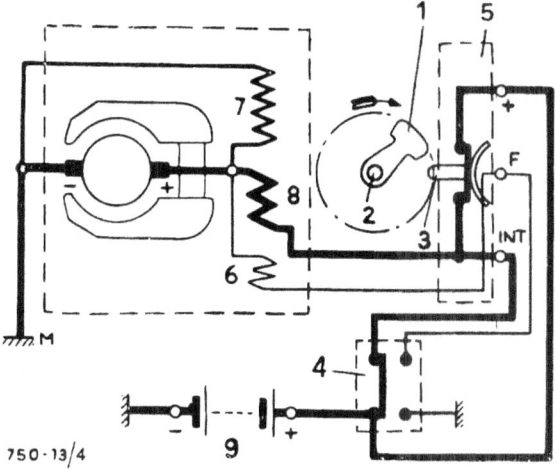

Fig. 4 - Diagram of the electric circuit and of the end-of-stroke stop on the Marelli windscreen wiper, model TGE 41 A.

1. Control switch shoe - **2.** Crank pin - **3.** Push-button - **4.** Commutator - **5.** End-of-stroke switch - **6.** End-of-stroke winding - **7.** Shunt winding - **8.** Series windings - **9.** Battery.

2 - MARELLI WINDSCREEN WIPER, MODEL TGE-41 A

Description and operation

This wiper comprises a motor the rotary action of which — after suitable speed reduction — is transmitted to a crankshaft and from the crankshaft to the levers which actuate the wiper blades.

The unit is provided with a blade end-of-stroke device ensuring perfect visibility of the driver.

Diagram 4 shows the electric circuit with the wiper end-of-stroke stop device.

Commutator **4** (main switch) is closed in the diagram; current passes through the commutator and the windscreen wiper operates.

In this way the end-of-travel switch **5** remains cut out of the feed circuit and is therefore independent of the position of shoe **1** in relation to the push-button **3**.

When the commutator **4** is opened, the motor remains fed by the switch **5** until the moment when the latter opens under the action of the shoe **1**. The feed to the motor is therefore cut off only at the instant when the wiper blades reach the end of their operating stroke.

In order to prevent the wiper blades from travelling beyond the said limit by the force of inertia, an electrical braking device is provided for the armature. This is effected by adding a third winding **6** to the two orthodox field windings.

The operation of the commutator **4** (in addition to opening the main circuit) causes the third winding **6** in parallel with winding **7** to come into operation.

The greater field excitation caused by the intervention of the third winding **6** and greater amount of current which passes through the winding **8** together determine a reduction of the speed of rotation of the motor without any reduction of the torque.

At a second stage, at the instant when the end-of-travel switch **5** opens, the motor acts as a dynamo (the braking winding also operates as a loading resistance) and the kinetic energy is transformed into heat with a considerable braking torque as a result of which the motor (and thereby the wiper blades) stop almost instantaneously.

Tracing faults in operation

Such faults may be causes by:

— incorrect fitting to the body;

— an inefficent motor induction unit.

Incorrect fitting to the car body can lead to the twisting of the carrying plate for the windscreen wiper unit; this in turn will prevent the free movement of the rods driving the arms.

It can cause uneven movement of the wiper blades on the shafts; the oscillation angle of the shafts is 115".

In like manner, incorrect fitting of the blades on the shaft can cause blade flutter at the windscreen edges;

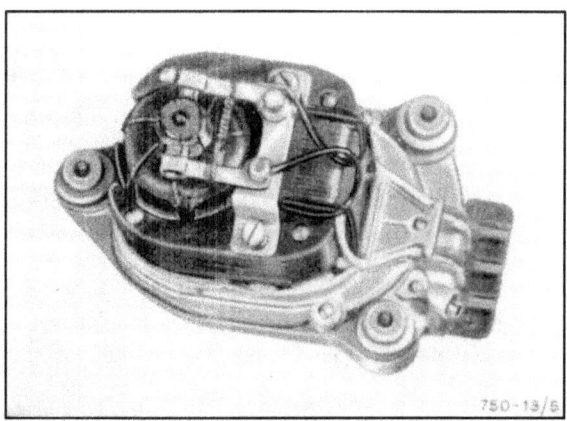

Fig. 5 - Marelli windscreen wiper motor.

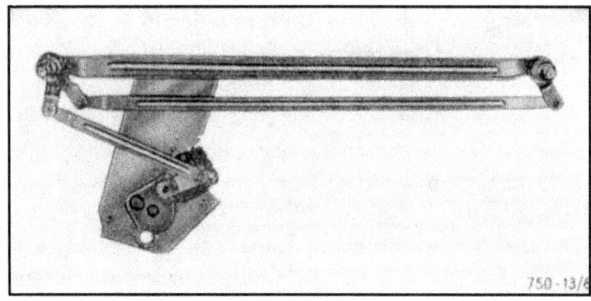

Fig. 6 - The Marelli TGE 41 A windscreen wiper unit.

this flutter is accompanied by shocks to the gear-wheels and the possibility of the blades stopping in a position where the driving motor remains under current although operating the switch, since the end-of-stroke shoe has not yet opened the feed circuit.

In such cases, in order to avoid burning out the motor (and as it is not sufficient to place the switch in the « stop » position) it will be necessary to disconnect the lead to the positive terminal.

If the windscreen wiper unit has to be removed from the car body, care should be taken when refitting it to make sure that the following instructions are observed:

— rubber water seals: these seals must be fitted over the pins and caused to adhere to the body so as to constitute water-proof joints;

— nuts for locking the pins: these nuts should be tightened sufficiently but not excessively or the rubber seals will become damaged;

— the wiper blades must be fitted while taking care that they are fully pressed home on the taper end and well tightened, as any slackness can cause the windscreen wiper to stop in a position that will cause the armature to burn out for the abovementioned reasons;

— the pressure of the blade on the glass (measured between the glass and the edge of the steel wiper back) must be 225 grams;

— the motor bracket must be tightened in position without causing any deformation of the bracket;

— it the connections are properly made, operation of the switch will cause the motor to stop in such a way that the wiper blades stop in the "at rest" position.

If the windscreen wiper is properly and completely assembled, any trouble which still persists must be looked for in the motor.

The spring clip on the crank-pin must then be unhooked and — after removal of the lever — the motor must be removed from its bracket and inspected. As a general rule the wiper motor should be replaced.

One cause of faulty wiper operation (due to excessive wear) is the result of an excessively sharp angle of inclination of the wipers in relation to the surface of the glass. In this case, and in order to prevent the metal members which hold the rubber blades from rubbing against the window surface and this cause any grooving which cannot possibly be removed, replace the blades complete.

3 - AVOG WINDSCREEN WIPER

Description and operation

The electric circuit diagram is shown in fig. 7 which also shows the end-of-stroke stop device.

By closing the switch **1**, the motor **2** is fed via terminal **3**.

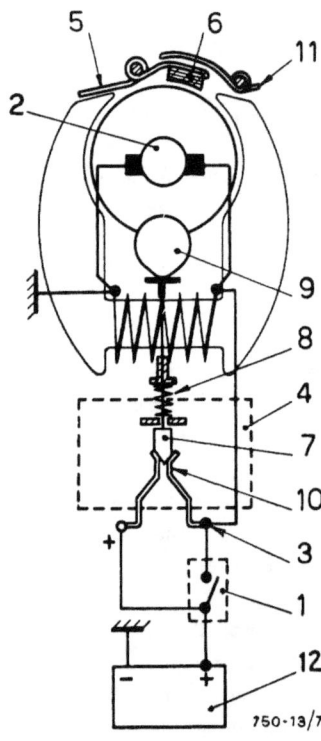

Fig. 7 - Diagram of the electric circuit and of the end-of-travel stop device on the AVOG windscreen wiper.

1. Switch - **2.** Electric motor - **3.** Terminal - **4.** End-of-travel stop device - **5.** Armature - **6.** Brake shoe - **7.** Contact point - **8.** Contact point return spring - **9.** Cam operating the contact point - **10.** Spring contacts - **11.** Braking shoe return spring - **12.** Battery.

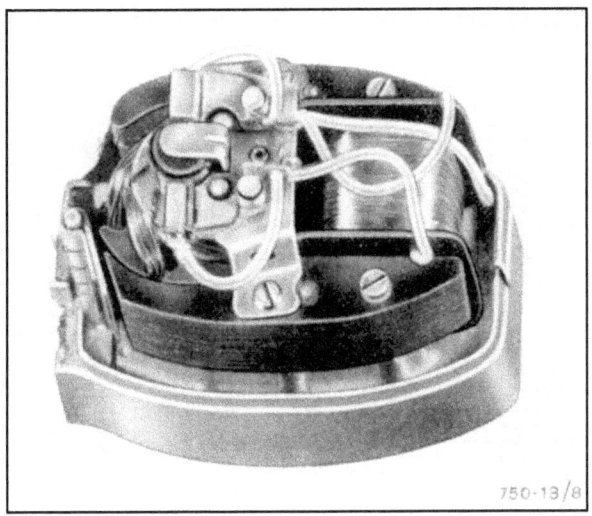

Fig. 8 - The Avog windscreen wiper motor.

The wiper parking unit **4**, while continuing to operate mechanically, remains ineffective in practice.

When current is fed to the motor, the armature **5** is attracted by the magnetism created in the stator pole-piece and thereby frees the rotor from the breaking effect of the shoe **6**.

The automatic parking arrangement — after switch **1** is opened — takes effect as a result of the breaking of the circuit by the metal contact point **7** which, under the influence of the spring **8**, follows the contour of the cam **9** fitted on the motor speed-reduction shaft; it is therefore synchronised with the movement of the wipers.

When switch **1** is opened, the motor continues to operate since current is fed to it by the spring contacts **10** and the contact point **7** until the contact point — following the contour of the cam **9** — moves away from the spring contacts and thereby breaks the circuit.

At the same time, and as the attraction of the magnetic field on the armature **5** ceases, the shoe **6**, under the action of the spring **11**, rubs on the rotor and quickly stops the motor.

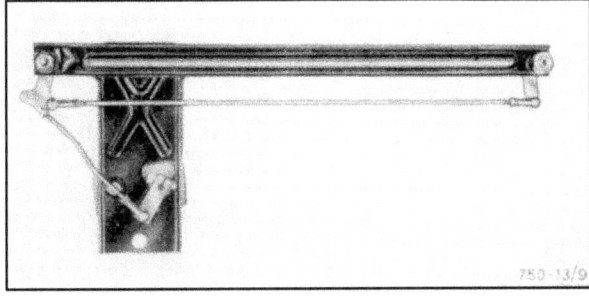

Fig. 9 - The Avog windscreen wiper unit.

Maintenance

Particular care must be taken to prevent oil from reaching the outer surface of the rotor, as this would reduce the braking effect of the shoe, thus permitting the rotor to continue spinning by inertia and causing the stopping zone to pass beyond the cam, thus closing the circuit between the contact point **7** and the spring contacts **10**, and starting up the motor.

If that happens it will be impossible to stop the motor. A similar problem arises if the brake shoe is worn or if only a small shoe area rubs on the rotor.

This trouble is particularly noticeable when the motor operates at maximum speed, that is, when the windscreen is very wet and when the motor operates under a high voltage of 14-15 V.

The position in which the cam is fitted to the motor shaft must be very carefully determined, as any slip results in an alteration in the stopping position.

4 - SWF WINDSCREEN WIPER, MODEL BSW

Description and operation

The diagram in fig. 10 shows the electric circuit in respect of the motor.

By closing the switch circuit **1** via the terminal **10**, the electromagnet **2** is excited and attracts the armature **3** which, by means of a rod attached to the plate **4**, releases the steel band **5** which acts as a brake and thus frees the rotor from the braking action. At the same time the contacts **7** close and the motor starts up.

By opening the switch **1** the electromagnet **2** is de-excited but the motor continues to rotate until the cam **8**, keyed onto the projecting shaft in such a position as to stop the wiper blade in the desired position, prevents the plate **4**, under the influence of the spring **9**, from opening the contact **7**; in this way the current supply to the motor is discontinued. At the same time the band brake **5** stops the rotor and eliminates any possibility of its continuing to rotate by inertia or its coming to a stop in any other than the desired position.

If the motor fails to stop, the cause may lie in a broken band brake or in its defective braking action due either to stretching of the band itself or to grease on the braking portions; in this case it will be found that the wiper tends to slow down in the stopping zone but then recovers its normal operating speed; this is because the inertia of the rotating mass is sufficient to overcome the stopping zone on the cam and as a result, when the contact **7** close, the motor resumes operation.

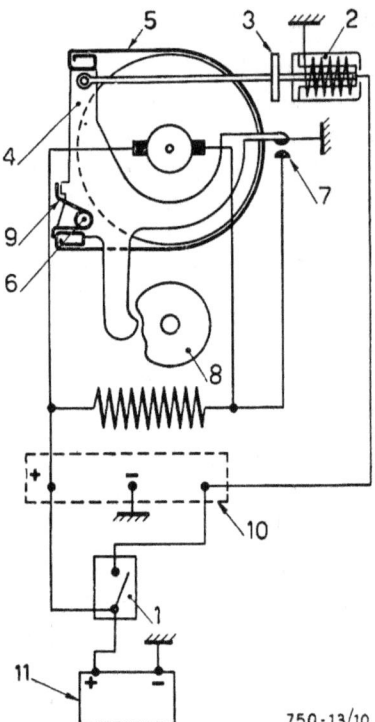

Fig. 10 - Diagram of the electric circuit and the end-of-travel device in respect of the SWF model BSW windscreen wiper.
1. Switch - 2. Electromagnet - 3. Armature - 4. Plate - 5. Band brake - 6. Pin on plate 4 - 7. Contacts - 8. Cam - 9. Return spring - 10. Terminal plate - 11. Battery.

If the wiper driving spindle becomes disconnected it is possible that the stem itself will stick and that the motor will be locked in other than the " stop " position; it will then be necessary to cut off the current supply to the positive terminal immediately in order to prevent the motor from burning out; **it is not sufficient** merely to open the control switch.

5 - PANEL INSTRUMENTS

A) ON THE GIULIETTA BERLINA AND T.I.

The instruments on the panel proper (see Fig. 13 and 14) are:

A speedometer: the scale is graduated from 20 to 140 km/h (Berlina cars) and from 20 to 160 km/h (t.i. cars) and shows the maximum speed limit which must not be exceeded in the various gears after the running-in period.

A total mileage indicator

A tripping mileage indicator: this device can quickly be reset at zero by means of the appropriate flexible control.

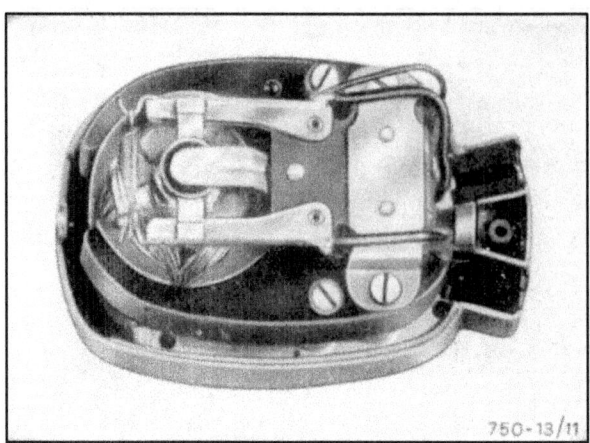

Fig. 11 - SWF windscreen wiper motor, model BSW.

A petrol level gauge with a low-level tell-tale: this gauge operates only when the ignition is switched on with the appropriate key. The red tell-tale lamp lights up when the fuel level in the tank is down to 6/7 litres.

An oil-pressure gauge

A red tell-tale, located in the centre of the speedometer dial, which lights up when the direction-indicators are working.

The instrument panel is lit by a 2.5 W bulb located in the centre of the speedometer dial.

B) ON THE GIULIETTA SPRINT AND SPIDER

The Giulietta Sprint and Spider have the same instruments at those described above, but they are located in separate frames. In this case an engine speed indicator and an oil-water temperature gauge are also fitted (see Fig. 15).

6 - LIGHTING EQUIPMENT

The lighting equipment comprises the two headlamps with double filament bulbs (45 W for the main beam

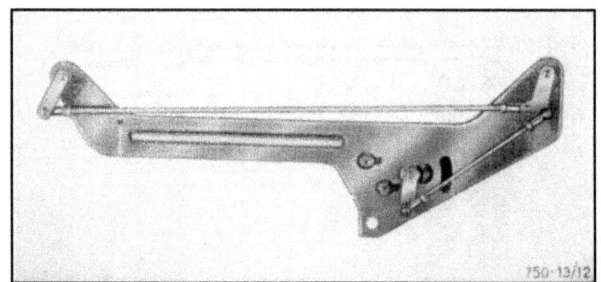

Fig. 12 - SWF windscreen wiper unit, model BSW.

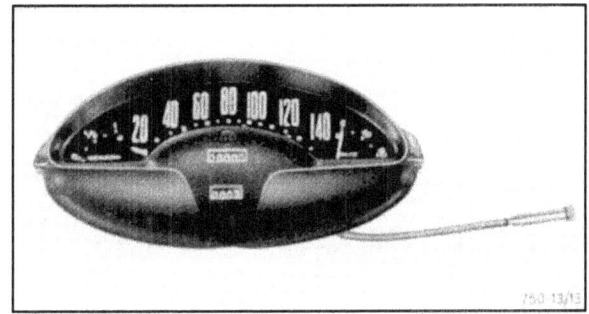

Fig. 13 - Giulietta Berlina and t.i. instrument panel.

and 40 W for the dipped beam), front parking and direction indicator lamps, triple-unit rear side lamps (parking lamp, direction-indicator lamp and "stop" lamp), a reversing lamp, a rear number-plate lamp, an instrument-panel lamp and a ceiling lamp.

The side and head-lamps (dipped and main beam) and the number-plate lamp are operated by a switch on the dash-board; a green tell-tale glown when they are switched on.

When the switch is moved to its first position, the front and rear parking-lamps and the number-plate lamps are switched on.

Whit the switch in the second position, and with the dip-switch in the normal position (i.e. when the lever beneath the steering-wheel is in the top position) the dipped headlamp filaments are lighted. To switch on the main beam this lever should be turned downwards.

The secondary front lamps (white glass) for town-driving and direction indication are fitted with double-filament bulbs (3 W for town-driving and 20 W for the flashing direction-indicators).

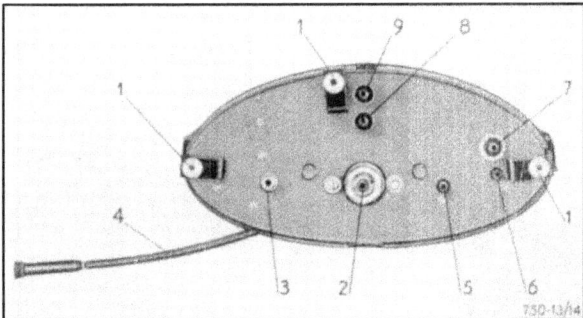

Fig. 14 - Rear view of the Giulietta Berlina and t.i. instrument panel.
1. Knurled retaining nut. - **2.** Terminal for the flexible speedometer cable - **3.** Terminal for the oil-pressure tube - **4.** Flexible control for re-setting trip mileage indicator - **5.** Electric terminal for the fuel gauge - **6.** Electric terminal for the fuel level indicator - **7.** Electric terminal for the low-level tell-tale - **8.** Lamp-holder for panel lighting bulb - **9.** Direction indicator tell-tale.

The rear side-lamps each contain three bulbs as follows:

1) the top (direction-indicator) bulb is protected with a orange-coloured glass and consumes 20 W.

2) the second or centre double filament bulb (under red glass) has a 3 W filament for parking and a 20 W filament which lights up when the car brakes are applied.

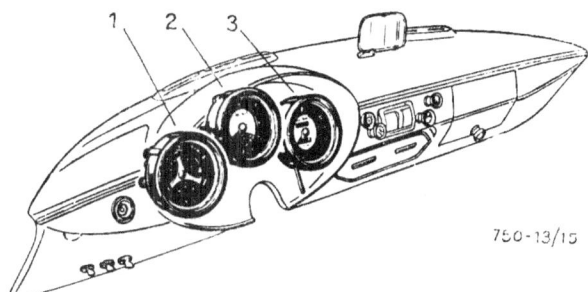

Fig. 15 - Giulietta Sprint instrument panel.
1. Unit containing the oil and water temperature gauge, the petrol gauge, head-lamp tell-tale, direction-indicator tell-tale and petrol low-level tell-tale - **2.** Engine speed indicator and oil pressure gauge - **3.** Speedometer, dynamo tell-tale, heater tell-tale.

3) the third bulb, also under a orange coloured glass, has a 20 W filament which lights up when reverse gear is engaged.

The front and rear direction-indicator winking lamps are operated by means of a two-position switch fitted beneath the steering wheel. A tell-table on the instrument panel glows when this control is in operation.

Two additional winking lamps with 5 W bulbs are also located at the side of the car.

Fig. 16 - Head-lamp.
1. Lever to open the lamp - **2.** Adjusting screw for beam adjustment.

Fig. 17 - Exploded view of a headlamp.

The number-plate lamp fixed to the centre of the luggage compartment comprises 2×5 W bulbs. These two bulbs illuminate the boot interior through a suitable orifice in the lid.

A ceiling light with built-in switch is fitted in the centre of the car and uses a 5 W bulb.

The instrument panel is lit by a 2.5 W bulb for which the switch is located beneath the dashboard.

Replacing head-lamp bulbs

First of all remove the pressure-fitted reflector rim; the lever located at the bottom of the lamp case should then be moved outwards through 90°; the reflector can now be drawn off. Lastly pull off the spring which fixes the lamp-holder to the reflector and take out the bulb (Fig. 16).

WARNING:

— Whenever bulbs are replaced, the new ones must always be of the same type. More powerful bulbs mean a current consumption beyond the charging capacity of the dynamo, and would lead to the gradual discharge of the battery.

— When reassembling the reflector take care that the mirror surface is not touched or soiled in any way.

Cleaning should only be attempted with either an air blast or a feather duster.

Head-lamp beam adjustment

When lamps have been removed from the bodywork, they should be aligned in the following way after re-fitting (Fig. 18):

— position the car on level ground 5 m. (16 ft.) for cars with normal headlamps and 10 m. (32 ft.) for cars with asymmetrical headlamps, from a white screen or a light-coloured wall, making sure that the centre line of the car is at right angles to the screen;

— draw a vertical line on the screen in line with the vertical centreline of the car and make four crosses according the following dimensions:

Normal headlamps

	A	B
	m.	m.
Berlina and t.i.	1.20	0.63÷0.64
Sprint and Sprint Vel.	1.20	0.60÷0.63
Spider and Spider Vel.	1.20	0.58÷0.60

	C	D	L
	m.	m.	m.
Berlina and t.i.	0.31÷0.32	0.77÷0.78	5
Sprint and Sprint Vel.	0.53÷0.55	0.70÷0.71	5
Spider and Spider Vel.	0.55÷0.57	0.64÷0.65	5

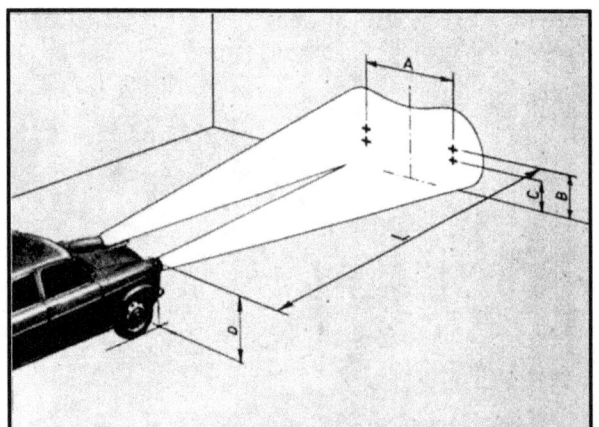
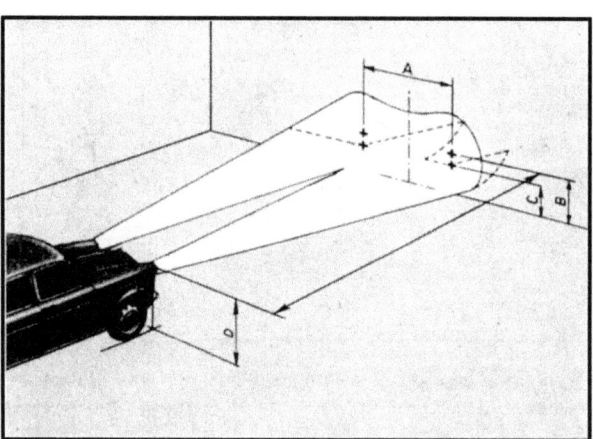

Fig. 18 - Headlamp beam checking arrangement.

a) Beam diagram with normal head-lamps. b) Beam diagram with asymmetrical head-lamps.

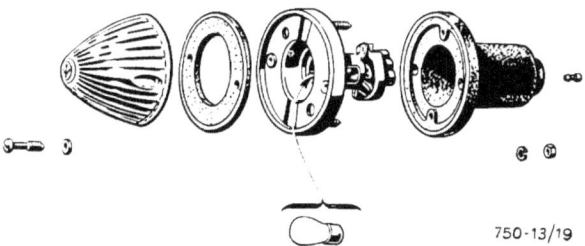

Fig. 19 - Exploded view of the secondary front lamps.

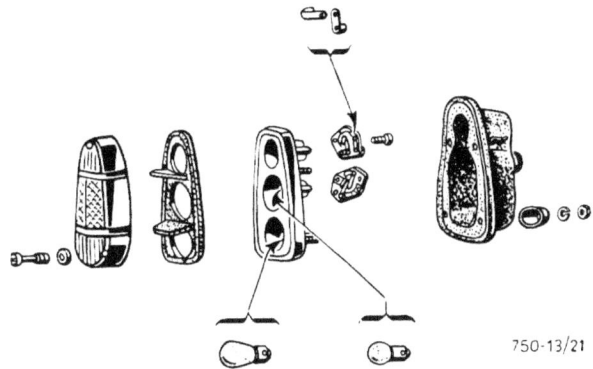

Fig. 21 - Exploded view of the rear lamp unit.

Asymmetrical headlamps

	A m.	B m.
Berlina and t.i.	1.20	0.73
Sprint and Sprint Vel.	1.20	0.44
Spider and Spider Vel.	1.20	0.40

	C m.	D m.	L m.
Berlina and t.i.	0.53	0.77÷0.78	10
Sprint and Sprint Vel.	0.30	0.67÷0.69	10
Spider and Spider Vel.	0.26	0.61÷0.62	10

Any necessary correction should be made by means of the three screws located on the reflector rim (Fig. 16).

Secondary lamps

When it is necessary to replace a bulb in a secondary front lamp (i.e. a parking and direction-indicator lamp), the plastic cover should first be taken off by removing the screws fixing it to the lamp body.

The same instruction applies in the case of the rear lamps (i.e. those containing three bulbs for parking, direction-indicator, stopping and reversing.

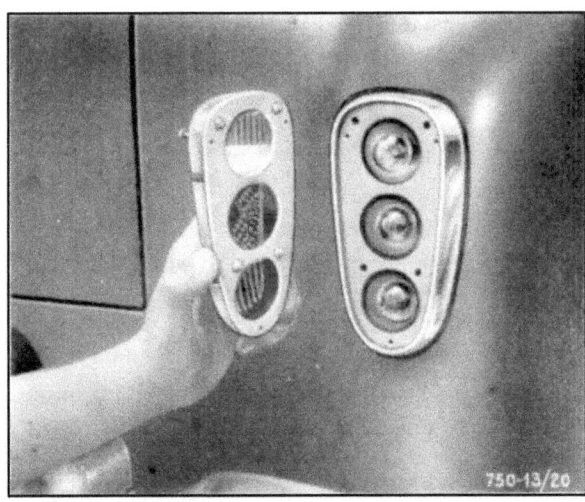

Fig. 20 - The rear lamps.

7 - CAR INTERIOR HEATING AND AIR-CONDITIONING EQUIPMENT

BERLINA AND T.I. CARS

Ventilation

The natural ventilation is ruled by operating the knob **7**, on which it is marked the letter **A** (Fig. 22).

When the knob is drawn the throttle ruling the air inlet in the car is closed, for which no air gets in.

On the contrary when the knob is resting (completely pressed) the throttle is open and air comes inside the car through the heat exchanger **2** and flow ports.

The forced ventilation is assured by the fan **1** inserted at the end of the air adducting pipe; operating the switch **5** the fan motor is put into action and the same blows air inside the car. With speeds over 50-60 kms/h (31-37 miles/h) it is possible to leave out to put the fan into operation being the dynamic force of the air sufficient enough for a good ventilation.

Heating

In order to make hot air to get inside the car pull the knob **8** on which it is marked the letter **T**. With said operation it is opened the thermostatic valve **9** establishing the flow of hot water of engine into the heat exchanger **2** inserted under the cowl: the thermostat housed in the valve **9** rules the flow of the water in order to keep the air temperature unaltered also with the change of temperature of the water in the engine.

The heated air flows inside the car through the ports placed at windshield base as well as through the bottom port that may be opened or closed as one likes operating the door **3**. Modifying the stroke of the knob **8** (**T**) it is ruled the temperature of heating air.

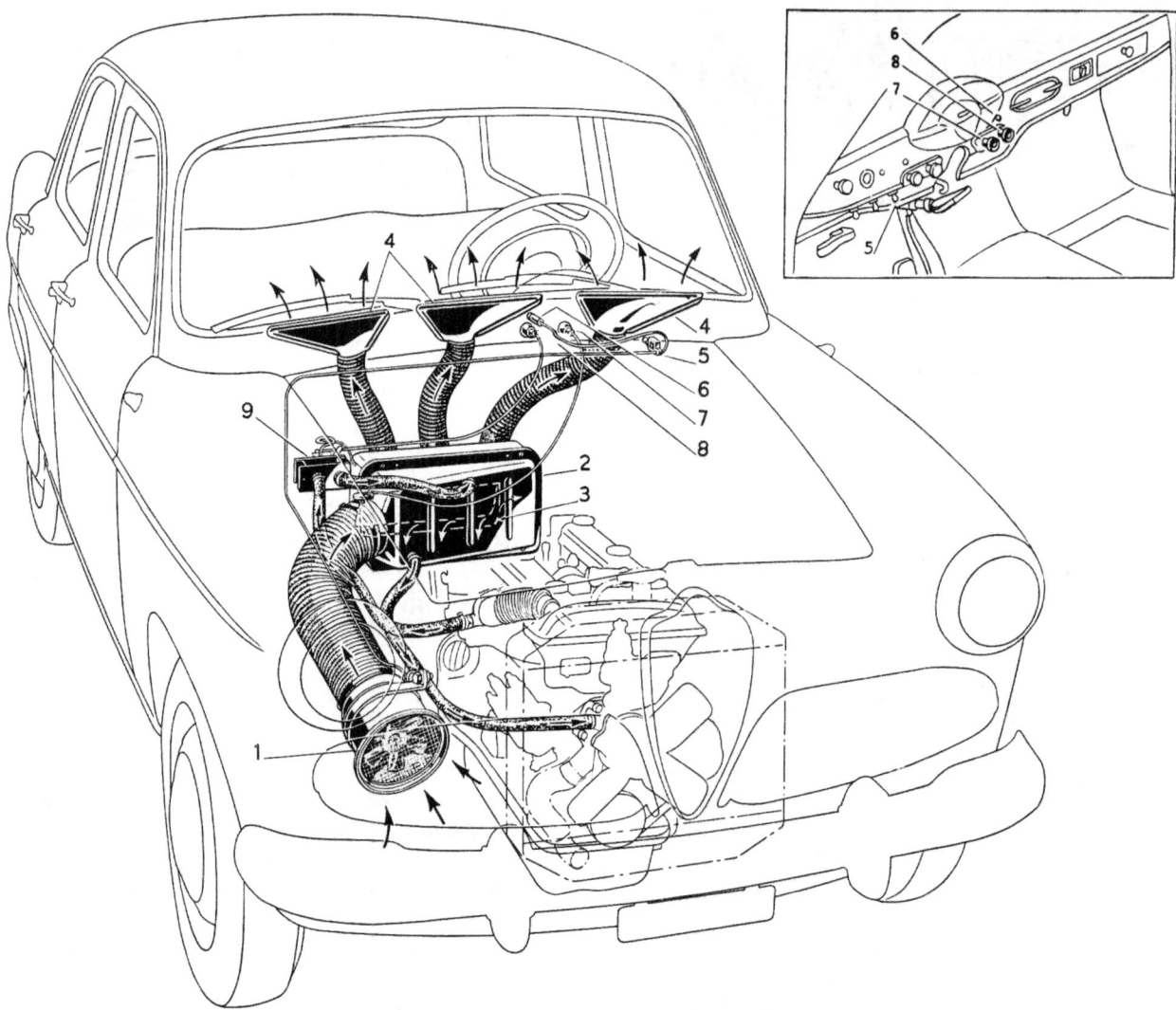

Fig. 22 - Diagram showing the heating and air-conditioning equipment on the Giulietta Berlina.
1. Fan motor set. - **2.** Heat exchanger - **3.** Shutter of air flow lower port - **4.** Air flow ports on the windshield - **5.** Heater motor switch - **6.** Motor insert tell-tale - **7.** Throttle control knob ruling air inlet in the car (**A**) - **8.** Control knob of water intake valve with thermostatic adjustment (**T**) - **9.** Thermostatic valve.

Equipment control

Circulation of hot air:

— extract the knob **8 (T)** as one likes;

— keep the knob **7 (A)** pressed either inserting or not inserting the fan (switch **5**);

— close or open the door **3** about it is wanted to convey air on the windshield only or also inside the car.

Circulation of cold air:

— keep knob **8 (T)** pressed and either insert or not insert the fan (switch **5**).

SPRINT, SPIDER, SPRINT VELOCE AND SPIDER VELOCE CARS

The heating equipment (Fig. 23) is compound by a radiator-fan group and by air inlet and distribution ducts. For the heating the group utilizes part of water of engine while a suitable electric motor, with low consumption, put the fan into action.

Heating

— Open the tap **7** to admit water of engine;

— start the fan motor by turning the control knob **2** to right. Remember that turning the knob on a first time the motor runs at maximum range (pointed out by the tell-tale **3**) and continuing to turn the knob it is inserted the regulating rheostat with consequent reduction of revolutions;

— pulling the knob **4** there is opened the throttle valve and the air intaken from outside passes in the heater where it is warmed, blown on the windshield and, if shutters on the heater are opened, blown also inside the same car;

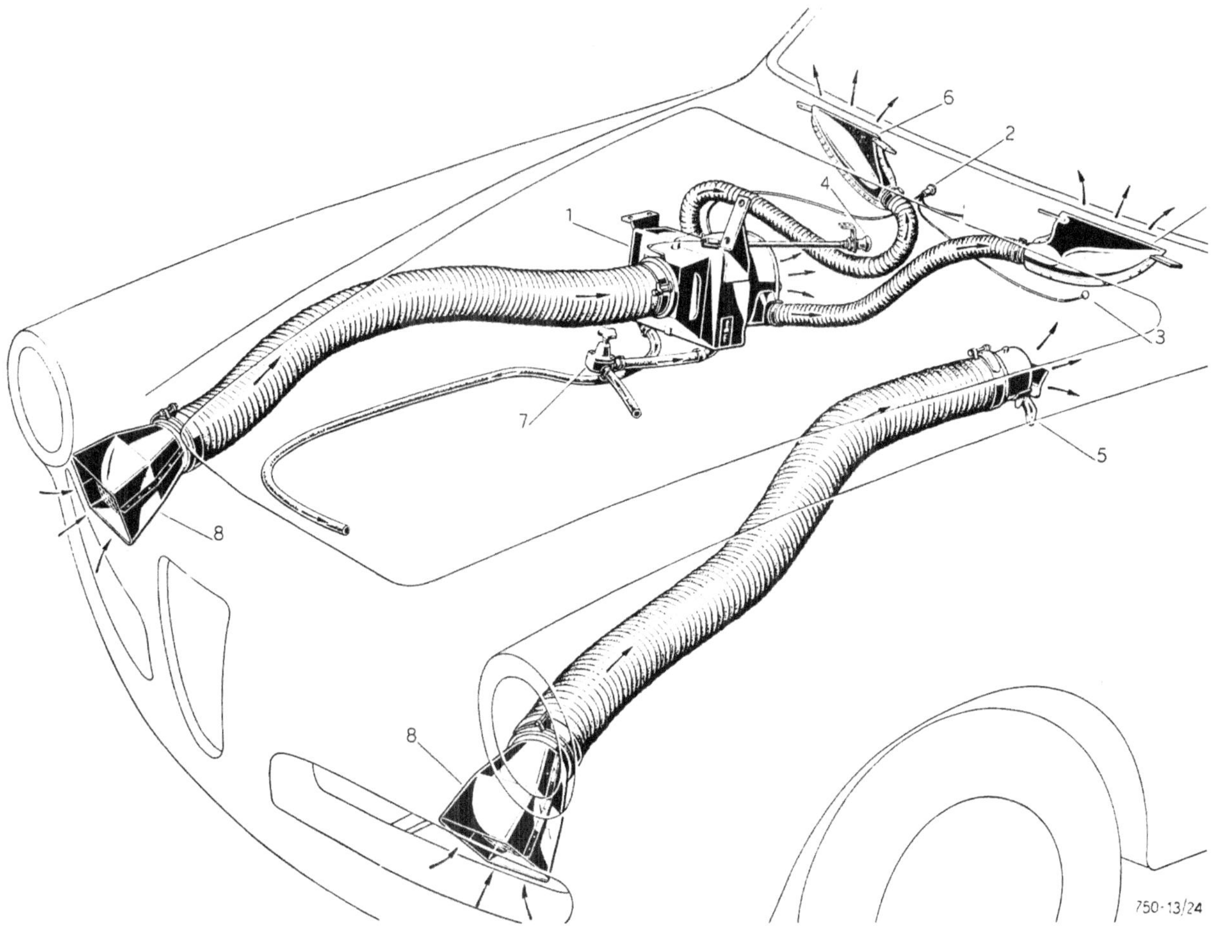

Fig. 23 - Diagram showing the heating and air-conditioning equipment on the Giulietta Sprint.
1. Radiator-and-fan unit - 2. Fan motor control knob - 3. Fan motor tell-tale - 4. Air inlet control knob - 5. Air inlet control lever - 6. Air supply to the windscreen - 7. Tap admitting hot water to the radiator-and-fan unit - 8. Air intake at the front of the car.

— with car running at high speed it is possible to leave out to put the fan motor into action.

Ventilation

The air for ventilation is taken from front side of the car through two conduits (one of them belongs to the heater). Opening and closing the shutters placed below the cowl the air is intaken or not intaken in the car.

Forced circulation is obtained by putting the fan into action, shutting of course the water tap.

Note - The heating plant on the Sprint Veloce and Spider Veloce cars is supplied only upon request.

8 - WINDSCREEN WASHING UNIT

The windscreen washer consists, as shown in Fig. 24, of a water tank, a pump and two jet nozzles.

When the pump is operated two jets of water are directed onto the windscreen. The windscreen wipers can then be started and the windscreen effectively cleaned.

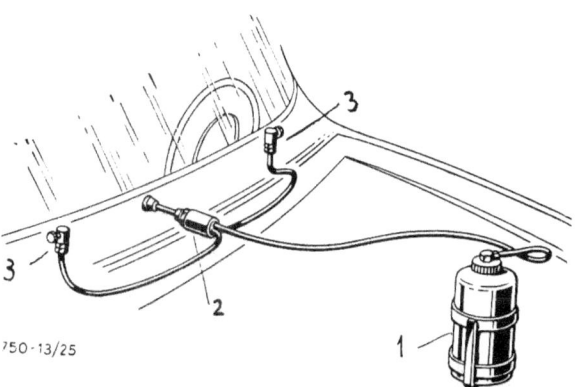

Fig. 24 - Windscreen washer diagram.
1. Tank - 2. Pump - 3. Jet nozzles.

INFORMATION SHEET REFERENCE

ASSEMBLY	DATE	SHEET N.	SUBJECT

PART 14

SPECIAL TOOLS AND EQUIPMENT

Group 1: Engine . . . . page 263

» 2: Clutch and gear-box . . . . » 267

» 3: Propeller shaft . . . . » 271

» 4: Rear axle . . . . » 271

» 5: Front suspension - Front and rear wheels . . . . . . » 274

» 6: Steering-system . . . . » 276

» 7: Brakes . . . . » 277

» 8: Body . . . . » 278

PART 14

SPECIAL TOOLS

Note - The numbers marked with ═══ show the minimum requirements for authorized workshops; the numbers with
* ═══ show the first requirement for the new authorized workshops.

GROUP 1: ENGINE

* 6121.18.021

16 mm. spanner for induction manifold nuts.

* 6121.18.041

16 mm. spanner for generator fixing-bolt nuts.

* 6121.18.055

Spanner for crankcase drain cock.

6121.18.338

Spanner for air intake case fixing-nuts to the carb.
(for engines with 40DC03 Weber carb.).

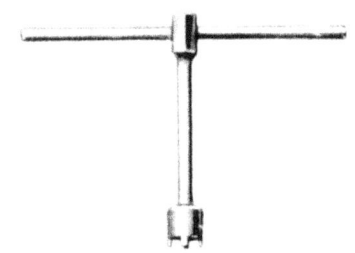

* 6121.20.039

Spanner for castellated lock-nuts for the fan.

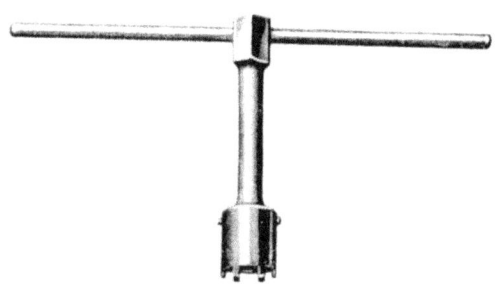

* 6121.20 040

Spanner for crankshaft pulley-wheel castellated lock-nuts.

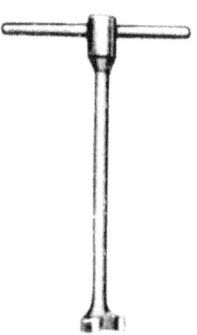

6121.23 026

Spanner for lower nuts fixing manifold to the slip joints
(for engines with 40DC03 Weber carb.).

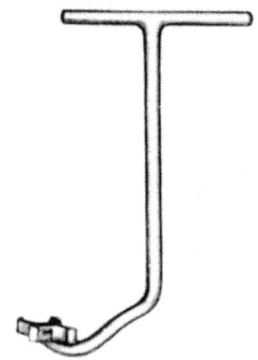

6121.23.027

Spanner for upper nuts fastening carburetters to the slip joints (for engines with 40DC03 Weber carb.).

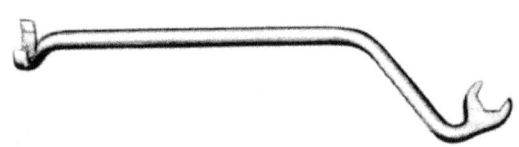

6121.23.028

Spanner for upper nuts fastening carburetters to the slip joints (for engines with 40DC03 Weber carb.).

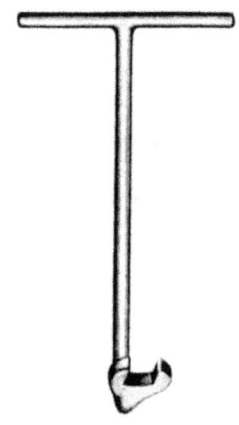

6121.23.029

Spanner for lower nuts fixing carburetters to the slip joints (for engines with 40DC03 Weber carb.).

6121.24.012

Spanner for rotating the distributor cam-shaft for timing purposes.

6121.04.002

Tool for extracting front and intermediate crankshaft bearing caps. On request (also used for the 1900 cars).

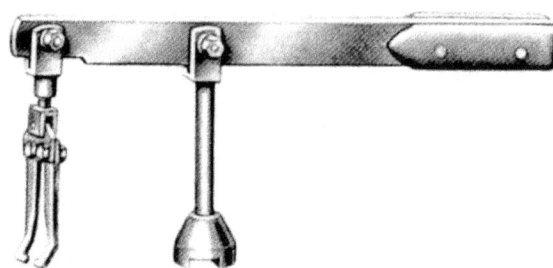

6121.11.004

Tool for extracting crankshaft rear bearing cap with central notches.

6121.11.006

Tool for extracting crankshaft rear bearing cap with lateral notches.

6121.12.093

Tool for drawing the flywheel off the crankshaft.

6121.13.012

Tool for extracting the shaft with impeller from water pump casing (also used for the 1900 cars).

6121.01.177

Device for securing the cylinder liners during engine assembly.

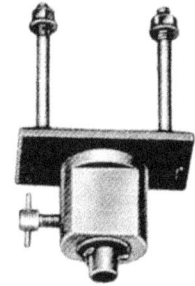

6121.01.274

Device for fixing the cylinder head in a vice.

6121.06.002

Tool for inserting the rubber seals in the crankshaft rear bearing cap.

6121.07.090

Device for fitting the water-seal ring in the pump body.

6121.07.293

Device for fitting the crankshaft rear oil seal.

6121.07.294

Device for fitting the oil seal in the front cover.

6121.07.295

Tools for inserting bearings and ring in the braket for the chain tensioning device.

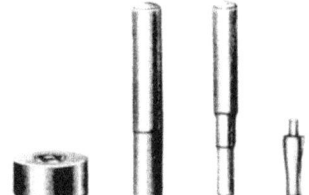

6121.07.308

Device for inserting bearing and distance-piece in the water-pump body (for pump bearing with outside diameter of 32 mm.).

6121.07.430

Device for inserting bearing and distance-piece in the water-pump body (for pump bearing with outside diameter of 35 mm.).

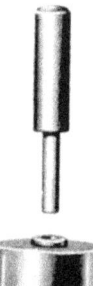

6121.07.312

Device for inserting the front seal ring in the water-pump body.

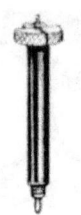

6123.41.008

Tool for T.D.C. check.

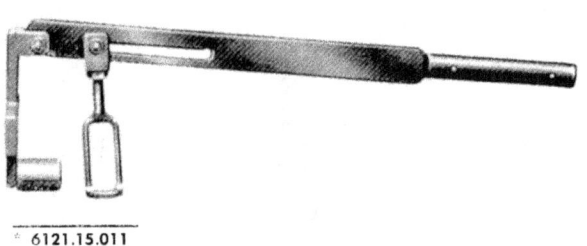

6121.15.011

Tool for fitting and removing the valve cotters.

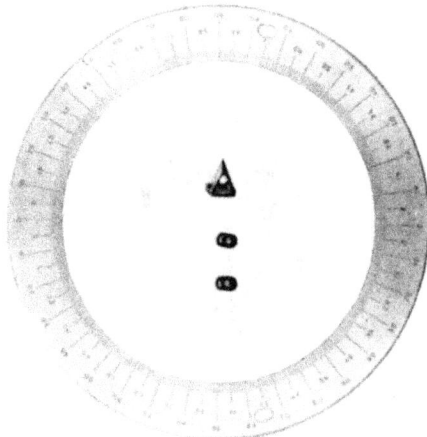

6123.45.003

Graduated ring for timing the engine.

6121.90.011

Tool for grinding valves by hand.

671.3153

Differential plug gauge for valve guides.

6121.41.008

Mandril to hold the valve seat grinder.

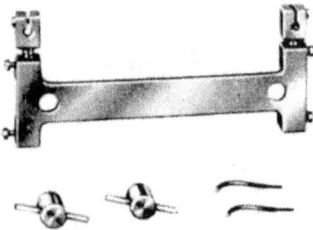

6123.01.053

Tool for engine timing check (on request).

672.5768

Ring gauge to check housing diameter of connecting road bearings with inside caliper.

672.5769

Ring gauge to check cylinder-liners diameter with inside caliper.

C2.0003

Special tool check valves tight (also used for the 1900 cars).

6549.557

Tapered grinding wheel for valve seats.

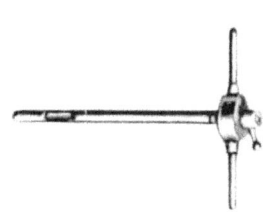

U2.0001

Reamer for valve guides hole.

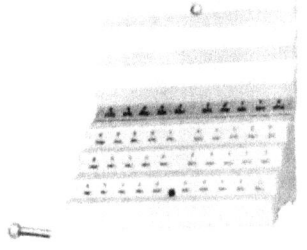

Arr. 2.0001

Box for valves adjusting caps.

GROUP 2: CLUTCH AND GEAR BOX

6121.19.025

32 mm. spanner for the rear fork securing pin.

* 6121.20.024

Spanner for the rear nut on the lay-shaft.

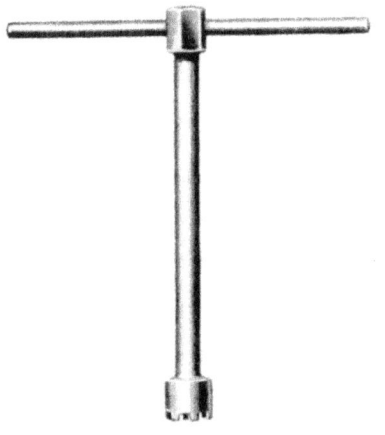

6121.20.038

Spanner for the front nut on the lay-shaft.

6121.22.041

17 mm. spanner for securing the cages holding the balls for positioning the gear control rods.

* **6121.12.092**

Extracting tool for removing the shafts from the gear-box front bearings.

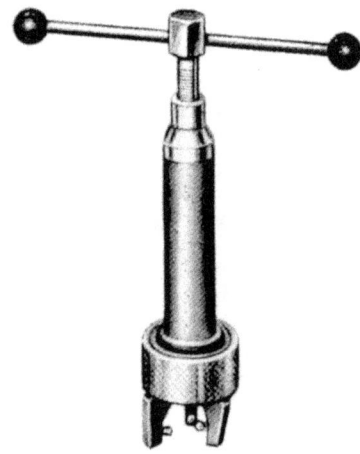

6121.12.045

Extracting tool for the synchronising hub for the 3rd and top gears. (also used for the 1900 cars).

6121.01.178

Block for supporting the primary shaft during assembly of the gear-wheels for third gear.

6121.01.179

Block for supporting the primary shaft during assembly of the gear-wheels for first and second gears.

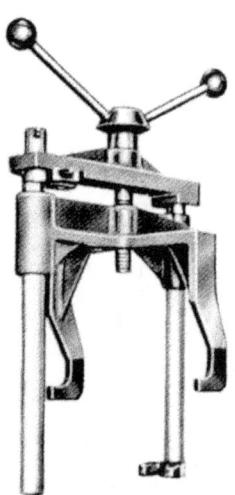

6121.12.091

Extracting tool for the gear-box intermediate flange.

6121.01.181

Plate to retain the lay-shaft while the front nut is being secured with spanner. 6121.20.038.

6121.04.014

Device for inserting and extracting the front-cover silentbloc.

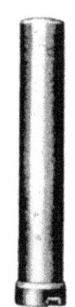

6121.07.237

Device for fitting the first and second gear hub on the primary shaft.

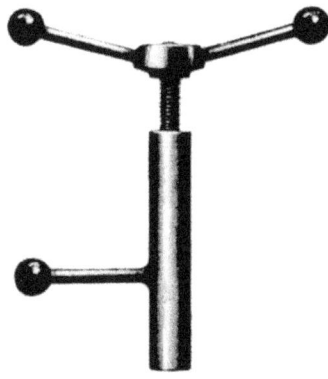

6121.05.016

Tool for fitting the reverse gear-wheel on the primary shaft.

6121.07.238

Device for inserting and extracting the ball-bearing in the gear box. (For bearings with hole diameter of 25 mm.).

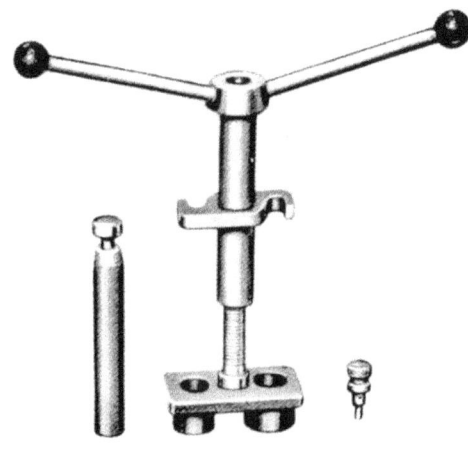

* 6121.05.036

Assembly for inserting the shafts, with the intermediate flange, into the gear-box.

6121.07.239

Device for inserting and extracting the ball-bearing in the gear box. (For bearings with hole diameter of 30 mm.).

6121.07.236

Device for fitting the third and top gear hub on the primary shaft.

6121.07.240

Device for inserting the roller-carrying box on the top-gear shaft.

6121.07.247

Device for inserting the oil seal in the front cover.

6121.07.274

Tool for inserting the oil seal for the gear-selection shaft in the real cover.

6121.07.275

Tool for inserting the oil seal for the primary shaft in the rear cover.

6121.12.062

Tool for withdrawing the reversing gear from the primary shaft.

Equipment for balancing the clutch unit:

6123.10.052

Clutch supporting plate (also used for the 1900 cars).

6123.13.001

Knife-carrying square.

672.5300

Gauge for determining the thickness of the shim located between the distance piece and the primary shaft rear bearing.

270

GROUP 3: PROPELLER SHAFT

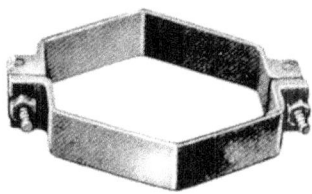

6121.01.291

Tool for assembling and dismantling the flexible joint on the propeller shaft front fock (for Berlina cars).

6121.01.069

Ditto ditto for t.i., Sprint and Spider (also used for the 1900 cars).

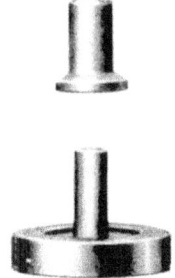

6121.07.327

Device for inserting the bearing in the front propeller-shaft bracket.

6121.07.328

Tool to insert the bearing with support in the forward half of propeller shaft.

GROUP 4: REAR AXLE

6121.18.047

Spanner for the lock-nuts on the right-hand left-hand rear-axle tubes.

* 6121.20.035

Spanner for the lock nuts securing the fork to the bevel pinion.

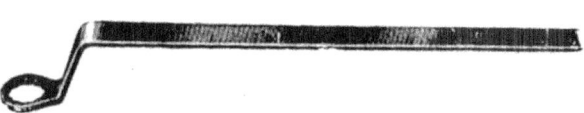

6121.18.049

Spanner for the lock-nuts securing the triangular member to the rear axle.

* 6121.20.036

Spanner for the lock-nuts securing the ball-bearings on the rear-axle shafts.

6121.19.024

17 mm. off-set spanner for the bolts fixing the ball-bearing cover on the rear-axle shafts.

6121.12.052

Tool for extracting the roller-bearing inner race from the differential housing.

6121.12.054

Tool for extracting the outer race of the bearing from the left-hand axle tube.

6121.12.087

Tool for extracting the rear-axle shaft bearings.

6121.12.055

Tool for withdrawing the rear-axle shafts from the axle casing (for rear-axle shafts with a hole in the centre of the wheel-securing flange).

6121.13.019

Device for extracting the inner race of the bevel pinion rear bearings.

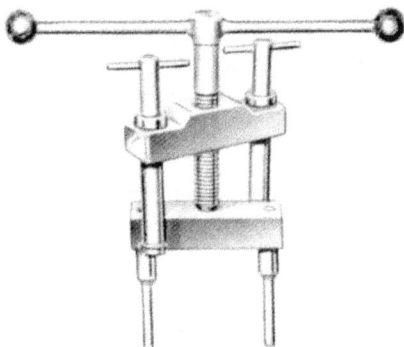

6121.01.166

Device for locking the bevel pinion sleeve.

6121.12.111

Tool for withdrawing the rear-axle shafts from the axle casing (for rear-axle shafts without a hole in the centre of the wheel-securing flange). - Also used for the 1900 cars.

6121.12.057

Tool for extracting the bevel pinion front bearing outer race from the differential bracket (for the front-wheel inner bearing outer race also used for the 1900 and 1900 t.i. cars).

6121.04.015

Tool for inserting and extracting the outer races of the bevel pinion rear bearing and the front oil-seal ring.

6121.07.141

Tool for inserting the outer race of the left-hand bearing and to extract the right-hand outer race from the differential bracket.

6121.07.217

Tool for inserting the inner races of the bearings on the differential box.

6121.07.220

Tool for inserting the inner race of the rear bearing on the bevel pinion.

6121.07.221

Tool for inserting the inner race of the front-bearing on the bevel pinion.

6121.07.222

Tool for inserting the outer race of the right-hand bearing on the differential bracket.

6121.07.223

Tool for inserting the front oil-seal ring in the differential bracket.

6121.07.366

Tool for inserting the oil-seal ring in the rear-axle tubes.

6121.07.287

Tool for inserting the outer race of the bevel pinion front bearing in the differential bracket.

Tools to determine the thickness of the shims to be inserted between the bevel pinion and its rear bearing:

6123.26.217

Tool for correcting the comparator gauge.
(Also used for the 1900 cars).

6123.27.028

Tool to measure the distance between the plane of the bevel pinion and the axis of the crown wheel.

6123.41.111

Tool to carry the comparator gauge.
(Also used for the 1900 cars).

* 6123.15.006

Lever for checking the pre-load value of the differential unit bearings.

6123.27.025

Tool for adjust the backlash between bevel and crown wheel and the bearings pre-loading in the differential box.

670.1654

Gauge for determining the thickness of the adjusting washer to be inserted between the left-hand rear-axle tube and the differential box.

6123.27.052

Tool for adjust the backlash between bevel and crown wheel and the bearings pre-loading in the differential box (only for bearings of rear axle with adjustment shims under R. and L. tube flanges).

670.1655

Gauge for determining the thickness of the adjusting washer to be inserted between the right-hand rear-axle tube and the differential box. (Only for adjustment of bearings clearance of the rear axle with adjustment shims under R. and L. tube flanges).

GROUP 5: FRONT SUSPENSION - FRONT AND REAR WHEELS

6121.25.009

Spanner fitted with two studs, for turning the locknut on the lower track-rod joint.

6121.12.057

Tool for extracting the outer race of the front wheel-hub inner bearing (can also be used for the outer race of the front bearing on the differential bevel pinion).

6121.12.063

Tool for extracting the front-wheel hub from the stub axle.

6121.12.066

Tool for extracting the inner race of the stub-axle inner bearing.

* **6123.15.007**

Lever for checking the pre-load values of the front-wheel hub bearings.

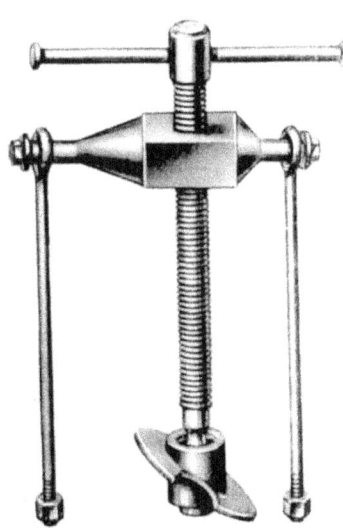

6121.04.016

Tool for fitting and removing the front-suspension springs.

6121.05.041

Tool for fitting the left-hand wheel hub to the stub axle. (Also used for the 1900 cars).

6121.05.042

Tool for fitting the right-hand wheel hub to the stub axle. (Also used for the 1900 cars).

6121.07.265

Tool for inserting the sealing cup in the outer bracket of the lower track rod.

6121.07.266

Tool for inserting the sealing cup in the inner bracket of the lower track rod.

6121.07.267

Tool for inserting the sealing cup in the inner bracket of the upper track rod.

6121.07.268

Tool for inserting the sealing cup in the outer bracket of the upper track rod.

6121.07.276

Tool for inserting the oil-seal ring in the front-wheel hubs.

6121.07.277

Tool for inserting the outer race of the outer bearing in the front-wheel hubs.

6121.07.278

Tool for inserting the outer race of the inner bearing in the front-wheel hubs.

671.3204

Plug gauge for bushes of front suspension lower arms.

671.3206

Plug gauge for bushes of front suspension upper arms.

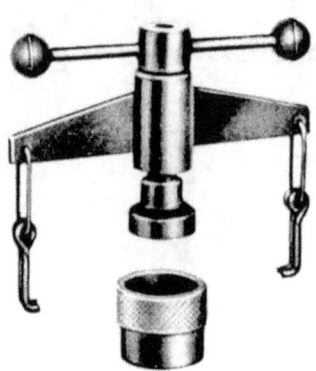

6121.12.099

Tool for extracting the brakes drums.

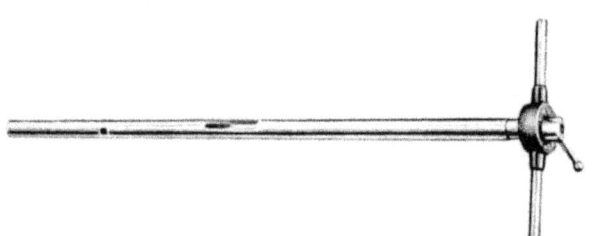

U2.0002

Reamer for bushes of front suspension upper arms.

U2.0003

Reamer for bushes of front suspension lower arms.

GROUP 6: STEERING SYSTEM

6121.16.002

Hexagonal jointed spanner for tightening ball joints.

* 6121.06.007

Tool for extracting the head-lamp flashing button on the steering wheel.

* 6121.12.085

Tool for extracting the steering arm.

6121.12.086

Tool for extracting the steering ball-joints.

6121.12.090

Tool for removing the steering-wheel.

GROUP 7 : BRAKES

6112.01.323

Tool for re-grinding real-wheel brakes, with linings fitted.

6112.01.330

Tool for re-grinding front-wheel brake-shoes with linings fitted.

6121.70.009

Tool for rivetting the linings to the front-wheel brake shoes.

6121.70.011

Tool for rivetting the linings to the rear-wheel brake shoes.

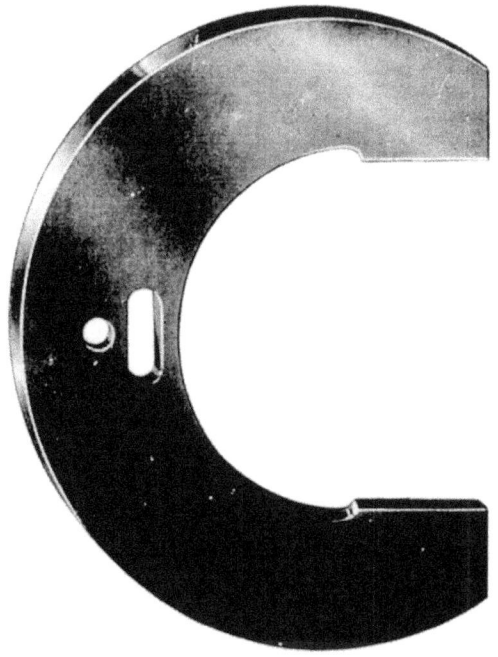

672.5031

Gauge for checking front-wheel brake shoes.

672.5316

Gauge for checking rear-wheel brake shoes.

6123.29.020

Tool for ensuring that the brake linings are square to the wheel axis.

GROUP 8: BODY

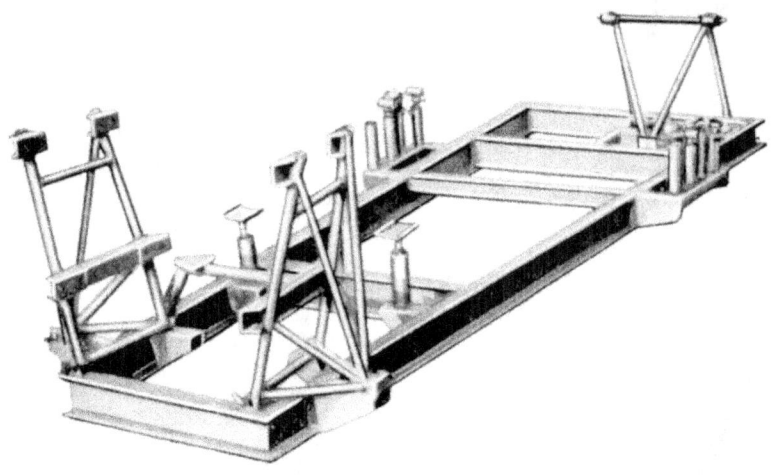

6123.91.001

Workshop chassis for body inspection, complete.

Note - The chassis with grey-painted rear triangle is used for Berlina cars up to n. 1488.04200, Sprint n. 1493.03000, Spider n. 1495.00800; with yellow-painted rear triangle is used for Berlina cars from n. 1488.04201, Sprint n. 1493.03001, Spider n. 1495.00801.

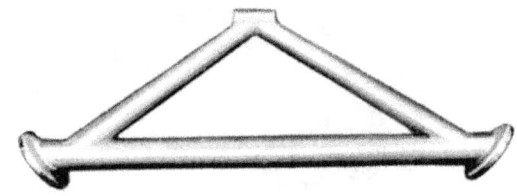 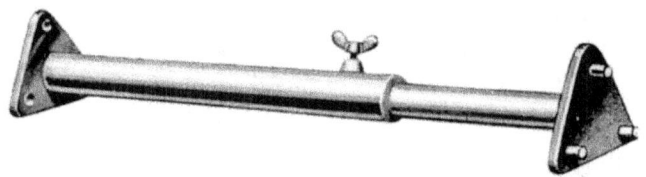

6123.91.002

Tool for checking the alignment of the engine-gear box-propeller shaft assembly.

6123.91.003

Tool for checking the attachment holes for the steering-box and idler arm (Giulietta Berlina).

6123.91.004

Tool for checking the attachment holes for the steering-box and idler arm (Giulietta Sprint, Spider, sprint Veloce and Spider Veloce).

6121.06.014

Tool for fitting up rubber strip on the front and rear glasses (also used for the 1900 cars).

6121.06.015

Tool for fitting up by cord the front and rear glasses (also used for the 1900 cars).

NUMERICAL INDEX

Tool Number (numerical order)	Page	Tool Number (numerical order)	Page	Tool Number (numerical order)	Page
670.1654	274	6121.07.247	270	*6121.18.041	263
670.1655	274	6121.07.265	275	6121.18.047	271
671.3153	266	6121.07.266	275	6121.18.049	271
671.3204	276	6121.07.267	275	*6121.18.055	263
671.3206	276	6121.07.268	275	6121.18.338	263
672.5031	277	6121.07.274	270	6121.19.024	271
672.5300	270	6121.07.275	270	6121.19.025	267
672.5316	277	6121.07.276	275	*6121.20.024	267
672.5768	266	6121.07.277	276	*6121.20.035	271
672.5769	267	6121.07.278	276	*6121.20.036	271
6549.557	267	6121.07.287	273	6121.20.038	267
6112.01.323	277	6121.07.293	265	*6121.20.039	263
6112.01.330	277	6121.07.294	265	*6121.20.040	263
6121.01.069	271	6121.07.295	265	6121.22.041	268
6121.01.166	272	6121.07.308	265	6121.23.026	263
6121.01.177	265	6121.07.312	266	6121.23.027	264
6121.01.178	268	6121.07.327	271	6121.23.028	264
6121.01.179	268	6121.07.328	271	6121.23.029	264
6121.01.181	268	6121.07.366	273	6121.24.012	264
6121.01.274	265	6121.07.430	265	6121.25.009	274
6121.01.291	271	6121.11.004	264	6121.41.008	266
6121.04.002	264	6121.11.006	264	6121.70.009	277
6121.04.014	269	6121.12.045	268	6121.70.011	277
6121.04.015	272	6121.12.052	271	6121.90.011	266
6121.04.016	275	6121.12.054	272	6123.01.053	266
6121.05.016	269	6121.12.055	272	6123.10.052	270
*6121.05.036	269	6121.12.057	272	6123.13.001	270
6121.05.041	275	6121.12.057	274	*6123.15.006	274
6121.05.042	275	6121.12.062	270	*6123.15.007	275
6121.06.002	265	6121.12.063	274	6123.26.217	273
*6121.06.007	276	6121.12.066	275	6123.27.025	274
6121.06.014	278	*6121.12.085	276	6123.27.028	273
6121.06.015	278	6121.12.086	277	6123.27.052	274
6121.07 090	265	6121.12.087	272	6123.29.020	277
6121.07.141	273	6121.12.090	277	6123.41.008	266
6121.07.217	273	6121.12.091	268	6123.41.111	274
6121.07.220	273	*6121.12.092	268	6123.45.003	266
6121.07.221	273	6121.12.093	264	6123.91.001	278
6121.07.222	273	6121.12.099	276	6123.91.002	278
6121.07.223	273	6121.12.111	272	6123.91.003	278
6121.07.236	269	6121.13.012	264	6123.91.004	278
6121.07.237	269	6121.13.019	272	Arr. 2.0001	267
6121.07.238	269	*6121.15.011	266	C 2.0003	267
6121.07.239	269	6121.16.002	276	U 2.0001	267
6121.07.240	269	*6121.18.021	263	U 2.0002	276
				U 2.0003	276

Note - The numbers marked with ═══ show the minimum requirements for authorized workshops; the numbers with * ═══ show the first requirement for the new authorized workshops.

INFORMATION SHEET REFERENCE

ASSEMBLY	DATE	SHEET N.	SUBJECT

APPENDIX

**Transmission supplement from 1957 manual
(Publication Number 611) that was omitted from
this 1958 manual (Publication Number 637)**

Page 282

**Enclosure to the (Giulietta) shop manual 'Technical Characteristics'
(Publication Number 854 - November 1962)**

Page 294

**Giulia (101 Series) 'Technical mCharacteristics'
for the 1600cc T.i. Spider & Sprint
(Publication Number 955 - October 1963)**

Page 311

**Giulia (101 Series) 'Technical Characteristics'
for the 1600cc Spider Veloce
(October 1964 Publication)**

Page 331

> THIS 12 PAGE SUPPLEMENT WAS INCLUDED IN THE 1957 FACTORY WORKSHOP MANUAL NUMBER 611. FOR UNKNOWN REASONS IT WAS OMITTED FROM THE 1958 MANUAL NUMBER 637 INCLUDED IN THIS PUBLICATION

APPENDIX

INSTRUCTIONS FOR OVERHAULING GEARBOX

(Berlina from No. 1488.20801 - t.i. from No. 1468.8501 - Sprint and Sprint Veloce from No. 1493.7301 Spider and Spider Veloce from No. 1495.4811)

1 - REMOVING THE GEARBOX FROM THE CAR

Drain the oil completely from the gearbox and then:

Remove

— The front propeller-shaft joints, the intermediate bearing bracket and take off the shaft;

— the exhaust pipe supporting arm on the gearbox;

— the speedometer flexible shaft;

— the clutch link rod from the corresponding control lever;

— the lower cover of the clutch housing;

— the exhaust pipe from the manifold;

— the gearbox link rods.

Note

— On the cars with a ball-type gearshift lever remove:

— the carpet over the gearbox cover plate;

— the gearshift lever bellows;

— the gearshift lever from the engagement and selection rocker.

Unscrew:

— the bolts fixing the rear cross member to the chassis sufficiently to allow the unit to tilt so as to facilitate the subsequent operations;

— the nuts fixing the gearbox to the rear plate on the crankcase and remove the unit complete with the cross member;

— the bolt fixing the supporting cross member and remove the latter.

Re-fitting the gearbox on the car is performed in the reverse order; after re-fitting adjust the external controls.

2 - DISMANTLING THE GEARBOX ON THE BENCH (See Fig. 25)

a) **Removal of the gearbox components**

— Set the unit on the overhaul trestle;
— unscrew the ring nut **1** fixing the fork **2** of the flexible joint (prevent the fork rotating by turning one bolt of the joint until it abuts against the cover) and draw off the fork;
— unscrew the nuts **3** securing the rear cover **4** and remove it.

WARNING - For gearboxes with ball-type gearshift lever it is necessary to engage the third gear to remove the cover.

— unscrew the bolt **5** securing the reverse-gear engagement fork sufficiently to allow the corresponding control rod to slide until it releases the gear engagement lever **6**;

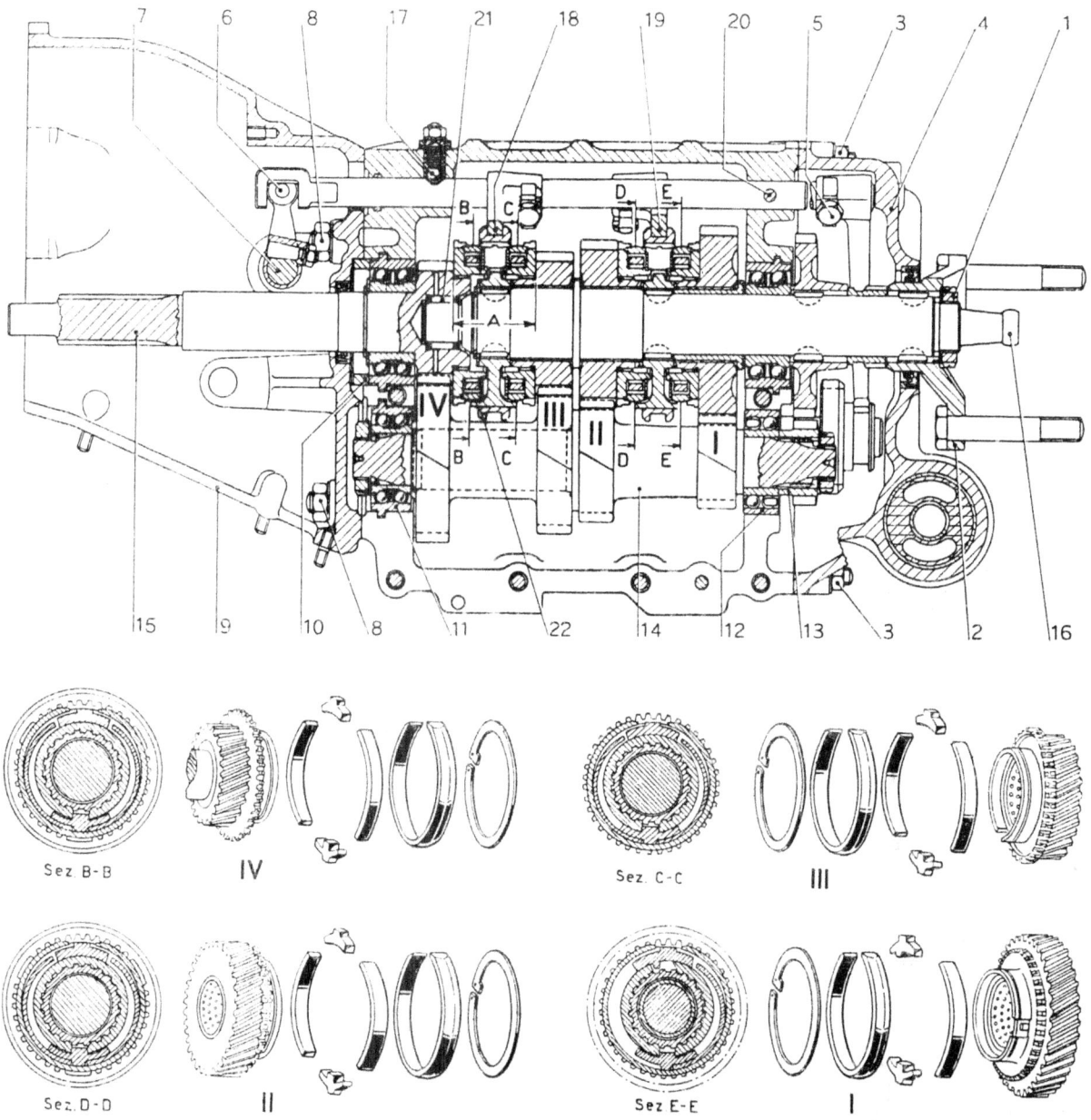

Fig. 25 - Longitudnal section - synchronisers

1. Ring nut securing transmission fork - **2**. Transmission fork - **3**. Nuts securing rear cover - **4**. Rear cover - **5**. Bolt securing reversing fork - **6**. Inner gear engagement lever - **7**. Pin for inner gear engagement lever - **8**. Nuts securing clutch housing - **9**. Clutch housing - **10**. Centring ring for half gearcase - **11**. Front bearing for layshaft - **12**. Rear bearing for layshaft - **13**. Reversing gear-wheel on layshaft - **14**. Layshaft - **15**. Direct-drive shaft - **16**. Main shaft - **17**. Gear-release mechanism - **18**. Control fork for third and fourth gears - **19**. Control fork for first and second gears - **20**. Safety pawls for rods - **21**. Retainer with rollers - **22**. Synchroniser sleeve, third and fourth gears.

— dismantle the gear selection lever spindle;

— remove the circlip retaining the spindle **7** of the gear engagement lever;

— dismantle the gear engagement lever **6** from the spindle and slide the spindle from the gearcase;

— unscrew the nuts **8** securing the clutch housing **9** and remove it together with the centring ring **10**;

— loosen the ring nuts retaining the bearings **11** and **12** and the reversing gear **13** on the layshaft **14** (**at the same time** engage a forward gear and the reverse gear to prevent rotation of the shaft);

— unscrew the nuts securing the half-casings and separate them by tapping them lightly with a wooden or plastic mallet;

WARNING - Take care not to damage the mating surface of the half-casing and of the covers, as these must seal securely without the interposition of a gasket.

— remove the direct-drive shaft **15** attached to the main shaft **16** and then the layshaft **14**;

— unscrew the nuts securing the retaining plate of the gear release device **17** and remove the retainers, the springs, and the relative balls;

— unscrew the bolts securing the forks **18** and **19** to the rods, withdraw the rods and remove the oval safety pawls **20**.

WARNING - When a single control rod has to be extracted, shifting of the pawls and the balls must be prevented by inserting an auxiliary rod.

— separate the main shaft from the direct-drive shaft, take off the roller-bearing housing **21**, and remove the third and top gear synchroniser sleeve **22**.

b) **Dismantling the direct-drive shaft** (See Fig. 26).

— Remove the circlip retaining the bearing **23** and remove the shim washer;

— take out the bearing **23** with a suitable extractor.

c) **Dismantling the main shaft 16** (See Fig. 26).

— Fix the main shaft in the lead-jawed vice, gripping it over the seat of the bearing that couples it to the direct-drive shaft;

— remove the speedometer driving gear-wheel **24** and the corresponding key;

— take out the reversing gear **25** and remove the relative key;

— take out the bearing **26**, withdraw the shim washers **27**, the 1st gear gearwheel **28** with its centring bush, and the synchroniser sleeve **29** for first and second gear;

— take out the first and second gear synchroniser boss **30**;

— remove the keys and withdraw the second gear gear-wheel **31**;

— turn the main shaft over and grip it in the vice;

— remove the circlip retaining the third and fourth gear synchroniser boss **32**;

— take out the synchroniser boss;

— remove the keys and withdraw the third gear gear-wheel **33**;

— remove the circlip retaining the synchronisation devices **34** mounted on the various gearwheels and take the device itself to pieces.

d) **Dismantling the layshaft 14.** (See Fig. 26).

— Fix the shaft in a vice with lead jaws;

— unscrew the rear ring nut retaining the reverse gear-wheel **13**;

— take out the reverse gear-wheel;

— take out the rear bearing **12**;

— turn the shaft over and unscrew the ring nut retaining the front bearing **11**;

— extract the front bearing from the shaft.

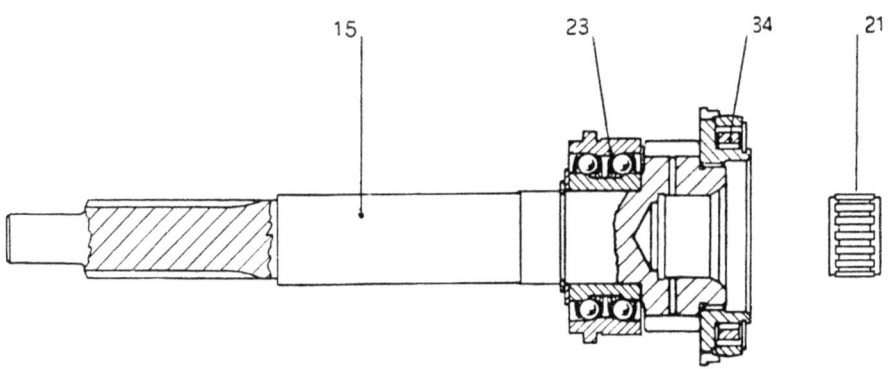

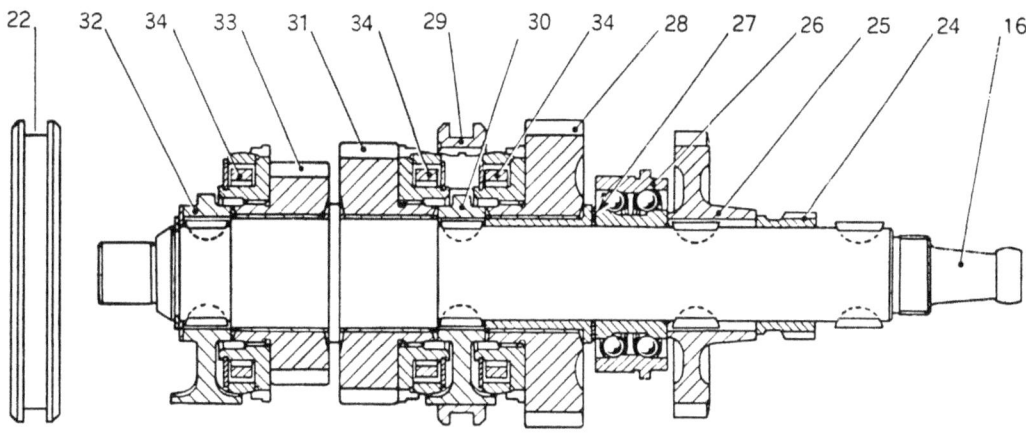

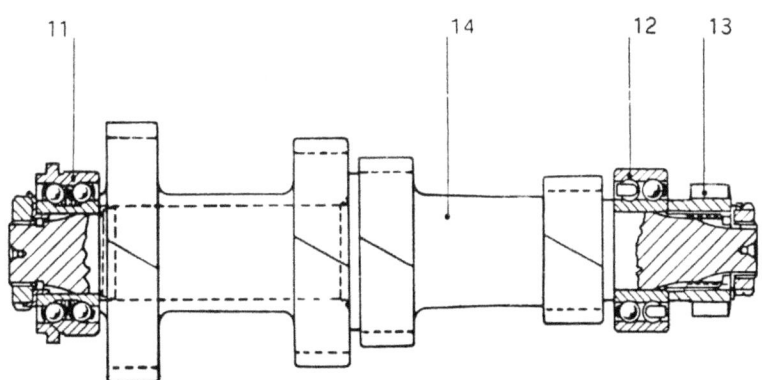

Fig. 26 - Direct-drive, main, and lay shafts

11. Front bearing, layshaft - **12.** Rear bearing, layshaft - **13.** Reversing gear on layshaft - **14.** Layshaft - **15.** Direct-drive shaft - **16.** Main shaft - **21.** Retainer with rollers - **22.** Synchroniser sleeve for third and fourth gears - **23.** Bearing, direct-drive shaft - **24.** Speedometer drive - **25.** Reversing gear on main shaft - **26.** Bearing, mainshaft - **27.** Shim washer - **28.** First gear gear-wheel - **29.** Synchroniser sleeve, first and second gears - **30.** Synchroniser boss, first and second gear - **31.** Second gear gear-wheel - **32.** Synchroniser boss, third and fourth gears - **33.** Third gear gear-wheel - **34.** Synchronising devices.

3 - INSPECTIONS AND CHECKING

— Check that the working surface of the main shaft, in line with the driven gears, shows no signs of seizing.

— Verify that the rolling surfaces for the rollers on the front end of the main shaft, and the surface of the recess of the direct-drive shaft are free from indentation and signs of seizing.

— Check the alignment of the main shaft by mounting it between points; any off-set measured with a gauge

must not exceed 0.02 mm

— Verify:

— that the working surfaces of the gear-wheel teeth show no signs of seizing and excessive wear;

— that the synchroniser sleeves slide freely on their bosses;

— that the radial clearances of the driven gears do not exceed the following permissible limits of wear.

First gear : **0.15 mm.**
Second and third gears : **0.12 mm.**

— that all the synchroniser parts are in good condition:
the circlips must show no signs of excessive wear;
the stop quadrants must be free from indentation at the points of contact with the circlips and the gears.

— Make sure that the driven gear-wheel for the bottom gear and its stop quadrant are of the modified type, i.e.

gear-wheel No.   10100.13027.03
quadrant No.   10100.13229.01

— Check that the working surfaces of the sliding shoes of the forks and of the sliding sleeves show no signs of seizing or excessive wear;

— Verify that the side clearance between the sliding shoes of the forks and the peripheral grooves in the outer sleeves of the synchronisers is kept within the prescribed limits:

Clearance, new: **0.4 to 0.5 mm.**
Permissible worn clearance: 0.7 mm.

— Check that the safety pawls slide freely in their seatings and that the working surfaces of the pawls and the rods are perfectly smooth.

Note - Should a pawl impression be found, increase the fillet radius of the sliding grooves with a suitable file.

— Verify that the springs for the gear-release balls are tensioned as follows:

Length when released: 14.9 to 15.5 mm.
Length under a load of 4.70 to 5.07 kg. 10 mm.

— Verify that the balls and their seatings on the rods are in good condition.

— Check that all the bearings are efficient.

— Verify that the mating surfaces of the half-gearcases, of the rear cover, and of the clutch housing are not distorted.

— Make sure that the seatings of the outer races of the bearings in the half-gearcases are in perfect condition (they must not show any signs of scoring caused by rotation of the outer race of the bearing).

4 - REASSEMBLING THE GEARBOX ON THE BENCH

Follow the sequence of dismantling operations in the reverse order and comply with the following rules:

— The synchroniser bosses must be shrunk on (heat to about 150° C).

— The circlips for the bearing **23** on the direct-drive shaft and on the third and top gear synchroniser boss **32** must prevent any axial movement of the said components; should there be any movement, insert a suitable shim.

— The maximum permissible clearance for the driven gear-wheels on the main shaft, **checked with all component parts assembled and with ring nut tightened by a torque wrench at 7.5 to 8 kgm,** is as follows:

for the first gear gear-wheels: 0.24 mm.
for the second and third gear gear-wheels: 0.21 mm.

— After having re-assembled the main and direct-drive shafts, proceed as follows:

— temoprarily assemble the fork **2** of the flexible coupling on the main shaft and tighten the ring nut to the prescribed torque rating;

— position the unit comprising the two shafts in the half-gearcase and with the help of a sliding gauge make sure that the dimension **A** (see Fig. 25) is as prescribed:

A = 42 to 42.2 mm.

If not, fit a new shim washer **27** of suitable thickness between the first-gear bushing and the inner race of the rear bearing on the main shaft;

— Before fixing the control forks on the relative rods, make sure that the forks themselves, **when in**

neutral, are perfectly centred in relation to the two corresponding sinchronising rings.

With this in mind, verify that the forks, when in neutral, **are equally spaced** from the stop steps on the gear-wheel leading teeth.

— After fixing refit the stop plates accurately.

— The oil seals and safety plates must be changed each time the gearbox is re-assembled.

— The securing ring nuts must be tightened with a torque wrench

at a torque load of 8 kgm

— Before joining the half-gearcases, position the centring ring **10** of the casings in its seating on the half-casing housing the gear-wheels.

— Carefully tighten the nuts fixing the half-gearcases, starting from the centre and working diagonally outwards.

Note - On gearboxes with ball-type gearshift levers, check that the lower end of the selection and engagement rocker in the idling position is centered on the third and top gear control rod; if it is not so centred, dismantle the device and check the various component parts.

5 - CHECKING AND ADJUSTMENT OF THE EXTERNAL GEARBOX CONTROLS

a) **Inspecting the gear selection control** (See Fig. 27)

— Engage first or second gear and verify that the control lever can still travel further towards the steering wheel;

— engage reverse and verify that the control lever can still travel further towards the dashboard;

— verify that both amounts of additional travel are about the same.
Should the travel towards the steering wheel be nil, or less than that towards the dashboard, **shorten** the tie rod **35** by means of the adjustable ball-point **36**.

If, on the other hand, the travel towards the dashboard is nil or less than that towards the steering wheel, **lengthen** the tie rod **35** by means of the adjustable ball-joint **36**.

b) **Inspecting the gear engagement control.** (See Fig. 27).

— Engage one of the **odd** gears (first or third) and verify that the control lever can still travel beyond the gear engagement position;

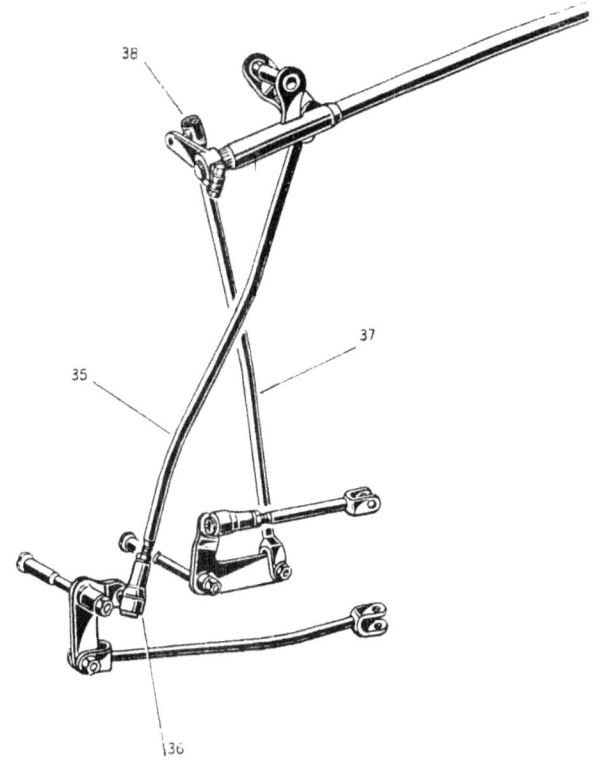

Fig. 27 - External gearbox controls

35. Gear engagement link rods - **36.** Adjustable ball-joint for selection link rod - **37.** Link rod, gear engagement - **38.** Adjustable ball-joint for gear engagement link rod

— engage one of the **even** gears (second or fourth) or reverse and verify that the control lever can still travel beyond the gear engagement position;

— verify that the play in both free travel have about the same value.

Should the amount of free travel, with the **odd** gears engaged, be nil or less than that with **even** or reverse gears engaged, **shorten** the tie rod **37** by means of the adjustable ball-joint **38**.

WARNING

2,000 kilometers after the overhaul, drain the gearcase completely, while hot, and refill to the correct level with fresh oil.
Prescribed lubricants: BP Energol Gear Oil SAE 90. Shell Dentax 90.

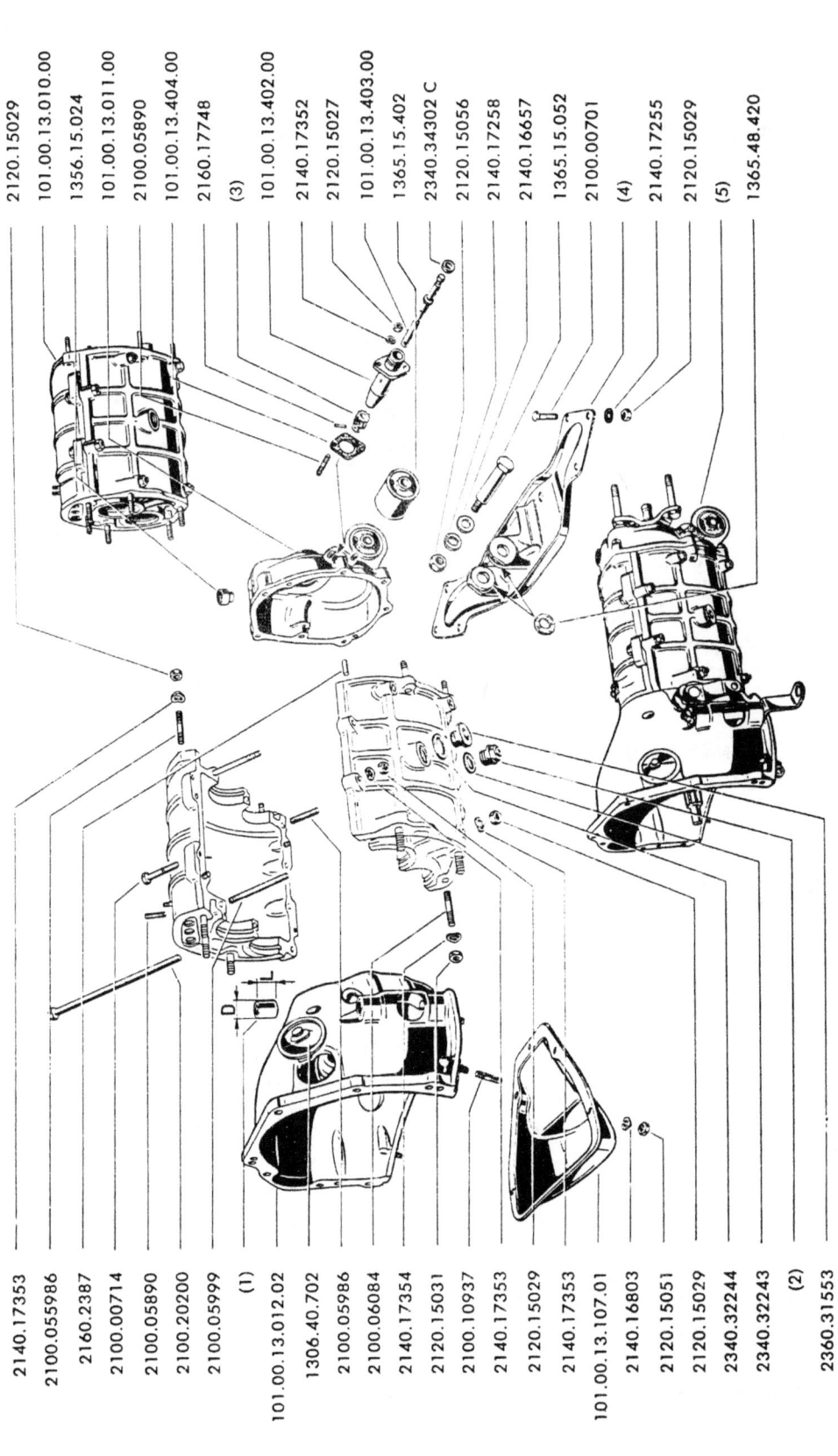

Fig. 28 - Gearbox shells and covers

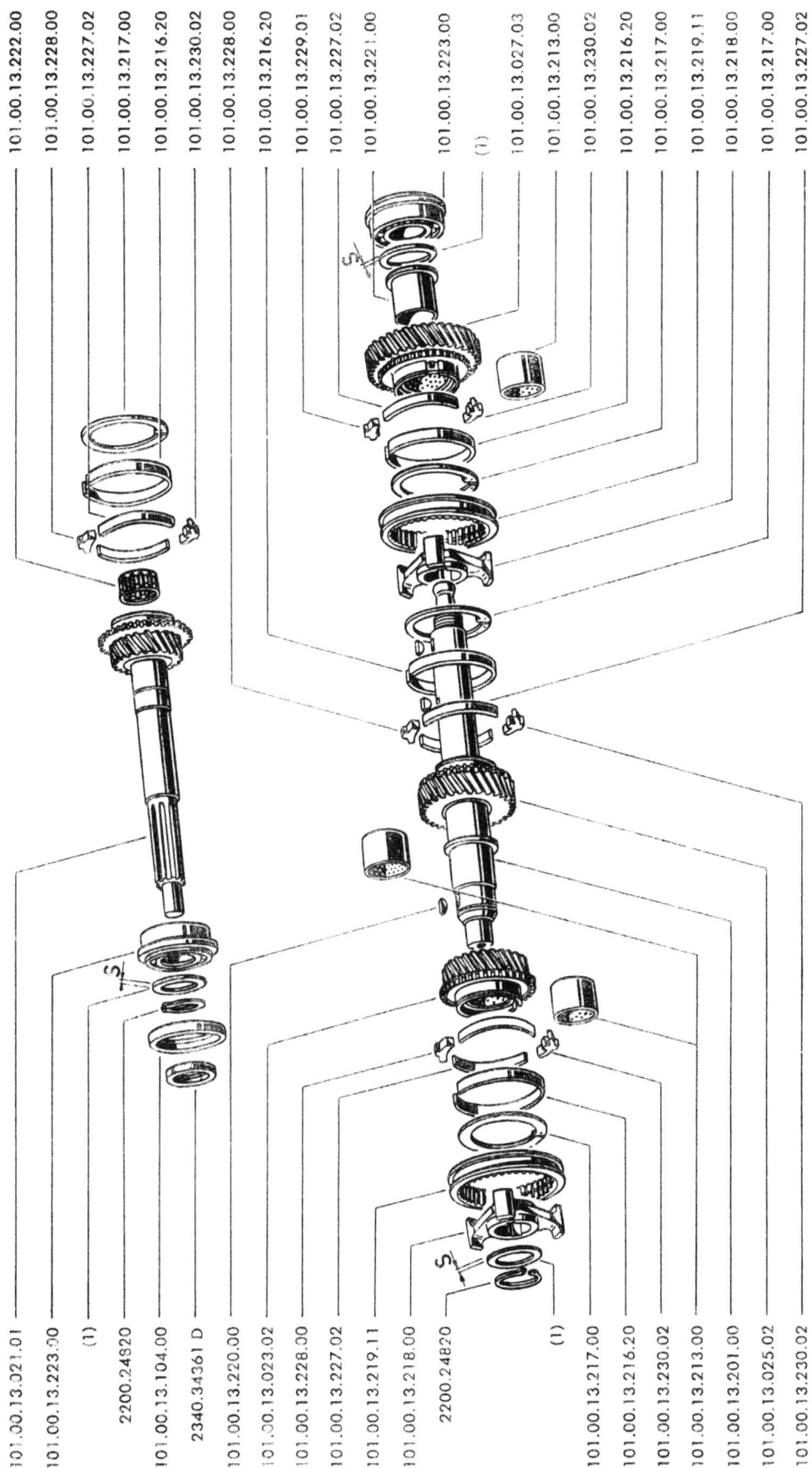

Fig. 29 - Direct drive and main shaft assemblies

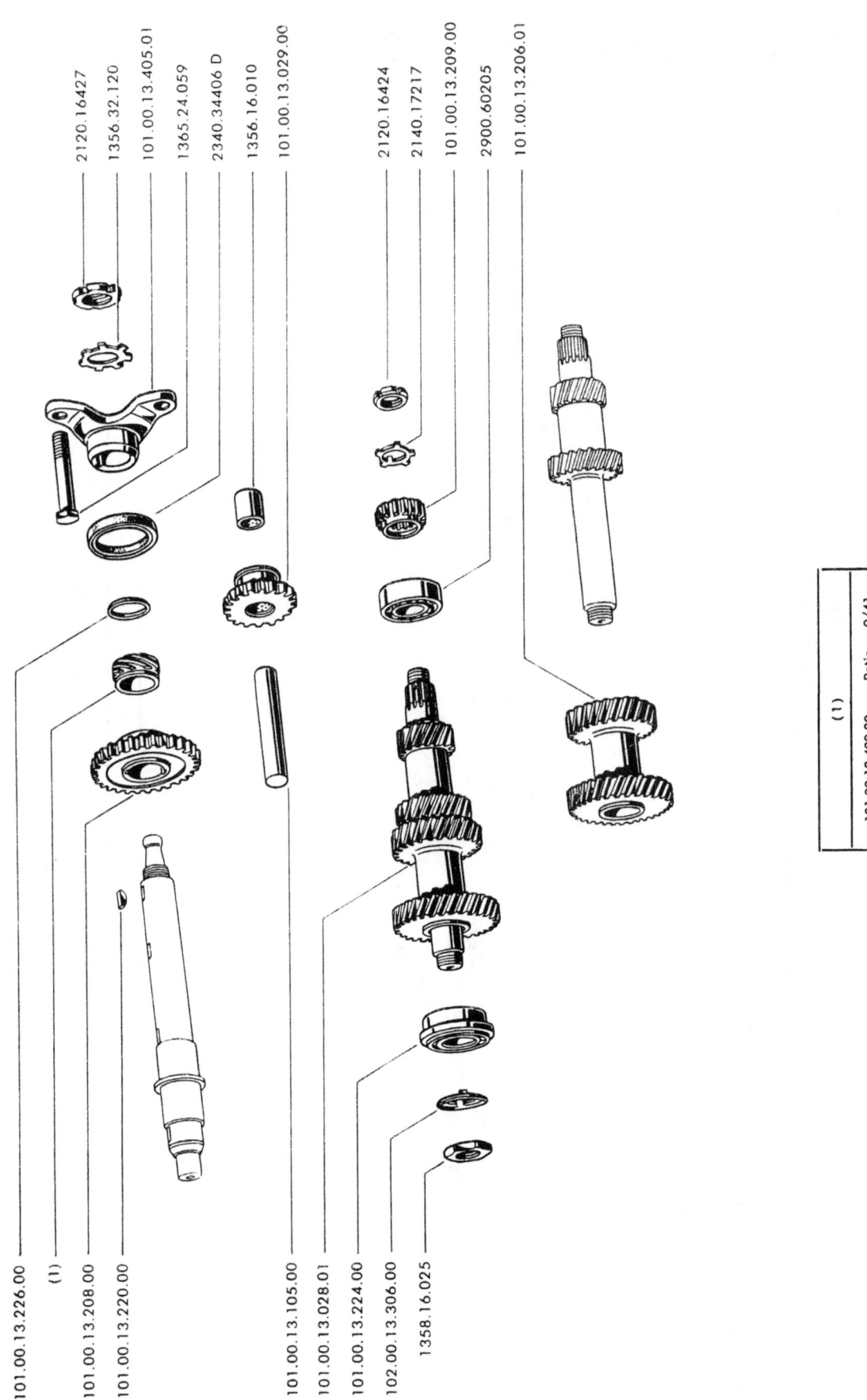

Fig. 30 - Layshaft and reverse-gear shaft assemblies

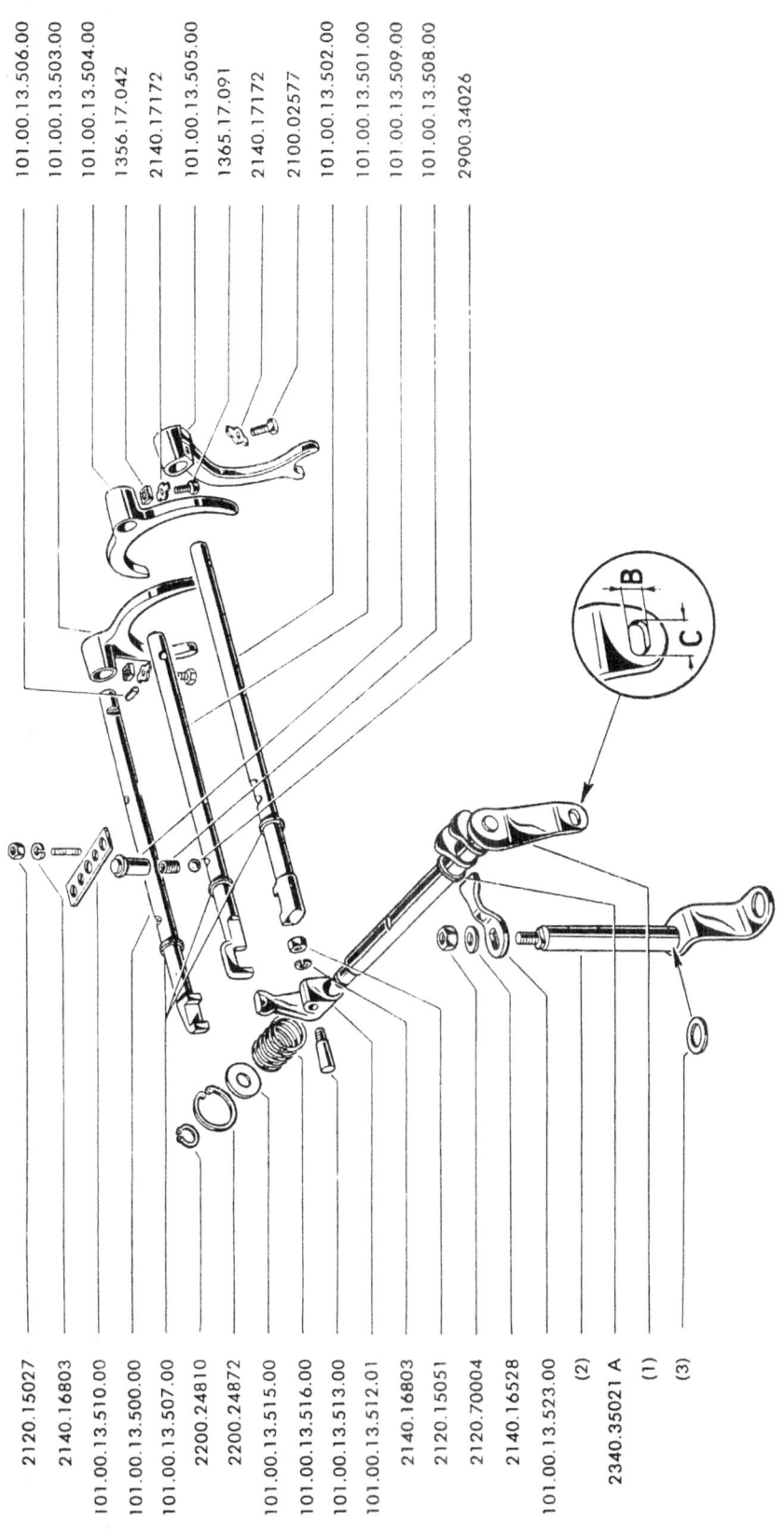

(1)		(2)		(3)	
101.00.13.051.02 - B - 8 mm; C - 11 mm		101.00.13.052.01 dia = 16 mm		101.00.13.529.00 - 0.30 mm thick	101.00.13.529.06 - 0.60 mm thick
101.00.13.051.04 - B - 16 mm; C - 18 mm		101.00.13.052.02 - dia = 15.875 mm		101.00.13.529.01 - 0.35 »	101.00.13.529.07 - 0.65 »
				101.00.13.529.02 - 0.40 »	101.00.13.529.08 - 0.70 »
				101.00.13.529.03 - 0.45 »	101.00.13.529.09 - 0.75 »
				101.00.13.529.04 - 0.50 »	101.00.13.529.10 - 0.80 »
				101.00.13.529.05 - 0.55 »	

Fig. 31 - Internal controls

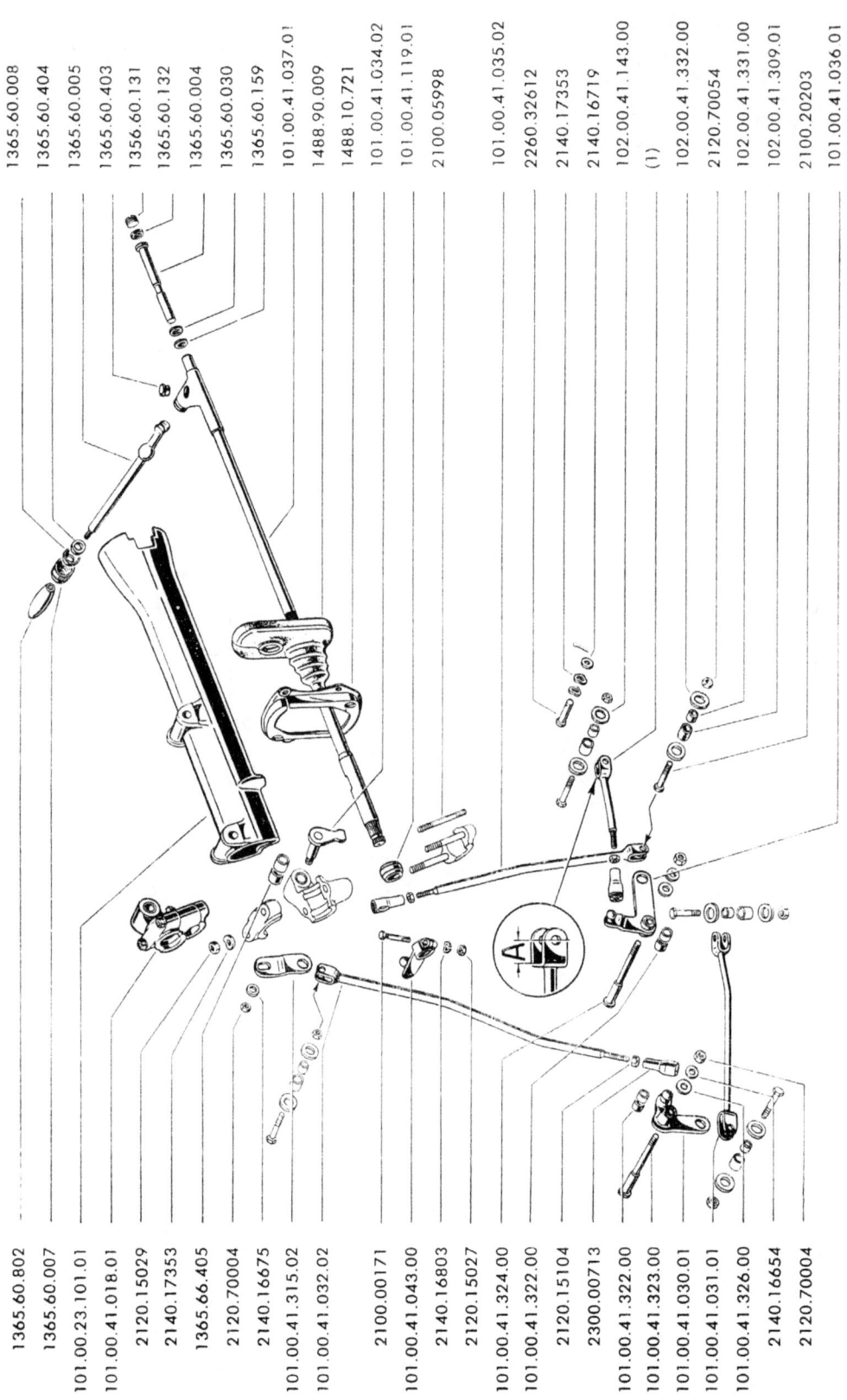

(1)	
101.00.41.033.01	- A - 19 mm
101.00.41.033.02	- A - 27 mm

Fig. 32 - External controls

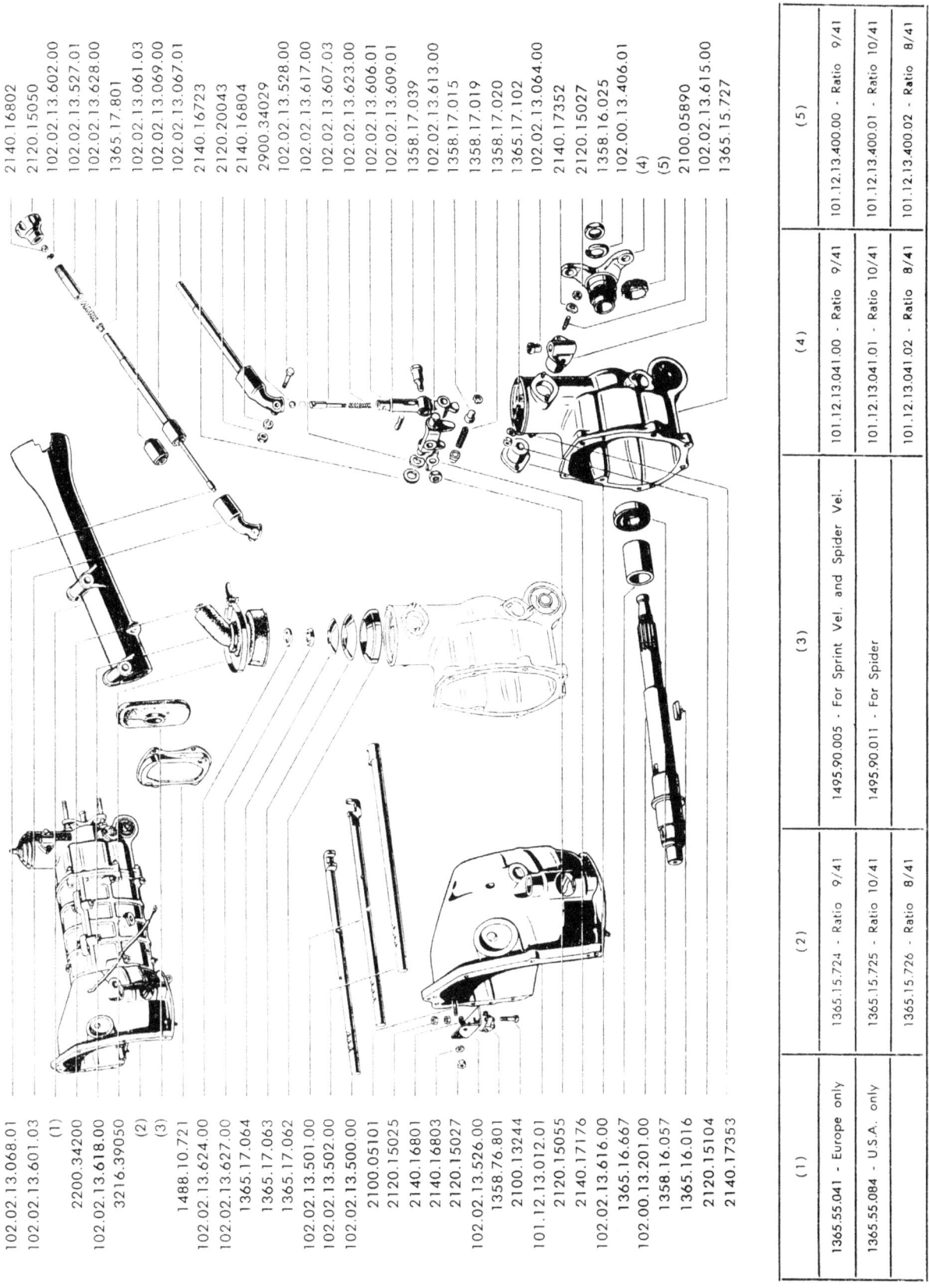

Fig. 33 - Gearbox with ball-type gearshift lever

(1)	(2)	(3)	(4)	(5)
1365.55.041 - Europe only	1365.15.724 - Ratio 9/41	1495.90.005 - For Sprint Vel. and Spider Vel.	101.12.13.041.00 - Ratio 9/41	101.12.13.400.00 - Ratio 9/41
1365.55.084 - U.S.A. only	1365.15.725 - Ratio 10/41	1495.90.011 - For Spider	101.12.13.041.01 - Ratio 10/41	101.12.13.400.01 - Ratio 10/41
	1365.15.726 - Ratio 8/41		101.12.13.041.02 - Ratio 8/41	101.12.13.400.02 - Ratio 8/41

Giulietta

Enclosure to the SHOP MANUAL
technical characteristics

Note: the specifications in this booklet refer to the following models:
Berlina (101.28) - t.i. (101.29) - Sprint (101.02) - Spider (101.03)
Sprint veloce (101.06) - Spider veloce (101.07) - S.S. (101.20) - S.Z. (101.26)

S. P. A. *Alfa Romeo* MILANO

DIREZIONE ASSISTENZA CLIENTI

INDEX

TECHNICAL CHARACTERISTICS

Principal characteristic data	Page	2
Tires	"	3
Performances	"	3
Refillings	"	4
Prescribed oils and lubricants	"	4
Valve timing	"	5
Carburetion	"	5
Ignition	"	5
Electric system	"	6
Spark plugs	"	6
Electric system main unit specifications	"	7
Electric system main unit adjusting data	"	8
Tightening torque specifications	"	8

PRINCIPAL INSPECTION SPECIFICATIONS

Camshaft journals and journal bearings	Page	9
Valves and valve guides	"	9
Valve cups	"	9
Valve springs	"	9
Cylinder barrels	"	10
Connecting rods	"	10
Pistons	"	11
Piston pins	"	12
Compression and oil scraper rings	"	12
Crankshaft	"	13
Clutch	"	13
Gearbox	"	14
Propeller shaft	"	14
Rear axle	"	14
Front suspension	"	15
Rear suspension	"	15
Brakes	"	15

TECHNICAL CHARACTERISTICS
Principal characteristic data

Number of cylinders			4
Bore and Stroke		mm	74 x 75
Total cylinder capacity		cc	1290
Maximum power	Giulietta berlina at 6000 rpm	HP	62
	Giulietta t.i. at 6200 rpm	HP	74
	Giulietta sprint & spider at 6300 rpm	HP	80
	Giulietta sprint & spider veloce at 6500 rpm	HP	90
	Giulietta S.S. & S.Z. at 6500 rpm	HP	100
"Potenza fiscale" (in Italy)		HP	15
Track	front	mm	1292
	rear	mm	1270
Wheel base	Giulietta berlina & t.i.	mm	2380
	Giulietta sprint & sprint veloce	mm	2380
	Giulietta spider & spider veloce	mm	2250
	Giulietta S.S. & S.Z.	mm	2250
Minimum turning radius	Giulietta berlina & t.i.	mm	5500
	Giulietta sprint & sprint veloce	mm	5500
	Giulietta spider & spider veloce	mm	5000
	Giulietta S.S. & S.Z.	mm	5000
Number of seats	Giulietta berlina & t.i.		5
	Giulietta sprint & sprint veloce		2 + 2
	Giulietta spider, spider veloce, S.S., S.Z.		2
Fuel consumption per 100 km (Italian Cuna Std. Spec.)	Giulietta berlina	liters	8.3
	Giulietta t.i.	liters	8.5
	Giulietta sprint & spider	liters	9
	Giulietta sprint veloce & spider veloce	liters	11
	Giulietta S.S. & S.Z.	liters	11.5
Weight of the car	Giulietta berlina	Kgs	915
	Giulietta t.i.	Kgs	920
	Giulietta sprint	Kgs	880
	Giulietta spider & S.S.	Kgs	860
	Giulietta sprint veloce	Kgs	895
	Giulietta spider veloce	Kgs	865
	Giulietta S.Z.	Kgs	770

Overall dimensions	Maximum length mm	Maximum width mm	Maximum height mm
Giulietta berlina	4033	1555	1405
Giulietta t.i.	4106	1555	1405
Giulietta sprint & sprint veloce	3980	1535	1320
Giulietta spider & spider veloce	3900	1580	1250 lowered top / 1335 raised top
Giulietta S.S.	4120	1660	1245
Giulietta S.Z.	3920	1540	1250

Tires 155 x 15

Pressures of inflation in kgs/cm^2

Car model	Pirelli Rolle front	Pirelli Rolle rear	Michelin S.D.S. front	Michelin S.D.S. rear	Pirelli cinturato front	Pirelli cinturato rear	Michelin X front	Michelin X rear
Berlina	1.4	1.5	1.5	1.5	1.4 (1) 1.5 (2)	1.5 (1) 1.6 (2)	1.4	1.5
t.i.	-	-	-	-	1.5 (1) 1.6 (2)	1.6 (1) 1.7 (2)	1.4 (1) 1.5 (2)	1.5 (1) 1.6 (2)
Sprint	-	-	-	-	1.5	1.6	1.5	1.6
Spider	-	-	-	-	1.5	1.6	1.4	1.5
Sprint veloce	-	-	-	-	1.6 (3) 1.8 (4) 2 (5)	1.7 (3) 1.9 (4) 2-2.1 (5)	-	-
Spider veloce	-	-	-	-	1.5 (3) 1.7 (4) 1.9 (5)	1.6 (3) 1.8 (4) 2 (5)	-	-
S.S. & S.Z.	-	-	-	-	1.5 (3) 1.8 (4) 2.1 (5)	1.6 (3) 1.9-2 (4) 2.2 (5)	-	-

(1) For touring use and small loads
(2) For sports use and full loads
(3) For road use, up to 100 m p h
(4) For road use, over 100 m p h
(5) For race track use

Performances after running in period

Car model	bevel drive	Gear	Speed Km/h	Gear	Speed Km/h	Gear	Speed Km/h	Gear	Speed Km/h	Gear	Speed Km/h	Gear	Speed Km/h
Berlina	9/41	1st	44	2nd	72	3rd	107	4th	145	--	---	REV.	44
t.i.	9/41	1st	47	2nd	78	3rd	114	4th	over 155	--	---	REV.	47
Sprint & Spider	9/41	1st	50	2nd	83	3rd	121	4th	165	--	---	REV.	50
Sprint veloce & Spider veloce	10/41	1st	55	2nd	90	3rd	132	4th	180	--	---	REV.	55
S.S. & S.Z.	9/41	1st	52	2nd	86	3rd	126	4th	171	5th	200	REV.	52

Refillings

		Berlina & t. i.	Sprint & Spider	Sprint Veloce	Spider Veloce	Sprint Speciale Sprint Zagato
Water (engine & radiator)	liters	7.5	7.5	7.5	7.5	7.5
Oil — Engine (pan & filter)	about Kgs	5.5	5.7	6.25	6.25	6.25
Oil — Gearbox	" "	1.350	1.650	1.650	1.650	1.650
Oil — Rear axle	" "	1.250	1.250	1.250	1.250	1.250
Oil — Steering box	" "	.250	.250	.250	.250	.250
Fuel tank capacity	liters	40	53	80	53	80

Prescribed oils and lubricants

Unit	(**) API - SAE - NLGI Number	BP	SHELL
Engine (*)	API MS SAE 20 W 40	BP Energol Visco-Static	SHELL X - 100 20 W 40
Gearbox	SAE 90	BP Energol gear oil SAE 90	SHELL Dentax 90
Steering box Differential	To avoid damage, the SAE 90 oils prescribed for the gearbox unit should not be confused with oils of the same grade but different in type, EP, which are prescribed for steering box and rear axle units. — SAE 90 API EP	BP Energol gear oil SAE 90 EP	SHELL Spirax 90 EP
Front and rear suspension ball joints Front suspension arm pins Propeller shaft universal joints Steering linkage joints	NLGI - 1	BP Energrease A 1 BP Energrease A 0	SHELL Retinax G SHELL Darina Grease A X
Front wheel bearings Ignition distributor	NLGI - 2/3	BP Energrease L 3 BP Energrease L 2 Multipurpose	SHELL Alvania Grease 3
Front & rear suspension shock absorbers	SAE 5 W	BP Energol shock absorber oil	SHELL Donax A 1
Solex 35 APAI-G carburetor throttle counterweight damper	SAE 20	BP Energol HD SAE 10 W	SHELL Rotella 20
Brake fluid reservoir	SAE 70 R 3	BP Energol brake fluid	SHELL Donax B 70 R 3 SHELL Super Safety brake fluid

(*) In the event the recommended "multigrade" engine lubricating oil is not available on the market, it can be replaced by the following oils:
- Above 10°C (50° F) BP Energol SAE 40 or Shell X-100 M.O. 40
- Below 10°C (50° F) BP Energol SAE 30 or Shell X-100 M.O. 30.

In countries where the recommended lubricant is not found, it is possible to replace it with products of other lubricant manufacturing Companies provided that in accordance with the prescribed specifications.

(**)
- SAE - Society of Automotive Engineers
- API - American Petroleum Institute
- NLGI - National Lubricating Grease Institute

Valve Timing

Adjusting data Car models	Valve clearance with cold engine		Intake valves		Exhaust valves	
	Intake	Exhaust	Opening starts	Closing ends	Opening starts	Closing ends
Berlina, t.i., Sprint, Spider	.475 - .50 mm	.525 - .55 mm	before TDC 25° 20'	after BDC 68°	before BDC 61° 20'	after TDC 18° 40'
Sprint veloce Spider veloce	.375 - .40 mm	.535 - .56 mm	before TDC 34°	after BDC 63°	before BDC 63°	after TDC 30°
Sprint speciale Sprint Zagato	.275 - .30 mm	.475 - .50 mm	before TDC 46°	after BDC 65°	before BDC 65°	after TDC 34°

Carburetion

	Berlina	t. i.		Sprint-Spider		Sprint veloce - Spider veloce Sprint speciale - Sprint Zagato
	Solex 32 PBIC	Solex 35 APAI-G		Solex 35 APAI-G		Weber 40 DCOE 2
		1st chamber	2nd chamber	1st chamber	2nd chamber	
Choke tube	25	24	24	24	24	29
Main jet	130	125	145	115	160	110
Main air gauger	160	180	110	150	160	200
Idler jet	50	40	-	40	-	50 (with axial hole 150)
Idling air gauger	100	100	-	100	-	120
Starter jet	130	160	-	160	-	60 - F 5
Acceleration pump jet	45	60	-	60	-	35

Ignition

Car model	Ignition distributor	Fixed advance AF	Maximum advance AM
Berlina, t.i.	Marelli S 71 B	8°	43° ± 3° at 5000 rpm
Sprint, Spider	Lucas DM 2	8°	43° ± 3° at 5000 rpm
Sprint veloce Spider veloce Sprint speciale Sprint Zagato	Marelli S 73 A	5°	46° ± 3° at 5000 rpm

12 Volt Electric System

1) Main units

Unit	Berlina, t.i., Sprint, Spider	Sprint Veloce - Spider Veloce Sprint Speciale - Sprint Zagato
Generator	Marelli DNA 44 E	
	Lucas C 39 PV 2 Bosch L/J/GEG/160/12/2500 R	---
Voltage regulator	Marelli IR 32 B	Marelli IR 32 A
	Lucas RB 106/2 Bosch RS/TBC/160/12	---
Starting motor	Marelli MT 40 B	
	Lucas M 325 BZ 2 Bosch AL/EDD 0,5/12 R	---
Coil	Marelli B 200 B	
	Lucas LA 12 Bosch TK 12 A 4	---
Ignition distributor	Marelli S 71 B	Marelli S 73 A
	Lucas DM 2 Bosch VJU 4 BR	---
Windshield wiper	Marelli TGE 63 A (berlina & t. i.)	Marelli SW 133 (Sprint Speciale, Sprint Zagato)
	Lucas DR 2 (Sprint & Spider)	Lucas DR 2 (Sprint Veloce, Spider Veloce)
Battery	Capacity 38 Ah	

Note: with LUCAS or MARELLI Electric System the battery positive terminal is grounded on models: Berlina, t.i., Sprint and Spider. On models: Sprint Veloce, Spider Veloce, SS and SZ the negative is grounded.

2) Spark plugs

Car model	Plug Type	Electrode gap (mm)
Berlina	Spica-Lodge HLN	.5 - .6
t.i.	Spica-Lodge HLN	.5 - .6
Sprint & Spider	Spica-Lodge 2 HLN/G	.55 - .65
Sprint Veloce & Spider Veloce	Spica Lodge RL 47 / Spica Lodge 2HLN/G	.38 - .46 / .55 - .65
Sprint Speciale & Sprint Zagato	Spica-Lodge RL 47	.38 - .46

Electric system main unit specifications

Battery

Capacity	38 Ah
Specific gravity, fully charged	1.28 (32° Bé)
Specific gravity, half charged	1.23 (27° Bé)
Specific gravity, flat	1.11 - 1.14 (15° - 18° Bé)
Voltage	12 V

Spark plugs

Make	Lodge
Type	RL 47 2 ULN LN
Thread	14 mm

Lights

Headlights	45/40 Watts
Stop, direction indicator and reverse lights	20 "
License plate light	5 "
Dashpanel light	2.50 "
Parking lights	5/20 "
Ceiling light	3 "

Generator

	LUCAS C. 39 PV 2	MARELLI DN 44 E
Min. rev. for battery charging (headlights out)	1050-1200 rpm 13 Volts	1350 rpm 12 Volts
Max. charging capacity	1900-2150 rpm 19 Volts	1900 rpm 18.3 Amps - 12 Volts - 220 Watts
Armature resistance	about 6 Ohm	4.9 - .1 Ohm

Starting motor

	LUCAS M 325 BZ 2	MARELLI MT 40 B
Terminal voltage	at 1000 rpm 8.5 Volts	free 1500 rpm: 11.6 Volts with 25 Amps under load 3200-3500 rpm: 10 Volts with 100 Amps
Short circuit torque	8 ft-lbs 350 Amps 8.5 Volts	at zero rpm .75 Kgm: 7.5 Volts with 300 Amps
Torque	at 1000 rpm 4.7 ft-lbs	at 3200-3500 rpm: .15 Kgm

Distributor

	LUCAS DM 2	MARELLI S 71 B	MARELLI S 73 A
Load on contact-breaker arm	511-680 grammes	550-650 grammes	800 - 50 grammes
Condenser capacity	.18 - .22 mmF	.18 mmF	.18 mmF

Electric system main unit adjusting data

Generator

	LUCAS C 30 PV 2	MARELLI DN 44 E
Load of spring on brush	625 - 710 grammes	400 - 500 grammes
Min. load of spring on brush	425 "	400 "
Min. length of spring	8.5 mm	8 - 10 mm

Voltage regulator

	LUCAS R.B. 106/2	MARELLI IR 32 A - MARELLI IR 32 B
Under-voltage trip:		
Cut-on voltage	12.7 - 13.3 Volts	11 - 12.5 Volts
Cut-out voltage	8.5 - 11 "	8 - 10 "
Reverse current	3.5 - 4.5 Amps	2 - 4.5 Amps
Voltage regulator (at 20°C):		
Regulating voltage	at 1500 rpm 15.6 - 16.2 Volts	at 3500 rpm { free 15.1 - 15.7 Volts / under load 12.6 - 13.5 Volts }

Starting motor

	LUCAS N 325 BZ 2	MARELLI MT 40 B
Load of spring on brush	800 - 900 grammes	550 - 700 grammes
Brush length	10 mm	8 - 10 mm

Distributor

	LUCAS DM 2	MARELLI S 71 B	MARELLI S 73 A
	Berlina - t.i. Sprint - Spider	Berlina - t.i. Sprint - Spider	S.S. - S.Z.
Contact breaker point gap	.35 - .40 mm	.42 - .48 mm	.42 - .48 mm
Centrifugal advance	at 375 rpm 0° ÷ 1° at 500 " .5° - 2.5° at 1500 " 8.5° - 10.5° at 2375 " 16° - 18°	at 400 rpm 0° ÷ 1° LINEAR at 2500 rpm 18°	at 400 rpm 0° ÷ 1° at 500 " 5° at 700 " 11° at 1500 " 14° at 2500 " 18°
Vacuum advance	635 mm Hg 5° - 7.5° 355 mm Hg 5° - 7.5° 304 mm Hg 2.5 - 5°	275 mm Hg 0° 400 mm Hg 6.5°	no vacuum advance

Tightening torque specifications

	Berlina - t.i. - Sprint - Spider	Sprint Veloce - Spider Veloce Sprint Speciale - Sprint Zagato
Cylinder head with cold engine	5.4 - 5.6 Kgm	5.4 - 5.6 Kgm in oil
Main bearing caps	3.2 - 3.5 Kgm	3.2 - 3.5 Kgm
Connecting rod bearing caps	3.4 - 3.6 Kgm	3.6 - 3.9 Kgm

PRINCIPAL INSPECTION SPECIFICATIONS

Note: if not otherwise specified the following values are common to all models.

Camshaft journals and journal bearings

Camshaft journal diameter	26.959 - 26.980 mm
Camshaft journal bearing diameter	27.000 - 27.033 mm
Clearance when new, between camshaft journal and their seats	.020 - .074 mm
Clearance between above members at maximum wear	.10 mm
End play between camshaft and thrust bearing	.065 - .182 mm

Valves and valve guides

Valves		SANTAMBROGIO	ATE
Diameter	intake	37 - 37.15 mm	-
	exhaust	34 - 34.15 "	34 - 34.20 mm
Stem diameter	intake	8.962 - 8.987 "	-
	exhaust	8.935 - 8.960 "	8.935 - 8.960 "
Total length	intake	108.80 - 109.20 "	-
	exhaust	108.35 - 108.75 "	108.35 - 108.80 "

Valve guide	Inner diameter with guide assembled	9 - 9.015 mm
	Outer diameter with guide removed	14.033 - 14.044 mm
Clearance between guide assembled in cylinder head and valve stem	when new (and assembled) intake	.013 - .053 mm
	when new (and assembled) exhaust	.040 - .080 mm
	max. wear intake	.10 mm
	max. wear exhaust	.13 mm
Diameter of seat on cylinder head for valve guide		14 - 14.016 mm
Interference between seat and valve guide		.017 - .044 mm

Valve cups

	standard	enlarged
Cup diameter	34.973 - 34.989 mm	35.173 - 35.189 mm
Cup seat diameter	35 - 35.025 "	35.2 - 35.225 "
Play when first assembled	.011 - .052 mm	
Play at maximum wear	.06 mm	

Valve springs

Outer spring	length	free	50.57 mm
		under a load of 31.5 - 32.5 Kg	28 mm
Inner spring	length	free	46.47 mm
		under a load of 19.5 - 20.5 Kg	26.5 mm

Diameter of the cylinder barrels

	Class A (Blue)	Class B (Rose)	Class C (Green)
Normal	73.985 - 73.994 mm	73.995 - 74.004 mm	74.005 - 74.014 mm
1st oversize	74.185 - 74.194 "	74.195 - 74.204 "	74.205 - 74.214 "
2nd oversize	74.385 - 74.394 "	74.395 - 74.404 "	74.405 - 74.414 "
3rd oversize	74.585 - 74.594 "	74.595 - 74.604 "	74.605 - 74.614 "

Elongation and taper of barrels
- with new barrel .... .01 mm
- with worn barrel (maximum permissible limit) .05 mm

Clearance between cylinder barrel and piston

Car model	Piston make		
	MAHLE	BORGO	K. S.
Berlina, t.i., Sprint, Spider	.051 - .069 mm	.045 - .064 mm	.050 - .069 mm
Sprint Veloce, Spider Veloce, Sprint Speciale, Sprint Zagato	.140 - .159 "	.065 - .084 "	---

Wear limits
- Berlina, t.i., Sprint, Spider .... .12 mm
- Sprint Veloce, Spider Veloce, Sprint Speciale, Sprint Zagato .18 mm

C o n n e c t i n g   r o d s

Length between center line of big end and center line of small end of connecting rod .... 132.955 - 133.045 mm

Inner diameter of the big end of connecting rod .... 20.005 - 20.015 mm

Clearance between small end bearing bore and piston pins ....
- specified .005 - .020 mm
- max. wear .05 mm

Diameter of bearing seat .... 48.658 - 48.671 mm

Bearing thickness
- for standard crankshaft ... 1.822 - 1.829 mm
- for 1st re-grind of crankpins 1.949 - 1.956 mm
- for 2nd re-grind of crankpins 2.076 - 2.083 mm

Radial clearance between pins and bearings .... .025 - .064 mm

Axial clearance between con-rods and their crankpins .... .2 - .3 mm

BERLINA - t.i. - SPRINT - SPIDER

MAHLE PISTON

	Class A (Blue)	Class B (Rose)	Class C (Green)
Normal	73.925 - 73.934 mm	73.935 - 73.944 mm	73.945 - 73.954 mm
1st oversize	74.125 - 74.135 "	74.135 - 74.145 "	74.145 - 74.155 "
2nd oversize	74.325 - 74.335 "	74.335 - 74.345 "	74.345 - 74.355 "
3rd oversize	74.525 - 74.535 "	74.535 - 74.545 "	74.545 - 74.555 "

BORGO PISTON

	Class A (Blue)	Class B (Rose)	Class C (Green)
Normal	73.930 - 73.940 mm	73.940 - 73.950 mm	73.950 - 73.960 mm
1st oversize	74.130 - 74.140 "	74.140 - 74.150 "	74.150 - 74.160 "
2nd oversize	74.330 - 74.340 "	74.340 - 74.350 "	74.350 - 74.360 "
3rd oversize	74.530 - 74.540 "	74.540 - 74.550 "	74.550 - 74.560 "

K. S. PISTON

	Class A (Blue)	Class B (Rose)	Class C (Green)
Standard diameter	73.925 - 73.935 mm	73.935 - 73.945 mm	73.945 - 73.955 mm
Oversized diameter	1st oversize 74.135 - 74.145 mm	2nd oversize 74.335 - 74.345 mm	3rd oversize 74.535 - 74.545 mm

SPRINT VELOCE - SPIDER VELOCE
SPRINT SPECIALE - SPRINT ZAGATO

MAHLE PISTON

	Class A (Blue)	Class B (Rose)	Class C (Green)
Normal	73.835 - 73.845 mm	73.845 - 73.855 mm	73.855 - 73.865 mm
1st oversize	74.035 - 74.045 "	74.045 - 74.055 "	74.055 - 74.065 "
2nd oversize	74.235 - 74.245 "	74.245 - 74.255 "	74.255 - 74.265 "
3rd oversize	74.435 - 74.445 "	74.445 - 74.455 "	74.455 - 74.465 "

BORGO PISTON

	Class A (Blue)	Class B (Rose)	Class C (Green)
Normal	73.910 - 73.920 mm	73.920 - 73.930 mm	73.930 - 73.940 mm
1st oversize	74.110 - 74.120 "	74.120 - 74.130 "	74.130 - 74.140 "
2nd oversize	74.310 - 74.320 "	74.320 - 74.330 "	74.330 - 74.340 "
3rd oversize	74.510 - 74.520 "	74.520 - 74.530 "	74.530 - 74.540 "

Hole in piston for pin

Car model	Color	Piston MAHLE	Piston BORGO	Piston K. S.
Berlina, t.i., Sprint, Spider	White	19.999 - 20.002 mm	20.003 - 20.005 mm	20.0025 - 20.005 mm
Berlina, t.i., Sprint, Spider	Black	19.996 - 19.999 mm	20.00 - 20.002 mm	20.00 - 20.0025 mm
Sprint Veloce, Spider Veloce / Sprint Speciale, Sprint Zagato	White	19.997 - 20.00 mm	20.003 - 20.005 mm	--
Sprint Veloce, Spider Veloce / Sprint Speciale, Sprint Zagato	Black	19.994 - 19.997 mm	20.00 - 20.002 mm	--

Piston pins

(for all car models)

BLACK Color	WHITE Color
19.997 - 20.00 mm	19.994 - 19.997 mm

Clearance between piston pin and hole

Car model	Color	Piston MAHLE	Piston BORGO	Piston K. S.
Berlina, t.i., Sprint, Spider	White	.005 to - .001 mm	.003 - .008 mm	.0025 - .008 mm
Berlina, t.i., Sprint, Spider	Black	.005 to - .001 mm	.003 - .008 mm	.003 - .0085 mm
Sprint Veloce, Spider Veloce / Sprint Speciale - Sprint Zagato	White	.00	.003 - .008 mm	---
Sprint Veloce, Spider Veloce / Sprint Speciale - Sprint Zagato	Black	.00	.003 - .008 mm	---

Wear limit - .04 mm

Compression and oil scraper rings

Thickness of rings.................................... compression 1.972 - 1.984 mm
oil scraper 3.958 - 3.970 mm

Height of seat in piston for compression rings and oil scraper ring (for all car models):

Piston	Compression ring seat	Oil scraper ring seat
Mahle	2.025 - 2.040 mm	4.015 - 4.030 mm
Borgo	2.022 - 2.047 mm	4.006 - 4.031 mm
K. S.	2.022 - 2.047 mm	4.006 - 4.031 mm

Axial clearance between seats and rings:

Piston	Compression rings	Oil scraper rings
Mahle	.041 - .068 mm	.045 - .072 mm
Borgo	.038 - .075 mm	.036 - .073 mm
K. S.	.038 - .075 mm	.036 - .073 mm

Crankshaft

Diameter of main journals	Normal	59.960 - 59.973 mm
	1st undersize	59.706 - 59.719 mm
	2nd undersize	59.452 - 59.465 mm
Diameter of connecting rod pins	Normal	44.963 - 44.975 mm
	1st undersize	44.709 - 44.721 mm
	2nd undersize	44.455 - 44.467 mm
Diameter of seat for main bearings in crankcase		63.657 - 63.676 mm
Thickness of main bearings	Normal	1.829 - 1.835 mm
	1st undersize	1.956 - 1.962 mm
	2nd undersize	2.083 - 2.089 mm
Diametrical play between pins and main bearings (specified)		.032 - .057 mm
Length of central journal	Normal	30.000 - 30.035 mm
	1st oversize	30.127 - 30.162 mm
	2nd oversize	30.254 - 30.289 mm
Thickness of thrust rings for central journal	Normal	2.311 - 2.362 mm
	1st oversize	2.374 - 2.425 mm
	2nd oversize	2.438 - 2.489 mm
Axial clearance of thrust rings for central journal (specified)		.111 - .228 mm
Axial clearance of connecting rods (specified)		.20 - .30 mm
Fillet radii of main journals and of connecting rod pins		1.7 - 2.1 mm

Clutch

Inside diameter of the driven plate		130 mm
Outside diameter of the driven plate		200 mm
Clearance between the thrust ring and the disengaging ring	specified	2 mm
	minimum limit	1 mm
Thickness of the driven plate (with new facings)	free	9.8 - 10.1 mm
	engaged	9.1 - 9.4 mm
wear limit		6 mm
Thickness of the clutch facing		3.5 mm
Clearance between the flywheel and the thrust ring face		59 - 59.8 mm
Clearance between the thrust ring face and the plane of the outer face of the cover		25.28 - 26.72 mm
Number of springs		9
Free length of springs		43.5 - 45.5 mm
Length of springs under load of 45/49 kgs		29 mm
Pedal free travel		23 mm
Distance between the end of hub on engine side and driven plate bearing surface	with new facing	5 mm
	with worn facing	6.5 mm

Gearbox

Ratios (for all car models) ....
- 1st gear ... 1 : 3.258
- 2nd gear ... 1 : 1.958
- 3rd gear ... 1 : 1.357
- 4th gear ... 1 : 1
- 5th gear ... 1 : .854 (only for S.S. and S.Z.)
- Reverse Gear . 1 : 3.252

Length of springs for gear release balls ....
- free .... 15.2 mm
- installed ..... 12 mm (Kg 2.88 - 3.12)
- under oprtng load . 10 mm (Kg 4.67 - 5.05)

Propeller shaft

Maximum eccentricity of the rear shaft .... .2 mm

Maximum eccentricity of the intermediate bracket bearing seat .... .03 mm

Maximum permissible out of squareness between the rear shaft and the face of the front flange (measured at the flange extremities) .... .05 mm

Maximum permitted out of balance of the rear shaft .... 10 gr.cm

Rear axle

Type of bevel drive .... Hypoid

Type of rear axle shafts .... semi-floating

Backlash, pinion/crown wheel .... .13 - .18 mm

Maximum crown wheel eccentricity .... .025 mm

Bevel drive

Car model	Bevel drive	
	Standard	On request
Berlina, t.i., Sprint, Spider	9/41	8/41 10/41
Sprint Veloce, Spider Veloce	10/41	8/41 9/41
Sprint Speciale, Sprint Zagato	9/41	10/41 (only Sprint Zagato)

Overall ratio
Transmission-Axle

Bevel drive	Gear	Ratio	Gear	Ratio	Gear	Ratio	Gear	Ratio	Gear	Ratio	Gear	Ratio
8/41	1st	1: 16.697	2nd	1: 10.173	3rd	1 : 6.954	4th	1 : 5.125	--	---	Rev.	1: 16.656
9/41	1st	1: 14.844	2nd	1: 9.045	3rd	1: 6.181	4th	1 : 4.555	5th	1 : 3.890	Rev.	1: 14.814
10/41	1st	1: 13.357	2nd	1: 8.138	3rd	1: 5.563	4th	1 : 4.100	--	---	Rev.	1: 13.333

Front suspension

Wheel camber .... 0°

Toe-in (measured at rims) .... 3 mm

King-pin caster angle .... 8° 35'

Steering angle .... { inner . 36°
                                                          { outer . 28° 30'

Car model	Spring free length	Length under static load
Berlina - t.i.	405 mm	274 mm (521 - 553 Kg)
Sprint - Spider - Spider Veloce	394 mm	267 mm (490 - 520 Kg)
Sprint Veloce - Sprint Speciale - Sprint Zagato	377 mm	267 mm (485 - 515 Kg)

Rear suspension

Car model	Spring free travel	Length under static load
Berlina - t.i.	479 mm	250 mm (255.1 - 270.9 Kg)
Sprint	414 mm	230 mm (189.15 - 200.85 Kg)
Spider - Spider Veloce	410 mm	230 mm (185.25 - 196.75 Kg)
Sprint Veloce	405 mm	240 mm (190.1 - 201.9 Kg)
Sprint Speciale - Sprint Zagato	393 mm	230 mm (165.87 - 176.13 Kg)

Brakes

	Berlina - t.i. - Sprint - Spider	Sprint Veloce - Spider Veloce	Sprint Speciale - Sprint Zagato (three-shoe front brakes)
Drum inner diameter	front 266.6 - 266.8 mm rear 254 - 254.1 mm	front 266.7 - 266.8 mm rear 254 - 254.1 mm	front 266.7 - 266.8 mm rear 266.7 - 266.8 mm
Brake shoe diameter	with { front 265.64 - 266.24 mm lining { rear 254 - 254.12 mm	front 265.64 - 265.94 mm rear 254 - 254.12 mm	front 265.94 - 265.64 mm rear 265.94 - 265.64 mm
Lining type	Ferodo MZ 41	Ferodo MZ 41	Ferodo ARZ
Lining working width	front 57 mm rear 44.45 mm	front 57 mm rear 44.45 mm	front 70 mm rear 57 mm
Lining wearing thickness	front 2.6 - 3 mm rear 2.6 - 3 mm	front 1.8 - 2.2 mm rear 1.8 - 2.2 mm	front 2 - 2.2 mm rear 2 - 2.2 mm
Master cylinder plunger dia.	25.4 mm	25.4 mm	25.4 mm
Wheel cylinder plunger dia.	front 25.4 mm rear 22.22 mm	front 25.4 mm rear 22.22 mm	front 22.22 mm rear 22.22 mm
Brake pedal working travel	120 mm	120 mm	120 mm

NOTES

GIULIA 1600 cars

t. i.
spider
sprint

 alfa romeo

technical characteristics and principal inspection specifications

INDEX

TECHNICAL CHARACTERISTICS

PRINCIPAL CHARACTERISTIC DATA	Page	3
Performances	"	3
Tires	"	4
Refillings	"	4
Prescribed oils and lubricants	"	4
Carburetion	"	5
Valve timing	"	6
Ignition	"	6
Spark plugs	"	6
Electric system	"	7
Tightening torque specifications	"	8

PRINCIPAL CHECK-UP SPECIFICATIONS

Camshafts	Page	9
Valves and valve guides	"	9
Valve seats	"	9
Valve cups	"	10
Valve springs	"	10
Connecting rods	"	10
Piston pins	"	10
Pistons and cylinder barrels	"	11
Compression and oil scraper rings	"	11
Crankshaft	"	12
Clutch	"	13
Gearbox	"	13
Rear axle and suspension	"	14
Front suspension	"	15
Brakes	"	16
Wheel alignment	"	18

TECHNICAL CHARACTERISTICS

PRINCIPAL CHARACTERISTIC DATA

	T I	SPRINT	SPIDER
Number of cylinders	4	4	4
Bore	78 mm (3.072")	78 mm (3.072")	78 mm (3.072")
Stroke	82 mm (3.23")	82 mm (3.23")	82 mm (3.23")
Total cylinder capacity	1570 cc	1570 cc	1570 cc
Maximum power	92 CV (DIN) 104 HP (SAE) at 6000 r.p.m.	92 CV (DIN) 104 HP (SAE) at 6200 r.p.m.	92 CV (DIN) 104 HP (SAE) at 6200 r.p.m.
Front track	1310 mm (4'3")	1292 mm (4'2 7/8")	1292 mm (4'2 7/8")
Rear track	1270 mm (4'2")	1270 mm (4'2")	1270 mm (4'2")
Wheel base	2510 mm (8'2 7/8")	2380 mm (7'9 1/2")	2250 mm (7'4 1/2")
Minimum turning circle	10,900 mm (35'9")	11,000 mm (36'1")	11,000 mm (36'1")
Maximum length	4140 mm (13'7")	3980 mm (13'3/4")	3900 mm (12'9 5/8")
Maximum width	1560 mm (5'1 11/32")	1535 mm (5'3/8")	1580 mm (5'2 5/32")
Maximum height (empty weight)	1430 mm (4'8")	1320 mm (4'4")	1335 mm (4'4 3/4") (raised top)
Weight, empty, with tools and jack	1000 Kgs (2,204 lbs)	905 Kgs (2,000 lbs)	885 Kgs (1,870 lbs)
Number of seats	6	2 + 2	2
Tires 155 x 15	PIRELLI Cinturato S MICHELIN XA	PIRELLI Cinturato S MICHELIN XA	PIRELLI Cinturato S MICHELIN XA
Fuel consumption per 100 Km (62 miles) (Italian CUNA Standards)	10.4 lt 2.28 Imp. gals 2.74 U.S. gals	9.4 lt 1.97 Imp. gals 2.48 U.S. gals	8.8 lt 1.93 Imp. gals 2.32 U.S. gals

Performances after breaking in period - Maximum speeds.

Gear	T I Bevel drive 41 : 8		SPIDER-SPRINT Bevel drive 41 : 8	
	Km/h	mph	Km/h	mph
1st	40	25	41	26
2nd	66	41	69	43
3rd	97	60	102	63
4th	131	81	137	85
5th	165	103	172	107
Rev.	44	27	46	28

Tires
Inflation pressures (with tire cold)

TIRE	T I	
	Front wheels	Rear wheels
PIRELLI 155 x 15 Cinturato S MICHELIN 155 x 15 XA	1.6 to 1.8 Kg/cm^2 22.7 to 25.6 psi	1.7 to 2.1 Kg/cm^2 24.1 to 29.8 psi

- Inflate to the lower pressure for use with low load and short peaks in speed
- Inflate to the higher pressure for use with full load and maximum speeds.

TIRE		SPRINT-SPIDER			
		Front wheels		Rear wheels	
		Kg/cm^2	psi	Kg/cm^2	psi
PIRELLI 155 x 15 Cinturato S	Touring riding up to 160 Km/h (100 mph)	1.6	22.7	1.7	24.1
	Sport riding above 160 Km/h (100 mph)	1.7	24.1	1.8	25.6
	On track	2	28.4	2.1	29.8
MICHELIN 155 x 15 XA	Touring riding up to 160 Km/h (100 mph)	1.7	24.1	1.7	24.1
	Sport riding above 160 Km/h (100 mph)	1.9	27.0	1.9	27.0
	On track	2.1	29.8	2.1	29.8

Refillings

				IMP.	U. S.
Water (engine & radiator)			lts 7.5	1.65 gals	1.98 gals
Fuel		(T I)	lts 46	10.1 gals	12.1 gals
		(Sprint-Spider)	lts 53	11.7 gals	14.0 gals
Oil	Engine (pan & filter) to min. level	(T I)	Kgs 3.25	3.2 qts	3.8 qts
		(Sprint-Spider)	Kgs 3.70	3.6 qts	4.3 qts
	to max. level		Kgs 5.75	5.7 qts	6.8 qts
	Gearbox		Kgs 1.650	3.2 pints	3.8 pints
	Rear axle		Kgs 1.250	2.5 pints	3.0 pints
	Steering box		Kgs 0.250	.5 pint	.6 pint

Prescribed oils and lubricants

Part	API - NLGI - SAE number	Recommended commercial equivalents
Engine	SAE 20 W 40 API MS	BP Energol Visco-Static Shell X-100 20 W 40
Gearbox	SAE 90	BP Energol Gear Oil SAE 90 Shell Dentax 90
Steering box and rear axle	SAE 90 API EP	BP Energol Gear Oil SAE 90 EP Shell Spirax 90 EP
*Front suspension arm ball joints *Front suspension arm pins Propeller shaft universal joints *Steering linkage joints	NLGI 1	BP Energrease A 1 BP Energrease A 0 Shell Retinax G Darina Grease A X
Front wheel bearings	NLGI 2/3	BP Energrease L 3 Shell Alvania Grease 3
Brake fluid reservoir	SAE 70 R 3	BP Energol brake fluid (green) Shell Donax B 70 R 3 (red)

(*) For Sprint and Spider models only.

Carburetion

T.I : Solex 32 PAIA 7 Carburetor

	1st barrel	2nd barrel
Choke tube (Venturi)	23	23
Main jet	125	130
Main air gauger	190	190
Idler jet	45	70
Idling air gauger	100	60

Acceleration pump jet = 45
Starter jet = 120
Inlet valve of acceleration pump = 40
Starter air gauger = 500
Needle seat diameter = 1.75 mm (.069")
Spacer under needle-seat = 1 mm (.039")
Distance of fuel level from bottom of float chamber = 12 mm (.47") (with a pressure of 2 mts (6'6") H_2O upstream the needle-seat)
Delivery of acceleration pump = 4 to 6 cc for every 20 pump strokes
Clogging pressure measured upstream the needle seat = 6 to 7 mts (19'8" to 23') H_2O
Weight of float = 7.2 grammes
Minimum engine RPM = 500 to 600

SPIDER - SPRINT : 32 PAIA 5 Solex Carburetor

	1st barrel	2nd barrel
Choke tube	23	23
Main jet	125	135
Main air gauger	220	200
Idler jet	45	70
Idling air gauger	100	60

Acceleration pump jet = 45
Starter jet = 120
Starter air gauger = 500
Inlet valve of acceleration pump = 40
Needle-seat diameter = 1.75 mm (.069")
Spacer under needle seat = 1 mm (.039")
Distance of fuel level from bottom of float chamber = 12 mm (.47") (with a pressure of 2 mts (6'6") H_2O upstream the needle-seat)
Delivery of acceleration pump = 4 to 6 cc every 20 pump strokes
Clogging pressure measured upward the needle seat = 6 to 7 mts (19'8" to 23') H_2O
Weight of float = 7.2 grammes
Minimum engine RPM = 500 to 600

N.B.: For the adjustment of carburetors see the instructions given in the "Instruction Books" Giulia 1600 T.I. and Giulia 1600 Sprint and Spider.

Valve Timing

T I - SPIDER - SPRINT

Checking of valve opening-and-closing angles

Clearance (with cold engine) between the unlobed profile of cam of camshaft and the cup ceiling:

inlet	.475 to .500 mm (.0187 to .0197")
exhaust	.525 to .550 mm (.0206 to .0216")

Opening of inlet valve:

linear displacement of cup	.20 mm (.008")
corresponding to angle value ..... before T D C	6°

Closing of inlet valve:

linear displacement of cup	.20 mm (.008")
corresponding to angle value ..... after B D C	54°

Opening of exhaust valve:

linear displacement of cup	.15 mm (.006")
corresponding to angle value ..... before B D C	54°

Closing of exhaust valve:

linear displacement of cup	.15 mm (.006")
corresponding to angle value ..... after T D C	6°

Angle values of the actual diagram of valve timing system with cold engine (clockwise rotation direction of the crankshaft seen from the front side):

opening of inlet valve ..... before T D C	24° 40'
closing of inlet valve ..... after B D C	72° 40'
opening of exhaust valve ..... before B D C	66°
closing of exhaust valve ..... after T D C	18°
inlet stroke	277° 20'
exhaust stroke	264°

Ignition

T I - SPIDER - SPRINT

Firing order = 1 - 3 - 4 - 2 (No 1 cylinder is that at the fan side)
Opening of contact points of ignition distributor = .35 to .40 mm (.014 to .016")

Values of advance of ignition distributor

Fixed advance F Before T D C	Maximum Advance M Before T D C
3° ± 2°	43° ± 3° at 5000 rpm

Spark plugs

Lodge 2HLN

Electrode gap = .55 to .65 mm (.022 to .025")

Electric system

Units	T I	Sprint - Spider
Electric system	\multicolumn{2}{c}{12 Volts}	
Battery	40 Amp. hours	50 Amp. hours
Generator	\multicolumn{2}{c}{Bosch LJ/GEG 200/12/2700 R. 32 mr}	
Voltage regulator	\multicolumn{2}{c}{Bosch RS/VA 200/12 A 2}	
Starting motor	\multicolumn{2}{c}{Bosch AL/EEF .7/12 R 11}	
Coil	\multicolumn{2}{c}{Bosch TK 12 A 3}	
Ignition distributor	\multicolumn{2}{c}{Bosch VJU 4 BR 41 mk}	
Windshield wiper	TGE 93 A Marelli	DR 2 Lucas

Power in watts of the electric system bulbs

	T I	Sprint - Spider
Inner headlights (high beams)	40 x 45	45 x 40
Outer headlights (low beams)	40 x 45	45 x 40
Front parking lights	5	5
Front lights - direction indicators	20	20
Side lights - direction indicators	2.5	2.5
Rear lights - parking & stop	5 x 20	5 x 20
Rear lights - direction indicators	20	20
Reserve light	20	20
License plate light	5	5
Inspection light	10	10
Engine compartment light	5	5 (Sprint only)
Dome light inside the car	5	5 (Sprint only)
Light in luggage compartment	5	-
Lighting on instrument panel	3	3
Tell-tale for parking lights	3	3
Tell-tale for direction indicators	3	3
Tell-tale for generator	3	3
Tell-tale for choke control	-	3 (Sprint only)
Tell-tale for gasoline supply	3	3
Tell-tale for heaters	3	3
Tell-tale for headlights	-	3

Tightening torque specifications

	Kgm	ft. - lbs	Manner of tightening
Nuts of cylinder head — after repairing, when cold	6.2 to 6.4	44.8 to 46.3	Slacken and retighten without lubricating
Nuts of cylinder head — when hot	6.6 to 6.7	47.7 to 48.4	Lock without slackening the nut
After 500 Km (300 mi.) from replacement of gasket, when cold	6.2 to 6.4	44.8 to 46.3	Slacken a 1/4 turn and retighten
Nuts of the camshaft caps	2 to 2.25	14.5 to 16.3	in oil
Nuts of main bearing caps	4 to 4.2	29 to 30.3	in oil
Nuts of the connecting rod caps	5 to 5.3	36.2 to 38.3	in oil
Spark plugs	2.5 to 3.5	18.1 to 25.3	With graphite grease, when cold
Nuts flywheel on crankshaft	4.2 to 4.5	30.4 to 32.5	in oil
Nut of gearbox main shaft	12	86.8	dry
Nuts of gearbox layshaft	8	58	dry
Screws to secure ring gear to differential case	4.5 to 5	32.6 to 36.1	dry
Ring nut securing yoke on bevel drive pinion shaft	8 to 14	58 to 101.2	dry
Nuts to secure steering levers to knuckles	4.5 to 5.8	32.6 to 41.9	dry
Screws to secure brake shoe backplates to knuckles	4.5 to 5.8	32.6 to 41.9	dry
Screws to secure brake shoe backplates to rear axle	4.5 to 5.8	32.6 to 41.9	dry
Nuts to secure rear axle reaction trunnion body (T.I.)	4.2 to 4.7	30.4 to 33.9	dry

PRINCIPAL CHECK-UP SPECIFICATIONS

Camshafts

Diameter of journals	= 26.959 to 26.980 mm (1.0614 to 1.0622")
Diameter of journal bearings	= 27.000 to 27.033 mm (1.0630 to 1.0642")
Radial clearance between journals and bearings	= .020 to .074 mm (.0008 to .0029")
End play of camshaft in thrust bearing	= .065 to .182 mm (.0026 to .0071")

Valves and valve guides

		intake	exhaust	
		SANTAMBROGIO	SANTAMBROGIO	ATE
Valves	Diameter of valve poppet	41.0 to 41.15 mm (1.614 to 1.620")	37.0 to 37.15 mm (1.4567 to 1.4625")	37.0 to 37.2 mm (1.4567 to 1.4645")
	Diameter of valve stem	8.96 to 8.987 mm (.3527 to .3538")	8.935 to 8.960 mm (.3518 to .3527")	8.935 to 8.960 mm (.3518 to .3527")
	Total length	106.63 to 107.03 mm (4.1981 to 4.2137")	105.90 to 106.30 mm (4.1693 to 4.1850")	106.05 to 106.15 mm (4.1753 to 4.1791")

N.B. - The Santambrogio - ATE exhaust valves are alternate supply

Valve guide	Outside diameter with guide removed	= 14.033 to 14.044 mm (.5528 to .5529")
	Inside diameter with guide assembled in cylinder head	= 9.000 to 9.015 mm (.3544 to .3549")
Clearance between guide assembled in cylinder head and valve stem	intake	= .013 to .053 mm (.0005 to .0020")
	exhaust	= .040 to .080 mm (.0016 to .0031")
Diameter of valve guide seat on cylinder head		= 14.000 to 14.018 mm (.5512 to .5518")
Interference between seat and valve guide		= .015 to .044 mm (.0006 to .0017")

Valve seats

		intake	exhaust
Outer diameter of the valve seat	normal	42.597 to 42.648 mm (1.6771 to 1.6790")	38.597 to 38.648 mm (1.5196 to 1.5215")
	oversized	42.897 to 42.948 mm (1.6889 to 1.6908")	38.897 to 38.948 mm (1.5314 to 1.5333")
Diameter of housing in the cylinder head for valve seat	normal	42.472 to 42.497 mm (1.6722 to 1.6731")	38.472 to 38.497 mm (1.5147 to 1.5156")
	oversized	42.772 to 42.797 mm (1.6840 to 1.6849")	38.772 to 38.797 mm (1.5265 to 1.5274")

Interference between valve seat and housing in cylinder heads = .100 to .176 mm / .0039 to .0069"

Valve cups

Diameter of cup .... { normal ... = 34.973 to 34.989 mm (1.3773 to 1.3775")
                                              { oversized.. = 35.173 to 35.189 mm (1.3848 to 1.3853")

Diameter of cup seat in cylinder head .... { normal ... = 35.000 to 35.025 mm (1.3779 to 1.3789")
                                                   { oversized.. = 35.200 to 35.225 mm (1.3859 to 1.3868")

Clearance between seat and cup .... = .011 to .052 mm (.0005 to .0020")

Valve springs

	Free length	Length under test load	Test load
Inner spring............	46.5 mm (1.83")	26 mm (1.02")	21.20 to 23.16 Kgs (46.7 to 51.1 lbs)
Outer spring............	51.3 mm (2.02")	27.5 mm (1.08")	35.6 to 37.1 Kgs (78.5 to 81.8 lbs)

Connecting rods

Length between center line of big end and center line of small end of connecting rod .... = 147.955 to 148.045 mm (5.8250 to 5.8285")
Inner diameter of the big end of connecting rod .... = 53.695 to 53.708 mm (2.1140 to 2.1144")
Inner diameter of bushing in the small end of rod .... = 22.005 to 22.015 mm (.8664 to .8667")
End play of the connecting rods on the pins of crankshaft .... = .200 to .300 (.0079 to .0118")

Thickness of connecting rod bearings .... { standard .. = 1.829 to 1.835 mm (.0720 to .0722")
                                                    { 1st oversize. = 1.956 to 1.962 mm (.0770 to .0772")
                                                    { 2nd oversize. = 2.083 to 2.089 mm (.0820 to .0824")

Radial clearance between crankshaft pins and bearings for big end of connecting rod .... = .025 to .063 mm (.0010 to .0024")

Maximum out of parallelism between center line of big end hole and center line of small end hole measured on a distance of 100 mm (3.94") .... = .05 mm (.0019")

	Black color	White color
Piston pin-to-small end hole clearance................	.008 to .021 mm (.0003 to .0008")	.005 to .017 mm (.0002 to .0007")

Pin and hole in piston

O.D. of pin .... { Black color.. = 21.994 to 21.997 mm (.86590 to .86602")
                                     { White color.. = 21.998 to 22.000 mm (.86606 to .86614")

		Black color	White color
I.D. of hole in	Borgo piston..	22.000 to 22.002 mm (.86614 to .86621")	22.003 to 22.005 mm (.86626 to .86633")
	Mahle piston..	21.996 to 22.002 mm (.86599 to .86621")	

		Black color	White color
Pin-to-hole clearance	Borgo piston..	.003 to .008 mm (.00012 to .00030")	.003 to .007 mm (.00012 to .00027")
	Mahle piston..	.001 to .008 mm (.00004 to .00030")	.004* to .004 mm (.00015* to .00015")

(*) interference fit

Pistons and cylinder barrels

Diameter of pistons to be measured to square with the hole for piston pin and at a distance of 12 mm (.472") from the lower border of skirt for Borgo piston and 11 mm (.433") for Mahle piston.

BORGO Piston

	Class A (BLUE)	Class B (PINK)	Class C (GREEN)
Normal	77.920 to 77.930 mm (3.0677 to 3.0681")	77.930 to 77.940 mm (3.0681 to 3.0685")	77.940 to 77.950 mm (3.0686 to 3.0688")

MAHLE Piston

	Class A (BLUE)	Class B (PINK)	Class C (GREEN)
Normal	77.945 to 77.955 mm (3.0687 to 3.0690")	77.955 to 77.965 mm (3.0691 to 3.0694")	77.965 to 77.975 mm (3.0694 to 3.0698")

Cylinder barrels

	Class A (BLUE)	Class B (PINK)	Class C (GREEN)
Normal	77.985 to 77.994 mm (3.0703 to 3.0706")	77.995 to 78.004 mm (3.0707 to 3.0710")	78.005 to 78.014 mm (3.0711 to 3.0714")

Clearance between cylinder barrel and piston
- with Borgo piston .. = .055 to .074 mm (.0022 to .0029")
- with Mahle piston .. = .030 to .049 mm (.0012 to .0019")

Projection of barrels from cylinder block .... = .000 to .060 mm (.0000 to .0024")

Compression and oil scraper rings

Height of grooves in piston for compression rings
- normal .... = 1.775 to 1.790 mm (.0699 to .0704")
- chromium-plated ... = 1.785 to 1.800 mm (.0703 to .0708")

Height of groove in piston for oil scraper ring .... = 4.015 to 4.030 mm (.1581 to .1586")

Thickness of compression rings .... = 1.728 to 1.740 mm (.0681 to .0685")

Thickness of oil scraper ring .... = 3.978 to 3.990 mm (.1567 to .1571")

End play of rings in grooves
- compression rings
  - normal .... = .035 to .062 mm (.0014 to .0024")
  - chromium-plated ... = .045 to .072 mm (.0018 to .0028")
- oil scraper rings .... = .025 to .052 mm (.0010 to .0020")

Gap of rings to be inspected in ring gauge or in cylinder barrels .... = .300 to .450 mm (.0012 to .0017")

Crankshaft

Diameter of main journals	Normal	= 59.960 to 59.973 mm (2.3606 to 2.3611")
	1st undersize	= 59.706 to 59.719 mm (2.3506 to 2.3511")
	2nd undersize	= 59.452 to 59.465 mm (2.3407 to 2.3411")
Diameter of connecting rod pins	Normal	= 49.987 to 50.000 mm (1.9680 to 1.9685")
	1st undersize	= 49.733 to 49.746 mm (1.9581 to 1.9585")
	2nd undersize	= 49.479 to 49.492 mm (1.9480 to 1.9485")
Thickness of main bearings	Normal	= 1.829 to 1.835 mm (.0720 to .0722")
	1st oversize	= 1.956 to 1.962 mm (.0770 to .0772")
	2nd oversize	= 2.083 to 2.089 mm (.0820 to .0822")
Diameter of seat for main bearings in crankcas		= 63.657 to 63.676 mm (2.5062 to 2.5069")
Lenght of central journal	Normal	= 30.000 to 30.035 mm (1.1811 to 1.1824")
	1st oversize	= 30.127 to 30.162 mm (1.1861 to 1.1874")
	2nd oversize	= 30.254 to 30.289 mm (1.1911 to 1.1924")
Thickness of thrust rings for central journal	Normal	= 2.311 to 2.362 mm (.0910 to .0929")
	1st oversize	= 2.374 to 2.425 mm (.0935 to .0954")
	2nd oversize	= 2.438 to 2.489 mm (.0960 to .0980")
End play of crankshaft		= .076 to .263 mm (.003 to .010")
Diametrical play between journals and main bearings		= .014 to .058 mm (.0005 to .0022")
Fillet radii	main journals	= 1.7 to 2.1 mm (.069 to .082")
	pins of connecting rods	= 1.7 to 2.1 mm (.069 to .082")
	pin on flywheel side	= 3.7 to 4.1 mm (.146 to .161")
Maximum elongation of main journals and connecting rod pins		= .007 mm (.00027")
Maximum taper of main journals and connecting rod pins measured on their full length		= .01 mm (.00039")
Maximum error of parallelism of main journals and connecting rod pins measured on their full length		= .015 mm (.00059")
Maximum misalignment allowed between main journals		= .01 mm (.00039")

Clutch

Pedal free travel	23 mm (.9")
Distance between the fingers of the clutch toggle arms and the reference sleeve of tool 6123.28.026	1 mm (.039")
Squareness of the clutch driven plate assembled on the direct drive shaft of gear shift	.50 mm (.020")
Driven plate inner diameter	129 to 131 mm (5.08 to 5.15")
Driven plate outer diameter	199 to 201 mm (7.84 to 7.91")
Driven plate thickness — with new facing — free	9.8 to 10.1 mm (.385 to .397")
Driven plate thickness — with new facing — engaged	9.1 to 9.4 mm (.358 to .370")
Driven plate thickness — wear limit	6 mm (.236")

Gearbox

Transmission ratios — 1st gear	3.304 : 1
Transmission ratios — 2nd gear	1.988 : 1
Transmission ratios — 3rd gear	1.355 : 1
Transmission ratios — 4th gear	1.000 : 1
Transmission ratios — 5th gear	.791 : 1
Transmission ratios — Reverse Gear	3.010 : 1
Maximum eccentricity of main shaft	.05 mm (.020")
End play between forks and sleeves — of assembly	.25 to .50 mm (.010 to .020")
End play between forks and sleeves — limit of wear	.7 mm (.027")
Calibration of springs for selector rod balls — free length	15.2 mm (.600")
Calibration of springs for selector rod balls — length under load	10 mm (.390")
Calibration of springs for selector rod balls — check load	4.67 to 5.05 Kgs (10.30 to 11.13 lbs)
Maximum end play of the main shaft gears — for 1st speed gear	.24 mm (.009")
Maximum end play of the main shaft gears — for 2nd speed gear	.21 mm (.008")
Maximum end play of the main shaft gears — for 3rd speed gear	.21 mm (.008")
Distance between outer planes of the engaging teeth of 3rd and 4th gears	42 to 42.2 mm (1.65 to 1.66")
Distance of the rear band (on propeller shaft side) of synchronizer sleeve of the 5th gear, in position of "neutral", from rear plane of engaging teeth of driven gear	12.5 mm (.492")

Rear axle and suspension

Transmission-axle overall ratios-with bevel drive 41 : 8 ....
- 1st gear = 16.933 : 1
- 2nd gear = 10.188 : 1
- 3rd gear = 6.944 : 1
- 4th gear = 5.125 : 1
- 5th gear = 4.054 : 1
- Rev... = 15.426 : 1

Maximum eccentricity of axle shaft .... = .10 mm (.0039")

Clearance between teeth of planetary gears .... = .05 mm (.002")

Clearance between teeth of bevel drive gears .... = .05 to .10 mm (.002 to .004")

Checking of shock absorbers on test bench

Calibration data (when cold)

	T I		SPRINT - SPIDER	
	Extension	Compression	Extension	Compression
High speed	135 to 165 Kgs (298 to 363 lbs)	50 to 65 Kgs (110 to 143 lbs)	137 to 171.5 Kgs (302 to 378 lbs)	45 to 59.5 Kgs (99 to 131 lbs)
Low speed	19 to 30 Kgs (42 to 66 lbs)	12 to 22 Kgs (27 to 48 lbs)	27 to 45.5 Kgs (59 to 100 lbs)	7 to 15.5 Kgs (15 to 34 lbs)

Checking of suspension springs

	T I	SPRINT	SPIDER
Free length	461 mm (18.15")	414 mm (16.30")	410 mm (16.10")
Length under static load	252 mm (9.9")	230 mm (9.0")	230 mm (9.0")
Test load	341.5 to 362.5 Kgs (753 to 799 lbs)	189.15 to 200.85 Kgs (417 to 442 lbs)	185.25 to 196.75 Kgs (408 to 433 lbs)

Front suspension

Pre-load of the bearings of wheel hub

	Kgmm	in. lbs	Weights to be placed in the proper holes of tool C.5.0109	
			Kgs	lbs
a) pre-load for assembly preparation	330	28.6	1.5	3.3
b) definitive pre-load of assembly	112	9.7	.5	1.1
c) test pre-load after functioning	62.5	5.4	.5	1.1
d) final pre-load of re-assembly	57.5	5.0	.5	1.1

Checking of suspension springs

	T I	SPIDER	SPRINT
Free length	310.5 mm (12.2")	394 mm (15.5")	394 mm (15.5")
Length under static load	200 mm (7.8")	267 mm (10.5")	267 mm (10.5")
Test load	896.20 to 952.80 Kgs (1976 to 2100 lbs)	490 to 520 Kgs (1080 to 1145 lbs)	490 to 520 Kgs (1080 to 1145 lbs)

Checking of shock absorbers on test bench

Calibration data (when cold)

	T I		SPRINT - SPIDER	
	Extension	Compression	Extension	Compression
High speed	150 to 182 Kgs (330 to 401 lbs)	55 to 70 Kgs (121 to 154 lbs)	137 to 172 Kgs (302 to 379 lbs)	45 to 59 Kgs (99 to 130 lbs)
Low speed	25 to 42 Kgs (55 to 92 lbs)	13 to 22 Kgs (28 to 48 lbs)	29 to 44 Kgs (64 to 97 lbs)	9 to 14 Kgs (20 to 30 lbs)

Brakes

Pedal travel adjustment

Before actuating the brake master cylinder, the brake pedal must be moved through a free travel corresponding to a master cylinder push rod stroke of 1-1.5 mm (.04 to .06").

Three-shoe front brakes

Brake drum specifications
- Drum inside dia., when new . . . . = 266.7 to 266.8 mm (10.499 to 10.503")
- Max. grinding depth beyond new drum inside dia. . = 1 mm (.04")
- Max. eccentricity . . . . = .045 mm (.0018")
- Max. elongation . . . . = .045 mm (.0018")
- Max. taper . . . . = .03 mm (.0012")
- Surface roughness . . . . = 40 to 60 microinches

Maximum diameter of lathing of brake shoes . . . . = 265.94 mm (10.470")

Calibration of brake shoe springs
- free length . . . . = 137.35 mm (5.4")
- length under load . = 151.1 mm (5.9")
- test load . . . . . = 50 to 60 Kgs (110 to 132 lbs)

Values of the chamfer to be made on linings
- A = 7 to 9 mm (.28 to .35")
- B = .5 mm (.02")

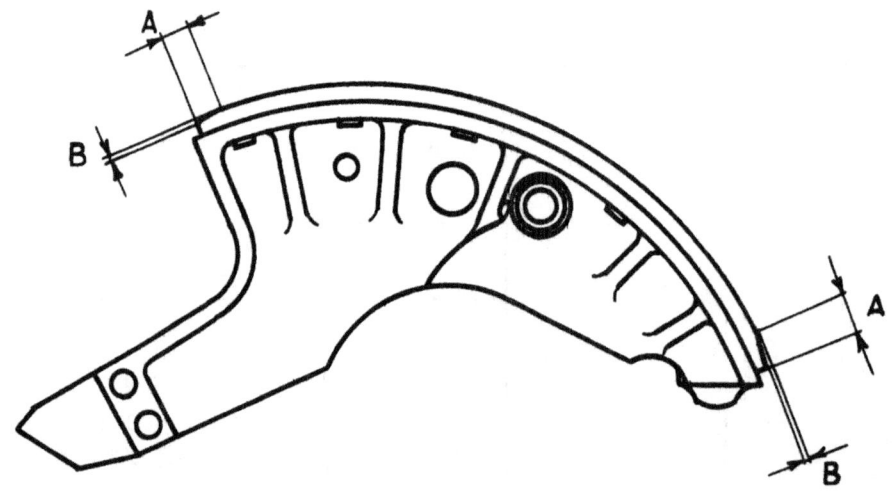

Two-shoe rear brakes

Brake drum specifications:
- Drum inside dia., when new = 254 to 254.1 mm (10.000 to 10.004")
- Max. grinding depth beyond new drum inside dia. = 1 mm (.04")
- Max. eccentricity = .045 mm (.0018")
- Max. elongation = .045 mm (.0018")
- Max. taper = .03 mm (.0012")
- Surface roughness = 40 to 60 microinches

Max. diameter of lathing of brake shoes = 252.984 to 253.340 mm (9.960 to 9.974")

Calibration of brake shoe springs:
- free length = 121.4 mm (4.78")
- length under load = 134 mm (5.3")
- test load = 18 Kgs (39.7 lbs)

Values of the chamfer to be made on linings:
- A = 6 to 7 mm (.24 to .27")
- B = 1.5 to 2 mm (.06 to .08")

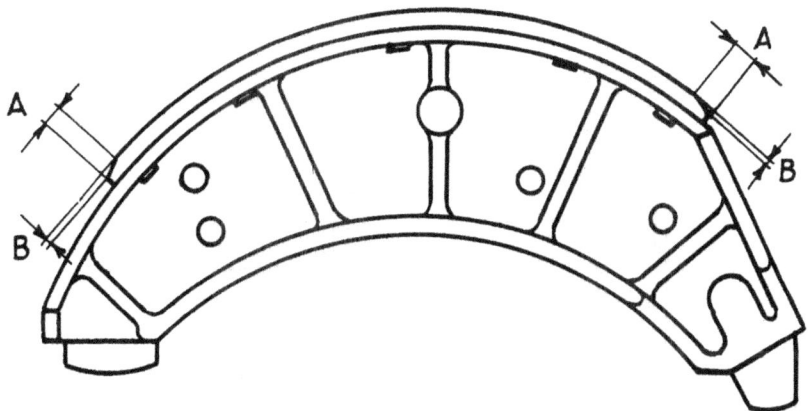

Wheel alignment

Conditions of load for checking the wheel alignment (with fuel tank full, spare wheel, complete equipment of tools)

SPRINT - SPIDER . . . . {2 weights of 50 Kgs on front seats
2 weights of 20 Kgs on flooring where feet rest

T I . . . . { front seats { 1 weight of 50 Kgs on each seat
2 weights of 20 Kgs on flooring where feet rest
rear seats { 2 weights of 50 Kgs on seat
2 weights of 20 Kgs on flooring where feet rest

50 Kgs = 110 lbs   20 Kgs = 44 lbs

Distance of front suspension lower arms from a reference level

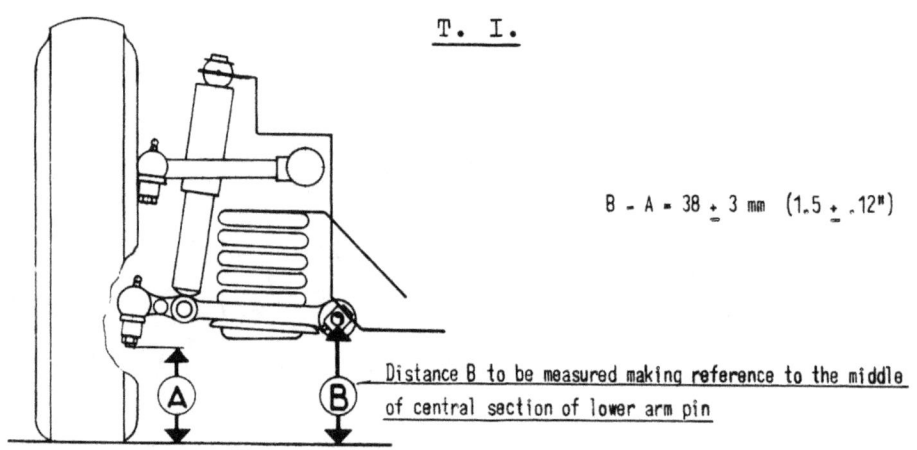

T. I.

$B - A = 38 \pm 3$ mm $(1.5 \pm .12")$

Distance B to be measured making reference to the middle of central section of lower arm pin

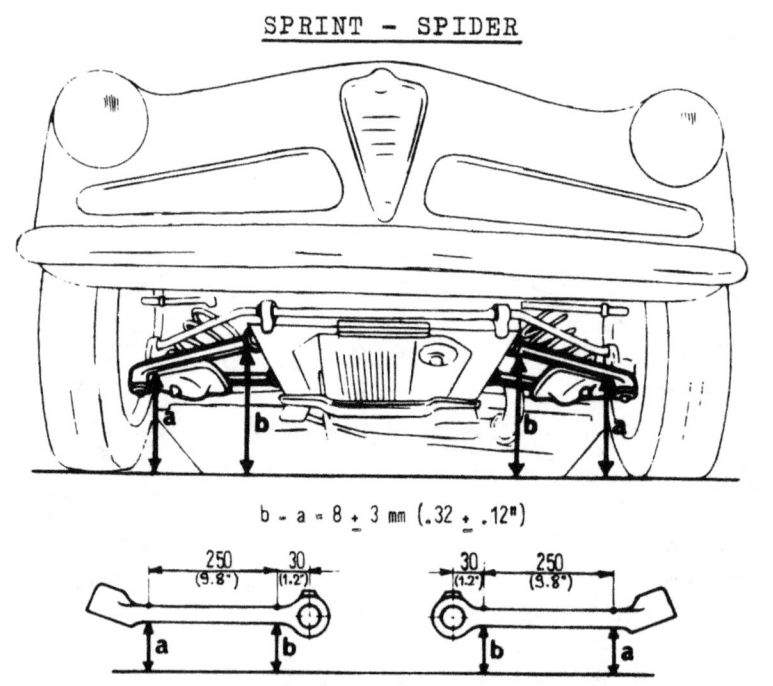

SPRINT - SPIDER

$b - a = 8 \pm 3$ mm $(.32 \pm .12")$

250 (9.8")   30 (1.2")   30 (1.2")   250 (9.8")

Clearance of rear axle from limit buffers

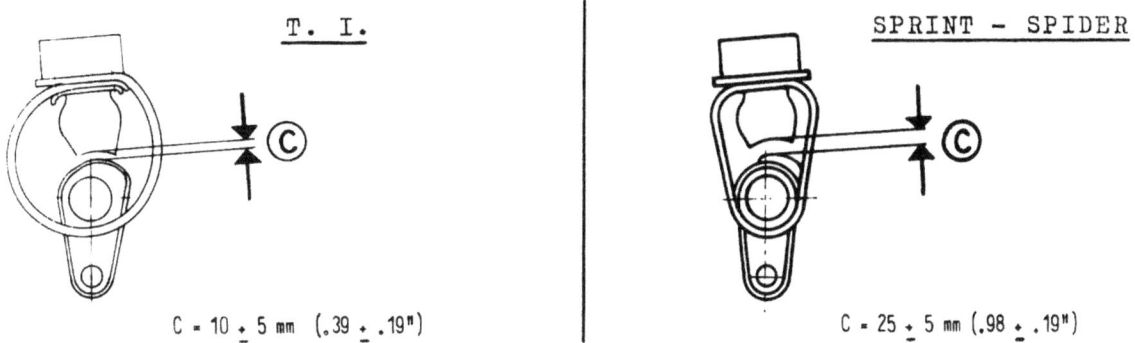

T. I.   C = 10 ± 5 mm (.39 ± .19")

SPRINT - SPIDER   C = 25 ± 5 mm (.98 ± .19")

King pin caster angle

T.I. .... 1°
SPRINT-SPIDER .... 40'   } Allowance .... ± 30'

Difference in caster angle between R.H. and L.H. king pins should never exceed 0°20'.

Adjustment of caster angle on T. I. model

The t.i. model is provided with a caster angle adjuster.
To perform this adjustment, loosen the lock nut and rotate the tie-rod properly.

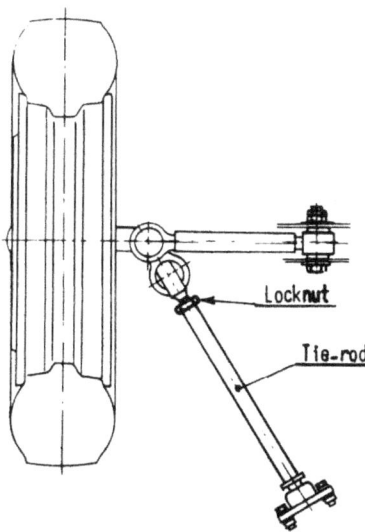

Inspection and adjustment must be performed on cars in the specified loading conditions and with shock absorbers detached from one end.

N.B. - Before checking the caster angle shake the front end of car in order to allow the silentblock on the front tie rod to bed down properly.

Front wheel camber

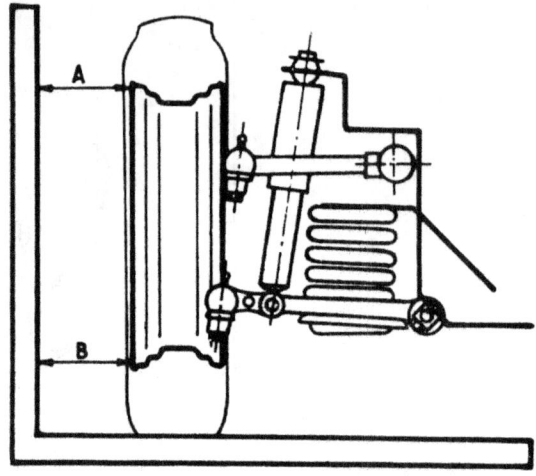

With the car loaded as prescribed the camber should be:

TI .... $B = A + 5$ (.19")
SPRINT-SPIDER ..... $A = B$

Front wheel toe-in

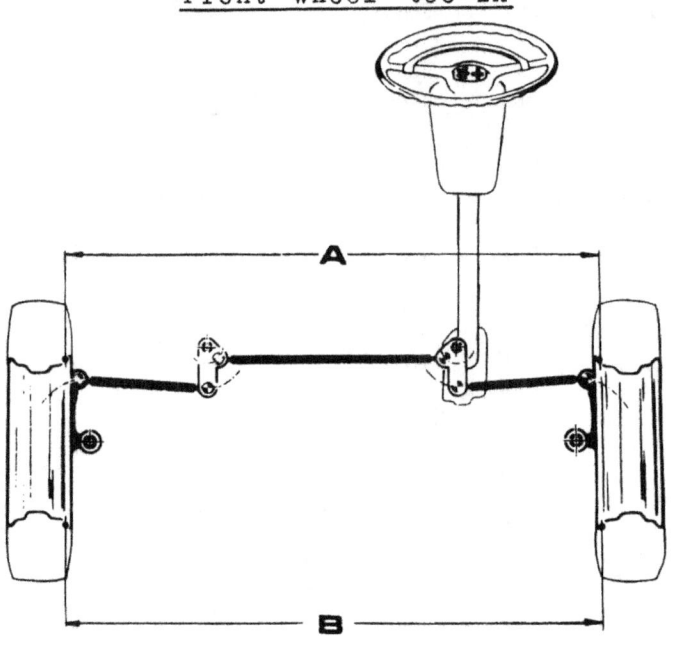

Between the inner edges of rims:

$A = B + 3$ (.12")

Length of rods measured between the centers of joints:

TI .... { lateral rods = 283 to 293 mm (11.2 to 11.5")
            { track rod = 530 to 550 mm (20.9 to 21.6")

SPRINT-SPIDER .... { lateral rods = 265 to 285 mm (10.5 to 11.2")
                { track rod = 470 to 490 mm (18.5 to 19.3")

GIULIA SPIDER VELOCE

Description and technical characteristics

TECHNICAL FEATURES

Engine

Number and layout of cylinders	4 in line
Bore and Stroke	mm 78 x 82
Displacement	1570 c.c.
B.H.P. at 6500 r.p.m.	HP 112 (DIN) / HP 129 (SAE)

Car

Track — Front	1292 mm (4' 2 7/8")
Track — Rear	1270 mm (4' 2")
Wheelbase	2250 mm (7' 4 9/16")
Turning circle	10000 mm (32' 10")
Overall length	3900 mm (12' 9 9/16")
Overall width	1580 mm (5' 2")
Max. height (with hood)	1335 mm (4' 4 9/16")
Dry weight	885 Kg (17 3/4 cwt)
Number of seats	2
Tyres: Michelin XA / Pirelli Cinturato S	155-15

Performance after "Running in" (Max. Speeds)

With final drive of 41 : 8

	K/H	mph
1st	49	30
2nd	81	50
3rd	119	75
4th	160	100
5th over	180	112
reverse	53	33

Do not exceed the maximum speeds shown in order to avoid serious damage.

The figures shown refer to use of the car in normal central European climatic conditions.

Petrol Consumption

At touring speeds, fully laden:

about 11.5 lts;   25 mpg GB;   21 mpg US;

Fill-Up Data

Water (Engine + Radiator)	7,5 lts	13 pts GB	15,5 pts US
Fuel: only use petrol with an octane ratio of not less than 92 (R.M.)	53 lts	11,5 gals GB	13,8 gals US
Fuel Reserve	6-7 lts	1 1/4-1 ½ gals GB	1,5-1.8 gals US
Oil – Engine (Sump + Filter) Max. level*	5.8 Kgs	5.7 qts GB	6.8 qts US
Oil – Engine (Sump + Filter) Min. level	3.25 Kgs	3.2 qts GB	3.8 qts US
Oil – Gearbox	1.65 Kgs	3.2 pts GB	3.8 pts US
Oil – Rear axle	1.25 Kgs	2.5 pts GB	3.0 pts US
Oil – Steering box	.25 Kgs	.5 pt GB	.6 pt US

*The capacity shown is that needed for regular changes; the total amount of oil in the circuit (sump, filter and passages) is 6.6 Kg - 6.5 qts GB - 7.8 qts US.

Attention for the first 3000 Km (1900 miles)

To obtain the gradual "bedding in" of the various parts of the car and especially the engine, gearbox and rear axle, it is necessary to have a period of "running in" during which you are asked to use great care. Do not exceed the speeds shown in the table.

Max speeds	Gear	1st		2nd		3rd		4th		5th	
		Kmh	mph	Kmh	mph	Kmh	mph	Kmh	mph	Kmh	mph
	Up to 1000 Km (600 mi)	31	19	52	32	76	47	103	64	131	82
	From 1000 to 3000 Km (600 to 1800 mi)	39	24	64	40	94	59	127	79	161	100

RECOMMENDED LUBRICANTS

Part	Standard No.	Recommended commercial equivalents	
		Agip	Shell
Engine	SAE 20 W 40 - API MS	F.1 Multigrade	X-100 20 W/40
Gearbox	SAE 90	F.1 Rotra SAE 90	Dentax 90
Differential & Steering box	SAE 90 API EP	F.1 Rotra Hypoid SAE 90	Spirax 90 EP
Propeller shaft sleeve & universal joints / Steering linkage joints / Upper & lower King pins / Front suspension joints / Rear axle reaction trunnion ball joint	NLGI 1	F.1 Grease 15	Retinax G
Front wheel bearings	NLGI 2/3	F.1 Grease 30	Retinax AX
Brake fluid	Castrol Girling Brake Fluid Amber		

N.B. - SAE - Society of Automotive Engineers
API - American Petroleum Institute
NLGI - National Lubricating Grease Institute

DESCRIPTION

ENGINE

Block: light alloy.

Cylinder liners: cast iron, water-cooled, detachable.

Cylinder head: light alloy, water-cooled, with valve seat inserts.

Crankshaft: forged in steel, counterbalanced on five main bearings.

Connecting rods: steel forgings, with small-end bronze bushing and big-end half shells.

Pistons: light alloy, two compression rings, of which the top one is chromium-plated and one oil control ring.

Main and connecting rod bearings: thin-wall shell bearings, steel with antifriction lining.

Timing: two overhead camshafts driven by duplex chain. Valves, two per cylinder, vee-positioned, directly operated by camshafts through oil bath cups.

Valve clearance with cold engine	intake	.425 - .450 mm (.0167 to .0177")
	exhaust	.475 - .500 mm (.0187 to .0197")
Intake valves	Opening starts	29° before TDC
	Closing stops	66° after BDC
Exhaust valves	Opening starts	64° before BDC
	Closing stops	27° after TDC

To adjust the valve clearances, shims are available to fit over the valves stems in a series of thickness ranging from 1.3 to 3.5 mm (.051" to .137") in increments of .025 mm (.001").

Fuel Supply by a mechanical pump and two twin horizontal Weber 40 DCOE 2 carburettors.

Carburettor jet Specifications

Venturis	30
Main jets	120 winter
	115 summer
Idling jets	55 (with axial hole 150)
Main air metering jets	180
Idling air metering jets	120
Acceleration pump jets	35
Choke jets	65 F 5

Air Filter

The air filter is fitted with a silencer and dry filtering element, which is pleated so that the filtering area is increased.

Ignition is by battery and distributor with centrifugal advance.

Firing order: 1 - 3 - 4 - 2

Contact-breaker point gap: .35 - .40 mm (.0137 - .0157")

Degrees of advance:

Static advance Before T.D.C.	Maximum advance Before T.D.C.
5° ± 2°	46° ± 3°

The timing marks are on the crankshaft pulley.

Sparking plugs Lodge RL 47

Regularly clean the electrodes and adjust the gap to .38 - .46 mm (.015 to .018 in.).

Lubrication: pressure by gear pump, with pressure relief valve.

Oil sump made in light alloy.

Full-flow oil filter in series with delivery circuit, fitted with a valve that by-passes the element if it should become clogged.

Cooling by means of a radiator and a fan. Forced by a centrifugal pump. Thermostatic temperature regulator.

Starter - 12 Volt, electric motor.

CLUTCH

Single dry plate. Smooth take-up is ensured by 9 coil springs.

The pedal travel should be about 1" before disengagement of the clutch.

GEARBOX

The gearbox, in unit with the engine, has 5 fully synchronized gears.

The box containing the gears and shafts is made in two halves to facilitate dismantling.

Ratios

Gears		
	1 st	3.304 : 1
	2 nd	1.988 : 1
	3 rd	1.355 : 1
	4 th	1.000 : 1
	5 th	.791 : 1
	Reverse	3.010 : 1

PROPELLER SHAFT

The propeller shaft is divided with flexible intermediate bearing attached to the frame.

The first half is fitted with a rubber coupling at the rear of the gearbox; the second half is fitted, at each end, with a universal joint.

REAR AXLE

The rear axle is attached longitudinally to the supporting structure by means of two beams with rubber bushes at the ends; transverse attachment is effected by means of an upper reaction triangle with arms hinged to the body and to the rear axle through rubber bushes.

The final drive is of the hypoid type.

Overall ratios

Gears		
	1 st	15.049
	2 nd	9.055
	3 rd	6.172
	4 th	4.555
	5 th	3.603
	Reverse	13.710

FRONT SUSPENSION

Independent suspension is provided for each front wheel; the wheels are secured to the body by transverse arms.

Coil springs and double-acting hydraulic telescopic shock absorbers are located between the lower arms and the body.

The suspension system is completed by a transverse stabiliser rod which improves the stability of the vehicle on bends.

Upwards rotation of the arms is restricted by pads in the shock absorbers.

Rotation downwards is restricted by a rebound cable one end of which is connected to the body and the other to the lower arm.

REAR SUSPENSION

The rear suspension is by means of helical springs and large diameter hydraulic telescopic shock absorbers coaxial with the springs.

The upward movement of the axle is limited by rubber buffers and the downward by fabric and rubber straps.

STEERING

The steering gear is of the worm-and-roller type.

Stable steering requires that:

there is no abnormal play in the steering gear (the bearings in the steering box, the worm-and-roller coupling and the ball joints);

the front wheels are perfectly balanced and the tire inflation pressures are as prescribed;

the front suspension members are in perfect conditions.

        Side rods   265-285 mm (10.4-11.2 in.)
        Center track 470-490 mm (18.5-19.3 in.)

BRAKES

Front:

Disc type: self-adjusting; the friction pads are directly actuated by the cylinders integral with the calipers.

Rear: drum type-with helical cooling fins; the two shoes have large working surface and are self-centering.

Hand brake: (emergency and parking)

It is mechanically-operated and acts on the rear brake shoes.

Usally the adjustment of parking brake control is performed only when brake shoe adjustment is required for lining wear or, exceptionally, for cable slackening.

To adjust the travel act on the slack adjuster.

If the parking brake is properly adjusted, the rear wheels should become locked when the lever is moved through half its total travel.

TYRES

PIRELLI Cinturato S

MICHELIN XA

Pressure	Front		Rear	
	Pirelli	Michelin	Pirelli	Michelin
Touring riding up to 160 Km/h (100 mph)	1,7 Kg/cm^2 (24.1 p.s.i.)	1,7 Kg/cm^2 (24.1 p.s.i.)	1,8 Kg/cm^2 (25.6 p.s.i.)	1,7 Kg/cm^2 (24.1 p.s.i.)
Sporting riding over 160 Km/h (100 mph)	1,8 Kg/cm^2 (25.6 p.s.i.)	1,9 Kg/cm^2 (27.1 p.s.i.)	2,1 Kg/cm^2 (29.8 p.s.i.)	1,9 Kg/cm^2 (27.1 p.s.i.)
On track	2,3 Kg/cm^2 (32.7 p.s.i.)	2,3 Kg/cm^2 (32.7 p.s.i.)	2,5 Kg/cm^2 (35.6 p.s.i.)	2,6 Kg/cm^2 (37 p.s.i.)

ELECTRIC SYSTEM

Battery 60 Ah

Generator BOSCH LJ/GEG/200/12/2700 R 32 mr.

Distributor BOSCH VJ 4 BR 35 mk

Coil BOSCH TK 12 A 3

Starter Motor BOSCH AL/EEF 0.7/12 R 11

Voltage Regulator BOSCH RS/VA 200/12 A 2

Windscreen wiper motor LUCAS DR 2

NOTES

VELOCEPRESS MANUALS - MOTORCYCLE

1930'S BRITISH MOTORCYCLE CARBS & ELEC COMPONENTS (BOOK OF)
1930'S BRITISH MOTORCYCLE ENGINES (OVERHAUL & MAINTENANCE)
1930'S BRITISH MOTORCYCLE GEARBOXES & CLUTCHES (BOOK OF)
AJS 1932-1948 SINGLES & TWINS 250cc THRU 1000cc (BOOK OF)
AJS 1945-1960 SINGLES 350cc & 500cc MODELS 16 & 18 (BOOK OF)
AJS 1955-1965 SINGLES 350cc & 500cc (BOOK OF)
ARIEL UP TO 1932 (BOOK OF)
ARIEL 1932-1939 PREWAR MODELS (BOOK OF)
ARIEL 1933-1951 (WORKSHOP MANUAL)
ARIEL 1939-1960 4 STROKE SINGLES (BOOK OF)
ARIEL 1958-1964 LEADER & ARROW (BOOK OF)
BMW R26 R27 (1956-1967) FACTORY WORKSHOP MANUAL
BMW R50 R50S R60 R69S (1955-1969) FACTORY WORKSHOP MANUAL
BRIDGESTONE 90 SERIES FACTORY WSM & PARTS CATALOGUE
BRIDGESTONE 175 SERIES FACTORY WSM & PARTS CATALOGUE
BRIDGESTONE 350 SERIES FACTORY WSM & PARTS CATALOGUES
BSA BANTAM ALL MODELS FROM 1948 ONWARDS (BOOK OF)
BSA SINGLES & V-TWINS UP TO 1927 (BOOK OF)
BSA SINGLES & V-TWINS UP TO 1930 (BOOK OF)
BSA SINGLES & V-TWINS UP TO 1935 (BOOK OF)
BSA SINGLES & V-TWINS 1936-1939 (BOOK OF)
BSA OHV & SV SINGLES 250-600cc 1945-1959 (BOOK OF)
BSA OHV & SV SINGLES 250cc (ONLY) 1954-1970 (BOOK OF)
BSA OHV SINGLES 350 & 500cc 1955-1967 (BOOK OF)
BSA TWINS 1948-1962 (BOOK OF)
BSA TWINS 1962-1969 (SECOND BOOK OF)
CYCLEMOTOR (BOOK OF)
DOUGLAS 1929-1939 PREWAR ALL MODELS (BOOK OF)
DOUGLAS 1948-1957 POSTWAR ALL MODELS FACTORY SHOP MANUAL
DUCATI 160cc, 250cc & 350cc OHC MODELS FACTORY SHOP MANUAL
HONDA 50 ALL MODELS UP TO 1970 INC MONKEY & TRAIL (BOOK OF)
HONDA 90 ALL MODELS UP TO 1966 (BOOK OF)
HONDA 125-150cc TWINS C/CS/CB/CA FACTORY WORKSHOP MANUAL
HONDA 250-305 TWINS C/CS/CB FACTORY WORKSHOP MANUAL
HONDA 450 CB/CL 1965-1974 K0 TO K7 WORKSHOP MANUAL
HONDA C100 SUPER CUB FACTORY WORKSHOP MANUAL
HONDA C110 SPORT CUB 1962-1969 FACTORY WORKSHOP MANUAL
HONDA TWINS & SINGLES 50cc THRU 305cc 1960-1966 (BOOK OF)
HONDA TWINS ALL MODELS 125cc THRU 450cc UP TO 1968 (BOOK OF)
INDIAN PONYBIKE, BOY RACER & PAPOOSE ILL PARTS LIST & SALES LIT
J.A.P. ENGINES 1927-1952 & MOTORCYCLES 1934-1952 (BOOK OF)
LAMBRETTA 1947-1957 ALL 125 & 150cc MODELS (BOOK OF)
LAMBRETTA 1957-1970 LI & TV MODELS (SECOND BOOK OF)
MATCHLESS 1931-1939 ALL MODELS 250cc THRU 990cc (BOOK OF)
MATCHLESS 1945-1956 350 & 500cc SINGLES (BOOK OF)
MATCHLESS 1955-1966 350 & 500cc SINGLES (BOOK OF)
NEW IMPERIAL ALL SV & OHV FROM 1935 ONWARDS (BOOK OF)
NORTON 1932-1939 PREWAR MODELS (BOOK OF)
NORTON 1932-1947 (BOOK OF)
NORTON 1938-1956 (BOOK OF)
NORTON 1955-1963 MODELS 19, 50 & ES2 (BOOK OF)
NORTON 1955-1965 DOMINATOR TWINS (BOOK OF)
NORTON 1957-1970 TWINS FACTORY WORKSHOP MANUAL
NSU PRIMA 1956-1964 ALL MODELS (BOOK OF)
NSU QUICKLY 1953-1963 ALL MODELS (BOOK OF)
PANTHER 1932-1958 LIGHTWEIGHT MODELS 250 & 350cc (BOOK OF)
PANTHER 1938-1966 HEAVYWEIGHT MODELS 600 & 650cc (BOOK OF)
RALEIGH MOPEDS 1960-1969 (BOOK OF)
RALEIGH MOTORCYCLES 1919-1933 (BOOK OF)
ROYAL ENFIELD 1934-1946 SINGLES & V TWINS (BOOK OF)
ROYAL ENFIELD 1937-1953 SINGLES & V TWINS (BOOK OF)
ROYAL ENFIELD 1946-1962 SINGLES (BOOK OF)
ROYAL ENFIELD 1958-1966 250cc & 350cc SINGLES (SECOND BOOK OF)
ROYAL ENFIELD 736cc INTERCEPTOR FACTORY WORKSHOP MANUAL
RUDGE 1933-1939 (BOOK OF)
SUNBEAM 1928-1939 (BOOK OF)
SUNBEAM 1946-1957 S7 & S8 (BOOK OF)
SUZUKI 50cc & 80cc UP TO 1966 (BOOK OF)
SUZUKI T10 1963-1967 FACTORY WORKSHOP MANUAL
SUZUKI T20 & T200 1965-1969 FACTORY WORKSHOP MANUAL
SUZUKI TWINS 1962 ONWARDS 125-500cc WORKSHOP MANUAL
TRIUMPH 1935-1939 PREWAR MODELS (BOOK OF)
TRIUMPH 1935-1949 (BOOK OF)
TRIUMPH 1937-1951 (WORKSHOP MANUAL)
TRIUMPH 1945-1955 FACTORY WORKSHOP MANUAL
TRIUMPH 1945-1958 TWINS (BOOK OF)
TRIUMPH 1956-1969 TWINS (BOOK OF)
VELOCETTE 1925-1970 ALL SINGLES & TWINS (BOOK OF)
VESPA 1951-1961 (BOOK OF)
VESPA 1955-1963 125 & 150cc & GS MODELS (SECOND BOOK OF)
VESPA 1955-1968 GS & SS (BOOK OF)
VESPA 1963-1972 90, 125 & 150cc (THIRD BOOK OF)
VILLIERS ENGINE UP TO 1959 INC. 3 WHEELERS (BOOK OF)
VILLIERS ENGINE UP TO 1969 (BOOK OF)
VINCENT 1935-1955 (WORKSHOP MANUAL)
YAMAHA 1961-1967 YA5 & YA6 (WORKSHOP MANUAL & ILL PARTS LIST)
YAMAHA 1971-1972 JT1& JT2 (WORKSHOP MANUAL & ILL PARTS LIST)

VELOCEPRESS TECHNICAL BOOKS – MOTORCYCLE

CATALOG OF BRITISH MOTORCYCLES (1951 MODELS)
MOTORCYCLE ENGINEERING (P.E. Irving)
MOTORCYCLE ROAD TESTS 1949-1953 (Motor Cycle Magazine UK)
SPEED AND HOW TO OBTAIN IT (Motor Cycle Magazine UK)
TUNING FOR SPEED (P.E. Irving)

VELOCEPRESS MANUALS - THREE WHEELER'S

BSA THREE WHEELER (BOOK OF)
VINTAGE MORGAN THREE WHEELER (BOOK OF)

VELOCEPRESS MANUALS - AUTOMOBILE

ALFA ROMEO GIULIA WORKSHOP MANUAL 1300 TO 2000cc 1962-1975
ALFA ROMEO GIULIA TECH MANUAL CARBURETED CARS FROM 1962
ALFA ROMEO GIULIA TECH MANUAL FUEL INJECTED CARS FROM 1969
ALFA ROMEO GIULIETTA & GIULIA 750 & 101 SERIES 1955-1965 WSM
AUSTIN-HEALEY SPRITE & MG MIDGET WORKSHOP MANUAL 1958-1971
BMW 600 LIMOUSINE FACTORY WORKSHOP MANUAL
BMW 600 LIMOUSINE OWNERS HAND BOOK & SERVICE MANUAL
BMW 2000 & 2002 1966-1976 WORKSHOP MANUAL
BMW ISETTA FACTORY WORKSHOP MANUAL
CORVAIR 1960-1969 WORKSHOP MANUAL
CORVETTE V8 1955-1962 WORKSHOP MANUAL
FIAT 500 FACTORY WORKSHOP MANUAL 1957-1973
FIAT 600, 600D & MULTIPLA FACTORY WORKSHOP MANUAL 1955-1969
JAGUAR E-TYPE 3.8 & 4.2 SERIES 1 & 2 WORKSHOP MANUAL
JAGUAR MK 7, 8, 9 & XK120, 140, 150 WORKSHOP MANUAL 1948-1961
METROPOLITAN FACTORY WORKSHOP MANUAL
MGA & MGB OWNERS HANDBOOK & WORKSHOP MANUAL
MG MIDGET TC, TD, TF & TF1500 WORKSHOP MANUAL
PORSCHE 356 1948-1965 WORKSHOP MANUAL
PORSCHE 911 2.0, 2.2, 2.4 LITRE 1964-1973 WORKSHOP MANUAL
PORSCHE 911 2.7, 3.0, 3.2 LITRE 1973-1989 WORKSHOP MANUAL
PORSCHE 912 WORKSHOP MANUAL
TRIUMPH TR2, TR3, TR4 1953-1965 WORKSHOP MANUAL
VOLKSWAGEN TRANSPORTER, TRUCKS & WAGONS 1950-1979 WSM
VOLVO 1944-1968 ALL MODELS WORKSHOP MANUAL

VELOCEPRESS TECHNICAL BOOKS - AUTOMOBILE

FERRARI 250/GT SERVICE AND MAINTENANCE
FERRARI GUIDE TO PERFORMANCE
FERRARI OWNER'S HANDBOOK
FERRARI TUNING TIPS & MAINTENANCE TECHNIQUES
HOW TO BUILD A FIBERGLASS CAR
HOW TO BUILD A RACING CAR
HOW TO RESTORE THE MODEL 'A' FORD
MASERATI OWNER'S HANDBOOK
OBERT'S FIAT GUIDE
PERFORMANCE TUNING THE SUNBEAM TIGER
SOUPING THE VOLKSWAGEN
SOLEX CARBURETORS (EMPHASIS ON UK & EU AUTOMOBILES)
SU CARBURETORS (EMPHASIS ON UK AUTOMOBILES)
WEBER CARBURETORS (EMPHASIS ON ALFA & FIAT)

VELOCEPRESS BOOKS & GUIDES - AUTOMOBILE

ABARTH BUYERS GUIDE
COMPLETE CATALOG OF JAPANESE MOTOR VEHICLES
FERRARI 308 SERIES BUYER'S AND OWNER'S GUIDE
FERRARI BERLINETTA LUSSO
FERRARI BROCHURES AND SALES LITERATURE 1946-1967
FERRARI BROCHURES AND SALES LITERATURE 1968-1989
FERRARI OPP, MAINTENANCE & SERVICE H/BOOKS 1948-1963
FERRARI SERIAL NUMBERS PART I - ODD NUMBERS TO 21399
FERRARI SERIAL NUMBERS PART II - EVEN NUMBERS TO 1050
FERRARI SPYDER CALIFORNIA
HENRY'S FABULOUS MODEL "A" FORD
MASERATI BROCHURES AND SALES LITERATURE

VELOCEPRESS BOOKS – RACING

CARRERA PANAMERICANA - MEXICAN ROAD RACE (BOOK OF)
DIALED IN - THE JAN OPPERMAN STORY
IF HEMINGWAY HAD WRITTEN A RACING NOVEL
VEDA ORR'S NEW REVISED HOT ROD PICTORIAL

AUTOBOOKS WORKSHOP MANUALS & BROOKLANDS ROAD TEST PORTFOLIOS

FOR A COMPLETE LISTING OF THE AUTOBOOKS & BROOKLANDS TITLES THAT WE CURRENTLY HAVE AVAILABLE, PLEASE VISIT OUR WEBSITE.

www.VelocePress.com

www.ingramcontent.com/pod-product-compliance
Lightning Source LLC
Chambersburg PA
CBHW060245240426
43673CB00047B/1878